SOCIAL AND CULTURAL ANTHROPOLOGY

The Key Concepts

Social and Cultural Anthropology: The Key Concepts is the ideal guide to this discipline, defining and discussing its central terms with clarity and authority. Among the concepts explored are:

- Cybernetics
- *Ecriture Feminine*
- Gossip
- Human Rights
- Alterity
- Stereotypes
- Kinship
- Thick Description
- Violence

Each entry is accompanied by specific cross-referencing and there is an extensive index and bibliography. Providing both historical commentary and future-oriented debate *Social and Cultural Anthropology: The Key Concepts* is a superb reference resource for anyone studying or teaching anthropology.

Nigel Rapport is Professor of Anthropological and Philosophical Studies at the University of St Andrews and the author of numerous books on anthropology, including *Transcendent Individual: Essays Toward a Literary and Liberal Anthropology* (1997) and, with Anthony P. Cohen, *Questions of Consciousness* (1995), both published by Routledge. **Joanna Overing** is Professor and Chair of Social Anthropology, also at the University of St Andrews. She is the author of many publications on Amazonia and on anthropological theory. She was editor of the volume *Reason and Morality* (Routledge, 1985).

ROUTLEDGE KEY GUIDES

SOCIAL AND CULTURAL ANTHROPOLOGY

The Key Concepts

Nigel Rapport and Joanna Overing

Routledge
Taylor & Francis Group

LONDON AND NEW YORK

First published, 2000 by Routledge
11 New Fetter Lane, London EC4P 4EE

Simultaneously published in the USA and Canada
by Routledge
29 West 35th Street, New York, NY 10001

Reprinted 2003, 2004

Routledge is an imprint of the Taylor & Francis Group

© 2000 Nigel Rapport and Joanna Overing

Typeset in Bembo by Keystroke, Jacaranda Lodge, Wolverhampton
Printed and bound in Great Britain by
MPG Books Ltd, Bodmin, Cornwall

British Library Cataloguing in Publication Data
A catalogue record for this book is available from the British Library

Library of Congress Cataloging in Publication Data
has been applied for

ISBN 0-415-18155-0 (hbk)
ISBN 0-415-18156-9 (pbk)

CONTENTS

ABOUT THE BOOK

This is a book of some sixty essays each of which deals with an important term in the toolbox of contemporary anthropological studies. The aim is to provide a concise repository of explanatory statements covering a number of the major concepts that professional anthropologists might use.

'Explanation' here includes argumentation concerning the diversity of ways in which anthropologists have understood the key concepts of their discipline and the way these have changed over time and might be expected to change in future. The volume is both overview and polemic, intended as a study guide as well as a research tool for original writing.

The 'cultural anthropological' tradition originating in North America and the 'social anthropological' tradition of Europe are combined in the book, reflecting the growing similarity of what is taught in university courses around the world.

Key Concepts would write anthropology into a changing environment of academic disciplines – their changing interrelations, methodologies and epistemologies – in the light of the current ('post-modern', 'reflexive') blurring of generic divisions and challenge to established verities. The volume draws on a range of disciplinary sources (including philosophy, psychology, sociology, cultural studies, literary criticism and linguistics), so situating anthropology within a broadly conceived notion of the humanities.

★ ★ ★

A book of key anthropological concepts is something of a departure. There are a number of introductions to anthropology (*Social Anthropology* (Leach 1982), *Other Cultures* (Beattie 1964)), also dictionaries (*The Dictionary of Anthropology* (Barfield 1997), *Macmillan Dictionary of*

Anthropology (Seymour-Smith 1986)), encyclopaedias (*Encyclopedia of Social and Cultural Anthropology* (Barnard and Spencer 1996), *Encyclopedia of Cultural Anthropology* (Levinson and Ember 1996)), and a companion (Ingold 1994a); but there have not been many attempts to distil 'anthropological wisdom', theoretical, methodological, analytical and ethnographic, by way of key concepts.

Of the two most comparable volumes, Robert Winthrop's *Dictionary of Concepts in Cultural Anthropology* (1991), and *South African Keywords* edited by Emile Boonzaier and John Sharp (1988), Winthrop's rather particular emphasis on 'cultural anthropology' as the description and interpretation of 'culturally patterned thought and behavior' (1991: ix) means that there are few overlaps – 'community', 'interpretation', 'network', 'urbanism', 'world-view', – between the eighty concepts he highlights and those selected here. Boonzaier and Sharp, meanwhile, analyse thirteen key words which they take to be instrumental in the construction, representation, objectification and interpretation of South African apartheid, both by anthropologists and by politicians. While less ethnographically focused than Boonzaier and Sharp's volume, the present book attempts likewise to look askance at the 'culture and society' of anthropology as an academic discipline and relate its conceptual tools to wider philosophical and folk discourses.

It echoes Boonzaier and Sharp too in claiming kinship with, and drawing inspiration from, an original project of the Marxian critic and theorist of culture, Raymond Williams. In 1976, Williams produced a book of *Keywords* in which he attempted to isolate certain significant landmarks in Western social and cultural discourse. The approach had been made famous in Germany, since the Second World War, under the title, *Begriffsgeschichte*, or 'conceptual history'; shifts and discontinuities in conceptual formation, it was argued, were an index of wider socio-cultural change as well as being instrumental in the shaping of such change. Through an assemblage of 'keywords', Williams explained (1983a: 15), he sought to delineate and detail a complex and broad land-scape of the Western imagination. Here were 131 words, he suggested, which forced themselves on his attention because of their general sociocultural import: their indicativeness of certain abiding values or forms of thought, and their connection to certain fundamental activities.

The key concepts signalled in this book are to be regarded in a comparable way: they are discursive nodes from which a broader, interconnected landscape of anthropological work and understanding should become apparent. The dictionary defines 'concepts' as 'things formed through the power of the mind', also 'general notions, fancies, thoughts and plans' (Chambers 1966). More technically, one might wish to identify by 'concepts' the specific things that human beings think about, the meaning(s) of those things at particular moments, and the relations between those things and various other things in a classificatory array (cf. McInnis 1991: vii). Each concept-entry in this book sets out to define an aspect of anthropological thought, therefore, to describe something of the range of a concept's meaning-in-use, and to offer pointers towards other entries with which the concept can be seen to connect.

Raymond Williams's espying of a landscape of Western sociocultural discourse was an inevitably partial exercise; also, partisan, subjective, programmatic and open-ended. At the same time as it claimed to espy it also created a landscape; seeking to compass a vocabulary it succeeded, above all, in generating further discussion. The enterprise of *Keywords* w..s to provide an argument more than an encyclopaedic lexicon. This book would offer no more and no less than that. It is imbued with the perspective of its authors; it is the landscape of anthropology as they see and interpret it. Indeed, the authors would argue that the notion of an academic discipline (as with any other institution) whose workings and use are intrinsically perspectival, contingent, subjective and situational matters, and in that sense anti-disciplinary, is in itself an inherently 'anthropological' notion.

★ ★ ★

The key concepts adumbrated by this book figure as some sixty essays, as mentioned. These range in length from approximately 500 words to 5000, as the significance of the concepts varies and as they give on to discussions of variable complexity. The concepts also cover a range of types: ontological ('Agent and Agency', 'Consciousness', 'Gender'), epistemological ('Cybernetics', 'Kinship', 'World-View'), methodological ('Culture', 'Methodological Individualism and Holism', 'Literariness'), theoretical ('Community', 'The Unhomely', 'Urbanism'), and ethnographic ('Home and Homelessness', 'Myth', 'Tourism').

The essay format is intended to give sufficient space for the history of usage of the concept to be addressed and the argumentation surrounding it, also the way that conceptual meanings change over time and according to author and context. Besides the labelled concept-entries, however, there is a detailed Index to this book which can be used to inquire more immediately of precise features in the discipline's discursive landscape. Finally, there is an extensive Bibliography of sources which directs the reader to further, specialized readings.

★ ★ ★

Amid the diversity and range of the volume, its partiality and open-endedness, it is intended that its dual authorship will tend towards a consistency of ethos and continuity of voice in the whole – at the least, towards a consistency and continuity of narrative tension.

A number of other voices have nonetheless ably assisted the authors in composing their text. For their support and advice the authors would like very much to thank Anthony Cohen, Andrew Dawson, Alan Passes, Marnio Teixeira-Pinto and Jonathan Skinner; Elizabeth Munro and Napier Russell; also their editors at Routledge, Roger Thorp and Hywel Evans, and copy editor Michael Fitch.

NJR and JO
St Andrews 1999

LIST OF CONCEPTS

Agent and Agency
Alterity
Auto-Anthropology
Children
Classification
Code
Cognition
Common Sense
Community
Consciousness
Contradiction
Conversation
Culture
Cybernetics
Dialogics and Analogics
Discourse
Ecriture Feminine
Ethnomethodology
Form and Content
Gender
Gossip
Home and Homelessness
Human Rights
Humanism
Individualism
Individuality
Interaction
Interpretation
Irony
Kinship

Liminality
Literariness
Methodological Eclecticism
Methodological Individualism and Holism
Moments of Being
Movement
Myth
Narrative
Network
Non-Places
Post-Modernism
Qualitative and Quantitative Methodologies
Reading
The Rural Idyll
Science
Situation and Context
Society
Stereotypes
Thick Description
Tourism
Transaction
The Unhomely
Urbanism
Violence
Visualism
World-Making
World-View
Writing

AGENT AND AGENCY

The concepts of agent and agency, perhaps related most closely to that of power, are usually deployed in debates over the relationship between individuals and social structure. They also pertain, however, to the nature of individual consciousness, its ability to constitute and reconstitute itself, and, ultimately, the extent of its freedom from exterior determination.

Agency and structure

Agents act, and agency is the capability, the power, to be the source and originator of acts; agents are the subjects of action. Weber suggested that acts be distinguished from mere (animal) behaviour on the basis of acts being seen to entail a number of features of human rationality: consciousness, reflection, intention, purpose and meaning. He felt that social science should be an interpretive study of the meanings of human action and the choices behind them. G.H. Mead sought to clarify the Weberian notion of meaning, and its social-scientific understanding (*Verstehung*), by differentiating acts into: impulses, definitions of situations, and consummations.

On a Durkheimian view, however, what was crucial for an appreciation of human action were the conditions under which, and means by which, it took place; also the norms in terms of which choices between acts were guided. Over and against action, therefore, were certain structures which implied constraint, even coercion, and which existed and endured over and above the actions of particular individuals, lending to individuals' acts a certain social and cultural regularity. What social science should study, therefore, was how such formal structures were created and how precisely they determined individual behaviour. To the extent that 'agency' existed, in short, it was a quality which derived from, and resided in, certain collective representations: in the social fact of a *conscience collective*; only in their pre-socialized, animal nature (a pathological state within a socio-cultural milieu) were individuals able to initiate action which was not predetermined in this way.

Much of the literature on agency since the time of Weber and Durkheim has sought to resolve these differences, and explore the limits on individual capacities to act independently of structural constraints. Despite attempts at compromise, moreover, the division does not prove an easy one to overcome. Either, in more individualistic or liberal vein, one argues that structures are an abstraction which individuals create and

1

which cannot be said to determine, willy-nilly, the action of their makers. Or else, in more collectivist and communitarian vein, one argues that structures are in fact *sui generis* and determine the very nature of individual consciousness and character; so that individuals' 'acts' are merely the manifestation of an institutional reality, and a set of structural relations.

Numerous claims to compromise have been put forward, nonetheless, most famously by Parsons (the theory of social action and pattern variables, e.g. 1977), by Berger and Luckmann (the theory of the social construction of reality, 1966), by Giddens (structuration theory, 1984), and by Bourdieu (the theory of practice and the *habitus*, 1977). In each case, however, the theorist can be seen to end by privileging one or other of the above options; the compromise is hard to sustain. Hence, a division between social structure and individual agency is collapsed in favour of either a liberal or a communitarian world-view – and more usually (certainly regarding the above claimants) the latter (cf. Rapport 1990).

For example, for Bourdieu, to escape from vulgarly mechanistic models of socio-cultural determinism is not to deny the objectivity of prior conditions and means of action and so reduce acts' meaning and origin to the conscious intentions and deliberations of individuals. What is called for is a more subtle approach to consciousness where, in place of a simple binary distinction between the conscious and the unconscious, one recognizes a continuum. One also recognizes that the greater part of human experience lies between the two poles, and may be called 'the domain of habit': most consciousness is 'habitual'. It is here that socialization and early learning put down their deepest roots; it is here that culture becomes encoded on the individual body, and the body becomes a mnemonic device for the communication and expression of cultural codes (of dress and gender; of propriety and normalcy; of control and domination). Competency in social interaction is also to be found in the habitual domain between the two poles: individuals act properly by not thinking about it. In short, the wide provenance of habit in human behaviour is a conduit for the potency of processes of exterior determination and institutionalization. Objective social structures produce the '*habitus*': a system of durable, transposable dispositions which function as the generative basis of structured, objectively unified, social practices. Such dispositions and practices may together be glossed as 'culture', an acquired system of habitual behaviour which generates (determines) individuals' schemes of action. In short, social structures produce culture which, in turn, generates practices which, finally, reproduce social structures.

In this way, the 'compromise' which Bourdieu provides ends up being a structurally causal model based on reified abstractions and materialist determinations. While claiming to transcend the dualism between structure and agency Bourdieu remains firmly rooted in a communitarian objectivism. While claiming to reject deterministic logic which eschews individual action, what there is of the latter (the intentionless convention of regulated improvisation) is merely a medium and expression of social-structural replication; what (habitual) subjectivity is allowed for in Bourdieu's portrayal is heavily overdetermined by social process. Agency is reduced to a seemingly passive power of reacting (habitually) to social-structural prerequisites (cf. Jenkins 1992).

Creativity and imagination

What social science often effects when faced with irresolvable opposition is a change in the terms of the debate. Thus, fresh purchase is gained on the relationship between social structure and individual agency when 'creativity' is introduced: the creativity of an individual agent in relation to the structures of a socio-cultural milieu.

Extrapolating from processes of fission and fusion (of 'schismogenesis') among the New Guinean Iatmul, Bateson concluded that each human individual should be conceived of as an 'energy source' (1972: 126). For here was something fuelled by its own processes (metabolic, cognitive and other) rather than by external stimuli, and which was capable of, and prone to, engagement in its own acts. Furthermore, this energy then imposed itself on the world, energizing certain events, causing certain relations and giving rise to an interaction between things organic and inorganic, which were then perceived to be 'orderly' or 'disorderly'.

Human individuals were active participants in the world, in short. Indeed, inasmuch as their energy determined the nature of certain relations and objects in the world, individuals could be said to be creators of worlds. For what could be understood by 'order' or 'disorder' were certain relationships between certain objects which individuals came to see as normal and normative or as abnormal and pathological; here were some from an infinite number of possible permutations of objects and relations in the world, whose classification and evaluation were dependent on the eye of the perceiver. But there was nothing necessary, objective or absolute about either designation; 'disorder' and 'order' were statements as construed by individual, purposive, perceiving entities and determined by individuals' states of mind. Between these latter there was great diversity, however, both at any one time and place and between times and places. What was random or chaotic for one perceiver may be orderly and informational for another, which in turn gave rise to the disputational, conflictual and ever-changing nature of social relations and cultural arrangements.

Bateson's commentary was widely appreciated, taken on, for instance, by psychiatrist R.D. Laing, and his definition of a person as 'an origin of actions', and 'a centre of orientation of the objective universe' (1968: 20). Strong echoes of Bateson also occur in Edmund Leach's alluding to the imaginative operations of the individual human mind and its 'poeticism': its untrammelled and unpredictable and non-rule-bound nature (1976a: 5). 'You are your creativity', Leach could conclude (1976b).

It is useful also to broaden the focus and remark upon the convergences between Bateson's ethnographic conclusions and Existentialism's philosophic ones. As Sartre famously put it, 'being precedes essence': each human being makes himself what he is, creating, and recreating continually, himself and his world. Of course, individuals are born into certain socio-cultural situations, into certain historical conditions, but they are responsible for the sense they (continue to) make out of them: the meaning they grant them, the way they evaluate and act towards them. Indeed, individuals are for ever in the process of remaking their meanings, senses, evaluations and actions; they negate the essence of their own creations and create again. They might seem to be surrounded by the 'actual facts' of an objective historico-socio-cultural present, but they can nonetheless transcend the latters' brutishness, and hence surpass a mere being-in-the-midst-of-things by attaining the continuous possibility of imagined meanings. Between the (structurally) given and what this becomes in an individual life there is a perennial (and unique) interplay; individual experience cannot be reduced to objective determinants (cf. Kearney 1988: 225–41).

Imagination is the key in this depiction: the key resource in consciousness, the key to human being. Imagination is an activity in which human individuals are always engaged; and it is through their imagination that individuals create and recreate the essence of their being, making themselves what they were, are and will become. As Sartre put it, imagination has a 'surpassing and nullifying power' which enables individuals to escape being 'swallowed up in the existent'; it frees them from given reality, and allows them to be other than how they might seem to be made (1972: 273). Because of imagination, human life has an emergent quality, characterized by a going-beyond: going-beyond a given situation, a set of circumstances, a status quo, going-beyond the conditions that produced it. Because of imagination, the human world is possessed of an intrinsically dynamic order which individuals, possessed of self-consciousness, are continually in the process of forming and designing. Because they can imagine, human beings are transcendentally free; imagination grants individuals that margin of freedom outside conformity which 'gives life its savor and its endless possibilities for advance' (Riesman 1954: 38).

Imagination issues forth into the world in the form of an ideally 'gratuitous' act, gratuitous inasmuch as it is seemingly uncalled for in terms of existent reality: unjustifiable, 'without reason, ground or proof' (*Chambers Dictionary*). For here is an act which surpasses rather than merely conserves the givenness in which it arises, which transcends the apparent realities of convention, which seems to resist the traditional constraints by which life is being lived. The gratuitous act appears to come from nowhere and pertain to nothing, something more or less meaningless in terms of the sense-making procedures which are currently instituted and legitimated; what is gratuitous is beyond debt and guilt, beyond good and evil.

Finally, then, it is the gratuitousness of the creative act of human imagination which makes it inherently conflictual; for, between the imagination and what is currently and conventionally lived there will be a constant tension. The indeterminacy of the relationship between individual experience and objective forms of life – the dialectical irreducibility of conventional socio-cultural conceptualizations on the one side and conscious individual imaginings on the other – means that the becoming of new meanings will always outstrip the present being of socio-cultural conditions. For, while what is currently lived is itself the issue of past imaginative acts of world-creation, and dependent on continuing individual practice for its continuing institutionality, inevitably, present imaginative acts will be moving to new possible futures; in the process of creating a new world, existing worlds are inexorably appropriated, reshaped and reformed. Or, to turn this around, the continuity of the conventional is an achievement and a conscious decision (not a mindless conformity) which must be continually worked for – consensually agreed upon or else forcibly imposed.

Anthropology and creativity

The essence of being human, Leach argued, is to resent the domination of others and the dominion of present structures (1977: 19–20). Hence, all human beings are 'criminals by instinct', predisposed to set their creativity against current system, intent on defying and reinterpreting custom. Indeed, it is the rule-breaking of 'inspired individuals' which leads to new social formations and on which cultural vitality depends. Nevertheless, the hostility of creativity to systems as are, means that its exponents are likely to be initially categorized and labelled as criminal or insane – even if their ultimate victorious overturning of those systems' conservative morality precipitates their redefining as heroic, prophetic or divine.

Narrowing the discussion of the existential imagination to more strictly anthropological work once more, Leach's is a good place to start. That of Victor Turner provides another (1974, 1982a). Abstracting from the ritual practices undertaken in the liminal period of Ndembu rites of passage, Turner could understand the entire symbolic creation of human worlds as turning on the relation between the formal fixities of social structure and the fluid creativity of liminoidal 'communitas'. Drawing on Sartre's dialectic between 'freedom and inertia' (as Leach drew on Camus's 'essential rebellion'), Turner theorized that society could be regarded as a process in which the two 'antagonistic principles', the 'primordial modalities', of structure and creativity could be seen interacting, alternating, in different fashions and proportions in different places and times. Creativity appeared dangerous – anarchic, anomic, polluting – to those in positions of authority, administration or arbitration within existing structures, and so prescriptions and prohibitions attempted precisely to demarcate proper and possible behavioural expressions. But, notwithstanding, ideologies of otherness (as well as spontaneous manifestations of otherness) would erupt from the interstices between structures and usher in opposed and original behavioural proprieties for living outside society (ritually if not normatively) or else refashioning in its image society as such.

Or again, in his *Someone, No One. An Essay on Individuality* (1979), Kenelm Burridge formulated a theoretical model similarly based on a processual relationship between social structure and individual creativity. If 'persons' were understood to be products of material (socio-historico-cultural) conditions, and lived within the potential of given concepts – feeding on and fattened by them, killing for and being killed by them – so individuals existed in spite of such concepts and conditions, seeking the disorderly and the new and refusing to surrender to things as they were or as traditional intellectualizations and bureaucratizations wished them to be. For to 'become' an individual was to abandon self-realization through the fulfilment of normative social relations, and to concentrate one's individual intuitions, perceptions and behaviour instead on the dialectical relationship 'between what is and what might be' (1979: 76).

Moreover, 'individuality' might be how one identified the practice of moving to the status of being individual, Burridge expounded, something of which each 'organism' was capable. What individuality did, in effect, was to transform the person, a social someone, into a social no-one – an 'eccentric' at least. However, if others were willing to accept for themselves – as new intellectualizations, a new morality – the conceptual creations of the 'eccentric' individual, then the move from someone to no-one culminated in their becoming a new social someone, a new 'person'. That is, persons were the endpoint of 'heroic' individuals, individuals who had persuaded (or been mimicked by) others into also realizing new social conditions, rules, statuses, roles; for here, individuality dissolved into a new social identity. Indeed, Burridge concluded, the cycle of: 'someone' to 'no-one' to 'someone', was inevitable, and individuality a 'thematic fact of culture' (1979: 116). Here was the universal instrument of the moral variation, the disruption, the renewal and the innovation which were essential to human survival, whether for hunters-and-gatherers, pastoralists, subsistence agriculturalists, peasants, village people, townsfolk or city-dwellers. Different material conditions may eventuate in situations which variously allowed, encouraged or inhibited moves to the individual and moments of creative apperception, but over and above this, individuals' creativity meant that they continually created the conditions and situations which afforded them their opportunity.

In sum, there were ever individuals who were determined to be 'singletons': to interact with others and with established rationalizations in non-predefined ways, to escape from the burden of given cultural prescriptions and discriminations, and so usher in the unstructured and as yet unknown. Whether courtesy of (Aborigine) Men of High Degree, (Cuna) shamans, (Nuer) Leopard-Skin Chiefs, (Hindu) Sanyasi, or (American) hippies, new intellectualizations were always being proffered by way of the agency of new individuals.

Anthropology and agency

The new social structures to which individual creativity gives rise soon petrify. In gaining independence from their individual creators, structurings of the world congeal into fixed, objectified, generalized, institutionalized cultural forms. However, all the while, the creative impulse, the active drive to individuality, goes on. It is the fate of individual agency ever to find itself threatened (and possibly stultified) by structure which is inappropriate to its creative needs – even a structure of its own one-time creation – and yet, the tension between the forms of social life and its creative processes provides the dynamic of cultural history.

For Burridge, the very same dynamic pertains to the world and writing of social science. Individual creativity provided the apperceptions which made an anthropological world-view possible, but then routine anthropological analysis tends to fix, objectify, generalize and institutionalize its socio-cultural object. Individuals become transformed into persons, events into categories, and the continuous vicissitudes of life into a constraining and stultifying, logical and orderly structure.

It has seemed, therefore, that individual creativity has remained a submerged strand in anthropological elucidation, drowned out by social-structural rigours and demands. The latter, especially in their 'deep' French manifestations (Lévi-Strauss, Godelier, Dumont), but also their 'conventional' Anglo-Saxon ones (Radcliffe-Brown, Fortes, Gellner), have been seen as more or less *sui generis* mechanisms which determine relations between elements of a society – indeed, to an extent determine those elements (their being and behaviours) *tout court* (cf. Park 1974). Individual agency has come to be buried under the vast weight of the collectivity. But then, contemporary ethnography, and a disinterring of a line of thought (from Bateson to Leach and Barth, Turner and Burridge, and on) which recognizes (*à la* Existentialism) an intrinsic agency to human being whereby individuals possess the power to be self-caused and free, does serve as a corrective.

For example, defining creativity as 'human activities that transform existing cultural practices', activities that, courtesy of a 'creative persona', emerge from traditional forms and yet move beyond them and reshape them (Rosaldo *et al.* 1993: 5–6), the volume *Creativity/Anthropology* (dedicated to Victor Turner) brings together cases of creative 'eruption' from different societies and cultures: the !Kung (Shostak), for instance, the Cochiti (Babcock), and Asturias (Fernandez). Here is social structure understood as 'discursive idiom' (Jackson 1989: 20): a shared language which may provide the basis (the form) of individual interpretation, which may articulate, mediate and typify individual experience, but which cannot be taken at face value as encompassing, capturing or determining that experience (cf. Parkin 1987: 66). Social structure, here, is not *sui generis*, and does not exist through inertia; it depends on the continuing, conscious, concerted activity of different individuals to intend, produce and sustain it (cf. Holy and Stuchlik 1981: 15–16). Furthermore, social structure does not inexorably give rise to homogeneity, stability, consistency or communication. As a discursive idiom, a fiction, it is always subject to creative interpretation, to individual manipulation and re-rendering, to 'alter-cultural action' (Handler and Segal 1990: 87).

In this way, anthropology has begun more concertedly to fill in the gaps in the ethnographic record of relations between convention and creativity, social structure and individual agency.

See also: **Consciousness, Individuality, Transaction, World-Making**

ALTERITY

The concept of alterity has only recently, in the 1990s, acquired an important place within the vocabulary of anthropology. This more general acceptance of the notion of 'otherness' as a major concern for anthropological consideration comes in the wake of innumerable writings over the past two decades that have been seriously engaged in a critique of all those grand 'isms' of modernist thought (evolutionism, functionalism, structuralism, and so forth) that are implicated in Western civilization's imperialist and capitalist past. A striking characteristic of this literature is that it consistently blurs the boundaries normally held between such disciplines as philosophy, sociology, anthropology, history. For instance, the writings of Zygmunt Bauman, a 'sociologist', are relevant to all the neighbouring fields of study within the human sciences, and also those of literary and cultural studies. Two very interesting and significant results of such crossing of disciplinary boundaries are that (1) unless one is 'in the know' it is often very difficult to pinpoint the author's disciplinary attachment, and (2) the traditional boundaries between the social sciences and the humanities are being systematically dissolved. The reason for the latter is that the primary resolve of this recent talk about 'alterity' – about, in other words, the concept and treatment of the alien objectified other – is to shake the foundation of the objectifying thrust of the human sciences, along with all its claims of scientific authority and objectivity.

Anthropology and the imperialized other

By definition anthropology's primary object for study has been the Western imperialized other (while sociology has had the task of objectifying the West's own internal subaltern classes). Thus, as anthropology is the academic discipline most *overtly* involved in an objectified imagery of otherness, it has become the obvious target of much post-colonial critique (e.g. Asad 1975; Said 1978; Thomas 1994; de Certeau 1997;

9

Bauman 1995; Fabian 1983). The incorporation of the concept of alterity into anthropology itself reflects a strong contemporary awareness within the discipline of the iniquities of its past, its own particular programme of scientific objectification. It must face its own centrality in the provision of constructions of otherness central to the vision of modernity (cf. di Leonardo 1998). Having lost its innocence, anthropology is now in an 'age of self-reflection', a process through which it often joins other post-colonial voices in a critique of the grand narratives of modernism. This exercise of addressing the past engagement of the discipline (whether naive or otherwise) in the creation of colonial agendas can be painful, especially when addressing what the political implications of some of our narratives of otherness have been for the great majority of peoples who have been marginalized in the name of the dogma derived from them. One thing is certain. The programme of decolonizing our ways of thinking about otherness means that the anthropology practised today is not the same as yesterday's.

The irony is that because of its historical expertise in the study of otherness, its specific voice can be a strong one raised against the dark side of colonialist excess. It has strengths unparalleled by other traditional fields of study, except perhaps history, in that it understands the importance of the *particular*, and thus the *local*, over against the universalist and the global. Anthropologists *contextualize* specific lifeways by keeping intact the systems of values and practice to which each is tied. Careful anthropologists do not usually go around making global, universalist sweeping statements. The cultural relativism of anthropology has been subjected to major attack by all those defensive defenders of universalist modernist models of human nature (cf. Hollis and Lukes 1982), and conversely praised by defenders of more humanist, perspectival concerns (MacIntyre 1985; Taylor 1985). Ever since Malinowski's famous work with the Trobriand Islanders in the South Pacific in the second decade of the twentieth century, the claim has also been that a major aim is to understand 'the native's' point of view, which provides, it would seem, a multi-perspectival framework for all analysis and conclusions. In other words, anthropologists should know well how to understand the perspective of the other, and to refrain from creating a fantasized other easily digestible for Western colonialist and scientific consumption. So where did things go wrong?

The birth of anthropology and Europe's intellectual climate

The fact is that anthropology had its birth as an academic discipline in the late nineteenth and early twentieth centuries, during what we might label the height of modernist thought – and at the apex of Western imperialist endeavours. Modernist and imperialist ways of thinking about things go very deep, and since anthropology could but be the child of its times, the intellectual and political climate of those times is deeply implicated in its own development. This is why present-day anthropology is mainly involved in a scrutiny of its own discourse on the primitive other, an ongoing deconstruction of its major concepts toward the end of uncovering the intellectual effects of the imperialist, Enlightenment and post-Enlightenment thought, and the practical, political implications of them.

The brand new science of anthropology was faced at the turn of the century with the necessity of claiming its own intellectual space, over which it could be the guardian of truth and objectivity. It needed to produce its own object (cf. Fabian 1983). It was Malinowski, cited above as the promoter of 'the native point of view', who set the standards, the rules and norms, for modern ethnographic writing. Ethnography is the recording of an *ethnos*, and, as Peter Mason phrases it (1990: 13), 'a form of translation and reduction'. 'All ethnography', he goes on to say (*ibid*.), 'is an experience of the confrontation with Other set down in writing, an act by which that Other is deprived of its specificity'. He notes that such writing conforms to particular stylistic and literary conventions. It must meet certain expectations. In producing a discourse on the Trobrianders, 'Malinowski was creating a work which is of the same substance intellectually as, say, James Joyce's Bloomsday' (Mason 1990: 13; cf. Ardener 1985: 57). Thus there is a sense in which 'the Trobrianders' as presented through this discourse do not have empirical reality, for, being the product of the ethnographic scientific discourse, they are but fiction.

The rhetorical genre which Malinowski created led to what Mason calls (1990: 13) 'the naturalist or realist' monograph. It was a form of anthropological writing that was followed throughout the period of modernism, which Ardener (1985) situates between 1920 and 1975 for anthropology. In short, this *realist* genre through which the ethnographer presented his or her object (as an example of the West's colonized other of the South Pacific, Africa, or Australia) followed the naturalist pattern set by other *studies of nature*, those of the flora and fauna of far-flung parts of the world. Mason quite rightly classifies (1990: 6, 15–17) 'the objects' of such studies of humans as the stuff of *imaginary worlds*, or the world of myth. Through the realist rhetoric of the anthropologist, the Trobrianders were *naturalized*, and thereby belong to one of those worlds transcended by modern civilization to be marked as an uncivilized part of nature, something which, to the modern spirit, was to be dominated and tamed. To objectify is to naturalize, and therefore to create distance between self and the object, whether it be animate or inanimate, human or stone. This ability of the scientist to move away from and transcend the object of enquiry is a measure of its arbitrariness, and thus lack of reason (cf. Bauman 1995: 163). We see then that anthropological realism is not an innocent, value-free task, for it is a highly coloured presentation of a very specific kind. As such it is a *creation* of 'the reality of the other', and not a *representation*; as a creation it has its own 'reality effect' (cf. Mason 1990). Such presentations acquire their special signifying power by taking their place within a network of other imaginary worlds also created in the modernist spirit by the rest of the human sciences as they made their fit with the natural sciences. Within all these fields of human studies our own historically contingent and local values, truths and practices were usually raised to absolute principles from which all deviance was judged, dismissed, or, even worse, ignored. For example, the eighteenth-century value upon a particular type of logic and reasoning became the defining attribute of human nature.

Eurocentrism and the inferiorization of excluded others

It is probably a truism that all peoples are ethnocentric. It is also more than likely that ethnocentric constructions of the stranger always follow a process through which alterity is reduced to a familiar form that is easily accessible to self. All systems of otherness are structures of identity and difference that have more to do with the establishment of *self*-identity than with the empirical reality of the other – whether their neighbours, trading partners, enemies, conquered peoples, or spirits that populate other worlds. This does not mean that we should consider all ethnocentrism or concepts of difference as the same, or as following an identical structure. Strangers might often be considered monsters; but peoples' concepts of the monstrous are not only splendidly diverse, they also have considerably different implications for the ways in which the self can interact with them. In all systems of alterity there is at least some interplay of the principles of *inclusivity* and *exclusion* which together provide the rules and norms for such interaction. In this play, the nature of the boundaries designating otherness varies tremendously from one people to the next: for some, who give weight to inclusivity, they are highly permeable, while for others they are rather rigid, which speaks of a more exclusivist set of values.

The literature on Western systems of alterity is now enormous, for Western civilization's treatment of the other throughout its modernist phase of development and expansion is the mainstay of all post-colonialist writings today. The stress time and again is that Western creations of difference and images of otherness are *products of a process of exclusion* (e.g. see Todorov 1987; Pagden 1982; Hulme 1986; Mason 1990; Lindqvist 1996 [1992]; Bauman 1995; Corbey 1991; Karstens 1991; de Certeau 1997; Duerr 1985; Fardon 1995a; Hiller 1991a; Thomas 1994; Said 1978; Bhabha 1994). The exclusivist ideology, which assumes the superiority of self *vis-à-vis* all others, is a very good strategy through which to disempower others. In the writings of Todorov, Pagden and Hulme, we have been presented with highly interesting discussions of the development during the conquest of the Americas of the European imagery of, and discourse on, the 'radical otherness' of the New World's indigenous peoples, especially those of the Caribbean and Amazonia. In colonial discourse the populations of the Americas appeared for the most part as the exotic and pathological antithesis of what the conquerors thought themselves to be. Through a principle of *inversion*, the difference between self and other was understood to be absolute. The most virulent argument for the inferiority of the American Indian was given by the lawyer, Sepúlveda, in his debate conducted in Valladolid in 1550–51 with the priest, Bartolomé de Las Casas, on the question of whether the indigenous peoples were human (see Hanke 1959; Pagden 1982: 117–18; Mason 1990: 52–3). Sepúlveda's characterization of the Indian was of a creature who was child-like, irrational, savage and incontinent as an animal, to be contrasted with the adult, rational, cultured, tame (gentle) European. Through the principle of inversion, the cultures of America became defined as an ensemble of negations to be contrasted with the civilized and cultured society of the developing ruling classes of Europe.

An insightful observation of Mason (1990: Ch. 2) in his discussions of Eurocentrism is that the imagery of the exotic that was used for the American Indian was but a projection of the imagery signifying both lack and excess already in use by the European upper classes for their own *internal* other. In other words, the Europeans, in conquering the Americas, in particular Amazonia, fixed the status of Native Americans at the level of the lower echelons of their own society, placing them alongside the Jew, the mad, the wild, the child, the peasant, the Gypsy and the witch. Incorporated into this language of alterity used to characterize both domestic and foreign European others was the rich imagery of the non-European monstrous and fabulous races depicted in Greek and Roman travel lore and described in Pliny's *Historia Naturalis*, a text that had great appeal throughout the Middle Ages and that also enjoyed considerable popularity during the sixteenth century

(Mason 1990: Ch. 3). The imagery of the brutish giant – the naked, bestial, and cannibalistic wild man – along with his cohort, the sexually profligate, cannibalistic wild woman especially caught the imagination of medieval Europe. These images, applied to Europe's internal subaltern classes, were transported to the New World and utilized for its inhabitants, as evidenced, for instance, by Sir Walter Raleigh's giant and headless Ewaipanoma, a people of the Guianas, who Raleigh says had 'eyes in their shoulders, and their mouths in the middle of their breasts' (in Mason 1990: 108). The image of the sexually deviant and monstrous cannibal heathen (with his or her culinary, religious and sexual perversions) covered both Europe's internal and external others (Mason 1990: 44).

Such 'inferiorization' of excluded others became a constant throughout the development of European thought. It developed by the nineteenth century into a unifying discourse upon alterity that was structured further by the increasingly popular language of evolutionism. With its stress upon the progressive move of humankind from the primitive to the civilized, such imagery had clear and powerful implications for the colonial enterprise (Corbey and Leerssen 1991; Lindqvist 1996 [1992]:104). If it can be argued, as Edward Said has done, that the Orient is a product of a Western hegemonic exoticism, the same can certainly be said for Native America as it too became the primitive other to Europe's civilized self (see Said 1978; Overing 1996a). Anthropology, as evidenced by its technical vocabulary on the primitive, has hardly been exempt from the encroachment of the prevalent European language of exoticism, and certainly not from the rhetoric which signifies and stresses lack. Peter Rivière (1984), commenting on the state of Amazonian ethnography, notes that through it Amazonian peoples are best known, not for what they are, but for what they *are not* – stateless, with no government, no lineages, no descent groups, no structure, no. . . .

Two solutions to alterity: anthropophagia and anthropoemia

Lévi-Strauss, in the chapter entitled 'A Little Glass of Rum' in *Tristes Tropiques* (1961), discusses the contrast between two solutions for neutralizing the dangers of the other, the anthropophagic versus the anthropoemic strategy (cf. Bauman 1995: 179–80). He notes that the first, the strategy of cannibalism, is repellent to Western sensibilities as the most barbaric of all customs. It is, however, a widely spread notion of native Amazonia that the powers of the self acquire their human potency only by assimilating the powers of dangerous others (Overing Kaplan 1981). For some Amazonian peoples the process must be literal, through the ingestion of the ground-up bones of a relative (otherness itself is a highly ambiguous state in Amazonia), as among the Yanomami, or the eating of a fragment of an enemy corpse as occurred among the Tupinamba. For others, it is the *idea* of 'cannibalism' (at least from our point of view) that frames their understanding of human life (see Overing 1996a). Thus to marry fits within this structure (one marries a stranger who becomes absorbed physically and socially as kin), as too does the eating of meat and vegetables (they both were human at the beginning of time). The ideal is to *assimilate* the other, and in order to achieve a life that is human this process of incorporation must be constant. There is the widespread Amazonian message that alterity is the hallmark of this-worldly *social* living: the achievement of the social state itself, and hence of the world of the interior, requires the force and creative powers of those different from self. Without consuming the powers of others, there can be no fertility and no productive capacity. Such an *anthropophagic* strategy of dealing with alterity follows the *inclusivist* route: we incorporate the powers of the other into our own body – and body social.

Lévi-Strauss comments (1961: 386) on our own ethnocentrism in being appalled on moral grounds by either actual or ritual cannibalism. To condemn cannibalist practices implies for instance a belief in bodily resurrection, which would be compromised with the material destruction of the corpse. This would be a religious belief of the same order as those in which ritualized cannibalism is practised. He suggests that there is no good reason why one belief should be preferred over the next. Lévi-Strauss also proposes that our own strategies would in turn appear highly *un*civilized, repugnant and barbaric to the native Amazonian. He gives as example our own judicial and penitentiary customs which neutralize the powers of dangerous others through a process of *anthropoemia* (from the Greek *emein*, to vomit). As Lévi-Strauss says (*ibid.*), our judicial procedures 'expel these formidable beings from the body public by isolating them for a time, or forever, denying them all contact with humanity, in establishments devised for that express purpose'. This is the *exclusivist* strategy, which severs all *social* links with the other. For the Amazonian this solution is an outrageous denial of humanity.

As a postscript to Lévi-Strauss's observations, we might add that the West has a history of its own *anthropophagic* practices, the reasoning for which being very similar to those of indigenous peoples of the Americas, i.e. that they revitalize and give health! Medicinal cannibalism in

Western medicine has a long history, and was especially popular in the sixteenth and seventeenth centuries when Paracelsian medical philosophy was followed. According to Beth Conklin (1998; cf Gordon-Grube 1988), Europeans consumed human blood, fingers, hands, fat and liver, bones and bone marrow as treatments for arthritis, sciatica, reproductive difficulties, skin problems. The public executions of criminals were a main source of blood and other body parts – blood drunk from people who died violently was considered especially potent. According to Peacock (1896: 270–1, and see in Conklin 1998), epileptics were reported to 'stand around the scaffold in crowds, cup in hand, ready to quaff the red blood as it flows from the still quavering body'. It is probable that the indigenous peoples of America would have found some of such practices exotically fascinating. Whether they would regard the anthropophagic practice in the West today of transplanting hearts, kidneys, lungs and livers as exotically monstrous is another question.

Inclusivity and exclusivity as political solutions

Overing argues (1996a) that the contrast of an emphasis on either inclusive or exclusive solutions for dealing with otherness can relate respectively to egalitarian and hierarchical political strategies, and to a difference between social philosophies that stress social symmetry and those that are attached to social asymmetry. As mentioned, native peoples of Amazonia were identified with Europe's subaltern classes. The signifying quality of otherness in Eurocentrism, certainly as it was elaborated as political and colonial discourse, was first and foremost that of inferiority. The gaze was that of the conqueror who took for granted a natural order premised upon conquest and the relations of super-ordination and subordination that might emerge from it. So extreme was the strength of this notion of the inferiority of the other that the divide between the self and other easily slipped into the opposition of the human and the non-human. The Eurocentric discourse, born within a hegemonic and totalizing rhetoric of hierarchy, is deeply exclusive in its view of humanity. It allows might to the conquerors alone. In contrast, the ethnocentrism of indigenous Amazonian discourse can best be understood as being based upon a rhetoric of equality, and its expressions of alterity are much more inclusive in its categorization of humanity. Here power does not accrue to self alone.

The indigenous peoples of Amazonia have no 'lower echelon' classes, and for most of its indigenous social groupings, certainly those of the Guianas, where the persistent destabilization of hierarchy in personal relations is the norm, it would be a misconstrual to identify specific social divisions or whole categories of people within them as inferior or subordinate to others (cf. Overing 1993a; Thomas 1982). Since the *right* to domination is alien to the understanding most native people have of proper social relationships (cf. Clastres 1977), they would not judge external others, even if monstrous, as *inferior* beings who were *therefore* rightfully subject to their domination. Instead we find a certain tolerance of difference (as well as a fascination, fear and strong desire for it). Moreover, the boundary between self and other tends to slip and slide; it is difficult to draw, as too is the distinction between human and non-human. Among the Piaroa of the Venezuelan Guiana, the root metaphor for alterity in their rhetoric was the lascivious and monstrous cannibal other – a character ironically very similar to the Spanish conquerors' imaginary other (Overing 1996a; cf. Mason 1990). However, for the Piaroa such an image did not preclude in any complete sense themselves. The 'cannibal other' devours people; the Piaroa cook and eat animals and plants which are transformed humans. There is always an ambiguity to the Piaroa language of alterity, for their stress is upon the plight of human existence as might generally be the case (for both self and other), and therefore upon the potential for the irrational and the villainous, as well as the positive strengths in human power; whereas in the European vision evil and danger are usually assumed to come from without, not from within.

It is true that in the nineteenth century, many European authors, influenced by the Romantics' rebellion against the rationalism of the Enlightenment, also stressed in a positive way the non-rational, emotional and wild aspects of a creative interior self. However, by contrast, psychoanalytic theory was to be put to the service of taming the neurotic, the uncontrolled, aggressive and lascivious beast within. As Raymond Corbey has so convincingly argued in his essay on the role of alterity in the architecture of psychoanalytical theory, Freud's understanding of the monstrous primal man within civilized man was in accordance with a nineteenth-century discourse on savagery and civilization and its pervasive association of prehistoric or contemporary 'primitives' with the wild, the impulsive, the childish and the excessive (Corbey 1991: 49). It was a discourse that operated with the same polar opposites used by Sepúlveda in the sixteenth century: the opposition between contemporary and primitive society, culture and nature, man and beast, men and women, white and black, adult and child. These were distinctions used in a *privative* way (cf. Karstens 1991: 78–81). All of the second pole of opposites lack essentially what is of quality in self: women, beasts, primitives and children lack reason, civilization and control. They are but inversions of self. A convinced Lamarckian, Freud assumed that the nature and experience of prehistoric humans were still relevant to the understanding of modern 'civilized' man: the primitive still lives within us, internalized, as a sort of lascivious and violent monster that it is the tragedy of modern civilized man to have to control. As Corbey concludes (1991: 55–6), 'The world within as Freud constructed it is intricately related to that of a nineteenth-century civilizatory discourse on races, sexes, classes and empire, and the wild other who inhabits this world within turns out to be an avatar of the colonial and sexual others constructed in this discourse'. This is also the discourse that anthropology inherited, and with which it still is having to contend.

See also: **Gender, Humanism, Post-Modernism, The Rural Idyll, The Unhomely**

AUTO-ANTHROPOLOGY

The concept of auto-anthropology was defined (deliberately ambiguously and tautologically) by Marilyn Strathern as: 'anthropology carried out in the social context which produced it' (1987: 17). More generously, the concept covers the notions of an anthropological study of one's own, one's home and one's self, and explores that murky ground, at once physical, phenomenological, psychological, social and personal, which 'an anthropology at home' gives onto.

Auto-anthropology is situated at the confluence of a number of important debates in anthropology, concerning the very nature and status of the anthropological project: 'Is anthropology politically correct as an undertaking?'; 'Is anthropology better undertaken in certain geo-physical settings than others?'; 'Is anthropology necessarily undertaken in certain existential states of mind?'; and 'Is anthropology best seen as a universal attitude towards social life, an ethnomethodology in the construction of social relations?'. These questions all pertain to the place of reflexivity both in the life of a professional, primarily Western and university, discipline such as anthropology, and also in the lives of those whom anthropology has undertaken to study.

Is anthropology politically correct as an undertaking?

In a political situation very different from that in which modern anthropology was born, a situation in which erstwhile relations between the 'West and the rest', between Euro-American cultures and societies and others (of the 'South', the 'under-developed', the 'Second, Third and Fourth Worlds'), have come to be described and decried as colonialistic, exploitative and imperialistic, the project of anthropology has itself been called into question. Is it possible to see anthropology as anything but a set of Western discourses and practices? Is it not irremediably tainted both by its birthplace and history and by its continuing intent to translate and compare (define and circumscribe) otherness?

One thing which an auto-anthropological awareness has instigated in the discipline, therefore, is an attempt to elucidate the unspoken analytical givens, concepts and techniques, historical and proximate, socio-cultural and personal, which the anthropologist inevitably brings to the work of engaging with others. Here is a reflexive awareness that 'adequate anthropological accounts cannot be crafted without acknowledging the forces – epistemological and political – that condition their writing' (Whitaker 1997: 470).

Such reflexivity had always been an implicit part of the modern discipline – Malinowski having been plagued by questions concerning why he was doing what he was doing, and how valid his data were – but now it becomes explicit, and linked to issues of ethics and power. Such a 'reflexive' turn was perhaps first noted by Bob Scholte (1969), in the context of a consideration of the politics of fieldwork undertaken by Americans in the wake of the Vietnam War, and in the face of local distaste at thus being studied. Anthropologists, Scholte advised, must always be aware of the political asymmetries which their activities presuppose; also how these are implicated in the epistemological privileges of so-called objectivity and neutrality. Fieldwork and analysis are in the end one praxis, and what is reflexively called for is a critical emancipatory exercise which would liberate the discipline from the vestiges of value-free scientism.

Matters came to a head in 1986 with the publication of two volumes, *Writing Culture. The Poetics and Politics of Ethnography* (edited by George Marcus and James Clifford) and *Anthropology as Cultural Critique. An Experimental Moment in the Human Sciences* (by Marcus and Fischer), and a flurry of intellectual activity which came to be known as 'The Writing Culture Debate'. This gave onto three central resolutions: (1) the scientific epistemology on which anthropology had been hitherto based – that anthropology would one day evolve the perfect language for describing 'real human nature' or 'real cultural essences' – was in fact a provincial, and politically unsavoury, Western specificity; (2) all writing was rhetorical, so any claims made by anthropologists about the others they studied spoke less of incontestable givens and more of the hegemonies of political and professional scriptural practice; (3) all so-called grand or meta narratives of knowledge and progress might be called into question and, by juxtaposing them against the equally specific narratives of diverse other cultures, deconstructed.

Anthropologists remain divided, however, on the matter of where this leaves the anthropological enterprise. Some (Prattis 1985) feel empowered reflexively to stand back and consider those discursive constraints on perception and knowledge production – others' as well as our own – and, by use of 'pragmatic methodologies', still make translations across cultural and personal boundaries (1996: 1073). Even if every language is partial and relative, unable to describe the diversity of human realities, then notwithstanding, a reflexive anthropology can hope to escape such tautology and unite observer and observed together in a new intersubjective space: a space of universal human being lying beyond language and culture. For some, in short, reflexivity shows the way towards a poetics by which we may access each other's individual experience beneath a multiplicity of cultural surfaces.

For others, a reflexive awareness points up the impossibility of ever studying 'others' except as a means further to define oneself – reducing otherness to a limiting space within one's own construction. There is no possibility of attempting to repair anthropological representation merely by being more self-conscious about it. 'Proper' representation can only ever be that effected from within a home environment, and all anthropology can properly attempt is an enabling or advocating of local voices; at most, anthropology can cause an accession of local voices to global platforms.

For still others, an eschewing of generalization and comparison, even of a description of otherness, tends towards a radical relativism which simply plays into the hands of conservatism and reaction. The so-called 'new' insights into the production of anthropological knowledge which reflexivity provides are simply partial reiterations of old Marxian ones, now redrafted into an elitist language which disables action and possible critique.

Is anthropology better undertaken in certain geo-physical settings than others?

Leaving aside questions of epistemology for a moment, the politics of post-colonialism has also meant that the geo-physical setting of much anthropological fieldwork has changed of late, and that many anthropologists are focusing on their own or home societies. This is not a wholly new situation (cf. Little 1948; Frankenberg 1957; Warner 1959), but more now than before anthropologists routinely find themselves (in Cheater's formulation (1987)) at once 'investigator and citizen'.

This situation has a number of causes and a number of consequences. As Jackson puts it (1987: 12), after a 'century-long flirtation with exotic fieldwork', anthropology has returned home (and seems home to stay) because research there is easier to access, cheaper and faster. More distant climes have become harder to reach due to decreasing Western funding, and due to suspicion elsewhere over Western research into local 'primitivism' or 'tribalism'; to hark back to a (pristine) tribal past is to practise a present intellectual neo-colonialism. At the same time, anthropologists have discovered a long-standing ignorance concerning their own Western societies – their histories and cultures – and the extent to which they are home to a diversity of socio-cultural practices and world-views. Surely there is a place for the micro-social methodology and specialism of anthropology in disinterring the underlying nature of life in the West?

As a consequence of work in Western societies, moreover, genuine theoretical advances, of relevance to all locations of anthropological study, have been made. For instance, anthropology at home brings to cognizance the true extent of individual mobility and social change in a milieu, and the way in which boundaries between cultural groupings are in constant flux. It has been an anthropological orthodoxy since the time of Malinowski that societies and cultures may be associated with bounded locations, and that thereby isolated and somehow timeless communities could be imaged and imagined in which anthropologists were to do their work. And yet it is now clear that anthropological places and regions can be constructed in this fashion only by way of arbitrary and political exclusions; Malinowski's Trobriand Islands were self-contained tribal isolates only at the expense of rendering others (White administrators, missionaries, traders, *et al.*) invisible. In fact, boundaries between separate cultures cannot be demarcated and areas are always interconnected; place is never coterminous with identity, geo-physical regions are never homogeneous, and any cultural groupings are only ever provisional.

For this reason, Okely (1996) would describe the erstwhile anthropological privileging of the study of 'other', exotically constructed regions, to the neglect of its 'home', as the discipline's worst example of exclusivity and elitism. Excluding study of its own centres of power, defining Europe, for instance, as outside its professional brief – because 'easy' or 'known' or the provenance of other disciplines – anthropology has missed both commonplaces elsewhere and exotica close by; it has mistakenly constituted itself as a regional as opposed to a theoretical specialism.

Anthropology 'at home', in short, has unique lessons to teach, concerning cultural ambiguity, hybridity and heterogeneity. The anthropologist of the West recognizes it as customary not exceptional, for instance, for a diversity of ways of thinking and being, a multiplicity of cultural realities and worlds, to co-exist in the same place. As anthropologists learn another language in the words of their mother tongue they see how surface similarities of form may hold contrary and subversive meanings (cf. Messerschmidt 1981).

On the other hand, anthropology at home has its own difficulties and dangers. It may not always be possible to gain that distantiation which has been the hallmark of anthropological method – so-called 'culture-shock', by which the conventions of local life are seen as strange and thereby calling for translation, if not 'explanation', by the anthropological observer. The anthropologist at home must sometimes work harder not to take things for granted and to make himself view things as a stranger might. Then again, as a citizen, the anthropologist expects to engage more mediately, not to say politically, with the socio-cultural milieu he is studying. Even if he does not see his writings as referring explicitly to the political situation of governance and the deployment of material and non-material resources, still those in power may make such direct links between the constructions of local intellectuals such as anthropologists and the workings of government policy. It may not be so easy for anthropologists at home to separate their academic from their more public pronouncements, and difficult, as Cheater puts it, to be a 'part-time citizen' (1987: 176). Nevertheless, as more 'indigenous anthropologists' (albeit usually Western-trained) set about undertaking research in their home communities – in New Guinea, Brazil, India, Africa and the erstwhile Communist world, as well as the West – this is a situation in which more find themselves.

There is an awareness now abroad, in sum, that anthropology dare not overlook its own, usually 'Western' space – Western exoticism and multiplicity – in some banal occidentalism (cf. Carrier 1995). Studying 'at home', in fact, can lead to an awareness and a promotion of anthropological disciplinary expertise as an enterprise theoretically and experientially (rather than geo-physically or regionally) validated and based.

Is anthropology best seen as a universal attitude towards social life, an ethnomethodology in the construction of social relations?

Powerful anthropological voices continue to be raised against an anthropology 'at home' in the West, nevertheless, even one practised alongside that of more 'exotic' locales. This opposition is both epistemological and political. It is said that many Western-based academic disciplines shine their light upon Western society and culture, from the humanities through the social sciences to the natural sciences, but only anthropology has taken as its central plank the decentring of the West, and the appreciating of other 'literatures', 'cultures' and 'sciences' (cf. Bloch 1988). At a time of Western retrenchment, in terms of the financing of research and of charitable aid overseas, and of a certain smugness concerning 'the end of history' and the domination of a Western model of national-democratic polity, it is all the more important that anthropology remain as flag-bearer of non-Western interests, in all possible senses.

Coincident with this is an argument that only via the radical disjunction of culture-shock is it at all possible to gain perspective either on oneself or on others. Anthropology at home in one's own culture is impossible because anthropological insight only derives from that 'contact zone' (Hastrup 1995b) which is set up when members of different cultures interact. As Ardener elaborates (1987), people's heads are full of concepts and categories 'generated by the social', and they spend their lives projecting these latter 'back upon the social'. But in ordinary circumstances, as 'native' actors, people do not perceive this, do not recognize this as representing their everyday experience and practice, because for them social space and the cultural worlds it contains are not objects of contemplation. Only the shock of the strange – the arrival of an anthropologist in an exotic community – breaks the quality of routine and automatism, both for the anthropologist and the locals, and makes what is normal unfamiliar; only then does one know whether one is 'at home' or not.

This makes 'anthropology at home' of only limited provenance and relevance, Strathern elaborates (1987). For all such reflexive or auto-anthropology can mean is rendering people's conception of themselves back to themselves. Anthropology is a folk discourse of the West (or, at least, an academically distilled and derived one), dealing with notions of 'society', 'culture', 'class', 'socialization', 'roles', 'relationships', 'community' and so on, because this is how a certain Western discourse has historically developed. Anthropology at home can only mean a recycling of these notions in a tautological fashion, and in no wise reaching an epistemological position from which they could be deconstructed (explained and critiqued). The only way beyond cultural discourses, concepts, categories, notions and genres, is via other such discourses: by setting up a contact zone as a *tertium quid* between radical differences.

In fact, this is what anthropology has done all along, and continues to do even when it claims to be working 'at home' in the West. Western anthropology is only possible because the anthropologist sets himself apart from his fellow 'citizens' and creates a discontinuity between his accounts of them and their accounts of themselves. And he is able to do this only by courtesy of the comparative ethnographic record: by his reading in other cultures and his drawing upon concepts and discourses which do not belong to the milieu under study. To this extent, inasmuch as such anthropological accounts set aside indigenous framings, accounts of the West are not so different from those of, say, Melanesia.

To recap, auto-anthropology is limited in its provenance on this view, not to say oxymoronic, because culture members cannot get a conceptual grasp of the conditions within which their lives are routinely lived except via radical cultural disjunctions. But such disjunctions rarely occur naturally. To the extent that anthropology sets itself up as the comparative study of cultural membership, then, its project is a strange one (is one concerning strangers) which will always distance it from the discourse of natives. There must always be this differentiation and a distance between the anthropological investigator and investigated because the latter are at home with certain kinds of discursive premises about social life while the former is at home in always attempting to displace such premises in a continuous round of tricksterish playing the *vis-à-vis*: anthropology offers 'an orgy of defamiliarization' to those at home in any one cultural world (Boon 1982). Moreover, anthropology achieves its aims only via specific disciplinary practices, namely the culture-shock of fieldwork – a new bodily becoming via immersion in new habitual practices – followed by writing up the experience in a theoretical language which is neither here nor there but both at once. While these practices may differentiate them from natives, they serve to link anthropologists together in a 'conversational community' of shared meanings, ideas and morals to which all belong. Finally, such an 'anthropological culture' can constitute a 'force field' which offers a site of resistance against Western givens and draws attention to the silent, embodied and inarticulate, collective memories of other cultures (Hastrup 1995b).

What is at issue here is the nature of culture and the place of reflexivity in everyday social life. For the above critics of reflexive or auto-anthropology, culture represents a discourse within which human life can but be lived, so that the anthropological employment of a concept of reflexivity neither brings the investigator closer to the investigated nor situates either in a cognitive space beyond or outwith cultural determinism. As Strathern comments (1987: 31), it is merely 'mystification' to claim that auto-anthropology, understood as 'techniques of self-knowledge', constitutes a universal class of phenomena; reflexively elucidating culture or society is not part of the way in which most people experience their everyday lives. Hastrup concurs (1995b): cultures ground people in socially constraining holistic worlds; all human beings are thus natives in a particular cultural world of which they have experience but only tacit knowledge.

Strathern has little time, therefore, for bland claims, such as those of Giddens (1984: 335), that all social actors are social theorists ('scientists', in Kelly's appellation (1969: 144)), able to reflect upon their socio-cultural milieu in order to direct their purposive action within it. Techniques of knowledge-production and theorization are themselves culturally specific and mediated, and one only transcends such cultural situatedness by way of a diversity of other cultures' situations.

From a somewhat different ontological perspective, however, cultural techniques, practices and discourses are merely the superficial clothing in which universal human capabilities and proclivities express themselves in different places. However different the cultural grounding, then, cognitive reflection on self and other is ubiquitous and its outcome possibly transcendent. How else would universal human communication, never mind global anthropological analyses, be possible? On this view, the person who leads an unexamined life (who cannot explain his own socio-cultural practices better than an anthropologist) does not exist and never has done (Shweder 1991a: 14). Human beings have never been prisoners of linguistic, social or cultural worlds from which they are unable to detach themselves so as to turn their attention elsewhere and concern themselves with their own inwardness and selfhood (Ortega y Gasset 1956: 166–7).

As Paul Rabinow sums up (1977: 151–2):

> This is the ground of anthropology: there is no . . . valid way to eliminate consciousness from our activity or those of others.
> . . . We can pretend that we are neutral scientists collecting unambiguous data and that the people we are studying are living amid various unconscious systems of determining forces

of which they have no clue and to which only we have the key. But it is only pretence.

Is anthropology necessarily undertaken in certain existential states of mind?

Once reflexivity is allowed as a universal part of human consciousness, a means and a practice by which people everywhere come to look askance at the particular socio-cultural milieux and languages in which their self-expressions find overt form, then, as Rabinow puts it above (1977: 151–2), auto-anthropology comes into its own. Here is not merely an instrument of political correctness, or a technique or location for better anthropological representation of otherness, but something fundamental to the potentiality of the anthropological enterprise as such.

Near the end of his professional life, Edmund Leach made a number of statements which were treated as almost scandalous in the pre-Writing Culture era of British anthropology; Leach himself provocatively described his revelations as 'Glimpses of the Unmentionable in the History of British Social Anthropology'. What Leach suggested (1984: 22) was that every anthropological observer can be expected to recognize in the field something which no other observer will see: a projection of his or her personality. Since this personality 'distorts' the interpretation and analysis of that fieldwork experience, what is to be discovered in published anthropological accounts is a record of their authors' reactions to the situations in which they were acting; here are texts full of possible implications and layers of particular meaning, intended and otherwise, rather than items that give onto a pristine or objective, external world. As in a novel, Leach elaborated (1989: 137–8): features of anthropological accounts 'are derived from aspects of the personality of the author. How could it be otherwise? The only ego I know at first hand is my own. When Malinowski writes about Trobriand Islanders he is writing about himself; when Evans-Pritchard writes about the Nuer he is writing about himself.' In short, 'cultural differences, though sometimes convenient, are temporary fictions' (*ibid.*).

Since Leach's death, and The Writing Culture Debate, such thinking has become more widespread, and its implications more followed through. If cultural integrity is a fiction behind which sits the individual personality, then this is as true for those investigated by the anthropologist as for the investigator himself. To understand otherness is therefore to attempt to gain access to other minds, for socio-cultural institutions cannot be understood except via the individuals who populate and create them (cf. Cohen and Rapport 1995); furthermore, 'the only way we have of understanding another man's condition is through ourselves, our experience and emotions' (Naipaul 1987: 220). As Okely pithily phrases it, 'the personal is theoretical' (1992: 9), and far from being relegated to the periphery of the anthropological enterprise, or pejoratively contrasted with impersonal, generalizable truth, the biography and autobiography of fieldwork selves must be written into an inclusive narrative of analysis and experience.

Cohen elaborates (1992a, 1994). Whether anthropologist or lay-person, it is the self which is used to understand the other. Making sense of the world is an interpretive project which begins not with a *tabula rasa* but with all the specificity of sense-making apparatuses contained within discrete individual bodies; hence, every version of an 'other' is a construction of a self (cf. Rapport 1997a). As well as being a universal feature of human social life, this is also our most potent anthropological resource. '[E]thnography is an ethnographer-focused art' (Cohen 1992a: 225), and anthropology should now seriously begin to exploit the intrusive self as an ethnographic resource.

This means, first, that in contradistinction to a traditional anthropological view of the individual self as a socio-cultural construction and as inexorably other-directed, we recognize that the sense of personal identity has a certain absolute, self-driven quality to it which is not contingent or relative. Individuality is ubiquitous, and it is upon their consciousness of self that a person's consciousness of things socio-cultural is built. Secondly, individuals are members of socio-cultural milieux through their deployment of certain sets of collectively shared symbols. Nevertheless, these symbols are ever perceived and interpreted in discretely (and often discreetly) individual ways. Not only do individuals remain members of socio-cultural groupings as individuals, then, but there may remain great incongruencies between different individuals' perceptions, and between how these symbols are publicly, conventionally, or hegemonically treated and how they are privately known: between self-knowledge and social knowledge (cf. Rapport 1993a). We know very well from personal experience the great discrepancies that can occur between the two, the fallacies with which others can construct the self, and we must use our knowledge of the complexity of our own selves to resist the temptation to generalize or simplify those of others. We should use our experience of our own selves to elicit and describe the thoughts and sentiments of others whom we otherwise risk glossing over in terms of the inadequate and crude generalizations we retrieve from conventional, collective social categories: 'tribes', 'castes', 'cultures', 'ethnic groups', and so on. In this way we can avoid privileging the social over the personal, and eliding others' individuality with their membership of a social or cultural group. The idea of individual as social cell or cultural clone may be convenient but it is not experientially authentic. Our own self-experience should tell us that others cannot be treated as mere ciphers of a collective socio-cultural condition; to employ a collective set of symbols is not to think or feel collectively or alike, while public identity is a transformation of the individual self rather than an equivalent expression of it. In short, we none of us passively conform to or reflect a social milieu and its forces, and '[i]f we do not do descriptive justice to individuals, it is hard to see how we could do it for societies' (Cohen 1992a: 229).

This is not to say, of course, that others' self-knowledge, as opposed to the superficial and formal knowledge which their use of symbols would flag, is at all easy to access. However, the auto-anthropological resolution would be that the discipline cannot continue to be practised as if self-knowledge did not exist, or were irrelevant, or somehow less important or less anthropological than collective knowledge. 'People's knowledge of themselves is of *critical* importance to us for without it we misunderstand them', Cohen concludes (1992a: 230). Again, our best methodology is our experience of ourselves: our self-realization that we must no more deny the self as too difficult to access anthropologically than, as participants in social milieux, we accept the versions of ourselves which others hold of us.

Towards this end, Okely (1996) proposes that nothing of the fieldworker's self should escape his or her consciousness in the process of analysing data, or be dismissed as private, taboo or improper – any more than parts of local life were traditionally excluded from a holistic analysis. Even the anthropologist's unconscious self might be accessed, psychoanalytically, so as to explore that of informants.

As long ago as 1961, David Pocock nicely summed up what has become, in the reflexive or auto-anthropological turn, a revaluation of the entire anthropological enterprise: only in appreciating the totality of one's 'personal anthropology' and its consequences, he recommended, can the anthropologist expect fully to perceive others'.

See also: **Ethnomethodology, Literariness, Qualitative and Quantitative Methodologies**

CHILDREN

The child is, in many ways, the paradigmatic 'other': 'the child', its attributes and identity, is something that adults and anthropologists have constructed in dialectical relationship to their own senses of world and self. Perhaps for this reason, anthropological work on children and childhood has been extremely diverse and long-lived without being particularly coherent (cf. James and Prout 1990). In conjunction with a common conceptualization of the child as an asocial or pre-social putty (a throwback to Durkheimian notions of animalistic human individuals who are perforce socialized into a collective moral consciousness), the study of children and childhood has, until recently (cf. James *et al.* 1997), reflected approaches and problematics from other anthropological spheres rather than generating its own theorization. Over and above this, however, the study of 'the child' presents us with a problematic of its own (which is at the same time exemplary): how to apprehend a research subject whose being is a continuous becoming? More generally, the study of children and childhood raises the vital question of how anthropologically to approach and accommodate the continuities of existential identity which lie beyond the reductive stasis of socio-cultural categories and classifications.

Children as indices

The appearance of children as indices of extraneous (adult), anthropological concerns makes for a long list. Among the latter concerns might be included the following:

Cultural relativism: Mead (1928) and Benedict (1938) both employed children and youth in an argument in favour of privileging the influence of culture over biology. Hence, less adolescent stress and more altruistic (nurturant–responsible) behaviour were to be found in 'other cultures' than in the competitive and egoistic (self-seeking) West. Derek Freeman (1983) succeeded in casting aspersions upon a Meadian approach, but controversial claims continue to be made, such as that women may withdraw from the mother–child bond in the event of the cultural estimation of scarce resources (Scheper-Hughes 1985).

Neo-Freudianism: Childhood practices in different societies have been compared, sometimes in large numbers (Whiting and Child 1953), in terms of Freudian assumptions concerning the way adult character is a reflection of childhood conflicts (cf. Erikson 1977). In an extended study, Du Bois (1944) argued that maternal neglect of young children on Alor was responsible for affective shallowness, suspicion and instability among Alorese adults, for a folklore which stressed aduit–child frustrations and hatred, and a cosmology of suspect deities. Spiro similarly introduced Freud into Trobriand and kibbutz childhoods (1958, 1982).

Neo-Darwinism: Child-rearing practices have been studied from the point of view of their instantiating a customization of environmental pressures and features. Parental investments in large numbers of children, then, may reflect life-threatening instabilities in the environment, whereas having fewer children and investing more time and energy in each (allowing each to be more demanding) furthers their survival chances in more socio-economically complex environments (cf. LeVine 1982).

Developmental psychology: From Piagetian notions of universal stages of human cognitive development, anthropologists have explored how children constitute their understandings of the world first through a manipulation of concrete objects and then through more abstract, logico-moral reasoning (cf. Dasen 1994). While from Vygotskian notions concerning how universals of developmental biology are mediated through particular historico-cultural contexts and everyday social processes, anthropologists have produced ethnographies of: Hausa children learning purdah (Schildkrout 1978), Tahitian children learning gentleness (Levy 1978), and Japanese children learning homesickness (Goodman 1993).

Role play: In studies of the relational nature of social life, of the way identities are elicited in terms of a mutuality of interconnected instrumentalities, 'children' and 'adults' are explored anthropologically as roles that give rise to one another. Through children, adults learn to be parents (Harkness and Super 1996); by fostering children, adults learn to be kinsmen (Goody 1982); by feeding children, adults learn to be co-villagers (Carsten 1991). Relatedly, of course, the differential attributes of parenthood give onto very different 'children'.

Self-consciousness: Consciousness, according to Ong (1977) is something that grows through time. This is true both phylogenetically and ontogenetically. Hence, with each succeeding generation, humankind relates to the cosmos and to itself with more conscious control, while the child enlarges its storehouse of conscious experience and knowledge as it moves from primitive unconsciousness to adult reflexivity.

Social policy: In a number of works dealing with deprivation and disadvantage in contemporary societies (and often oriented towards their alleviation), anthropologists have focused upon children's lives as markers of levels of social welfare and manifestations of social care (cf. Ennew 1986). Here are studies of disadvantaged children in school situations (Lacey 1971; Heath 1983), of social support systems beyond the school (Weisner 1989), of sibling caretaking (Weisner and Gallimore 1977), and of children with developmental abnormalities (Weisner *et al.* 1996).

Social critique: After Gramsci or Bourdieu, children figure in a range of works whose intent is a disinterring of the reproduction of hegemonic discourses of socio-cultural inequality. Inasmuch as hierarchical structures of socio-cultural milieux are seen as being reproduced through the agency and the false-consciousness of individual actors – even those with least to gain by the hierarchy – the teaching and learning of children to maintain exploitative relations is an important process. Here, then, are children who learn to live with poverty (Jenkins 1982), who learn to labour (Willis 1978), and who learn to die (Scheper-Hughes 1992). Seemingly, the best such children can hope for is escape into a subculture of abandonment or denial (Jenkins 1983; Hebdige 1979).

Children as agents

Something of a revolution in the anthropological study of children has been recently brought about, however, by the rise of more interpretive, phenomenological and literary approaches. Here is a realization that children might be looked to for their own accounts of experience, of participation, activity and relationship in socio-cultural milieux and beyond, as distinct from an adult's construction or interpretation of these (cf. James 1993). Children's social and emotional dependence do not mean that they may be regarded as mere passive recipients of adult expectations and knowledge – pawns in a process of conditioning socialization – or that adult assumptions and preoccupations provide the best basis for entering into or understanding worlds which may be built upon very different premises (cf. Amit-Talai and Wulff 1996). Unlike other 'exotics' whom anthropologists study, children might not have a formally distinct language (although this too is debatable), and they are taught to know and tell of themselves in (conventional) adult terms. Nevertheless, this ought not to detract from an appreciation of the way that children's utilization of conventional forms and meanings is reformatory and idiosyncratic; whether through innocence (ignorance) or expertise (rejection), it is as much a matter of creation as of learning (cf. Bruner and Haste 1987).

In an important pair of studies, for instance, Briggs (1970, 1998) elucidates how, far from being givens, 'Inuit children' make 'Inuit culture', its institutions, rules, practices, values, habits of interaction and meanings, through processes whereby individuals experience themselves as agents engaged in emotionally charged conflicts with others. Individual Inuit children and Inuit culture are thus mutually created. Moreover, the process is ongoing; Inuit individuals never stop being 'children' creating their culture and their identities (Briggs 1992). Adult cognitions, in other words, can be expected to be as fluid, and contextually embodied, as those of children (Toren 1993).

Rather than treating fixed socio-cultural categories, then – 'child' and 'adult', 'society' and 'culture' – what needs to be anthropologically examined are those interactions in which concepts, behavioural forms and meanings are created, recreated and acquired, and individuals become committed to their acquisitions (cf. Bluebond-Langner 1978). Pertinent studies of children as dynamic agents who learn (create) culture and society in interaction with other children and with adults would then include how Nepalese children's understandings of caste, gender and the future at once reflect, resist and reinterpret adult conceptions (Skinner and Holland 1996), and how English children learn how to 'belong' to an English village milieu by creating public but individual identities for themselves (James 1986).

As Hockey and James conclude (1993), to appreciate children as actors in their own right is to convey a sense of individuals partaking in a number of ongoing tensions. To be a 'child' is to be both an agent *and* part of a world of socio-cultural structures run by adults: to be both an actor with an identity of its own *and* something which comes into its own only by a recognition of its difference from certain consociated others; to be both a symbol of change in a socio-cultural milieu *and* an aspect of continuity in socio-cultural reproduction; and to be both a phenomenon of local diversity in the world *and* one of global generality.

See also: **Agent and Agency, Alterity, Liminality**

CLASSIFICATION

The human practice of classifying the world into distinct objects and relations is a cognitive accomplishment: the means by which human beings create order and identity in an environment, making it socio-cultural. It also embodies a paradox and tension. Classification is the activity of assigning people, things, concepts, relationships, forces and so on, to different categories; human beings are perhaps unique among animals for the extent to which they manipulate the physical realities of their environs in terms of the categories they impose upon them – and for the extent to which they depend upon such creative cognitive manipulations for the procuring of a stable environment in which to live. Classification is essential to our human ability to think about and know the world, and to think about and know our own place and that of our activities within it. At the same time as our classifying the world empowers us to act and to know, however, it also limits us, because what we can know, what we anticipate, and recognize, and intend, and regard as orderly and work towards, are all in a way pre-given by classificatory schemata which we are employing.

In philosophical deliberation, the tautological or circular nature of human interpretation has become known as 'the hermeneutic circle'. For human beings, there is nothing that is necessarily or simply 'there' in the world besides the entropy of matter, or flux. What is there is a matter of what we anticipate to be there, and only by courtesy of a system of anticipations do we make meaningful interpretations and hence 'fix' our world. Hence Gadamer's conclusion: 'it is our prejudices that constitute our being' (1976: 9). In other words, classification gives onto definition and order which are also an impoverishment and a constraint. For one way of seeing the world, of making it orderly and humanly livable, tends to preclude our simultaneous appreciation of other ways; we are limited by our definitions. As succinctly put by Karl Mannheim (1952: 20): 'The fact that we give names to things which are in flux implies inevitably a certain stabilisation. . . . It excludes other configurational organisations of the data which tend in different directions.'

But then the complexity of our human relationship with the accomplishment of categorial order in the world must also be taken into account. If classification is the means by which human beings become (human), then it is also what they endeavour to overcome. The labour of the categorial division of the world comes to be recognized not only as an achievement but also as a burden; division thus entails the wish for, and the promise of, conjunction. Moreover, human systems of classification are ever uncertain and contingent because in the diverse assemblage of classificatory possibilities, each system contests the others, and each shows up the others as arbitrary and partial.

'Primitive Classification'

Anthropological interest in classification can fairly be dated from the publication by Durkheim and Mauss of the book *Primitive Classification* in 1903. If human beings classify the world by matching up perceptual images, words and concepts, then, for Durkheim and Mauss, it is the collective cultural representations of a society which supply all three; to the extent that people are members of a society, they will share in the *conscience collective* (the collective consciousness) of the whole, and thus partake of the same classificatory system. In short, as emanations of 'the collective mind' of society, classifications 'express the very societies in which they were elaborated' (1970 [1903]: 85, 66).

To unpack this conclusion somewhat, for Durkheim and Mauss, a society or culture amounts to an orderly, integrated and harmonious human space which extends over time. Such order is secured and denoted by classificatory schemata, often conceived symbolically, in terms of language; and this order is modelled on society. Each society propounds a certain model of order in the world and the order envisaged is a reflection of those structuring principles by which life in society is itself ordered and arranged. If the world is conceived of as having certain classes of being, then this is because society has such classes (houses, lineages, status groups, say). If the world is conceived of in terms of divisions of space and time, then this is because society has such divisions (between habitations, between annual festivities, between age-grades). And if the world is conceived of as party or prey to certain relations and certain forces, then this is because society is home to relations and forces too (hierarchy, cause-and-effect, power and authority). For Durkheim and Mauss, in sum, society was the elemental model for logical classification, and only gradually did such schemata come to dissociate themselves (for example, science) from social realities, social functions and social needs.

Even in the latter cases, however, there would be a relationship to trace (however implicit and indirect) between the society and how the wider world was humanly conceived. This was inevitable because, in itself, the human mind lacks any innate capacity to construct systems of classification: hence the diversity of the latter. Furthermore, giving rise to the systems of classification by which the world was known was one of the chief mechanisms by which societies maintained their own existence. The world as reflection of the social made the latter seem more natural and inevitable, hence legitimate. While having societal members all share in one and the same schema of classification provided for social solidarity even if those members were seen as occupying different categories within the schema. Hence, members of a society come to classify alike, and to represent and act upon their classifications alike. Via socialization into a system of classification, the shape of the individual mind comes to be collectively derived. One society means one collective manifestation of a precise and, where possible, once-and-for-all division and conjunction of people and things in the world.

For many years after Durkheim and Mauss wrote, anthropologists who regarded it as their 'first task' to 'discern order in a sociocultural milieu and make it intelligible' (Needham 1970: 40) took what Durkheim and Mauss had propounded as the paradigm of their efforts. There might have been some fine-tuning of the model (cf. Gluckman 1959, 1963a; Douglas 1966; Leach 1968), but it was generally assumed that systems of classification .were social in origin, were intrinsically logical and non-contradictory, were singular and shared in any one time and place, were part-and-parcel of social solidarity, and were what mediated between individual cognitions and collective actions.

Even seemingly revolutionary advances were grounded in the Durkheim–Mauss orthodoxy. Thus, Lévi-Strauss (1969a) explored the logical–universal life to which he claimed collective systems of classification could be seen to lead. If Chomsky could argue for underlying grammatical structures of which every language and every speech-act might be said to be transformations, then Lévi-Strauss determined that comparably unconscious, deep structures of symbolic classification, albeit now culturally derived, inhabited the minds of socialized human individuals. A structural anthropology might chart the vast network of transformations and variations by which the classificatory systems of different cultures and times were linked and the transformatory principles (such as binary opposition) by which this was effected.

Benjamin Lee Whorf (1956), meanwhile, proposed that language was the key to cognition inasmuch as the different classificatory structures of different languages would determine different ways in which speakers of those languages would perceive and think as well as speak. If it was through the (arbitrary and historico-culturally specific) indices of verbal labels and syntactical constructions that human beings recognized and ordered the objects of their worlds, then the ways in which different languages cut up the flux and continua of reality into discrete categories, things and relations (objects, persons, events) would cause different language-users to live in different worlds of perception and experience. People thought through linguistic categories, and did not think outside them, and so their understandings (of themselves and their environments) would be structured by their grammar; taxonomies thus gave onto knowledge.

Victor Turner (1982a), finally, argued for an oscillation, cognitive and social, between the classificatory and the non-classificatory as constituting a universal dynamics of human life. Human beings oscillated between inhabiting structure and anti-structure, between division and homogeneity, but human culture must be seen as comprising both.

Everyday life, then, was characterized by a status-bound social order: persons and things differentiated according to their positions and roles in a segmentary symbolic system. However, at periodic intervals human beings resorted and reverted to an antithetical, indeed primordial, modality of relationship characterized by '*communitas*' or total communion. Here was a recognition, however fleeting, of a generalized social bond between all human beings, and between them and the world, not yet fragmented into a multiplicity of structural divisions and ties; via this generic bond (beneath all differentiation, hierarchy and conflict) human beings related to one another freely and as totalities. From the point of view of the structural, such *communitas* appeared anarchic because it was marginal and unclassifiable in terms of everyday criteria. And yet, both modalities of human relationship were necessary for societal continuity; equally, individuals needed to alternate between the two experiential states. For, the creative power of *communitas* fashioned the being of individuals and communities in liberating, potentiating ways, while the routinization of this creative togetherness into norm-governed distinctions and relations afforded a stability conducive to taking stock and taking action.

Post-Durkheimian classification

'We have not truly got rid of God if we still believe in grammar', Nietzsche tersely concluded (1979), and anthropologists are now, finally, getting to grips with dismantling a Durkheim–Mauss framework to classification. *Contra* the latter emphasis on the almost superhuman determinations of a classificatory system upon, and ramifications through, human life, comes the allowance that 'there is absolutely no captivity within a language' (Gadamer 1976: 16), nor, by implication, within any particular hermeneutic schema *per se*. Here is a loosening of the hold which classificatory schemata can be said to have upon human life – an appreciation of the diversity of relations possible between human beings and this most human of creations – and an exploration of the diverse nature of the schemata as such. Not only may classifications vary according to what content is assigned where, then, but also what kind of content: from physical things, to attributes of things (colour, weight, shape, size, sound), to synthetic things, to abstractions. Not only may classifications vary according to the scope of categorial content but also the complexity of the latter's definition: from monothetic or common denominations, to polythetic denominations or 'family resemblances' (Wittgenstein 1978). Finally, different categories may relate to one another in a variety of ways: as parts of taxonomic or hierarchical wholes certainly, but also as opposites, by analogy or other metaphoric transformation (cf. Ellen 1997).

Rodney Needham, for example, who was responsible for translating the Durkheim–Mauss text into English, has also furbished trenchant critique concerning the symbolic nature of human classification, and the relations between classification and action (e.g. 1979, 1985). Durkheim and Mauss would have us see symbolic classifications amounting to collective philosophies concerning things and relations, to commonly held values, upon which social groups and the constraints of membership depend. But much that is classified is not symbolized; much that is important in the way of socio-cultural knowing is not represented or made explicit but held implicitly, subconsciously, by group members (cf. Sperber 1975: x–xi). In this way, classification can be seen as preceding language (the symbolization of words and labels) and as proceeding outwith what is overtly known or expressed; categories, things and relations can exist without there being words for them.

Furthermore, classificatory systems and their antitheses (structures and their so-called polluting anti-structures) can be viewed as going together, as aspects of the same world-view. Schemata of classification are not threatened or broken down by indefinable anomalies or transitions, and one need not view ritual or other intervals in classificatory order as somehow transcendental moments. Human ingenuity allows for anything to be made to fit a classificatory schema if this is desired, and thus anomalies and ambiguities should better be seen as special parts of such a schema: parts to which people wish to give a special value – of respect, or distrust, or comedy, or indifference, as well as of danger or fear (cf. Geertz 1983: 80–5). Structure and anti-structure, order and pollution, belief and scepticism, belief and practice, should better be seen as parts of the same form of life, not as a classification and its threatened overcoming (cf. Heald 1991).

Furthermore, it is not necessary to posit a classificatory schema so as to explain behaviour. Sometimes people have reasons for their actions and sometimes not; in either case it might be better if anthropologists were to view behaviours (some at least) as meaningless, with no significance beyond themselves. Their 'meaning', purpose and effect is in the performance, which itself makes them 'the right thing to do'. In other words, where a classificatory schema is enunciated it need not evince a degree or level of explanation more inclusive than the behaviours which it accompanies.

Finally, Needham (1970) has questioned the tenability of the Durkheim–Mauss notion that classificatory systems find their roots in social institutions and functions, and have nothing to do with cognitive *a prioris* or universals. How might we suppose that individuals may apprehend spatial, temporal, socio-cultural distinctions, or whatever, if there were no innate individual capacity for or tendency towards classification, and these latter were pure and simple reflections of social organization? Inasmuch as the same categories and relations recur among different people, and inasmuch as one would wish to avoid the Lévi-Straussian fallacy of granting classificatory schemata their own transformatory and *sui generis* facticity, one would have to conclude that classification reflects certain general underlying principles of human cognition. Much recent anthropological work, then, has gone towards elucidating what form such human universals might take (e.g. Berlin and Kay 1969; Berlin 1992). As Ellen concludes (1993), we classify as we do because we possess certain innate cognitive skills, and because we organize our perceptions by cultural means such as language. Occasionally the logic of our classifications can be derived simply and directly from the logic of the cultural medium (from linguistic grammar, for example). More usually classificatory schemata can be seen to derive from an interplay between individual experience, linguistic form, cultural tradition, social context, material circumstance and metaphoric transformation. Far from being rooted in the socio-cultural, classificatory function and form are grounded in the individual human body (its rhythms, somatic states and formal constitution) and in a bodily experience of the environing world.

Fernandez has argued, in this vein, that classificatory schemata are a kind of hypothesis which people bring to bear on what they otherwise experience as somatically inchoate, 'as problematic [because] not precisely defined' (1982: 544). Classification serves the need for more concrete identification by people of their bodily circumstances, their selves and those of significant others; natural analogies, perhaps, are used to make more concrete, graspable, and therefore resolvable, what is inchoate in psycho-social experience and relationships. Systems of classification are thus embodiments of certain elemental vectors of human existence: ways in which we project what are initially psycho-somatic experiences of the body onto the world. Here are individual bodily concerns ramifying, via cultural media, into social strategies of boundary and identity. For this reason, classificatory schemata could be said to be inherently perspectival (*à la* Nietzsche), matters of projection from individual points of view, and matters of the moment, as new bodies continually come along with projects to complete by which the inchoate becomes identifiable.

Nietzschean classification

> We set up a word at the point at which ignorance begins,
> at which we can see no further, e.g., the word 'I', the word 'do',
> the word 'suffer': – these are perhaps the horizon of our
> knowledge, but not 'truths'.
>
> (Nietzsche 1968: no. 482)

Anthropological work on classification began with the Durkheim–
Mauss thesis which posited the sources of classification as being the
social group, the purposes of classification as being the socialization and
integration of group members, and the consequence of classification as
being the objectification of a collective life-world which all share. Here
was an imaging of a one-to-one relationship between a social group, its
language-world, and that language's meanings: language as determinant
of a single and consistent classificatory schema (cf. Berger and Luckmann
1969: 66). What has been argued for since is a freer appreciation of the
relations and the potential among system of classification, language,
group membership, world-view and behaviour. There is no necessary
one-to-one or once-for-all relationship between classificatory schema
and language, between language and world-view, between classificatory
schema and behaviour.

Relationships, here, are understood far more as complex, fluid and
purposive: matters of interpretation not mechanics. Classifications as
used in a socio-cultural milieu may not be singular, or neat, or consensual, or collective, or coercive, or holistic, or final, or even systemic.
Classifications can be consciously multiple, even contradictory, and
individuals can practise denying or deeming true different schemata
over time or at the same time. Moreover, a classificatory schema need
not be synonymous with social organization, and neither need account
for the pragmatic and rhetorical manoeuvrings by which individuals
organize and enunciate their passages through life.

This kind of anthropological appreciation owes its origins to an
Existential or Nietzschean imaging: to a perspective on classification
which includes the conscious and self-conscious individual agent, and
which ties the classificatory firmly to the cognitive constructions of
creative minds in interaction. Deriving from developing individual
cognitions, the function of classifications of the world would appear
to be a series of ongoing individual constructions of order (of self,
other, beauty, and hierarchy) for the fulfilment of a series of individual
purposes. In place of Durkheim and Mauss's understanding that a
formally similar and singular societal language translates, via a shared

system of classification, into social solidarity, anthropology has moved to a more reflexive understanding whereby linguistic practice need say nothing about the possible (inconsistent) classifications expressed within it or outside it. Language is rather envisaged as a medium for an attempted exchange of a surfeit of ongoing, individual orderings, the assumption being that there will exist a diversity of such orderings within the individual person and within the social milieu at any one time as well as over time (cf. Rapport 1993a, 1997c).

Finally, inasmuch as we create systems of classification which are arbitrary, multiple, momentary, contested and inconsistent, what are the phenomenological implications of living with such diversity and provisionality? In a system of classification we construct a bulwark against ignorance, Nietzsche suggested, and yet at the same time we admit that our concepts and categories are inherently and unavoidably ambiguous: they are singularities which stand for actual multiplicities. That is, human beings recognize that the world is actually multiple – subject to a diversity of actual and potential cognitive constructions – and that any one system of classification is only a pretence at overall orderly encompassment. We recognize that there is a contradiction at the very heart of the classificatory process: the practice of giving a name (however provisionally) to a diversity. We classify, we categorize, conscious of the logical impossibility of so doing once-for-all, and thus we continue to make 'the world as a work of art' (Nietzsche 1968: no. 796).

But if this is the case, if the categories and concepts of classificatory schemata are recognized to be attempts logically to define, make singular, limited and congruous what *at the same time* we know to be multiple, unlimited and incoherent, then why do we continue with the practice? Because we recognize our human products as aesthetic or poetic ones, and that this production is what makes us human. We recognize that it is through the conscious ongoing creation of a plurality of inconsistent systems of classification that we become individual human beings living within social milieux and also experience ourselves as such. To gain analytical vantage upon these cognitive processes, in turn, calls for what Nietzsche described as a poetic or aesthetic, rather than mechanical or structural, understanding.

See also: **Cognition, Contradiction, World-View**

CODE

Code and codification are important concepts which lie at the interface of anthropological theories of communication, knowledge, translation and community. The concepts deal with questions of media of information, of the forms in which information is packaged, conveyed and expressed, and the way in which the form and the content of information are mutually influential, even constitutive: codes 'control both the creation and organization of specific meanings and the conditions for their transmission and reception' (Bernstein 1973).

At the same time, the concepts deal with translation, with the transcription and transition of information between domains or levels, contexts or situations – translating different perceptions, different generalities, different societies and cultures – and questions of the extent to which information remains 'the same' through the translation process. Finally, code and codification have themselves been treated by anthropologists as concepts of different levels of generality, referring to: sets of rules for the transcription of one experiential domain into another; communicational devices; and types of discourse which are swopped in accordance with social circumstances such as degree of formality.

Codes and knowledge

Codification, Gregory Bateson explains (1951), refers to the transition between events in the external world and their life as perceptions, propositions and ideas in socio-cultural milieux; codification is the process whereby the latter come to stand for and substitute for the former. However, a system of codification is not only a network of perception, it is also a system of communication. Codification gives onto messages about the external world and their passage between those who share knowledge of the code. In short, codification enables communication about the world, and it entails two translations: between the world and a code, and between one user of the code and others. A 'codification system' (Bateson 1951: 175) can be understood as the way in which a universe of objects, relations and events is transformed into communicable signs.

For codification to work in these dual ways calls for a certain systematization, so that there is a consistent relationship between certain events and certain elements of code. Hence, codification usually represents an analogic mirroring of relations among one set of phenomena ('events') in another set ('symbols'). The latter can then consistently be read as signs, as symbolizing certain events and the actions that might follow. This is necessary both for the initial perceiver of events to know what he is seeing – his code orders and generalizes his perceptions – and necessary for his possible communication of information about his perceptions to others; decodification of messages is not possible if the code contains too many random elements.

Codes must also carry information, however implicitly, concerning what kind of information they contain, who it is for, and what is to be done with it. Besides information about external events, therefore, the messages in a codification system also convey information about the system itself and those who are using it. Hence, not only do the messages communicate information, they are also communications about communication, or 'metacommunications' (Bateson 1951: 209). In fact, 'every statement in a given codification is an implicit affirmation of this codification and is therefore in some degree metacommunicative' (1951: 214). In some circumstances, the metacommunication 'We are communicating' may be the most important thing that is being exchanged, more important than the overt contents of the message.

Metacommunications may be divided into two main kinds: those concerning the system of codification, and those concerning the interpersonal relations of those who share the system of codification and seek to communicate through it. Hence, terms of courtesy or respect, intonations of condescension or dependence, are metacommunicative cues: statements about the relations between users of a code contained in the way the code is used. Other cues will indicate what is jocular, what is ironic, what is secret, what is informal, and so on. Levels of regress, meanwhile, may be endless; 'This is me communicating to you that we are communicating about communicating . . . '.

In short, codes are to be understood as specific symbolic systems in given socio-cultural milieux, containing information about the world and also information on how to interpret and treat the information contained. Simply to participate in an exchange affirms the fact that rules of codification are shared, and hence codes are at once communicative and metacommunicative.

Codes and community

From this Batesonian basis, we might see much of the anthropological work on codes as concerning an elucidation of the types in use in different social situations and cultural contexts, and the ways in which these are shared, imposed, developed, exchanged, switched between and translated.

This has found perhaps most formal expression in the work of Gumperz and Hymes (e.g. 1972). Social groups, they begin, amount to 'speech communities' which share a repertoire of regular ways or 'fashions of speaking' (Whorf); any focus on the regularity and diversity of ways in which human beings codify the world and communicate their codifications, therefore, should centre on 'a community sharing rules for the conduct and interpretation of speech, and rules for the interpretation of at least one linguistic variety' (Hymes 1972: 54). As Gumperz continues (1972), a social group may be wider than a speech-community (one social group may consist of more than one speech-community), but within each such community, members will have shared knowledge of communicative options and constraints, and will share the rules governing conventional communicative strategies in a significant number of social situations. This will include the proper encoding and decoding of social meanings in symbolic forms – knowledge which derives from members' social networks and their frequency, longevity and intensity of contact. To the extent that group members of different status or age or gender or wealth or occupation or recreation come into more or less contact with one another, a variety of different speech-communities may develop.

However large or open a speech-community, certain choices will be made concerning appropriate codification and limits set on the conventional repertoire. More precisely, as a discrete social grouping, a speech-community will be responsible for coordinating the appropriateness of different members' 'speech styles' with different 'speech situations'. There will be many conventional speech situations recognized by the group (such as ceremonials, fights, hunts, meals, love-makings) and in each rules of speaking will be part-and-parcel of the setting. Indeed, competency in knowing appropriate styles of speaking may represent one of the primary determinants by a community of its full members. Making up different speech situations will be 'speech events' – the different parts of the different role-players – and constitutive of speech-events will be individual 'speech-acts'. These latter too will be formalized within the group context so that form and content will gel with setting and scene, speaker and addresser, addressee and audience, purpose and goal, 'key' (tone, manner or spirit) 'channel' (oral or written) and genre (prayer, say, poem or lecture). In this way, even individual speech-acts may be given general, causal explanations (related to the social structure as such) and treated not only in terms of the conditions of their origin but also their maintenance, development and change. '[W]e are never not in a situation', in the words of literary critic Stanley Fish (1972: 250), never outwith a situational frame or structure of expression and interpretation by which meaning, symbol and setting are socially conjoined; hence, 'a set of interpretive assumptions is always in force' (1972: 257).

Leavening the collectivist tenor of the above analysis, Gumperz and Hymes have also attempted to introduce the strategic individual speaker–hearer of code. While an individual's choice is subject to grammatical restraints (whereby only some codifications are intelligible to fellow users) and social restraints (whereby only some codifications are considered pukka), still there will likely be a range of possible, acceptable formulations within a speech-community, each with a subtly different effect. Thus the individual's selection from the repertoire is akin to a choice of weapon from an arsenal (Gumperz 1970). It is important, moreover, not to underestimate the extent to which individual speaker–hearers can strategically deploy their competencies, switching between repertoires, grammars and speech-communities, creating anew, and having their innate differences of voice socially celebrated, exaggerated or ignored (Hymes 1979). In short, it is important not to over-emphasize the homogeneity of a speech-community or the uniformity of its ideal speaker–hearers.

Leavening the functionalism of the work of Gumperz and Hymes still further have been studies which examined the development and exchange of codes between socio-cultural groups. Werbner (1989), for example, argues against the one-to-one matching of code and community and uses African ethnography to show people happily using several at once. Of these, the analyst might describe one as a 'source code' and others as 'pidgins' or 'creoles' which have developed from it. Locals might class one as their 'traditional' indigenous code, one as that of strangers which they have nonetheless imported, and one as 'universal' which pertains to all social groups in the region. To switch between such codes is, then, an opportunity for speaker–hearers to meta-communicate that their identity transcends any one group; to import strange codes is to meta-communicate that the speaker–hearers have privileged access to exogenous sources of power.

Finally, leavening the formalism in Gumperz and Hymes are approaches which emphasize the inevitable loss of meaning in processes of codification (cf. Rapport 1993a). As Bateson argued, between the external world and its symbolization, and between the senders and receivers of symbolic communication, there is an inevitable process of 'entropy' or disordering. In other words, any attempt to say the same thing in a different way (to symbolize the world, or have two people share the same symbol) can be seen ultimately to amount to saying a different thing (cf. Hough 1969: 4). And it is for this reason, as Leach observed (1977: 11), that when one appreciates what people actually do as opposed to what they are supposed to do (how they actually speak, say, rather than how the social group would have them speak), most neat categorial distinctions (such as 'speech-communities') leading to an orderly framework for our social thinking, whether as group members or as analysts, disappear.

Put more sociolinguistically, the concept of a normal or standard idiom of encoding or decoding must be treated as an analytical and social fiction, because each speaker–hearer possesses a 'personal lexicon' (Steiner 1975: 46). No 'language system' is a 'singular entity' since 'it exists only as individual language systems in individual brains; and these systems and these brains are all in some ways different' (Martin 1983: 428). More precisely (Steiner again (1975: 46)): 'the language of a community, however uniform its social contour, is an inexhaustibly multiple aggregate of speech-atoms, of finally irreducible personal meanings'. In using a code, therefore, we find speaker–hearers drawing upon a more or less common vulgate and also upon a more or less private thesaurus, an idiolect, making contingent connections in unpredictable ways. Individual experiences and intentions and social contexts and conventions mix in irreducibly specific ways.

As Fillmore elaborates (1979), individual differences in codification point to both different competencies – different internalizations of grammar – and different performative practices – different strategies of use which individuals prefer to employ. Even if they were to try to be ideally representative speaker–hearers, sharing both competencies of use and performances with fellow members of social groups, individuals' different personalities, memories, skills and experiences – in a word, their different consciousnesses – would make them codify differently. If different patterns and styles of codification exist in different situations, therefore, then this is as likely to be a matter of individual interpretation of context than it is of social definition, perhaps more so. Individuals, as Leach reminds us (1977: 9), will cross social boundaries (and sociolinguistic systems of codification), and thereby make cultural distinctions fuzzy, no matter the conventions and laws instituted to stop them.

Codes and communication

Much anthropological work has gone into identifying particular types of code and charting their use. Most famously, perhaps, Bernstein, as part of a wider exploration of how speech may be regarded as 'the major means through which the social structure becomes part of individual experience' (1964: 258), identified two different ideal-types of codification in everyday use. One is a highly coded form of language, impersonal and ritualistic, and suited to an explicitly authoritarian and reactionary social structure; the other is a more open and fluid 'now-coding' language suited to the ongoing realization of personal identities. The former Bernstein called 'public language' or 'restricted code', and the latter 'formal language' or 'elaborated code' (1964, 1972).

More precisely, in elaborated code language is specifically and newly formed to fit a particular referent (situation and speaker), to serve as an individuating factor in experience and to describe individual experience; language is used explicitly to clarify meanings, and acts as a mediation of complex personal sensation and cognition. It exemplifies analytical thought processes, and fine gradations of measured cogitation and subjective sensitivity. Elaborate code accords, in sum, with 'organic solidarity' (Durkheim): with differentiation and ambiguity surrounding the changing relations between a diversity of creative individuals and their perceptions.

In restricted code, a referent is designated using ready-made terms and phrases from a common repertoire, put together quickly and automatically in a well-organized sequence. Syntax is rigid, grammar simple and sentences predictable; likewise the type of content, if not the specifics of what the sentences contain. Meaning is implicit, largely impersonal, and ritualistic, even tautological. The effect is the symbolizing, establishing and reinforcing of the normative arrangements and relations of a social group; it is social not individual symbols that are expressed and exchanged. In short, restricted code expresses concrete thought processes and a high degree of affect concerning a restricted range of significant subjects and assumptions held in common by the group. It accords with 'mechanical solidarity' (Durkheim): with loyalty, passivity and dependency in a social group characterized by inclusive homogeneous relations.

While emphasizing that these were ideal types, and that individuals moved between codes according to social context, nevertheless, Bernstein further argued that particular social contexts could be seen to be dominated by one or other of these codes. Their usage was a function of subculture and of particular forms of social relationship (rather than individual psychology). Hence, restricted code pertained to 'position-oriented' social milieux and relations – armies, prisons, age-grades, long-established friendships and marriages – while elaborated code pertained to 'person-oriented' ones. In particular, the two codificatory usages differentiated the working class from the middle class; the 'genes' of working-class sociality and solidarity were transmitted by restricted code, while the genes of middle-class sociality and individuality were transmitted by elaborated code.

Bernstein's differentiation between restricted and elaborated code has been highly influential, and anthropologists have gone on to identify versions of it, even if they have sought too to loosen 'the straitjacket of ideal dichotomous propositions' and speak of restricted or elaborated 'situations' rather than social groups (Paine 1976: 74). Fillmore, for instance, describes how 'an enormously large part of natural language is formulaic, automatic and rehearsed, rather than propositional, creative, or freely generated' (1976: 9). A large part of an individual's ability to get on with any social system of codification will depend on his or her mastery of and facility with such formulaic expressions as clichés, bromides, proverbs, politeness-formulae and leave-takings (cf. Goody 1978). Individuals will learn and memorize these in close association with the often very specific situations in which their use is called for. Cultures and social groups will vary, however, according to the situations for which the formulaic is especially required. In the USA, for example, funerals represent a routine social context (a speech-situation) in which exchange is most fluent when it is most formulaic; beyond formulae people find themselves tongue-tied even when they desire to give comfort (Fillmore 1979).

For Bloch (1975), meanwhile, political oratory among the Merina of Madagascar takes place in a restricted code in which the vocabulary, syntax and style, intonation, loudness, sequencing and illustrations of the speaker are institutionalized. Such oratory may be said to lie at the end of a spectrum of Merina codifications, between the formal or polite and the informal or everyday. Nevertheless, power resides in the use of this formal language, and it conveys the traditional authority of those with the status to use it. For the hearers' response is equally institutionalized and polite; to employ such oratory is to coerce an audience whose only alternative is to revolt against the code altogether. Hence, Merina oratory may be described as a form of social control, and an expression of a hierarchical relationship. At the same time it is a highly ambiguous and impersonal codification of expression. Since they are known in advance, utterances in this code cannot be tailored to particular cases or relationships or policies or personalities; conventional order and role are emphasized above all. Thus the skilful politician combines more and less formal codes in the exertion of his personal power.

Paine (1976) begins with Bernstein's assumption that codes control 'both the creation and organization of specific meanings and the conditions for their transmission and reception', but seeks to combine this with a more individually strategic approach to linguistic transaction.

In particular he is mindful of Bateson's notion that coded messages are tailored by their senders to fit their intended receivers and hence might represent a 'metacommunicative attack'. Paine thus examines the individual selection of types of code as means of gaining and expressing power; different sorts of code will impart different sorts of control, by senders, over different sorts of message in different sorts of relationship. The closed messages of restricted code may therefore be said to be tailored to exerting a uniform control over a social group organized in terms of status and consensuality of interpretation. While the open messages of elaborated code may be said to be tailored by their senders to exert control over a social group organized in terms of individuals' autonomous motives and intentions. Hence, a leader with 'traditional authority' (Weber) will control a retinue by emotionally rousing them to do their ritual duty, while a leader claiming 'rational authority' will control a citizenry by convincing them intellectually of their best interests. Alternatively, a group of individuals seeking to formalize their relations as a group might turn to a restricted code, an argot of some sort, as a means of signalling (to themselves as well as to others) the restrictions on properly loyal and purposive communication which they now intend to instigate (cf. Rapport 1994b).

Codes and translation

If restricted code is a closed form of communication in which meaning is implicit (and largely non-verbalized), and in which exchange is largely a matter of expressing and maintaining the positions and boundaries of a social group, then, Paine wonders (1976), what might be the consequences for translation and understanding between such codes? More broadly, might not types of codes be differentiated according to the extent to which they serve as vehicles of self-enclosure or social distantiation, giving onto a privatization of meaning (Arendt)? Or is it the case that since every code is a matter of learning, practice and use, translation is a hazardous procedure whatever the code's nature; so that disagreements ramify as people talk past one another in elaborated code, while non-communication prevails as people resist outsiders' efforts to engage in restricted code?

As intimated earlier, such questions of translation, of the inexorable loss of meaning between different individual speakers of code, go to the heart of language usage: of the use by human beings of symbolic systems to represent their experience. Theorists of translation, such as George Steiner, will argue that individuals must translate whenever they receive others' messages: 'all communication is translation' (1975:

238). Furthermore, guaranteed translation requires guaranteed access to the unique idiolect of the individual interlocutor – something which is never achievable and never demonstrable. Hence, codificatory exchange is always ambiguous and 'indeterminate' (Quine). No two individuals' experience is the same and any translation between them must involve inventive interpretation. Translation, Felstiner concludes, remains 'the art of loss' (1994).

Considering these ideas more anthropologically, Roy Wagner (1991) admits that the perceived world is always the reaction to the world by an individual: a refracted world, deflected through the prism of the self. Moreover, while 'nothing could possibly be more clear, distinct, concrete, certain, or real than the self's perception of perception, its own sensing of sense' (1991: 39), such subjective perceptions can only be elicited in others via codification in iconic–symbolic forms: a process from feeling to felt meaning to intended meaning which is inexorably entropic. Moreover, the meaning which an iconic–symbolic trope elicits is hermetically sealed within the personal microcosm: there is a perennial uncertainty as to whether one's 'green', one's 'Prince Hamlet', is another's. Meaning is a personal, subjective, internal perception, and the extent to which intuitively apprehended subjective experience can be objectively described is a question without solution.

The way in which people do try to '[do] justice to internal self-perception with external means' (Wagner 1991: 39) is the subject of a formidable body of work by James Fernandez (1971, 1977, 1982) which centres on metaphor and has become known as 'trope theory'. It is not just anthropologists who struggle against the fundamental solipsism and loneliness of incomprehensible individual lives, Fernandez begins, for individuals do so themselves. The elemental vectors of human existence are simple: we project what are initially psycho-somatic experiences of the body out into the world. However, these experiences are 'problematic and not precisely defined' even for the individuals concerned; in a word, they are 'inchoate' (1982: 544). Using cultural codes, then, is a means by which individuals attempt to make more concrete, graspable and therefore resolvable what is otherwise barely comprehensible in their experience and relations with the world. More precisely, people employ the analogies of metaphor and other linguistic tropes (metonym, simile, synecdoche) so as to try to figure out what their lives are like; then, they build up these tropes into narratives which are recounted amongst others in attempts to compare their compositions of their experiences with others'. The codification of experience as trope can be understood as a kind of hypothesis which is being brought to bear on an inchoate subject out of a need for more concrete identity and understanding. In particular, via natural analogies with the physical human body and its concrete circumstances, individuals are better able to grasp their inchoate experiences and those of significant others; hence, the centrality of the body as a symbolic construct.

In order to approach the experiential 'sensorium' in which other minds are enmeshed (1992: 135), Fernandez advises, the anthropologist must hope empathetically to approach the phenomenological subjectivity of others via the tropes they employ. To discover what others' lives are like is to accede to the appropriateness of their metaphors. Indeed, this is the only access anyone ever has to the experience of others. Even an individual's closest socio-cultural consociates know him in terms of the metaphorical associations he brings into play and their feeling of rightness: 'perhaps the best index of cultural integration, or disintegration . . . is the degree to which men can feel the aptness of each other's metaphors' (Fernandez 1971: 58).

But then is metaphorical usage so statically descriptive? Beginning from an attempt to codify and share experience, does not the employment of tropes itself give onto new experiences, new inchoateness (and an infinite deferring of intended meanings being communicated)? This was certainly the conclusion of linguistic theorist Mikhail Bakhtin (1981) for whom two embattled tendencies characterized the life of language-in-use. On the one hand there was the fixed unity of language which continually convinced its fellow-users that there existed an abstract grammatical system of denotative forms through which their common world-views might find expression. But on the other, there was the continuous becoming of language into something new, something deriving from ongoing perceptions of its users and the contingency of those moments in which the schemata lead its socially charged, intentioned and accented existence.

In their study of codes and codification, and of metaphor in particular, anthropologists tend to have emphasized one or other of these Bakhtinian tendencies. For Fernandez, then, metaphorical communication amounts to a movement between different semantic domains within a culture's shared 'quality space' (1977: 459–61); this 'cross-referencing' provides a sensation of experiential fixity and of cultural integration. And Michael Jackson agrees: metaphor reveals unities between the intelligible, the sensible and the social; to use metaphors is to make the domains of the personal, the social and the natural co-extensive, and thus achieve a sense of a cosmic 'wholeness of being' (1989: 152–5). If all metaphoric correspondences were 'discovered', Berger concludes, one would secure proof of the indivisible 'totality of existence' (1984: 97).

On the other hand, for Paine (1981: 188), metaphor is the trope which most develops and extends thought. As Ricoeur elaborates (1981: 180–1), the essence of metaphor is the crossing and the breaking of boundaries, the transcending of ordinary usage within any one semantic domain by bringing it into unusual relationship with others. Hence, the most important feature of metaphor is its nascent or emergent character; here, in the provision of previously unapprehended combinations of thought, is an enlarging of the circumference of the imagination. In nascent metaphorical usage, Steiner concludes (1975: 23), is a new mapping of the world and a reorganization of the experiential habitation of reality.

Taking these battling emphases together we can perhaps conclude that metaphorization, as a process in the codification of experience, both serves as a means by which individuals seek to formulate and convey their prior perceptions and is itself a significant source of future perceptions to be conveyed.

See also: **Classification, Cybernetics, Discourse, Interaction**

COGNITION

'Cognition' concerns the knowledge which people employ so as to make sense of the world, and the ways in which that knowledge is acquired, learnt, organized, stored and retrieved. More loosely, it covers the major modalities of human experience: the ways in which people think, feel and sense, and so make their lives meaningful and more or less ordered.

Cognition as culture

Clearly there are overlaps between cognition as broadly conceived and the concept of 'culture'. In this sense, there never has been a time when cognition was not a major anthropological focus. One may recall here, the early debate between Levy-Bruhl and Malinowski concerning 'how natives think'. For Levy-Bruhl (1985), 'primitive' people were characterizable in terms of a pre-logical or mytho-poetic apperception of the world: a mentality governed by emotion, magical contagion and incoherency, and a belief in mystical connectedness. For Malinowski (1948), on the other hand, all people were equally rational and could recognize the same logical principles, and all people applied these principles in their everyday worldly dealings; it was not as if primitives inhabited something akin to enchanted dream-worlds from which modern man's technological practices divorced him. In a later version of this debate, Lévi-Strauss (1966) posited that 'savage thought' was characterized by 'a science of the concrete' while modern thought was more abstract. Primitives (including their modern-day craftsmen descendants) made meaning and solved problems by way of employing extant and concrete objects and analogizing from them: so that differences between people may come to be conceived of as those between different animal species (totemism), while dreams were explained in terms of spirit-doubles at large in equivalent other worlds. Moderns, meanwhile, were less imaginative in their thought-processes, less wild, and content to solve problems on the basis of reasonable, intellectual models.

The question of the so-called 'psychic unity' of humankind lived on in 'the rationality debate' (cf. Wilson 1970). The issue was now re-formed as one concerning whether the logic of reasoning perforce took one universal form or whether, following notions of Wittgenstein (and Winch 1970), people in different cultures could be said to reason within the criteria and terms of diverse 'forms of life'. As Evans-Pritchard famously concluded concerning the witchcraft beliefs of the Azande of Sudan, and the rationality of maintaining those beliefs in daily practice: within the conditions and confines of their belief system, the Zande reason perfectly well, but they could not and did not reason beyond or against them (1950). In similar vein, the project of 'ethnoscience' (cf. Frake 1980; Atran 1993) set out to collate native categories of thought as constituted in particular places. From elementary 'units of meaning' (equivalent to phonemes, the elementary units of meaningful sound), a cultural grammar for normatively constituting the world could be disinterred: from elementary terms for kinsfolk, plants and diseases, say, to the lineaments of social life.

In this way, issues of cognition and rationality also came to merge with those of cultural relativism, and questions concerning the nature of cultural difference as it pertains to individual members' experiences and mentalities. It is worth noting here, therefore, the challenge to cultural-relativist notions (Boasian and Whorfian) of the direct effects of culture on individual psyches posed by more recent work on innate cognitive tendencies. The Chomskian revolution in language-acquisition, for instance, has substituted a focus on common human genetic programming for earlier (say, Saussurean) ideas of predetermining cultural matrices, so as to delineate how individuals learn and continually transform what they know. More particularly, in opposition to Whorfian notions of colour-words determining colour-cognitions Berlin and

Kay (1969) have convincingly argued for an understanding of people's perception of colour not in terms of a physical spectrum of light being arbitrarily and differently divided up per culture, but a matter of the same cognitive principles being applied with only limited variation.

Similarly, from assertions of ethnoscientific diversity, anthropology has moved to an appreciation of underlying, universal principles in human cognitive structurings of the individual or person, of self and other, of relationships and causality, of recognition and classification, of narration, and of space and time (cf. Sperber 1985). This is not to say that people will not differ vastly in their cognitions; (indeed, transformative differences may represent the only permanency and sameness in human cognition). But the logic of difference is a common and human rather than cultural and particular issue. As Jack Goody concluded (1977), neither binaristic not relativist theorizing will suffice in accounting for the patent universalities in human intellection and intuition.

Cognition and practice

Since the rise of symbolic or interpretive anthropology, from the 1970s onwards, debates over cognition have shifted somewhat. Cognition now becomes part of the continuous process by which the world is symbolically constructed: the focus is on the precise knowledge held by individual actors within a socio-cultural milieu, their 'systems of meaning' (Geertz 1973), and the contexts in which that knowledge is practised. The key issue is less whether cognition is a matter of cultural variation than the extent to which individual members of a social group could be said to partake in a social consensus concerning the structure and content of the way they knew the world.

As Holy and Stuchlik (1981) elucidate, social life is a matter of intention and performance: the impacting of meaningful, goal-oriented actions upon the world so as to maintain or change a status quo. Cognitive models are responsible for constituting the worlds of human being (through the application of given criteria of evaluation), while actions taken in the light of those models are responsible for continuously reconstituting the worlds of human being. Anthropological analysis must encompass both: intention and performance, model and action. Even though only the enacted or performed is visible, anthropology must study the relationship between it and the intentioning cognitive models if the social structures which emerge from performance are to be understood.

Two central questions now arise: how to gain access to those cognitive models by which individual members construct social reality, and how to explain the forms the models take over time. As Toren warned (1983), while the interface between individual cognition and observable practice is the key to anthropological knowledge, a yawning gap could open up between anthropological interpretations and those to whom the practice, as symbolic vehicle, belonged. Symbolic meanings could be imaginatively construed in potentially limitless ways; anthropologists needed a conceptual guide by which they could model and typify the way local imaginations and cognitions tended to operate.

The notion of cognitive 'schemata' or 'scripts' had been developed by the psychologist F.C. Bartlett, working in Cambridge in collaboration with the anthropologists Rivers and Bateson earlier in the century (1932). Memory and mind, Bartlett suggested, work by way of mental representations of prototypical events, behaviours and things. These define for the person the nature of any situation in which they are likely to become involved, including the emotions they might feel there and the goals they might attain. The representations are simple and simpli-fied models but they significantly frame and inform perception and knowledge. If nothing else, it is the taken-for-granted background anticipations which enable the person to take more notice of less predictable aspects of life.

These ideas have been significantly developed in social psychology since then by the likes of Neisser (1976), and have remained influential with anthropologists. Perceiving, imaging, thinking, remembering and speaking are skilful exploratory activities, Neisser suggests, which are directed by certain pre-existing cognitive structures or schemata. The latter prepare the person to anticipate, perceive and accept a certain kind of reality (and the meaningful events of which it is composed), while remaining open to certain modifications on the basis of exact information which is received. Cognition therefore represents a dialectical relationship with an environment, wherein schemata assure a certain continuity over time but are themselves in a continuous process of change; perceiving changes the perceiver while at the same time what is perceived is a matter of what has already been perceived. Schemata may be more or less general ('anticipate someone laughing at a joke', 'anticipate Uncle George laughing cynically'), more or less overarching ('win in life', 'win this football match'), and more or less proactive (involving patterns for action as well as patterns of action), but people will possess many and these will be related together in complex ways.

Ordinarily, anthropologists have read work on 'schemata' as means of both generalizing cognitive norms to collectivities and explaining social reproduction. Gellner, for instance, has claimed (1970) that schemata (and the concepts and beliefs which are their individual elements) can be treated like other social institutions. They exist in the context of people-in-society not in isolated individual minds, and they provide a fairly permanent coercive frame, independent of any one individual, within which conduct takes place (cf. Zijderveld 1979). Hence, the anthropologists can chart their correlations with other institutions, and, indeed, must do so for their use to make sense; through such activities as religious rituals they can examine the ways in which society endows its members with conceptual schemata and imposes their acceptance.

But then, examining another activity in which it might seem as though societies were simply 'endowing and imposing' schemata – child-rearing – Toren (1993) shows how schemata are actually transformed and reconstituted in the process of their being made available and learned. It is never a simple matter of individuals' being taught by others how to experience, think, feel and know within certain social configurations and historical conditions, then, for children end up constituting their own ideas of themselves and their worlds, and changing these equally idiosyncratically over time (cf. James 1993).

Cognition as personal construct

This introduces a more individually oriented approach to cognitive schemata, such as has been psychologically championed by the likes of George Kelly (1969). Kelly has urged an understanding of schemata as 'personal constructs': as *ad hoc* anticipatory frameworks, reference axes, contexts, plots, criteria of judgement and identity which each person devises for and by her- or himself. Personal constructs are properly seen to be neither dictated by environmental events, nor a property extracted from them, but as beholden to the person; they are psychological, not logical, abstractions and they have no existence independent of the person whose cognition they characterize. They are the outcome of individuals' defining their own stimuli, and also determining their own responses, in contexts of their own devising. Individuals thus confront themselves with people and events of their own creation, and their behaviour amounts to an experiment made in terms of their created cognitions.

For nature is open to an infinity of constructions, and human environments derive from the particular constructions placed upon it: 'Man develops his ways of anticipating events by construing – by scratching out his channels of thought. Thus he builds his own maze' (Kelly 1969: 86). Only human imagination sets limits to the constructions which can be employed to this effect. Moreover, since human beings are intrinsically active – since human lives, as such, are forms of movement or process – personal constructs are always changing. Not only do these systems of anticipation link past to future, then, they are also being transformed and created anew: in relation to what is construed, and often in terms of what is already known, but also possibly *ab initio*. Finally, this implies that no two persons are likely to share the same construction system, the same cognitive schema. Communication between the 'private universes' of personal constructs is, therefore, a matter of time, effort and chance: a matter of developing an empathetic understanding of another person's constructs by endeavouring to 'share' experiences with them.

An ethnographic exploration of cognitive schemata as personal constructs is provided by Rapport (1993a; also cf. Ewing 1990; Briggs 1992). In a micro-social analysis of the interaction largely between two individuals in an English village, Rapport attempts to identify personal constructs in the process of being used – as they are put into practice or enacted – and also to describe the individual worlds (the 'world-views') from which they derive.

Exploring cognition as a matter of personal construct in an empirical setting, a number of general points are arrived at (cf. Rapport 1993a: 150–8). First, individuals can be found defining themselves in relation to a wide array of 'others' – things, people and events – in the universe around them. The individual self becomes the hub, the anchoring point, of a constellation of other objects; this practice both provides individuals with contexts (social and physical) in which to act and also a measure of significance for their actions. Individuals claim significance for themselves by construing the possible relevance of their actions for these others and vice versa. The denser the relations, the more the evidence of the individuals' own existence, the greater its importance and the more precise its nature. In sum, individuals place themselves within full social-cum-natural environments and so construct for themselves meaningful identities and satisfyingly full, rich and varied social lives.

Not only do individuals construe personal relations between themselves and a host of others but they also 'realize' these relations; the things, people and events they construe become part of their real experience. Thus do individuals' abstract personal constructs have concrete consequences. Indeed, it is by claiming a relevance which a host of others has for them, and which they have for others, that individuals' own selves become real to them. Cognizing and naming objects in the universe is to give them shape and stability, to impose form upon an otherwise 'entropic' universe and so to create 'information' (in Bateson's terms (1951: 217)), and acting with their selves upon their assumptions is for individuals to vitalize both. Individuals' selves are fleshed out and animated in terms of a populous environment of relevant others with which relationships have been effected or could be, if desired, in future.

To realize one pattern of things, however, to configure one order of people, things and events in the universe, is to exclude and eschew other ones; every concept and organization of information represents a type of taboo against other potential orderings and meanings. For individuals to realize one set of identities, therefore, is to negate others those same individuals might have assumed. Not only that, existing schemata tend to act as canalizing devices for what is cognized in future. The schemata serve as self-fulfilling prophecies, their meanings self-sustaining. Hence, individuals can usually be found seeing what they expect to see, reaffirming objects in the universe which their cognitive schemata have led them to expect all along; perceiving familiar things from preconceived perspectives, hypotheses about environments are reconfirmed and cognitive schemata come to be reinforced. In short, produced in compliance with prior expectations, the features of the universe which individuals 'recognize' around them usually come to seem not only obvious but inevitable.

However, if individuals come to see largely what their personal cognitive schemata lead them to expect, then there is a sense in which this makes for satisfaction. For, to find in new situations echoes and reflections of old ones is both to have one's prior assumptions and evaluations vindicated, and to reaffirm that the world around one is governed by principles which are consistent and amenable to one's reason and comprehension. Of course, fulfilled expectations do not necessarily mean pleasant ones and often, indeed, occasion anxiety. Nevertheless, the 'discovery' of worrying scenarios still brings with it a kind of security; for, the disharmony is of a certain, expectable kind, of which the individual has past experience. By way of an individual's personal constructs, 'familiarity breeds content' (Young and Wilmott 1974: 116).

See also: **Consciousness, Stereotypes, World-View**

COMMON SENSE

In a famous formulation, Alfred Schuetz (1953), building on the phenomenological insights of Husserl, argued that individuals regularly and habitually apprehend the world around them courtesy of a set of 'background expectancies' which typify their experience and make it comprehensible. However concrete, obvious and natural the facts of an individual's everyday life seem, these facts are, 'in fact', already constructs. All thinking involves constructs, Schuetz claimed, as well as bodies of rules concerning how thinking with such constructs is to proceed. Abstractions, idealizations, generalizations and formalizations thus always intercede between human beings and the world, pre-selecting and pre-interpreting it for us.

Background expectancies are taught and learnt from birth, thereby becoming intersubjective norms which are shared by members of a socio-cultural milieu; not only socially derived, they are also socially approved, controlled, maintained and institutionalized. Indeed, Schuetz suggested that group membership be analytically conceived of in terms of its members' sharing of a set of common background expectancies by which the world was properly to be typified and known.

Background expectancies also come in different types, Schuetz theorized, perhaps the most important being that which typified behaviour, motivations and goals which were deemed sensible, reasonable and rational on an everyday basis; he called such expectancies 'commonsensical'. Schuetz claimed that these pointed up a type of cognition, a set of constructs, which most people employed most of the time: 'the paramount reality of human experience is an everyday world of commonsensical objects and practical acts' (1953). Of the many different kinds of socially imposed rules and recipes for typical sense-making, it was common sense that provided human beings with their fundamental grounding in the world, that which made the everyday world an obvious 'natural' and 'concrete' reality. '[C]ommonsense knowledge of the world', Schuetz concluded, 'is a system of constructs of its typification' (*ibid.*).

Schuetz's work, in turn, has provided the foundation for much anthropological thinking on the everyday realities which people construct for themselves and the sense of naturalness with which these realities come to be invested. Geertz, for instance (1983), has elaborated upon the workings of common sense 'as a cultural system'. Common sense, Geertz begins, claims to apprehend reality matter-of-factly; it is but the immediate deliverances of experience, what 'anyone in their right mind could see'. However, cross-cultural comparison of what is 'matter-of-fact' and to be taken-for-granted quickly reveals that here is a specific cultural system: an ordered body of considered thought, a set of symbols and messages taught and learnt, whose practice is as much an accomplishment as reciting a theological covenant or following a logical proof. Common sense is as dogmatic as religious knowledge and as ambitious as scientific knowledge, Geertz argues, affording a totalizing frame of thought with which to access the ways of the world.

While the content of common sense varies greatly between socio-cultural milieux, however, there are certain stylistic, attitudinal and tonal features which make people's commonsensical constructions of everyday reality everywhere comparable. There is what Geertz calls a 'commonsensical voice', with five distinctive features. First, common sense claims to identify things which are 'natural': inevitable, intrinsic to the world. Second, common sense claims to be a superlatively practical wisdom for getting things done. The forms it takes are anecdotes, jokes, maxims and proverbs; together these may amount to a disparate, heterogeneous, even contradictory, pot-pourri, but they also provide practical advice for engaging with life in all its multifariousness. Third, common sense claims that the truths of the world which it enunciates are obvious, patent and plain; it is what anybody who is sober can see. Fourth, common sense provides immediate wisdom that fits the moment. Finally, common sense promises wisdom which is accessible to all, needing no expertise or special powers, only maturity and some worldliness. These features, to repeat, demarcate a mode of everyday knowing and being-in-the-world which is universal, however it may locally be dubbed; (the term 'common sense', and its distinction from 'religion', 'science' or 'sociology', is merely a Western framing).

In another place (1971: 91ff.), Geertz adds a further distinctive feature to commonsensical knowledge: its limitedness. Common sense, he explains, may be handy and economical but it is also insufficient to deal with all of human experience and to make sense; always and everywhere it needs supplementing and superseding by other, more theoretical, more specialized, forms of knowledge, often within the provenance of experts. Religion, science, sociology, art, law, medicine might all be described as provinces of specialized knowledge which grow out of common sense and go beyond it: transcending, completing, transforming it. Most of the time and for most purposes common sense might be sufficient but periodically there are occasions when answers are needed which common sense fails to supply; mundane routines are effaced by the advent of random, marginal, chaotic and otherwise disorderly happenstance. At this time, the paramount reality of everyday life is left behind and an explanation for the commonsensically inexplicable (disaster, miracle, dream, dispute, disease, death) is sought elsewhere (cf. Berger 1969: 23–4). Again, Geertz is keen to emphasize that substantively, the content of what is inexplicable is wholly socio-culturally contingent; only the cognitive move from common sense to specialist knowledge is universal. And even here Geertz injects a note of caution. It may be that some milieux are more dominated by a non-specialist 'colloquial' culture than others; it may be that only some cultures square off areas of particularly systematized, 'studied' expertise (1983: 74). Nonetheless, whatever the extent of the specialization of knowledges, it will always be true to say that the deficiencies of common sense are episodically made up for by cognitively resorting to the religious expertise of shamans and priests, the medical expertise of doctors, the legal expertise of adjudicators, the scientific expertise of chemists, and so on.

Finally, inasmuch as common sense and more specialized forms of knowledge are complementary to one another, the particular substantive qualities of common sense in any one time and place also give rise to the particular substantive qualities of expertise. If religion and science, alike, provide wider causal understanding than can common sense – breaking common sense down into componential aspects, relating these to a wider universe of forces, and so extending its limited causal vision (Horton 1967) – then common sense provides the grounds from which they grow. Another way of saying this is that, whatever their ideology and mystique, specialist knowledges are not worlds apart. Religion, science, sociology, art, whatever, have a history which sees them not only growing out of the mundane worlds of common sense but also designed in specific ways to supersede them (cf. Schuetz 1953: 3; Latour and Woolgar 1979: 21). Perhaps, Geertz concludes, a comparison of the ways and extents by which common sense is periodically replaced by other modes of thought provides a better way of considering the differences between socio-cultural milieux than to talk of one being more 'traditional', 'modern' or 'post-modern' than another.

See also: **Ethnomethodology, Science, World-View**

COMMUNITY

The concept of community has been one of the widest and most frequently used in social science. At the same time a precise definition of the term has proved elusive. Among the more renowned attempts remains that of Robert Redfield (1960: 4), who identified four key qualities in community: a smallness of social scale; a homogeneity of activities and states of mind of members; a self-sufficiency across a broad range of needs and through time; and a consciousness of distinctiveness. Nevertheless, in 1955, Hillery could compile 94 social-scientific attempts at definition whose only substantive overlap was that all dealt with people (1955: 117)! To overcome this problem, community is often further specified by a qualifying or amplifying phrase: the 'local community', the 'West Indian community', the 'community of nations' or 'souls'. But this would seem only to beg further questions.

Traditional anthropological approaches

In anthropology, one might usefully isolate three broad variants of traditional approach. 'Community' is to be characterized in terms of: (i) common interests between people; or (ii) a common ecology and locality; or (iii) a common social system or structure.

Taking these (briefly) in turn, Frankenberg (1966) suggests that it is common interests in achievable things (economic, religious, or whatever) that give members of a community a common interest in one another. Living face-to-face, in a small group of people, with common interests in mind, eventuates in community members' sharing many-stranded or multiplex relations with one another; also sharing a sentiment towards the locality and the group itself. Hence, communities come to be marked by a fair degree of social coherence.

For Minar and Greer (1969), physical concentration (living and working) in one geographical territory is the key. The locale will throw up common problems and give rise to common perspectives, which lead to the development of organizations for joint action and activities, which in turn produces common attachments, feelings of inter-dependence, common commitment, loyalty and identity within a social group. Hence, communities come to exhibit homogeneity: members behaving similarly and working together, towards common aims, in one environment, whatever their familial or generational differences.

For Warner (1941), meanwhile, a community is essentially a socially functioning whole: a body of people bound to a common social structure which functions as a specific organism, and which is distinguishable from other such organisms. Consciousness of this distinction (the fact that they live with the same norms and within the same social organization) then gives community members a sense of belonging. So long as the parts of the functioning whole (families, age-sets, status-groups, or whatever) work properly together, the structure of the community can be expected to continue over time.

Whether it be in terms of interests, ecology or social structure, then, anthropologists have traditionally emphasized an essential commonality as the logic underlying a community's origination and continuation. Communities have been regarded as empirical things-in-themselves (social organisms), as functioning wholes, and as things apart from other

61

like things. This was in turn the logical basis of 'the community study': the tradition in anthropology of basing research on what could in some sense be treated as a bounded group of people, culturally homogeneous and resident in one locality, because this 'community' would provide a laboratory for the close observation of the interrelations, the continuing interfunctioning, between interests, sub-groups and institutions; and also serve as a microcosm of a bigger social picture which might prevail as societies grew in size and complexity. Anthropologists convention-ally studied communities (villages, tribes, islands) because these were regarded as the key structural units of social life: what the elementary structures of kinship gave onto; what the complex structures of society were composed of.

Symbolic approaches

As varieties of functionalism and structuralism have come to share space in the anthropological armoury with approaches which emphasize the extent to which cultural reality is negotiated and contested, its definition a matter of context and interpretation, and as anthropologists have come to regard social life as turning on the use of symbolic not structural logics, so notions of 'community' have changed. Conceptions of something reifiable, essential and singular have been replaced by a focus on how 'community' is elicited as a feature of social life, on how membership of community is marked and attributed, on how notions of community are given meaning, and how such meaning relates to others. In place of the reified notion of community as a thing-in-itself, then, comes the realization that, as Gregory Bateson put it succinctly: things are epiphenomena of the relations between them (1951: 173); or as Barth elaborated, social groups achieve an identity by defining them-selves as different from other such groups and by erecting boundaries between them (1969). In terms of their field research, anthropologists have come to admit a distinction between the locus of their study and their object of study: they may study *in* villages (on islands, in cities, in factories) but not villages *per se*.

Applying these ideas fruitfully to the concept of community has been Anthony Cohen (1985). Community, he argues, should be seen as a symbolic construct and a contrastive one; it derives from the situational perception of a boundary which marks off one social group from another: awareness of community depends on consciousness of boundary. Hence, communities and their boundaries exist essentially not as social-structural systems and institutions but as worlds of meaning in the minds of their members. Relations between members represent not a set of mechanical linkages between working parts so much as 'repositories of meaning' (1985: 98), and it is these which come to be expressed as a community's distinctive social discourse. In short, membership consists not so much of particular behavioural doings as of thinking about and deliberating upon behaviour in common; here is attachment to a common body of symbols, a shared vocabulary of value. Moreover, it is the ambiguities of symbolic discourse which allow members to unite behind this vocabulary when facing what they perceive to lie beyond their boundaries but also, when facing inward, to elaborate upon differences in its interpretation and hence affirm a variety of cherished individualities. Community is an aggregating device which both sustains diversity and expresses commonality. Thus it is that community comes to represent the social milieu to which people say they most belong; community, its members often believe, is the best arena for the nourishing of their whole selves.

Furthermore, to say that any understanding of 'community' must be situational, that the concept is a matter of contingent symbolic definition, is also to talk about 'community' in relation to other types or levels of sociation. Here, Cohen continues, community can be understood to represent that social milieu – broader than notions of family and kinship, more inclusive, but narrower, more immediate, than notions of society and state – where the taken-for-granted relations of kinship are to be put aside and yet where the non-relations of stranger-ness or the anti-relations of alien-ness need not be assumed; community encompasses something in between the closest and the furthest reaches of sociation in a particular context. Hence, the notion of community encapsulates both closeness and sameness, *and* distance and difference; and it is here that gradations of sociality, more and less close social associations, have their abiding effects. For, members of a community are related by their perception of commonalities (but not tied by them or ineluctably defined by them as are kinsmen), and equally, differentiated from other communities and their members by these relations and the sociation they amount to. In short, 'community' describes the arena in which one learns and largely continues to practise being social. It serves as a symbolic resource, repository and referent for a variety of identities, and its 'triumph' (Cohen 1985: 20) is to continue to encompass these by a common symbolic boundary.

Evolutionary approaches

For many social scientists, the problem of defining community is to be explained not by its situational qualities, however, but its anachronistic ones. Community is said to characterize a stage in social evolution which has now been superseded, and the problems of definition arise from the fact that what is seen as 'community' now is a residue or throwback to a mode of relating and interacting which was once the norm but has now all but been eclipsed by more modern notions of contractual relations in complex society (cf. Stein 1964). Such formulations are by no means new; indeed, they can be seen to imbue the evolutionary schemata of such nineteenth-century luminaries as Maine, Durkheim and Marx. In particular they are associated with the work of the German sociologist Ferdinand Toennies, who, in 1887 [1957], posited the transcendence of 'community' (*Gemeinschaft*) by 'society' (*Gesellschaft*). What he hypothesized was that the traditional, static, 'naturally' developed forms of social organization (such as kinship, friendship, neighbourhood and 'folk') would everywhere be superseded (in zero-sum fashion) by associations expressly invented for the rational achievement of mutual goals (economic corporations, political parties, trade unions). This was not an unmixed blessing, for while community relations might be moral, sentimental, localized, particular, intimate, ascribed, enduring, conventional, consistent, and based on intrinsic attachments (to blood, soil, heritage and language), societal relations were artificial, contractual, interested, partial, ego-focused, specialized, superficial, inconsistent, fluid, short-term and impersonal. And yet, community was inevitably (and absolutely) losing out to the advancing society of capitalism and individualism.

'Community' in current usage

Whatever the evolutionary prognosis, needless to say, (whatever 'advances' capitalism may have made over the past century) 'communities' have continued to flourish; as an idea, community has continued to possess both practical and ideological significance for people. Indeed, recent decades have seen an upsurge in 'community consciousness', 'community development and rebuilding' and 'community values and works' (at the same time as there has been a vaunting of migrancy and globalization). Whether that community is defined in terms of locality, ethnicity, religion, occupation, recreation, special interest, even humanity, people maintain the idea that it is this milieu which is most essentially 'theirs', and that they are prepared to assert their ownership and membership, vocally and aggressively, in the face of opposing ideas and groups (cf. Anderson 1983). Thus, anthropologists have continued to be interested in this idea in use, while Robert Redfield's counsel (1960: 59) remains timely:

As soon as our attention turns from a community as a body of houses and tools and institutions to the states of mind of particular people, we are turning to the exploration of something immensely complex and difficult to know. But it is humanity, in its inner and more private form; it is, in the most demanding sense, the stuff of community.

Anthropologists, in short, continue studying 'community' (Pitt-Rivers 1974; Meillassoux 1981; Cohen 1987) because this is what their subjects inform them that they live in and cherish.

It is perhaps sufficient to say, in sum, that, however diverse its definition, community ubiquitously represents a 'hurray' term (Cranston 1953: 16). Whether 'community' represents a togetherness of the past (Toennies), contemporary behavioural commonality (Frankenberg, Minar and Greer, Warner), political solidarity (ethnic, local, religious), or a utopian future (a rural idyll, a world order), here is a concept of always positive evaluation and evocation, whose usage expresses and elicits a socio-cultural grouping and milieu to which people would expect, advocate, or wish to belong.

See also: **Home and Homelessness, Non-Places, The Rural Idyll, Urbanism**

CONSCIOUSNESS

Consciousness has been of modern philosophical concern since René Descartes (1596–1650) formulated what became known as the *cogito*: 'I think therefore I am'. Thereafter, the centre of philosophical gravity shifted from the cosmos to the individual human being; forces which controlled human behaviour and destiny were felt to arise more and more from within the individual, while belief in the spiritual life and activity previously felt to be immanent in the world outside – gods, planets, herbs, humours, church ritual – grew feebler. Philosophers began to work outwards from the thinking self rather than inwards from the cosmos to the soul; and John Locke (1632–1704) adopted the new word 'consciousness' to mean: 'perception of what passes in an individual's own mind'. Consciousness came to be seen as fundamental to human behaviour, society, language and knowledge.

However, anthropological interest in consciousness is relatively recent, particularly in the UK. In North America, Franz Boas's work helped the early formation of a psychological anthropology which was concerned with the mode in which the mind of the individual became 'enculturated'. Sigmund Freud's legacy led to a psychoanalytical–anthropological focus (on the European continent and in America) on the relationship between consciousness and unconsciousness, as elucidated via 'ethnopsychoanalysis' and the analysis of dream and myth. Finally, G.H. Mead's emphasis on relocating the mind of the individual in the experience of social order led to symbolic–interactionist writing on the corresponding identities of *ego* and *alter*.

In much British (and European) anthropology, notwithstanding, a Durkheimian legacy, which insisted on a separation of the sociological and the psychological, and posited a social realm which was subject simply to social forces and hence home purely to social facts, caused individual consciousness to be seen as irrelevant, irretrievable or non-existent. Instead, a 'collective conscience' was posited in which all members of a society were said to partake via 'collective representations'. To the extent that individuals were recognized as possessing consciousness, this latter was identified with the structural logic of that individual's social or cultural circumstances: to live in group X or class X or role X was to possess X consciousness. Anthropologists thereby provided themselves with a foolproof means of defining away the problematic of consciousness; only in pathological or deviant cases need it be questioned whether people who 'shared' culture or were located within common social structures did not also share similar kinds of consciousness. Anthropologists were content with the generalization of thought and belief to whole societies and the subordination of individuals to these collective thought-regimes.

Recent anthropological work has brought the relationship between individual consciousness and collective conscience into sharper focus, however (cf. Cohen 1994; Cohen and Rapport 1995). There is an increasing appreciation that attending to consciousness is not to privilege the individual over society but rather is a necessary condition of a sensitive understanding of social relations: of society as composed of individuals in interaction. Social reality cannot be described as other than a matter of ongoing interpretation by conscious individuals; there are perceiving, interpreting, intentioning, creative, imaginative – in a word, conscious – individuals within role-players, within language-speakers, within social functionaries, within culture members.

That is, anthropologists have come recently to recognize that an inner/outer dichotomy was in the past being employed as a methodological avoidance strategy. By arguing that anthropology could deal only with what was empirically manifest (the outer), and must be content to treat anything else (such as 'inner' feeling) as either a matter for imagination (fiction, philosophy), or else for other disciplinary investigation (psychology), questions of consciousness were simply pre-empted. As genres have blurred, however, following anthropology's literary turn, so that it has become proper for anthropologists to write reflexively, personally and politically, so, correspondingly, it has come to seem inadequate to write as if the outer life of symbolic forms, institutions and norms was all there is, or as if an outer life of overt behaviours somehow spoke for itself or was intrinsically meaningful: a social fact somehow independent of the ongoing consciousness of the individual. It is necessary to connect up (however partially) the ideational and sensational world of the experiencing individual with the outer world of publicly exchanged behaviours.

In short, anthropologists in the UK and Europe, as in America, have increasingly come to a recognition that to approach other societies and cultures is to approach other conscious minds – albeit through the medium of their own. The consciousness of the anthropologist is, thus, inextricably implicated in those of his or her subjects since it is only in terms of the former that the latter come to be known. Hence, consciousness comes to be seen as not only a central plank of anthropological enquiry but also as a method which necessarily undergirds that enquiry as such.

Approaches to consciousness

To elaborate upon Locke, consciousness may be defined as denoting: 'the movement of the mind both in recognizing its own shape and in maintaining that shape in the face of attack or change' (Ellmann 1977: 1). It includes sensations, perceptions, moods, emotions, propositional-attitudinal states, and narrative structures (Flanagan 1992: 213), and it is embodied: there can be no mind without a body. Perhaps the dia-critical feature of consciousness is its awareness of itself: we are conscious about being conscious. It is this, some have argued, which distinguishes human-like awareness (including, perhaps, that of the higher mammals) from animalistic awareness. All animals possess a 'primary consciousness', a present awareness deriving from the mental imaging, the perception and categorization, of things and events in time. But human beings also possess a 'higher-order consciousness' which entails the ability to model the world free of present awarenesses: to report on, correlate and study subjective states and phenomenologies, and to model such internal states free of time. As Focillon concludes: '[t]he chief characteristic of the mind is to be constantly describing itself' (cited in Edelman 1992: 124).

Nevertheless, such definition should not be allowed to gloss the diversity of opposing hypotheses and conclusions concerning the nature of consciousness. For the sake of convenience, contemporary explanations of consciousness (whether empirical or philosophical) might conveniently be plotted as a continuum. At one pole is found a 'closed' view of consciousness which sees nothing that is not ultimately reducible to materialist explanation: to a physical theory of mind in an objective world. At the opposite pole is found an 'open' view which emphasizes the unconfined scope of the imagination and the potential infinity of linguistic expression, and concludes that there is a unique subjective quality to conscious experience which transcends a purely objective accounting (cf. Cornwell 1994: 10/4–10/6). Traversing the continuum, a sample of such studies might include the following:

1   Francis Crick, *The Astonishing Hypothesis. The Scientific Search for the Soul* (1994): conscious awareness, sentience, feeling and intellectualization derive from the assembly of nerve cells in the brain, their networks and oscillation (at 40 hertz). Neurons fire and consciousness results; humans are no more than the sum of their molecules.

2   Hans Moravec, *Mind Children* (1988), or Colin Blakemore, *The Mind Machine* (1988): the brain amounts to an evolved, biologically programmed computer which gives merely the impression of free will. There is no substance to the 'mind' and it should simply be identified with some of the faculties, states and activities of the body.

3   Roger Penrose, *The Emperor's New Mind* (1989): mechanical computation could not possibly propagate consciousness. But the latter could be an outcome of microcosmic physics: the effect of quantum gravity in the brain.

4   Daniel Dennett, *Consciousness Explained* (1991): the brain is an 'anticipation machine', working on a principle of 'parallel distributed processing'. Consciousness is an illusion, a series of shifting 'multiple drafts' with no 'centre of narrative gravity' and no continuity. There is no Cartesian theatre where 'I am' comes together; moreover, the *qualia* of experience, the way things seem, are far from ineffable or merely subjective.

5   Colin McGinn, *The Problem of Consciousness* (1992): consciousness is an intractable problem which Dennett (*et al.*) explain away rather than explain. Accounting for the presence of consciousness in a world of physical objects and processes, understanding the self, free will, meaning and knowledge, simply transcends our natural powers;

it is too great a problem for human intellect ever to surmount. Or Patricia Churchland, 'Can Neurobiology Teach us Anything about Consciousness?' (1994): despite the spectacular advances in neuroscience made this century, and even if we eschew the mind–body dualism, how human consciousness emerges from networks of neurons yet escapes scientific understanding.

6   John Searle, *The Rediscovery of the Mind* (1992): to insist on treating 'objectively observable phenomena' alone is to ignore the mind's essential features. Hence, while we might accept that both consciousness and intentionality are biological processes of the brain, we need not accept a materialist orthodoxy which would either eliminate consciousness – because it is observer-relative, or because it is really something else (language, environment) – or else reduce it to something more basic (such as computation). Rather, we must insist that consciousness and intentionality are both intrinsic and ineliminable. We all have inner subjective qualitative states of consciousness; we all have beliefs, desires, intentions, perceptions *et al.* which are intrinsically mental.

7   Gerald Edelman, *Bright Air, Brilliant Fire* (1992): to reduce a theory of an individual's behaviour to a theory of molecular interactions is simply silly. The way the brain develops and works (before as well as after birth) is more like an object undergoing natural selection in an ecological habitat than a computational system, hence the ceaseless novelty, creativity and change of our mental processes. Consciousness is a habitat ultimately beyond the physical, and science will never ultimately explain the human individual.

8   David Chalmers, *The Conscious Mind* (1996): consciousness arises from the mind but is intrinsically beyond the material facts of the world. The 'hard problem' of consciousness, what it feels like for an individual to be looking out at the world from the inside, is beyond the ken of science.

9   John Eccles, *How the Self Controls Its Brain* (1994): a purely materialist explanation for consciousness is by no means inevitable; some form of dualism is inevitable. For, through language, consciousness transcends its own biological bases, becoming conscious of the latter and even exerting some control over them. As 'mind', dead matter is transcended.

Given the importance of consciousness, and the diversity of competing claims concerning its nature, one might expect anthropology to have been insistent long ago on making its own contribution. And for this to have been welcomed. For, as historian of science, Roy Porter, recently concludes: the hard sciences still tell us far less about the aspects of the 'soul' (the self, personality, individual identity) that really matter – about the details of the subjective nature of consciousness, and about 'the stupendously complex dialectical interplay of subjectivity, self and society' – than those first-hand observations of the 'moral narratives' by which meaningful lives are lived (1994: 7).

Conventionally, however, as has been explained, *après* Durkheim, the anthropological appreciation of the problem of consciousness has been somewhat narrow. Even in the work of Clifford Geertz, responsible for an interpretive anthropology which recognized that the conscious imposition of meaning on life was the major end and primary condition of human existence, and that 'becoming human was becoming individual' (1973: 52), still consciousness is seen solely as a collective phenomenon which pertains to the culture or the social group. For Geertz postulates that we become individual only in the context of 'cultural patterns': under the guidance of historically created systems of meaning 'in terms of which we give form, order, point and direction to our lives' (*ibid.*). Even though individuals are ever making interpretations, these are determined by the systems of significant symbols and particular cultural contexts in terms of which they are expressed. In this way, Geertz claims human thought to be 'out in the world'; it represents merely an 'intentional manipulation of cultural forms', of systems of symbols of collective possession, public authority and social exchange (1983: 151). Moreover, such thought is publicly enacted: tied to concrete social events and occasions, and expressive of a common social world. In short, giving meaning to behaviour is not something which happens in private, in insular individual heads, but rather something dependent on an exchange of common symbols whose 'natural habitat is the house yard, the market place, and the town square' (1973: 45). The symbolic logic and the formal conceptual structuring of this thought may not always be explicit, but they are socially established, sustained and legitimized. Cognition, imagination, emotion, motivation, perception, memory and so on, are thus directly social affairs, while outdoor activities such as ploughing or peddling are as good examples of 'thought' as are closet experiences such as wishing or regretting.

In Geertz's adumbrating of 'an outdoor psychology' (1983: 151), then, culture (as systems of historically transmitted symbols) is constitutive of mind, while individual experience and memory of the social world are both powerfully structured by deeply internalized cultural conceptions, and supported by cultural institutions; life in society entails a public traffic in significant cultural symbols. Geertz concludes that the webs of significance we weave, the meanings we live by, achieve a form and actualization only in a public and communal way. There can be no private (individual, unique) symbolizations for mind is 'transactional': formed and realized only through participation in cultures' symbolic systems of interpretation. Furthermore, different 'individual' minds within the culture are neither opaque nor impenetrable to one another, for they think in terms of the same shared beliefs and values, and operate the same interpretive procedures for adjudicating reality. To construe a system of cultural symbols, in sum, is to accrue its individual members' subjectivities.

In this way, Geertz's interpretive anthropology may be aligned with preceding anthropological approaches to consciousness. In Durkheimian (or Saussurean) terms, individual interpretation is prefigured by a set of collective representations, while individual consciousness as such is a manifestation – temporary, episodic and epiphenomenal – of a collective conscience; the particularities of conscious individual expression (or *parole*) simply depend and derive from an enabling collective language (or *langue*).

Consciousness as movement

It is the 'terrifying feature' of studying consciousness, as Searle has put it (1992: 16), that the ontology of mental states is a first-person phenomenon while the epistemology and methodology is third-person. It seems that we know what consciousness is for ourselves – our consciousness is ineluctably ours, however all-encompassing, diaphanous, momentary, multiple and impossible to circumscribe it also seems – but we can judge its existence in others only by inference. As we have seen, Geertz's 'outdoor psychology' obviates this problem of knowing other minds by regarding 'minds' as consisting of nothing more than publicly exchanged symbols. Notwithstanding, other methodologies do suggest themselves by which consciousness can be treated more humanistically and individually and still be approached ethnographically. These centre on notions of movement: on the movement of consciousness, and on consciousness as movement.

A good place to begin is with William James's (1961 [1892]) conclusion that consciousness is not so much a substance as a process, continuous and yet always changing. In existentialist writing of later periods, too, there has been an appreciation that individual consciousness is a matter of an ongoing (and never completed) project. The process of consciousness, in short, entails the continuous 'writing', rewriting, erasing and developing of a narrative of being and identity.

The individual continually defines and composes the story of his or her life, and it is in the composing and in the telling (to themselves and to others) that consciousness arises and dwells. Consciousness comes to know itself in and through the movement between different points of view in time and space. Moreover, this involves directedness or intention: relating consciousness to itself and to otherness for the purpose of coming to know it, and be it, in relation to others. Consciousness is thus both inner- and outer-directed; it possesses 'open closure', in Ong's words (1977: 338). Moreover, being a process of becoming, something which attains to knowledge via cognitive movement between 'itself' and what is 'other', consciousness offers at least potential access from outside; as a narration of otherness, consciousness is more observable than if it were an unchanging substance or thing.

An early anthropological appreciation of this relationship between consciousness and movement is to be found in the work of Gregory Bateson (1951, 1972). The human brain, Bateson begins, thinks and knows in terms of relationships: all knowledge of external events is derived from the relationship between them (1951: 173). Indeed, things and events are epiphenomena of the relationships which the brain conceives between them. Moreover, to conceive relationships (and so create things) is to move or cause to move things relative to the point of perception (the brain) or relative to other things within the field of perception; subject and object, perceiver and perceived are thus intrinsically connected. Movement is fundamental to the setting up and the changing of relations by which things gain and maintain and continue to accrue thingness. And since one of the 'things' that thus comes to exist as an identifiable thing is 'oneself' (the perceiving brain as objectified 'out there'), movement is also fundamental to the thingness, the identity, of the self.

There are a number of implications of these conclusions. The first is that the things which derive from cognitive movement in this way – differences, relations and things – are material and immaterial alike. Ponds, pots and poems, are all the outcome of engineering movement relative to a point of perception; to cause to move relative to a point of perception is to construct an ambient environment that is both 'natural' and 'cultural'. All experiential phenomena in human life are, thus, 'appearances', that which is perceived to be.

A second implication is precisely that the mind is 'individual' in its constructing. Bateson describes the individual as an 'energy source' (1972: 126), responsible for the movements which underlie the perception of difference, as well as the point of perception *per se*, and thus responsible too for energizing the events in the world; it is not that the mind is merely being impacted upon by environmental triggers. More generally, each human individual is an 'energy source' inasmuch as the energy of his or her acts and responses derives from his or her own metabolic processes, not from external stimuli. It is with this energy, through this movement, and by this construction of relations and objects, that individuals create order and impose it on the universe.

A third implication, then, is that what can be understood by 'order' is a certain relationship, a certain difference, between objects which an individual mind comes to see as normal and normative; it is one of an infinite number of possible permutations, and it is dependent on the eye of the individual perceiver. Furthermore, this may not be what others perceive as orderly. 'Order' and 'disorder' are statements of relations between an intentioning perceiver and some set of objects and events; they are determined by individuals' states of mind.

In exploring the relationship between movement and consciousness, then, what Bateson established (at least: translated into an anthropological environment from an existential one) was the fundamental relationship between such movement and perceived order in the world, and between such order and individuality.

The evolution of consciousness

An appreciation of movement of another kind characterizes anthropological work which approaches consciousness from the vantage point of human evolution, both phylogenic and ontogenic. In the latter vein, Gerald Edelman (1989, 1992) has argued for an ontogeny of individual consciousness in terms of activity in the world; the individual brain evolves during its lifetime by selecting between different ideas and behaviours.

Much conventional thinking about the brain, Edelman explains, has been either instructionist or programmatic in intent; the characteristics of the brain are seen as being either produced in response to the environment or else written into a computer-like programme which is in-born or learned. Edelman, however, suggests a selectionist model wherein characteristics are seen as originally appearing in the brain randomly, and independent of their possible usefulness or use, and are then selected for by an experimenting human organism which moves through life solving problems. The model has come to be known as 'neural Darwinism'.

For Darwin's theory of selection, diversity was the key – the diversity of species, the diversity of individuals – and how such diversity was selected from. Even tiny differences, independently occurring, could affect the environmental viability of the organism. Edelman's model has it that selection, on a different time-scale also operates within the individual body. Comparable to the immune system, adapting the body on a time-scale of hours and minutes so that new antibodies come to be selected for, the brain adapts the body in seconds: by selecting for new ideas and behaviours.

The grounds of Edelman's model are three: (1) There is initial diversity in the brain, spontaneous and intrinsic, which exists independently of the environment and how it is changing (the brain has 100 billion nerve cells, with a possible million billion connections, and each is responsible for causing a potentially different idea or behaviour). (2) From this initial diversity, variant forms of idea and behaviour are experimented with as means to encounter and interact with the environment; sensory signals (visual, auditory, etc.) then relay information back to the brain concerning the 'success' of the idea/behaviour in gaining a favourable, 'hedonic' result. (3) Those patterns of brain connections which produce a favourable result are 'strengthened'. The successful movements come to be 'valued' more highly than the failures by cellular 'value systems' located in the brain stem which chemically amplify certain cellular connections over others which have been tried. The behaviour is then 'learnt', the idea 'remembered'.

In this way, human beings can acquire complex skills without being pre-programmed – and without the need to conceive of the brain as a logical machine or the plaything of socialization. (Programmaticist thinking has the brain merely rearranging what has been put in, while instructionist thinking must posit a cause-and-effect relationship between environment and human activity.) It is through experimental activity in the world that individuals build up more and more abstract cycles of thought and action, every action suffused with value, with some goal that has been achieved; by interacting with the world from the moment they are born (if not before), individuals select the perceptions that work and discard those that do not.

What this is doing, moreover, is ordering the world and locating the owner of the brain as an individual actor *vis-à-vis* that order. The human brain is thus not so much a passive receptor of information from the world as an active constructor of it. There may be a real world out there (with cultural and social as well as natural lineaments) but individual experience of it does not involve neat parcels of information waiting to be unwrapped. Rather, the world is diverse, ambiguous and entropic, and it is out of unstructured and incoherent impressions which it receives that the brain makes distinction and actively generates information. The brain does not copy boundaries of the world so much as impose them on the world, and the way the latter is perceived and organized depends on the individual organism doing the work. In short, individual organisms construct their own versions of the world and generate their own action within it.

The facts speak to Edelman, in short, (as they did to Bateson) of an individuality of consciousness. First, '[t]he forms of embodiment that lead to consciousness are unique in each individual, unique to his or her body and individual history' (1992: 136). Second, not only is there an enormous diversity and individuality of brain structure, but each brain interacts with the world in a unique way, motivated by its own system of 'values', of what has worked 'successfully' for it over time in the past. Finally, each consciousness also gives on to a unique future. It is impossible to prescribe how an individual will in future behave, even with the knowledge of his or her 'strong values' in the present. For the inherent spontaneity of the brain's activity always throws up new variations for possible experimentation. Here is the creativity, the 'extraordinary imaginative freedom' (Edelman 1992: 170), whereby each individual, each day, says and does and thinks things never done or said or thought before, by them or anyone else, and may judge their success and value with equal novelty.

In terms of the phylogenetic evolution of humanity, the 'higher-order consciousness' described above, Edelman would regard as a relatively recent organic development. 'Primary consciousness', meanwhile, has a far longer inheritance. It arose, possibly, as a means by which animals (and plants?) might differentiate, coordinate and retain information on two vital kinds of perceptions and the relations between them: that of the outside world and that of the body's internal homeostasis and well-being. Self/not-self and inside/outside were two of the most fundamental things for an animal to recognize; it was necessary to know where one's self ended so that one could preserve oneself and not eat oneself when hungry, and so that energy was not wasted saving enemies or 'the world'.

In human beings, primary consciousness became enhanced by the evolution of a memory with which to retain hypotheses about what things had hedonic value for the self and then to project these hypotheses onto the future. The human brain thus became able to experiment with a multitude of different generations of simulations of events – without overt trial and error, and using innocuous remembered environments – in milliseconds. The human brain became an 'anticipation-machine' (Dennett 1991) which would track, memorize and plot its environment, surmising self and world and anticipating action: zillions of idea germs competing for space in a final draft of future likelihood.

To early hominids, such anticipation may have been a crucial adaptive advantage, assisting their survival despite their size and relative defencelessness. Engendered by conscious control, a plasticity of environmental response would have greatly increased hominid fitness. A significant part of this environment, moreover, for the hominid, would long have concerned others of its own kind: family and friends, strangers and enemies beyond the self. Anticipating their movements, predicting their behaviour, would also confer adaptive advantage. Hence, anthropological work has recently concerned the relationship between a phylogenetic evolution of consciousness and human sociation (Ingold 1990).

As Humphrey elaborates (1983), in the same way that our self-knowledge or self-awareness contextualizes our behaviour within an orderly flow of events which meaningfully connects our past life with our future, so we imaginatively write the narrative of the lives of others. Our imagination connects us together and enables us to conceive of others' different experiences. While the biological integrity of the human body and the way our sensory apparatus connects with our brains means that we each have our own, and only our own, mental experiences, still we can hope to understand one another: not by taking on one another's experiences but by imaginatively taking on one another's points of view. In short, others might be seen as acting as they do because of where their lives have come from and where they are directed towards; this movement also affords insight into how they might be expected to act in future. Furthermore, in the same way that we are aware of the subtle discrepancies between appearance and reality where our own behaviours are concerned, how an outward display does not necessarily coincide with an inward sensibility, so we can imagine the possibly labyrinthine layers of intrigue between behavioural form and meaning in the lives of others.

In sum, the phylogenetic evolution of consciousness may have represented a human adaptation of enormous consequence. One's experience of one's own bodily routines and changes could be projected onto the environment as a means of anticipation and control; furthermore, using self-knowledge one could hope to get beneath the skin of others. Here were imaginative projections giving onto constructions of the world of great explanatory power.

The modalities of consciousness

A further understanding of the movement of consciousness, of consciousness as movement, concerns the study of individual memory.

Memory is seen as an important key to consciousness and as that which gives coherence to experience. This is because memory orders the images drawn from experience in a temporal or narrative form (cf. Crites 1971). Memory represents a lasting chronicle (not without its gaps or lacunae) of the temporal course of experience: experience as a succession.

Another way of saying this is that consciousness grasps its objects of attention (of intention) in an inherently temporal way. Past, present and future are the universal modalities of our experience. Or, as Augustine famously phrased it (1907: XI/xxviii): consciousness 'anticipates, attends and remembers'; what it anticipates passes through what it attends to become what it remembers.

Remembering, nonetheless, is not the same as knowing. To know something is more than the simple recital of the chronicle of memory, of its succession of images. Rather, our experience is illuminated by 'recollecting' from the memory: knowledge is recollection. When we narrate the ongoing story of our lives, we recollect particular images, stopping the flow of memory's stream at certain points, slicing off segments or abstracting certain general features and elements from it. To know (ourselves and our lives) is to re-collect the images lodged in memory, the 'memory stream', into particular configurations, continually ordering and reordering past experiences into different presents.

Then again, memory is only one of three modalities of our experience. The second, oriented to the future not the past, is anticipation. Like memory, anticipation has an elemental narrative form. We actively plan and resolve and project and make guesses and predictions of what may happen, and in doing so we write a series of narrative scenarios. Albeit more vague and 'thin' than memory, we dream and worry and wish a future; then we act by improvising on this. If memory is the present of things past, then anticipation is the present of things future.

But then, memory and anticipation are more properly seen as tensed modalities of the present. That is, the above two stories are not separate but exist as a tensed unity in the present; an ongoing story absorbs the chronicle of memory and the scenario of anticipation into the thick description of an embodied present, so that our identity remains continuous (even if not coherent). The present becomes the decisive moment in our story of self and other, the moment of decision, and of crisis, between the remembered past and the anticipated but undetermined future. If memory represents the depth of our experience, and anticipation the trajectory of its action, then in the present, action and experience meet.

77

Finally, by participating in and observing this present, by taking account of the storifying process by which individuals continue to write their lives into a narrative whole, the anthropologist can hope to gain access to the consciousness of others as it moves from past awareness to future (cf. Tonkin 1992; Hastrup 1995a). It is their memory and their anticipation that individuals express and perform in their use of cultural symbols and social institutions.

An anthropology of consciousness

The anthropologist seeks the subtleties of intimate knowledge: knowledge behind the ideal-types, categories, generalities and abstractions of public exchange. The quest is for the knowledge which animates these collective forms, forms which far from revealing this knowledge may well mask it beneath the vagaries of symbol or conventional idiom. For much of its history, social anthropology has lived with the comforting notion of collective representations. However, to continue to resign itself to the inaccessibility of consciousness is for anthropology to abide by a view which it knows from experience to be false: that behaviour can be taken at face value, and that what people appear to do equates with what they do do and what they think. Anthropology cannot be concerned solely with what is public or revealed, for this is, or may be, mere gloss on what is concealed or not obviously apparent. To gloss consciousness either by notions of society or by culture, so that an individual experience is treated as if it were simply identical to or derivable from that of the collectivity to which he or she supposedly belongs, is to deny or, at best, misrepresent individuality and selfhood by gross simplification. Moreover, with the collapse or redundancy of the old positivistic orthodoxy which stipulated a strict difference between the anthropologist and the anthropologized, consciousness has certainly become more accessible to valid study than previously. It is no longer acceptable (*à la* Durkheim, or Mauss (1985)) to claim a consciousness for ourselves which we deny to others.

In a sense, of course, this is not so much a new departure in anthropology as a matter of rediscovering what its practitioners have always enjoined; anthropology has been concerned with consciousness (as a method and a subject) since Malinowski first wrote in his field dairy in 1917: 'Principle: along with external events, record feelings and instinctual manifestations; moreover, have a clear idea of the metaphysical nature of existence' [1989: 130]. Anthropologists have long made claims about other people's consciousness and their grasp of it, and ethnographic reports have been replete with imputations of belief, thought, knowledge and emotion to members of the societies and social groups with which they were concerned; anthropologists have sought to make sense of what they have seen and heard, and have taken this latter as evidence of conscious sense-making beings. Of late, however, they have been more prepared to admit that this is necessarily the case, in studies of consciousness as this pertains to: creativity (Fernandez 1993), individuality (Rapport 1993a), childhood (James 1993), psychopathology (Littlewood 1993), healing (Kapferer 1983), spirit possession (Stoller 1989a), or altered states (Lewis 1971).

Ultimately, an anthropology of consciousness translates into a 'decolonizing' of the human subject: a liberation both from over-determining cultural conditions and overweening social institutions (discourse, collective representation, social relationship, *habitus*, praxis), and from their social-scientific commentator–apologists. This is not because of a desire to change anthropology's object from society to the individual, but because anthropology can no longer rest content with traditional assumptions that social behaviour originates or resides in forces (social, historical, cultural) beyond and 'outside' the individual.

See also: **Cognition, Individuality, Narrative, World-View**

CONTRADICTION

In an influential collection of essays (1990), the philosopher Isaiah Berlin elaborated upon the Kantian aphorism that 'Out of the crooked timber of humanity no straight thing was ever made'. Between the supreme values, the true answers and the final ends as construed within the diverse world-views of different individuals and societies there can be expected no necessary commensurability, no final reconcilability and no true synthesis. 'Great goods' can always be expected to collide for there is no determinate means of putting different 'goods' together, no single overarching standard or criterion available to decide between or harmonize discrete moralities. Moreover, this is so not merely in the case of the values of a succession of civilizations or nations, persons, times and places, but also of contemporaneous ones. Every social milieu, in short, can be said to be grounded in incompatibility and contradiction. These, indeed, are perhaps the only non-contradicted human realities.

Anthropologists have had cause to consider the contradictoriness of social life, the 'disharmony of ends' (Douglas 1966: 140) of which individuals and societies are in pursuit, in a number of contexts. First, there is what Malinowski perhaps first enunciated, the contradictions which come to be contained in an anthropologist's field notes. The field-journal, 'in which everything is written down as it is observed or told', amounts to 'a chaotic account' (Malinowski, cited in Wedgwood 1932–4: notebook 18 May 1932). In part, this can seen to be due to an elision of the spoken with the written. Oral exchange involves 'the flow of speech, the spate of words, the flood of argument', and here 'inconsistency, even contradiction' can prosper in ways which appear chaotic when seen through the 'critical scrutiny', 'explicitness' and 'fixity' of the written (Goody 1977: 49, 37; also cf. Clifford 1990: 64). The field-journal contains a chaotic aggregation because of recontextualization: because the grammar of oral exchange, and the rubrics of intelligibility and consistency, are not those of written exchange (cf. Rapport 1997a: 93–105).

Secondly, anthropologists have sought to avoid a recontextualization of local notions of rationality; what appears 'chaotic' in their data, illogical and contradictory, may well evidence an alien logic and way of ordering matter which does not accord with Western notions. In debates over rationality, therefore (Wilson 1970; Hollis and Lukes 1982; Overing 1985a), anthropologists have sought ways of avoiding construing their data via the empirically based truth conditions and formal rules of logic of the West. Alien truths may contradict our own and in our terms may seem self-contradictory, but this is something that we can neither ignore nor explain away as 'poetry': as examples of figurative or analogic or metaphoric thinking which exist still within the bounds of a (necessarily universal) Western account of human reason and reasoning (Overing 1985b: 152).

Perhaps the central issue, however, concerns the question of consistency which the anthropologist can expect to encounter both within and between the people they are investigating. Are individuals and the societies they come to constitute likely to be characterized by contradictory thoughts, words and actions? Should the anthropologist expect, and expect to recognize, a certain non-contradictory consistency in the social milieux they are investigating?

Sybil Wolfram (1985: 72–3) has warned anthropologists that logicians often distinguish between 'contradiction' and 'inconsistency'. Two things are contradictory if they are of opposite truth-value, so that one is true if the other is false, and vice versa; two things are inconsistent, however, if they cannot both be true, but both could just as well be false. Anthropologists, notwithstanding, are usually satisfied to use the terms interchangeably, and to understand by 'contradiction' something whose existence appears to deny the possible simultaneous existence of something else: both/and rather than either/or (cf. Rapport 1997c).

A Durkheimian treatment of contradiction

Early on, Malinowski appreciated that:

> arguing by the law of logical contradiction is absolutely futile in the realm of belief, whether savage or civilised. Two beliefs, quite contradictory to each other on logical grounds, may co-exist, while a perfectly obvious inference from a firm tenet may be simply ignored.
>
> (1948:194)

However, to the extent that, conventionally, social-anthropological theorizing has followed the lead of Durkheim rather than those of, say, Simmel, Weber or Marx, the above wisdom has been undervalued. Hence, it has been an anthropological orthodoxy that human beings symbolically classify the world in such a way as to eschew contradiction, and follow social practices which call for, and ultimately maintain, consistency in thought and behaviour.

Primitive Classification (Durkheim and Mauss 1970 [1903]) was an important volume for drawing attention to the fact that order in human life is procured through the construing and imposing of systemically related symbolic categories. As Durkheim and Mauss expounded, complex systems of classification characterize every socio-cultural milieu: discrete things arranged in distinct groups and categories, separated by clearly determined lines of demarcation and hierarchy, standing in fixed relationships to one another and uniting to form single, congruous wholes. These classificatory systems are necessary to human understanding. They make intelligible the relations which exist between things, they connect ideas and they unify knowledge.

Moreover, Durkheim and Mauss insisted that classificatory systems were cultural products, derivative of, modelled on and expressive of, society. Such a view came to be widely shared, laying the foundation for much social-anthropological appreciation of the social-structural ordering of human things, from Radcliffe-Brown through Evans-Pritchard and Fortes to Gluckman. It found perhaps its most elaborated expression in Douglas's *Purity and Danger* (1966).

There is a human 'yearning for rigidity', Douglas begins (1966: 162), a longing for 'hard lines and clear concepts', and all such epistemologies are to be found anchored to ongoing social realities. Each culture comes to represent a universe to itself, and members come to view their social environments in common as consisting of people and things joined and separated by boundaries that are socially sanctioned and must be respected. Here are indubitable, coherent systems from which the contradictory, the incoherent and the arbitrary are banned. However, having constructed symbolic classifications of the world, Douglas admits, we human beings have to 'face the fact that some realities elude them, or else blind ourselves to the inadequacy of the concepts' (1966: 162). That is, any systemic ordering and classification of matter inexorably rejects certain elements as inappropriate: it must do this in order to arrive at clean lines of division between matter. An inevitable by-product of a system of symbolic classification, therefore, is 'dirt': that which contravenes the ordering. Hedged about with taboo, the dirt which threatens the clear-cut ordering of the world, which would 'pollute' its cleanliness, is eschewed; while the notion that something is polluted serves to protect cherished principles and categories from contradiction. The only exceptions are certain extraordinary, ritual situations. For while the disorder which such dirt represents is a threat, it is also recognized as powerful. Unrestricted by existing categories and order, it ushers in new possibilities. Ritual, therefore, represents a venture out of social order and control in an attempt to tap an extraordinary power which is seen to inhere outside the everyday nomos of human life and to belong to the supernatural cosmos. Here is a surmounting of conventional differentiations, Douglas concludes, and a confronting of ambiguity and contradiction: an expression of a common human desire 'to make a unity of all their experience and to overcome distinctions and separations in acts of at-onement' (1966: 169).

However, if the universe of human experience is a purely socio-cultural universe, and that universe is necessarily coherent and unitary, on the Durkheimian view, it is not quite clear where and how those 'dirty realities' intrude: how categories come to fray at the edges and so how individuals come to 'see' the contradictory. Seeking to marry Durkheim and Mauss to a Marxian critique which placed contradiction, via competition and contrast, at the centre of the societal model, therefore, was the work of Max Gluckman. Gluckman described 'social systems' as replete with ambivalence: as fields of tension, cooperation and struggle (e.g. 1963a: 135–6). There were inherent tensions between principles of social-structural organization, between institutions, and between individuals. Nevertheless, some control of these tensions was achieved through their cathartic expression in ritual. Rituals effected an institutionalized expression of conflict and protest which worked paradoxically to renew, strengthen, and even sacralize, the established system; here were public statements of rebellion against, and hostilities within, the established social order, dramatizations of conflict, and annulments or reversals of hierarchy, whose regular, routine and normative staging served as a prelude to their nomic reinstatement. 'Rites of reversal' and 'rituals of rebellion' (1959), in short, were extraordinary, topsy-turvy stages which removed the significance and, to an extent, the cognizance of the contradictory in ordinary social life so that the tensions (social and psychological) which derived from these contradictions came to be dissipated. Hence, while a social system may no longer be conceived of in terms of a stable equilibrium, at least dynamic equilibria persisted. In a more radical appreciation of this dynamism, Leach (1954) theorized that this might entail societies in continuous change, swinging, pendulum-like, between contradictory ideal-typical versions of how, symbolically, social life was to be conceived of and lived.

It remained unclear, in the Durkheimian picture, however, just why recognition and embrace of the contradictory should be cordoned off in, and only cognized as, the extraordinariness of ritual. Upon this, Victor Turner sought to elaborate (1964). If symbolic behaviour 'created' society, then ritual performances could be described as dynamic moments in social groups' creative practices wherein symbolic creations adjusted to internal or external pressures for change. The symbols in terms of which rituals were structured provided points of junction, and enabled compromises to form, between social needs of classification and control on the one side, and innate (anarchic) human drives on the other. For what symbolic formulations afforded, Turner theorized, were unifications of disparate, contradictory significata; ritual symbols brought together, in condensed form, what was otherwise divided and kept apart. They juxtaposed ideological against sensory meanings, the normative against the emotional, and the cognitive against the affective. Symbols thus effected an interchange of qualities such that what appeared tense, contradictory and potentially anomic in the everyday came to seem a unity. As a result of ritual catharsis, normative social classifications were revitalized.

In sum, the anthropological orthodoxy which began with Durkheim problematized contradiction to the extent that it saw social order as wedded to an everyday eradication of symbolic contrarieties. Societies, as social facts, as things-in-themselves, were unitary and orderly; the institutional structuring of societies took place in non-contradictory fashion; and individuals, as members of societies, cognitively mirrored the institutional structures in which they were habitual role-players. At best, contradiction was recognized in this formulation as pertaining between the states of order and disorder or un-order – between different social-structural episodes, between structure and ritual – but not as a state in itself.

What is absent from this line of thought is an appreciation of the possible ubiquity of contradiction: people saying and doing and thinking inconsistent things as a matter of course; people employing multiple, contradictory symbolic classifications at the same time; people able to construe classificatory systems which are in themselves contradictory. In a well-known example provided by Foucault (1973), a Chinese encyclopedia suggests the following division of animals:

> a) belonging to the Emperor, b) embalmed, c) tame, d) sucking pigs, e) sirens, f) fabulous, g) stray dogs, h) included in the present classification, i) frenzied, j) innumerable, k) drawn with a very fine camel-hair brush, l) et cetera, m) having just broken the water pitcher, n) that from a long way off look like flies.

It is with cognitive-symbolic contradiction of this kind (not either/or but both/and) that anthropology has come slowly to recognize it must deal.

A Nietzschean treatment of contradiction

Inasmuch as Durkheimian notions of social order were in sympathy with nineteenth-century natural-scientific notions of homeostasis and an emphasis on the conservation of energy, an appreciation of the ubiquity of contradictoriness in human social life coincides with a post-Einsteinian emphasis on the contingency of order, its pertaining to perception and perspective, and on entropy (cf. Bateson 1951: 246ff.). There is now a far more reflexive anthropological appreciation of the implicatedness of human beings in the order they construe and the uncertainty this gives onto; constructions are situated and diverse, and constructions change. Even as human beings seek meaning and order in themselves and their world, their lives remain unpredictable – to themselves as to others – even chaotically so (cf. Abrahams 1990; Prigogine 1989).

Part of the reflexive revolution which anthropology has embraced of late concerns the implications of its own expectations for the socio-cultural realities it 'discovers'. '[E]thnographic reality', in Dumont's words (1978: 66), is something 'actively constructed, not to say invented'; while 'other cultures' might be understood as anthropological imaginings of plausible explanations of what other people seem to have been doing (Wagner 1977: 500–1). If anthropology has traditionally eschewed contradiction, then, this is so because of the dogmatic, axiomatic and doctrinal nature of its own analytical discourse and not the nature of socio-cultural reality. Perhaps now, other discourses should be chosen for anthropological analysis, ones more 'commonsensical', in Geertz's terms (1983), than specialized, technical or theoretical, and so closer to those employed in the everyday by informants. Is it not now possible to imagine an anthropological way of looking, knowing and inscribing which is heterogeneous and self-contradictory, even wildly so, a way which transcends what Kundera refers (1990: 7) to as that '"either-or" [which] encapsulates an inability to tolerate the essential relativity of things human, an inability to look squarely at the absence of the Supreme Judge'? Perhaps only a pot-pourri of disparate analytical notions is capable of grasping the vast multifariousness of human social life (Geertz 1983: 90–1).

As Marilyn Strathern puts it (1990a: 6), the 'diversity and multiple character' of phenomena (including their contradictoriness) need not necessarily give way, in analysis, to any more systemic representation; one can imagine an anthropological account which specifies complexity without simplifying it. Moreover, any one anthropological account can flag its own provisionality, insist on its own perspectivity and timeliness (Cohen 1992b); while the contradictions between such accounts serve merely to point up the fluidity and multiplicity of human social life and classification, and the aggregation of 'limitless discursive perspectives' (Parkin 1987: 66) to which the latter amount.

Kundera's reference, above, to 'the absence of the Supreme Judge' alerts us to the essentially Nietzschean nature of the new anthropological dispensation concerning the contradictory (cf. Shweder 1991b: 39). For Nietzsche, human society and culture are above all poetic projects, art-works, and it is to artistic models and aesthetic evaluations (and not scientific assessments and rational judgements) that one may best turn for an understanding of them. Like an art-work, human worlds are something constructed and something requiring interpretation in order to be understood – made livable, mastered – by their inhabitants; being the joint product of ineffable matter and human interpretation, there is no absolute truth about the world, and it possesses no independent character. Moreover, the world can be interpreted equally well in innumerable, vastly different and deeply incompatible ways. The 'death' of God (as hero and author) means that the world is not subject to a single interpretation – God's will or intention; it is something, instead, with 'no meaning behind it, but countless meanings' (Nietzsche 1968: 267). This being the case, there could never be a 'complete' theory or final interpretation of the world or anything else, merely an array of succeeding perspectives.

Human beings may themselves be part of the world, may be viewing it from situated, interested and partisan perspectives, but nonetheless, it is they who create the world, create themselves and their perspectives in their interpretations. They construct the world as they interpret it; and their constructions add further to the complexity and multi-fariousness and indeterminacy of the art-work that continues to be interpreted – by others, by themselves – in the present and future. Amidst the profusion of versions and forms of construction of the world, there is only one singularity: the continuation of their profusion. Interpretations continue to be made because to interpret is to be human, and to be individual, and because the human world has no objective character, no underlying or overarching structure, system or regularity to it. Moreover, with the death of God, one might expect the relation-ship between the profusion of interpretations to be anything but a clear-cut one; instead, it is indirect, tangential and contradictory.

In brief, a Nietzschean emphasis on the artistry of symbolic classifi-cation provides an approach to the latter which allows for contradiction, its poetic import and creative promise, in a way which Durkheim's insistence on singularity and system does not. With the 'literary turn' in anthropology, moreover, the value of Nietzschean aestheticism in the depiction of society has begun to be celebrated.

The contradictoriness inherent within socio-cultural milieux, and its phenomenological appreciation, has also begun to be emphasized in contemporary ethnography (Moore 1987; Ewing 1990; Rapport 1993a, 1997c). Here is a recounting of contradictory thoughts, beliefs and behaviours both between people and within people. Individuals are seen apt to construct and maintain a diversity of perspectives for them-selves, each contradictory in terms of the elements, relationships, va!ues, norms, desires, expectations and so on of all the others. Contextualizing their lives in terms of these perspectives, individuals can think, speak and act in any number of contradictory ways. The aggregation of these individual perspectives can also alter with time, as new ones are constructed, current ones developed and old ones sloughed off; and as the aggregation changes so does the array and range of assembled contradictions.

This diversity of perspectives, of world-views and identities possessed by an individual can be more and less conscious, the deployment of contradictions in thought, speech and action more and less strategic. Contradiction may be disguised by the momentariness of life, by the way that conscious existence turns on momentary thoughts, feelings, apprehensions, emotions, on what Virginia Woolf refers to as 'moments of being' (1976). Hence, while contradictory in their interpretations of the world, in the meanings they imparted to people and events, nevertheless, the contradictoriness of individual lives may be swallowed up by the experiential intensity of each moment – by the absoluteness of order which one particular perspective leads them to attribute to that moment – and by the constant movement of their conscious lives from moment to moment.

Then again, contradictoriness (as duplicity or hypocrisy) can be employed as a vehicle for all manner of purposive social gain: pleasing an electorate, confusing an enemy, being polite to a guest, keeping in with a friend, insulting, provoking, misleading, mystifying another or oneself. While between the more and less deliberate uses of contradictions are beliefs and assertions which might be described as vague or fuzzy, such that contradictoriness is not always so self-evident. One can envisage a graded scale, Wolfram suggests (1985: 72–3), between blatant and non-blatant, self-evident and fuzzy contradictions, such that the complexity of an individual's relationship with his or her contradictory representations of self and world is given full analytical measure. One thing that is clear, however, is that, as Hollis puts it (1982: 72): 'Mankind could hardly survive without beliefs which are incoherent, unlikely, disconnected or daft'. Or again: 'private paradoxes can be allowed to stand indefinitely' (Kelly 1970: 12).

When the private becomes public, when contradictory individuals interact, the situation does not become any simpler, more coherent or consistent. The opposite, in fact, as the self-contradictory meanings of the thoughts, beliefs, words and actions of one individual meet those of others. That is, interaction between individuals and their variegated cognitions does not somehow give rise to 'social systems' which are consensual, coherent, coercive, or without contingency – or which are particularly singular or systemic at all. The picture is rather one of 'chaotic relativism' (Rapport 1993a) in which a diversity of individual perspectives influences a diversity of others in all manner of indirect, incidental, contingent, changeable – and contradictory – ways. Moreover, the ambiguities and abbreviations of public systems of symbolic exchange, of language and behaviour, are such that the contradictions and inconsistencies need not become apparent. Symbolic forms mediate between the words and actions of one individual and the thoughts, beliefs and cognitions of others, so that, as Sapir concluded (1956: 153): 'the friendly ambiguities of language conspire to reinterpret for each individual all behavior which he has under observation in terms of those meanings which are relevant to his own life'.

In short, an appreciation of contradiction gives onto a modelling of human social life not as something coherent, rather as a muddling through. Socio-cultural milieux are neither systemic nor singular, for they are constituted by the aggregation of a multiplicity of private symbolic–classificatory orders which collide, abut, overlap, and need not consistently coordinate or coincide. Furthermore, the muddle is ongoing, brought on by interacting individuals continuing to influence one another and themselves in all manner of possibly unintentional ways.

From the traditional Durkheimian image of singularity, coherency and consistency, of symbolic–cognitive classifications expressing the structural–functional solidarities of their societal origins, we have arrived at a rather different conclusion. Here is an image of a diversity of contradictory symbolic realities or perspectives in use at any one moment and between moments, even in the 'same' sociolinguistic milieu, and in no necessarily singular, clear, uncontested or coherent relationship one with another. Individuals may live in a diversity of constructed world-views and identities, their contradictory cognitions giving existence to a plurality of social worlds in any one time or place. This, it can be argued, represents a more authentic picture of ethnographic reality, of individual and society, than a denial of the contradictory or its sidelining as something extraordinary if not pathological.

Muddling through the myriad of versions of symbolic reality in use in a socio-cultural milieu may not make experience easy or comfortable. Notwithstanding, there is an inexorable relationship between symbolic order and the contradictory, and perhaps it is in the latter that there is to be found evidence of our human being and becoming, its creativity and artistry. In the symbolism of society and culture, things can be both/and because human worlds run along poetic lines, and in terms of momentary cognitions. Both/and amounts to a cognitive norm, and it points up the constructed, provisional nature of the social worlds which we inhabit and for which we are individually responsible.

See also: **Classification, Cognition, Methodological Eclecticism**

CONVERSATION

For Michael Oakeshott (1962), conversation is what human cultures accomplish and what human societies inherit. Conversation is a meeting of individual voices speaking in different idiom or mode. Science, poetry, practical activity and history are such modes of speech, different universes of discourse. It is the very diversity, the manifold of different voices, speaking in different idioms or modes, which 'makes' conversation. The voices need not compose a hierarchy, and the conversation need not amount to an argument; the diverse voices may differ without disagreeing, and they may appear to be saying the same without agreeing. Hence, conversation is not an inquiry or contest, exegesis or debate; it does not set out to persuade, refute, or inform. Conversation has no truth to discover, no proposition to prove, no conclusion to seek; reason is neither sovereign nor primary, and there is no accumulating inquiry or body of information to safeguard. Instead, as 'thoughts of different species take wing and play round one another' – responding to and provoking one another's movement, obliquely interrelating without assimilating – so their individual thinkers engage in the 'unrehearsed intellectual adventure' of socio-cultural life (1962: 198). Going on in public and inside themselves, a conversation between individuals ultimately contextualizes every human activity and utterance.

For anthropology, perhaps the key characteristic of conversation is that it gives onto socio-cultural reality; '[i]n every moment of talk, people are experiencing and producing their cultures, their roles, their personalities' (Moerman 1988: xi). Conversation is a kind of interaction in which human reality – a constructed reality which does not objectively exist beyond the consciousness of its individual agents – is continually created and recreated. A sensitivity to the micro-processes of conversational interaction is a growing anthropological concern (cf. Bauman and Sherzer 1974; Bruner 1983).

Conversation and anthropological accounts

Conversation as focus, theme and image is no stranger to anthropological representation. It is expected that the anthropological text will convey conversation between informants; oratory, disputation, curing and cursing might all elicit precise reportage of the verbal and other expression and exchange in the field (cf. Favret-Saada 1980; Rapport 1987; Cohen 1989). Similarly, it has come to be acceptable, even expectable, for there to be conversation recounted between informant and anthropologist; as the anthropologist enters into relations in the field, verbal and other, so that field takes shape for him, is indeed shaped by his interactions (cf. Briggs 1970; Dumont 1978; James 1993). Likewise, the anthropological text may be expected to engage in conversational exchange between the writer and his academic reference group; as the anthropologist makes sense of the field so his sense-making is informed by accounts he has read before, and mediated by the effect he would wish his writing to have on others (cf. Rabinow 1977; Clifford

1986; Campbell 1989). Finally, it is anticipated that the anthropological account achieves its effect only through engaging in conversation with its reader; as objective and positivistic representation no longer persuades – is denigrated as epistemologically mistaken and morally questionable – so the reader is expected to make sense through an evocation and performance of the text (cf. Bruner 1986; Tyler 1986; Brady 1991b).

What might be added to the above varied appreciation of conversation is an emphasis on conversation as perhaps the fundamental ground on which social life rests. We use conversation as anthropological focus, theme and image because of the 'naturally occurring' importance of conversation; conversation is a feature of every socio-cultural milieu, and its practice radically affects the nature of both social exchange and cultural process.

Conversation as naturally occurring

An awareness of the significance of naturally occurring conversation (albeit more sociological than anthropological) is nothing new in social science. Symbolic-interactionism (Blumer), ethnomethodology (Garfinkel) and sociology-of-knowledge (Berger and Luckmann) approaches all make it central to their projects. As Blumer would put it, if individuals act towards things on the basis of the meanings that the things have for them, and these meanings are the *sine qua non* of the socio-cultural existence of things *per se*, then it is in conversation with their fellows, in the processes of interaction, that this construction of meaning takes place (1969: 3). For Garfinkel, meanwhile, it is in conversation that the shared but implicit competency, knowledge and common-sense assumptions of culture members comes into play; it is here that members do the work of artfully (if contingently and unwittingly) apprehending order and reasonableness in social life (1972: 323). And again, for Berger and Luckmann, just as social reality is a precarious human construction, an ongoing everyday work in the face of encroaching entropy and threatening anomy, so conversation is the most important vehicle of reality-maintenance; working away at his conversational apparatus, the individual protects and confirms the consistency of his world (1966: 140).

For each of the above theses, furthermore, conversation gives onto, and can be treated in terms of, an epistemic singularity. In each case, conversation connects with (is preceded and followed by) a single social structure and a consensual culture. Through (Blumerian) symbolic interaction and mutual indication, then, a group of common objects emerge for a group of people, objects which bear the same meaning;

conversation eventuates in shared perspectives, in a high degree of consensus over what people call 'reality'. This consensus then enables group members to define and structure in common most situations in which they meet, and to act alike (Blumer 1972: 187). Meanwhile, by complying with (Garfinkelian) common background expectancies of interpretation in conversation, the stuff of everyday life gains not just an accountable and 'methodical' but also common character; thanks to the stable social structures underlying the processes of unconscious interpretation, cultural systems thereby replicate themselves: a world its members know in common and take for granted (Garfinkel 1964: *passim*). Finally, the conversation which (*après* Berger and Luckmann) ongoingly maintains a construction of reality against chaos also serves to structure subjective perceptions into a typical, intersubjective, cohesive and universal social order. This constrains what individuals experience in terms of what they can communicate, since conversation cannot but accommodate itself to the edifice of coercive categories and objective norms that is a society's language (Berger and Luckmann 1969: 66).

Epistemic diversity

Epistemic singularity arising out of conversation might now be regarded as questionable. Indeed, it has become a commonplace of contemporary anthropological reportage that today's world ('globalized', 'post-modern') is characterized by a diversity of discourses, narratives or epistemes per socio-cultural milieu with no necessary consensus or synthesis between them (cf. Tyler 1986: 132). No single locale is possessed of just one local (symbolic or structural) order of things through which the world is understood and normalized, and rather than any overarching ideological totalism, the locale is home to the intersecting of a multiplicity of systems of meaning. It is recognized, in short, that conversation gives onto epistemic diversity and interaction, with individuals negotiating their ways between competing centres of philosophical gravity and the shifting balances of their power, playing off one episteme against another as different existential strategies at different moments (cf. Jackson 1989: 176–86).

Furthermore, it can be argued that there is nothing particularly new (or 'post-modern') in this condition, and that cognitive and practical manoeuvring between a plurality of socio-historically situated epistemes has ever been characteristic of human life. Epistemic conversation is something which individuals practise everywhere, and have always practised, part-and-parcel of our 'human realities' (Fernandez 1985:

750). Inasmuch as the world is constructed on an ongoing (*ad hoc*, contingent, conjectural, contesting, 'poetic') basis by individuals exchanging cultural forms in social interaction, a conversation between a diversity of epistemes can be seen to be the natural condition of human life.

See also: **Discourse, Interaction, Literariness, Methodological Eclecticism**

CULTURE

Cultural pluralism versus culture in the singular

Given the fact that anthropology has usually been defined as the study of other cultures, it is not surprising to find 'culture' to be one of the most crucial concepts of the discipline. The focus of anthropology is upon the diversity of ways in which human beings establish and live their social lives in groups, and it is from this diversity that the anthropological notion of culture, at least in the twentieth century, is derived. This idea of the plurality of culture contrasts with the idea of culture in the singular, an interpretation that began its development in eighteenth-century European thought (see Williams 1983a), and became predominant in the nineteenth century. Framed through the social evolutionary thought linked to Western imperialism, culture in the singular assumed a universal scale of progress and the idea that as civilizations developed through time, so too did humankind become more creative and more rational, that is, people's capacity for culture increased. The growth of culture and of rationality were thought to belong to the same process. In other words, human beings became more 'cultivated' as they progressed over time intellectually, spiritually and aesthetically. De Certeau (1994: 103) notes that such a model, which proclaims culture as a defining feature of 'cultivated' human beings (other people have something called 'tradition'), can have a strong political agenda, and in the hands of empires it has served a rather useful tool for introducing elitist norms wherever they imposed power.

In contrast, the modern anthropological stance, on the side of cultural relativism and in confrontation with racism (cf. Boas 1911), has been startlingly liberal in its insistence that culture must always be understood in the plural and judged only within its particular context. Very early on, Franz Boas firmly placed all cultures on equal par, and scoffed at notions that wed technological might with social and cultural superiority (Boas 1886). In this view Chinese culture is different from, and equal to, that of the African Nuer, or the Amazonian Yanomami. Each culture pertains to a specific, historically contingent, way of life, which is expressed through its specific ensemble of artefacts, institutions and patterns of behaviour. Another and related use of the term within anthropology states that culture pertains to that huge proportion of human knowledge and ways of doing things that is acquired, learned and constructed, that is, not innate to a newborn child. Thus while the capacity for language may be inborn, the specific language that the child learns to speak is not, and as learned knowledge its particular grammar and idiosyncratic classifications of the world become a crucial part of his or her own cultural heritage.

There is nothing straightforward about any of these meanings, including the anthropological notion of culture in the plural. Probably most of us apply the term across a range of overlapping meanings, depending upon the approach being used, the questions being asked, and increasingly the political point we wish to make. From its inception, anthropology has been engaged in active controversy over the meaning of the term, and in recent years there has been an ongoing, virulent debate over the propriety of its very use. Thus today, even in the most 'liberal' of hands, the term is so fraught with complications that what we might individually decide to include as 'belonging' to the category of culture becomes a flag-waving gesture, a throwing down of the gauntlet. Edwin Ardener noted (1985) that important concepts tend to go through periodic stages of hot debate, and they do so whenever a field of study is on the verge of a strong epistemological break. The concept about which he was speaking was 'rationality', and the epistemological rupture that he foresaw was an abrupt shift away for anthropology from the high modernist era of the anthropological grand narratives of Marxism, structural-functionalism and structuralism. Ardener's discussion was over a decade ago, but the present-day controversy over the concept of culture is to a large extent a continuation of the same remarkably perplexing chore of extricating ourselves methodologically, epistemologically and politically from the powerful categories of modernist thought.

Below will be discussed some of the more interesting aspects of the controversy over culture, such as questions about the status of culture's reality (does culture in fact exist?). If there is a reality to culture, where does this culture reside? does it dwell in the mind or is it a matter of practice? to what extent is culture shared? through which approach (cognitivist? phenomenological? materialist?) can 'it' best be understood and translated? These are large issues, and none of course has been resolved. To do so would entail agreement over just what culture is, and also over just what it is that anthropology does. It is probably because an agreement with respect to either endeavour would be most unlikely that controversy over culture will remain electric, and thus continue to play an essential role toward creating an anthropology that is relevant (and we hope acceptable) to the academic and political concerns of the twenty-first century. As will be made obvious, the big question revolves around the ways in which anthropology can best persevere toward the end of extricating itself from its nineteenth-century colonialist and grand narrative beginnings.

The critique of cultural homogeneity, and culture's objective reality

While anthropologists have insisted upon the plurality of cultures, they have also tended to view a given culture in the singular. Although Boas was the most important force in introducing the idea of the plurality of historically conditioned cultures into anthropology, the discipline has not always followed his insistence that culture itself is an ongoing *creative process* through which people continually incorporate and transform new and foreign elements. Boas argues further, still within his romanticist and anti-evolutionist perspective, that it is through such adaptations that a culture arrives at an *integrated spiritual totality*. Although his observations on the creativity and openness of the cultural process tended to be ignored, Boas's notion that cultures become manifest as distinctive coherent systems has had considerable influence. A more up-to-date version would be the notion of the aesthetic autonomies of cultures. The idea that culture refers to a systematically harmonized whole with each therefore comprising a *shared and stable system* of beliefs, knowledge, values, or sets of practices held sway for a very long time in anthropology. It is a notion strongly embedded in all functionalist, structural-functionalist and structuralist thought. Thus this notion of the homogeneity of culture flourished and developed through many versions, but in the direction that assumed (unlike Boas) the fixity, coherence and boundedness of cultures. In what Fabian (1998: x–xi) refers to as this 'classical modern concept', a position of 'ontological realism' is assumed with respect to culture which understands tradition as something real, to be found outside the minds of individuals, and objectified in the form of a collection of objects, symbols, techniques, values, beliefs, practices and institutions that the individuals of a culture share.

It is a position that has much at stake, for in portraying cultures as having objective reality over and beyond individual agency, the foundation is set for what is thought to be the development of a true science of anthropology. The major bequest of Durkheim (1966 [1895]) to the discipline was the idea that the discovery of the social sciences' own distinctive object ('the social fact') would provide the upstart human sciences with a competitive edge – i.e. the methodological procedures through which human behaviour could be explained. With this achievement the social sciences would acquire scientific respectability *vis-à-vis* the natural sciences. There have been important voices taking exception to such a goal. We have Evans-Pritchard in his Marett Lecture of 1950 (see Evans-Pritchard 1962) hotly debating that, because anthropology's distinctive subject matter pertains to conscious, thinking human beings, the methodology of the discipline should be situated within the humanities, and *not* the natural sciences. On the whole, however, we see that Boas's most important argument, that creative process, historical contingency, and learned, socially transmitted behaviour are not in conflict, has not been widely explored until fairly recently. We find instead that the notion of culture as a coherent, bounded, and stable system of shared beliefs and actions has been a powerful twentieth-century idea that has been very difficult to shift. As intimated above there were reasons for such neglect.

The crisis in representational theories of meaning

In the 1960s there was a move away from the earlier emphasis upon culture as customary or patterned behaviour, to a stress upon culture as idea systems, or structures of symbolic meaning. Each culture was understood in this later view to consist of a shared system of mental representations. As David Schneider saw it, culture consists 'of elements which are defined and differentiated in a particular society as representing reality – the total reality of life within which human beings live and die' (1976: 206). In this view culture is not just shared, it is intersubjectively shared (cf. D'Andrade 1984). Such a Parsonian/Weberian systemic, 'symbol- and meaning-centred' concept of culture became the centrepiece of a 'unified theory of action' designed to provide a mighty and authoritative theoretical linkage between all the social sciences (see Fabian 1998: 3–4, 6). Culture, as a conceptual structure made up of representations of reality, was understood to orient, direct, organize action in systems by providing each with its own logic. Culture gave purpose to the social system, and ensured its equilibrium. Behaviour out of sync with the system's cultural valuations was said to be abnormal, deviant, dysfunctional, with the implication being that it was aculturally, or anticulturally, driven. It took some time for this powerful law-and-order (as Fabian dubs it) concept of culture to be seriously questioned.

However, over the past couple of decades anthropology has increasingly been involved in a crisis over its representational theories of meaning, and at the same time expressing deep regret over its former misdirected scientific hopes – those as envisioned by our more sociologically oriented masters, who used the natural sciences as the yardstick for judging our own success. What is particularly being called into account is the understanding of cultural (collective) representations as a template for social action, with its related unfortunate effect – all those anthropological portrayals of cultural dopes who act unconsciously in accordance to underlying structures of shared symbolic meaning. The world of meaning, as Roy Wagner insists (1986, 1991), cannot articulate with a natural science format, which must by the very nature of its task (of objectification) ignore, mystify, disdain, *doubt* personal invention and concrete imagination. Wagner, one of the most persuasive in his critique of the idea of shared, stable systems of collective representations, suggests that cultural meanings are not constituted of the signs of conventional reference, but instead 'live a constant flux of continual re-creation'. He goes on to say that 'the core of culture is . . . a coherent flow of images and analogies, that cannot be communicated directly from mind to mind, but only elicited, adumbrated, depicted' (Wagner 1986: 129).

Any fieldworker who has worked carefully with the telling and learning of myths, or the performance of rituals, should recognize the wisdom of Wagner's insight into the poetics, creativity, individuality, inconsistencies, contradictions of such cultural processes (also see Dell Hymes (1981) on the poetics of the American North West Coast telling of myths, and Overing (1990) on the tropes and performance of Amazonian myths). As Ingold says (1994b: 330, his italics), 'what we do *not* find are neatly bounded and mutually exclusive bodies of thought and custom, perfectly shared by all who subscribe to them, and in which their lives and works are fully encapsulated'. What we *do* find can be much more challenging, and, as one antidote to the treatment of culture through the lens of representational theories of meaning and other grand theory, many anthropologists today are focusing upon the dialogics and poetics of everyday behaviour. In so doing the primary concern is with living, experiencing, thinking, affectively engaged human beings who follow (in varying degrees and a myriad of manners) particular lifeways. It is antagonistic toward all those attempts to create 'objective' abstract structures that have the effect of dismissing much of what the rest of the world has to say.

The question of practice

There is much, it would seem, that representational theorists omit in the experiencing of culture (also see Ingold 1994b). First, while it is meaning systems that is their primary concern, it is cogent to stress that these systems are creations of the anthropologist, and not of the people who supposedly 'follow' them. The usual claim is that, for the people, the 'system' and the mental representations that comprise it are unconsciously followed. Thus the meaning-creating, speaking, socially occupied person (whether from Chicago, Italy or Timbuktu) is omitted. As too is all practice in which he or she engages, and this by definition since the symbolist view of culture excludes behaviour.

What, we may ask, *is* the relation between meaning and practice? between mind and body? concept and performance? The present trend is to oppose the representational view of the body as a passive instrument, and thus time and again we find in today's literature across a range of disciplines – in anthropology (e.g. Wagner 1986, 1991; Fabian 1983, 1998; Ingold 1994b), cognitive psychology (e.g. Shanon 1993), philosophy (e.g. Meløe 1988a, 1988b) and culture theory (e.g. de Certeau 1997) – the plea to recognize *embodied* meaning, that is, to wed concept and practice, the perceiving with the acting agent. We might say that there is no such thing as 'a culture', or rather that 'culture should not be a noun, but a verb: "to culture", or "culturing"' (Overing 1998; also see Friedman 1994: 206). As Ingold notes (1994b: 330, his italics), 'it might be more realistic . . . to say that people *live culturally* rather than they *live in cultures*'. For most people around the world, culturing is an endless and ever ongoing, overt activity, which ill fits the social scientist's categories. From the Amazonian perspective culture time and again refers to the *skills for action*, which conjoin (independent) thinking and a sensual life, that individuals have, mould and use to live a particular human life. However, to reunite the body, the sensual, acting, feeling, emotive aspects of self, with the thinking, language-knowing self creates havoc with most modernist versions of culture. As should only be expected, debates today on the implications of a more phenomenological approach to culture for the future development of anthropology have a certain edge, a passion and often a political as well as academic challenge to them.

The politics of culture

The breeze of post-colonialism

Today, the politics of the use of the concept of culture is such an explosive topic that no anthropologist can afford to remain naive about the issues involved. Anthropology is not an innocent endeavour – a point the debate makes abundantly clear. At the same time it raises questions that appear to threaten the very political and academic viability of the discipline – at least as practised in modernist guise. Post-modernism has taken its deconstructive toll, while the voices of post-colonialism have been even more devastating, though in many ways fair, in their criticism of the grand narratives of anthropology. Combined, this is a literature that has played an important role in implementing certain major shifts of focus in the ethnographic 'eye'. One thing is certain: anthropology today is not what it was a decade ago. To a certain extent the subject is now in a period of confusion, indeed breast-beating, as each new post-colonialist treatise is published: we find within such literature the anthropologist replacing the missionary as the 'bad guy' of the Western world. For many of us the breezes of post-modernism and post-colonialism have been refreshing. Be that as it may, there is no simple answer to the accusations that anthropology has served as handmaiden to colonial conquest and government, and for the most part was developed within intellectual frameworks distinctly modernist in design (see Ardener 1985). Although most anthropologists working among the colonized have viewed their programme as one to alleviate the weight of colonialism by reducing its mistakes, anthropology – at least to the extent it has considered itself a social science and not of the arts – has nevertheless inadvertently served colonialism's aim. It has also served the hegemony of modernist programmes of development and ways of thinking. How did this occur?

The creation of the exotic other, or cultural relativism gone wrong

The claim is that in its representations of other cultures, anthropology has transformed the 'other' into anthropological object, and in so doing has reified, homogenized and exoticized the lives of other peoples. Within this gaze it is difficult to glimpse real, living, experiencing, meaning-making human beings who follow particular lifeways. Rather, such lives are reduced to the 'objective' abstract structures created by the anthropological expert, and the people who live them are thereby silenced. Anne Salmond suggests (1995: 41) that in this act of silencing the other, the ethnographic other becomes as object, a resource for the self. As she notes, objects have negative properties in Western thought, for they cannot speak, think, or know. In their describing and their measuring, anthropologists have, in her words (1995: 23), produced 'others' as 'exotic curiosities for European consumption'!

Thus we see that the liberality of the notion of cultural pluralism within modernist constructions is now being strongly contested. What was considered to be the healthy route of cultural relativism is being reinterpreted as the weedy path of a diseased exoticism. For instance, McGrane argues (1989) that the idea of the superiority of Western culture, particularly its spectacular scientific success, became the potent and decidedly unliberal yardstick through which anthropologists assessed the accomplishments of other cultures. There is the superior Western culture, and then there are all the rest as contrast. A sharp divide is created, with epistemological privilege always on the side of the West. In general, the process of exoticizing other cultures has been intensified through this tendency of characterizing their salient features in contrastive frames to our own (cf. Ingold 1994b: 331). The content varies somewhat in accordance to context, but in each contrastive frame, we find lurking the underlying idea that 'unsophisticated' technology is understood to entail weak religion, weak thought, weak ritual, weak politics, weak economics. Thus, we have science, they have magic; or we have history, they have myth; we have high-tech agriculture, they have subsistence practices; we have priests, they have shamans; or we have scientists, they have shamans; we have philosophy, they have beliefs; we are literate, they are illiterate; or we have writing, they have oral literature; we have theatre, they have ritual; we have government, they have elders; we have rationality, they are pre-logical; we have individualism, they have community – and so on through a myriad of cultural traits that are suggestive of a thesis long popular in the history of Western thought that equates 'simple' technology with simple minds. Such contrasts do indeed play havoc with the original tenets of cultural relativism, where understanding and judgement were meant to be relative to local context.

Part of the problem has been methodological, for anthropologists have steadfastly used as analytical categories such concepts as science, religion, economics, politics, kinship, society. Such Western classifications, while highly relevant to our own highly compartmentalized existence and history, have proven to be very clumsy tools through which to understand the perspectives of other peoples. Moreover it means that the very vocabulary that anthropology has used for analysis, its own definitional terms, have carried a perverse and hidden agenda: the other's local was to be understood within the context of our local, which in the end became a universal standard, not only of judgement, but for description as well. This has placed the other in a true double-bind situation. The relativist (and humanist) intention that insisted upon respect for the local could hardly be achieved through such a methodology.

The politics of exotica

Thus there is little wonder that the post-colonialists accuse anthropology of the production of fictionalized exotica. Its use of the concept of culture has well served the purpose of distancing ourselves – politically, epistemologically, morally, technologically, mentally – in time and space from all other peoples of the world (see Fabian 1983; Ardener 1985). Through modernist classification, a powerful 'primitivism' has been created that freezes most of the peoples of the world within a time (neolithic, medieval) and space (Asia, Africa, Amazonia) a hopeless distance from our own. As Johannes Fabian says (1983), it would be impossible to achieve a *conversation* with the other, one based upon mutuality and respect, through such a programme of study that so relishes exotic difference. The 'catch-22' (Heller 1961) for anthropologists has been that it would only be through establishing such coeval conversations that we could learn the discipline's prejudices: without the conversations, we could not come to know the prejudice; while, because of the prejudice, we could not know the benefits of conversation! This has been an important step for anthropology – to recognize the *necessity* of achieving a mutual, coeval exchange to the endeavour of under-standing other perspectives on ways of living.

The political implications of this process of creating exotic cultures are truly awesome. Just think of being frozen in neolithic time, and your chances of dealing equitably with those who recognize only themselves as existing today! Exoticism provides impetus to 'first-world' development projects, though which 'inferior' forms of life can 'assimi-late' the knowledge of a 'superior' sort of people in order to live a 'better life'. Exoticism plays into the politician's hand by reinforcing and contributing to Western antipathies toward other peoples of the world (cf. Said 1978 on the effects of Western Orientalism). Culture and difference have become the most powerful political paradigms fuelling political action in the modern world (cf. Eller 1997), where for instance a common strategy of nation-states is the fixing of cultural identities (in the name of ethnicity) within its territorial boundaries toward the end of centralized control and domination. We know all too well the dangers of these notions of ethnic purity and ethnic separation.

Many people are driven to conceive of themselves in this way, and thus to devise and proclaim their own cultural distinctiveness (cf. Eller 1997). As Sahlins remarks:

> the cultural self-consciousness developing among imperialism's erstwhile victims is one of the more remarkable phenomena of world history in the late twentieth century. 'Culture' – the word itself, or some local equivalent – is on everyone's lips . . . For centuries they may have hardly noticed it. But today, as the New Guinean said to the anthropologist, 'If we didn't have *kastom*, we would be just like white men'!
>
> (Sahlins 1994: 378)

In Amazonia, people who never lived before within a bounded universe are today instructed by national governments to devise boundaries for themselves – and to live in accordance to their 'authentic' cultures; many peoples who had no singular self-denominations are now creating them in order to deal with national governments, and are recognized by government agents only insofar as they display the practice of their 'authentic' culture, such as through the wearing of indigenous dress and their lack of political savvy in dealing with these self-same agents. The notion of culture is a true monster, if we agree with Abu-Lughod who argues (1999: 13) that the concept of culture is always contaminated (as is the concept of race) by the politicized world.

It is because the notion of culture can so easily be used in pernicious ways that Abu-Lughod argues for the abandoning of its use in anthropology. However, it is for that very reason – its prevalence in everyday and political talk – that anthropology should not turn its back on the concept. As Cerroni-Long argues (1999), times demand that anthropologists actively counteract the dangers of 'cultural fundamentalism', in all its colours and practices. Multi-culturalism, transculturalism, transnationalism are phrases in the air, so to speak. The strength of anthropology is that we appreciate *multi-perspectivism*: there are a multiplicity of colonial discourses and post-colonial ones, and a plurality of potential and active subversions of both. Our recognition of this universe of pluralities is surely anthropology's real competence. We should therefore remain firmly and reflectively engaged with the concept of culture, so as to *resituate* it so as to play into our strengths, one of which is the possibility of destabilizing all those grand narratives that underpin ongoing relationships of cultural domination. It is not the word 'culture' that is at fault. The *word* is not responsible for the sins of its academic and political use. Rather, the problem has been the modernist paradigms of knowledge within which it has been placed, which entail very specific relationships of domination and subordination. Insofar as anthropologists collude with the postulates that provide weight to such frameworks of knowledge, the anthropological task is hardly innocent.

See also: **Classification, Community, Myth, Post-Modernism, Society, Stereotypes, The Unhomely, World-View**

CYBERNETICS

Cybernetics might be described as: the 'elucidating of patterns in recursive, nonlinear systems' (Harries-Jones 1995: 3). More generally it deals with the patterned nature of the world: with the connectedness of phenomena and the connections between things; with the way patterns of connectedness both relate spheres of life and experience that might circumstantially seem unrelated, and are ultimately responsible for the existence of those seemingly unrelated phenomena in the first place. Cybernetics takes seriously Whitehead's counsel (1925):

> [T]he misconception that has haunted philosophical literature throughout the centuries is the notion of 'independent existence'. There is no such mode of existence; every entity is to be understood in terms of the way it is interwoven with the rest of the universe.

Cybernetics is the elucidation of the circuitry of the world, and how that circuitry can best be appreciated and maintained for the future existence both of human societies and their relation to the natural environment.

One of the founders of cybernetic thought was the anthropologist Gregory Bateson. It is with his work that we begin here, therefore, before exploring briefly how others have applied cybernetic thinking since.

Gregory Bateson

In his intellectual biography of Bateson (1904–80), Harries-Jones describes him as 'the most brilliant holistic scientist of this century' (1995: 3). Holism was a key word for Bateson; an understanding of our human part in the whole 'living system' that was the world he saw as crucial for our earthly survival. Furthermore, anthropology had to be a non-specialist, 'interdisciplinary discipline' because only in a holistic (however seemingly seeming amateurish) use of all manner of information could it expect to tackle the 'vast intricacies' of the worlds of cultural construction and social interaction (Bateson 1959: 296). Hence the need for an anthropological understanding to connect up with ethnology, ecology, biology, philosophy, aesthetics and psycho-analysis. This might then give onto a new ecological world-view where aesthetics and consciousness combined to form a 'sacred' recognition of the one-ness of life, of life's ontological monism.

Holism called for a new language, one which transcended the long tradition in Western metaphysic of positing dualisms: between human and animal, between nature and culture, between mind and body. In this search, Bateson was variously inspired: by the English poet William Blake, by his naturalist father, by his own fieldwork among the Iatmul of New Guinea (1936). Significantly, he was also inspired by the new theme of 'cybernetics', as coined by the American mathematician Norbert Wiener. Wiener's realization that the social-scientific concept of 'information' and the natural-scientific concept of 'negative entropy' were in fact synonymous represented, for Bateson, 'the greatest single shift in human thinking since the days of Plato and Aristotle' (1951: 177). Or, in Wiener's own words (1949: 18):

> The notion of the amount of information attaches itself very naturally to a classical notion in statistical mechanics: that of entropy. Just as the amount of information in a system is a measure of its degree of organization, so the entropy of a system is a measure of its degree of disorganization: and the one is simply the negative of the other.

Let me backtrack, however, and offer nine basic steps to a Batesonian appreciation of the 'recursiveness', the circuiting, of life on earth.

I: 'Maps are not territories'

According to Bertrand Russell's theory of logical types, there is an inevitable discontinuity between a class and its members; the term used for the class belongs to a different level of abstraction from the terms used for members. Bateson borrowed this Russellian insight and made it fundamental to his conceptualization of the universe of human behaviour. Logical types and levels, for Bateson, characterize, differentiate, hierarchize and interrelate world, biosphere, society, body and mind; and there is an infinite regress of such contexts. For example, there is a world of material objects, of things-in-themselves, which is distinct from (which is known differently to) the world of human bodies, of metabolic supplies and channels, which is in turn distinct from the world of the mind, of narratives, thoughts and ideas. The mind can thus be said to be made of parts and processes which are not themselves mental but metabolic, while consciousness represents a transformation of unconscious metabolic processes.

Linking one logical level or context to another is a complex network of meta-relations. Moving from the world of one logical type or level to another always entails, for Bateson, a transformation of knowledge: a re-codification of how and what is known. Between distinct logical types or levels, however, there can be no direct knowledge and no 'complete' communication. Hence, the metabolic processes which give rise to the rich content of consciousness are not themselves subject to direct introspection or voluntary control. Similarly, 'maps are not territories'; the worlds of human experience are distinct from a noumenal world of external things, of things-in-themselves. There are no rocks, trees, or even people in the human mind, Bateson is wont to say, there are only ideas of rocks, trees and people. Things enter the human world of experience, of meaning and communication, by our ideas of them − whatever else they may be in their thingish world. Ideas are the only things human beings can know and we cannot otherwise imagine the world 'as it is'.

Ideation, the processes of perceiving and thinking and communicating about perceiving and thinking, involves a transformation or codification (translation or substitution) which might variously be described as 'symbolic classification', 'naming' or 'mapping'. We attribute names and qualities to things and so 'produce' them by reproducing them in a world of human experience. Ideation Bateson describes as itself an operation of logical typing; but since direct communication between logical types remains impossible, the 'things' that enter our minds as ideas are at best guesses at the things-in-themselves. For the mind as such is a no-thing, existing only in ideas, while ideas are also no-things; they are not the things they refer to. What occupies the mind, in short, is an abstract account of a concrete external world which otherwise remains itself, distinct and mysterious.

What ideas do involve are differences.

II: 'Information is difference which makes a difference'

The mind operates with and upon differences; differences are the unit of psychological input. So that if minds are aggregates of ideas, then what minds contain are differences: ideas and differences are synonymous. For to perceive something, to recognize a thing, is to recognize a difference between it and some other thing or some other perception. Things are thus defined by and through their differences. To the extent that things enter the world of human experience they do so as aggregates of their differences.

Another way of saying this is that human thought is relational. We perceive and think in terms of relationships – difference is a relationship – and not in terms of things-in-themselves. Things enter the world of human experience (are seen as separate and real) only through their interrelations; they are epiphenomena of the relations to which we perceive them to be a party: relations to ourselves, to other things, and to themselves in other contexts.

Information about the world Bateson then defines as differences which make a difference, which human beings see, and see as relevant, at a particular time. Information is 'news of difference' (1980: 37), while maps are organizations of news of difference.

III: 'All phenomena are appearances'

Since the mental worlds of human beings are about maps, and maps of maps, and not about things-in-themselves, all human phenomena can be said to be abstractions, their truth-value turning upon appearances. The Berkeleyian motto, 'To be is to be perceived', therefore applies to all human behaviour, for the human universe has no objective features. Even so-called natural-scientific knowledge shares this character; Euclidean geometry, for example, is not about space as it exists but as it is defined by a human perceiver or imaginer. There is an infinite number of potential or latent differences and relations between and within things in the external world but only some of these become 'effective', meaningful or manifest in the world of human ideation – differences which have made a difference and become information. Hence, we create the world we perceive, editing and selecting from the noumenal universe so that it conforms with our beliefs, with our vision of 'order': of the orderly relations between objects.

To this extent, objects (as well as their being experienced) are subjective creations. Indeed, all thinking and all human experience can be said to be subjective: a matter of the images our brains make about the 'external world', a matter of the mediation of our sense organs and neural pathways. Even pain is a created image. And while nineteenth-century science founded itself on the claim that this subjectivity was 'in fact' objective, it was the latter which was illusory. Human knowledge and conditions of knowledge are always, and inevitably, personal; knowledge is a relationship in the eye of the beholder. As Bateson pithily phrases it (1951: 212): 'man lives by those propositions whose validity is a function of his belief in them'.

In this way, the subjective viewer and the personal world which he or she creates can be seen as one; since things-in-themselves never enter the mind, only complex transforms of these, there is a one-ness between the perceiver and the things perceived. Rather than subjects and objects there exist subject–objects and perceiver–perceiveds: always the purposive organism in interaction with its created environment; always the territory of things and objects filtered into a mental world of subjective images and maps. Bateson talks of the 'mental determinism' immanent in the universe (1972: 441).

In this way too, worlds are multiple. If order is defined as the privileging of one or more of an infinite number of possible relations between objects and events, between things in the world, then the perception of any two viewers, or the same viewer at different times, need not overlap. Even two individuals in interaction have a freedom regarding how they interpret: both how they codify the world and how they act upon their codifications. And differences multiply. Because to assert one thing, privilege one pattern of relations, is to deny something else.

Finally, visions of order are self-fulfilling. Human individuals live in worlds of their own perceiving, codifying, creating, imagining, because they set out to establish a correspondence between what is in their heads and what is outside them, and in large measure they succeed. They see what they want to see and want to see what they see. Or, as Bateson puts it, value is a determinant of perception, and perception a determinant of value; evaluation and codification are aspects of the same central mental phenomenon. We must wish things to be as we see them, and vice versa, or our actions will bring us frustration and pain instead of success. In short, in the perception of a particular set of relations between things, a particular order in the external world, value and information meet.

IV: *'Patterns connect'*

While there are discontinuities between logical types and levels, between classes and members, Bateson also posits the existence of corresponding patterns between the components of particular types and levels which connect those types and levels. Similar relations between parts evince meta-patterns: shapes and forms of an aesthetic kind. The process of recognizing connecting patterns between logical types and levels, Bateson calls 'abduction'. He finds it in metaphor and in dream, in parable, allegory, poetry, totemism, and comparative anatomy, and he believes that what he calls 'abductive systems' characterize great regions of nature and human life, linking the body and the ecosystem (1980: 158).

For example, stereoscopic vision, provided by two eyes which are logically discrete but perceive corresponding patterns between the component parts of the worlds they perceive, amounts to an abductive system. Similarly, a routine relationship of exchange between two people is an abductive system: a relationship Bateson describes as a double view of something or a double description. Not internal to a single person, a relationship is based on the recognition by the parties concerned of corresponding patterns of behaviour and response on each side. Or again, an abductive system characterizes the process of perceiving an environment. A difference between a standing and a falling tree is transformed into a difference between neurons in the human brain; the physical event is translated into an idea, a piece of information, which bears a commensurate pattern between component parts. The mental process entails a sequence of interactions between neuronal parts, which is a coded version, a transformation, of events perceived in the external world. There is a relationship of commensurate difference which connects the two.

V: 'Mental processes are recursive'

A clear emphasis in Bateson's understanding of how we come to perceive both difference and sameness is upon the movement inherent in mental processes. We come to know difference by cognitively moving between two or more things, or moving ourselves relative to a thing, or moving between two of our cognitions of a thing. And we come to know sameness by abducting, by moving between patterns of relations between things and appreciating the meta-patterns that they share. Knowing entails cognitive movement.

And we remember these movements, Bateson next argues. If we value the information which they provide us, then the cognitive movement is reinforced and comes to be habitual: a habitual pattern or pathway between neurons in the brain, a habitual association of ideas in the mind. These remembered, habitual movements, Bateson calls a 'cybernetic circuit' or 'system': a pathway, and network of pathways, along which information and transformations are transmitted (1972: 434). He also calls them 'circular (or more complex) chains of determination': a dynamic processing of information in recursive patterns of relations between neuronal components of the brain and ideational components of the mind (1980: 102). Even the simplest cybernetic circuit possesses such memory, Bateson insists, based upon the travel of information; and as the mind matures, so it comes to consist of habituated loops of thought and networks of such loops: a total completed circuitry. Hence, an appreciation of this circuitry is essential for an understanding of human behaviour, for this is how we think, this gives onto what we know.

This also reveals how we know that we know, how we become self-conscious. It is recursive circuitry which produces an organism's autonomy and its self-control. For by getting messages about messages, a repetitive spiral is entered into, which eventually results in the crossing of a threshold: to awareness. Thus, an organism comes to know itself. It can correct itself and make choices – to change or stay the same. Through the process of recursion it is *as if* the differences between certain parts of the brain and mind – 'transmitters' – caused other parts to become 'receivers' (a 'sensory end-organ'), responding to the differences between them (1980: 106). In fact, there is no 'ghost in the machine' of this kind, no Cartesian *res cogitans*, it being simply an effect of recursion: of the reaching of a level of complexity (and hierarchy) of circuitry which causes the organism to perceive its own prior perceptions. And Bateson concludes that this is how one might define something as having consciousness: something which is turned in on itself, acts on itself and is able to control itself through recursion.

VI: 'Knowledge is both evolutionary and tautological'

The notion of memory, of habit and reinforcement, which Bateson introduces to explain the process of recursion, whereby a maturing body and mind will contain an increasing number of cybernetic circuits – habitual pathways between neurons in the brain, between ideas in the mind – also introduces the equally important notions of development, stasis and change over time. The knowledge which the organism possesses is not fixed. Being a matter of recursion, of cybernetic circuitry, movement is indeed inherent in its nature. But more than this, the circuitry of the brain and the mind is not fixed. Habit is certainly a fixing process, but not everything in human life is habit, and habits themselves change. As individual organisms die and are replaced in a population, whole networks of habits die and come to be replaced too.

Habits are not everything and habits change, Bateson now explains, because new relations between things in the world, new pathways between neurons in the brain, new associations between ideas in the head, are always being created by the individual. Each individual human body is an 'energy source' (1972: 126), and the energy of its metabolic processes translates as a constant perception of possible new relations in the world, and hence new objects. In his quest to see the meta-patterns between logical types, Bateson refers here too to the Second Law of Thermodynamics, the law of entropy, whereby 'the randomness of probability will always eat up order and pattern in the world'. That is, while each purposive organism will have created an order for itself by selecting a set of possible relations between possible things in the world (and defining it as 'order', or 'law' or 'custom' or 'norm'), still its world will tend towards entropy because any number of other possible permutations of relations are likely to occur to it in future. Order and pattern in the world are eaten up by the organism shuffling and recombining the relations between components of circuits and networks of circuits in its body and mind – ideas and neurons – and shuffling and recombining the relations between components of its external world – objects and events. In short, proceeding alongside the habituation of life is a degree of entropy: relations between the components of an aggregate being mixed up, unsorted, random, unpredictable, unorderly.

The organism deals with entropy in two contrasting ways. Bateson calls them evolutionary versus tautological: an embracing of the implications and ramifications of possible change versus a homeostatic eschewing of them. The watchwords of the latter tautological process (also to be known as 'epigenetic' and 'embryological') are: coherence, steady state, rigour and compatibility. The process acts as a critical filter, demanding certain standards of conformity in the perceiving and thinking individual. Left to itself it proceeds towards tautology: towards nothing being added once the initial arbitrary axioms and definitions of order have been laid down. Hence, the first test of a new idea is: is it consistent with the *status quo ante*? is it entirely latent in the original axioms which supply the 'proof' of its correctness? In the tautological procedure, in short, every 'becoming' is tied back to existing conditions.

Contrastively, the evolutionary process is exploratory, creative and stochastic, feeding on the random to make new designations of order. From the steady supply of random perceptions, from 'no-things', new information is made, new 'some-things', by a non-random selection process which causes some mutations of prior order to survive longer than others and so be maintained and taken into the future. Here is an ongoing, endless trial and error with new things and relations, setting off down new, randomly presented pathways, some of which are then chosen as components of a new order. Collecting new mutations, new imaginations, evolutionary thought gathers new 'solutions' to the problems of meaning in the world, empirically testing these solutions according to new cybernetic circuiting.

If the tautological process is seen in terms of the DNA of an embryo which will determine how that organism will develop over time only in accord with latent, originary genetic terms, then the evolutionary process is one of genetic mutation where random changes will continually throw up potential alternative pathways of adaptation. And Bateson deliberately juxtaposes the patterns of these different logical levels. Tautology operates alike at the logical level of the individual organism and at that of thought in its cranium, at the level of cultural patterns and again in terms of ecological systems. Evolution occurs in the mind as in the brain and as in the gene pool of the population.

VII: 'Evolution and Tautology are dialectically linked'

If there are two realms, that of tautology (whose essence is predictable repetition and replication) and that of evolution (whose essence is creativity, exploration and change), then life entails an alternation, a dialectics, between the two. As mental processes and phenomenal happenings the two may be adversarial, but a zigzag between them whereby each determines the other would appear to be necessary for the continuation of life. Homeostasis and adaptation, structure and process, form and function, status and learning, conservatism and radicalism, quantity and pattern, homology and analogy, calibration and feedback – these are 'dialectical plural necessities of the living world' (1980: 237). The survival of life involves the marriage of random mutation, completely independent of existing ordered environments, and environmental demands, the regularities of functioning systems (minds, bodies, social systems, ecosystems). The procedure of life runs continuously between disruption and self-healing consistency.

VIII: 'Social processes can be seen as recursive systems of relations'

Traditional modelling of the world in the West has employed a linear dynamics: external forces act on things, cause reactions, and so give rise to events; order derives from maintaining these factors in balanced equilibrium. Cybernetic models of order in the world, however, are based on inherent circularities and oscillations, and on dynamic thresholds. Cause is circular and reticulate, a matter of mutual feedback.

Instead of 'things', then, there are relations between the parts and the whole of systems; instead of facts there are messages; instead of externalities *per se* – objects, forces and events – there are mutually implicating structures: patterns of constant and habitual interaction between co-dependent members of communicational systems.

Relationships, like ideas, are founded upon differentiation; only the distinct can be related. Once differentiation has occurred, however (and a relationship has been construed between distinct 'individuals' or 'clans' or 'nations' or 'species'), relations can proceed on the basis either of similarity between the partners or of difference. Moreover, since entropy always eats up the fixed orders of life, such relations between partners do not stay the same for long. Hence, two processes can be observed: schismogenesis, where partners become increasingly distanced from one another, and integration, where they become increasingly close.

Schismogenesis itself can be of two kinds. If relations between partners is based on similarity, then a kind of schismogenesis can occur which Bateson calls 'symmetrical': each tries to outdo the other by adhering closer and closer to the common terms of their relationship. This is how nations get involved in arms races and Kwakiutl bigmen in *potlatches*. If relations between the partners is based on difference, then another kind of schismogenesis can occur: 'complementary'. Here the progressive change in relations takes the form of different partners becoming more and more different or polarized in their behaviour. This is how class divisions and exploitations deepen, and how people become immured in sado-masochistic exchanges.

In the same way that 'cumulative interaction' (Bateson 1936: 175) between partners to a relationship can lead to a process of schismogenetic differentiation – each reacting to the reactions of the other and so causing exponential changes in relations which follow simple mathematical laws – this might also lead to increasing integration. If partners' relations are based on their similarity, then a kind of integration can occur which Bateson calls 'peripheral'; here is a league of nations, or a valley of farmers, whose community is nurtured by a sense that 'the more you give the more you get back'. If relations between the partners are based on difference, however, then another kind of integration can occur: 'centripetal', where increasingly complex divisions of labour or systems of welfare are engendered by people having their differences organized, say by a central administrative authority.

Schismogenesis and integration Bateson recognizes to be ideal-types. Ordinarily as social relations develop through time, and as habit counteracts entropy, so there will be a mixing: people getting both closer and further apart, tensions rising and falling. Two things, nonetheless, remain the same: there is always change, and there are always relations of cumulation. Only in terms of recursive circuiting can social relations – whether dyadic partnerships (between individuals or groups) or complex assemblages – be comprehended. They are communicational systems between co-dependent members whose habitual interaction is characterized by circularities, oscillations, dynamic thresholds, and feedback.

IX: 'The biosphere is a mutually causal living system of communication'

The natural world of living forms, too, becomes a matter of organized communication. Living forms are not separate from nature but in recursive relationship with it. Indeed, living forms are coupled not only to their conceptualizations of environments and environmental order but also to embodiments of their ways of thinking about these and acting upon them in interactions within environments. Hence, all organisms contribute to the ordering and organization of the biosphere, and the perceptions held concerning the natural environment are part of their natural fitness.

Organism-plus-environment modify and generate each other, and just as there are no agents independent of interactions (and vice versa) so there are no organisms independent of environments (and vice versa). Natural order and a human or animal construction of it are, in short, inseparable. Instinct and culture can be understood alike as sets of propositions about the world by which different species communicate with the world; both are processes of adaptation. Life on earth concerns ecosystems wherein the material and the ideal are combined; the 'ideal' of conceptualization and information speaks of material events, is carried by material signals, and has material consequences. Information and natural order (negative entropy) are one.

If the organization of the biosphere should be considered a communicative recursive order rather than a material one, then to study it is aesthetically to appreciate pattern, context and meaning. Quantitative analysis may be sufficient for an abstract study of physical particles, but for a study of living forms, cultural, biological or ecological, a qualitative epistemology is called for; it makes no sense to attempt to factor in 'energy', 'power' and 'control' as isolated material phenomena. Indeed, the human aesthetic appreciation of the ubiquity of circuitry is vital for ecological survival; we are born of our world-views, their validity is a matter of our belief, but if they do not map correctly onto the environment, we can destroy it and ourselves. In this way, the subjectivity of the world, its subjectivation, should be understood in non-idealistic terms: it has real ramifications.

The complexity of ecosystems, moreover, may be enormous; always in states of dialectical oscillation, often characterized by multiple levels and circuits of oscillation between as well as within levels, usually containing contradictions, needful of reflexive homeostatic monitoring yet sometimes giving rise to cycles of escalation, the passing of thresholds, and the onset of 'runaway' and system disintegration. Little wonder that from the Ancient Greek 'Eco' to the modern 'Gaia', its apprehension has been seen as a matter of divine mystery. But in fact there is no mystery, only beauty: patterns which map onto patterns which map onto patterns; patterns which connect. If there is something here which pertains to the 'sacred', then it is that the appropriate world-view is characteristic of those which preceded the Enlightenment, and eschews those dualisms which have plagued Western philosophy since – distinguishing humanity from nature, life from death, subject from object. What is necessary for ecological maintenance are correct ideas about ecosystems: namely, an apprehension of their systematization, of the recursive (meta-)patterns which connect all into a unified biosphere.

Anthropological applications

The influence of the above thinking has been enormously widespread, even if its attribution has remained implicit. R.D. Laing's famous theory of the 'divided self' (1976), on the mutual constitutionality of separateness and relatedness, and the alienation and madness that can ensue from being unable to integrate into the self others' paradoxical, logically incongruent and conflicting messages, owes much to Bateson's ideas on schizophrenia as a communicational 'double bind' (1974). Goffman's work, meanwhile, on how social structure and reality are maintained via a process of socially sanctioned, situational 'encounters', or 'situated activity system[s]' (1972: 85) has a distinct cybernetic ring; that obligations are fulfilled and expectations realized is a matter, Goffman concludes, of people jointly participating in 'closed, self-compensating, self-terminating concrete circuits of interdependent actions'.

Equally, there are cybernetic overtones in *structuraliste* notions of societies as systems of communication by which cultural messages of a binary kind are ever in the process of being conveyed. Indeed, Lévi-Strauss can be said to have adapted the cybernetic work which underlay the advances in computer science – computers as reflexive 'thinking systems' – in his exploring of the coded combination and recombination of communicational units that went to make up socio-cultural phenomena as diverse as mythologies, economic exchanges and kinship terms (1963, 1969a).

Strathern (1990a), meanwhile, employs the science-fiction figure of the 'cyborg' – part-human, part-machine; part-body, part-tool; part-self, part-other (the Six Million Dollar Man, the Cybermen, Robocop) – in order to overcome the false mathematics of seeing entities either as a series of discrete atoms or as parts of a monolithic, static whole. What is crucial is our appreciation of 'the relation' (cf. Strathern 1995); and how the nature of things in the world is an effect elicited by the ongoing (circuiting) reciprocal relationship between partners at a particular point in time and space.

Paine (1976) marries Bateson to a more transactionalist approach to social exchange by exploring how communicational circuits can be strategically managed and become political resources. As communication is wont to involve messages on more than one logical level – messages and also tailored information on how to interpret or decode the message – the so-called factual nature of human worlds is always entwined with matters of mediation, evaluation, rhetoric and power. It becomes impossible to differentiate between pure 'information' and socially intelligible 'communication', and truth becomes a matter of conviction.

Taking a more ecological perspective is the work of Rappaport (1968), for whom culture as a whole can be understood as a cybernetic system for regulating relations between people and their environment. Thus, the periodic cycles of ritualized warfare and peace among the Tsembaga of New Guinea, for instance, represent a strategy for the perpetuation of balanced, systemic relations between people, pigs and such natural resources as cultivatable land and wildlife. Or again, for Harries-Jones (1991), a cybernetic appreciation is necessary for negotiating our way out of an increasingly schismogenetic ecological predicament. Only 'a recursive vision' which points up how interpretations have consequences, continually entering into, becoming entangled with, and re-entering the universe they describe, provides such insights as are necessary for the survival of our human species-plus-natural environment.

Finally, Ingold (1992) adapts a Batesonian (-cum-Heideggerian) appreciation of our embeddedness in the world to give fresh under-standing to human technological competency. It is a mistake, he argues, to abstract and objectify the techniques we use in relating to the world – to make an object out of our making of objects and relations. For what the Greek word *techne* should alert us to is the artistry, the expressiveness and the aestheticism inherent in crafting a world, and the bodily skills of practising within it. A 'technologist', then, is not someone who mechanically applies an objective system of rational principles and rules, but more properly a being wholly immersed in the rational nexus of an instrumental coping-in-the-world.

See also: **Code, Consciousness**

DIALOGICS AND ANALOGICS

The Dialogic Imagination was the title given to a highly influential collection of posthumously published articles written by the Russian literary critic Mikhail Bakhtin (1981). Anthropologists have borrowed the term 'dialogic', and set it against the term 'analogic', so as to convey a certain understanding of the way language is used, knowledge is accrued, and ethnographic data is represented.

Mikhail Bakhtin

In *The Dialogic Imagination* Bakhtin made a number of salient points. Only as an abstract grammar could a language be conceived of as a unitary whole. In the concrete it was inexorably 'heteroglot': an inter-section and an expression of a multiplicity of different social, ideological, occupational groups and individuals, past and present, all co-existing as speakers of a language. *Contra* Saussure's notion that the meaning of words in use is fixed by their relationship to others in a singular matrix as defined by an abstract system, *la langue*, Bakhtin appreciated that meaning is contextual and contested; it is open to continual redefinition within the meetings between different social classes, status groups and individuals. All words become assimilated to the specificities of their users' conceptual systems, worlds of objects and emotional expressions. Words came to have 'the "taste" of a profession, a genre, a tendency, a party, a particular work, a particular person, a generation, an age group, the day and hour', being constantly enriched by new elements and shot through with the intentions, contexts and contents by which they 'lived [their] socially charged life' (1981: 293).

This also meant that the ownership of words was contested, with some words resisting appropriation and use as the property of one group of speakers because of its close association with (even over-population by) the accents of others. What this came down to was language's 'dialogic' nature, its betweenness and emergent quality. Language lay on the borderline between self and other, between speaker and audience, between past and present; also between centripetal and centrifugal forces. As a living thing, an instrument of contradictory ideologies, world-views, belief systems and histories, a language and every utterance within it was party to two tense, battling tendencies: the expression of an abstract unitary whole of denotational forms, and the expression of a heteroglossia of contextual, contested connotations. And what was true of the form was true of the content: what was known through language was equally dialogic and heteroglot.

When it came to representing sociolinguistic reality in a written text, moreover, Bakhtin also advocated dialogism (1984), à la Dostoevsky, say, and his attempts to capture the polyphonic interplay of characters engaged through an incoherent multiplicity of discourses, in preference to (a Tolstoyan) monologism, and the subordination of a diversity of characters' voices to the single viewpoint of the author. By making the ground of scriptural style dialogic and diverse, one captured the truly open-ended, indeterminate, playful ('carnivalesque'), interactive and perspectival nature of social life.

Anthropological dialogism

An early anthropological borrower from Bakhtin was Dennis Tedlock (1979, 1983). Anthropological knowledge exists in a contact zone on the frontier between an anthropologist and his or her informant, Tedlock asserts (cf. Hastrup 1995b: 2–5). This betweenness is the world of dialogue; it is through the performance of dialogue that anthropologist and informant negotiate grounds of their meeting. The knowledge that emerges from their conversation is something new to both of them: a shared world or a shared understanding of the differences between their two worlds.

In accounting for anthropological knowledge, therefore, it is important to provide an account of its dialogic coming-into-being. And yet, traditionally, this has rarely been done. Not one native speaks in Lévi-Strauss's concoction of South American myths, while the transformations in which he indulges makes them unrecognizably exogenous. Even Geertz's claims to present field conversations are meta-phoric, collectivized and generalized. Instead of dialogics, traditional anthropology has practised 'analogics'. It has treated others in a closed, presumptive way, attempting to understand them via *a priori* reasoning; instead of having knowledge emerge from local dialogue, traditional anthropology employed extraneous analogies which derived from its own system of rationality. It then presented its data in a monologic, so-called objectivist fashion.

Taking this critique further, James Clifford (1988: 39–46) has reviewed the new paradigms of dialogue, collaboration and polyphony which have arisen of late (cf. Rabinow 1977; Dumont 1978; Crapanzano 1980; Dwyer 1982); these should be seen as attempts to retain in the anthropological text the process of dialogue from which a (shared) understanding of ethnographic reality derives. Discourse in the field is shot through with multiple subjectivities in specific contexts, and meaning derives from intersubjective interlocution, and yet anthropological texts have a tendency to become monovocal and decontextualized, Clifford argues. Field events and experiences become patterned, simplified narratives, separated from their discursive occasions of production and, seemingly, not in need of being understood as the communication of specific persons. The narratives become evidence, rather, of a new englobing and integrating, generalizing and totalizing, context called 'cultural reality'. With ambiguities and diversities airbrushed out, the dialogic and situational features of the field encounter are allocated only exemplary topoi (at best) in the textual account.

To open up this textualized fabric of anthropologist and informant, to displace, even if not wholly eliminate, the former's monologic authority, is to recognize the contemporary heteroglossia of socio-cultural milieux. We are now all part of a world of 'generalized ethnography', an ambiguous, multivocal world in which everyone interprets everyone else in a bewildering diversity of idioms (Clifford 1988: 23). Language becomes an interplay and struggle of dialects, argots, and individual speaker–hearers, while culture becomes 'an open-ended creative dialogue of subcultures, of insiders and outsiders, of diverse factions' (1988: 46). Language and culture are revealed as non-homogeneous and non-integrated wholes.

See also: **Code, Literariness, Movement, Situation and Context**

DISCOURSE

'Discourse', at its broadest, can be understood to mean ways of speaking which are commonly practised and specifically situated in a social environment: 'speech in habitual situations of social exchange'. The significant elements contained in this definition are regularity, conventionality, propriety, diversity and context. The philosophical term to which discourse most closely approximates is probably Wittgenstein's notion of the 'language-game' (1978); here is a type of speech-making, of variable complexity and length, in which people habitually engage, and which is accompanied by particular habitual actions. 'Language-game' is an attempt to convey the embeddedness of speech-making in routine social relationships and behaviours, the formulaic way in which speech accompanies everyday social inter-action and amounts to a whole 'form of life' (cf. Rapport 1987: 170ff.). What the concepts of discourse and language-game share is their insistence on intrinsic ties between speech and behaviour, between the linguistic and the socio-cultural, and between individual speakers and social conventions.

Discourse analysis

The analysis of discourse has been undertaken in a number of different ways (cf. Brown and Yule 1983). Wittgenstein has already been mentioned, while Alfred Schuetz, influenced by the phenomenological insights of Edmund Husserl, influenced in his turn by the ethnomethod-ology of the likes of Harold Garfinkel. Garfinkel (1967) explored the ways in which everyday conversation was mediated by a set of common background expectancies which speakers shared; so that an engagement in habitual discourse maintained and reinforced a common world-view and a common set of social structures in whose terms speakers lived.

More strictly anthropological has been the work of Dell Hymes (1972), emphasizing both the regularity of ways of speaking which human beings practise in particular times and places, and the manner in which ways of speaking and, more generally, ways of behaving and interacting, are closely tied; language and society are perhaps indistinguishable. Hence, Hymes suggests the composite term 'speech-community' for those who share rules concerning the conduct and interpretation of speech: a speech-community will determine particular proper ways of speaking which its competent members will practise. These ways will involve 'speech styles' which are set in certain 'speech-situations' (ceremonies, fights, meals, hunts), making up particular 'speech-events', and comprised of individual 'speech-acts'. In this fashion, Hymes prescribes a systemic analysis of discourse – the form, content, channels and setting of everyday speech, its addressers, addressees and audience, its goals and outcome, its history and development – and its systemic relating to the rest of the social structure of a group.

Another important anthropological approach to discourse has been the work of Robert Paine (and others) on political rhetoric. Paine distinguishes rhetoric as a particular kind of discourse, arguing that while most speech-acts concern 'speech about something', the kernel of rhetoric is that 'saying is doing' (1981: 9). In this, rhetoric most resembles music or drama, for there too the doing and the effect are inseparable. The effect which rhetoric most often intends is persuasion, in particular the persuasion of an audience by a speaker – although a speaker might also be found to be persuaded by his own voicing of his words – and this is perhaps most clearly seen in the realm of politics. Rhetoric can be seen as an instrument by which a speaker gains or increases control over a political environment. And once this control becomes routinized, institutionalized, then control over language, over the right to speak, may be defined as an essential base of power and authority. So that those with power are those who control others, in part at least, via the medium of speech, and those in power are those with the right and duty to decide who speaks when and how (cf. Goldschlaeger 1985).

While it was in the eighteenth century that Giambattista Vico's *Scienza Nuova* first propounded a systematic link between the study of rhetoric and the study of cultural forms and effects, it is more recent thinkers such as philosopher J.L. Austin and critic Kenneth Burke who have inspired an anthropological focus on the power of speech to affect others. For Austin (1971, 1975), speech should be appreciated as having meaning, force and effect. In particular, an important range of speech-acts, 'performative utterances', do not merely describe the social world ('declarative') but give it form and content too. Here is speech with the 'illocutionary force' to create social happenings, speech as an instrument of social action with significant social consequences. For Burke (1973), symbolically mediated and interactionally coordinated forms of behaviour (speech, gesture, dress) can be studied for the ways they are used artfully so as to influence others' beliefs and attitudes. In particular, the effects of such successful rhetorical usage may be to cause an audience to achieve a state of 'identification' with a speaker, whereby aspects of the social identity or being of the people involved in the rhetorical encounter come more closely to approximate one another. Hence, Paine's definition (1971) of a patron as someone whose power is to have values of his own express choosing affirmed by others – those who come to identify themselves as clients.

As a development of the above focus on speaking and power, perhaps the most popular approach to discourse in anthropology of late has been that influenced by the French philosopher of systems of thought, Michel Foucault (and other post-structuralist theorists). In *The Archaeology of Knowledge* (1972) Foucault set forth a programme for what he called 'the pure description of discursive events'. This was important, he claimed, because there were inexorable links between forms of communication, knowledge and power. Discourse was a key determinant of social life and exchange, for particular cultural discourses maintained both conventional ways of knowing the world and a network of power relations among those who did the knowing. Discourse amounted to certain conditions and procedures regulating how people may communicate and what and how they may know.

Insofar as Foucauldian concerns have become anthropological ones, the key questions are whether it is true that formulaic limits to routine and conventional ways of speaking in a social milieu need be said similarly and necessarily to limit what is known (thought, experienced and imagined) by individual speakers, and the extent to which this formulaicism elicits hierarchies of power, knowledge and belonging which speakers can but barely escape (cf. Bauman and Briggs 1990).

A Foucauldian anthropology of discourse

'Discourse' is perhaps Foucault's key conceptual term, but it also figures as part of a broader post-structuralist imaging of social life as the playing out of impersonal and largely unconscious systems of signification: anonymous, depersonalized networking of images (cf. Kearney 1988: 13–14). Here, collective discourses or forms of life are seen to cause to be true or 'real' certain constructions of the world and its components, as well as instituting a set of knowledge-practices with inevitable ties to a mastery of power. In other words, it is language which 'discourses', not individual speakers, and they only speak to the extent that they respond to (and correspond with) the conventional discursive forms of their language. In this anti-idealist and anti-humanist vision, linguistic expression is the fount of knowledge and of power (of 'power-knowledge') while its human speakers and their subjectivities, their selves and societies, are the 'effects' of expression. Individual speakers are not responsible for the expression and constitution of identities effected through their speaking; discourse deprives the human subject of any alleged status as 'source and master of meaning' (Culler 1981: 33).

The wider intent is to displace (dissolve and decentre) the individual speaker from analysis so as to make room for the hierarchy of 'subject-positions' which a particular discourse is seen to articulate. Here is an exploding of humanist notions of what it is to partake of speech – including subjective inwardness and originality, sequential development of topic, coherent expression of narrative. As Foucault sums up (1991: 118): 'In short, it is a matter of depriving the subject . . . of its role as originator, and of analysing the subject as a variable and complex function of discourse'. To enter into discourse is seen perforce to comply, however artfully, with certain collective structures (hypograms, matrices, codes) of signification (cf. Riffaterre 1978: 164–6). The symbolic process of linguistic expression and the social practice of speaking are both regarded as part-and-parcel of a *conscience collective* which classifies the world in terms of certain subject-positions and prescribes proper relations between them. Occupying particular subject-positions in particular discourses, human beings are said inevitably to find themselves viewing the world and being viewed by it in certain partisan, interested and power-laden ways.

At once verbal and behavioural, collective and coercive, discourses are seen as inhabiting the body and habituating the mind; so that it is in terms of particular discursive constructions of the world that individual human beings come to be socialized. Human beings are 'bodies totally imprinted by history' (Foucault 1977). The only partial transcendence involves the move from one discourse to another: subverting one power relationship by playing it off against others, as discourses develop and change, abutting against and jockeying with each other, through time. But this is no real escape, since it is still a matter of individuals' coming to consciousness in terms of one particular system of discursive classification, one particular set of unequal power relations, or another. Thus do individuals find themselves 'being spoken' by unconscious, preconditioned linguistic codes and knowledge-practices. Far from speakers' employing discursive measures for the effecting of original or even intentioned ends, here is 'mimesis without origin or end' (Kearney 1988: 6). Indeed, were it not for the subject-positions which discourses offer, human consciousnesses would not exist as human as such. Discourses create our humanity.

An ethnographic example of a Foucauldian approach to discourse is provided by Lila Abu-Lughod's work on Bedouin love poetry (1990a), specifically on a traditional genre of oral lyricism known as *ghinnawa*. Love poetry is a highly cherished and privileged art-form among the Awlad 'Ali Bedouin (of Egypt's Western Desert) which is thought of as distinctly Bedouin and associated with a noble past of political autonomy, strength and independence, and Abu-Lughod explores its status as 'social text'. Her particular intent is a critique of 'mentalist models' of individual thought and emotion – of individual consciousness as private – and she argues that it is discourse which informs individual experience and constitutes the realities and truths by which individuals live. Far from *ghinnawa* being an expressive stage for individual emotionality, and far from this representing an inner state, therefore, the conventional poetic form must needs be regarded as rhetorical usage which itself constructs emotions as legitimate social phenomena, as social facts. Emotionality is routine discursive practice. Moreover, it is of and about social-structural conditions that emotional expression, and poetry about emotion, speaks; formed in and by a certain social ecology and political economy, the emotion of *ghinnawa* necessarily reflects the form of society (the hierarchical Bedouin social structure, the relations of power) in which the genre lives, which gave rise to it and for which its expression has practical consequences.

'Fathalla', for instance, Abu-Lughod describes as a young Bedouin man whose plans to marry 'his beloved' are thwarted by her father, his uncle. In this situation, Fathalla resorts to expressing 'his' feelings of love and regret in *ghinnawa*. For while this poetic genre is very much part of daily life, and often interspersed in the middle of ordinary conversations with intimates, the sentiments which he may properly express in conversation and in *ghinnawa* are very different. Thus, it is legitimate for Fathalla to express a feeling of love (to feel love) in the poetry while continuing to express (and feel) very different emotions in the conversational discourse which precedes and follows it. For Fathalla, we are informed, appropriate emotionality and proper discursive practice are one and the same.

Ghinnawa is not resorted to by all of Bedouin society alike, furthermore; it is primarily associated with young men and women. For these latter are the disadvantaged dependants of the social structure, and the sentiment of love which *ghinnawa* constitutes represents a subversion of the sentiment of modesty and an adherence to the social-structural status quo. The *ghinnawa* is a conventional discourse of defiance to the authority of the elders. And yet, those, like Fathalla, who compose *ghinnawa* are not disapproved of, even by the elders themselves. In fact, cassette-tapes have been made of Fathalla reciting his poems in a 'moving and pained' voice, and it was on the car cassette-player of her (elder) host that Abu-Lughod was introduced to them. Elders 'clearly admired this young man for his passion and for his ability to express it in poetry. They were moved by his poems and awed by the power of his words' (1990a: 36).

In people's approval of *ghinnawa*, Abu-Lughod concludes, in their discomfort with its emotions in ordinary conversation and their glorification of them in conversation's interstices, can be read a fundamental paradox in Bedouin life between the ideals of equality and the everyday practice of hierarchy. The fact that the Awlad 'Ali Bedouin may be frequently 'moved' by *ghinnawa* poetry pertains in no necessary way to individual qualities or subjective states, however. For, here are people far removed from Western habits of contemplation, interpretation, understanding, from what Foucault describes as the 'psychologizing' projects of the Western 'individual'. Rather, *ghinnawa* emotionality concerns the public construction and exchange of cultural behaviours and concepts: the playing out of an emotional discourse and a discourse on emotion. It is this discourse, moreover, which is the proper object of anthropological enquiry, for its very playing out constitutes Fathalla and his audience as social actors, tells them what (and when and how) they can 'think and feel'.

An anti-Foucauldian anthropology of discourse

Notwithstanding the modishness of Foucauldian approaches to discourse in anthropology, in particular for an uncovering of relations of power and their links to what is known and said, for some, Foucauldian imagings remain unhappy and unconvincing (cf. Sahlins 1996). This is not simply a signalling of the 'antihumanism' of the imaging, but an asserting that any such impersonal accounting for social life is unconvincing primarily because of its inaccuracy and unsubtlety: its distance from the details of the ongoing work of social interaction, work by individuals in conjunction, creating themselves and their social relationships. To miss reporting this individual work and to substitute the dead hand of determinism – to replace, as does the Foucauldian, individual mentalities by conventional and collective 'governmentalities' – appears a travesty of both a political and an empirical kind. If there is to be found a discourse in shared cultural concepts in a social milieu, then there must also be an account of individual usage and interpretation. For, it is the agency of each individual which is ever responsible for animating discourse with significance (and so maintaining its role as the major synthesizing process of social life), without which discourse would simply remain inert cultural matter. To claim for discourse its own animating force is a hypostatization, with possibly dangerous (totalitarian) political consequences.

Two bases of the anti-Foucauldian argument, then, are that discourse is not the same as consciousness: that the form and the content of discursive expression must needs always be analytically distinguished, and that communication between people is, thus, never simply a matter of an exchange of conventional verbal or behavioural forms. Secondly, socialization within a set of discursive forms of expression and exchange is never 'completed' (Berger 1969: 31), in the sense of those discourses being learned alike by different people, or those people becoming alike through an unconscious identification with the discourses.

As formulated by George Steiner (1975: 170–3), discourse can be seen always to exhibit a dual phenomenology: a common surface of speech-forms and notations, of grammar and phonology, beneath which is to be found a concurrent flow of articulate consciousness. The conventional surface of collective public exchange thereby rests upon a base of possibly private meanings and associations, meanings which derive from the 'irreducible singularity' of personal consciousness and sub-consciousness, from the singular specificity of an individual's somatic and psychological identity (cf. Rapport 1993a: 161–77). As Steiner concludes (1975: 46): '[t]he language of a community, however uniform its social contour, is an inexhaustibly multiple aggregate of speech-atoms, of finally irreducible, personal meanings'. While there may be discursive rules and routines (concerned, say, with the proprieties of the expression of emotion in public exchange), affected by, even effecting, differentials of power, it is surely impoverishing of description and analysis to suggest, then, that when people speak (when Fathalla persuasively recites his poetry) the playing out of a language-game is the only thing occurring. Public and social-structurally situated discourses certainly afford links between the individual and the collective and effect avenues of social exchange, but it is surely unperceptive to claim that their enactment is all or most that their individual participants are or can be engaged with.

More broadly, engagement in a discourse need in no way translate as that discourse achieving agency, determining or causing meaning, eliminating the interpretive work of the individual speakers and hearers. Conventional discourses provide means of expression but they do not determine what is meant by them (cf. Knapp and Michaels 1982, 1988). Rather, it is the individual who animates discourses by the imparting to them of personal meaning; individuals personalize discourses within the context of their own discrete perspectives on life, using them to make and express a personal construction of the world, a possibly original language-world, a sense particular to them at a particular time.

Discursive exchange, moreover, is never unmediated by a creative individual improvisation of its conventions. Individuals at once partake of discourses' rules and routines, take part in the continuing constitution of socio-cultural milieux which such exchange gives onto, and make these instruments of their own understanding and use. Indeed, it is individuals' personalization of discursive structures that causes them to remain alive: here are structures granted contemporary relevance, validity and significance, by being imparted with personal meaning and intent. For this reason, too, there can be worlds of difference between shared grammatic-cum-paradigmatic competency on the one hand and shared cognition or mutual comprehension on the other. For individuals in interaction can be seen to be both assisting in a continuing collective performance and, at the same time, creating, extending and fulfilling ongoing agendas, identities and world-views of their own. The sense made of the discourse by its speakers and its hearers need not coincide, therefore, because each is responsible for instigating their own process of originating meaning, imparting a possibly uncommon order to the discourse's common forms; the individual makes personal sense in interaction, alongside others doing similarly. Hence, even if the various senses made of the discourse are complementary – even possibly consensual – this is something achieved through individual interactants' work (and by chance) rather than something carried in on the back of the discourse *per se*. To adapt Hymes (1973a: 25–6), the 'communicative event' of the discourse becomes a question of its manifold construals.

One can say, in sum, that without a fund of discourses the individual would not have the means of making sense, but without this work of interpretation, this individual use, discourse would not achieve animation in public life. Indeed, for Searle (1977: 202–8), the two necessarily presuppose each other; there is an infinitude of content possible within a finitude of linguistic expression *because* there is conventionally iterated verbal and syntactical form on the one hand and conscious, intentional individual activity on the other. Certainly, such duality should neither be sundered nor compounded in anthropological accounting.

In an eminently sensible counsel, Victor Turner eschewed all mystifications which would obscure the fact that human beings possess the consciousness and sophistication to transcend their own institutions (cited in Ashley 1990: xix). In an anthropological appreciation of discourse, it would appear a mystification not to see the individual speakers and hearers behind the conventional roles allotted them – the so-called 'subject-positions' or 'discursive sites'. For here are persons who cannot help themselves from periodically standing back from the social routines in which they are engaged and reflecting on them ironically: making sense of them in ways which may subvert the totalizing effects of those routines and in ways which reveal those persons to be able to adopt cognitive positions beyond the domain and determinism of those routines.

Whatever the order and sense propounded by the logic of the routines as such, the persons taking part in those routines, animating them by their mental and bodily, verbal and behavioural, presence in those routines, are able to (are destined to) write their own sense. They compose their own personal narratives which include them saying: 'Here I am partaking of a particular discourse, playing a language-game'.

Sometimes the game is played better than at other times, sometimes the playing is more trying than at other times, but there is surely no moment at which individuals do not experience the mixed emotions of both recognizing what the language-game expects of them and knowing precisely where they stood – emotionally, cognitively – in relation to it. It may not always be an easy matter determining how to reconcile these positions – what to say, how to act, how to seem – and it is always a far harder thing to know where one's interlocutors stand *vis-à-vis* the discourse, but it is never difficult for the individual to see her- or himself both present and absent: a conscious player in the game (however reluctant and formally disempowered) but never unconsciously played by it.

See also: **Code, Common Sense, Ethnomethodology, Irony**

ECRITURE FEMININE

Ecriture feminine, or 'women's writing', is a term coined by Luce Irigaray (1985) to convey a notion of female symbolic expression which can overcome a hegemony in current linguistic structures which is not just masculine but positively phallocentric and patriarchal, and which renders specifically female expression silent. As employed by Irigaray, and by the likes of Hélène Cixous (1990) and Julia Kristeva (1984), the concept amounts to a heady concoction of linguistics and psychoanalysis. There is no overall agreement between the above on the extent of biological determinism or essentialism in female experience, but all draw upon its bodily nature: '[B]eyond the classic opposites of love and hate . . . lies this perpetually *half-open* threshold, consisting of *lips* that are strangers to dichotomy' (Irigaray 1993).

Ecriture feminine draws on the works of Saussure, Freud, Lacan and Derrida, but owes its ethos, perhaps, to the writings of Nietzsche, and his attempts self-consciously to develop a philosophy based on irony, critique and revaluation. 'Suppose Truth is a Woman', Nietzsche advises, as part-strategy towards an ongoing 'revaluation of all values'; *écriture feminine* takes this to heart (cf. Irigaray 1991).

Language and identity

Social inequalities between the sexes derive from deep ideological structures, it is argued, in particular the play of language upon the unconscious. These make 'the subject', the *ego*, whether in language or

126

in the developments of science, religion or law, inevitably masculine; the truly feminine is erased in a network of lies. Women cannot know or love themselves, therefore, because language is foreign to them, rather than home to them, and merely mirrors their lack; women are in a state of 'dereliction', and hence commonly suffer psychosis (Irigaray 1993).

What is called for is to establish a presence in language which goes against and disrupts conventional norms and does not begin from the repressed, lacking and markedly 'other' nature which characterizes the feminine in contemporary structures and symbolizations. The feminine is more than simply a container of the masculine codes of everyday life, and yet the truly feminine represents something unnameable and inexpressible, at present. Women must speak like men and be attached to men in order to achieve a social status, to engage in social relations, and to acquire cultural capital. According to masculine parameters of identity, subjectivity, truth, meaning and value, women can only know themselves as inferior (castrated) versions of men.

The challenge is not to eschew language for, as poesis, this symbolization is a source of liberation, social, individual, spiritual and imaginative. However, to go beyond 'the Name and the Law of the Father', it is necessary to rewrite the woman beginning from that feminine fullness within the woman; not to mimic the male or seek to play a part in his social contracts (not to aim for a male-imitation identity, status or publicity) but to draw on feminine experiences which lie beyond and before conventional languages. Such a 'feminine idiolect' might emphasize, and give form to, multiplicity, fluidity, rhythm, difference and becoming, in place of the masculine verities of singularity, linearity and fixed (binary) oppositions. It is a matter of experimenting with poetic styles and achieving new discursive forms (cf. Irigaray 1991). For instance, maybe the rhythmical babblings of the child, before it learns linguistic structures could be adapted so as to write over and against language with voice, body and song. At present, these rhythms merely remain in language as echoes: as gaps, pauses and silences within the linear sequence.

A feminine God is yet to come – indeed, she would always be the God of becoming as such – but a specifically feminine language (also law and philosophy) can still be imagined. Above all, the writing of the feminine could entail an exploding of the definite singularities, distinctions and oppositions of Western thought: body/mind, subject/object, affect/intellect, substance/form, nature/culture, *alter/ego*. For every one of these binarisms reduces to feminine versus masculine: Western civilization is built on patriarchalism. Instead, two (or more) could be imagined as simultaneously one: a unity derived from a marriage of differences. If autonomy and equality were the masculine discoveries of the past century then difference might be a feminine addition in a future one: the equality of differences.

Anthropological resonances

Much of the above resonates, in ethos, with contemporary 'feminist' writings within anthropology and their 'passion for difference' (Moore 1994a). To focus on one such, Strathern (1991) describes the new aesthetic in which anthropology finds itself; here the old verities of singular fieldworkers becoming singular authors, in the translation of singular societies or cultures into singular objects of study, no longer convinces. Rather, there is an anticipation of the complexity of phenomena being retained in anthropological analysis without giving way to any more systematic representation of division and conjunction. Complexity might be specified without being simplified: complexity might be analysed without treating that analysis as anything but a controlled and convenient fiction.

One way to maintain a sense of the provisional and tentative nature of anthropological accounting, Strathern elaborates (1988), is through polemics: the continual overthrowing of extant analytical categories, so that the social world is continually apprehended anew. For example, inasmuch as conventional anthropological theories of symbolic classification are imbued with a Western folk conception of society as intrinsically plural and collective, as a gathering together (ordering, classifying and unifying) of irreducible individual persons, it is fruitful polemically to juxtapose against these notions Melanesian-infused anthropological theories which conceive of society as singular and its components as plural and 'dividual' (1988: 13). Here, the singular person is imagined as a social microcosm, as containing a generalized sociality, so that the bringing together of many persons is just like the bringing together of one.

In a sense, the plurality of the person and the singularity of society can be imagined to be 'the same' (namely, homologues of one another), just as Melanesian- and Western-inspired anthropologies are 'the same' (namely, opposites of one another). Melanesian- and Western-inspired anthropologies are contradictory accounts (classifications) of individual and society whose contradictoriness is an enabling factor which extends each. The contradictions enable one to see the provisionality of each account, and enable one to envisage social life as consisting in 'a constant movement from one state to another, from one type of sociality to another' (Strathern 1988: 14). It is through such movement, moreover, that anthropological analysis can hope to retain the flexibility and multiplicity of its socio-cultural objects of study; for here is the fixity and singularity of classification swallowed up in a plurality of classifications, each a displacement and extension (a contradiction but not a refutation) of what has gone before. Here is anthropology as a palimpsest of fictional analyses.

The future hallmark of social science, Strathern envisages, might be a regenerative overthrowing of fixed analytical categories and single symbolic classifications such that ever new meanings and viewpoints are born (cf. Moore 1988: 186). Not only would this include displacing the category 'social science' in its opposition to, say, 'literature', but also the 'domestic' *vis-à-vis* the 'politico-jural', the 'public' *vis-à-vis* the 'private' (cf. Caplan 1987), the 'observatory' *vis-à-vis* the 'contributory' (cf. Grimshaw 1992), the 'vocal' *vis-à-vis* the 'corporeal' (cf. Callaway 1992), and the 'dominant' *vis-à-vis* the 'subordinate' (Ardener 1975).

See also: **Contradiction, Cybernetics, Dialogics and Analogics, Gender, Literariness**

ETHNOMETHODOLOGY

Peter Berger and Thomas Luckmann once opined (1966: 140–1) that if human social reality is a precarious construction in the face of chaos, then conversation with consociates is our most important vehicle of reality-maintenance. Hence, an individual's everyday life can be seen to represent the working-away, in collaboration with significant others, at a conversational apparatus by whose 'realizing efficacy' the world continues to make sense, possesses regular coordinates and is filled with meaningful objects. Moreover, since language, according to Saussure (1983), is a 'social fact', the reality which conversation gives onto is a collective and intersubjective one; by partaking of conversation, Berger and Luckmann conclude (1969: 66), individual consciousness is structured in terms of the common-sense assumptions and norms, of the taken-for-granted values and categorizations of the social group as a whole.

Ethnomethodology, a school of social analysis associated in particular with the work of Harold Garfinkel, Aaron Cicourel, Harvey Sacks and others, elaborates and complexifies the above ideas, demonstrates them in micro-social practice, and draws out their macro-social implications. Bringing together Durkheim's belief that the consciousness of members of a social group will be steeped in collective representations, Saussure's theory that the everyday *parole* of language-speakers partakes of the unitary *langue* of the social whole, Husserl's methodology that social wholes must be approached via the phenomenology of individual experience, and Schuetz's notion that our experience is influenced inexorably (if implicitly) by common background expectancies which we learn to share as culture members . . . Garfinkel *et al.* focused on the everyday conversational 'work' by which people everywhere continue to give their lives and worlds a 'methodical' and shared character.

If our lives in society are structured, then this is not because social reality has a *sui generis* or even objective existence beyond social agents, the ethnomethodologist argues. Rather, social reality is something worked at methodically and collectively, courtesy of certain common systems of reasoning, comprehending and accounting, with which individuals have been socialized. It is constructed via an ongoing, face-to-face exchange of talk. Moreover, common background expectations of the world lead individuals to interpret the structure of both conversation and reality in routine ways; emerging out of this collaborative work is the continual reconstituting of social structures (cf. Coulter 1979). The project of ethnomethodology is to build models of the background knowledge and methods of interpretation which local actors ordinarily bring to bear in everyday situations.

While his writings are not always the most accessible or succinct, Garfinkel's work (1964, 1967, 1972) epitomizes the 'school' and is used below to set out its chief tenets. Ethnomethodology, Garfinkel summarizes (1967: 11), is: 'the investigation of the rational properties of indexical expressions and other practical actions as contingent ongoing accomplishments of organized artful practices of everyday life'.

Garfinkel's thought

Persons are members to organized social settings and affairs, to everyday moral orders which are taken-for-granted as natural facts of life. Nonetheless, such moral orders are something which members of a society are in the process of continually effecting, in collaboration with one another in face-to-face interaction. They are able to effect this because they share the same 'background of common understandings' and the same 'socially structured conditions' of the production of expression (1964: 233); the moral orders can be understood as the 'contingent accomplishments of socially organized common practices' (1972: 323).

That is, people are intent on determining and demonstrating that their lives are arranged in rational, coherent, consistent, chosen, clear, knowable, planful and uniform ways. Moreover, as members of social groups they have common methods for achieving this and providing themselves with rational (etc.) accounts of their lives and activities. The common methods consist of recourse to conventional norms, tasks and troubles, methods which are employed collectively and continually. Hence, 'every claim by practitioners of effectiveness, clarity, consistency, planfulness, or efficiency, and every consideration for adequate evidence, demonstration, description, or relevance obtains its character as a phenomenon from the corporate pursuit of this undertaking' (1972: 323).

Ongoing moral orders still demand work, however; acts of individual interpretation are necessary if prior, background, social-structural conditions are to be taken forward as members' common social properties into the future. True, the conditions will tend towards certain interpretations fulfilling themselves and certain classifications, analyses, understandings and identifications in the world being prescribed. However, the underlying disorder and unpredictability of human life still calls for continuous '*ad hoc*-ing' by members: filling in the gaps and sorting out the ambiguities of knowledge according to certain shared inferences, expectations and anticipations. Moreover, there is an inherent incompleteness or vagueness in the common understandings which members of a society share and employ, a vagueness which is a necessary adaptive feature if the understandings are to remain relevant and viable for long. Hence, much of everyday practice in society can be said to entail the serious task of carefully managing and negotiating the production of rule-bound, organized social activity by selecting among a communal set of alternative possible explanations, causes, senses, objectivities and facticities. In short, it is through a continuing negotiation of accounting practices – an 'artful (if unconscious) accomplishment' (1972: 323) – that members continue to make the familiar, commonplace activities of their everyday lives recognizable to themselves as familiar and commonplace.

This all means that the paramount reality in which members live is a commonsensical world of everyday expectations, activities and interpretations. However, this everyday world also serves as a point of departure and return for occasional modifications of normal life – in such phenomena as play, ceremonial, theatre, theory, dream and mortification. For instance, individual identity and status are resultants of communal negotiations based on common grounds of expected behaviours; fellow members will reason how and why an individual should act. However, there are also instances – 'status degradation ceremonies' (1968: 205) – where the public identity of a member is temporarily or permanently lowered in status and he or she is shamed. This act of shaming may have the purpose and effect of making the social structures of members' everyday activities more observable to themselves; stepping beyond the everyday, members look reflexively askance at it, becoming momentarily 'lay sociological researchers' and strangers to themselves (1967: 78).

Similarly, by deliberately causing disruption to everyday routines, social analysts ('professional strangers') have the best chance to watch the *ad hoc* work of repairing and reconstituting normal reality.

Ethnomethodology in action

An apt illustration of the above thinking is provided by Sacks (1974) regarding a seemingly innocuous and casual piece of 'natural language'.

A study of natural language shows how Garfinkel's 'everyday practical reasoning' is employed, Sacks begins, for it is in communicative acts that social norms are maintained. Grammatical norms govern members' interpretation of meaningful speech, while social norms govern members' interpretation of meaningful events; members' implicit social knowledge is thus revealed in their making of sentences and part-sentences into coherent and structured social texts. It is knowledge of shared norms which enables members to perceive actions as intelligible, conversation as meaningful and events as orderly. A common social structure enables members to understand conversation, in short, whose shared understanding replicates social structure.

Take, for instance, the minimal verbalization (Sacks 1974: 226): 'The baby cried. The mommy picked it up.' Among culture members a number of observations can be made. First, it is likely that members assume that the mother in question is that of the baby. Next, they assume that the event described in the second sentence took place after that described in the first sentence; indeed, they will presume a causal relationship such that the mother picked up the baby because it cried, and with a mind to soothing it. Finally, these sentences are recognized as a possible general description of a state of affairs without knowing which particular mother and baby are involved. These two sentences represent a complete story, and the 'shared cultural device' of grammar means that members have access to a common world of meaning and value.

Members are able to interpret in the above fashion, Sacks continues, because 'the fine power of a culture' is such that it 'fills the brains' of culture members 'so that they are alike in fine detail' (1974: 218).

Members share the same 'categorization devices' of objects in the world and how these might be properly expected to occur in their lives, in what sequence and with what ramifications, and conjoined with what activities: 'babies' can be expected to 'cry' and 'mommies' can be anticipated 'to pick them up'. Once members have perceived a possible eventuality, the *ad hoc* meaningfulness they have arrived at may divert them from testing other possibilities. However, the latter are equally prescribed. Members will share the same lexical system such that a range of possible alternatives is also supplied for different points in the meaningful sequence of events: 'infants' also cry, and 'fathers' also do the 'picking up'. Rules of relevance per situation will tell members which lexical ranges to expect to hear when.

Fellow travellers

Clearly there are overlaps between the issues which Garfinkel *et al.* are treating and their ways of proceeding and other schools' and social analysts'. Berger and Luckmann's portrayal of 'the social construction of reality' has already been referred to, and mention might also be made of attempts by Anthony Giddens and Pierre Bourdieu, and other so-called 'action theorists' to account for the continuing structuration of social milieux without recourse to Durkheimian notions of social facts as *sui generis* – to notions of social arrangements reproducing themselves without the mediating effects of individual agency (cf. Rapport 1990).

But more particular overlaps and borrowings between ethnomethodology and anthropological work might justifiably be alluded to. In Clifford Geertz's theory of common sense (1983), for instance, there is a parallel debt to Schuetz. Common sense is a taken-for-granted set of matter-of-fact assumptions, Geertz begins, which claims to be the immediate deliverances of experience and known by anyone in their right minds, but which is better understood as an ordered body of considered thought, a cultural system of learnt symbols. As such it will differ from one society to another. Nevertheless, its style, its way of knowing, the attitude to life which it engenders, the tone in which its wisdom is expressed – these may have a universal quality. To wit, common sense is a totalizing, ambitious and dogmatic frame of thought, claiming to strike at the heart of how things are. It pretends to knowledge which is natural and inevitable, practical and easily accessible, plain, obvious and earthy. Moreover, it is where most people in most places spend most of their social (intellectual and emotional) lives. Only intermittently do human beings see their lives in other than practical down-to-earth ways. And even then, more theoretical, religious, scientific, or aesthetic perspectives only come into play to make up for certain insufficiencies in the explanatory force of common sense. In most situations of human life, the cultural system of common sense, employed together with one's peers, is sufficient for making life meaningful. At certain non-everyday moments – a ritual, for example – a different cultural system of meaning, mood and activity can be brought to bear whereby everyday happenstances become recontextualized – perhaps in 'ultimate', sacred terms. Nevertheless, this non-everyday light thrown on the commonsensical serves to elucidate and thereby bolster the latter, so that members return to its system of significations and significance more solidly rooted. Indeed, it is out of the commonsensical that all more theoretical systems of meaning have grown, and they retain a dialectical relationship to it; in transcending common sense, they complete and maintain it (cf. Geertz 1971: 90–112).

In the work of Esther Goody *et al.* (1978), there is a recognition that it is from seemingly trivial, micro-social, linguistic forms and processes that the building blocks of social structure are made. At the same time, social interaction is shaped by general 'goals and constraints anchored in the wider social structure' (1978: 2). Indeed, each culture will possess a predominant interactional style and ethos, and prescribe a certain 'interactional systematics' (1978: 288); here will be 'patterns that are daily replicated by countless individuals' (1978: 245). Hence, the dialectic: interactants behave according to a common set of rules concerning how properly to proceed, and successful interaction serves to reinforce this repertoire of culturally standardized strategies of expression and representation. Under the aegis of such rules, moreover, meanings come to be successfully negotiated and managed, and selves presented.

Part of the interactional systematics of a culture will be what John Gumperz and Deborah Tannen call 'frames' and 'contextualization cues' (1979: 307–8). These amount to a constellation of surface features of interactional style which direct participants into interpreting the content of conversation in particular ways and as particular types of activity. Contextualization cues channel interpretation so that some common background knowledge is unconsciously brought to the fore and some reserved for other occasions. Hence, there exists a conventionalized co-occurrence between such features of conversation as: prosody, phonology, lexical choice, turn-taking, interjection, rhythm, timing, breathiness, volume, tone, somatics, formulaicism and thematic progression.

A further part of a culture's interactional systematics will be what Kenneth Pike calls 'emic units' (1964: 55). Cultures, he explains, cut up and classify the world into 'emes' – units of information and behaviour – and thus cause their members to perceive and expect certain possible experiences; culture members will share a knowledge of 'emic spots' at which certain unit behaviours and their class of alternatives are likely to occur. Conversation becomes a matter of negotiating which objects of experience are being represented, and their possible alternatives, and which behaviours are appropriate. Since the verbal and the non-verbal are inextricably bound, since emic units of language seamlessly give onto 'behaviouremes' (1964: 58), the emes of a culture are part-and-parcel of a unified phenomenon of behaviour, of thought, speech and action, through which all purposeful human activity is socially structured alike.

Ethnomethodology and ethnography

One difficulty in applying ethnomethodological analysis more widely to ethnography is the knowledge demanded by the analyst of his or her informants' language. Few anthropologists working outside their mother tongue will have the competency to subject their data to the requisite micro-social focus.

One attempt explicitly to treat non-Western ethnography according to ethnomethodological tenets, however, is provided by Moerman (1988) who compares Thai conversation with American. Moerman's intent is a 'culturally contexted conversation analysis' from which may issue a scientific account of how experienced moments of social life are constructed, and the ongoing operation of the social order is organized. '[I]n every moment of talk', he explains, 'people are experiencing and producing their cultures, their roles, their personalities' (1988: xi).

Moerman sets out his case using 58 pages (out of a total of 214) of transcripted and annotated conversational segments between both Thai and American speakers. These he describes as 'interactive processes' which speakers enact largely unconsciously. They are acquired schemes of expression for: 'the intentionless invention of regulated improvisation' (Bourdieu 1977). So encompassing and coercive are members' common interactional systems – whether Thai or American – that in both cases they routinely make 'single sayable somethings' with exact timing and without error. In both cases, their conversations derive from and by-and-large replicate common worlds of sense, orientation and experience.

See also: **Code, Common Sense, Discourse, Interaction**

FORM AND CONTENT

This conceptual distinction is most usefully introduced by reference to the seminal work of Georg Simmel (e.g. 1971, 1980).

Any social phenomenon has two inseparable elements, Simmel suggests (echoing a Kantian distinction between appearance and actuality): form and content. The *form* of something is its structure, its skeleton, its grammar. Forms amount to categories and collections of categories, taxonomies, schemata, languages, rotas, systems of classification. Moreover, the world and its aspects only become possible matters of experience and knowledge when constituted by forms. Forms negate the continuity of matter by introducing the distinctions that make things separate. Thus, forms specify the conditions under which it is possible to have a certain kind of experience and acquire a certain kind of knowledge. Forms, in short, are objects and the relations between them: objects like morality, sexuality, flirtation, prostitution, eroticism, love, household, society, history, bourgeoisie, drama, religion, death, science, art, literature and anthropology; and relations like hierarchy, complementarity, symmetry, correspondence, obviation, metaphor and metonymy. Forms mediate the human experience of the world: the human world can be said to be formally constituted.

Furthermore, forms are synthesizing processes. Forms are the means by which individuals come together, negotiate continuing relations and affiliate into groups. Through a sharing of language and other formal, classificatory systems, individuals are able to meet in regular and routine interaction: are able to make 'society'. Society represents individuals interacting under the aegis of common forms, individuals using forms in conjunction and compatibility with other individuals; and one can think of an amalgam of different types of society as forms are used among members: in precisely the same way or with marked differences, in cooperation or in opposition, with complementarity or with mutual exclusivity, with simultaneity or with sequentiality, in face-to-face settings or at a distance, with mutual knowledge or without.

Perhaps a definitive human characteristic is the multiplicity, the diversity and heterogeneity of forms which are used to mediate human relations with the world, however. For forms are humanly invented, and a plurality of languages, perspectives, conceptual and mechanical schemes serve to constitute a plurality of worlds of human invention. No one form or set of forms possesses a privileged logical, ontological or epistemological status over any other, and use of particular forms is a matter more of contingency, of tradition, of rhetoric, of strategy, of power and of practical implication. A particular set or fund of forms, linked over time, might be described as a 'culture', and to belong to a culture is to share a knowledge of the normal use and proper practice of a fund of forms. Moreover, as with the amalgam of types of society, one can imagine a continuum of types of culture members, in time and space, running between those who share all, some and none of the same cultural fund of worldly forms.

The discipline of anthropology, for example, would represent a particular culture (as would any number of other 'ologies' and 'isms' (Boon 1982: 231)), its members possessing alike knowledge of such formal objects as: fieldwork, functionalism, ethnography, Azande witchcraft, the Kachin, Clifford Geertz; and knowledge of such relations as: procuring a set of informants, writing up fieldnotes into a thesis, publishing a literature review, getting the *Current Anthropology* treatment, representing the Manchester School (and everything else down to page-formatting (Brady 1991b: 13)). Those who use these cultural forms adequately, compatibly and in conjunction with other members at a particular time and place, can be said to belong to an 'anthropology society'.

In the Simmelian portrayal, then, a fund of cultural forms provides a medium of interaction through which individuals come together; the fund is their means of sociation, of setting up a society between themselves and claiming to share a symbolic reality. To belong to a society means to use the same cultural forms for the construction of reality.

Cultural funds, however, are never static. For forms are in perpetual historical processes of variation and transformation, so that cultures amount to sets of objects and relations in constant flux. To understand why is to appreciate *meaning* or *content*. Forms are invented, we have said. In fact, they are the products of individually intentioned mental and physical activity, of individual agency. Individuals create the forms by which worlds come to be made and experienced, and by which 'others' come to be met. This they do in order to satisfy any number of different drives and secure any number of ends. Individuals make and use forms so as to fill them with a diversity of personal meanings; they give them sense and significance particular to their own lives: their purposes, interests, desires, needs, beliefs, values, and so on. It is this which makes up the content of their forms. Moreover, it is this individual usage which causes their collective exchange; individuals continue to bring cultural forms to social life, continue to make society and share culture, for the purpose of expressing their individual meanings. And yet, since content is fundamentally distinct from form, the same content is able to find expression in many different forms, and the same form is able to house any number of different contents. Hence, no two individuals may impart

137

meanings to cultural forms alike; so that at the same time as they are exchanged in interaction between individuals, indeed serve to make that meeting possible, they may be being used and interpreted in a diversity of ways.

Notwithstanding the free play between form and content, individuals make new forms because they continue to find that their desired meanings are not expressible within existing ones. To understand, in turn, why this is so, is to appreciate that once invented by individuals to house and express certain contents, forms become to some extent autonomous. Once an individual has made his or her word, fact, icon or car, they cannot as easily be unmade; they have lives (in dictionaries, in encyclopaedias, in films, in churches, in garages) which are independent of their makers. Moreover, they function according to their own mechanisms and capacities (cars cannot be used to write poetry, words cannot be used to drive to Cardiff). And, finally, once invented, their individual inventor has slight chance of controlling their effect on or use by others, or the hypostatization and institutionalization that they might undergo. In short, forms may achieve a certain independence from their creators and their moments of creation, acquiring a certain self-sufficiency, stability, even objectivity, whereby they fix the world.

It is not that they acquire their own power or force; this point must be made clear. Forms do not become things-in-themselves; they do not live their own lives. Rather it is individuals who continue to lead their lives through them. Forms are inert: they embody inertia, not momentum. Words in dictionaries, cars in garages, facts in encyclopaedias, icons in churches, call for continuing human agency for them to work and move, to have continued relevance in human lives. Forms continue to depend on individuals' bringing them to interaction, habitually relating them together, routinely exchanging them, regularly using them in mental, physical, spiritual contexts.

The point is that, while lumpen and inert, cultural forms are still difficult to ignore. Dictionaries and encyclopaedias, garages and churches, make for cluttered (not to mention institutionalized) worlds, and individual users of these forms must carefully manoeuvre with and around them if they are to express themselves normatively and with propriety (and so join synthetically with their fellows in socio-cultural milieux). Indeed, manoeuvring around cultural forms, leading routine lives of habitual exchanges, can take up the whole of life of a society's members. Moreover, as cultural forms pass between many hands, are used in many different interactions, so their shapes and qualities are reduced: smoothed, flattened, drained, distilled by common denomination. Words become clichés, facts become common sense, machines become furniture, icons become dogma. The clutter of forms can rigidify interaction, petrify further imaginative agency, estrange individuals from their creativity.

More historically usual, however, is the situation of formal inertia and individual invention proceeding side by side. Hence, as cultural forms 'congeal' and become independent, detached from the energies which produced them, and fill the world with habit, individuals are also creating new forms, and causing a world of further heterogeneity and flux. New energies, not incorporatable within old forms, create new forms. This happens as, first, amid the clutter of forms, individuals have the possibility of choosing between a number of often competing options (religion and science; Freudian and Jungian psychoanalysis; Jaeger, Armani and St Michael tailoring; Manchester City, Man. Utd, Wolves and Hibernian football); and also of putting these forms together in a sequence and frequency which amounts to a new *bricolage* (Lacanian psychoanalysis; Punk tailoring). Secondly, as individuals may find that no existing forms suit their purpose, feel right, fit what they have in mind, so they invent new ones both for their own use and for possible later inclusion into the collective fund: new words ('spliff'; 'byte'), new facts (time is relative; one in ten children is sexually abused), new machines (aeroplanes; faxes), new icons (white witchcraft; electric guitars).

In sum, Simmel's picture is one of inert forms and 'energetic' contents. The former are produced by the latter, but then the former stand still, become autonomous, objectified and institutionalized, while the latter progress and change – thus producing a potential tension and conflict between them. Creative energies, moreover, are in individual possession, while the inert forms come to be collectively owned. And so new individual subtleties are continuously coming into conflict with old collective formalities. Simmel described this as the sociological 'tragedy': the common forms of cultural exchange facilitating wide-spread communication and also making it practically ineffective; the routine exchange of objectified cultural forms acting as an impediment, a constriction, to the individual subjectivity which seeks continuing expression through them; individual creativity being threatened by the very forms it has produced. But then again, it is these tensions which are responsible for the dynamism of social life and for cultural development and change. Here, in sum, is a picture of society neither simply as something of systemic imposition or objective determination, nor as the mere momentary impulses of subjective states of mind, but as the coming together of collective, autonomous objects and relations with continuing individual creativity. To a fund of common forms individuals impart experiences of social life which are multiple, fragmentary, idiosyncratic, inexorably conflictual and endlessly processual.

Simmel and anthropology

The Marxian critic Georg Lukacs once dubbed Simmel the theoretician of Impressionism and advocate of Transitionalism (cf. Gassen and Landmann 1958: 171–3); here is a vision of culture and society stressing not the systemic requirements and normative constraints of Marxism (or functionalism, or structuralism), so much as the equivocation and polyphony of interaction and the phenomenological contingency of those individual minds where interactions are experienced and hence 'occur'. But then it is precisely to Impressionism (as represented by Cezanne's six variant portraits, *Still Life with Apples and Oranges*) that David Parkin turned (1987: 64–6) to furnish anthropology with an image of contemporary cultural life as composed of potentially limitless perspectives: a vast variety of visions and versions, complementary to one another but without any underlying structure of common denomination, any circumscribed set of generative principles, any single controlling logic. More generally, it is to the line of thought from Impressionism through Cubism to Dadaism that Parkin would now have anthropology look to for its social models; here is a mocking of the possibility of thinking in terms of fixed structures and certainties, to inspire in us new key metaphors of incompleteness, perspective and creativity (cf. Moore 1987: 729–30).

Nor is this anthropological meeting with a Simmelian ethos exclusively of recent vintage. Edmund Leach, after all, argued that the essence of our humanity was to be found in our continuous rebellion, as individuals, against received collective structures, laws, rules, customs and controls, and our creating of something new. Leach saw structure and creativity, tidiness and vitality as being in inevitable contradiction, and implicated in an inexorable dialectical process (1977: 19). While Victor Turner's adaptation of the Weberian dialectic of routine versus charisma into a universalizing theory of structure versus anti-structure, turned, essentially, on the same tension. Symbolic behaviour constituted society, Turner elaborated, and society as a process involved the uniting of structure and anti-structure in variable proportions. Moreover, it was the anti-structural which was prior to and creative of the structural, while remaining antithetical in character and embroiled in a continual struggle for individuals' true loyalty (1974: 231–69, 1982a: 96–129).

What is demonstrated is how (Simmelian) form-and-content offers anthropology an apposite way of conceiving of creativity, diversity and ambiguity in social life (cf. Rapport 1993a: 161ff.). This conception entails an appreciation of the diverse individual use of collective cultural forms (objects and relations, institutions and grammars): the diverse constitution of forms, combination of forms, and imparting of meaning to those forms.

See also: **Culture, Discourse, Interaction, Society**

GENDER

The 'problem of women'

In 1972 Edwin Ardener published an article entitled 'Belief and the problem of women'. In it he illuminated a methodological predicament of ethnography of the greatest magnitude, namely, the absence of speaking, thinking, believing, knowing women within ethnographic texts. In the anthropological writings of the 1960s, unlike those of earlier decades, there appeared almost always only the voices of men, whereas, whether the ethnographer be male or female, women were 'muted', erased as conscient beings. While the behaviour of women might be observed (they married, tended children, cooked, farmed), they were 'effectively missing in the total analysis or, more precisely, they were there in the same way as were the Nuer's cows, who were observed but also did not speak' (Ardener 1975: 4).

Ardener concludes his article by warning female ethnographers to resist 'expressing the "maleness" of their subject when they approach the women of other societies' (*ibid.*: 15). In short our own dominant (male) models about the workings of society, within which women are viewed as outsiders, invalidated even for the female anthropologist the very possibility of the worth and importance of the perspectives of women on the procedures and lifeways of their communities. Ardener challenges women ethnographers by remarking that 'it may well be, too, that their positive reluctance to deal with the "problem of women" [the silencing of them] is the greater because they sense that its consideration would split apart the very framework in which they conduct their studies' (*ibid.*).

The reappearance of women

Ardener's prophecy about the implications of a female rebellion was brought home with a vengeance. In the 1960s, ethnographic publications with 'women' in the title did not sell, while today the section on gender in any reputable academic bookshop is healthily large. This change of attitude, however, has to do with far more than the popularity of the *topic* of women, or the female perspective on things; for gender studies within anthropology, as in its sister disciplines, have played, along with the forces of post-modernism and post-colonialism, a salient role over the last two to three decades in a major critique of the grand narratives of the human sciences. This dawning recognition of 'the problem of women', not only in anthropology but in many of its sister studies as well, served as one of the major impetuses for the redrawing of sacred academic boundaries, visions and concerns.

Thus, the reason for this particular consciousness-raising exercise, or 'the problem of women', having such momentous effect, has been that gender blindness was but the tip of an enormous iceberg formed by the cold procedures of Western juridical, political, economic and academic thought and practice which have created all those other inequalities – beyond those between men and women – of class, race, ethnicity, nationality and sexual preference. Once women were firmly inserted *within* the parameters of 'establishment' discourse, either as objects of social research or as subjects conducting such inquiry (having shed their previous status of honorary males), the consequences were, as Edwin Ardener predicted, a true 'Kuhnian' paradigm shift. The epistemological and methodological foundations of 'the disciplines' are indeed shaken when females, fifty per cent of the world's population, finally enter the picture. In the words of Seyla Benhabib (1992: 178, her italics), 'the definition of the *object domain* of a research paradigm, its units of measurement, its method of verification, the alleged neutrality of its theoretical terminology, and the claims to universality of its models and metaphors are all thrown into question'.

Once recognized, the 'question of women' did then play a large part in upsetting established ways of thinking and practice in the human sciences. Those systems and institutions once viewed as just, egalitarian and progressive came to be understood as unjust, unequal and regressive. Previously all those suffering from the inequities of dominant structures had been both unheard and unseen, for the most potent strategy of Western establishment ways of seeing, whether for political or academic intent, was *not to see* all those who had been categorized as not just like self, that is, the white, middle-class, propertied male (Benhabib 1992). Thus to recognize women as agents in the world has meant to actually *see* an other. The undermining by feminists, post-modernists and post-colonialists alike of hallowed paradigms has led to the recognition of this *difference*.

This discovery of the fact of difference – and with it the acceptance of the full humanity of all those different others – has been a subversive activity, defiant of many of the universalist traditions that the human sciences have held as sacred (Benhabib 1992: 191). For feminist theory, as for other major critiques of grand narrative logics, the unravelling of the implicit ideological construction of otherness in Western academic thought, and the explication of its *social* and *historical* constitution, have become the central chores. The *local* nature of our constructions of truth, reason and humanity needed to be *de*constructed. As these are tasks for a *social* theory that is centred in the art of social contextualization, the anthropological studies of gender relations which have been carried out over the past two decades can be understood to be especially crucial to the development of this rebellious interdisciplinary task.

The early writings on the female voice in anthropology, and their contributions

The impact of feminist studies upon anthropology seems to have made its mark a good decade before similar intrusions were felt in the other human sciences. For instance in psychology, Carole Gilligan's groundbreaking study, *In a Different Voice*, which questioned the premises of a Piaget and Kohlberg developmental model of moral capability, was published in 1982. Within anthropology a series of volumes, which became mainstream, centring on 'the question of women' and expressing dissatisfaction with the androcentric bias in anthropology were published in the 1970s (cf. Strathern 1981: 167). Among these were: Michelle Rosaldo and Louise Lamphere's edited collection, *Women, Culture and Society*, in 1974, and Shirley Ardener's *Perceiving Women* in 1975. The latter volume had both female and male contributors, yet another indication of mainstream acceptance of the issues. In addition, during the 1970s well-received ethnographic monographs by women anthropologists that focused upon the women of particular societies began to enter the literature; among these were Marilyn Strathern's 1972 publication of *Women in Between* and Annette Weiner's *Women of Value, Men of Renown* in 1976, both based upon research in New Guinea.

These early writings made two major contributions to the development of gender studies. The first was to make the discipline of anthropology itself clearly aware of its exclusion of women as a topic for study, and how such oversight was moreover linked to the male bias of dominant theoretical and methodological assumptions of the discipline. In *Women, Culture and Society*, its authors show how women, like men, trans-culturally 'are social actors whose goals and strategies are intrinsic to the processes of social life' (Rosaldo and Lamphere 1974: 11), and that 'even in situations of overt sex role asymmetry women have a good deal more power than conventional theorists have assumed' (*ibid*.: 9). It became quickly obvious that disciplinary presuppositions and procedures needed to be radically reconsidered in order to include the agency of women. The second contribution was that the anthropological treatment of the female question was from a cross-cultural perspective, rather than being situated within the Western context alone. It was especially this sensitivity to cultural and social difference that provided one of anthropology's important gifts to the development of gender studies across disciplines in the 1980s and 1990s, for from its early writings on 'the woman question' it emerged that the ways in which women and men related to each other, and the manner in which each of the sexes was conceptualized, varied considerably from one people to the next. In other words, gender and its attributes are not givens. As Rosaldo and Lamphere conclude, 'different forms of social and cultural organization have provided women in different places with very different powers and possibilities, so our [own] contemporary situation renders any "natural" ranking or differentiation of the sexes altogether obsolete' (*ibid*.: 14).

By the early 1980s, the concept of 'gender' came to be used to designate the social construction of differences between men and women, to contrast with the notion of 'sex' which refers to their biological difference (cf. Pine 1996). It was 'gender' as a *symbolic construct* that became a major focus of interest in the 1980s (cf. Strathern 1980), along with the exploration of the ways in which such constructs might variously relate to practice. There are those today (e.g. see Benhabib 1992; Moore 1994b) who would argue that the notion of 'sex', or the nature of the 'biological' make-up of men and women, is likewise a social construction. In other words, what is recognized as a physically distinct sexed body is not so straightforward a matter as once thought. Certainly in Amazonia, some peoples have no concept of 'body', and most consider a person's capabilities for reproduction to have an other-worldly source, that is, not to be a 'biological' matter. What we understand as a biological 'given' may well conflict with other peoples' ideas about physical reality (cf. Strathern 1992b; Overing 1996a).

The early debate on the 'subjugation of women': the vestiges of Western values

Despite their crucial role in rectifying the anthropological erasure of female agency in ethnographic writings, the early writers upon 'the problem of women' tended to raise as many questions as they answered. In large part this was due to the fact that extrication from the received paradigms of power and authority could not be a quick process, nor was it easy to shed the penchant for subscribing to the universalisms underpinning them. For instance, many of the feminists of the 1970s and 1980s used Marxist models of power relations to interpret their findings, a Western paradigm of power *par excellence*. The result was that there was a tendency to universalize the woman question in terms which, while highly relevant and useful to the project of unfolding misogynist bias within their own society, were perhaps not so perspicacious when it came to understanding the complexity of the situatedness of the gender relations among other peoples.

For more than a decade the most chosen generalization was that women were universally dominated, and everywhere men tended to have more prestige (e.g. Rosaldo and Lamphere 1974: 9). Indeed, Ortner and Whitehead (1981: x; also see Collier and Yanagisako 1987) *defined* gender as a form of social inequality, and they therefore viewed the study of gender as 'inherently a study of relations of asymmetrical power and opportunity' (Ortner and Whitehead 1981: 4). As a second generalization it was argued further, most forcefully by Sherry Ortner (1974; also see Rosaldo 1974: 41), that women are universally devalued because of their reproductive capacities, which place them culturally on the side of nature, the emotions, the particular, the domestic, the private, and *thus* the irrelevant.

As was also pointed out by certain writers (e.g. MacCormack 1980; Strathern 1980, 1984; Jordanova 1980), the second of these assumptions, the linkage of the female gender to the domain of 'nature' is a salient myth of the West. However, the extent that *either* assumption (including the notion of gender as a major framework for the playing out of inequalities) might hold elsewhere is always another question (cf. Overing 1986; Strathern 1992b). If we can accept the *local* quality of these 'universals', 'the problem of women' as some of these early writers phrased it, can be seen as integrally linked to Western ideology and a Western paradigm of power relations. The idea that women are devalued and dominated because they are seen to be on the side of nature, the ignorant, the uncontrolled and the domestic was the powerful myth about gender relations associated with both the rise of science (Jordanova 1980: 61, 64) and of capitalism (cf. Benhabib 1992) in the West. Nature, a category including other peoples and societies, was to be a realm upon which European man acted and which he controlled; women, perceived as part of nature, are a man's property – or an object of man. As Marilyn Strathern notes (1980: 217): 'It is our culture which sets up males as creators and inventors and females therefore as perilously near objects, for we define "culture" itself as manifested in things which are made and are alienable'. Women within such a scheme, being viewed as objects, are then treated as a *natural* resource.

As Overing (1986) and others (especially Strathern) have argued, the 'problem' of gender when placed within a comparative framework, becomes in large part one of not taking the rhetoric and claims of Western science and society at face value. In the meantime, we have learned in the process of our mistake a good deal about Western images and evaluations of gender, its moral judgements about it, while the ethnographic evidence supports the view that this particular package of values is hardly a universal. It is also clear that our own understanding of gender in the West is tied to notions not just about the relations between the sexes, but to more general ideas about how culture is different from and superior to nature. At the core of this construction of the relation of culture to nature is also a theory about power and the political, which includes very specific notions about relations of domination and subordination, exploitation, coercion, control and, of course, inequality. Western academic notions of order and rationality favour the play of dominance and subordination. However, the perils of ethnocentrism go further. On one powerful level these relationships are envisaged in scientific thought as having amoral content, that is, humankind's relation to the environment is understood as an exploitative one without the limits of a higher morality to order it; the scientist's truths, free from value, are amoral ones (cf. Overing 1985b). It can be said without stretching the truth too much that our theories of power and the political, and also of gender relations, tend to reflect this bias toward the amoral forthcoming from the world of science.

Still, the understanding of Western science both of truth and of the proper relationship of humans to the environment contrasts sharply with the ideas held by many other peoples who see both truths and relationships of human beings to the environment to have moral, social and political value. Their understanding of gender relations are as enmeshed as our own within wider networks of meaning, and thus their images of gender can be framed against the backdrop of ontological concerns radically different from our own. As Gillison comments (1980: 172), other peoples have their own obsessions, and to underrate the complexity of indigenous cosmologies would be to deny this to be true. Following this line of thought we should expect theories of personal agency and power relationships for many peoples to differ substantially from our own. However, the theoretical implications for the cross-cultural study of gender relations of such rich ethnography as that by Gillison on indigenous theories of power, and the place of gender relations within it, of the Gimi of Highland New Guinea, has only slowly left its mark (see especially Gillison 1993; also see McCallum 1989, Belaunde 1994, Guss 1989 on Amazonian peoples). Why then did universalist theories of gender relations hold sway for so long?

The Marxian argument and the 'catch-22' of gender relations

The Marxian argument of Meillassoux (1981) provided one of the strongest assertions of the universal domination of women by men. It also was a point of view highly favoured by both women and men throughout the 1970s and 1980s in their anthropological writings on gender relations: women because they were disgruntled and infuriated with Western gender asymmetries, men because the view supported what they already assumed. Meillassoux argues that it was the formation of the sexual division of labour, itself, that led to the socio-political subjugation of women, and thus made 'the woman (or slave) a servant of men' (Meillassoux 1981: 21). Kinship institutions are the culprit, for it was through their development that the subjugation of women was achieved. Marriage, conjugality and paternal filiation, all were imposed upon women by men to be the means through which men could constrain women. Through the regulations of kinship, men gained control over both the means of reproduction and female labour in society (*ibid.*: xii–xiii, 20).

Since much ethnographic work until recently has been within what anthropologists once referred to as 'kinship-based societies', the reader can understand the implications of such a Marxian argument: women *as social beings* are first and foremost trapped and exploited as victims of ideological hegemony, and most obviously so among those peoples about whom anthropologists write the most. This is a view, however, predicated upon certain precarious Western assumptions about civil society through which gender becomes defined from the start as a structure of inequality. It is assumed that notions about gender are universally about male superiority and female inferiority, and that gender relations are therefore always enacted through modes of exploitation and domination. It is taken for granted that it is universally the case for women's activities to pertain to a denigrated, restrictive world of the 'domestic', while men tend to their own prestigious political (and economic) affairs within a wider realm of relationships. Because this male domain of politics is assumed to be always a more valued sphere of activity than the 'domestic' domain of women, the status of females is always judged as inferior to that of men.

Overing has argued (1986) that when the anthropological gaze is through the lens of such Western paradigms of power females are universally placed in a position of 'catch-22'. As Joseph Heller in his novel *Catch-22* tells of air force regulations, 'there was only one catch . . . and that was Catch-22': you are damned if you do and you are damned if you don't. A similar absurdity was evident in much of the early literature on gender, where *any* piece of ethnographic information on women's activities was taken as evidence of female degradation. The catch to Meillassoux's judgements of male and female tasks is clear. He asserts (Meillassoux 1981: 28–9) that in societies where hunting and *therefore* war is valued (an unwarranted assumption itself) women are correspondingly devalued and made inferior because of their social vulnerability, and thus 'put to work under male protection and given the least rewarding, the most tedious and *above all*, the least gratifying tasks such as agriculture and cooking' (*ibid*.: 19, my italics). We find that by the ethnographer's definition, the work, ritual, obligations and pain of men are all tribute to their high status as controllers of society, while women's work, ritual, obligations and pain become evidence of their subordinate status and exploitation. If women follow menstrual taboos, have children, tend gardens, prepare and cook meat and vegetables, bake bread, spin cotton – all these activities are taken as signs of woman's exploitation by men and of their demeaned status. Similarly, if they do not hunt, go to war, make political speeches, play sacred flutes and drums, make canoes, cut down trees – each such omission also provides yet one more example of woman's lowly position.

Attempts such as that of Meillassoux, to achieve a viable unified Marxian theory of gender relations (and of social inequalities more generally) have proven to be based on too uncertain a ground. As Keesing notes (1987b: 59), anthropological theory, including the Marxian attempt, has not developed a concept of ideology that is sufficiently sensitive to allow for adequate generalizations about the force of cultural symbols or constructs cross-culturally. The achievement of such a unified theory would, at any rate, be highly unlikely in that the Marxist notion of culture-as-ideology acquires its saliency within a particular history, and that is a Western one. As such it carries all the baggage of this specific history which makes it risky to use as a lens for understanding even those other systems that manifest blatant inequalities, and for which such concepts as 'subordination', 'exploitation' and 'oppression' are too bluntly crude (cf. Strathern 1988; Keesing 1987b; Overing 1986).

The question of coercion, and its evaluation

The Western notion of the political tends to be highly restrictive, being attached to ideas about coercion and the control of labour and the products of it. Also, embedded in it are all those ethnocentric assumptions about what work is, what constitutes personhood, agency, power, what subjects and objects are, and what property is (cf. Strathern 1980, 1984, 1988). It is assumed that women's work, the products of their labour, and their reproductive capacities are controlled by men. But equality and inequality can be very difficult to judge, and there is a serious methodological question with regard to how we as ethnographers recognize exploitation among other peoples. Roger Keesing remarks (1987: 59–60) that attempts to find the mystification, false consciousness and oppression lurking within other peoples' practices, and their constructs of gender, rely too often upon hazardous assumptions about what constitutes inequality, domination and exploitation, or about what equality means and what a just and liberated society would be like.

From a cross-cultural perspective the equation between public leadership and dominance is questionable. What does one mean by 'dominance'? Does it designate coercion? Or control over 'the most valued'? 'Political' systems may be about both, either, or conceivably neither. The idea of 'control' would be a bothersome one for many peoples, as for instance among many indigenous peoples of Amazonia where all members of a community are fond of their personal autonomy and notably allergic to any overt expression of control or coercion (cf. Clastres 1977; Thomas 1982; Rivière 1984; Overing 1993a). The conception of political power as a *coercive* force, while it may be a Western fixation, is not a universal. It is very unusual for an Amazonian leader to give an order. If many peoples do not view political power as a coercive force, *nor as the most valued domain*, then the leap from 'the political' to 'domination' (as coercion), and *from there* to 'domination of women', is a shaky one. As Marilyn Strathern (1981: 167–8) has remarked, the notions of 'the political' and 'political personhood' are cultural obsessions of our own, a bias long reflected in anthropological constructs. We should be wary of projecting our own value of 'the political' upon others.

Given this difficulty of defining 'the political' within a cross-cultural framework, it would be facile to assume that women are not political beings, nor powerful actors within their own societies. It should be noted that for many peoples it would be difficult to draw the line between what we might separate as 'religious' and 'political' domains.

In early feminist literature the general idea was that while boys at puberty receive esoteric privileged knowledge, girls only suffer prohibitions and restrictions at their initiation. This is an area where later ethnographic attention has greatly enriched and enlightened our view, particularly on the topic of the privileged knowledge of women (e.g. Keesing 1987; Descola 1994, 1996; Ardener 1975; Hugh-Jones 1979). As Overing has noted (1986), the meaning of gender, its cultural construction, is often associated with highly complex theories of energy, fertility, and power in the universe. Thus to reduce the meaning of such idea systems to the political one of male dominance over women would be foolish. David Guss writing on the Yecuana of the Orinoco Basin notes that privileged knowledge, or ritual activity, permeates every cultural function, whether centred on males or females. Women, who are masters of the domain of gardens, own powerful magical herbs which 'are the paramount expression of women's sacred knowledge and ritual independence' (Guss 1989: 35). Some of these plants heal children or initiate women, others 'ease menstruation, aid or prevent birth, cure or produce fever, frighten snakes, stop rains, secure lovers, induce sleep, dispel ill humor, deter evil spirits, protect travellers, and cause death' (*ibid.*). For the Yecuana, power vacillates between men and women through the endless inter-play of dualistic structures: female and male, inside/outside, house and garden; female outside/male inside; female inside/male outside. There is therefore a strong relativity to Yecuana gender politicking, which is also ritually played out, where women, and not just men, take their respective centre positions.

The relationship between the genders among Amazonian peoples is often highly egalitarian by anyone's standards, and an emphasis, for instance, on 'hidden' control mechanisms that might allow for male dominance can too easily lead one to miss the more socially prevalent institutions that create equality. There is by now a large amount of ethnography telling of indigenous peoples among whom the women, both ideologically and in practice, control their own labour, and the products of it (see much of the contemporary literature on Amazonia). On the other hand, values – and the structures of equality and inequality linked to them – may well not be so straightforward, but ambiguous, as among the Hagen of New Guinea (Strathern 1981, 1988) where there is constant play between egalitarian and hierarchical principles. There are also by now many ethnographic examples showing that the quality of the relations between the genders may well be subject to perspective, where females have a very different view from males of the strengths of their respective roles and participation within the social life of the community (cf. Ardener 1975; Keesing 1987b).

The problem for the ethnographer is that because of *our* gender politics a particular kind of inequality is presumed to be the predominant mode of existence.

A plurality of voices, and the artful skills of everyday life

Anthropology, in its self-reflection upon its treatment of the 'problem of women', and subsequent attempts to rectify its sins, has, because of its cross-cultural perspective, much to offer its sister disciplines. The most difficult set of assumptions of all to shift within anthropology has been those having to do with the Western distinction between the 'private' and the 'public', and the immensity of the implications of its ensnarement of our judgements are only beginning to be appreciated. The dichotomy of the 'domestic' and the 'private' has been noted time and again in gender studies more generally to have special saliency within Western political and moral thought and evaluations, and it is therefore with its intricacies and iniquities that much of the more recent feminist literature has been concerned.

The distinction assumes that women are imprisoned within the domain of the private and the domestic, and therefore devalued by the male public and political arena. One of the chief contributions of feminist thought to political theory, psychology and moral philosophy is to question this line that divides the public and the private (cf. Gilligan 1982; Benhabib 1992; Baier 1994). Women, being bound to the domain of the private, have been confined beyond the pale of justice where they take an invisible place within contemporary theories of justice and community. As Benhabib says (1992: 12–13), 'the norms of freedom, equality and reciprocity have stopped at the household door'. The moral reasoning of women has been denigrated as they are shown to be lacking in their acceptance of universals of justice, and more attentive in their moral judgements to context, details of relationships and narratives (Gilligan 1982). Some feminists are attempting to wed the traditional male theories of justice and contract theory with what they understand to be the female concerns of care and nurturance (cf. Benhabib 1992; Baier 1994). In other words they are trying to find ways in which 'the public' can responsibly include the female domestic matters of child-rearing and all the other normal concerns and responsibilities with which we are daily and intimately most concerned. These writers assume 'the domestic', and the concern for care and trust, to be largely a matter of gender, of interest to females but not males. For them, the genders have different moral outlooks: while men tend to phrase morality in terms of obligation, contract and justice, women are most concerned with a morality relevant to the bringing up of children, engendering of love, care, trust and cooperation.

Anthropologists, however, may well question the cross-cultural relevance of the Western case, where males and females appear to be opposed in moral outlook in accordance to their respective separation of domains of activity. There are peoples who do make a strong separation between the public and the domestic, and others who do *not* (cf. Overing 1986). Or, conceptually, the distinction may not make a fit with our own. For instance the notion of 'the private' may well pertain to the person, and not a domestic group. Among many indigenous peoples, female performance as primary actors, listeners, or provocative commentators is as public as that of the men (cf. Passes 1998). Moreover, there are peoples, certainly in Amazonia, who prize 'the domestic' over the political, as that informal, intimate domain where the art of everyday maintenance and artful skills for social life reign. In such cases that is what social life *is* about, the care of children and the trust in relations of interdependency related to such care. Here neither a gender distinction in moral outlook, nor a distinction between 'public' and 'private' domains, is relevant (cf. Overing 1989, 1999). Until recently, because of the dominant strand in Western political theory, from which anthropology has not been totally exempt, that excludes domesticity and the everyday relations of the ordinary moral agent, this type of Amazonian sociality was not seen, much less understood. By listening to the women, the messages of the men could be understood in a different light, for these are peoples whose social organizations make no sense without the full inclusion of the social acts of their women.

In short, it *has* made all the difference to the ethnographic endeavour to include the subject of women and especially women's voices. In the process we have time and again discovered a rich symbolic world that demands an understanding of the *interplay* of men and women, and their respective knowledges, that makes a travesty of the simplistic 'male only' models of yesteryear. It is only by understanding both male and female (often complementary) perspectives that gender relations among another people can begin to be comprehended. As gender studies progressed, it became absolutely clear that the peremptory voice of the ethnographer was insufficient, as too that of the male informant. Nor can we speak from the perspective of a generic female, for there is no such thing. There is ever a plurality of voices, a seemingly helter-skelter chiming, that provides, *significantly*, rich layers of evaluative contextualization, the recognition of which has in the end transformed our anthropological visions of culture and society.

All those kinship structures through which men established important relationships with each other through the exchange of their muted women, which became the model of 'society'; all those 'political' roles and statuses through which men who controlled the political domain became the knowledge-holders of their culture – these were the topics that once were recognized as primary anthropological concerns. The recognition by gender studies of the critical importance of allowing the authorship of a multitude of voices has led to energetic debate over the epistemological foundations of anthropology, which in turn has transformed the question, the topics and the methodology of the discipline – and in the end its own self-image as having the right of authorial privilege.

See also: **Ecriture Feminine**, **Kinship**, **Moments of Being**, **Post-Modernism**, **Qualitative and Quantitative Methodologies**, **Society**, **The Unhomely**

GOSSIP

In any socio-cultural milieu, people may be occupied in gossip for a substantial part of their every day. Recognizing, since Malinowski, that studying the world of the everyday is the key to an understanding of how people behave, anthropologists have long appreciated the significance of gossip.

Nevertheless, sustained analysis of gossip *per se* remained intermittent (cf. Radin 1927; Herskovits 1937; Colson 1953) until the 1960s, when three broadly distinct approaches emerged: the functionalist, the transactionalist and the symbolic-interactionist.

The functionalist approach is exemplified by Max Gluckman (1963b). Gossip, Gluckman begins, is a culturally determined and sanctioned process, a social fact, with customary rules and with important functions. Notably, gossip helps maintain group unity, morality and history. For, the essence of gossip is a constant (if informal and indirect) communal evaluation and reaffirmation of behaviour by assessment against common, traditional expectations. Furthermore, gossip enables groups to control the competing cliques and aspiring individuals of which they are composed; through gossip, differences of opinion are fought out behind the scenes (through customary innuendo, ambiguity and conceit) so that outwardly a show of harmony and friendship can be maintained. Finally, gossip is a hallmark and a privilege, even a duty, of group membership. A group gossips, gossip is group property, and to be a member is to gossip – about other members.

The transactionalist approach, spearheaded by Robert Paine (1967), eschews the presumptions of seeing groups as united and equilibrated, and social-structural convention as being always geared towards this end. Paine argues that it is more apposite to see gossip as a means by which individuals manipulate cultural rules and to see individual gossipers as having rival interests (in power, friendships, networks, *matériel*) which they seek to forward and protect. Individuals, not groups, gossip, and they gossip primarily not about group values but individual aspirations, others' and their own. Indeed, any appeal to group unity should rather be seen as a managing of self-interest: an attempt to have a particular definition of a social situation prevail. In short, gossip allows the moral order to be bent to individual purpose. It is instrumental behaviour which uses a genre of informal communication for the partial effecting of competition between individuals through the selective imparting and withholding, the manipulating, of information.

To an extent, the above dichotomy between group- and individual-oriented analyses is collapsed in the symbolic-interactionist approach. Here (Haviland 1977; Heilman 1978) the emphasis is on how, through everyday talk, cultural reality and social relations are continually being represented and debated; in gossip, individuals can be seen actively speculating together on the nature of their lives and world. Hence, gossip provides individuals with a map of their social environment and with current information about happenings, inhabitants and their dispositions. This then provides the resource by which they can devise a programme of action. Also, gossip is the means by which individuals align their actions: negotiate between themselves the scope and import of cultural rules and the social behaviours to which they apply. Gossip is essentially a meta-communicative process: an activity through which individuals examine and discuss together the rules and conventions by which they commonly live. Moreover, since rules are relative and ambiguous in their application, such interpretation is never final or consensual. Hence, gossip at once disassembles, evaluates and reconstitutes the everyday world.

See also: **Community, Ethnomethodology, Interaction, Narrative**

HOME AND HOMELESSNESS

Anthropologists have long been interested in migratory processes, often of people in search of work (possibly later followed by their families) and often from rural areas to urban ones, and from relatively or seemingly deprived areas to less deprived ones. Indeed, the complexities of the relationship between labour migration and (momentous) social, cultural, economic and political change, and the numbers of people involved or affected by such movement in search of a better 'quality of life', have been a major conceptual concern (cf. Kearney 1986).

Hence, there have been studies of communities of poor rural labourers in overcrowded cities (cf. Parkin 1969; Scheper-Hughes 1992), and the networks of contacts by which people move and move again in search of work, and information moves with them (cf. Mitchell 1969; Gardner 1995). There have also been studies of the traditions of labour migrancy that can flourish as generations of men and women move from their homes (cf. Lloyd 1979; Marx 1987), and the problems that can accrue as returners hope to find their original homes again (cf. Gmelch 1980; Ballard 1987). Migratory processes have been seen to cast significant light on questions of socio-cultural reproduction and development, both concerning those who move and those who stay put (Redfield 1960; Meillassoux 1981), and on the relationship between individual (migrant) actors and global (modernizing) processes (Frank 1965), and to call for an elucidation of the meanings imparted to migratory processes by those who move and those who 'host' them (Lewis 1961; Grillo 1985).

At the same time, inequalities in the distribution of wealth, resources and power have led to migrations which may be described as less than voluntary; hence the anthropological interest in the 'exile' and the 'refugee' alongside the labour migrant. Exile has been explored (*après* van Gennep 1960) as a rite of violent disaggregation from a home community which pitches refugees into a liminal zone (for example, the refugee camp) and which can only be overcome by a corresponding rite of reaggregation into new identities (Conquergood 1988). Exile has also been explored as a categorial anomaly, a 'pollution' (*après* Douglas 1966), which derives from the collision of cultures and their incompatible systems of symbolic classification (Malkki 1995). In particular, anthropological study has focused upon a mediation between the definition of 'refugees' under international law – being those who have fled their country of former habitual residence out of fear of persecution on the grounds of race, religion, nationality, political opinion or membership in a specific social group – and the experiences on the ground of the exiles themselves and those agencies set up to deal with them (cf. Gilad 1990; Harrell-Bond 1986). Finally, as exile experiences extend over the years, anthropologists have explored the cultural adaptations exhibited by long-term refugee communities, and the tensions involved in their self-identification: not 'acculturation' to new identities so much as a practising of a permanent in-betweenness or transnationalism (Hirschon 1989; Gonzalez 1992).

In this way, study of migratory processes also includes an appreciation of diasporas. Originally a term referring to the exile and dispersions of Jews from the land of Israel following persecution in Classical and pre-Classical times (and thence the migration of Jewish communities around the Gentile world for ensuing millennia), the term has since been applied more widely to include those populations separated from an erstwhile home and scattered around the world who nevertheless retain a sense of themselves as present strangers. Armenians (Amit-Talai 1989), Italians (Gans 1965) and Greeks (Moskos 1989), for example – like Jews (Avruch 1981) – seek to maintain an ethnic unity, a cultural continuity, and a sense of peoplehood across the globe. They retain distinctive practices, a myth of their uniqueness, memories of their past home, and a hope of eventual repatriation: ' . . . Next year in Jerusalem'.

Migration and 'home'

It may be argued, however, that the labels 'migrant', 'refugee', 'exile', 'expatriate', betray differences in evaluation and orientation, differences in strategic dealings with the phenomenon of migration, more than differences in the migratory process as such. By 'expatriate', then, is conveyed a sense of wealth and voluntary detachment, by 'migrant' a hope for upward mobility, by 'exile' a sense of loss, and so on (Tedlock 1996: 341). Beyond these labels, however, lies the migratory process whereby people operate as 'transnationals' – ever transgressing so-called socio-cultural borders rather than operating strictly within circumscribed fields.

It was a thesis of Edmund Leach's (1977) that individuals spent their lives crossing socio-cultural boundaries – whatever the norms might have prescribed and law-keepers sought to realize in terms of their closure. Hence, Leach posited, most categorial distinctions (the orderly frameworks behind socio-cultural routinization) evaporated when anthropologists observed what people did as opposed to what they were supposed to do. Recently, this has found more general anthropological favour. The thesis of 'transnationalism' (Schiller *et al.* 1992) signals a move away from the notion of bounded socio-cultural units of analysis in favour of an appreciation of individuals who move cognitively and physically through their lives: who throughout their lives move shorter and greater distances across the globe, and who imagine communities of belonging (and invent their traditions) on their way (cf. Anderson 1983; Hobsbawm and Ranger 1983). It is as a result of this shift in anthropological sensibility that an analytical focus on home and home-lessness becomes timely.

'Home' did not much figure in traditional anthropological concep-tualizations, except perhaps as a synonym for 'house' or 'household' (cf. Carsten and Hugh-Jones 1995). Here was 'home' as stable physical space, and a place which amounted to an 'embryonic community' (Douglas 1991: 289), in which territory and time were structured functionally, economically, aesthetically and morally; so that even if the potential mobility of home was attested to – the tent of the nomad, say – still the focus was on the necessary routinizing of time and space. As Douglas elaborated, home could be defined as a pattern of regular doings, furnishings and appurtenances, and a physical space in which certain communitarian practices were realized. Homes began by bringing space under control and thus giving domestic life physical orientations: 'directions of existence' (Douglas 1991: 290). Homes also gave structure to time and embodied a capacity for memory and anticipation. In short, homes could be understood as the organization of space over time, and the allocation of resources in space and over time.

Then again, the routinization of space–time was also aesthetic and moral; it provided a model for redistributive justice, sacrifice, and the common, collective good. Homes were communities in microcosm which coordinated their members by way of open and constant commu-nication, a division of labour, rights and duties, a commensal meal, and a rotation of access to resources. They encompassed total-prestatory systems which exerted possibly tyrannous control over their members' minds, bodies and tongues in their search for solidarity.

However, to understand homes in this way – as being synonymous, in microcosm, with Durkheimian notions of solidary communities and coercive institutions – is anachronistic and provides little conceptual purchase on a world of contemporary movement. A broader under-standing is possible and necessary, and one concerned less with the routinization of space and time than with their fluidity and with individuals' continuous movement through them (cf. Minh-ha 1994: 14). A conception of home is required which transcends traditional ways by which identity is analytically classified and defined (according to locality, ethnicity, religiosity or nationality) and is sensitive to allocatings of identity which may be multiple, situational, individual and paradoxical. As a concept, 'home' must encompass cultural norms and individual fantasies, representations of and by individuals and groups; it must be sensitive to numerous modalities: memory and longing; the conventional and the creative; the ideational, the affective and the physical; the spatial and the temporal; the local and the global; both positive evaluations and negative (cf. Wright 1991: 214). As Simmel sums up, 'home' may be said to provide a 'unique synthesis': 'an aspect of life and at the same time a special way of forming, reflecting and interrelating the totality of life' (1984: 93–4). A working definition for charting the morass of ambiguities and fluidities of contemporary identity may be of 'home' as 'where one best knows oneself' (Rapport and Dawson 1998) – where 'best' means 'most', even if not always 'happiest'.

Such an understanding of home is also apposite for coming to terms with the movement inherent in social life, for charting the intrinsic migrancy of identity. Increasingly, individuals are seen as moving between homes, erstwhile to current, or as moving between multiple present homes. More precisely, the thesis of transnationalism implies a radical change in the conceptualization of relations between movement and home: not only can one be at home in movement, but that movement can be one's very home.

This is certainly the explicit thesis of John Berger. For Berger, the realization of a world of movement gives onto radically different ideas of home – and also of homelessness. A far more mobile notion comes to the fore, ideational and behavioural: home as something to accompany people whenever they decamp. For a world of travellers – labour migrants, exiles and refugees – home comes to be located in a routine set of practices, in a repetition of habitual social interactions, in styles of dress and address, in memories and myths, in stories carried around in one's head, in the ritual of a regularly used personal name. People are more at home nowadays, in short, in 'words, jokes, opinions, gestures, actions, even the way one wears a hat' (Berger 1984: 64).

It might seem, as Heidegger pronounced, that 'homelessness is coming to be the destiny of the world', but it is rather that there is a recognition that we possess another sense of being-in-the-world (cf. Chambers 1994b: 246). (It is not that there cannot be a sense of homelessness – far from it – but that a sense of home or of homelessness is not necessarily related in any simple or direct way with fixity or movement.) One dwells in a mobile habitat and not in a singular or fixed physical structure. Moreover, as home becomes seen as more mobile so it also becomes more individuated and privatized; everyone chooses their own, and one's choice might remain invisible (and irrelevant) to others (cf. Rapport 1995). As Berger concludes, 'no longer a dwelling', home can be conceived of as 'the untold story of a life being lived' (1984: 64). A sense of homelessness perhaps derives, paradoxically, from a reaction against movement, a refusing of fluid boundaries; hence the clamouring by the homeless for renascent 'particularisms': primordial places for which they are willing to kill and die (Auge 1995: 35).

To traverse the globe with their informants, then, is for anthropologists to record the 'moving' homes of various kinds, behavioural and ideational, which individuals construct and enact. Here are routine practices and narrations which do not merely tell of home but represent it: serve, perhaps, as cognitive homes in themselves. As Gaston Bachelard puts it, the human imagination always builds 'walls' of impalpable shadows, comforting itself with the illusion of protection, and so carries 'the notion of home' into any 'really inhabited space', whether cognitive or physical. Thus it is that 'we ever bring our lares with us' (Bachelard 1994: 5; also cf. Rykwert 1991: 54).

Homelessness?

And yet, for Berger, there is still that sense in which many people are at home in 'untold stories'. This is by no means the same as being 'homeless' – as being without a moving account of one's passage across boundaries and through life – but it is a recognition that, as individual, mobile and private, the homes of many remain invisible. Many people in movement across the globe today do not have the resources (temporal, financial) to exhibit their homes and make them formally or widely known; and even if they did their homes would remain invisible inasmuch as they would clamour for attention alongside millions of others'; while those in a position to publicize these multiple versions of home attempt deliberately to suppress them, or at least ensure that it is only their own versions which are exhibited, held up as models and recorded for posterity (cf. Berger 1975).

Superficially, this conclusion comes close to that drawn by Peter Berger and his collaborators in the premonitory text *The Homeless Mind* (1973). They agreed with a portrayal of modern social life as a plurality of social life-worlds between which individuals were in inexorable migration. Every day, they argued, individuals transgressed between a variety of divergent, discrepant, even contradictory, social milieux; so there was no consistency concerning what was experienced as 'right' or 'true' between different contexts and life-stages. However, rather than appreciating that individuals may be in possession of their own cognitive homes and itineraries which gave their transgressions a sense of consistency and direction, Berger *et al.* defined this migratory process as a 'spreading condition of homelessness' (1973: 138).

Their ideas derive from a sense of loss: that in the modern world there has been lost a traditional home of fixity and physical centredness, of absolute values and a unified reality. Now uprooted from this first and 'original' socio-cultural milieu, no succeeding one becomes truly home. Individuals are in transit between a plurality of life-worlds but come to be at home in none. Berger *et al.* describe this condition as at once normative, spiritual and cognitive: the anomy of social movement correlates with a metaphysical sense of homelessness in the cosmos which correlates with personal alienation on the level of consciousness.

Moreover, the 'homeless mind' is hard to bear, and hence there is widespread nostalgia for a condition of being 'at home' in society, with oneself, and with the universe: for homes of the past which were socially homogeneous, communal, peaceful, safe and secure. 'De-modernization' movements of various kinds (socialism, localisms, religious cults and fundamentalisms) therefore promise new homes where individual members are reintegrated within all-embracing, meaningful structures of social, psychical and metaphysical solidarity. There are also growing attempts by those with the wherewithal to reconstruct homes in private, closed havens which shut out the present and serve as subjective refuges of the self. Nevertheless, Berger *et al.* conclude, before the cold winds of homelessness, nostalgia proves to be fragile defence; de-modernization schemes which are not institutionalized and society-wide are mostly precarious buffers, given the finitude and mortality of the human condition. Thus, in a modern world in which 'everything is in constant motion' and where 'the life of more and more individuals [is] migratory, ever-changing, mobile', homelessness represents a deepening global effect (1973: 184).

The Homeless Mind remains a challenging thesis, but it is steeped in a communitarian ideology which would decry modern 'ills' (individualism and pluralization, alienation and anomy) so as to posit an idyllic past of unified tradition, certainty, stasis, and cognitive and behavioural commonality, But this latter is highly questionable; the existence of an 'original life-world' of traditional absoluteness and fixity (where the individual may said to be first and 'truly' at home) is without empirical foundation (Phillips 1993: 149–56; also cf. Geertz 1995: 15–16).

Furthermore, not only does the thesis of cognitive homelessness involve a mythic past, it also remains ethnographically ungrounded in the present. Even as individuals lead their lives in and through movement (cognitive and physical) and refrain from finally and essentially affixing their identities to places, the empirical evidence points to the resilience of people's achieving of 'homes' (however these may come to be defined) and the inexorability of their home-making. *Contra* Berger *et al.*, there is no necessary relation between fixity and physical centredness and the accruing of absolute values and a unified reality. Individuals are quite able to maintain the latter in continuous movement. Being 'at home' and being 'homeless', in short, are not as such matters of movement, of physical space, or of the fluidity of socio-cultural times and places. One is at home when one inhabits a cognitive environment in which one can undertake the routines of daily life and through which one finds one's identity best mediated – and homeless when such a cognitive environment is eschewed (cf. Silverstone *et al.* 1994: 19).

Paradoxes of home-making

Certain paradoxes surround the concept of home, however, which are not easily ignored.

First, there is the paradox, already alluded to, that an increase in move-ment around the world, and the freeing-up of restrictive boundaries to travel, is accompanied by an increase in renascent particularisms. In Hobsbawm's terms (1991), home as an essentially private and individual routine, fantasy, memory, longing or presence – *Heim* – is impacted upon by *Heimat*: an attempt publicly and collectively to impose home as a social fact and a cultural norm to which some must belong and from which others must be excluded. Hence the 'exiles' and 'refugees'; and hence, too, the tramps and 'bag-people' expelled from the ranks of those felt deserving of combining house and home.

There is also the paradox that it is by way of transience and displacement that one achieves an ultimate sense of belonging. As Kateb puts it (1991: 135), to be at home 'in one's own place' it is necessary to become alienated and estranged to some degree, mentally or spiritually. Exile is a resource inasmuch as it gives onto that vantage-point from which one is best able to come to know oneself, to know oneself best. It is for this reason too that home 'moves' us most powerfully as absence or negation (Hobsbawm 1991: 63).

Finally, there is the paradox concerning whether the movement to which home is party is linear or circular. Chambers (1994a) (*à la* Heraclitus) is definite that the migratory processes of the world are linear, since no returns are possible or implied. The journey of our lives is not between fixed positions and there is no itinerary affording routes back again. And yet, while it may be true that 'the destiny of our journeys' is not circular, still home represents both 'the place from which we set out and to which we return, at least in spirit' (Hobsbawm 1991: 65). We engage in ongoing transgression partly out of a desire to overcome it, and find our end in our beginning.

Perhaps it is part-and-parcel of an appreciation of the way that individuals live in movement, transition and transgression, that its conceptualization, as 'home', should be similarly paradoxical and trans-gressive.

See also: **Irony, Movement**

HUMAN RIGHTS

In the past fifty years, human rights has become 'one of the most globalised political values of our times' (Wilson 1997: 1). And yet, most anthropological literature has isolated itself from mainstream discussion of these values; it has tended to regard the legalistic language and the nation-state frameworks of much discussion as falling outside its professional scope (cf. Messer 1993), and questions of better or worse socio-cultural practice as value-judgements which go against its pro-fessional ethos (cf. Wolfram 1988). While 'human rights', as discourse and as international law, has enjoyed enormous growth, anthropology has therefore remained aloof, if not sceptical.

Even when they find themselves, perforce, within the human rights arena, anthropologists have been loath to pass judgement on what might be meant by such notions as the right to 'life', to 'adequate food, shelter, health care and education', to 'privacy and the ownership of property', to 'freedom from slavery and genocide', to 'freedom of movement', to 'freedom of speech, religion and assembly'. Even a practice such as 'female circumcision' (clitoridectomy and infibulation), anthropologists have insisted, must needs be regarded by those affected as a 'problem' before cultural outsiders may intervene and provide information for change. Little wonder that, as Richard Wilson puts it, anthropology is often viewed by human-rights theorists and activists as 'the last bastion of cultural absolutism' (1997: 3); as if somehow believing that cultures contain an inherent moral rectitude, whereby one might always expect 'underlying cultural values' ultimately to assuage immoral political systems (American Anthropological Association 1947: 543).

This stance can be seen as anachronistic if not irresponsible and reactionary. In a 'post-cultural' world (Wilson again), a world where '[t]he 'fantasy' that humanity is divided into [discrete groups] with clear frontiers of language and culture seems finally to be giving way to notions of disorder and openness', anthropologists remain committed to a romantic communitarianism and relativism (Wilson 1997: 10). They continue to believe that, as canonized by the 1947 statement of the American Anthropological Association executive board (penned chiefly by Melville Herskovits), it is upon 'a respect for cultural differences' that respect for all other social and individual differences should be based (1947: 541).

The logics of human rights

A number of ideal-types of 'competing normative logics' (Falk 1980) concerning human rights may be identified. For much of the past two centuries in the West, the prevailing logic has been what might be termed 'statist'. That is, nation-states have demanded the right to their own sovereignty and their own juridical and political equality; as such, the rights of their citizens are internal or domestic matters, and it is outwith the prerogative of members of other states to intervene. Statist logic was a development out of 'hegemonic' logic. This is the reasoning that 'virtue' is a manifestation of power, 'might is right', and it is the right of the more powerful to interfere in the affairs of the less powerful so as to maintain their interests and their (more virtuous) version of right. In its turn, however, statist logic has had to vie for its privileged position, in political debate of recent decades, with a number of other logics. There is a 'supra-national' logic, which lodges judgement of rights with institutions such as the United Nations, NATO, or the European Union; it is they now which claim the power to determine the rightness of states. There is also a 'transnational' logic pertaining to non-state, non-governmental organizations such as Amnesty International, Human Rights Watch, or the Worldwide Fund for Nature, which yet claim the right to monitor behaviour on a global scale whoever the protagonist. Then again, there is a 'populist' logic which rejects the necessary authority of states – if not all such self-perpetuating institutions – and seeks to derive rights instead directly from 'the people'; this might span a range of manifestations, from Bertrand Russell's pacifist War Crimes Tribunal to fundamentalist and terroristic organizations such as The Red Brigades or *Hizbollah*. Finally, there is what Falk refers to as a 'naturalistic' logic of rights, claiming that they inhere in human nature and therefore should be recognized universally and take precedence over all other (institutional) claims.

While the longevity of the above logics may be placed in a historical framework, it is important to recognize that all continue to contest for space and allegiance on a world-political stage today. And while the criteria for distinguishing between their appeals are many, perhaps the crucial one for present purposes concerns the units in which they see rights as inhering and to which harm can be done: from groups and collectivities on the one hand to persons and individuals on the other. As an ideal-type, statist logic sets out to protect collectivities from infringements against their rights while naturalistic logic is focused on individuals. This distinction then correlates with a further important one, that between relativism (statist) and universalism (naturalistic).

Human rights and anthropological relativism

Inasmuch as anthropology has seen its pedagogic mission as the further-ance of respect for 'other cultures' – has argued for the rights to cultural difference, and posited cultural differences as the grounds for all others – it can be seen to have adopted a collectivist and relativistic logic.

The thinking behind anthropological relativism is well rehearsed (cf. Crawford 1988; Downing and Kushner 1988). It is said that ethnog-raphy evinces no universal notion of humanity, and no commonality among those notions that do exist concerning the distribution of rights, duties and dignity. It is further said that there is no universal 'individual' – that unified human subject with a knowable essence whom a naturalistic logic posits as the bearer of rights – only socially constructed persons. Those notions of 'human nature' and of 'rights' which derive from the fact of being human are historically and culturally bounded, it is argued; there can be no essential characteristics of human nature or rights which exist outside a specific discursive context. In particular, the United Nations' Universal Declaration of Human Rights of 1948 was a charter of European, post-Enlightenment, liberal–humanist and idealist, political philosophy which came to be formulated in the wake of the Second World War and the Holocaust. It can be seen as a continuation of Kantian attempts to establish an Archimedean point that provides rational foundations for universal norms of justice; and it must be understood as part-and-parcel of the rise of capitalism – a means for individual profiteering enterprises to proceed unencumbered by communitarian obligations, traditional custom or a localized morality. In its application – in Western interference in moral issues internal to other cultures – the Universal Declaration has been responsible for a particular normative blindness towards indigenous peoples and their collectivist narratives of land ownership, political determination, selfhood and so on. Meanwhile, Western governments, such as that of the USA, feel free to pull out of UN bodies, such as UNESCO, when they feel too much emphasis is being placed on collective rights of peoples; a strengthening of group interests at the expense of the human rights of individuals is decried as the so-called 'socialist bias' of non-democratic societies.

But then what are the so-called human rights and freedoms of individuals as distinct from rights which people practise in the context of cultural, national and spiritual communities? To enjoy individual human rights requires community rights; individual rights cannot be exercised in isolation from the community – individual rights to join a trade union or to enjoy their culture, for instance, necessitate rights of groups to preserve their trade unions or their culture. Even in a laissez-faire Western democracy, individual rights are not absolute or immutable: they are balanced by the rights of others and by the interests of society, so that freedom of expression, of association and assembly, for example, are subject to the maintenance of national security, public order, and health and morals. In short, removed from his communities, 'man loses his essential humanity' (Moskovitz 1968: 169–70).

Hence, the truly anthropological proposition that cultural rights have been implicit in any other rights from the start. Furthermore, if there is today a demand or a desire for anthropology to exercise ethical judgements, then this need not be paralysed by an appreciation of cultural relativism. The latter simply demands that such judgements always be made in cultural contexts and take account of the local *habitus*. Rights cannot be seen as anything but particular cultural forms, and notions of human rights as somehow existing outside or beyond distinct cultural realms is logically and empirically impossible.

Nonetheless, most if not all societies have propositions concerning some rights or others, however differently they might be perceived and formalized, and the claims operationalized. Hence, one can say with anthropological accuracy that human rights propositions invoke claims to specific goods and privileges by specific groups in specific places and times. Moral judgements, similarly, pertain to particular socio-cultural contexts; European genocide is not equivalent to tribal head-hunting or infanticide, cannibalism or feuding, because questions of violence must relate to cultural logic, technology and scale.

More generally, anthropologists can support a devolution of power to less powerful yet culturally distinct groups, and advocate their being given fair treatment before the law, towards the aim of maintaining if not increasing cultural diversity. Anthropologists can support the rights of groups to reproduce their own culture, and argue that this be seen to be as fundamental as the right to genetic transmission. One might describe a right of Third World peoples currently to express themselves in nationalistic terms, for instance; in their so-called 'third generation rights' (cf. Prott 1988) are expressed collective assertions of the right to self-determination, to protection from genocide, to permanent sovereignty over natural resources, to socio-economic development and to peace and security which grow out of the senses of group solidarity of various Third World populations.

A variety of cultural logics might give onto a variety of notions of 'human rights', in short, but anthropologists can still support and defend the universal rights of cultures to those logics as such. Cultural relativism is after all based on the universalism that cultures are the foundational human right.

An alternative anthropology of rights

Equally well rehearsed are the arguments against relativistic thinking in anthropology. It has morally nihilistic, politically conservative and quietist consequences. It is also imbued with a relativistic meta-narrative concerning cultural difference which is logically inconsistent; for, cultural relativism must also include the relativity of the concept of 'cultures' *per se* (cf. Gellner 1993).

It further implies a modelling of society and of culture which many would now see as outmoded. That is, society and culture are depicted as *sui generis*: as reified and as ontologically secure. They are modelled as entities not processes: hermetically discrete and internally integrated; the basis of all similarities and differences between people, the ground of their being, the bank of their knowledge. This illusion of holism might have been legitimate currency in nineteenth-century nationalism and in Durkheimian sociology (cf. Barth 1992), but it is of little account in contemporary existential contexts. Mechanistic, social-structural notions of society and culture as organically functioning wholes must now give way to notions of human groupings as purposive and contingent political entities (ethnicities, religiosities, localisms, occupational lobbies) which live on as sets of symbols and interpreted meanings in the minds of their members. As Wilson sums up, 'bounded conceptions of linguistic and cultural systems' are out of place in a context where 'culture' may be characterized as 'contested, fragmented, contextualised and emergent' (1997: 9).

In this situation, 'culture' cannot be raised as a right-bearing entity over and against human individuals. Individuals may have rights to cultural attachment and belonging, rights to membership of one or more cultures (of their choosing), but cultures do not have rights over individuals or members. Hence, on this view, 'female circumcision' is a violation of: (a) the right to freedom from physical and psychological abuse, (b) the right to corporal and sexual integrity, and (c) the right to health and education (Boulware-Miller 1985: 155–77). More generally, the noble anthropological goal of seeking to understand others in their own terms cannot be employed as an excuse to avoid making moral and ethical judgements. Individuals have the right to resist and opt out of the norms and expectations of particular social and cultural groupings and chart their own course.

For instance, an individual's rights freely to choose a marriage partner take precedence over a group's rights to maintain cultural patterns of marital preferences – even if it is argued that these norms are basic to a definition of the group's identity. As the testaments of refugees and asylum-seekers attest, many women have recourse only to suicide in order to avoid being forced into an unwanted marriage, and it is the responsibility of the anthropologist to support those disenfranchised individuals who find themselves under the power of others (cf. Gilad 1996). However that power is locally framed and legitimated (as that of elder kinsmen, religious experts, or whatever), here are relations of domination which anthropology should oppose. Moreover, even though such conceptions of individuals taking precedence over groups, of individual freedom *contra* cultural hegemony, derive from Western liberalism, the United Nations International Bill of Rights which these conceptions have given onto (comprising the Universal Declaration of Human Rights (1948), the International Covenant on Civil and Political Rights (1966), and the International Covenant on Economic, Social and Cultural Rights (1966)) is the only framework we have by which to make decisions on globally appropriate action.

Finally, if the discourse and law of human rights are manifestations of liberalism as a modern political philosophy, then its opposition is no less political or ideological. To decry the seeming atomism of individually conceived human rights – as opposed, say, to notions of collective attachment, common good, public interest, patriotism, group loyalty, respect for tradition, and so on – is to extol the virtues of communitarianism: to wish to replace a politics of individual rights with a politics of common good, and an emphasis on collective life and the supreme value of the community. This has long had its (equally Western) social-philosophical exponents, from Toennies and Durkheim ('[T]o experience the pleasure of saying "we", it is important not to enjoy saying "I" too much' (1973: 240)), to MacIntyre, Taylor and Sandel today. However, as an ideology it can also be critiqued (cf. Phillips 1993). As with the aforementioned illusory notions of society and culture as *sui generis*, communitarianism can be said to represent a backward-looking myth of a situation of cognitive and behavioural commonality that never existed. In practice, communitarianism is often hierarchical, and always exclusionary with regard to those who do not belong – women and slaves, savages, pagans, Jews, Communists, homosexuals. In sociological usage, moreover, the ideology represents an attempt to 'colonize' the consciousness of individual members so that the latter are pressed into the matrices of perception of socio-cultural groupings and identify with them completely (cf. Cohen 1994). Hence, individuals come to be analytically treated as incidental to their social relationships and cultural institutions. This, as Cohen sums up, amounts to both flawed social science and complicity in processes of ideological hegemony:

> We must make deliberate efforts to acknowledge the subtleties, inflections and varieties of individual consciousness which are concealed by the categorical masks which we have invented so adeptly. Otherwise, we will continue to deny people the right to be themselves, deny their rights to their own identities.
>
> (1994: 180)

We must, as analysts, preserve individuals' rights to their own awareness and thus contribute to the decolonization of the human subject.

To say that it is impossible to consider individuals as bearers of rights independently of group memberships and identities, then, is to risk blinding oneself to those iniquitous failures of social arrangement from which liberalism has served as an escape, and to rob human beings of their best protections against abuses of power. On the other hand, to insist, as liberalism does, that the individual is the benchmark of justice, to believe the morally independent individual to be the ultimate source of value, is to direct the focus of attention to interpersonal ties not bounded groups: to 'personal communities', chosen by individuals, not ascribed ones. If community is important in people's lives, this must be seen to be a voluntary community – of friends, neighbours, family, co-workers, co-ethnics, co-religionists – from which individuals are free to come and go. '[I]t is attachment rather than membership that is a general human value' (Phillips 1993: 194); hence what is preferable is an anthropological philosophy which protects the rights of attachment and detachment *per se* rather than particular (types of) attachments.

This is 'post-cultural' inasmuch as it posits individuals as ontologically prior to the cultural milieux which they create and in which they dwell. A post-cultural wisdom recognizes the universal fact of individuality whatever the hegemonic community ideology concerning 'person-hood'. Individual actors are 'the anthropological concrete' (Auge 1995: 111) and they must remain free voluntarily to adopt or reject any number of cultural personae.

In short, it is important today for anthropologists to appreciate the right of the individual citizen to his or her own civil freedoms *against* cultural prejudices, *against* social statuses, and *against* the language embodied in their self-expressions. Hence, human rights have a universal relevance and resonance, and their advocation is a universal responsibility. In an interdependent, 'post-cultural' world, human rights represents a discourse offering shared standards of human dignity, with possible procedural implications for forms of global governance.

A comparative anthropology of human rights

If globalization finally bankrupts relativistic arguments, then this is not to say that the global situation becomes one of either standardization or Westernization. Rather, the situation is of global forms being animated, brought to social life and made culturally meaningful, by an endemic process of local and individual interpretation. Thus, out of global relatedness, new diversities are always being constructed.

Indeed, this is perhaps nowhere more visible than in the case of 'human rights'. In human rights discourse and law, a global form can clearly be seen to be given a diversity of local formulations. Two major transformatory processes are found to be at play: the vernacularization of a set of international legal institutions, and the globalization of local cases of dispute. In 'a confusion of legal tongues' (Geertz 1983: 220), local, national and transnational codes now overlap and intermix, such that there is no 'traditional culture' which is not an ongoing construction by people who find themselves in a pluralistic socio-cultural context.

It is precisely this tension between the local and the supra-local which a 'comparative anthropology of human rights' study sets out to study: 'how a transnational discourse and set of legal institutions are materialised, appropriated, resisted and transformed in a variety of contexts' (Wilson 1997: 23). Notions of human rights come to be seen as the results of concrete social struggles, embedded in local normative orders, while yet caught in translocal webs of power. Anthropologically to represent human rights violations, then, is not necessarily to ape the universalistic objectivity of legalistic declarations, nor yet to give in to absolute perspectivism where any representation is as good as any other. Rather, anthropology can judge the appropriateness of particular renditions of concrete examples of violation according to the context of their expression and intended reception. Thus a comparative anthropology of rights can contextualize without relativizing (cf. Clay 1988).

More specifically, according to Wilson (1997), an anthropology of human rights should provide thick descriptions of existential situations: should evidence how experiences of brute existence in particular contexts come to be translated into human rights narratives. Thus, anthropology can restore the richness of subjectivities immersed in complex fields of social relations which legalistic accounts of human rights often omit. Situating human rights within socio-cultural milieux, anthropologists can show rights to be grounded, value-laden features of social life and bound to purposive agents. Here are human rights not merely as instrumental mechanisms but as expressive too: constructing local identities, classifying and legitimating claims to self-determination and sovereignty, embodying relations of force and struggles for power between competing interest groups.

In short, anthropologists can chart how human rights are founded, possessed and transformed as complex strategic situations unfold. Hence, while the spread of human rights discourse might seem tantamount to the imperialistic interjection of a Western legal regime, a vibrant diversity and creativity undergirds this seeming globalization such that indigenous rights movements can be found appropriating the discourse as a suitable form for the expression of a vibrant local identity. In this way, the spread of 'human rights', albeit originally a liberal discourse, need not produce a historical process (or progress) which Western liberal theorists would immediately recognize. Nevertheless, human rights can be seen to afford a symbolic form of common denomination whereby many different individuals and groups can dialoguize.

Maybe the contextual multiplicity and openness concerning the operationalizing of human rights discourse holds lessons too for the reporting of human rights violations. At present, the genre of such reporting fails to capture the multiplicity of local narratives and subjective constructions of events. In order to produce globally consumable bits (and bytes) of information with an aura of neutrality, authority and legitimacy, decontextualized accounts impose meaning and coherence on what is chaotic and indeterminate; meanwhile, formulaic applications of international rights law can do as much harm as good to local conditions of sustainable fair government. Admittedly, a legalistic language and universal templates are an advantage for the persuading and pressurizing of nation-states. Nonetheless, if the power of human rights agencies is a discursive one, turning on the symbolic capital of certain types of information and denunciation, and if the wider audience for human rights reporting is a variegated one, then the genres of reportage should be carefully selected and likewise various. In this diversity of genres, in fine, existential anthropological accounts may have a large part to play.

Human rights in a post-cultural world

At the outset of *Anthropology as Cultural Critique* (1986: vii), Marcus and Fischer posed the provocative question: 'how is an emergent post-modern world to be represented as an object for social thought?'. Liberal–humanist notions of general humanity now take political precedence over a highlighting of autochthonous difference, while 'Orientalist' critique now challenges the perpetration of any form of 'othering'. Global penetrations of systems of communication and technology mean that the once distant 'exotic' informant and lay reader of anthropological texts become coevals, while the extensive movements of populations (labour migrants, refugees and tourists) make the cognitive landscapes of an increasing number of people a global one. To talk of 'culture' and 'intrinsic cultural difference' in this setting rather than of some form of 'global ecumene' could be seen, Marcus and Fischer concluded, as a romantic revelling in inessential minutiae or as an obfuscatory denial of the nature of contemporary social reality (1986: 39). It is not that the global ecumene is a homogeneous social space, rather that difference is more than ever an internal relation: of wealth, localism, ethnicity, religiosity, sex and gender within the single social arena or polity. The question for anthropology in this post-cultural environment is both how to write the meeting of internal differences and how to right it.

Perhaps an anthropology of human rights offers a way forward. For, in highlighting the discourse and the laws surrounding human rights as 'transnational juridical processes' (Wilson 1997: 9), anthropology can point the way towards an appreciation of such rights as perhaps 'the world's first universal ideology' (Weissbrodt 1988: 1). That is, human rights, as discourse and law, can be seen as a concrete form of political procedure on which a global liberal polity and justice is to be founded (cf. Rorty 1986). Here is a symbolic form in which the tensions between the global and local may be played out, in which differences between identities are not elided, without thereby losing sight of the ideal of reaching consensus concerning the freedom of individual practice and belief. Anthropology can show how 'human rights' is being adopted as a resource in manifold local situations: a means by which identities both come together and remain distinct.

While there is a flexibility in its interpretation, limits are still imposed beyond which 'violations of human rights' are identifiable. As a political procedure, 'human rights' might say little substantively about the fundamentals of belief which the discourse expresses, but it does not say nothing. As Wilson spells it out (1997: 8–9), it does not countenance the maintenance of 'inegalitarian and repressive political systems', it does not entertain 'international acquiescence in state repression', and it does not place culture on the level of supreme ethical value. To the contrary, in a 'post-cultural world', as we have seen, the focus is firmly upon culture as optional resource, as a trope of belonging, employed by individual actors on a global stage. In this situation, anthropological accounts, rich in subjectivities and social relations, can show how people the world over engage with human rights discourses and law for the effecting and expression of a diversity of identities. By writing existentialist narratives concerning human rights violations, anthropologists can complement other genres of reporting, thus 'restor[ing] local subjectivities, values and memories as well as analysing the wider global social processes in which violence is embedded' (Wilson 1997: 157). In an anthropological dissemination of narratives of human rights, we can play our part in effecting a global society of individuals free to believe in and practise a diversity of identities which they ongoingly create.

See also: **Individualism, Individuality, Literariness, Movement**

HUMANISM

'Humanism' is a nineteenth-century term for the values, practices and ideals which are associated with the European Renaissance of the fourteenth to sixteenth centuries, and its rediscovery of the texts of Classical Greece and Rome. The Renaissance appreciation of the latter, the so-called '*studia humanitatis*', as represented by the work of such diverse figures as Dante, Petrarch, da Vinci and Galileo, Erasmus, Montaigne, Bacon, Shakespeare and Milton, Cervantes and Copernicus, brought about a break with predominant medieval (Christian) perspectives on the nature of life. New emphases arose, a new image of humankind and its capacities. In particular, there was new faith in the power of learning and a desire freely to enlarge its bounds; a scepticism concerning the absoluteness of existing knowledge; a belief in the potentialities for creativity, growth, pleasure and action of the individual human being; and an interest in ascertaining the place of humankind in nature, of discovering the laws of nature, so that life on earth might be placed more within human control.

In succeeding centuries, the humanism of the Renaissance gave on to the Enlightenment and the rise of science, with its belief in rationality, as opposed to (religious) revelation, as an adequate source of human knowledge; also on to liberalism, and a belief in the inherent dignity of individuals and their right to freedom and self-determination; and also on to social science, and its belief in the possibility and necessity of applying knowledge about human affairs and individual relations to an improvement of the socio-cultural conditions of human life.

Anthropology and humanism

On this view, anthropology is a humanistic pursuit, with a heritage of rationality, liberalism and advocacy which many would see as legitimately continuing today (cf. Gellner 1993; also Berger 1963). For others, however, the case is more complex, and the relationship between anthropology and humanism is one which might be subjected to a more or less radical critique. Certainly, the humanistic tag is one that can be associated more with some names in anthropology (Paul Radin, Edward Sapir, Ruth Benedict, Robert Redfield, Raymond Firth, Edmund Leach, Victor Turner, Anthony Wallace, James Fernandez, Miles Richardson, Paul Friedrich, David Riches, Michael Jackson) than others, while some have positively decried it, linking it, historico-culturally to Western acts of imperialism (over nature and otherness).

When Eric Wolf (1974) writes that anthropology, as a discipline, is to be understood as: 'the most scientific of the humanities and the most humanistic of the sciences', it is clearly a more particular connotation of 'humanism' that he is dealing with. In fact, it is difficult to say what precisely the word 'humanism' denotes, and what conjoins its various expositions (the work of Erasmus and that of Milton, say, or that of Sapir and of Leach); even what it and they oppose ('supernaturalism', 'theology', 'fundamentalism', 'totalitarianism') has no singular essence. As Leach advised in another context (concerning the definition of the term 'marriage') it is best to treat humanism as a bundle of traits, a 'polythetic category' of concerns (Needham 1975), which are linked together by overlapping commonalities but have no one thing in common. Humanistic anthropology, then (cf. Fratto 1976; Wilk 1991; Brady and Turner 1994), would be expected to exhibit a range of characteristics (as follows), but not to show agreement, among its various exponents, concerning which characteristics properly belong nor how those that do ought to be prioritized.

Traits of humanism

1 Human beings are to be regarded as centres and subjects of experience; human beings have experiences, and treating these is a central concern.

2   Human experiences are important because of what they give onto
    – knowledge – and what they intrinsically demonstrate: a capacity
    for knowledge, beauty, pleasure, love, reason, emotion and self-
    awareness. Through their experiences, human subjects are sources
    of knowledge, and of knowledge about knowing.

3   There is, however, something mysterious in this knowledge and
    self-knowledge; human consciousness, the awareness of having
    experiences and of acting upon these, is a capacity and quality
    which makes human beings and their products (historical events,
    economic systems and literary works) unamenable, for the time
    being, to the kind of reductive, generalizing and objectifying
    analysis of certain brands of scientific materialism. The workings
    of human cognition and perception are at least qualitatively, if not
    ontologically, different from the material determinations which
    give rise to cause and effect in the physical world.

4   This gives human life and action a value above all else: an impor-
    tance and a dignity. It also makes human accomplishment, power,
    status and welfare a cause for celebration, while the finality of death
    is cause for the greatest sadness. For it would seem the end of
    consciousness beyond which there is nothing.

5   Together with a belief in the human capacity to know, and an
    expectation that knowledge can be reasonably applied to the
    solving of problems, there is a scepticism felt for knowledge
    which claims authority on the basis of tradition alone, as dogma
    or institutional truth. For knowledge to be authoritative it must be
    subjected to proof in the light of current experience. Moreover, as
    experiences change, so knowledge can be expected to too. Human
    consciousness is dynamic and there is an inexorable evolution,
    becoming and change to the world which human beings inhabit.

6   This is not to say that humanity cannot or will not accede to
    knowledge of certain eternal verities, rather that what is known
    to be true must always be treated sceptically and subjected to testing
    and critique. Continuous scholarship is the route to knowledge,
    as opposed to all manner of blind belief, doctrine or revelation. For
    human beings are responsible for discerning and defining the
    meaning of their lives on earth, through the critical exercise of their
    innate capacities to know, and so far as has been proven to date they
    are alone in this exercise; there is no superhuman guiding presence,
    and human capacities end at their bodily death.

7   This places great emphasis on the human body, its potentiality, its
    fragility, its individuality and its mortality. What human beings
    know, they know as mortal individuals, secured in discrete, if

permeable, sensory mechanisms (bodies and minds) which give rise to unique sensoria, unique awareness of the world around them. Individual bodies and minds are at once part of this world and the vehicles for distinct perspectives upon it (the mystery, again, of self-knowledge).

8   Faith in the human condition, optimism concerning human potential and a celebration of human achievement, is thus tempered with a recognition of the absurdity of the human position. So far as is currently known, humans are alone as a consciousness in a universe which has its laws but is otherwise meaningless and entropic beyond the range of the products with which human beings occupy themselves. In human terms the universe appears cruel, but this is simply a matter of perspective, and outwith human perspective nothing is certain. Moreover, what is human perspective but individual perspective? Nothing is known for certain outwith the bodily sensorium of human beings as individual entities.

9   Are not 'heroic' individuals who live with certain knowledge of the absurdity of life and of the inevitability of death, and yet work towards creating for themselves and others full and meaningful lives, deserving of respect? These lives of knowledge and accomplishment are examples for all; as potential sources of new knowledge and of beauty, indeed, they may offer tangible and direct help to others.

10 Hence the importance of individual liberty, freedom of thought and expression, by which individuals can be expected to make the best of their potential to know and create, and the importance of overcoming those circumstances by which individual creativity is threatened. In other words, the bodily individuality of human experience and knowledge gives onto a certain morality: a set of ethical values concerning the rights to free thinking and investigation, to freedom from constriction or oppression, and concerning the benefits to all which accrue therefrom.

11 Respect for human dignity and individual freedom and creativity also extends to the ways in which humankind is to be represented. Inasmuch as human beings gain self-knowledge, can gain vantage on their lives and reflect on what they know and do, they are able to express this self-knowledge in language and artefact and hope to communicate it to others; human beings continually compose narratives of their own lived-in worlds. Moreover, human beings also compose narratives of others' worlds, and, recognizing that much (if not most) true knowledge of others remains inexorably hidden and unsaid within individual selves, these narratives (whether scientific, social-scientific or literary) ought to be of a

175

certain character. Human beings should be seen to be in conscious control of their lives, creating the meanings and regularities by which they live and not subject to unconscious or determining forces, to independent causes and constraints. They should be described as possessing agency with regard to natural, social, cultural or historical phenomena. Above all, representational justice should be done to the complexities of human life: to its individuality and commonality, its idiosyncrasy, ambiguity and nuance as much as its conventionalism, its pleasures and glories as well as its cruelties and ignorances.

Anthropos versus ethnos

'Doing representational justice to the complexities of human life', the samenesses and the differences, introduces a problem for the humanistic anthropologist regarding the status of culture. Are human beings the same *inasmuch as* they all inhabit different cultural worlds or *over and against* their inhabiting such worlds? Do they become human within culture or does their humanity (consciousness, creativity, individuality, dignity) transcend cultural particularities? Geertz has called this anthropology's 'recurrent dilemma' (1973: 22): how to square generic human rationality and the biological unity of mankind with the great natural variation of cultural forms. George Stocking concludes that the entire 'history of anthropology may . . . be viewed as a continuing (and complex) dialectic between the universalism of "anthropos" and the diversitarianism of "ethnos"' (1992: 347). Anthropological humanists, in other words, have been both cultural relativists and existentialists, some describing human consciousness as essentially individual and free, others describing it as culturally determined.

Cultural relativism can be taken much further, however, and become a thoroughgoing anti-humanistic critique, as has recently transpired under the monikers of 'structuralism' and 'post-structuralism'. If consciousness, its form and content, are not prior to the symbolic discourses and social practices in which it is culturally embedded, then not only is identity – human, individual, whatever – subordinate to cultural matrices (which may remain unconscious), but the whole idea of humankind, humanism, human dignity, and so on, is a historically contingent cultural product: ethnocentric, mythical, teleological. 'Man', as Foucault put it, 'is only a recent invention, a figure not yet two centuries old' (1972: 115).

Whatever one makes of Foucault's history, the implication is clear: humankind and humanism are concepts to deconstruct and overcome.

Far from being transcendent, humanistic values, methods, truths are part of specific discourses which have created the world in a certain image so as to serve certain interests and ends. 'Humankind' – 'the subject' or, better, 'the subject-effect' – is ever, inevitably and inextricably enculturated: hence multiply and partially constructed, conditioned, elicited, motivated and gendered. Even the existential certainties of the Western humanist – whereby, in Lewis's words (1982: 55), 'My distinctness, my being me, is quite unmistakeable to me, there can be nothing of which I am more certain' – amounts to a culturally derived (and rather unusual) 'metaphysics of presence'.

Tactical humanism

There are a number of possible responses to this critique. One is simply to reassert an existentialist and rationalist position and say that cultural relativism and deconstruction are just plain wrong. Science, medicine, history, literature and travel prove the existence of a universal humanity, and the inherent individuality of consciousness and experience through which it is embodied (cf. Rapport 1994a, 1997a). Of course, this proof cannot force itself on those who would see otherwise – hence, the number of times the word 'belief' appears in the above exposition of (agnostic) humanistic traits. Nevertheless, it is believed that humanistic beliefs are subjected to the most critical attention and are accessible to all who approach with an open mind (cf. Popper 1966).

Another response, as adumbrated philosophically by Rorty (1992), is to admit to the historico-cultural specificity of the humanist perspective but to claim, nonetheless, that as a way of knowing the world it offers the best prospectus for a diversity of cultural world-views being able to live peaceably alongside and through one another.

In what she calls a 'tactical humanism' (1990b: 138), Lila Abu-Lughod would seem to arrive anthropologically at a similar position. Humanism, she begins, may be a local discourse (despite its erstwhile claims) but it still has more speakers, writers and readers than any other: it carries most moral force as a language of equality. Of course, the discourse has suffered from being misapplied and abused. In the past, celebrating the example of heroic individuals has co-occurred with an eschewing of others' systematic oppression; positing individuals' autonomy has co-occurred with a masking of the inequalities of power; placing humankind at the centre of the world has co-occurred with a justifying of an exploitation of nature; and respecting a universality of human dignity and individual integrity has co-occurred with a denying of humanity to specified 'others' (women, children, natives, slaves, Jews).

However, this abuse notwithstanding (and what discourse, finally, can protect itself from abuse?), humanism offers anthropology the best hope for describing both the universality and the universal particularities of human experience.

In particular, humanism offers anthropology an escape from imprisoning essentialisms such as 'culture', 'gender' and 'race'. For these concepts have operated in anthropological discourse as means of making alterity: creating differences between people and enforcing separations which have come to imply inevitable hierarchy and inequality. Sameness within the category ('culture', 'gender', 'race'), meanwhile, has come to imply inexorable homogeneity, coherence and determination.

To write 'against culture' and other such generalizing, fundamentalist–essentialist concepts is to produce humanistic 'ethnographies of the particular': narratives of particular individuals in particular times and places. For, human beings 'all live in the particular' (Abu-Lughod 1990b: 157), and this is something they have in common over and against their so-called cultural (etc.) differences. Ethnographies of the particular will tell of the struggle to make meaning, of flux, movement and contradiction, of pain and success, of practices, strategies, contests, choices, improvisations and interests (cf. Langness and Frank 1981; Watson and Watson-Franke 1985). Paradoxically, these are individual experiences and activities that generalities cannot convey.

See also: **Consciousness, Human Rights, Individuality, Literariness, Post-Modernism**

INDIVIDUALISM

Individualism should not be confused with individuality, difficult though it has been to separate their definition and implication in anthropologists' work. To attempt this as a starting-point here, individualism pertains to a particular historico-cultural conceptualization of the person or self. Included within this conceptualization would be notions of the ultimate value and dignity of the human individual, his moral and intellectual autonomy, his rationality and self-knowledge, spirituality, right to privacy, self-sovereignty and self-development, and his voluntary contracting into a society, market and polity (cf. Lukes 1990). Individuality, by contrast, refers to the universal nature of human existence whereby it is individuals who possess agency. Moreover, since individuals engage with others by virtue of discrete sense-making apparatuses (nervous systems and brains) – discrete centres of consciousness in discrete bodies – their agency necessarily accords with distinct perspectives on the world. Not only is an individual's being-in-the-world universally mediated by very particular interpretive prisms which distance him from it, then, but while intrinsically 'of the world', the individual also inexorably comes to know the world as 'other'. Finally, this individuality of consciousness and agency is current whatever the acceptance of individualism as a cultural norm.

In much anthropological writing on individualism, however, a conflation is apparent. The study of the conceptualization of the person and his behaviour in a particular socio-cultural milieu spills over into a positing of the nature of the individual actor, also socio-culturally specified. The society or culture to which the individual actor belongs is looked to as the source of his agency, the origin of action and its interpretation; individuality, in short, is depicted as much prone to the vagaries of socio-cultural fashion as individualism.

The root of the confusion lies in the nineteenth-century tradition of social thought from which twentieth-century anthropology derives. In attempting social-scientifically to come to terms with what were felt to be the grand-societal changes wrought by the French Revolution, the American Revolution and the Industrial Revolution (to discover their origins, predict their evolutions, in mimicry of the science of natural organisms) – as well as guarding against the radical and individualistic 'excesses' which these changes were seen as portending – 'sociology' was born as a popular explanatory paradigm. Grand changes could be seen to evidence grand forces and grand patterns. Hence, grand explanatory narratives were fashioned which turned on (and prescribed the natural-ness of) the workings of such collective organisms as Society (generally in Europe) and Culture (generally in North America).

While Boas and American anthropology owed debts to the writings of Spencer and Morgan (and later, Weber), perhaps the key nineteenth-century influence on the twentieth-century development of anthropological explanation – the key exponent of a collectivist narrative which subsumed the individual actor within grand-societal workings – was Emile Durkheim. It was from him that Radcliffe-Brown and Malinowski, Lowie and Kroeber adopted much of their theoretic programme and problematic, and it is from Durkheim's French followers, especially Mauss and Dumont, that a narrative which conflates individualism with individuality has been propagated and elaborated. Let us trace this development.

The Durkheimian individual

Durkheim conceived of human beings as *homo duplex*; on one side there was the biological and personal (comprising the individual body with its material senses and appetites) and on the other the mental and moral (the conceptual and conscientious). The individual thus led a double existence: one rooted in the physical organism and one (morally, intellectually, spiritually superior) in a social organism. And while the former was naturally egoistic and anti-social, the latter, accruing from society, effected by socialization, was able to be altruistic and impersonal. Between the two there was constant antagonism and tension, but through inculcation into a public language and culture, humankind was capable of rising above mean (animal) individuality and becoming part of a collective conscience in which the (sacred) traditions of a society were enshrined. Indeed, if individuals were conscious of themselves as individuals, then this too was a product of their socialization in a collective conscience. Thus, the Western centrality of the individual actor derived from the complexities of the collective division of labour in European societies, and could be traced back to the Christianity of the Enlightenment and to the rise of Protestantism. Individualism was a social product like all moralities and all religions.

Marcel Mauss (1985) took it upon himself to show in more detail how society exerted its force on the physiological individual: through collective representations and collectively determined habitual behaviours, submerged the individual within 'a collective rhythm'. Nonetheless, Mauss's account is confused. He begins with the un-Durkheimian pronouncement that there has never been a human being who was not aware of his own body, also of his spiritual and physical individuality. However, conflating such universal individuality with cultural individualism, he then proceeds to outline an evolution in how people in different ages and societies have been differently aware of themselves as individual beings, and how these differences can be traced back to different forms of social structuration. First, then, comes the tribal stage of *personnage*. Here individuals are conceived of as ephemeral bearers of a fixed stock of names, roles and souls in clan possession. Each name-holder is the reincarnation of an original mythical holder, and each is the locus in daily life of different rights and duties. But these individual name-holders have no existence independently of the clan and they possess no inner conscience. Here is the individual solely as a structural fact. Next comes the Classical stage of *persona*. Here individuals are conceived of as free and responsible, independent and autonomous citizens of a state; they are legal persons with civic identities. But still they have no inner life and no individual conscience. Then, with the rise of Christianity, comes the stage of *personne*. Here is the individual conceived of as indivisible and rational, with a conscience, indeed, with a unique sacred soul, who serves as the foundation of all political, economic and legal institutions. Finally, accompanied by modern schools of psychology, there is the peculiar Western stage of *moi*: the individual as a 'self' with an increasing self-interestedness and self-knowledge.

Louis Dumont (1986) agrees with Mauss that the Western notion of the individual – an autonomous actor, bearing supreme moral value – is an exceptional stage in the evolution of civilizations. Traditionally it is society as a whole which is thus conceptualized. Through a comparison with the archetypal holism of Indian society, therefore, Dumont attempts more precisely to plot the origination and progress of this odd idea. Looking (as a Durkheimian would) to religion as the cardinal element, it is Hinduism which provides the first clue. For despite the constraining interdependence ubiquitously imposed by Indian society on its members, in the Hindu figure of the 'world-renouncer' – he who seeks ultimate truth by forgoing the world in favour of his own independent, individual spiritual progress and destiny – one finds a Western-like individualist. For him, society is recognized as having lost its absolute reality. Instead, in throwing off society's fetters and becoming self-sufficient he is said to have discovered his own self. The crucial difference between the Hindu world-renouncer and the modern individualist is that the former can continue to exist only outside the everyday social world.

Dumont's second clue is that these same 'outworldly individuals' can be seen to be present at the birth and ensuing development of Christianity. For Christ's teaching that man possesses a soul of infinite worth and eternal value which absolutely transcends the world of social institutions and powers, which is absolutely individual in relation to God and meets others' only in Him, engenders a community of out-worldly individuals who meet on earth but have their hearts in heaven. The history of Christianity over the ensuing centuries then represents a triumphant overcoming of the dualism between the Christian and the societal so that life-in-society becomes synonymous with that of the outworldly individual. Initially through the institution of the Catholic church (with the fourth-century conversion of Emperor Constantine and thereafter the Roman Empire), and ultimately through the Protestant Reformation, the outworldly Christian message comes to repossess the world. Here is society run wholly along individualist lines, with modern Christians being both individuals and 'inworldly'.

Nevertheless, Dumont concludes, the evolution need not end here. The individualistic and the holistic represent two diametrically different conceptualizations of society, and although the former Western 'liberal' model is enshrined in the United Nations' Universal Declaration of Human Rights (recognizing the inherent dignity and equality and the inalienable rights of all individuals), it is the latter holistic conceptualization which still represents the common type. Indeed, through movements as diverse as multi-culturalism, nationalism, fascism and Islamic fundamentalism, the cultural future of individualism is, to say the least, unpredictable.

Anthropological applications

Characterizing the above line of thought (from Durkheim through Mauss to Dumont), then, is the idea that the individual actor of Western society is the result of a recent, particular and exceptional historico-cultural development. Nor is it surprising that, learned in this (or commensurate) thought, anthropologists have been prone to find a lack of individualism (and hence an absence of individuality) in their ethnographies of traditional societies (cf. Carrithers *et al.* 1985).

'The African', Roger Bastide pronounces, is someone who defines himself by his position: is conscious of himself only as member of a lineage, a genealogical tree, a general category (a race, people, family, corporation) (cited in Lienhardt 1985: 144). The New Guinean 'Gahuku-Gama tribesman', Kenneth Read (1955) asserts, lacks a concept of the individual person; hence, there is no 'friendship' between unique individuals, only relationships between socially defined positions, and if personalities are recognized as distinct, then this is merely the issue of unique combinations of social relationships.

In short, ethnographic exploration proves how the individual is unique to Western thought, Jean La Fontaine (1985b) concludes. The concept and its moral and social significance is absent in other societies, with no *a priori* differentiation being made between individual and role, self and society.

The Non-Durkheimian individual

Nevertheless, there have been exceptions to the Durkheimian expectation and conclusion: ethnographies and analyses which would distinguish between individualism and individuality, which build on individual agency, which deny the priority (ontological, developmental, historical) of the societal.

Notably, Alan Macfarlane (1978), tracing the 'origins of English individualism', spectacularly refutes those theorists (particularly Marx, Weber, Durkheim, Dumont) who would see individualism as a recent socio-cultural development, an issue (variously) of the Renaissance, the Protestant Reformation, the rise of capitalism, the Enlightenment or the Industrial Revolution, upon a previously holistic, collectivist, close-structured, traditional society. For, in England at least, historical records (local registers, legal text-books, court rolls, autobiographical journals) evidence an individualistic, open, egalitarian society with political and intellectual liberty, with private property rights, with legal rights of the person against the group, in existence since the 1200s if not long before. As Macfarlane summarizes: 'the majority of ordinary people in England from at least the thirteenth century were rampant individualists, highly mobile both geographically and socially, economically "rational", market-orientated and acquisitive, ego-centred in kinship and social life' (1978: 163). Here, at least, the traditional anthropological evolution towards individualism can be abandoned and the conventional anthropological eschewing of conscious individuality obviated, for one does not find a time when 'an Englishman did not stand alone . . . in the centre of his world' (1978: 196). Contrariwise, it is the individual and his nuclear family which may be looked to for originating those socio-cultural changes which traditionally have been taken to be causative.

Moreover, even focusing on non-Western areas of anthropological concern (as above), Godfrey Lienhardt (1985: 143–50) observes how 'African' literature celebrates individual eccentricities, inner consciousnesses, which defy and subvert collective judgement and behaviour. Meanwhile, drawing on his fieldwork in New Guinea, Kenelm Burridge (1979) describes how most people are 'individuals' and 'persons' in different respects and at different times, where 'persons' may be understood as those who realize the given and embody the categories which are prescribed by tradition and the social order, while 'individuals' are those who use their intuition and perception to create anew. If persons are created by current intellectualizations and moralities, then individuals are creative of new ones (including new persons); if persons are products of socio-cultural conditions, then individuals exist in spite of them. Moreover, each 'spatially bounded organism' is able to switch between the two: leave their person-hood behind and realize their individuality. This realizing may take a variety of ethnographic expressions, Burridge admits, and the Western recognition of individuality (conceptualized as 'individualism') may indeed originate with Christianity, but nevertheless, an expression is everywhere possible. Certainly, in 'New Guinea' there are individuals who seek in events a 'truth' which goes beyond established moralities and which transcends material conditions. Indeed, Burridge concludes, such individuality would seem constitutive of our very human being, deriving from a universal imperative which pre-exists culture.

Burridge's ethnographic summation is also commensurate with Edmund Leach's general theoretic stance (developing a somewhat submerged Malinowskian recognition of individual 'needs') wherein the essence of humanity is a ubiquitous individual proclivity to break with normative social structures, reinterpret cultural conventions and create afresh (1977: 19–21). Here it is the individual actor and not the social system which should be looked to as source and guarantor of cultural vitality and social process.

Leach's insights have been perhaps most famously developed in the work of his student Fredrik Barth (e.g. 1959) and the school of transactionalism with which his name came to be associated (along with Fred Bailey's, Robert Paine's and others'). However, an emphasis on the individual actor – an interest in individualism; an appreciation of individuality – also found expression in early anthropological theorists of consciousness and personality (such as Gregory Bateson, Anthony Wallace and Ward Goodenough), in the work of network analysts (such as John Barnes, Clyde Mitchell and Jeremy Boissevain), and more recently in the flowering of studies within symbolic anthropology which focus on the constructions and interpretations of symbolic realities as made by particular individuals (Edward Bruner, Anthony Cohen, Michael Jackson).

Imbuing all of these approaches, perhaps, is an insistence that, in Macfarlane's formulation, 'individuals and their attitudes, their assumptions and mental life' should not lose out to macro-social (statistical, material, collectivist) 'facts' (1970: 3).

Current approaches

In much mainstream debate, sensitivity to the individualistic is still denigrated as 'methodological individualism': as erroneously couching explanation in terms of characteristics of individuals, their behaviours and interests, and so procuring insufficient purchase on the broader and deeper conditions of socio-cultural 'realities'. The centre-ground of anthropology, in other words, continues to be a preserve of 'method-ological collectivism' – positing social phenomena as determined by factors which bypass individual rationality, and hence envisaging cultural development quite independently of individual consciousness. Here is a continuing insistence that the distinction between the individual and the societal is specific to the West and must be collapsed in favour of the latter – or at least of 'social relations' (cf. Strathern 1990b) – for anthropology persuasively to encounter cultural others.

On the other hand, there is a continuing insistence that it is a peculiar ethnocentrism for anthropologists to fail to 'extend to the "others" we study a recognition of the personal complexity which we perceive in ourselves' (Cohen 1989: 12). We are individuals and persons, role-players and rebels, conventional and creative. We may be self-contradictory, personally paradoxical, socio-culturally situated, but we are always interpretively (helplessly, proudly) autonomous and agential, inevitably and inexorably ourselves (cf. Rapport 1993a). It is not good enough simply to say that only Western culture valorizes the concept of the individual ('individualism') and therefore only in Western society do individuals act distinctively ('individuality'). For, whether it is socio-culturally confirmed or not, the individual is the crucial actor in every social situation and individual consciousness the crucial factor in the interpretation of any cultural artefact.

See also: **Agent and Agency, Individuality, Methodological Individualism and Holism**

INDIVIDUALITY

Individuality is tied inextricably to individual consciousness, to that unique awareness, and awareness of awareness, which is the mark of human embodiment. The body, and in particular the brain ('a supremely well connected system of processors [an individual arrangement of neurons and synapses] capable of more distinct states, by several orders of magnitude, than any system ever known' (Flanagan 1992: 60)), gives rise to knowledge of the world, to a perspective upon the world, which is inevitably individual. Human beings come to know themselves within the world by way of cognitions and perceptions, thoughts, feelings and imaginings, which are unique to them.

The concept of individuality also bespeaks a host of ambiguities. The physical matter of the human body is in ongoing process of birth and decay (so that the assemblage of cells has changed completely in some seven years), while the individual's sense and sensing of identity is continuous. The senses of the human body operate in terms of repeated, momentary apperceptions ('moments of being') which are singular and diverse, and from which the individual builds up a variety of different knowledges and perspectives, or world-views; and yet, one feels oneself to be consistent and coherent at any one time, and that one's views develop logically over time. Being born and coming to consciousness very much within the world – thrown into the middle of a mêlée of ongoing processes of life, organic and inorganic, human and non-human, natural and socio-cultural, personally focused and ambient (family life, politico-economic conditions) – the individual nevertheless looks out upon this environment from a point of view which is both originary and original; each individual's knowledge of the world is particular and discrete, and subject to its own perceptual mechanisms (or 'subjective').

In anthropology, recognition of these ambiguities takes a characteristic form. As Wallace has put it (1961: 131):

> The paradox [is] that cultures do exist, and societies do survive, despite the diversity of the interests and motivations of their members, the practical impossibility of complete interpersonal understanding and communication, and the unavoidable residuum of loneliness that dwells in every man.

While leading lives of unique experiences and interpretations of the world, individuals yet partake of routine interactions with others, and succeed in maintaining relationships (intellectual and emotional, human and animal, socio-cultural and environmental) which are symbiotic and (at different possible levels) communicational. It does seem possible, at some level, to overcome individual discreteness and exchange knowledge and perspectives which are commonly held; to what extent, therefore, is it possible to treat habitual interactions in socio-cultural milieux as objective? While human individuals are irreducibly distinct, is it legitimate to make generalizations concerning the relations and behaviour of individuals who regularly come together as members of communities, associations or partnerships? Even though it is individuals who originally create and ongoingly utilize and maintain the institutions and practices which come to characterize a socio-cultural milieu (common language, politico-legal arrangements, systems of marriage, socialization and health care, and so on), to what extent is it possible to treat these latter as things-in-themselves, as accruing an identity and a weight which makes them, in time, *sui generis*?

However much such questions are debated in anthropology (cf. Ingold 1997), it should not detract, as it has a tendency to do, from an appreciation of the concreteness of individuality. This latter is the human *a priori*, the physical–psychical basis on which all knowledge of the world and all human creativity within the world rests. Human consciousness is unavoidably and irreducibly individual, and all human constructs (including socio-cultural milieux and their socio-cultural anthropology) are shaped by and imbued with this truth (cf. Cohen 1994; Rapport 1997a).

Existential anthropology

The anthropology which has sought most deliberately to keep this truth in view has been termed 'existential' or 'phenomenological' (cf. Jackson 1989, 1996; also Douglas and Johnson 1977; Kotarba and Fontana 1984; Csordas 1994; Stoller 1997), after the philosophical traditions associated with such writers as Kierkegaard, Emerson, Nietzsche, Husserl, Jaspers and Heidegger. As adumbrated by Sartre (1997: 44–6):

> Our point of departure is . . . the subjectivity of the individual
> . . . not because we are bourgeois, but because we seek to base
> our teaching upon the truth. . . . And at the point of departure
> there cannot be any other truth than this, *I think, therefore I am*,
> which is the absolute truth of consciousness as it attains to itself.
> Every theory which begins with man, outside of this moment
> of self-attainment, is a theory which thereby suppresses the
> truth, for outside of the Cartesian *cogito*, all objects are no more
> than probable. . . . [T]here is [an absolute] truth which is
> simple, easily attained and within the reach of everybody; it
> consists in one's immediate sense of self.
>
> In the second place, this theory alone is compatible with
> the dignity of man, it is the only one which does not make man
> into an object . . . – that is, as a set of predetermined reactions,
> in no way different from the patterns of qualities and phenom-
> ena which constitute a table, or a chair or a stone. . . .
>
> Furthermore, . . . [there is] a human universality of *condition*
> . . . , all the *limitations* which *a priori* define man's fundamental
> situation in the universe. His historical situations are variable
> . . . [b]ut what never vary are the necessities of being in the
> world, of having to labour and to die there. These limitations
> are [at once] [o]bjective, because we meet with them every-
> where and they are everywhere recognizable: and subjective
> because they are *lived* and are nothing if man does not live them
> – if, that is to say, he does not freely determine himself and his
> existence in relation to them. And, diverse though man's

purposes may be, at least none of them is wholly foreign to me, since every human purpose presents itself as an attempt either to surpass these limitations, or to widen them, or else to deny or to accommodate oneself to them.

Some of Sartre's phraseology seems old-fashioned now, sexist and self-satisfied; it can appear the credo of the secure and resourceful bourgeois, able to reflect on the self, to determine 'his' relations to the conditions or circumstances of his life, and to lay claim to a certain lifesome dignity. Indeed, this has led some anthropologists to reject such an existentialist orientation *tout court*. However, such a reading is superficial, and mistaken; avoiding gender-specific linguistic formulations may still not be easy, but by his words Sartre succinctly points up a number of important truths. Let me elaborate upon a number of his phrases in turn.

(i) I think, therefore I am is the absolute truth of consciousness

Descartes's attempt to isolate a knowing subject as a foundation for a scientific exploration of the world has been heavily criticized in recent social science. The search for a *res cogitans*, a discrete substance and process of cognition, has been seen as responsible for setting up a number of misconceived dualisms, such as mind versus body, thinking versus feeling, reason versus emotion, thought versus action, individual versus environment, man (society and culture) versus nature. However, Descartes's description of consciousness can be easily improved upon without being discarded by adding such words as 'feel' and 'imagine', 'sense' and 'dream', 'evaluate' and 'experience', to 'think'; and by portraying the knowing being as always situated, as a body in a certain time and space. One thus retains Descartes's insistence on a discrete consciousness as the ontological essence of being human. Hence: 'I think and feel – I experience – at a particular moment, and therefore I am at that moment' (cf. Cohen and Rapport 1995).

(ii) Outside of the Cartesian cogito, all objects are no more than probable

What the individual knows with most immediacy, clarity and certainty is what his senses inform him, what he experiences first-hand. Indeed, this is the only thing of which he has certain knowledge. He knows what he senses but he cannot know the accuracy of those senses and measure them against an absolute standard because he 'is' his senses and not something over and against them. He can test, improvise and experiment with what his senses tell him, but these procedures also call upon his senses to effect and measure. He can compare what his senses tell him with what others' senses tell them but, still, these efforts entail his sensual interpretation of the information he gleans from (what he interprets to be) others'. In short, the individual's senses of self and world are the beginning and, in a way, also the end of knowledge. They are certainly the paradigm of knowledge, and give onto a sense of certainty that is never equalled in other forms of knowledge – however much they might inspire the wish for such comprehension. As Roy Wagner concludes (1991: 39):

> nothing could possibly be more clear, distinct, concrete, certain, or real than the self's perception of perception, its own sensing of sense. It is the very archetype, the inspiration, of everything we have ever imagined for the objective

And yet such knowledge remains hermetically sealed within the personal microcosm. Hence: 'I am certain of my own cognitions at a particular moment (and therefore I am) but I am not so certain about anything else'.

(iii) The necessities of being in the world, of having to live, labour and to die there, is a universal human condition

The notion of 'independent existence' Whitehead (1925) famously decried as a philosophical misconception since entities are more properly understood in terms of the way they relate with the universe. In the Heideggerian terms which have become popular in environmentalist anthropology, human beings can be said ever to dwell within worlds of nature and of socio-cultural exchange (cf. Ingold 1986; Weiner 1991). However, this dwelling does not detract from human beings' individuality. For our being-in-the-world courtesy of individual bodily mechanisms of cognition and perception is such as always to make of the world something other, always something interpreted. One comes to see, to construct, the world and its objects in certain ways which have proven personally 'valuable' over time (cf. Edelman 1989: 184), and one learns to recognize signs and symbols by which are expressed the experience of dwelling in the ('same') world of other sentient beings. But these signs and symbols remain ambiguous, and the world and its objects ever something refracted through the prism of a situated consciousness. Ambiguity, doubt, incoherence and multiplicity are the nature of the universal human (not to say animal) condition, dwelling alongside fellow sentient creatures, dependent upon one another and the remainder of the organic and inorganic universe for the environmental conditions of one's life (even for the transient agglomeration of chemicals that underwrite one's bodily existence), and yet never certain concerning one's meaningful construction of that universe, its rectitude or sharedness. Meaning is a personal, subjective, internal perception (cf. Rapport 1993a). Hence: 'I experience and become myself (I am) at particular moments while dwelling within environments comprised of other, similarly cognizing, beings and inorganic, non-beings; and while there is a relatedness, even a mutuality, to all this matter, I know of it only as an interpreted other'.

(iv) Being in the world and relating to its conditions is a subjective phenomenon because the world and its conditions are nothing if individuals do not live them

Whatever may be the ultimate nature of earthly physical reality, human beings gain access to it only through their senses. Moreover, this is not a passive or reactive exercise entailing the reception of external stimuli but rather the pro-active testing of original models and the adjudicating of consequences. To 'interpret' the world in this way is not only to give it meaning, then, but also form: to construct it, its objects and events in a certain way. In the world of human being, as Bateson has it (1958: 96), the Berkeleyan motto cannot be faulted: 'To be is to be perceived'. Moreover, it is important to emphasize that it is the individual who is the 'energy source' behind this act of worldly perception or interpretation (Bateson 1972: 126). Knowledge is individual and subjective, deriving from individuals' sensitive bodies, and the drive, the work and the habitude behind this are exemplifications of individual agency. This is especially important to recognize with regard to habit. Worldly order which they find valuable or satisfying, individuals tend to maintain. They also tend to maintain certain orders in common with those others with whom they dwell in 'an' environment – human and animal, organic and inorganic. (In a habitual way of farming, for instance, individuals will find themselves in symbiosis with human neighbours, with animals, domestic and wild, with crops and with soils.) However, these orders do not acquire their own energy or momentum; they are always inert unless continually worked and made meaningful by their individual users. Should they cease to be considered valuable, they cease to exist. These common orders (languages, social structures, ecosystems) are always ambiguous, always means by which a diversity of understandings and motivations are synthesized by common forms and practices which allow a diversity of gratifications. Moreover, they tend to be temporary and transitory, so that after a time individuals construct orders anew and old environmental arrangements and alignments die. Hence: 'I experience and become myself by dwelling at particular moments in particular environments; but those environments (and that self) exist only so long as I continue to construe them in a particular way and practise them as such'.

(v) Individuals are responsible for determining whether to attempt to surpass the conditions they construe around them or to accommodate themselves to them

Individuals construe the world as they take it to be; nothing is certain but their own consciousness of self, but they construct the world in a way which proves valuable (successful, meaningful) for them. Once they have done so, individuals must also determine how to react in relation to this world. This is a decision which nothing and no-one else can make for them, because the decisions and behaviours of others must still be cognized and perceived, interpreted and made meaningful, within the world-views of the individuals concerned. Hence, individuals can be affected by the decisions of others, if they are something of which they take notice, but not determined. There is no alternative to individuality, in short, no certain or direct access to another consciousness or to the world 'as is', and there is no other source of an individual's meanings but that individual himself. Hence his responsibility for deciding how to react to the world he has made: to do as before (maintain a habit) or to create anew; to try to fit in with what seem to be the expectations and aspirations of others (be a 'good family member', a 'loyal client', a 'pious co-religionist') or to cut a different path for oneself (as 'poet' or 'rebel' or simply 'Jean-Paul Sartre'). Objects and events which he construes within his environment may affect his decision – say the wishes, deeds and words of other individuals – but these cannot determine his decision; there can be no external determination because the world beyond the individual is always something other to him which he is ultimately responsible for construing. Even trying to fit in to a social group or accede to others' wishes is a creative act of individuality. The individual, as Sartre concludes, is inevitably 'free', of guidance as of determination (cf. Burridge 1979). Hence: 'I experience and become myself by dwelling in particular environments, and I am responsible at every moment for deciding how to act (and be) in relation to my cognitions, and where to take the world around me'.

(vi) This appreciation of individuality succeeds in not having humanity appear objectified

Human knowledge is something to which individuals subject the worlds they construe around them. There is no escape from individuality in human life, the latter being ever a subjective condition; human individuals are always subjects: always agents and always exercising their agency. Indeed, there is no other source of human agency but individuals. In search for relief from, or denial of, the burdens of responsibility in their lives, individuals sometimes imagine other sources – gods, ancestors, natural forces, linguistic grammars, cultural traditions, unconscious histories, social conditions – but these are fantasies, and serve as puppets in the hands of their individual users. This denial of responsibility and turning oneself into an object created, construed and controlled from without, Sartre calls 'bad faith': living one's life 'inauthentically'. What it is also important to say is that it too is an instantiation of individual agency and subjectivity; here are individuals making themselves into certain kinds of object. An existentialist appreciation of human life becomes 'humanist' at that point when it is felt that individuals can do better for themselves than spend their lives falsely objectifying the fantastical, and perhaps they can be influenced towards more truthful construals of their condition (cf. Rapport 1994a). Hence: 'I experience and become myself in particular environments at particular moments, and in recognizing my responsibility for the above I abide by my individual integrity: I accede to the dignity of my individuality'.

Anthropology and individuality

To become human is to become individual, Clifford Geertz once expounded (1973: 52), and we become individual in an environment of socio-cultural forms and patterns in terms of which we give form, order, direction and point to our lives. The crucial question which this begs is the precise relationship between socio-cultural forms and the individual lives lived by them. Becoming human and individual in an environment of socio-cultural forms is neither becoming 'the same' as others, or even necessarily comparable, nor is it becoming after a deterministic or directly influenced fashion. In becoming individual in certain socio-cultural milieux, energy, agency, intention and inter-pretation remain the property of the individual, self-conscious subject.

This seems often to be overlooked or negated in anthropological writings, where a system of forms is foregrounded to the almost total exclusion of their individual usage (creation, animation, interpretation, re-formation). Indeed, the intrinsic dichotomy between the individual and the world is often eschewed as a peculiarity of 'Western' socio-cultural milieux, and hence as methodologically and analytically inapplicable. This is indefensible. At best it confuses individuality with individualism; and while the latter might be said to describe a particular socio-cultural form of behaviour (the pursuit of self-distinguishment), the former concerns a condition which is a human universal: by virtue of a unique consciousness, each of us perforce engages with the world as other and is possessed of distinct perspectives upon it. Such individuality remains consequential whether or not individual consciousness is an item of collective discourse, whether or not individual reflection is publicly eschewed, and whether or not individual distinctiveness is something which the institutionalization of a fund of common behaviours does its utmost to obviate. No process of socialization or enculturation overcomes the separateness of the individual body and brain, the phenomenology of the ideating, acting, breathing, eating, mating, dying, birthing subject. Individuals experience and interpret (and interpret themselves interpreting) and therefore they are.

Treating individual distinction as a matter of socio-cultural discourse, however, has allowed much anthropology to pass over individual agency and responsibility even where diversity is admitted into the analysis. For the diversity now becomes that of opposed social-structural interests, of competing status groups, of contradictory mores, of situational roles, of circumstantial norms, of a disequilibriated social organization, of a complex system of values and beliefs, of a social system in change. It is collective socio-cultural systems which become the sources and guarantors of meaning, and socio-cultural forces to which individual 'members' perforce respond and of which their behaviour is an expression. That is, individual distinction and diversity disappear as individuals are decentred from analysis, dissolved into various systems of convention which are said to be operating through them, constituting their beings.

In short, individuals become collective constructs. Psyches become defined and realized by society: universes of discourse reflecting social positions (cf. Berger 1970: 375). Selfhood becomes allocated from socio-cultural repertoires for use in certain collectively structured worlds of experience: pegs on which items of collaborative manufacture can be hung for a time (cf. Goffman 1978: 245). Roles played become allotted and determined by society, representing bundles of obligatory activity (cf. Goffman 1972: 76–7). Even imaginative explorations become emanations of certain pre-given and pre-structured life-worlds of socialization (cf. Psathas 1973: 8–9): it is not individuals who think through their fantasies, then, but fantasies which think through them, unbeknownst and outwith their control (cf. Lévi-Strauss 1969b: 20). In short, diversity is socialized and enculturated, and thereby sanitized; it is not the individuals who are diverse so much as the working parts of the complex social systems of which they are components and conduits. Their diversity is itself governed and part of a replicated pattern. In fact their diversity becomes an absence of diversity, of individual difference, and a triumph of cultural order. For culture, on this view, is essentially a set of 'control mechanisms', as Geertz would have it (1983: 44–5): symbolic devices – plans, recipes, rules and instructions – which act like computer programs, reducing the breadth and indeterminateness of individuals' potential lives to the specificity and narrowness of their actual ones (cf. Gellner 1995a: 50).

Such modelling is existentially fallacious; it offers only a pale pretence at depicting the ambiguities inherent in human life and the complexities of individual interactions in socio-cultural milieux. Nor is it sufficient to say, as some apologists are wont, that social-scientific theorization is committed to holistic explanation and so is bound to seem out of place and 'vulgar' in the context of the individual and particular case (cf. Culler 1981: 16). Because it is surely from individuals that any comprehension of socio-cultural milieux must proceed, since it is they who provide what A.J. Ayer dubbed 'final testimony' to the existence of a common socio-cultural world (1968: 256–7): it is they who remain the 'anthropological concrete' (Auge 1995: 20).

Far from entities with mechanisms and dynamics operating in their own right, what is socio-culturally institutional and systemic is made up of a complex and continuous interlinkage of individual actions, deriving in turn from how individuals define and decide to meet the situations in which they find themselves. The large-scale system of cooperation or conflict (the community, kinship group, class-uprising, political confederation, or religious sect) may be broken down into smaller-scale interactions between interpreting individuals in any number of settings and situations. Even if, *in extremis*, the socio-cultural milieu has come to be seen locally as a machine, a super-organism with a separate existence, then this state of affairs should be described as the ongoing construction of the individuals who serve it. It is they who remain responsible for this 'phantasy' of groupness, as Laing depicts it (1968: 81), and for the 'bad faith' (Sartre) which is ever necessary for its maintenance.

To 'decolonize' the individual human subject from its common anthropological representations, in short, is to liberate it both from overdetermining cultural conditions and overweening social institutions (discourse, language-game, collective representation, social relationship, *habitus*, praxis), and from their holistic and hegemonically minded social-scientific commentators. Anthropological analysis should retain respect for individual cognitive processes and, to this end, apprehend that ambiguous interface between aggregation and individuality. It should take into account both the individual agency which brings socio-cultural milieux to life and also the common socio-cultural forms and practices by which individuals coordinate their activities and world-views within these milieux. In this way, an anthropological appreciation might be reached of socio-cultural milieux as encompassing and composed of individual difference, indeed, in a significant way constituted by it: by self-conscious individuals making an ongoing diversity of meaningful worlds.

See also: **Agent and Agency, Consciousness, Individualism, Methodological Individualism and Holism, World-View**

INTERACTION

Collective behaviour, as Anthony Cohen puts it (1994: 7), is a triumph; far from something mechanical it should be understood as the coming-together for particular purposes of a greater or lesser number of individuals, for shorter or longer periods of time, in more or less formalized and institutionalized fashions. Above all, it should be understood as an aggregative rather than an integrative phenomenon. Collective behaviour entails the meeting of individuals but not their elision, their being subsumed within some super-organism: a group mind, a collective conscience, a reified society, community or culture.

Interaction as synthetic

How precisely is collectivity possible? This was a question Simmel posed himself (1971), and the answer he suggested entailed an appreciation of interaction, its moments, situations and processes. Interaction represented a 'synthesizing phenomenon' whereby individual and often private purposes intersected with public institutions in a routine, negotiated fashion. This meeting then gave onto, and itself embodied, structures of social exchange and cultural practice held in common; through interaction, individuals created and maintained societies and cultures.

For something to be seen to exist, Simmel elaborated, contrast must be construed between it and other things distinct from, or opposed to, it; oppositional entities, processes and tendencies are, thus, ultimately complementary because a constitutive force inheres in the tension between them. In the social realm, we find this fundamental constitutive dualism in the opposition between individuals as members of societies and cultures and the routine socio-cultural behaviours, structures and institutions by which such membership is formalized. One can envisage the shared worlds of society and culture as a collection of common symbolic forms: languages; scientific, educational, historical and economic concepts; artistic, moral, religious and legal precepts. In interaction with one another, individuals come together and exchange these common forms, maintaining them in their usage. However, their usage is a personal and subjective one. As they employ or 'consume' the symbolic forms, so they personalize them; they incorporate them into their individual lives, deploy them in the development of a subjective world-view. Here are commonalities of interaction engaged in for the pursuit and fulfilment of personal, diverse and possibly contradictory individual ends. And the one feature or aspect is married inexorably to the other. Individuals express and realize their idiosyncrasies because they engage in routine social interactions, and routine interactions continue to take place between members of societies and cultures because of continuing individual idiosyncrasies. The social exchange is constituted by this inherent duality.

In any socio-cultural phenomenon, in short, purposes and institutions, meanings and forms, are distinct, opposed but intimately related. Indeed, they can be seen to constitute one reality. Interaction entails the coming-together of common forms and diverse meanings or contents. Divorced from their socio-cultural form, individual meanings would not achieve public expression, while emptied of content, separated from individual goals, motives, purposes and interests, thoughts and feelings, the languages of common forms would fall into desuetude. Hence, the relationship between form and meaning is one of interdependence and multifactoriality; individuals depend upon these common socio-cultural artefacts in order publicly to express themselves, while the vitality of the forms depends on individuals with meanings they endemically want to express through them. Forms are the shared vehicles by which individuals and their meanings come together; they represent a mode of exchange and of continuing association.

At one and the same time, then, interaction is routine and something shared – something owned together by those individuals who partook of its regular exchange – and yet something multiple and diverse. It represents at once something institutional and, in its symbolic regimen, possibly constricting of free expression, and also a vehicle of idiosyncrasy, of creative expression and escape. This was the source of beauty in social interaction, and also its potential drama, Simmel felt: the tension between the surface agreements of the exchange, the orderly interactional form precisely structured, painstakingly developed, and carefully maintained between members, and the unique visions, the limitless avenues of thought that were motivating and animating the exchange, causing its regular re-occurrence, but dancing invisibly around its expression. The ambiguity of everyday interaction is translated into both an uncertainty and a release.

Anthropology and interactionism

Such thoughts are not strange to socio-cultural anthropology. A number of years ago (1961), David Pocock was advising that society is a dialectical process between principles making for aggregation and principles making for individuation, and urging that their interaction be the object of anthropological study (1961: 103, 114). Indeed, a century of ethnographic exploration since Simmel wrote makes the latter's portrayal seem in some respects truistic and anthropologically unremarkable.

However, there is the question of emphasis, and the extent to which the implications of a viewing of society as symbolic interaction – that the collective structures of social reality can only be fully grasped through an appreciation of the way they are personalized in individual lives; that the objectification of cultural objects is only to be understood in terms of the subjective psychic processes of the individuals who use them in interaction, the intentions which they bring to that usage and the experiences they construe – are carried into practice. All too often, it seems, following Durkheim, Simmelian insights are deemed inapposite: eschewed as social psychology, or decried as psychologisms. That is, tending to privilege the abstraction of a system of forms to the exclusion of their individual negotiation and usage, anthropology has approached the regularities of social interaction as if they pertained to a reality external to the individuals responsible for constituting and re-constituting it, which could satisfactorily be described in their absence. Thus, various kinds of interactional determinism have been arrived at – structures of exchange responsible for formulating the thinking of individual members – while little or no account has been taken of the consciousness of those involved: of their ability to reflect on their own behaviour, make choices and construct meaning. It is rare to find a full appreciation of the dialectical interdependence between the institutionalism of interactional routine and the diversity of individual purpose.

For instance, in an influential treatise, *The Social Construction of Reality*, Berger and Luckmann described conversation as a most important vehicle by which the contours of a homogeneous social reality are maintained and developed; by way of conversation individuals are integrated within a set of social practices, and a common cultural world-view is objectified and crystallized (1966: 140). This is brought about by sharing in what Brown and Levinson (1978: 256) dub a culture's 'interactional systematics'. As elaborated upon by Gumperz and Tannen (1979: 307–22), partaking in a successful interaction is a matter of a subtle and complex coordination of conversational elements, such as: turn-taking, direction of gaze, establishment of verbal rhythm, cooperation to produce identifiable lines of thematic progression, orderly sequencing, and recognition of and assistance in formulaic routines. Participants in an interaction are called upon to identify familiar and conventional types of activity and styles of speech which 'frame' the words they hear and the behaviours they observe so that they are able to define habitual and shared 'speech-situations'. Finally, a combination of an understanding of semantic content and an appreciation of cues of contextualization within such formulaic routines enable the signalling and interpretation of shared meaning.

In short, the shared rules of conversational conduct are seen to entail common techniques of interpretation, and a constellation of features of conversational form are seen as directing fellow interactants into interpreting one another's words in the same way. Successful interaction is a manifestation (a resultant and a constituent) of an ongoing community born out of common expectations concerning conventionalized co-occurrence between potentialities of words' semantic content and aspects of discourses' surface style. The interaction becomes a joint activity, whose performance replicates part of the coherent and 'corporate' structures of the societies and cultures to which the individual participants belong. As Hymes sums up, shared rules for the conduct and interpretation of speech represent the primary determination by a community of the competence and belonging of its members (1972: 54–8; also cf. Garfinkel 1967: 11; Schegloff 1972: 350).

Symbolic interactionism

However, to appreciate the consciousness of individual participants as something distinct from the various structures of socio-cultural exchange in which they partake is to understand interaction as entailing both more and less than the above portrayal. More individual creativity may go into its negotiation, and less commonality or sharing be occasioned by its successful maintenance.

As Hymes would also recognize, then, what counts as a 'communicative event' is not something that can be predicted or even easily identified, for its status 'is entirely a question of [its] construal by a receiver' (1973a: 22–6). To identify a successful interaction and its socio-cultural ramifications – even to identify what passes for an 'interaction' as such – is a subjective judgement, a matter of what Winch has called 'internal relations' within a system of ideas or world-view (1970: 107). It is rash to extrapolate, therefore, from the seemingly orderly nature of an interaction between individuals, and the superficial systematics in which they partake, to the character and extent of a culture or society of sharing in which they are members.

This is the starting-point of Herbert Blumer's work (1969, 1972), and the furthering of an appreciation of 'symbolic interactionism' which had its roots in the thinking of the social theorist G.H. Mead. It is wrong, Blumer begins, to consider interaction as a medium through which socio-cultural determinants move so as to constitute the forms and contents of human behaviour; interaction is between individual actors, not factors imputed to them, and individuals' actions are a consequence of their interpretations of situations and the meanings that things hold for them, rather than an expression of socio-cultural forces. Lines of action are built up step by step, Blumer suggests, by a process of 'self-indication' or self-communication whereby people, relations, events, objects and situations are defined according to their possible significance to the individual concerned. Individuals communicate with themselves in this way continuously, indicating things to themselves, making sense, dealing with what they note, and moulding their behaviours. 'Instead of the individual being surrounded by an environment of pre-existing objects which play on him and call forth his behavior, the proper picture is that he constructs his objects on the basis of his on-going activity' (Blumer 1972: 182). Importantly, the process of self-indication stands over and against so-called external forces of the make-up of society and culture. Through self-designation and self-interaction, individuals manifest how they are pro-active, not passive or merely reactive: the nature of the interactions with others in which they partake consists of the meanings that they have for the individuals for whom they are objects of consciousness.

The picture of society, culture or community which emerges is neither of systems nor integrations but of aggregations of variable numbers of jointly occurring actions, of variable linkage, all pursued for their individual participants' interests, not a system's requirements. Society entails ongoing negotiation between individuals engaged in their own multitudinous activities and lines of action. Its study is the story of many individual lives recurrently intersecting in symbolic routines which exhibit shared forms and endlessly variable individual meanings. 'Interaction' conveys the sense in which actions carried on by, and belonging to, an aggregation of individuals come to be fitted together into a developing matrix or routine (cf. Watson and Watson-Franke 1985: 205–6; also Rapport 1997a: 12–29).

Socio-cultural life, Blumer says, is individuals interacting with one another. To the extent that there is joint action, group action or 'interaction', then, this can be seen as an interlinkage of individuals' separate acts, an articulation, a coming together, that is new in each instance. Initially, individuals coming-together in interaction do not know what to expect from others, so they test inferences and gradually identify one another as beings who behave according to certain rules. Interaction thereby becomes a form of mutual typification. From a routinization of this process of mutuality, of equivalent structures of individual interpretation, socio-cultural structures emerge. The process is ongoing, however, and constantly revised. It is often also precarious, for the negotiated norms of interaction depend on the reciprocal but distinct interpretations of the participants; the routines are adhered to only as long as they are separately felt to be meaningful or useful, or at least better keeping to than not.

In short, the process of mutual individual self-indication or interpretation, giving onto the construction of a socio-cultural reality of common structures of behaviour is never to be taken for granted (cf. Dreitzel 1970). Even while many instances of interaction will occasion a repetition of forms of coming together which have been negotiated in, and recalled from, the past, they still call for the work of individual management and interpretation; they are maintained because they continue to be worked by – and work for – the individuals involved. Socio-cultural structures and institutions do not work themselves.

It is important to emphasize this point. Routine interactions do not possess or assume an independent power, logic or life-force; nothing emerges from them which is greater than or distinct from the sum of the individual energies of which they are made up. Routine interactions are like inert moulds or masks in which, and behind which, individual meanings are made and interests pursued, and it is wrong to talk as if these interactions worked themselves, or had requirements; they are rather worked, serving as vehicles for individual users. Moreover, they may be seen to be worked, not as a machine which is switched on and off for the performing of a set task, but more as a piece of music which is jointly interpreted by an ensemble of instrumentalists. Different noises come together, different parts are played in the whole, different senses are made of the whole. The interaction, in short, does different jobs for different participants. It may be incumbent upon each to know and employ certain routine, even standardized, forms (musical, behavioural) in order to enter into the exchange, but these serve a diversity of ends; they are not a constraint. In the poet Shelley's formulation (1954: 281): 'a single word, even may be a spark of inextinguishable thought'.

Focusing more precisely on the nature of linguistic interaction for a moment, one can say that a shared language provides a fund of forms and cases which individuals adapt to their communicational requirements. However, past linguistic practice does not determine present communicational possibilities, and so interaction eventuates in varied and inconsistent usage, with the repetition of words and syntax regardable as only partial replication; the language becomes home to polythetic readings without end. In contrast to portrayals of structural determinacy, then, a linguistic grammar should be seen as neither overwhelming nor sacrosanct. Rules of grammar represent only very approximate and unstable summaries of past regularities, and aggregations of individual interactants need not assume any regimented sameness in their linguistic practices or competencies (cf. Steiner 1975: 204–5). Individuals continuously improvise, innovate and make meaning as best they can, and notions of linguistic predetermination make little sense in relation to their construings of acts of communication. Interaction represents a structure of exchange which individuals by and large make up, without convener or referee, as they go along (cf. Harris 1981).

Individuals do not engage in routine interactions willy-nilly. Rather, these linguistic and behavioural forms are available for implementation by those who choose to adopt them as instruments towards their own diverse ends. And while it is the case that not all interactions are equally freely entered into or followed through, still they do not run by themselves or for themselves, or in a realm separate from individual consciousness and will; interactional routines cannot force participants' compliance and, even when adopted, cannot determine individual users' states of mind.

Finally, the multitude of routine interactions under way in a socio-cultural milieu (constituting a milieu of greater or lesser density of networks of relations between people) should not be seen to eventuate in one, integrated, working system. Society and culture can be thought of as funds of interactional forms (linguistic and behavioural) from which individuals concoct their personal relations. But the way some individuals develop routine relations with one another need in no way constrain those same individuals in their negotiations with others. Far from operating together in equilibrium or integration, one routine may oppose another – in time, in style, in consequence – or have tangential relations or none at all. Far from enactants of deterministic socio-cultural structures and members of singularly integrative communities, individual interactants can be depicted as negotiators of routine exchanges whose most vibrant and significant communities may ultimately remain private to themselves: it is within the boundaries of their selves that their most significant truths are construed and reside. In sum, socio-cultural milieux amount at one and the same time to arenas in which there is an ongoing exchange of shared forms and a continuous construction of individual worlds of meaning.

Ego-syntonism

The question remains of how common interactional forms are able to serve the interests of a diversity of individual users, and here, the phenomenon of ego-syntonism, as sketched by Devereux (1978: 126), provides significant pointers:

> [B]oth organized and spontaneous social movements and processes are possible not because all individuals participating in them are identically (and sociologistically) motivated, but because a variety of authentically subjective motives may seek and find an Ego-syntonic outlet in the same type of collective activity.

Ego-syntonism is a process whereby a number of discrete consciousnesses come harmonically to interact one with another.

A great advance in the appreciation of the processes of sociation, of interaction and socio-cultural participation, Devereux felt, would be to recognize that the collective or joint act (the family meal, the clan ritual, the regional market, the national war) should not be construed in terms of either a homogeneous set of individual experiences or a single massive, social one. Instead, the collective act represented the embodiment of an institutional medium, a channel, an occasion, afforded by 'society' or 'culture' through which was achieved the public actualization, ratification and gratification (in different ways and to different extents) of any number of individual meanings and motivations

(1978: 127–8). The institutional medium or movement may be regularly repeated (weekly church-going) or rarely so (the 1956 Hungarian uprising), and may be revolutionary or conservative in consequence, but what is important is that differently motivated persons can come to perceive in that certain socio-cultural moment or event a suitable outlet for their various gratifications.

The crucial distinction here, for Devereux, is between collective action and the 'conglomerate' of individual motives underlying it: between public behaviour and its personal meaning. Certainly, the notion of ego-syntonism would appear a useful instrument for construing relations between the individual and the collective, between the personal and the public (cf. Rapport 1994b). For here is a recognition that joint social events need not be singular in order to be maintained, and need not eventuate in singularity either. Individuals need not be in agreement when they begin to interact, and constant interaction need bring them no closer to a joint or standardized consciousness, or an overcoming of their idiosyncrasies: a great deal of their interaction can go on in a situation of misperception or misinter-pretation of one another's meanings and motivations. As Devereux sums up, quoting the Latin aphorism with approbation: "'Si bis faciunt idem, non est idem'" (if two people do the same thing, it is not the same thing)' (1978: 125). A variable number of individual actors can come together in a group, form a public collectivity, and at precisely the same time remain apart, maintaining their discrete and diverse individualities. Indeed, in echoes of Simmel, Devereux recognizes how the two are dialectically conjoined; the development of collectivity and individuality takes place through a constitutive tension of opposition.

The key to ego-syntonism is the ambiguity of socio-cultural forms. For the latter to serve as significant synthesizing instruments by which the threads of different individuals' lives come to be interwoven, they must possess a basic indeterminacy. A language of common forms is the means by which individuals both come together and remain apart. Always mediating between the actions of one individual and the interpretations of another, the 'friendly ambiguities' of interaction, as Sapir put it (1956: 153), conspire to reinterpret for each the behaviour they observe in terms of 'those meanings which are relevant to his own life'. The ambiguity of common forms also adds to their inertia. Vague and superficial, they can be inherited intact by different generations and adapted to a variety of settings; they are ready-made formulae always capable of being substantiated and revived by new motivations and moods (cf. Propp 1968: 116): their inertia or conservativeness, their usefulness and prevalence, issue from their malleability in use.

Interaction in Wanet

The paradigmatic form of human interaction, Blumer asserted, is that between two individuals; larger instances of human association are based on this 'interactional atom'. Not only is the traditional micro-focus of anthropological study the strategic point of entry into a field, then, but the proper grounding of conclusive analysis. A number of well-known works have focused on the dyadic relations between anthropologist and key informant (Dumont 1978; Crapanzano 1980; Shostak 1983), and a number of others have sought to build up an analysis on the basis of small-scale, face-to-face relations between informants which gradually become more inclusive (Briggs 1970; Boissevain 1974; Cohen 1987).

In *Diverse World-Views in an English Village* (1993a), Rapport attempts to chart the relations between two long-standing neighbours in the English village of Wanet; by basing his analysis largely on interactions between the farmer Doris Harvey and the builder Sid Askrig, he seeks to construct an analysis of the diversity of interpretation and the ambiguity of interaction in a socio-cultural milieu in general. Doris and Sid are found partaking in interaction which is regular and routine and which both regard as appropriate and legitimate. They share, that is, notions of conversational propriety: of turn-taking, of politeness, of the use of space, and so on. Hence, their interaction can be described as a flowing sequence of mutual interpretings and part of a habitual talking-relationship which they maintain between themselves. At the same time, however, the 'contours of reality' (Berger and Luckmann 1966) which their interaction maintains and develops are seen to be far from shared or even compatible; Doris and Sid write themselves into often very different worlds. For, they use the conventional devices of expression in different ways. The behaviours they share and exchange prove ambiguous enough for each to impart to them their own meanings, and for each to house them in very different cognitive contexts or world-views.

More generally, the forms of behaviour in common use in Wanet village and beyond could be said to amount to polythetic categories rather than anything singular or common-denominational. While there are many forms of behaviour which people routinely employ in the locale – even regard as special to them in the locale – there are no standard definitions of what these forms mean. Rather, usage is individual, and connected to and expressed within particular relationships. A juxtaposition of these usages reveals a wide range of interpretations with possibly nothing in common other than their formal designation. In short, the forms which many would agree upon as common and proper to Wanet come to be mediated in use by a diversity of individual ends, and are the means for achieving satisfaction of a variety of kinds and amounts. Interaction in Wanet appears as both a uniformitizing phenomenon and a primary process in the development of individuality.

Aggregations of perspectives

Routine interaction should not be confused with common under-standings or a coming-together of individuals on anything but a superficial level. Interaction represents an aggregation of individuals who meet, initially at least, on the surface of their selves. In this dialectic between commonality and diversity, Simmel's notion of form versus meaning, or content, as a mutually constituent, co-present dualism of socio-cultural life is a significant conceptualization. Society and culture come to be seen as phenomena wherein, to paraphrase Simmel (1971: 24), the vitality of individual meanings attains the reality of common forms. The forms alone do not constitute society, do not determine social order, and severed from content they do not gain meaningful existence. But they do facilitate the imposition of individual world-views. Hence a society or culture can be conceived of as an aggregation of perspectives, possibly highly diverse, expressed and maintained in certain limited and common forms. In complex socio-cultural milieux, these forms can be expected to have a particular distribution, some common to certain individuals, relationships, families, neighbourhoods, occupations, statuses, more than others (cf. Bakhtin 1981: 293). But over and above what Bakhtin has called the 'heteroglossia' of formal usage, the way in which these forms are individually employed is the same; through their employ, people can be seen to be members of communities and living in individual worlds at one and the same time. Indeed, the two states may be inextricably related; people are able to manifest and develop their idiosyncrasies *because* they engage in habitual social interactions, and interactions exist in commonality *because* of continuing individual idiosyncrasies.

In any understanding of the systemics of socio-cultural interaction it is this highly complex relationship which must be grasped. To talk about the behavioural forms alone, abstracted from individual usage and context, is to produce something reified and sterile, to assign the forms a misleading metaphysic and reality. The necessary focus is instead on specific interactions where individuals regularly meet and interpret these forms – however manifold and intricate the analysis becomes, and however attractive a hypostatization of forms seems. Equally, to integrate these forms into a tight and objectified socio-cultural pattern is to decontextualize the realities of separate situations so as possibly to misrepresent them all. The more vital image is of the complicated and fragmentary: of a socio-cultural fund of forms amounting to a shifting collage of behaviours whose pattern no two members may configure quite alike (cf. Sapir 1956: 200–3).

Instead of describing society or culture as mechanisms of encompassment and control, they may be more properly seen as means by which a host of individual world-views come to be expressed and realized. For through the exchange of common cultural forms we can say that members of a society are able to build one another into characters in a multiplicity of different worlds, and influence one another in all manner of indirect, incidental, contingent, contradictory and changeable ways. And a culture comes to be represented not as an entity with a positable, objective significance but as the forms in which subjective worlds develop, interact and are fulfilled and maintained: forms which derive their quickness from individual creativity. It is with individuals' purposes and their reasons for coming together in interaction that the key to any understanding of the socio-cultural lies.

See also: **Code, Discourse, Form and Content, Network**

INTERPRETATION

In Nietzsche's phrasing, human socio-cultural worlds are like art-works, something which can be interpreted – read, written – equally well in innumerable, vastly different and deeply incompatible ways: something with 'no meaning behind [them], but countless meanings' (1968: no. 481). Indeed, like an art-work, a world requires interpretation in order to be understood, made livable, mastered, by its inhabitants. These inhabitants may themselves be part of the world, may be making interpretations from situated, interested and partisan perspectives, but nonetheless, it is they who create their world, create themselves and their perspectives, through their interpretations. In this way, human social worlds are worlds of human making, dependent upon human activity and symbolic practice for their existence. Human beings compose the world as they interpret it; and their compositions add to the complexity, multifariousness and indeterminacy of the art-work that then continues to be interpreted – by others, by themselves – in the future.

The form human interpretations take, Nietzsche continues, are various. The books of the philosopher, certainly, but also the various habitual practices and modes of life of others. Amidst the profusion of versions and forms there is only one singularity: the continuation of profusion. Interpretations continue to be made because to interpret is to be human; while to make individual interpretations, self-caused and free, and to have these develop and change as one moves through life changing one's perspectives, is to be an individual human being – likewise self-caused and free.

Nietzsche and anthropology

Nietzschean interpretation has been a major inspiration behind twentieth-century Existentialism, not to mention post-modernism (Nietzsche: 'there is no immaculate perception'; 'there are no facts, only interpretations'; 'truth is a mobile army of metaphors'), and also the philosophy of consciousness (Henri Foçillon: 'The chief characteristic of the mind is to be constantly describing itself' (cited in Edelman 1992: 124)); and anthropology did not miss out either. Indeed, Shweder goes so far as to say that the credo of modern anthropology – that society and morality derive from the projection of mental representations onto the universe and their imposition as symbolic forms; that socio-cultural reality is not other than the stories told about it, the narratives in which it is represented – derives from Nietzsche (Shweder 1991b: 39; also cf. Thornton 1991, 1992).

The most celebrated Nietzscheanesque title in anthropology is, perhaps, Clifford Geertz's *The Interpretation of Cultures* (1973). Geertz is also content to borrow a Nietzschean tag – *froehliche Wissenschaft* ('joyous wisdom') – to describe anthropology as a discipline (1986: 105). As he elaborates, if human beings make their worlds by making meaningful interpretations of them, then 'our [anthropological] constructions of other people's constructions of what they and their compatriots are up to' amount to a form of knowledge more akin to that of the literary critic than the cipher clerk (Geertz 1973: 9). Anthropological wisdom claims attention not on the basis of capturing exotic facts but of reducing puzzlement: bringing readers in touch with the lives of strangers in other cultures as these people involve themselves in seeking to reduce the puzzlement of their own lives (1973: 16).

However, belying its seemingly Nietzschean and Existentialist form, 'cultural interpretation' comes to have rather a different understanding for Geertz. For, 'culture' Geertz wishes to be seen as 'an acted symbolic document' wherein individuals interpret only courtesy of systems of significant symbols in a particular cultural context. Hence, while Geertz admits that 'becoming human is becoming individual', he posits that we become individual in the context of 'cultural patterns': under the guidance of the historically created systems of meaning 'in terms of which we give form, order, point and direction to our lives' (1973: 52). Thought thus represents an 'intentional manipulation of cultural forms', of systems of symbols of collective possession, public authority and social exchange. The symbolic logic and the formal conceptual structuring may not be explicit, but they are socially established, sustained and legitimized.

They are, moreover, 'out in the world' (1983: 151); tied to concrete social events and occasions, thought processes are publicly enacted and expressive of common social worlds. Giving meaning to behaviour is not something which happens in private, in short, in insular individual heads, but rather something dependent on an exchange of common symbols whose 'natural habitat is the house yard, the market place, and the town square' (1973: 45). Hence, outdoor activities such as ploughing or peddling are as good examples of 'individual thought' as are closet experiences such as wishing or regretting, while cognition, imagination, emotion, motivation, perception, memory and so on, are directly social affairs.

In Geertz's adumbrating of 'an outdoor psychology' (1983: 151), then, culture (as systems of historically transmitted symbols) is constitutive of mind, while individual experience and memory of the social world are both powerfully structured by deeply internalized cultural conceptions and supported by cultural institutions. Social life entails a public traffic in significant cultural symbols; individual consciousness comes about via the co-embodying of a world under the auspices of a common system of symbols: 'I think' via 'we name' (cf. Percy 1958: 640). Thus, while flagging Suzanne Langer's phrase that 'we live in a web of ideas, a fabric of our own making' (1964: 126), and seeming to adopt a Nietzschean (interpretivist–perspectivist) stance, Geertz concludes that the webs of significance we weave, the meanings we live by, achieve a form and actualization only in a public and communal way. There can be no private (individual, unique) symbolizations for mind is transactional: formed and realized only through participation in cultures' symbolic systems of interpretation; while different 'individual' minds within the culture are in fact neither opaque nor impenetrable to one another, for they think in terms of the same shared beliefs and values, and operate the same interpretive procedures for adjudicating reality. To construe a system of cultural symbols, in sum, is also to accrue its individual members' subjectivities (cf. Frake 1964).

Anti-Geertzian interpretation

An 'outdoor psychology' which is 'out in the world' – for all its apparent expansiveness and openness – turns out to be rather a confining metaphorization. It appears to deny any inner, private life and language which is not readily accessible to others who employ (are employed by) the same cultural system of formal symbolic signification. At one and the same time, Geertz appears to champion a humanistic appreciation of the human condition and the anthropological project: 'man is an animal suspended in webs of significance he himself has spun', whose analysis is 'not an experimental science in search of law but an interpretive one in search of meaning' (Geertz 1973: 5); but then he seems to fall foul of a most restrictive determinism: 'culture is best seen as . . . a set of control mechanisms – plans, recipes, rules, instructions (what computer engineers call "programs") – for the governing of behavior', and it is the 'agency' of these mechanisms which is responsible for reducing the breadth and indeterminateness of the individual's inherent capacity to live thousands of lives to the specificity and narrowness of his actual accomplishment in living one life (Geertz 1973: 44–5).

In short, the interpreting – imagining, constructing, writing – which Geertz foresees is intra-paradigmatic: contained within a certain encompassing, collective, public and shared cultural context. Initially, he appears to follow Langer's lead when she explains that 'at the center of human experience, then, there is always the activity of imagining reality, conceiving the structure of it through words, images, or other symbols' (1964: 128). But for Langer, this places the imagination at the source of all human insight, reason, dream, religion and general observation: the greatest force acting on our feelings, and bigger than the stimuli surrounding us. Not only, therefore, does imagination make our human worlds, framing, supporting and guiding our thinking, it also 'gives each of us a separate world, and a separate consciousness' (1964: 103). For Geertz, however, little leeway is left between the cultural patternings 'of' and 'for' social practice. Ultimately, Geertz would appear to sign up to a Saussurean–Durkheimian thesis wherein the varieties of individual interpretive *paroles* simply depend and derive from an enabling collective *langue*. Particular interpretive–linguistic performances are here prefigured by a structure of rules and possible relations, by a set of *representations collectives*, so that individual expressions within a socio-cultural milieu add up, at any one time, to a total and autonomous synchronic system of related parts, and so that individual consciousness is a manifestation, temporary, episodic and epiphenomenal, of a *conscience collective*.

Post-Geertzian interpretation

Geertz's part in the refocusing of anthropological interest from the measuring of social structure to the interpretation of meaning, and in the re-reckoning of the anthropological enterprise as 'fictional writing', has been found liberating and inspiring (cf. Myerhoff 1974, 1978; Cohen 1987; Rapport 1994a). Ultimately, however, and despite his Nietzschean (and Weberian) borrowings, Geertz can sound conventionally Durkheimian (and structuralist). For, like other well-known exponents of a symbolic anthropology which came to focus centrally on the meanings with which human beings invested their worlds (e.g. Schneider 1968; Sahlins 1976), he saw these meanings as amounting to a collectively held, coherent and singular system; this might be abstracted from individual sayings and doings as if it were *sui generis* and autonomous.

But this is unsubtle. Such an abstraction belies the actual, everyday work of interpretation which anthropologists witness in their individual informants – its complexity and agency – and the radical diversities that issue forth (cf. Keesing 1987a). If systems of symbols are 'vehicles for conceptions', as Geertz puts it, then the systems of meaning which they give onto will necessarily be individual and highly diverse (cf. Cohen 1985). More precisely, a system of symbols in common usage is possessed of an inherent duality: a common surface and a private base, in Steiner's phrasing (1975: 173). Beneath the publicly consensual symbols which label social life, there lies the individual consciousness which is responsible for animating those cultural symbols with meaning. Here are pan-human potentialities, capacities and processes, which begin at birth (if not before) and continue throughout life, by whose works 'the world' (cultural categories, images, stories and language; people, interactions, social selves and things) becomes endowed, invested, infused, with personal emotion, fantasy and affect. It is these psychological processes of sense-making, of interpretation, which are finally responsible for shaping and constituting human life and society, for creating and recreating culture as a meaningful phenomenon in the life of each individual; thus are systems of symbols ever made subjectively, personally, individually meaningful. As Chodorow states (1994: 4):

> People personally animate and tint, emotionally and through fantasy, the cultural, linguistic, interpersonal, cognitive and embodied worlds we experience, creating and interpreting the external world in ways that resonate with their internal world, preoccupations, fantasies and sense of self and other.

Rather than according the interpretation of symbolic realities a primarily collective and cultural ontology *à la* Geertz (*et al.*), then, and rather than conceiving of individuals being inscribed into pre-given cultural texts, a notion of 'the interpretation of cultures' might be seen to give onto individual world-views. For, in using the various symbol systems which a culture places at their disposal as tools of their writing, individuals personalize them – and hence make of the symbol-systems something 'of and for' themselves. Individuals consume cultural symbolic forms in the construction of their own systems of meaning, and in terms of their unique biographies and personal histories of intrapsychic strategies and practices. The contexts in which individuals fashion, speak and live their world-views may be seen to be ontologically internal to themselves (cf. Rapport 1995).

For Nietzsche, for individuals to 'find their own words' in the language of the community was an 'aesthetic' experience; it was a way of coming to terms with the intrinsic nature of the human condition (as meaningless and absurd beyond acts of interpretation and outwith the aesthetic appreciation of beauty), and also a source of dignity. It represented both an individual's particular responsibility to her- or himself and the foundation of a general human power. For, to interpret was to become who we were; and to change how we interpreted was to change who we were: to reconstitute our worlds and ourselves. Human history was the history of successive metaphors, Nietzsche suggested, and the important dividing line was not between falsehood and truth but between old and new interpretations of 'falsehood' and 'truth'.

There was nothing more powerful or important than ongoing interpretations, in sum, because these acts demonstrated that the notion of a single 'true' world was a fable; all human life was a construct of the particular individual employment of symbolic systems.

See also: **Classification, Consciousness, Discourse, Thick Description, World-View**

IRONY

Besides its literary meaning, of certain figures of speech (antiphrasis, litotes, meiosis) where there is an inconsistency or contradiction between what is said and what is meant or apparent, irony can be understood to represent a certain cognitive detachment from the world as is or seems, and an imagining of its infinite possible otherness. Nietzsche famously referred to this ironic imagining as a 'revaluation of all values', and he counselled its ongoing practice as the means of humankind's continuous 'coming-to-itself'.

Understandings of irony

Irony may be defined (ironically) as: 'never having to say you really mean it' (Austin-Smith: 1990: 51–2), or never accepting that words mean only what they appear to say. Treated more broadly, irony means being at home 'in a world without guarantees' – without an Archimedean point of reference or transcendental truth – and prepared to explore 'the tense truth of ambiguity' (Chambers 1994a: 98). Its definition may be said to include an ontological premise that human beings are never cognitively imprisoned by pre-ordained and pre-determining schemata of cultural classification and social structuration. They can everywhere appreciate the malleability and the mutability of social rules and realities, and the contingency and ambiguity of cultural truths. Hence, people always practise a certain detachment from the world-as-is for the purpose of considering alternatives. In unmasking the world as an ambiguous fiction, irony plays with the possibility of limitless alterity. Here is an ability and a practice, enduring and ubiquitous, by which people loose themselves from the security of what is or appears to be, and creatively explore what might be. Here is a process by which human beings render even the most cherished of their values, beliefs and desires open to question, parody and replacement. However momentary the impulse, irony represents an endemic reaction against 'final vocabularies' (Rorty 1992: 88), a celebration of the fictive nature of all such human inheritances and the imaging of other worlds.

Such a broad understanding is controversial, and arguments have certainly been made for the ironical stance or attitude's being historically and culturally specific. Ortega y Gasset (1956), for instance, suggests that the ability to become detached from the immediacy of the world and treat it ironically is a manifestation of the technological revolution in human civilization. Entering an intense, inner world in which ideas are formed which are then returned to the world as a blueprint for its re-construction represents a concentration which humankind has created for itself painfully and slowly. The growth of irony has followed a growth in science, and the freedom not to be obliged inexorably to concern oneself with reacting to things as they are but temporarily to ignore the latter in favour of a created self and a plan of action. In short, irony as that detachment by which the world becomes anthropomorphized, a reflection and realization of human ideas, is a technological by-product.

Oppenheimer (1989), meanwhile, attaches an ironic consciousness to certain literary forms. Irony was present in Socratic dialogue, then, and also in the poetics of Classical Rome but thereafter, through some seven centuries of the Dark Ages, it disappeared. Only with the rise of the sonnet in a twelfth-century Rome was there an ironic renaissance. The sonnet might be described, therefore, as the lyric of 'personality' and the 'private soul' for with its invention came a new way for people to think as and about themselves. Irony, in short, is a matter of that introspection and self-consciousness which the possible silent reading of the sonnet literary form made fashionable, conventional, esteemed, and hence possible.

Giddens (1990), however, makes an argument that only modernity – that recent sociological condition characterized by capitalism, industrialism, cosmopolitanism and the massification of complex society – is characterized by an ironic detachment. Indeed, the presumption of this reflexivity (including our sociological reflection upon our reflexivity) is an intrinsic part of modern social practice. We constantly examine and reform our practices in the light of incoming information about those practices, which thus alters the character and constitution of the practices we next examine. In short, irony is part-and-parcel of the process of structuration by which modernity reproduces itself and knows itself.

Finally, Appadurai (1991a) sees irony as part of the 'cultural economy' of contemporary globalization. The deterritorialization of ideas, images and opportunities brought about by mass communication enables people to lead complex lives more of projection and imagination than enactment or prediction. The balance between *habitus* and improvisation (Bourdieu 1977) shifts, such that fantasy becomes a social practice in even the meanest, poorest and harshest of lives, and conventional cultural reproduction succeeds only by conscious design and political will. People no longer view their existence as a mere outcome of the givenness of things, in short, but as an 'ironic compromise between what they [can] imagine and what social life will permit' (Appadurai 1991a: 199).

Notwithstanding the above, it can convincingly be argued that the cognitive displacement and detachment of irony is a universal human trait, capacity and cognitive resort. As John Berger sums up the case (1994): '[T]he human condition actually is more or less a constant: always in face of the same mysteries, the same dilemmas, the same temptation to despair, and always armed unexpectedly with the same energy.' Or, in more strictly anthropological vein: '[T]here were never any innocent, unconscious savages, living in a time of unreflective and instinctive harmony. We human beings are all and always sophisticated, conscious, capable of laughter at our own institutions' (Victor Turner, in Ashley 1990: xix). Always and everywhere one finds 'individuals engaged in the creative exploration of culture' (Goody 1977: 20), intellectually distancing themselves from the existing conceptual universe and looking at it askance. Any notion of a binary divide between those (intellectual individuals, times and places) with irony and those without, Goody concludes, is a nonsense (cf. Shweder 1991a: 14)..

An extended endorsement of this position is provided by Handler and Segal's (1990) anthropological examination of the writings of Jane Austen. Writing in and of a time and society (early-nineteenth-century England) where irony might seem a far cry from a stable, unambiguous, axiomatic and largely conventional way of life, Austen shows no ironic 'reticence'. Readily ironizing any claims of a homogeneous, integrated or bounded socio-cultural system to give onto a singular or unitary truth, she offers her readers an appreciation of the normative, the institutional and the principled in culture (here, the implicit cultural principles of genteel English society of marriage, courtship, rank and gender) as symbolic forms always subject to, and needful of, creative interpretation, and always affording independent manipulation and individual re-rendering. Handler and Segal call this 'alter-cultural action'. Clearly, for Austen, the schemata of cultural classification and social structuration, being arbitrary, and being recognized to be arbitrary, should be seen less to regulate conduct or ensure the unconscious reproduction of an established order than to give communicative resource, significance and value to what Handler and Segal dub her characters' 'serious social play'. Rather than norms which are taken literally, conventional etiquette and propriety become matters for meta-communicative comment and analysis; and hence come to be displaced in the process of individual constructions of situational socio-cultural order.

The writings of Jane Austen, Handler and Segal conclude, are a celebration of the 'fiction of culture', and of individuals' creative potential for alter-cultural world-making: of an enduring human disposition to render all socio-cultural norms ultimately contingent. Moreover, what is true for Austen's language can be argued as true for language as such: it is 'of its very nature, an ironic mode' (Martin 1983: 415), imbued with the multiple ironies of there being no certain or necessary accordance between the meanings of different individuals, or between those and the way the world is. Hence, what is true for Austen's age is true for all times.

Hutcheon notes (1994: 9) that the historical claim to be an 'age of irony' is a repeated one, but perhaps equally or more true is its denial;

for the socio-cultural milieux in which the cognitive freedom (scepticism, creativity, idiosyncrasy) which irony flags is welcomed (the will and the practice to complexify, multiply and call into question socio-cultural realities) are at least balanced by a blinkered absolutism or fundamentalism in which the substance of inherited verities alone is validated. But whether it is celebrated or negated on the level of public convention, irony exists as a cognitive proclivity and practice, embodying a certain imaginative movement from the world(s) as is, a certain reflection upon the latter and differentiation from it.

Non-ironic displacements

Not all such cognitive movement, reflection and differentiation need be identified as ironic as such, however. Irony amounts to cognitive movement as an endemic mode of being; it is a continuous process to treat the world ironically because every truth reached is recognized to be contingent and perspectival, and bound to be left behind in a progression of meaning which is without limit. Irony thus represents something of a royal road to recognizing infinite regress and contingency: a necessarily limitless revaluation of values. Certain other cognitions partake of part of this movement, then, but not its habituation. It might, however, be worth briefly referring to these so as further to isolate the ironic mode.

Conversion can be said to entail a cognitive shift or move such that one looks back at a position from which one has now become displaced – from which one has displaced oneself – due to an original sense of 'meaning-deficit' in one's life and a need for revitalization (Fernandez 1995: 22). This accords with the philosopher Kierkegaard's understanding of religiosity *per se*. As he explains, religious identity derives from believing something which is deeply offensive to reasoning, for it is the very difficulty of belief which provides its reward: the believer feels alive and singularly inspired in ways which believing something currently plausible could not achieve. The essence of religious belief, for Kierkegaard, is not being persuaded by the truth of a doctrine, but becoming committed to a position which is inherently absurd, which 'gives offence' to those criteria of truth which existed prior to the conversion.

This also applies to Gellner's understanding of cultural or ethnic belonging. As he succinctly puts it, a culture is a collectivity united in a belief: '[m]ore particularly, a collectivity united in a false belief is a culture' (1995b: 6). Truths, after all, are universal and available to all; but errors are culture-specific and define a continuity of faith and its believers. Hence, non-facts, the currently unproven or unprovable, tend to become badges of community and of loyalty. 'Assent to an absurdity identifies an intellectual *rite de passage*, a gateway to the community defined by that commitment to that conviction' (Gellner 1995b: 6).

Then again, this applies to various theorists who see consciousness – the coming to a consciousness of oneself – as something akin to a conversion experience. These theories have a Freudian tinge ('self-consciousness begins in frustration') inasmuch as they posit selfhood as deriving from a certain point in the maturation process when the individual achieves satisfaction only by repressing what he or she knows to be true. For Brodsky, then, the origin of consciousness is to be found in childhood lying (cited in Bruner and Weisser 1991: 132). Giving a deliberately false self-report, distancing himself from what he knows presently to be the truth, the child first appreciates his power to change the world and become himself as the source of its perceptions. Being oneself is, to an extent, then living one's lies. From Ortega y Gasset (1956) we hear something similar: 'Man is a sort of novelist of himself who conceives the fanciful figure of a personage with its unreal occupations'. The life of the self is then taken up with converting these fictions or lies into a believed-in reality.

As mentioned, the above conversions of identity – religious, cultural and individual – are seen to entail certain cognitive movements and displacements, certain distantiations from what is, but they do not amount to displacement as an ongoing cognitive resort, as a conscious way of being. They do not compass being as an endemic becoming. And yet this seems to be essential to irony; it is a living with displacement, a living in cognitive movement, and a refusing to take any value as final or absolute, as free from revaluation, except the value of revaluation *per se*.

Holding an ironic attitude towards one's current final vocabulary, Nietzsche argued, was tantamount to appreciating how the world was as full of final vocabularies as it was of other people. Choices could and should be made between these, as well as there being a recognition of the choice to compose a new vocabulary for oneself *ab initio*. This 'ironic' recognition was a resource which took an individual beyond any one final vocabulary, and indeed, beyond language as such.

From Nietzsche's prescriptions can be disinterred an anthropological appreciation of the human capacity to transcend present ontologies and epistemologies, present appearances, and insist on the reality of an individual's own being and becoming. Irony is part-and-parcel of this individual force which 'insists on itself' and proceeds continually to create and to live its own truth.

See also: **Consciousness, Interpretation, Movement, World-View**

KINSHIP

Studies in kinship, and the related institutions of marriage and the family, have until recently been central to anthropological investigation and debate. As Ladislav Holy remarks (1996: 1), 'if there was a subject which anthropologists could have rightly claimed to be their own, it was kinship', and thus the problem of handling the topic of kinship cross-culturally is the key to understanding the historical development of a large majority of anthropology's central analytic concepts, theories and methods. Deliberations over the puzzles of kinship and marriage gave rise to the discipline's most sophisticated technical and theoretical elaborations, and also its most virulent, ever-present controversies. It was also assumed to be the area of technical expertise, the most demanding of rigour of thought, through which anthropology could best defend its scientific respectability. The issue of kinship became therefore the topic through which the most able minds in the history of anthropology could display their erudition. As a result, kinship was that aspect of social life that became the linchpin for the unfolding of all the grand paradigms of thought within anthropology, whether it be Morgan's narrative of evolutionism (1871) or Malinowski's of functionalism (1930), Radcliffe-Brown's of structural-functionalism (1962 [1952]), Lévi-Strauss's of structuralism (1969a [1949]), or Meillassoux's of structural-Marxism (1981). As Robin Fox could comment in 1967 (1967: 10), 'kinship is to anthropology what logic is to philosophy or the nude is to art; it is the basic discipline of the subject'. The situation, however, has changed.

Today, anthropologists demonstrate such a decided *lack* of interest in the topic of kinship that it is tempting to declare it no longer to be a key concept. In 1984, David Schneider advised anthropologists to stop looking for 'kinship' which he claimed was but a vacuous and confused domain when applied cross-culturally. As he argues, there has been a drastic problem in the ways in which anthropology has treated the topic that takes us well beyond anthropology to the emergence and growth of the human sciences themselves, and to the modernist project through which they developed. Because kinship studies were the heartbeat of the discipline of anthropology, it is no wonder that 'kinship' can be dismantled as the emperor with no clothes, or rather the emperor fully clothed in grand-narrative imaginary dress. All the perils of the modernist stories through which anthropology developed as a field of study are highlighted in those passionate debates about the substance of 'kinship'. To now ask why kinship was once so predominantly prioritized will take us then to problems in the major presuppositions underlying anthropology's highly valued analytic constructs of kinship and society. The legitimacy of the topic came under scrutiny in the 1960s in a process that has since accelerated due to very basic epistemic shifts within anthropology in the wake of feminism and other modes of disciplinary self-inspection about its claims to knowledge. One prevalent conclusion forthcoming from such shifts is that much of received kinship theory is no longer seen as justifiable. The reasons are many.

The narrative of kinship: or law and order by another name

The primary puzzle for the anthropologist throughout the first half of the twentieth century was how to explain the maintenance of order within the 'simple societies' of far-flung regions where anthropologists conducted their research. Such societies lacked the basic law-and-order organizing institutions of Western society. They had no government to speak of, no law courts, police or armies, and not even the market place as we know it. It was clear that they did not compartmentalize their social life into the distinct and separate institutions that we recognize as kinship, economics, politics and religion. Anthropologists found instead that these peoples used the *idiom of kinship* to frame most of their activities, including those with political, economic and religious intent. Analytically, the step from this insight was to view kinship to be *the* major institution of 'tribal' societies, and the kinship tie to be the one that compelled all others in social relations. Kinship, as the strongest of social bonds, became seen as the basis through which 'primitive' societies *maintained order*; it was through kinship ties that people created relations of social solidarity. Thus '*social structure*', that is, those rules regulating the kinship, marriage and residential institutions of a people that endow social role and identity, and which therefore perpetuate societal relationships, became anthropology's proper object of inquiry (e.g. see Radcliffe-Brown 1965: 191). Everything else, a society's morals, law, etiquette, religion, politics and education, was to be studied as but an aspect of social structure (*ibid.*: 195), or in other words its kinship system.

The emphasis anthropologists placed upon the problem of 'societal order' cannot be stressed too much. As Firth comments, the perception of *order* was fundamental to their inquiry (Firth 1951: 19). An underlying concern was over what could replace the authority of government in 'simple' societies, and the answer was to view kinship as having this coercive power. This was seen to be the case because the kinship system became *defined* as the primary source for the rules and regulations providing for order and continuity of the 'native' society. Through such circular reasoning it was presumed that the status, role, rights, duties and obligations of a person in a 'simple' society were seen to be forthcoming from and ascribed by the person's place within the kinship system. The primary societal organization of these societies was then understood to be '*kinship-based*', and it was the 'kinship polity' (see Fortes 1969) forthcoming from either patrilineality or matrilineality that was the key concern. The slippage was simple: we have government, while they have the politics of kinship.

The evolutionist agenda underpinning such kinship theory is obvious, despite the functionalists' claim to the contrary. It was a bias that assumed that the history of humankind's social development discloses a progression that moved from a reliance upon the natural facts of kinship, and the cultural elaboration of them, to a Western style of development that increasingly compartmentalizes the societal institutional ordering of kinship, economics, politics and religion in such a way that kinship eventually becomes *de*prioritized. Anthropology's main object for study has been the modern West's alien other, all those 'primitive' peoples attached to worlds marked as an uncivilized part of nature to be transcended and dominated by modern civilization. In large part anthropology's technical vocabulary has denoted primitivism, and 'kinship' is no exception. First of all, the institution of kinship, more than any of the other primary domains of society, was understood to be the one most closely linked to the natural in human activities: while kinship can modify nature, it cannot transcend it. As Schneider argues (1984: 188), an axiom critical to kinship theory has been that the social and cultural attributes of kinship are *derivative* of the biological relations of reproduction. Thus if all those alien societies studied by anthropologists were *kinship*-based, and if for their people the idiom of kinship took priority over economics, politics and religion, their primitive status was further confirmed. The other reason so many anthropologists emphasized the underlying natural element of kinship is that this, of course, is the way we think about our own kinship relationships (where 'blood is thicker than water'). For us, kinship has been neatly shifted out of society proper into the domain of the domestic where it can be tidily contained and isolated from the true business of civil society where all roots of humans in the natural process can be transcended.

The plot thickens: the distinction between the domestic and the jural

The 'law and order' thrust of traditional kinship studies, which equated the kinship system (of 'primitives') to 'society' itself, also came to include the critical distinction between the 'domestic' and 'jural' domains of kinship. It was this separation of domains within kinship that imposed on 'native' peoples a similar demoted status for familial ties as found in the West, that is, the domestic being defined as that area of life that is to a large extent enacted beyond the ken of the important work of society (see Sahlins 1972). The realm of the domestic comprised relations of filiation between parents and children; it was the domain of the hearth, the family, the husband and his wife and children. In Fortes's terms (1969), it was the domain where the 'axiom of amity' reigned. In contrast, within the 'jural' domain the everyday relations of amity and filiation were for the most part irrelevant, for the principles of descent and lineage ruled its membership and provided the backbone for its jural structures of dominance and subordination. It was the jural domain that comprised the polity and thus provided society with its order and continuity. The prescriptions and regulations of the kinship polity (comprising its 'corporate descent groups') were what ruled and constrained 'primitive' people. A man's status, rights and obligations within society were in essence provided by his place within the lineage of his birth. Genealogy determined one's political status, and one's rights to land and other entitlements.

Given the above narrative of the place of kinship in 'native' societies, we can understand that the received wisdom of kinship theory until the 1970s was that unilineal descent systems were necessary as a sticking plaster of 'primitive' societal order – despite increasing evidence to the contrary. As Radcliffe-Brown asserts (1965: 48), 'unilineal institutions in some form, are almost, if not entirely, a necessity in any ordered social system'. Even Lévi-Strauss, in his major *critique* of descent theory in kinship studies, finds the existence of unilineal descent essential to the logic of his model of elementary structures of marriage exchange. He says that this is because the *social cohesion* of elementary systems of kinship that are premised on the notion of groups of men exchanging wives *require* a rule of descent, for the groups themselves must be *defined* by such a 'stable' rule of descent (Lévi-Strauss 1969a: 105). One should be aware, however, that Lévi-Strauss began his formidable attack upon the prevalent 'descent as societal order' view of primitive society in 1949 (Lévi-Strauss 1969a), and that his stress upon alliance (relationships through marriage) over descent as the *salient* ordering principle of 'primitive society' did not become part of mainstream debate until the 1960s (e.g. Leach 1961a; Needham 1964), but also see the earlier debate between Radcliffe-Brown (1953) and Dumont (1953) on the meaning of classificatory kinship terms. The concern of Lévi-Strauss, it is to be noted, was with creating a *minimal* model of *society* by showing the ways in which kinship (descent) groups were integrated through rules of marriage exchange, that is, he wished to demonstrate how classifications of kinship and marriage logically provided a broader level of *societal integration* than that achieved through rules of descent alone.

The chauvinistic reductionism of the structural-functionalist and structuralist grand paradigms of society and societal ordering, where the agency of women was ignored and society itself equated with male structures of domination and subordination – to be ordered through either descent or alliance - took another couple of generations to unveil and unravel.

The question of definitional rigour

A fuller ethnographic record in itself began steadily to undermine many of these major analytic constructs of kinship and societal order, particularly the idea that 'primitive society' was universally based upon exogamous, corporate, land-holding unilineal descent group structures. By the 1950s and 1960s reports of field research, especially from the Pacific, on kinship systems that were *not* premised on a unitary rule of unilineal descent became legion. It became clear that often people also followed instead cognatic, bilineal, ambilineal or double-descent principles in the ordering of various aspects of their social life (cf. Bohannan and Middleton 1968). The debate over the unitary view of unilineal descent was basically closed by the influential article by Scheffler (1966) who was able to demonstrate through ethnography by then at hand that notions of descent were used among different peoples, and even by the same people, toward highly varied ends, and not necessarily toward that of corporate group structure.

By the 1970s, for instance through the ethnography from Amazonia that began to enter mainstream debates on kinship and marriage, it became clear that the notion of descent itself could hardly be declared a universal principle of 'primitive' social ordering, for there were peoples who did not recognize a principle of descent as relevant for any social or intellectual purpose (e.g. see Rivière 1969; Overing Kaplan 1975). Even kinship and marriage as analytical constructs *per se* came under attack, especially the notion of achieving any sort of unitary definition of either (a point most energetically argued yet earlier by Leach (1961a) in his hatcheting of these sacred constructs of societal ordering). We find Rodney Needham (1971: 5) flamboyantly announcing that 'there is no such thing as kinship, and it follows that there can be no such thing as kinship theory'! He was referring to 'minimal' definitions of kinship when framed in the context of genealogically reckoned *jural rights*, such as their allocation and transmission from one generation to the next. Cross-culturally, the ethnographic evidence could not uphold a *totalizing* view that assumed a predictable relationship between the cultural constructs of kinship and its classification, social roles, rights and obligations, and the allocation of individuals to particular types of social groups. It was this unitary package of kinship as part-and-parcel of particular politico-jural orders that earlier anthropology had indeed upheld.

Even more courageous for the times are Rivière's (1971) queries into the analytic concept of marriage. He argues against *any* jural definition of marriage, and suggests instead that the institution of marriage be first viewed structurally, as one of many relationships conceived possible between men and women. It was his reading of the ethnographic literature that anthropologists had been defining institutions cross-culturally as 'marriage' when said institutions in fact had 'no feature in common other than that they are concerned with the conceptual roles of male and female' (*ibid.*: 70). In other words, to understand what marriage *is* for any given people the question of the cultural construction of gender relationships must be understood, rather than the jural relations between groups of men that entail their exchange of women.

It is significant that Rivière's fieldwork experience had been with indigenous peoples of Amazonia, for whom anything approaching a 'jural' relationship would be stretching the point, as too would be lineages and descent-group ordering as normally discussed in the literature. It was as difficult to find corporate land-holding groups among Amazonian people, as the elders who might rule them. There were no *groups* of men forming ties of alliance through the exchange of their women. Instead, ties of marriage, which *were* highly salient to Amazonian constructs of sociality, were more likely to be linked to a principle of cognation than descent. As a consequence, the contributions of Amazonian specialists, more in line with Dumont's reading of marriage alliance in India, has played a major part in the later reinterpretation and unravelling of both alliance theory as first formulated by Lévi-Strauss and descent theory as proposed by Fortes and Radcliffe-Brown.

It is by now obvious that we cannot achieve an analytic definition of the construct of kinship that would be both universally adequate and at the same time respectful of indigenous understandings and knowledges. In short, anthropology cannot, even if it wished, arrive at a universal definition of kinship. Part of the dilemma is of course linguistic insofar as most of the important analytic terms of anthropology have not only been highly abstract but also continued to carry the complex historical baggage of Western thought and practice. Terms such as *society, community, family, kinship, descent, lineage,* or *structure, function, system* are to be used at the peril of totally eluding another people's understanding of what they are doing socially – which is *the very raison d'être* of the anthropological task.

The structural analysis of kinship terminologies: or, where are all the people?

As anthropology slowly came to realize, any 'definitional rigour' to be achieved through the use of any of the above analytic concepts of society is well nigh impossible. Such constructs tend to sit within particular and forceful paradigms of social order, and therefore carry all the litter of such grand narratives. Structural-functionalism was followed by structuralism, and the structural analysis of kinship terminologies was a particularly obvious case of a paradigm so mighty that its highly reductive results killed for the time being the possibility of interesting further advances being made in kinship theory, the very area where anthropology was once so creative and rich in debate.

The overwhelming attraction of the structural analyses of kinship can be ascribed to the power of their methods which wed anthropology to advances in modern linguistics, a field considered to have become the most scientific of the human sciences. The methods and models of formal analysis gave the promise of a mathematical rigour that would transform anthropology into a 'true science', having a definitional clarity never before achieved. Their initial success (e.g. see Lounsbury 1968) was so stupendous that they made seeming child's play of previous attempts to provide order to the complicated structures of many 'native' kinship terminologies. Anthropologists were taught to be more rigorous in discerning the logical differences between systems. Such sophistication in method was greatly needed in anthropology, and for its example we can only be grateful.

However, as Overing has argued (1987), the method became confused with world-view. The logic of the method through sleight of hand became equated to the logic of terminological *use*, and thus also with indigenous understanding. As a result we arrived once more at the 'universal', to what Schneider so aptly derides as the anthropological 'doctrine of the genealogical unity of mankind' (Schneider 1984: 122–4), or the genealogical meaning of kinship terms. Kinship is everywhere first and foremost *about* genealogical relatedness (see especially, Scheffler 1978), a resoundingly uninteresting conclusion to come in the wake of the dazzling structuralist performances. It also was a conclusion that was suspect. It appears that the method itself allowed for no other interpretation, because the meanings of terms were made to fit not only the scientific value upon logical rigour, but also Western common-sense notions about what kinship is.

The demand itself of formal analysis for logical rigour reduces the character of its elements that account for meaning to very few: affinity as well as consanguinity can be allowed, but not the complications of what such notions might possibly mean from the indigenous point of view. Many anthropologists came to the conclusion that if future study were to be dependent upon such rigorous intellectual exercise that in the end gave so little reward *and said so little about the people* then why go to the bother? It was the niggling doubt over this issue (Where are all the people?) that drove many anthropologists away from the technical chore of analysing kinship logics. As Alan Campbell remarks (1989), the very abstract level at which structuralist analysis operates is about the tenth remove from anything going on in daily practice and thought.

Is there hope for kinship through new key concepts?

While we can heartily agree with Schneider's (1984) full-blown rampage against the anthropological treatment of the topic of kinship, such concordance does not entail the dismissal of the study of those social relationships, and their classifications, that were once more or less subsumed under the label of 'kinship'. People do bear children, and there is a social framework through which they do so, and through which these children are raised to become adult members of human social groups. The members of these social groups follow particular practices in the course of which relationships that are highly significant for them are developed, as too are very interesting ways of thinking about them. With all this we can agree. The overriding question still remains – how do we understand and translate such practices, relationships and ways of thinking?

Happily, anthropologists over the past twenty years have developed a myriad of different ways to approach subjects that would formerly have been classified under the general rubric of 'kinship'. While nowadays the *topic* of 'kinship' does not loom large in the literature, such key concepts as 'self', 'agency', 'gender', 'the life of values and affect', do. The topics of 'personhood', 'emotions' and 'aesthetics' are much more likely to take their place in the titles of doctoral theses than those of 'kinship', 'affinity' and 'jural rules'. Thus we see that the 'technical' language of anthropology has been transformed in the wake of the shifts of attention away from something we once called the 'jural–political' domain, with its contrast to something we labelled as 'the domestic group', and equally away from the notions of social structure and prescriptive behaviour, and those of 'rights' and 'obligations'. In their place, the idioms of equality and inequality are now being explored, and such values as nurture, sharing, pooling, generosity, and those of peace and violence. The stress is upon ambiguity, flux, the personal everyday, and the multiplicity of voices, rather than upon grand structures of mind and society, and societal rules and regulations. The emphasis tends to be upon context and the performative, and not underlying and hidden rules of practice and thought. Such shifts in direction have often been undertaken in a spirit of rebellion, by feminists but also many others, against the ethnocentrisms (e.g. the muted woman) underpinning the grand narratives of anthropology. The gain has been that anthropologists are presenting very different pictures, certainly in their richness, from those of yesterday of the ways other people view, act and experience the world of the social. These depictions in themselves are further enlightening of the previous 'sins' of reduction and prejudice.

Kinship by another name? Networks of relationships and personal-kind terms

We find that Schneider and Needham, as pioneers in the deconstructing of key concepts of kinship theory, were merely tapping the surface of a modernist creation for which the very notion of kinship was but one aspect of a complicated multi-faceted edifice filled with assumptions about society and the social order. These in turn were tied to networks of ideas about the relation of the family to other societal institutions, and the relationship between the sexes, between the private and the public, between the dominant and the subordinate, all of which were implicated further by ontological assumptions about natural kinds, the nature of human existence, and its progress, which in addition were premised upon a notion of the priority of reason over the emotions. So it continued through an enormous number of other dualisms and bundles of relations pertinent to the Western imagery of society and the world, and the elements of which they were comprised. Our notion of kinship carried with it the interarticulations of this entire structure.

The interesting lesson that has been more recently learned through changing the types of questions anthropologists ask is that *other* people's views of the social relationships of everyday life are as enmeshed as our own within wider networks of meaning. They also include ontological presuppositions about the nature of human existence and capabilities for sociality that are linked to bundles of relationships and arrays of ideas about the world that are as complex, but usually very different from, our own. It is not only we who have thought about such complexities and who have therefore developed the social theory to think about them. But how do we understand these other sets of linkages, so unlike our own? That has become a primary question. How do we understand a Bororo who says his 'brother is a parrot' (Crocker 1977), or a Piaroa who insists that 'the tapir is our grandfather' (Overing 1985c)? The quest for understanding *their* interconnections requires first of all an unpeeling of our own presuppositions about reproductory and biological processes, parenting, the nature of the material world and the interconnections of all of these things to what we call society (cf. Strathern 1992b). Anthropologists had been inadvertently reducing other peoples' rich interconnections of meaning by treating them as 'kinship relationships', or better expressed as kinship in the way *we* know it – cultural constructions of biological reproduction and the relations between humans relevant to such reproduction – that is, as the least intellectually interesting element of our own prime units of society, the royal four of kinship, economics, politics and religion.

Overing has suggested (1985c) that to understand better the complexity of indigenous social thought, we should change the label of what we have been calling 'kinship terms' to '*personal-kind terms*'. This involves a radical switch in perspective that concomitantly raises the conceptual status of these terms to one more closely aligned to the indigenous view and practice. As with many of our scientific constructs of 'natural kinds', 'personal-kind terms' are also highly abstract, philosophically important concepts that defy unitary definition. They share the openendedness and elusiveness that is typical of all abstract terms that comprise complex relational properties. The difference is that personal-kind terms do not refer to the world of nature, which is the Western domain of competence, but to qualities of *personal* relationships, the area about which indigenous people have opted for theoretical elaboration (cf. Horton 1979). For instance, toward the end of achieving health, wealth and safety, Amazonian peoples aim to master, not nature, but as many as possible of their *personal* relationships with other beings, human or otherwise, in the world. We unfortunately have reduced their personal-kind ('kinship') terms to our own very weak language of kinship, one that speaks of 'consanguinity', 'affinity', 'social category', 'amity', which is often a bad mistake.

In discussing the highly flexible use of the personal-kind ('kinship') categories among Piaroa of the Orinoco Basin, Overing shows (1985c) that the meanings of these categories incorporate (what for us is) an alien world of explanation and abstract theory construction about the possibilities for difference and similarity in modes of power or agency in the cosmos. The terms, *as used in everyday life*, have metaphysical weight that goes well beyond our Western notions of 'biological' relationship or a social relation through marriage. Each term in its application carries with it possibilities of sharing or not sharing a bundle of social, moral, or metaphysical qualities, and there is no *a priori* guarantee which will be salient to a given case. The *quality* of the relationship, as for instance one of nurturing, teaching, treachery, competition or predation, often overrides a more physical sort of relating. Will this man or woman work tranquilly with me, or have predatory designs on me that will make me ill?

Certainly in Amazonian ethnography, the emphasis today in investigations of peoples' use of relationship terminologies is often upon the metaphysical and/or moral loading of the classifications (also cf. Teixero-Pinto 1997; Viveiros de Castro 1992; Belaunde 1992). For instance Stephen Kidd writes about Enxet of Paraguay that:

> Their understanding of why they act as they do centres on their concept of the *waxok*, an aspect of the self that is both intensely private and inherently social. They insist that their social behaviour – both appropriate and inappropriate – can be explained by the physical – or metaphysical – state of the *waxok*. Furthermore, because the *waxok* is also the centre of cognition, people can also consciously transform it so as to enable themselves to act in either a self-centred or other-regarding manner. It is an explanation that, I believe, we should take seriously if we want to understand indigenous social life and it is one that finds its root in the practice of child-raising, in the creation of 'good/beautiful' people who have been taught not only how to think but how to feel. It is this *waxok*-centred combination of thinking and feeling that enables the Enxet to act appropriately and which, ultimately, guides them as they strive to generate sociality and engender tranquillity.
>
> (Kidd 1999: Conclusion)

For Enxet, kinship is about attaining a certain sort of affective life. These are people for whom the personal ties of parenting, nurturing, sharing and pooling are not so much based on a notion of 'biological linkage' or a 'linkage through blood', or membership within a jural group, but which instead are generated over time through consistent and processual action. Enxet kinship is about not making those with whom you live angry; it is about being generous. As such the personal quality of a relationship as made manifest through *everyday practice* is paramount to its classification as kin or not kin, or as a particular type of kin link.

More generally, the ongoing quality of an Amazonian personal relationship (as in the 'growing' of a child by a parent and child, the mutual care of brothers, or sisters, or of any other personal relation) may have generative value *in a material sense* that goes far beyond the minimal possibilities that are endowed through the act of sex (e.g. see McCallum 1989; Gow 1991; Lagrou 1998; Overing 1999). Teaching, feeding, working together tranquilly, all are generative processes pertinent to their personal idiom of kinship. For sure, the personal-kind terms that are here being applied to their nearest and dearest, and to those further afield, *are* about reproductory possibilities, but it is not 'reproduction' in the sense that the anthropologist conceptualized it in traditional kinship theory. To understand *their* language of reproduction, the anthropologist needs to turn to an anthropology of the emotions through which affect, thought and moral value can be highlighted, and to wed the pragmatics with the metaphysics of using the personal idiom of kinship.

Kinship is alive and well

In fact we can say that the area of kinship is as alive and well as ever in anthropology, in that the personal relationships and activities of parenting and nurturing and the whole process of generating and gendering of bodies into social adulthood hold central attention. Such studies are, however, unrecognizable as pertaining to the kinship theory of yesteryear. A similar reorientation of concentration is as clear in Melanesian studies as in those of Amazonia (e.g. see Strathern 1988; Gillison 1993) where personal relationships are discussed through categories very different from the former ones of prescriptive rule, roles and statuses, and social structure. Here instead, as among Amazonianists, talk is upon the indigenous understandings of such matters as gender distinctions, the content of the self and its mastery of them, and the construction of social bodies. It is about indigenous ambiguities over the nature of personhood and the various possibilities of agency in this world and others, and the elaborate relation of these issues to indigenous practice and metaphysics. In other words, a dialogue is being created between us, the anthropologists, and them, the peoples of New Guinea or Amazonia, over what it means to be human in this world (cf. Storrie 1999). What does it mean to be *social* beings in this world? And how do we go about attaining this state? If for other people the Western grand distinctions between society and nature do not hold, what other possibilities of an interesting kind are there? These are very different questions than were being asked in mainstream anthropology a couple of decades ago.

See also: **Agent and Agency, Common Sense, Culture, Gender, Moments of Being, Qualitative and Quantitative Methodologies, Society, The Unhomely**

LIMINALITY

The concept of liminality, from the Latin word for 'threshold' (*limen*) and implying all manner of interstitiality, of being betwixt and between, is most associated with the work of Victor Turner, and his extending of the original ideas of Arnold van Gennep; it has also been put to profitable use by Max Gluckman, Mary Douglas and Edmund Leach, and given rise to a host of spin-off applications. Through liminality, anthropology has found it possible to focus conceptually upon such phenomena as marginality, alterity, rebellion, ostracism, subalternality, pollution, eccentricity and deviance.

Rites of passage

'The life of an individual in any society', van Gennep observed (1960: 3), 'is a series of passages from one age to another': from baby to infant to child to adolescent; from kindergarten to primary school to secondary school to university; from maiden to wife to widow; from warrior to elder to ancestor. In *Rites of Passage* (1960 [1909]), van Gennep examined and compared the way that these passages and stages were socio-culturally constructed, marked and effected, by the practising of certain ceremonial, public rites: rites which accompanied every change of place, state, social position and age. Indeed, such 'rites of passage' seemed to represent the majority of ritual or ceremonial occasions in any socio-cultural milieu. They at once proclaimed movement from one state or category of recognized existence to another and brought this about.

Furthermore, rites of passage seemed to partake of a common, tripartite structure, to share a grammar of three distinct phases, even though these were possibly differently emphasized on different kinds of occasion (a birth versus a death). There was a 'rite of separation' or disaggregation by which the old identity, status or frame of mind, was sloughed off, followed by a middle, mediatory or liminal stage of rites of transition, where the protagonist undergoing the change (the initiate or neophyte) was neither one thing nor another but betwixt-and-between, followed by a 'rite of incorporation' or aggregation by which a new identity was assumed. While the symbolism accompanying the rites of separation and incorporation often bespoke death and rebirth, and the moving from one socio-cultural condition to another was often represented by physical movement out of and then back into socio-cultural space, the mediatory or liminal stage was far more complex and confused. For, having crossed the threshold beyond one status or identity while not yet having crossed into another one, the initiate was neither here nor there; beyond normal, everyday socio-cultural categories, beyond normal conceptions of routine identity, and also the conceptions of behaviour, rule, time and space that accompanied identity.

The liminal stage was a zone of socio-cultural non-identity, non-existence. In different socio-cultural milieux, van Gennep found the liminal stage of rites of passage to be treated with very different kinds of attention (or inattention) and gravitas: from the honeymoon period of an English married couple to the vision quest of a Comanche brave (cf. Hoebel and Wallace 1958); but there were interesting symbolic overlaps. Individuals in this stage were often removed from everyday sight, or else treated as if invisible. They were often spoken about as dead or as dissolved into amorphous, unrecognizable matter, or as unformed or embryonic. They were often involved in tasks and occupations which were never normally undertaken in the course of everyday life. They were often treated as unclean and polluting to those still going about their everyday lives; also as potentially dangerous, as possessing the power to harm those engaged in quotidian routines should there be unmonitored contact between them. Hence, initiates in the liminal stage were often the responsibility of certain ritual officers or experts who managed their lives until the rite of reincorporating them into socio-cultural space, time and identity was to be effected.

Anthropological applications

Since van Gennep's comparative work, there have been detailed ethnographies of initiation and socio-cultural renewal which have instantiated and commented upon the above schema (cf. Richards 1982; La Fontaine 1985a). Gluckman developed the idea of rites of passage as entailing behavioural irregularities or reversals to explore the seeming 'rites of resistance' or 'reversal' which accompanied such things as regal investitures in African kingdoms, and which had clear echoes in Classical European festivities such as Saturnalia and Bacchanalia. Here, amidst uncommon revelry and behavioural unrestraint, there was a reversal of normal formalities and hierarchies such that commoners, slaves and women would temporarily lord it over their socio-cultural 'betters'. For Gluckman, such rites of reversal represented preludes to the re-establishment of everyday relations of stratification (1963a). They were transitions between states of order which served in fact to bolster the systematization of inequality by periodically releasing tension and disquiet.

For Leach, as part of an exploration of the structures of communication by which socio-cultural milieux were maintained between individuals (1976a), liminal zones, stages and statuses made possible transitions between entities whose identity called on them to be at once discrete and bounded but not *incommunicado*. Lands must be divided between owners, worlds between gods and men, lives between bodies and souls, times between pasts and futures. In each of these cases (and others), ambiguous, liminal phenomena, partaking of the character of both sides of the divide, kept the identity of things both related and distinct.

Douglas, meanwhile, developed the van Gennepian notion that what was liminal and neither here nor there was at once polluting, dangerous and powerful. There is a human 'yearning for rigidity', Douglas began, a longing for 'hard lines and clear concepts' (1966: 162). Hence, each socio-cultural milieu came to be based on and to embody symbolic classifications of the world which were indubitable, coherent and systemic, and from which the contradictory, the incoherent and the arbitrary were banned. Nonetheless, any systematic ordering and classification of matter inexorably rejected certain elements as inappropriate: it had to do this in order to arrive at clean lines of division between matter (which is otherwise, in reality, continuous). Hence, an inevitable by-product of a system of symbolic classification was 'dirt': that which contravened the ordering. Hedged about with taboo, the dirt which threatened the clear-cut ordering of the world, which would 'pollute' its cleanliness, was eschewed; while the notion that something was polluted served to protect cherished principles and categories from contradiction. The only exceptions to this eschewing were extraordinary, ritual situations. For while the disorder which dirt represented was a threat, it was also recognized to be powerful. Unrestricted by existing categories and order, it ushered in the imagined possibility of new patterns. In certain rituals, therefore, one could observe efforts to harness this power; the rituals represented ventures outwith social order and control in an attempt to tap supernatural, 'cosmic' power inhering outside the everyday nomos of human life. In ritual one found an acceptance of the wholeness of the real in contradistinction to the partiality of everyday nomic categories, and a surmounting of conventional differentiations. Human beings possessed a 'common urge to make a unity of all their experience', Douglas concluded, 'and to overcome distinctions and separations in acts of at-onement' (1966: 169).

Victor Turner's limin(oid)al

Like Douglas, Victor Turner was to move from ideas concerning ritual liminality to a theory of socio-cultural life as such. Initially (1964, 1967), however, he focused upon initiation rituals among the Ndembu of Tanzania, as seen in a van Gennepian light. Here was an oscillation between the individual experiencing of society and culture as highly structured, and the episodic venturing into ritual situations which were transitional and ambiguous in ethos *vis-à-vis* the preceding and following structures, if not purposely anti-structural. If Ndembu society was conceived of as a structure and classification of positions, standards, behaviours, customs, rights and duties, then the ritual periods and processes amounted to inter- or extra-structural situations. The Ndembu moved from one social status (with its attendant proprieties, moralities and identities) to another and to another throughout their lives, the moves sometimes involving great changes in behaviour, world-view and expectation, by way of ritual periods which were themselves asocial, amoral, out of time, out of sight and out of mind.

Certainly, liminality was the main focus of ritual activity among the Ndembu. There were liminal initiates, liminal officiants and liminal activities, taking place in liminal spaces. These spaces were powerful, even dangerous, phenomena, through which the Ndembu could be expected to be visited by otherworldly creatures and forces. It was with the assistance of the latter, for instance, as spirit helpers, that ritual officiants managed the transitions between social statuses of Ndembu initiates. Initiates were regarded as being ground down or rubbed clean of their earlier identities, so that they entered a uniform, formless state of pure potential, from which they were fashioned anew. Initiates were shown fearful and mysterious sacred objects which shocked them out of their complacency within existing identities and prepared them to learn and adopt new perspectives on life and themselves. Often monstrous in form, Turner hypothesized that the sacred objects and experiences to which the initiates were subjected provoked them into reconsidering the world, its nature and relations; so that it and they became objects of their own reflection and fantasy. Here was, in Eliade's words (1959), a 'still centre' to the universe from which all the current classificatory trappings of the socio-cultural milieu could be looked at askance. However, being strictly managed by their officiant–keepers when in a transitionally amorphous and identity-less state, initiates' rebirth took the apposite and required directions; as far as possible, their reflections and fantasies were manipulated and directed (their bodies coerced, even humiliated), so that their new world-views were as appropriate to their statuses as their old ones.

Like Gluckman and Douglas, then, Turner, in this early work, enunciated a conservative vision concerning the structural nature of socio-cultural life, and the play of ritual liminality within this. It was not that the cake of custom was broken *per se*, so much as that individuals temporarily or permanently came to have their positions within the social structure changed. While rites of passage might radically affect initiates, the social system to which they returned remained, as a whole, unchanged; individuals may change, episodically, thanks to the creative processes of ritual, but the structures of social systems on the whole did not.

It was as if rituals carried health warnings. Human beings could not bear the (polluting) effects of supernatural power, of formlessness beyond human apprehension, on a routine basis or for too long. After their 'time-out', therefore, ritual participants were returned to social systems whose structures came to be validated afresh. Nevertheless, as a religious believer himself, Turner did wish to emphasize the favourable aspects of the ritual state. If everyday life was a matter of social-structural positions and identities, then the creativity of ritual process opened up an anti-structural recognition of life beyond such arbitrary distinctions. Washed clean of particular and parochial statuses, initiates had the opportunity temporarily to enter a state of pure being, to engage with one another as representatives of a generic humanity. Turner coined the term *communitas* to describe a sense of heightened togetherness which people might feel with one another once the superficial clothing of age, status, occupation, gender and other differences had been removed.

Then Turner came to broaden his focus, beyond the Ndembu and beyond rites of passage narrowly defined. He argued (1974, 1982a, b, 1986) that the phenomenon of liminality – or 'the liminoidal', as he came to call it by way of distinction – could be seen to apply to a great variety of institutions, practices, movements, situations, roles and persons: from churches to shrines and priests, pilgrims, monks and nuns, ascetics and hermits, even hippies, kibbutzniks, new-age travellers and revolutionaries. In different ways, extents and durations, all of these shared in a condition of 'sacred marginality', their nature characterized by something of the anti-structural, the transitional and processual, the creative and re-formative, the reversing, resistant and rebellious, the communal and communing. They stripped themselves of normative everyday identities and refrained from normal practices in order to achieve vantage-points from which the social structure could be critiqued and re-formed. They deliberately held the everyday social structures of others in abeyance, opting out of status-bound, position-oriented lives, even if this meant taking on the stigmata of the lowly, poor and unkempt, the vagrant and ostracized, the mad and simple. They voluntarily abstained from participation in and membership of those social structures within which most mainstream life was conducted so that they may replace social-structural obligation and differentiation with a sense of true human bonds, based on personal relations of love, equality, spontaneity and freedom.

From being a transitional passage between social states, then, the liminal developed in Turner's work and appreciation to being an ongoing (asocial) state in itself. Not only was this always and everywhere present, in some shape or form, in human socio-cultural milieux, but, for Turner, it represented the best of those milieux. It was where people related to one another as full human beings over and above their socio-cultural exclusivities, and it was where they distilled the creativity and energy with which they created and re-created society and culture, and returned to them reinvigorated, preparing to keep giving them another try. Refusing social-structural distinction, classification and hierarchy, fragmentation and compartmentalization, the limin(oid)al was always a threat, always polluting and undercutting, always presenting a view upon the global and cosmopolitan, the universal and eternal. Hence, the guardians of social structure always attempted to police the liminoidal, if not out of existence then out of sight (time, mind) and seriousness in terms of everyday life. The power of the liminoidal might be recognized as of periodic use by these policemen, but it was also something whose application and provenance had to be carefully controlled, whose representatives were to be co-opted, wherever possible, into (marginal) positions within the social structure.

However much co-optation occurred, though, Turner concluded, however much church or hippy or punk 'leaders' and the groups they 'represented' became institutionalized parts of the socio-cultural milieu (and spoke on behalf of the status quo rather than its re-formation), there remained the sense in which every socio-cultural milieu continued to be characterized by an ongoing dichotomy between structure and anti-structure. Every individual life, indeed, partook of this dichotomy in an oscillatory fashion. For while the creative and rebellious and personalizing and communitarian spark may light up some individuals' lives more than others', it was a potentiality inherent to them all; every individual life had the potential to see beyond the conventionally normative and divisive, and every individual life shared in the necessity to experience this otherness at some time and to some extent. All were rebels, poets, humanists at some moments; all felt the power of social authority, property, wealth, tradition, status and fashion, but all also recognized the potentially far greater power of human overcoming and at-oneness.

In imaging the co-optation and routinization of liminality, but also its dialectical rebirth, Turner comes to appear quite Weberian, where uncategorizable 'charismatic' authority episodically affords the insights whereby socio-cultural milieux advance but where this authority inevitably comes to be routinized, institutionalized, in a 'traditional' or a 'rational–legal' form. Perhaps this is also why Turner (1982a: 132–53) comes to soften the stark distinction between structure and anti-structure and talk of their similarities. Hence, there may be different kinds of *communitas* which liminality can give onto: 'existential', 'ideological' and 'normative'. These latter might initially sound self-contradictory – how could the generic human bond of *communitas* be conceived of in the same terms as ideologies or norms? – but what Turner has in mind is the way that the spontaneous *communitas* felt by those who together 'drop out' of the social system must evolve into something more routine (even if still voluntaristic and 'free') if it is to maintain itself over time. Hence, the Franciscan monastery, the hippy commune and the kibbutz.

Turner may be criticized for the religious underpinning and romantic overtones which he gives to the concept of limin(oid)ality. He may be taken to task for an overemphasis on everyday life as structured, static and inhumane, and on 'sacred marginality' as humanistic, spontaneous and creative. The institutions and officers of the sacred have, after all, the habit of being at least as hierarchical, divisive, formal, fixed, narrow and inflexible as those of the social-structural, and not necessarily so otherworldly in their orientations either (cf. Mandelbaum 1966; Stirrat 1984).

Nonetheless, Turner's exposition of a liminal cognition, identity and practice beyond the social-structural status quo has proved very fruitful. In the anthropological study of play (Schwartzman 1978), of performance (Hughes-Freeland 1997), of literature (Ashley 1990), of creativity (Rosaldo *et al.* 1993), of existential individuality (Burridge

1979), of celebration (Manning 1983), of pilgrimage (Eade and Sallnow 1991) and of deviant subcultures (Marsh *et al.* 1978), Turner's version of the liminal-cum-liminoidal can be seen to have offered significant leads.

See also: **Alterity, Children, Humanism, Irony**

LITERARINESS

Since the 1960s, an appreciation of the contingencies of anthropological representation has steadily grown. Since the 1980s, with the so-called 'literary turn', this has become a major preoccupation. Representation, it is said, inevitably serves certain interests and purposes. Furthermore, the means of construing representations is tantamount to a particular construction of data; socio-cultural reality *per se* is a matter of representation. Anthropologists, in short, have come to treat writings – their own as well as others' – as 'situated texts'.

Traditionally, anthropological texts purported, or at least aimed, to simply present a true and detached view of the world. But texts do not simply come from nowhere, and they do not give onto an unbiased reality; inevitably they represent historico-socio-cultural documents. Indeed, the very claim to truth represents a particular rhetoric, a narrative and stylistic technique, which has served to obscure the links between those representations, the 'knowledge' they construct, the relations of power they embody, and the interests they further. Far from a true view of the world, here is simply one institutionalized way of being which is not intrinsically better than any number of other ways; truth being a 'docile servant' (Goodman 1978: 18), there was no monopoly on ways in which a construction of reality might be seen to 'fit the facts'.

By way of the 'literary turn', then, there has been a move away from an innocent focus upon the analysis of 'others' to an analysis of the processes by which anthropology comes to order, express, disseminate – in a word, inscribe – its analyses of others to the point where, for some, the questioning and self-doubting has endangered the practice of the writing *per se*. Looked at more positively, however, an anthropological consciousness of its acts of writing has caused a freeing-up of those practices and a willingness to experiment: a seeking out of genres which does not pretend to disinterestedness but best serves certain interests. Through a mixing of genres, a 'blurring' of distinctions and connections between genres and disciplines, there has been more of an open embracing of the power, creativity and beauty potentially to be found in all genres of representation (cf. Geertz 1983: 19).

To continue this exposition, a narrative may be woven which begins from three important literary-anthropological texts: *Works and Lives. The Anthropologist as Author* by Clifford Geertz (1988), *Writing Culture. The Poetics and Politics of Ethnography* edited by George Marcus and James Clifford (1986), and *Anthropology as Cultural Critique. An Experimental Moment in the Human Sciences* by George Marcus and Michael Fischer (1986).

Works and Lives: I

"'What does the ethnographer do?'", Geertz asks himself rhetorically: '– he writes' (1973: 19). However, in *Works and Lives*, Geertz discovers a certain nervousness in the state of current anthropological writing, a lack of confidence and persuasiveness in its traditional claim to explain others. Engaging others in the field and then representing them in the academy has become far more visible, and is felt to be incongruous and uncomfortable. As Strathern puts it (1991: 8–11), anthropology finds itself in a new 'aesthetic' wherein the traditional fieldworker and author who claims authentically to translate his or her particular observations of a culture or society no longer convinces.

The nature of the difficulty is both moral and epistemological, Geertz continues. The moral difficulty concerns logistics of 'going there' which were laid largely in the context of colonialism, but whose power asymmetries can be seen to be replicated today; still anthropologists act as unrequested, lifelong spokespersons-cum-experts for groups of people with fewer Western 'resources', whom they briefly meet in some 'peripheral' environment. And yet, such colonialist trappings are a far remove from the reorganization of ethnic political relations in which many anthropologists would nowadays hope to see themselves involved. The epistemological difficulty concerns a questioning of what description of 'there' means. Words offer no transparent medium of representation, and anthropological analyses represent constructions which are not automatically more truthful or accurate or impartial or scientific or objective than native ones.

In short, where once the discipline of anthropology shared complex institutional connections with Western colonial expansion on the one hand, and a salvational belief in the power of pure science on the other, now anthropologists find they can no longer act convincingly either as transcontinental mediators or as transcultural theoreticians. Is anthropological representation of the other decent? Is it even possible?

Hence, the calls, in recent years, for new, non-canonical ways of writing: first-person narratives; reflexivity; rhetorical self-consciousness; linguistic play; heteroglossia; verbatim recording; performative translation. In Stephen Tyler's vision (1986), ethnography should become a dialogic and collaborative production which replaces the monologic 'rape' of a scientistic 'alienation' (with its synthesizing gaze, transcendent argument and final word) with a negotiated and cooperatively evolved text. This might hope to evoke in readers the therapeutic possibility of a new commonsensical reality, transformed, renewed, even sacralized.

Writing Culture

Writing Culture is introduced (by Clifford) with the claim that far from being objective, anthropological writings are literarily constructed accounts, in a word, inventions and fictions. They are fictions because any historically situated truth is only ever partial, and because every one telling of a story must deny the telling of another at the same time from another perspective. As Nietzsche (1911) put it: 'all constructed truths are made possible by powerful "lies" of exclusion and rhetoric'. Anthropologists, then, are those who traditionally have had the power to tell their story of other cultures, while silencing the voices of the actual members and pretending to tell an authoritative, objective story in an omniscient way (with personal details, purple prose and rhetoric eschewed). But, however much anthropological writing intends to be impartial, even advocatory (written on behalf of the natives, and critical of present power relations), it is still enmeshed in a world of power inequalities; and it enacts further power relations.

More precisely, anthropological writings are overdetermined:

1 contextually: by the social milieux in which the anthropologist lives while he or she writes;
2 rhetorically: by the expressive conventions of language which are used, which use them;
3 institutionally: by the specific academic discipline the texts feed into and the academic audience which reads them;
4 generically: by the genre they add to (monograph; thesis; edited collection; textbook) and set themselves against (novel; poem; religious tract);
5 politically: by the power they have to assume the authority to describe and analyse and publish 'a culture';
6 and finally historically: by the fact that all the above factors are changing through time.

In sum, the anthropologist must be constantly self-conscious when he writes: conscious of the historical situation which places him in the position of writing up accounts of others; conscious of possibly competing accounts; conscious of how he is constructing his text, so that while avoiding self-indulgent confessionals, he admits to the personal nature of his account.

Works and Lives: **II**

The way out of the moral asymmetries and discursive complexities, according to Geertz, is to admit that anthropology entails representing one sort of life in the categories of another (those of the writer), and to accept that anthropological texts are literary texts: to be looked *at* and not just *through*. Of course, this makes authorship more burdensome. For, it is art which is primarily involved in bringing anthropological texts to life and keeping them active, and such artistry cannot be displaced onto 'method' or 'language' or 'the people themselves'. Anthropological writing entails telling stories, making pictures, concocting symbolisms and deploying tropes: 'half-convinced writers trying to half-convince readers of their (the writers') half-convictions' (Geertz 1988: 139). Only by admitting this can claims that the enterprise is iniquitous or impossible be countered.

And yet one still finds great resistance to seeing anthropology as a kind of imaginative writing. It is regarded as improper for anthropologists to reflect upon such literary questions instead of surveying the external world: an unhealthy self-absorption; narcissistic and decadent; time-wasting and hypochondriacal (cf. Sangren 1988: 423; Spencer 1989). It is felt that anthropologists produce texts which do not warrant literary inspection: they are not aiming for distinct styles; they are not mixed up in the 'sharp practice' of rhetoric. Moreover, it is feared that disinterring how knowledge claims are rhetorically advanced will reduce their plausibility as serious knowledge.

To this, Geertz responds that reality privileges no particular idiom in which it demands to be described – literally, positivistically, or without fuss. Anthropological representation has always been an 'impure' business, of feelings and sentiments, deriving from a dialogue between anthropologist and informant which changes them both. Indeed, the 'classic' anthropological texts have always been stylistic *tours de force* (cf. Hymes 1973b). What is called for, then, is for anthropology to admit that its continuing genealogy is literary, not scientific, and that it is inappropriate to peddle scientific-sounding rhetoric concerning 'induction', 'reification', 'generalization', 'truth', or 'fact'.

After all, 'ethnographic reality is actively constructed, not to say invented' (Dumont 1978: 66). The anthropologist attempts to convey the multiplicity of voices and viewpoints which passed through his consciousness during his research, while knowing that his consciousness has inextricably transmogrified those viewpoints. Thus, anthropology should recognize its proper realm to be '"faction": imaginative writing about real people in real places at real times' – where the 'imaginative' and the 'imagined' need not be confused with the 'imaginary', the 'fictional' with the 'false', or the 'made-out' with the 'made-up' (Geertz 1988: 141).

Not that seeing anthropology as in important respects a literary vocation does not have its dangers. For then the enterprise may be seen as the seduction to intellectual positions through rhetorical artifice, with its central quarrels construed as conceptual ones, and its central value as aestheticism and the pleasures of a good read (cf. Marcus 1980).

Anthropology as Cultural Critique

The argument is taken on in *Anthropology as Cultural Critique*. Marcus and Fischer ask how precisely anthropological writing can be made more sensitive to its broader political, historical and philosophical implications. And their answer is: by questioning the conventions of representation and by seeing in a permeability of disciplinary borders – between social science and the humanities, between the textual and the contextual – a liberation from traditional (illegitimate-because-absolutist-and-essentialist) symbolizations of the world. We might rework traditional differentiations between disciplines and genres, and see them instead as analogous enterprises: as corresponding ways of treating social reality which can come into fruitful communication and complementary relationship.

As Pratt argues (1992), particular tropes and genres need not be seen as somehow natural or native to a discipline, and just as anthropologists have had recourse to particular ones in the past, so they might invent new ones now. Anthropological texts need not be so far removed from novels, from travel reports, memoirs and journalism, from avant-garde cultural commentary, where these are seen to be corresponding ways of 'writing social reality'.

Or again, in the same way that the so-called realist novel (which depended on a narrator whose insight into circumstances and subjectivities was omniscient) was superseded by the modernist text (highlighting dialogue between the narrator and the other characters, between the writer, his subjects and the reader, so as to achieve a reciprocity of perspectives), so dialogue and reciprocity between a multiplicity of legitimate voices and views, may be watchwords for a new way of writing anthropology. The anthropologist engages in dialogue with his informants, and this can be conveyed in the text – with the reader then engaging in further dialogue. The processes of writing and reading alike could be conceived of as a series of multivocal exchanges in which a juxtaposition occurs of manifold cultural assumptions. In place of one culture representing another in its own terms, then, there are cultures juxtaposed, each framing questions which challenge the others' preconceptions. After all, it is not only anthropologists who write socio-cultural reality, and by playing off of such realities against one another one may accrue (not 'the truth' but) fruitful dialogue without end.

Works and Lives: **III**

What is central to the anthropological text, Geertz urges, is the experience of its writer. If anthropological writings attempt to provide openings onto others' socio-cultural realities, then they persuade not through the facts they contain, nor through their stylistic elegance, but to the extent that they convey, in its fullness, the author's experience of travel between ways of life and worlds of meaning. In the conveyance of this, there might also be travel between ways of writing, between tropes and genres. Because not only does the reality anthropology approaches not demand one way in which it must truthfully be described, but, to the contrary, this reality is human reality – a necessarily experienced reality – and ever multiple. To travel between literary forms in one's efforts to represent human socio-cultural reality is to seek to do justice to this multiplicity.

'Factional' genres?

Genres have been defined as 'literary institutions, or social contracts between a writer and a specific public, whose function is to specify the proper use of a cultural artefact' (Jameson 1981: 106). To coin a term such as 'faction', as Geertz does, in order to refer to the 'literari-ness' of contemporary 'anthropological' writing, is at once to evince the relationship between academic disciplines and certain genres of representation, and to posit a destabilization of this relationship. Disciplinary boundaries between literature and anthropology should no longer disguise or subvert inter-disciplinary correspondences in their representation of socio-cultural realities.

Ordinarily, however, it is still the differences (of genre, institutionality, artefact) between the two disciplines which tend to be emphasized by their various apologists and exponents. Thus, the fictional is claimed to address the might-have-been, the should-be, the could-well-be, the would-never-be (and so on); so that when actual people and events gain ascendancy over invention then literature becomes what it is not (cf. Lodge 1977: 8). In anthropology, meanwhile, as Geertz reports, there is the broad claim that its writings may be speculative, and are probably inductive, but nevertheless they can, do and should aspire to being in true and direct relationship to the stimuli of an externally met world (to real people and events), and to representing themselves plainly and honestly.

More precisely, it is said that anthropology attempts something more than, or at least different from, literature, which lacks the realism of content of the anthropological endeavour, the expected rigour of research, method, theory and presentation. While literature takes cultural material and transforms it, exploits it, instead of presenting it for its own sake, the discipline of anthropology is based on the descriptive integrity of ethnography: a dedication to fact, not to the satisfaction of artistry; a holistic depiction of actual happenings in genuine settings, not an impressionistic fusion of idea and reality. Even if literature sets itself the goal of realism, then, this is not the same as descriptive accuracy because the idea will always come first and reality then be made to fit it (Erickson 1988).

Furthermore, the literary text is not beholden to a painstaking revelation of the steps in its argument, of the logic in its associations and extrapolations, so that conclusions can be reached which simply suit its opening ideas. The literary text is indirect and selective, introverted and self-oriented; it seeks to rivet attention on itself rather than seeking, as does the referential text in anthropology, to describe literally the external reality of an objective world (cf. Watt 1979: 306–8). Hence, anthropology remains a project well worth pursuing even by writers who will never achieve the artistry of literaryism and, indeed, might not aspire to it.

In sum, many anthropologists resist a 'literary turn' to their discipline when this is seen as a mooted change to their institutional practices and a threat to the tradition, ideology, training, purpose, prestige, in a word, the 'culture' of their discipline. For, here are ways of writing (of giving names to things; of orienting collective activity; of deriving meaning; of systematizing date; of configuring the truth) which are exclusive and exclusionary. They are incommensurable and irreducible, relevant in different ways, for different times, and different purposes. To take a 'literary turn', in short, is to surrender anthropology to its antithesis, to precipitate its demise.

But this can equally well be turned around. If anthropology would conventionally constitute itself through a contrast with literary 'otherness', then it cannot isolate or even separate itself either; it cannot exist without literature since it needs this other to describe the 'factual' nature of the problem it sets itself. If the latter has been called into question, then might not this ontology of self and other? Might not both come together as different versions of the one 'factional' project?

In their intent to produce realistic representations of social life, then, there is perhaps much in the anthropological and literary enterprises which might be seen to overlap. Certainly, between the anthropological fieldworker-cum-analyst and the 'social novelist' – Fielding, Dickens, Eliot, Forster, Woolf, Lawrence, Greene, and others 'concerned with detailed and prolonged observation and comment on the manners and mores of a social milieu in which he is at the same time a participant' (Rapport 1994a: 67) – there are compelling correspondences of a historical, methodological and experiential kind. If there is something fundamentally anthropological in cultural comparison and critique, then, equally, literature is grounded in a transcending of the apparent and a critiquing of the conditions of its own existence. The station of the novelist, as Graham Greene described it, is ever to be on the ambiguous borderline, promulgating an alternative world and providing novel insight into people's perceptions, evaluations and sensations (cf. Hoggart 1966: 247)

That is, looking beyond distinctive disciplinary and generic institutionality (at 'anthropology' versus 'literature') is to see the figure of the individual writer who puts these institutions to use in the writing of social reality. This writing, whether in anthropology or literature, is a poetic enterprise. It entails stepping back from experience, reflecting upon it, and then transforming this into orderly text. It also entails personalizing institutional verbal forms so that they may convey a novel individual sense of reality. To author a 'literary-cum-anthropological' text, in short, is to impart personality to language and to express a personal construction of the world. Both anthropology and literature come together under the rubric of what Leach dubbed 'divine inventiveness' (1969: 90). Indeed, the anthropological destination, for Leach (1982: 53), should be the insight which great novelists display: that quality of deep understanding into the behaviour of others.

Nor does such questioning and realigning necessarily threaten anthropology, or detract from its practical purpose or efficacy. These practices, in fact, could be seen to be intrinsically 'anthropological'.

Certainly, if anthropology, as cultural comparison and critique, is intent on juxtaposing one viewpoint and symbolic construction of the world against another and identifying their ongoing relations, then this applies to its own viewpoints and preconceptions, its own practice too; maybe especially so. There is perhaps a routine need for anthropology to be non-routine: through comparison and critique, to step outside its own symbolic constructions so as to contextualize and evaluate its relations with other disciplines. For, if anthropology is a discipline, then, to borrow Keith Hart's phrase, it is also a 'virtual anti-discipline' (1990: 10). It ought not to bound itself; it should recognize categorical differences (such as in ways of writing, in genres), but not be restricted by them in its search for as complex an appreciation of experience as possible. Anthropology was 'born omniform', as Geertz puts it (1983: 21), and should continue to be thus.

Individual writing

In *Works and Lives*, Geertz analysed the writings of four anthropologists – Malinowski, Benedict, Evans-Pritchard, Lévi-Strauss – and compared how they imparted their own identity and very personal signatures to their texts. Here we find individual writers bringing their 'creativity' (Parkin 1987) and 'imagination' (Finnegan 1977) similarly to bear upon the socio-cultural realities they find around them. The results are 'factions' which belong to the 'romancer' who created them.

'Imagination', 'creativity', 'faction', still do not sit easily as terms of anthropological self-description. We might grant that, in its way, literature can 'take stock of a culture', its efforts evincing a 'reflecting mind and feeling heart' (Turner 1976: 78); we might even admit that literary writing can be 'free-floating' – its meaning too flexible to be directly or closely tied to the social exchanges in which it appears, its life-in-use not rigidly bound by a socio-cultural environment (Finnegan 1977: 260). However, we are immeasurably more leaden when it comes to appreciating how our own writing works (is worked).

And yet we write in the same way. At least, when Malinowski, Benedict, Evans-Pritchard, Lévi-Strauss (Bateson, Leach, Wallace, Geertz) use 'fieldnotes', 'papers' and 'monographs' to write up their field experiences, their work is great in its individuality. In use, the cultural forms and social relations of anthropology are personalized and transformed: given meaning, brought to life, within the particular contexts of individual lives. In other words, anthropological writing is free-floating stock-taking too, for it can be bound (predicted, deter-mined, encompassed) neither by the field experience nor by the disciplinary genres which preceded it. Its greatness, perhaps, can be measured by the extent to which it rewrites both: 'explains' the other and 'extends' the discipline.

The American novelist Don DeLillo has described each writer as his or her own language, 'building himself word by word and sentence by sentence' (1991); it is here that the novelist and the anthropologist ultimately meet.

See also: **Movement, Science, Writing**

METHODOLOGICAL ECLECTICISM

In 1964, Max Gluckman and (economist) Ely Devons collaborated on a book entitled *Closed Systems and Open Minds: The Limits of Naivety in Social Anthropology*. Their topic was anthropological method; more precisely, given the complexity of that human reality which anthropology set out to investigate, their topic concerned how the investigator could both open himself or herself up to socio-cultural complexity and close off a manageable portion for presentation. The solution, Gluckman and Devons maintained (1964: 162–8), turned upon the notion of naivety; naivety was an anthropological duty, inasmuch as it was in naivety that openness and closure met. Open to all manner of socio-cultural complexity, the anthropologist circumscribed, delimited, incorporated, abridged, isolated and compressed his or her experience into a distinct narrative of interrelations which contained its own order: a closure which specialists of different particular fields may inevitably find to be naive.

Anthropology, the most humanistic of social sciences, the most comparative of humanities, thus could be said to make a specialism out of non-specialism. Anthropology was an interdisciplinary discipline which, through the exercise of an 'intellectual poaching licence' (Kluckhohn) and a seeming amateurish use of all manner of information, could expect to tackle the 'vast intricacies' (Bateson 1959: 296) of the worlds of human cognition, sociation, construction and interaction.

Descriptive eclecticism

There is, in Michael Herzfeld's formulation (1993: 184), a strong temptation to reduce social experience to single models. Indeed, the representation of social life may be fatally prone to simplistic reduction, inasmuch as singular texts stand for plural exchanges, and concepts replace complex processes of interpretation. However, to represent the diversity, the openendedness, the chaotic relativism that comprises cultural process is not necessarily to attempt to re-present a social milieu singly, steadily and as a whole, if one maintains the 'naivety' of a certain epistemological pluralism and narrational eclecticism. That is, the seeming closure of the anthropological account is ameliorated by its embodying a certain methodological eclecticism, such that the account itself implies conversation: between different systems of sense-making, different universes of discourse, in a word, different epistemes. If the bringing together in one text of the distinct, diverse and incompatible voices and epistemes of a socio-cultural milieu in such a way as to point up their irreconcilability and their interaction may be described as 'writing conversationally', then it may be possible to aver that 'the epistemological conversation of this anthropological text is a homologue of the everyday conversation of social life'.

Analytical eclecticism

To represent adequately the local conversation of epistemes is, to borrow from Feyerabend (1975: 18) to be epistemologically 'opportunistic' in one's analysis. This must be characterized by epistemological 'complementarity' (Claxton 1979: 415), and a refusing of epistemological resolution (cf. Simmel 1971: xii). For no theory or episteme or narrative which the social commentator might bring to bear could cover all the 'facts' which are alive and being exchanged in a social milieu and convey the latter's intrinsic complexity and diversity; while any attempt to force social life into one or other perspective ends in tautology and serves only to destroy the 'reality' under study. To eschew the endemic diversity of cultural construction in one's account – 'the maze of interaction' (Feyerabend 1975: 17–18), rich in content, varied, many-sided, lively and subtle – may indeed make for neatness, system, clarity, the contentment of order, but only at the expense of a totalizing dogma and a totalitarian depiction (cf. Louch 1966: 239).

To adopt an eclecticism of analytical narration and style is to free one's account from an obsessional Aristotelian combat between battling singularities. In such eclecticism – locating human behaviour in more than one frame of reference at once; locating such (often mutually exclusive) frames of reference in conversation with one another in the text – one finally escapes the notion that epistemic diversity can and should ultimately be 'resolved' in terms of a finite limit of possibility (Society; structure) or an ultimately determining and integrating code (God; grammar).

Eclecticism instanced

In modern physics, methodological pluralism or eclecticism has reached renown as a means of dealing with the mutual exclusivity of theories positing the nature of electrons as particles or as waves – as isolated material entities or as perturbations in a continuous field. The 'reality' of electrons is attested to by the plurality of explanations of which it admits (cf. Devereux 1978: 1–3). A direct corollary of this in anthropology might concern the dispute between theories of meaning. Is meaning a function of (isolated) individual intention at a particular moment, and an act which can wilfully alter or subvert any collective system that grounds it? Or is meaning a (continuous) collective fact, deriving from culturally determined codes and textual mechanisms which transcend particular volition?

An anthropological eclecticism of analytical style would allow for such mutual exclusions, as well as others one could name – instance versus category, performance versus competence, event versus structure, subject versus object – and more plural oppositions as well – functionalism versus symbolic interactionism versus Marxism versus structuralism versus post-modernism – all to appear within the same text. Indeed, analytical eclecticism would insist that this were the case: that a text be constructed out of a conversation between different epistemic realities.

For instance, in her account of contemporary Chagga social life – 500,000 people living on the slopes of Mount Kilimanjaro – Sally Falk Moore (1987) is cognizant, above all, of the 'fact' that the events of local life are not coherent instantiations of shared, pre-existing structures (normative, conventional, grammatical), rather they are revelations of multiplicity and indeterminacy, contestation and change. Hence, Moore determines that the 'event' of her text should not be characterized or informed by any single mode of knowing or interpreting. She decides to construct her anthropological narrative around the analysis of three 'chopped-off anecdotes' (1987: 734) which were told her (concerning the transfer of land), and to process (to converse) between and among their overlapping themes: the meaning of good and evil; the competition over a scarce resource; the contested powers and weaknesses of church and state. What the conversation of her text elucidates is that 'like a sunburst', the anecdotes can be seen to lead in all directions. They are shot through with ambiguity, with 'a contiguity of contraries'. Every anecdote carries concomitantly antithetical messages, every theme open to contradictory interpretations; every statement made by their protagonists, or by her, their reporter, could be shown to have kinds of 'self-subversive anti-statement' attached to it. At the very least, in their detailed exposition of interlocked social-organizational frameworks, of rich systems of symbolic categories, and of multiple modes of production and class distinctions, the anecdotes offer simultaneous grist to the explanatory mills of functionalism, structuralism and Marxism. But by the same token, any attempt at a totalizing truth-claim by any one such explanatory ideology may be easily deconstructed. As Chagga attachment to any single or consistent order and ordering of things is fragmentary and intermittent, so can be the anthropologist's attitude to any one episteme; the anecdotes reveal a multiplicity of epistemes, in creative combination, in terms of which anthropology, like the Chagga, should continuously construct the social world as meaningful and as new. In this way, the anthropologist might write an account which converses with itself in a plurality of different voices, each epistemologically calling into question the possible completeness of any other.

In sum, just as there is no single or coherent or common-denominatory social structure which underlies any one socio-cultural milieu (which explains, grounds, contextualizes or determines its goings-on), so the latter warrants no single or coherent or common-denominatory mode of interpretation. Instead the anthropologist might provide a description which represents the conversation of social life as it is (diversely) lived in individual interactions. In such 'provisional writing' (Cohen 1992b), the anthropologist might evoke in the reader a sense of the 'incomplete project' (James 1993: 234) that is both socio-cultural life and its representation.

An ethos of eclecticism

This gives to anthropological accounting a particular character. As Deborah Tannen puts it (1989: 197), the anthropological project is at once scientific and humanistic and aesthetic; it is fraught with tensions between knowledge, value and ethics which are ultimately irresolvable.

Philosopher Richard Rorty (1980: 357–72) has drawn a useful distinction between two kinds of disciplinary pursuit, one being essentially constructive and systematic, the other reactive and edifying. A systematic discipline seeks objectivity: a system of monologic explanation, argument and agreement, which will possess universal commensurability, which can become the paradigm of all cultural knowledge, which will last if not for all eternity then until it acts as the foundations of future progress. An edifying discipline, by contrast, distrusts the notion of essences and is dubious about claims that reality can be accurately, holistically, singularly or disinterestedly explained and described; for not only is there the contingency and diversity of existing epistemological regimes, there is also the poetry of the new. In the face of an essentialist inquiry, therefore, the edifying account seeks to maintain a conversation between different ways of being in the world, and eschews any singular, authoritative framing. It offers aphorisms, satires, parodies in the face of systematic arguments, and esteems the continuous metamorphoses of metaphor and poetry.

The edifying account does not only deal in conversation as subject-matter and style, it also makes for conversation to continue. In describing and analysing being-in-the-world it composes another chapter within it; it adds to the array of epistemic construction and interaction. As Rorty concludes (1980: 378): to be wise is to 'sustain a conversation' between epistemes, while 'to look for commensuration rather than simply continued conversation . . . is to attempt escape from humanity'.

Clearly, both the elucidation of the conversation of socio-cultural life and the representation of conversation in the account of socio-cultural life proposed above would make of anthropology an edifying pursuit. It is an edifying anthropology which endeavours to secure a representation of human beings not as singular and limited epistemic objects but rather as their own plural and limitless subjects.

See also: **Contradiction, Conversation, Literariness**

METHODOLOGICAL INDIVIDUALISM AND HOLISM

Holism and collectivism

Geertz once advocated viewing culture as 'a set of control mechanisms' – plans, recipes, programs, instructions – which reduce the individual potential for living thousands of lives to the narrowness and specificity of his or her actual accomplishments in one (1970: 57; also cf. Schneider 1968: 5–8). By virtue of this notion of culture, anthropologists could hope both to 'seek complexity, and order it' (Geertz 1970: 48). In this formulation he continued a long methodological tradition in anthropology which may be characterized by the term 'holism'. Whether arguing in terms of 'culture', as here, or 'society', 'social structure', 'community', 'class', or some other collective notion, the assumption persisted that both elucidation and explanation of socio-cultural phenomena – what precisely they were, what they meant, where they came from, what their implications were – could be derived only from an abstract and holistic contextualization. Socio-cultural phenomena, in the common shorthand, were to be known as 'greater than the sum of their constituent parts': individual actors and acts, individual lives, gave onto something other, something transcendent – onto the phenomena of socio-cultural wholes. Here were total systems, social or cultural, structural or symbolic, linguistic or behavioural, which might be seen to emerge out of everyday individual interactions but which were in fact ontologically prior to both actors and their exchanges, and overdetermining of them. To explain the individual and actual, in short, was to contextualize it within the general, the collective, the impersonal.

Indeed, there is a venerable tradition of regarding a 'methodological holism' or collectivism of this kind not merely as a virtue of social-scientific analysis but as a *sine qua non* of its verity. For Durkheim (1966 [1895]), the notion of a 'social fact', of an objective and institutional phenomenon which was external to, constitutive and coercive of the individual, encapsulated both the fundamental *explicans* and the *explicandum* of 'sociological' method. While the notion of a generalized, formal social reality above and beyond the actions, subjectivities, motives and intentions of individuals forms a central plank in Anthony Giddens's centennial reappraisal (1976). Social action becomes, for Giddens, an impersonal concept, pertaining to a holistic domain, to which interaction between individuals can be seen objectively to give rise – and which ultimately comes to embody the causal conditions and structuring force of that interaction (1976: 155–60).

Anthropology, as variously canonized (van Velsen 1967: 145–6; Pelto and Pelto 1978: 36; Peacock 1986: 83), has been a willing partner to the above Durkheimesque holism and impersonalism. In crossing what Fortes referred to as the threshold between description and analysis (1970: 130–3), anthropology has looked to overcome the complexities and untidinesses of actual individual lives and thereby accede to a level of generality, homogeneity and simplification where social forces and cultural practices take on their own form, logic and routine (cf. Gellner 1959: 200, 263). Hence, anthropology has reified certain epistemo-logical constructs – 'collective conscience', 'collective representations', 'social facts', 'the cult of the individual' – it has routinized and generalized certain forms of social interaction – 'joking relations', 'segmentary lineages', 'dynamic equilibria' – and it has hypostatized certain forces and powers which lead lives of their own determination, orientation and evolution – 'society', 'culture', 'kinship', 'ritual' and 'religion', 'political and economic relations', 'language'. Anthropology claims to gain access to sociological data (on 'suicide', on 'mechanisms of solidarity', on 'marital prescriptions and preferences') which, due to a lack of learning or impartiality or self-reflexivity or freedom of thought, are beyond the personal ken of actual individual participants in a socio-cultural milieu: the 'members' or 'role-players', if not 'tribesmen' or 'primitives' (cf. Lukes 1968, 1990; Bloch 1998).

Treated unsympathetically, it almost appears as if, for much of its history, actual actors and social interactions have been absent from this Durkheimian project: incidental if not departicularized, generalized into one impersonal (defining, limiting) category or another. The reductions that emerge amount to 'synthetic fictions' on this view, fictive matrices of uniformity. As Sapir once put it (1956: 200–7), ideas of societies and cultures as objectified patterns which provide each group with its own 'tidy table of contents' – with (à la Geertz) plans, recipes, programs, instructions – might be convenient, but they are fallacious, assigning 'society' and 'culture' to misleading metaphysical loci. This reductionism, Anthony Cohen more recently has expounded, is not merely dull and unambitious, redundant and intellectually barren, but arrogant and insensitive, discreditable (1989: 10–12, 1994: 5).

Reductionism is persistent, however, even where it is recognized as a failing, because of the way the Durkheimian project in social science was originally conceived. Hence, holism, 'impersonalism', the imaging, knowing and phrasing of the world and its features in terms which deny or devalue the individual, the particular and the personal, remain ubiquitous. Giddens, for instance, after initially criticizing the reductiveness of functionalist and structuralist notions of social process for their removal of individuals as competent and practical subjects, responsible for actively re-constituting social life, would still appear to conclude his *New Rules of Sociological Method* (1976), with a similar eschewing of individual agency, a divorcing of the micro and macro, and a disdain for micro-social mundanities in favour of institutional analysis of the 'macro' alone.

Briefly doffing his cap to individuals' constitutive agency in social life and their constructing of society through ongoing speech-acts, Giddens goes on to explain that since not all actions and outcomes are as individually intended, a concept of social action must needs be distinguished, whose sense and meaning is 'free' from notions of individual intention and reference. Moreover, the concept should properly be located in pure sociological realm where the 'triviata' of everyday interaction and ordinary exchange can be removed (1976: 15). Here, analytically juxtaposed with structures of social morality and power, action can fuel more incisive institutional analysis of macro-social form and process. For individuals' actions are transformed, unbeknownst to them, into instruments of social-structural replication, and thus merely serve to further the institutional historical conditions which *de facto* constituted those actions in the first place. Hence, individual cognitive processes achieve sociological relevance, if at all, as features of societal symbolic classifications; individual differences are swept under the carpet of collective and coordinated interactional identities. In this way, for Giddens, social-scientific generalizations can be arrived at, describing the societally reproduced alignments of the 'unintended' consequences of individual actions.

Methodological individualism

But this need not be the case. An impersonal holism need not be taken on board as an ontological or methodological postulate of human reality; at best, holism represents, in Jackson's phrasing, an instrumentality rather than a finality (1989: 1). The human world can be and certainly is made to seem 'impersonal', totalized and totalizing, but this is not its necessary or actual nature. Holism is a strategy, a rhetoric, an instrument to denaturalize the world; anthropology may set out to analyse the above impulses toward impersonalization and their working-out in a socio-cultural milieu without allowing itself to become party to them (cf. Rapport 1997a: 12–29).

For, if one looks beneath the impersonal (categorial, stereotypical, generalized) surface of such a world, one sees the complexity, the multiplicity and diversity, the inconsistency and contradiction of a congeries of personal relations abutting against one another. The actual nature of the human world is of individuals in interaction. This is its causation – the cause of there being human worlds of culture and society – and its manifestation. Ideologies may seek to obscure such facts, may transmogrify the personal into the impersonal, but, to borrow a phrase from E.M. Forster (1950: 26), 'personal relations are the real life'.

Moreover, knowledge of these personal relations is individual knowledge. There is nothing else that it can be. There are no collective knowing organisms to which human beings are party: cultures and societies, institutions and associations cannot know, only individuals have the minds and memories to know. Which means, furthermore, that personal relations may be known differently by their different individual participants. While it is true that human life is lived in personal relationships, and while human individuals depend on others (living and dead, real and imagined, particularized and generalized) for all manner of securities (physical, emotional, intellectual), nevertheless, individuals begin their knowing from different points (bodies, brains, consciousnesses) and, ultimately, they end there too. In short, the personal relations in which individuals live may eventuate in sharing and intimacy of a variety of levels and kinds, but not necessarily in a common or even consistent knowledge of the relations which are being practised. While the true nature of the human world is of individuals in interaction and of individuals contextualizing one another within socio-cultural worlds of action, the ultimate knowledge of these worlds is individual *per se*: the possession of individual bodies and brains.

The above insights may be pulled together under the approximate title of 'methodological individualism'. Here, as Popper advocates (1966: 91–8), is explanation which avoids a vulgar use of collective, impersonal terms (from '*Zeitgeist*' to 'state', 'nation', 'social group', 'institutional structure', 'division of interest' or 'labour', or 'asymmetry of power') in favour of explanation in more descriptive, individualistic terms. This does not deny the pertinence of notions of class or gender, role or status etc., but says that the meaning and effect of these latter must be derived from how they are constructed in situations of interaction. For it is use of these notions by interacting individuals which affords them social life – use which may be very far from consensual, homogeneous or uniform (cf. Blumer 1972: 185–7). Equally, this does not suggest that individuals' actions are free from constraint or deleterious outcome, or that their socio-cultural worlds are objects of their own making *ex nihilo* and *in vacuo*. It says that societal configurations are to be understood as resulting from the decisions, attitudes, dispositions, taken-for-granted expectations, relations and actions of specific individuals in specific situations, and the unintended consequences and repercussions of these; and that it is a misleading misconception to claim that notions of collectivity and constraint possess their own internal dynamic and obey their own laws, as if deriving from a separate sociological reality. It says that the meaning and effect of historical and structural conditions is never something immanent and unmediated but, even as action and outcome 'break free' of interactional setting and the moorings of the sender's intention, something always dependent on individual interpretation in order to arrive.

If individuals appear subject to 'general socio-cultural conditions', then upon closer inspection those conditions may themselves be seen to be constituted by networks of other individuals, acting with their own dispositions and interacting in their own situations. Hence, what seems impersonal and imposing and objective to one person is the personal of another; it is a matter of perspectives and distance, not of phenomenological thresholds and domains.

Methodological canons

To adumbrate a number of other methodological–individual canons, briefly, one might begin with MacIver (1961: *passim*):

> Generalisations are true or false in proportion as they represent or misrepresent all the individual doings and happenings. . . . 'The Book of the Recording Angel' may be regarded as the ideal limit to which [social science] approximates as generalisation tends to zero.

Since individual human beings are not mere theoretical postulates – they are met in the flesh – their description in social science is never merely for the convenience of supposition (as it is for 'societies', 'cultures', 'ethnicities', 'traditions' and 'spirits of the age') [*Simmel (1971: 27): a society may be informed by an extraordinary multiplicity and variety, but this is no reason to hypostatize or autonomize it*]. Moreover, it is the countless individual acts and doings of such individuals taken together which give rise to the 'stuff' of social science [*Simmel (1971: 27): society exists where a number of individuals enter into interaction; society is interaction*]. Hence, the ideal social-scientific text would tell the whole story of everything that ever happened to every individual, everything that every individual caused to happen. And while such an 'Book of the Recording Angel' remains a mythic ideal, the project of the social scientist can still be to précis a greater or lesser part of the Book while misrepresenting its contents, through generalization or reduction, as little as possible.

Such a précis, Watkins continues (1953), must configure the complexity of socio-cultural situations, institutions and events out of the particular situations, dispositions, beliefs, understandings, interrelations and resources of particular individuals [*Popper (1965: 37): sociological models and analyses must be constructed in terms of individuals' attitudes, expectations, actions and relations*]. For since individual human beings are the sole 'moving agents' in history, and since socio-cultural phenomena are nothing but the product, intended and otherwise, of the interaction of individual characteristics – individual knowledge and ignorance, individual action, reaction and inertia – it is to the latter that the social scientist must turn for insight [*Mill (1875: 469): the laws of social phenomena can be nothing but the laws (actions and passions) of individual human nature*]. No socio-cultural knowledge can be arrived at which is not also individual knowledge. A socio-cultural system is a collection of people 'whose activities disturb and influence each other' (Watkins

1959: 511), and no socio-cultural reality exists which could not be altered by appropriate and sufficient individual knowledge and desire [*Hayek (1969: 60): in social science, things are what individuals think they are*].

To talk of individual knowledge and desire is to talk of psychological processes and influences. And just as any general characteristics of a social situation must be derived from piecing together what is known of individual situations, so the socio-cultural derives from piecing together the psychological; there is no irreducible socio-cultural domain *sui generis* [*Simmel (1971: 32): a description of a social situation is an exercise in psychological knowledge*]. This is not to say that socio-cultural realities are direct reflections of individual psychological realities, are individual psychological realities writ large, because individual intentions often have unintended repercussions as these intentions are construed and reacted to by other individuals. Nor is this saying that individuals always operate with knowledge which is sufficient or appropriate to their desires; the outcome of action and interaction may be very different, opposite, or only vaguely related to the intentions of those involved. And nor is this saying that individuals do not run into obstacles and constraints which can frustrate, even destroy them. What it is saying, to return to where we began, is that one must eschew seeing routine collective phenomena as something possessing their own internal dynamic, obeying their own laws and having their own qualities and effects; eschew seeing individuals as the playthings of inhuman, impersonal, historicist, determinist conditions or tendencies; eschew seeing individuals as confronted and constrained by other than the desires, intentions, habits, loyalties, inertias, rivalries – also the miscarried plans – of other individuals [*Hayek (1946: 8): the only way to understand social phenomena is by understanding the actions of the individuals who compose them, actions directed towards other individuals and guided by their expectations of their behaviour*].

Even if, as Giddens reminds us, not all individual action is unconstrained and not all outcomes are as intended, it is only through an analytical appreciation of the niceties of individual practice that the constraints of power differentials and moral injunctions can be properly accounted for and understood; the indirection of individuals is also a matter of individual intention. Moreover, if such argument appears to partake of circularity or infinite regress, as Gellner charges (1959: 514), then perhaps this is something less to be 'corrected' than to be welcomed: the 'impersonal' and 'holistic', as viewed from one vantage-point, dissolving into yet another relationship between particular individuals when viewed more closely.

What methodological individualism guarantees, in short, is an affirmation of the mutuality of the individual and the socio-cultural, and a pertinent reminder of the need to understand how the socio-cultural and generalized is perceived and used by its individual recipients [*Weber (1964: 101): 'collectivities must be treated as solely the resultants and modes of organization of the particular acts of individual persons'*].

Overview

'What is the "social condition" that has nothing to do with an individual condition?', F.R. Leavis once rhetorized (1972: 53–4), 'what is the "social hope" that transcends, cancels or makes indifferent the condition of each individual? where is a condition, a life, to be located if not in individuals' lives – lives which cannot be generalized, averaged or compounded?' Due in large part to Durkheim and his followers, such generalizing, averaging and compounding has played a significant role in the holistic tradition in social anthropology, where identities and behaviours of individual actors have been derived from precisely such institutional contexts and conditions; individual selves have been invented in the image of the generalization 'culture', and as a replicate in miniature of 'society' (cf. Cohen 1994: 128).

Dealing with, and inferring individuals from, institutions and structures in this way maintained a reductionism and redundancy in anthropological analysis and comparison. Even the changes occasioned by a Geertzian emphasis on meaning and interpretation did not alleviate the privileging of the collective, to the detriment of the experientially individual. For, through an identification of the cultural with the collective and the holistic, the individual, here too, came merely to refract the conditions and characteristics of collective categories.

How different it might have been if anthropology had had more time for Mill or Simmel, or even for Weber, for whom the individual is 'the upper limit and the sole carrier of meaningful conduct' (1964: 101). Hence, Weber continues, it is in the understandable acts of such 'participating individual men' that social science must, without exception, deal: 'social science must proceed from the actions of one or more separate individuals and adopt strictly individualistic methods' (cited in Mommsen 1965: 25).

Nevertheless, the experience of some anthropologists (as individuals as well as fieldworkers among individuals) has led them to oppose a holistic orthodoxy dogma. A submerged line of individualistic methodology also has its history in anthropology, which recognizes that individuals are more than their membership of and participation in collectivities. Moreover, since the latter are themselves the products of their individual members, individual identities and explanations of individual behaviour cannot be derived from impersonal collective categories; the relationship between the two is rather one of great complexity and ambiguity.

The proper description of culture, as Sapir elaborated (1956), should involve not the reification of words and behaviours into patterns of social structure so much as an exploration of the individual interpretation and animation of words and behaviours in their personal interactions. Any simple generalization and integration of these elements into objective structures represents a reification of ideas and actions which actually appear in endlessly different patterns of meaningful use. Every element of the reification may be true in some situation, then, but the elision of situations causes something fictional; it creates a mechanical order which seems neat, but with a vitality which is misplaced. For it is not the cultural elements which are alive but their creative usage in different situational configurations by different individuals: it is individuals who bring socio-cultural categories and institutions to life.

Only via methodological individualism, in short, is one able to avoid the reductionism of an impersonal (and inhuman) socio-cultural world where a holistic collective grammar – a Durkheimian *conscience collective*, a Marxian infrastructure and superstructure, a Saussurean *langue*, a Bourdieuvian *habitus* – holds sway. To study collectivities is to treat individuals' consciousness of them.

See also: **Individualism, Individuality, Situation and Context**

MOMENTS OF BEING

In 1961, in a collection of essays considered particularly timely, Edmund Leach reflected upon the paradoxical nature of time. Time was something in our experience which was at once repetitive and non-repetitive; time was a human construction at once projected onto an environment via the collective structuration (and punctuation) of social life, and a matter of subjective experience, something relative to the consciousness and purpose of particular individuals (1961a: 125–35).

Reflecting upon similar experiential paradoxes concerning the way we temporally make sense of our lives, Virginia Woolf coined the phrase 'moments of being' (1976). Whatever we are, Woolf asserted, we are in moments. Being turns on momentary thoughts, feelings, apprehensions, emotions; we experience being in the world in distinct chunks. Not that we are necessarily always conscious of this, however. Rather, the conscious momentariness of our lives derives from our momentarily stepping back and forming mental images of what is to come and what has passed; we image momentary snapshots of past and future occasions. As Woolf described it in the case of emotion: 'one never realises an emotion at the time. It expands later, and thus we don't have complete emotions about the present, only about the past' (1980: 18 March 1925).

Furthermore, it is rarely the 'official', collective moments of crisis or celebration which are the crucial ones in personal experience. Instead, the moments which we look back on and forward to, the moments by which we experientially age, achieve their significance through judgements and criteria particular to the construer. Hence: 'it's not catastrophes, murders, deaths, diseases that age and kill us; it's the way people look and laugh, and run up the steps of omnibuses' (Woolf 1978: 82). The individual experience of individual lives seldom runs to institutional design.

Finally, if we construct individual moments of being, if we ever live in discrete experiential units, of time, of self, of individuality *per se*, then equally, such moments are a constant, for we are never not being in a moment of some kind and degree or other. Our lives may turn on moments of greater and lesser significance, but our reflection on our lives is never non-momentary (or non-momentous) and hence the moments of our lives are eternal.

Socio-cultural time

In the social-scientific literature, the particularity to the West (the cultural and historical specificity) of cutting up the passage of time into moments of progression is well attested (cf. Gell 1992). At least since the Enlightenment, it is explained, Western culture has, unusually, imaged time as inexorably linear: stable, unrepeating and oriented towards a becoming: an 'evolutive' time. Such notions, indeed, are said to inform the very (deep-structural) bases of Western society; from neatly and constantly sectioned intervals of varying duration, timeliness comes to impose a certain 'discipline' on everything from the individual body to the institutions of state (Foucault 1977: 151).

Hence, the experience of discrete temporal moments echoes equally discrete moments in ontological experience: we are babies, then infants, children, adolescents, adults and, finally, old-aged. We see time cut up into regular, precisely measured and constantly applied units of greater and lesser duration, and we see society segmented into a hierarchy of social levels and social beings of greater and lesser inclusivity. As seconds are parts of minutes, of hours, days and so on *ad aeternitatum*, so individuals are parts of families, of neighbourhoods, clubs, churches, communities, ethnic groups, nations and confederations which become larger and larger. As minutes can seem to amount to hours, so heroic individuals can seem to represent entire communities; as hours can appear to pass in minutes, so lifetimes of whole societies and epochs can appear as ephemeral as morbid individuals; and so on. Temporal sectionalization and progression, in short, can be seen to mirror the conceptualization of stages of a life-cycle and components of a social hierarchy (cf. Gellner 1998: 3).

The same effect is said to pertain in societies and cultures where time is circular or cyclical rather than linear, or possessed of some other rhythm. What is significant is that time always has a rhythmical (and hence momentary) quality and that, in Durkheim and Mauss's influential formulation (1970), it is seen as a representation and a manifestation of a *conscience collective*. As with other socio-cultural distinctions, that is, time can be seen as emanating from 'the collective mind' of society, and thus as coming to 'express' the socio-cultural milieu in which it is practised (Durkheim and Mauss 1970: 85, 66). The rhythm of temporal distinction penetrates the individual members of a society or culture and instils a pervasive 'anatomo-chronological schema of behaviour'; so that a correct use of time (thinking in momentary terms) precipitates a correct use of individual body and mind and the way they are conceived of (cf. Mauss 1985).

Moreover, the more temporal division is refined, it has further been argued, the more detailed the partitioning of experience into moments of individual being, so the more the activities of that individual, their stages, development and elaboration, may be subjected to detailed government. Foucault (1977) thus charts the rise in militaristic eighteenth-century Prussia of a modern, highly detailed structuring of time, an increasing refinement in the conventional recognition of minute temporal intervals, as that which also comes to determine an entire disciplinary regimen or discourse within which individuals live. Indeed, Foucault would tie in the genesis of this conception of time (the fetish for chronometry and timetabling) with the invention of the modern Western individual (and its 'cult status') as such. In the moments of being of an individual's life, then, time may be seen as a social-structural, functional and ideological imposition which places that individual – body and being – within a collective social framework at once totalizing, integrative and disciplinary (1977: 150–60).

In short, the social-scientific account of temporally sectionalized lives – lives classified into moments and statuses – has generally been impersonal and collective. A homology is posited between the structure of a society and the cognitive structures of its (individual) component parts, brought about by time's obligatory rhythm.

Phenomenological time

What is significant in Woolf's account of moments of being is its centralizing of the experiencing individual. She might live in moments as formal units of time just as those around her, and she might deal with these units as conventional forms in her interaction with others, but the experiential time of her life, notwithstanding, she construes and maintains independently of, and most likely differently to, others. Ultimately, the significant moments of her life are hers alone.

What makes these moments of being are encapsulation and juxtaposition. Moments make moments, in short, a viewing of the times of one's life from across an experiential boundary, from another time: one interaction, one holiday, one generation, status or identity, from another. The act of juxtaposition replaces a flowing continuity of lived-in time (an unconscious immersion within it) with a detached observation of it. Furthermore, since moments are constructed from outside, from across a boundary, their significance, their existence as 'moments of being', as moments at all, also varies according to the particular vantage-ground. Moments of being are contingent, therefore, upon their particular differentiation, connection and comparison with others.

What makes moments of being more or less significant is their felt intensity; also their unexpectedness as experiences. In comparison with the moments which juxtapose or encapsulate them, far more has happened within them. Here are, in Fernandez's words (1986: xi), 'moments of a sudden constellation of significances' which become '"revelatory incidents"'. There are crests to experience and there are troughs, in other words; and here too there is contingency. For, only afterwards, looking back on significant moments of being, can their heightened intensity (emotional, intellectual) be seen at some point to have begun and to have stopped. As moments and as intense experiences, moments of being are contingent upon individual acts of *post facto* construal.

In short, if it is a collective shadow which tends to fall across much contemporary social-scientific accounting of time, then 'moments of being' also calls attention to an individual phenomenology of experience over and against its formal sectionalization. As Woolf's contemporary, E.M. Forster, phrased it: 'man does not live by time alone' (1961: 199);

the significance and resonance of the experience of time is individually variable and not appreciable simply in terms of its external, measurable proportion. True enough, homologies can be drawn between the way we image social time in the West, say, and our image of individuals as components of society: between the logics of Time and Society as discourses in common usage. Notwithstanding, such formal overlaps between discursive logics do not necessitate cognitive overlaps, nor demand that these overlaps be used or experienced in a particular way. Human behaviour, after all, is less a matter of the formal properties of socio-cultural institutions such as discourse than of occasions of their individual interpretation.

What is evidenced ethnographically, then, is less the conventionality of temporal experience and its division than its personalization (cf. Crapanzano 1980; Campbell 1995). Individuals make their own significant moments, which are not necessarily others', nor even ones others are aware of as significant or as moments at all (cf. Rapport 1994a: 156–88). The morphological logic is no guide to the sense that is derived from it: the formal conventionalities of Time and the Individual in no measure point to the embedding and control of the former discourse in the latter's consciousness. Indeed, an emphasis on moments of being identifies those nature and the processes which make for an individual control over time; by conceptualizing their lives in terms of significant moments, moments of greater and lesser intensity, individuals gain a certain purchase upon their temporal experience. For, the idiosyncrasy and privacy of their moments of being, the fact that they do not involve collective participation or entail collective acknowledgement, mean that the moments become theirs to run and rerun, classify and reclassify, juxtapose and rejuxtapose, model and remodel, as they will; they become resources for facing the future (cf. Wallman 1992).

To cut up a life into moments of being, in sum, is for the individual to possess a means by which that life can be filled, shaped and reshaped in significant ways.

See also: **Cognition, Individuality, Narrative**

MOVEMENT

Movement conceptualized as a mode of human being ramifies into all manner of arguments concerning socio-cultural life and identity. The contemporary importance of the concept is forcefully stated by Paul Carter (1992: 7–8, 101):

[I]t becomes ever more urgent to develop a framework of thinking that makes the migrant central, not ancillary, to historical process. We need to disarm the genealogical rhetoric of blood, property and frontiers and substitute for it a lateral account of social relations . . . An authentically migrant perspective would, perhaps, be based on an intuition that the opposition tween here and there is itself a cultural construction, a consequence of thinking in terms of fixed entities and defining them oppositionally. It might begin by regarding movement, not as an awkward interval between fixed points of departure and arrival, but as a mode of being in the world.

Anthropological fixity

Paradoxically, perhaps, what has been conventionally assumed in anthropology is a relationship between identity and fixity. In the promulgation of essential cultures, societies, nations and ethnic groups (embodying ways of life which were coherent, homogeneous, and more or less long-lived), the traditional anthropological understanding has been that the cognitive environment in which human beings undertake their daily routines is a fixed one – if not stationary then at least centred.

Hence, anthropologists have come to depict environments as normatively fanning out around the perceiver in concentric circles of greater and lesser degrees of consociality, with the perceiver at the perspectival centre: from house to lineage to village to tribe to other tribes, perhaps (Sahlins 1968: 65). A language of classification has been seen to place the speaker reassuringly at the centre of a social space and fan out from there: from 'self' to 'sibling' to 'cousin' to 'neighbour' to 'stranger', perhaps; or else from 'self' to 'pet' to 'livestock' to 'game' to 'wild animal' (Leach 1968: 36–7). To be at home in an environment, in short, has been to situate the world around oneself at the unmoving centre, with 'contour lines of relevance' in the form of symbolic categories emanating from this magisterial point of perception (Schuetz 1944: 500–4). To know (oneself, one's society), it was necessary to gain a perspective on an environment from a single, fixed and homogeneous point of view.

Even if the subjects were nomads, their myths were regarded anthropologically as making of the environment through which they passed a known place, an old place, a proper place, not only fixed in memory but to which their belonging was stationary because permanent, cyclical, normative and traditional; cognitively, they never moved. And even if the subjects engaged in ritual journeys outside everyday space and time – rites of passage; pilgrimage; vision quests – in search of sacred centres to their lives (Eliade 1954: 12–20), these anti-structural events served in fact to fix them even more; as special, extraordinary, aberrant experiences, the rituals merely emphasized and legitimated an everyday identity which derived from fixity in a social environment. Ritual pilgrims used their moments of (imagined) movement to establish routinely fixed orientations to a world around them (cf. Yamba 1992). Similarly anti-structural and marginal, finally, were the passages undertaken between status-groups by individuals in hierarchically organized societies (between classes, between professions, between age-grades), for here was movement whose experiential purpose, whose successful conclusion, was eventual stasis. As Lévi-Strauss concluded, myths should be understood as machines for the suppression of the sense of passing time and space, giving onto a fixed point from which the world took and takes shape (1969b: 14–30); a conclusion Leach then extended to ritual acts in general (1976a: 44).

In short, under this traditional anthropological dispensation, movement was mythologized as enabling fixity. As cultures were rooted in time and space, so cultures were seen to root societies and their members: organisms which developed, lived and died in particular places. Finding a stationary point in the environment from which to engineer one's moving, perceiving, ordering and constructing was regarded as a universal necessity. Movement and travel, as Auge quipped (with Lévi-Strauss in mind), was something seemingly mistrusted by this anthropology to the point of hatred (1995: 86).

Movement and identity

Of late, however, there has been a conceptual shift in the norms of anthropological commentary. As Keith Hart begins (1990), socio-cultural fixity and stasis no longer persuade; the world is not divisible into framed units, territorial segments and the like, each of which shares a distinctive, exclusive culture, a definite approach to life. There are no longer traditional, bounded cultural worlds in which to live – pure, integrated, cohesive, place-rooted – from which to depart and to which to return (if there ever were), for all is situated and all is moving. Human society is fluid and inclusive, such that ways of life 'increasingly influence, dominate, parody, translate and subvert one another' (Clifford 1986: 22). There is a complex movement of people, goods, money and information – variously depicted as: 'modernization'; the growing global economy; the migration of information, myths, religions, icons, languages, texts, entertainments, imagery, cuisine, décor, costume, furnishing, fashions, above all, persons (Geertz 1986: 120–1); the new technologies of communication and 'knowledge engineering' exploding distinctions between localities, and between the local and the global (Schwartz 1987); the induced, often brutally enforced migrations of individuals and whole populations from 'peripheries' towards Euro-American metropolises and Third World cities (Chambers 1994a: 16) – all of which causes even the most isolated areas to belong within a cosmopolitan global framework of socio-cultural interaction. As Hart concludes: 'everyone is caught between local origins and a cosmopolitan society in which all humanity participates' (1990: 6).

In this context, John Berger makes the argument that movement around the globe be regarded as 'the quintessential experience of our time', while emigration, banishment, exile, labour migrancy, tourism, urbanization and counter-urbanization, are our central cultural motifs (1984: 55; cf. Minh-ha 1994: 13–14). Being rootless, displaced between worlds, living between a lost past and a fluid present, are perhaps the most fitting metaphors for the journeying, modern consciousness: 'typical symptoms of a modern condition at once local and universal' (Nkosi 1994: 5).

To bring different contemporary forms of movement together in this fashion, as Berger does, furthermore, is not inevitably to essentialize movement: to claim 'it' is phenomenally somehow always the same, or *sui generis*. Movement remains a polythetic category of experience: diverse, and without common denomination in its particular manifestations. Nor is it to underrate either the forces eventuating in large-scale population movement in the past (famine, plague, crusade, imperial conquest, urbanization, industrialization), or the forces arrayed against movement in the present (restrictive or repressive state or community institutions, state or community borders). To talk about the ubiquitous experience of movement is not to deny institutionalized power and authority, nor the differential motivations and gratifications in that experience which hierarchy might give onto. Rather, what Berger draws our attention to is the part movement plays in the modern imagination, and in our imaging of the modern; '[m]ore persons in more parts of the world consider a wider set of "possible" lives than they ever did before' (Appadurai 1991a: 198). Movement is the quintessence of how we – migrants and autochthones, tourists and locals, refugees and citizens, urbanites and ruralites – construct contemporary socio-cultural experience and have it constructed for us. Wandering the globe, as Iain Chambers puts it (1994a: 16), is not now the expression of a unique tradition or history; for the erstwhile particular chronicles of diasporas – those of the black Atlantic, of metropolitan Jewry, of mass rural displacement – have come to constitute the broad ground-swell of modernity; modern culture is practised through, and the work of, wandering.

Anthropological movement

In this context, anthropology has had increasing recourse to 'write movement'. Through such concepts as 'deterritorialization' (Appadurai 1991a), 'creolization' (Hannerz 1987), 'massification' (Riesman 1958), 'compression' (Paine 1992), 'hybridization' (Bhabha 1990), 'inter-referencing' (Clifford 1986), and 'synchronicity' (Tambiah 1989), it has sought to comprehend the processes that movement effects in socio-cultural milieux – and so to apprehend the relations between movement and identity.

This may be exemplified in the work of Drummond (1980), Hannerz (1987) and Paine (1992). For Lee Drummond, the culmination of some 400 years of massive global migration, voluntary and involuntary, of a continuous traffic in capitalist commodities, can be seen to have transformed most societies. However, the result of these transformations is neither new integrations of what were once separate societies and features of societies, now fitting neatly together as one, nor pluralities whereby old separate societies simply retain their cultural distinctive-nesses side by side. Rather, what results are socio-cultural continua or combinations: 'creolizations'. Rather than discrete social spaces with their own discrete sets of people and cultural norms, societies are basically creole in nature: combinations of ways of life, with no invariant properties or uniform rules. A series of bridges or transformations lead across social fences and cultural divisions between people from one end of the continuum to the other, bridges which are in constant use as people swop artefacts and norms, following multiple and incompatible ways of life. Here is a world in which there are now no distinct cultures, only intersystemically connected, creolizing Culture: a 'concatenation of images and ideas' (Drummond 1980: 363).

For Hannerz, the traditional picture of human cultures as forming a global mosaic must now be complemented by a picture of 'cultural flows in space', within a single field of persistent interaction and exchange (1993: 68). Through mass media, objects of mass consumption, and the mass movements of people, culture now flows over vast distances; here is a continuous spectrum of interacting forms, which combines and synthesizes various local cultures and so breaks down cultural plurality; indeed, it may be better to conceive of culture *tout court* as a flow.

Nevertheless, any new 'world system' results not in socio-cultural homogeneity but a new diversity of interrelations: many different kaleidoscopes of cultural combinations, amounting to no discrete wholes, only heterogeneous and interpenetrating conglomerations. For people now draw on a wide range of cultural resources in the securing of their social identities, continually turning the erstwhile alien into their own; they make sense to themselves and others by selecting from amongst a global inventory of behaviours and beliefs, ideas and modes of expression. Hence, each locality partakes in a global collage, a 'Kuwaiti bazaar' (Geertz 1986: 121), and speaks in a stuttering, creole voice (Chambers 1994b: 247). '[W]e are', in short, 'all being creolized' (Hannerz 1987: 557).

For Paine, however, such global movement among and between cultures is neither smooth nor is it singular. With individuals making different cultural selections and combinations – different from other individuals and different from themselves in other times and places; different in terms of particular items and their relative weighting, and different in terms of the willingness, loyalty and intensity of the selection – and with individuals combining cultural elements which were not just previously separate but are still incommensurable, so global movement can be expected to be volatile. Advocates of different selections, furthermore, can be expected to be exclusionary if not hostile. At the same time as there is globalization, therefore, and movement across the globe, between societies and amongst cultures, as never before – people treating the whole globe as the cognitive space within which they can or must imagine moving and actually do move, the space which they expect to 'know' – there is also 'cultural compression' (Paine 1992): an insistence of socio-cultural difference within the 'same' time and space; a piling up of socio-cultural boundaries, political, ritual, residential, economic, which feel experientially vital, and which people seek to defend and maintain. A dialectic is born (not to say a Batesonian schismogenesis) between global movement and local compression. So that even if travel is ubiquitous, and one is 'at home' on the entire globe, to travel within one's home is to encounter a world of socio-cultural difference; even to stay home is to experience global movement (cf. Featherstone 1990).

Moving from Drummond to Hannerz to Paine in this way is not to meet perfectly commensurable expositions of the contemporary world, then. There is disagreement over the extent to which a globalization of culture results in an ongoing formation of boundedness around social groups, as well as disagreement concerning the extent to which this globalization is experienced as colonial or post-colonial – as the imposition of a particular cultural way of being-in-the-world as opposed to the opportunity to constitute and reconstitute the set of cultural forms which go to make up one's lifeway (cf. Appadurai 1990). More significantly, there appears to be divergence concerning whether the thesis linking contemporary movement and identity is a historical one or a representational one. In particular, Drummond is happy to talk in terms of four centuries of change, while Paine's central motif is a comparison of could-be anthropological representations between E.M. Forster and Salman Rushdie. The historical argument would seem to be the harder one to make, and would also seem prone to the kinds of grand-historical reductionism which characterized conventional anthropology in its traditional dispensation (from 'fixity to movement' as from 'mechanical solidarity to organic', from 'community to association', from 'concrete thought to abstract', from 'hierarchy to individualism'). Certainly, the history and archaeology of frequent and global movement make generalizations about the uniqueness of the present foolhardy.

Movement and methodology

Where Drummond, Paine and Hannerz do meet is in a recognition of the contemporary significance of movement around the globe – its universal apperception, its ubiquitous relationship to socio-cultural identities. Now we have 'creolizing' and 'compressing' cultures and 'hybridizing' identities in a 'synchronizing' global society; there is a sense in which metaphors and motifs of movement are of the quintessence in the conceptualization of identity. Identity is seen as forming 'on the move': a 'migrant's tale' of transitions and heterogeneities (Chambers 1994a: 24).

'Settled arrangements' in socio-cultural milieux were always a story, Geertz admits (1995: 15–16), and things were always actually fluid and multiform. What is different now is that we recognize our traditional categories of comparison – 'parts', 'norms', 'practices' and 'wholes' – and the master-plots and grand pictures of culture they gave onto – causal forces shaping belief and behaviour to a generalizable, abstractable pattern – as impossibly illmade and unworkable. What is called for, therefore, is representation more attuned to hints, uncertainties, incompletions and contingencies: 'swirls, confluxions and inconstant connections'. Whether in folk commentary or in social-scientific, the personal myths and rituals that one carries on one's journey through life (that carry one through a life-course) need not fix one's perspective on any still centre outside one's (moving) self.

What is also called for is a pertinent methodology through which to address the ethnographic enterprise 'in a post-structuralist' era: how anthropologically to capture the sequentiality-of 'part-structures being built and torn down' (Moore 1987: 730). Since no overarching ideological totalism can any longer be said to characterize an ethnographic setting – if it ever truly could – anthropologists are witness to events which instantiated not *a priori* social structures or symbolic systems but structural and symbolic orderings continually in the process of being created and dismantled. Hence, a 'processual ethnography' is called for, of parts and pluralities in time, accounting for situations which are constantly transitional regarding social organization, scale and identity (Moore 1987: 736; also cf. Hastrup and Olwig 1997).

For a superficial sameness in cultural forms across the globe should not reduce to casual, homogeneous descriptions, or expected treatments of homogeneity (such as once characterized the work of theorists of 'world systems' (cf. Wallerstein 1974/1980)). As Drummond, Hannerz and Paine each argued, the dismantling of what were once conceived of as the structural(–functional) bases of discrete societies and cultures, and the prevalence of globalism as a popular motif, should not translate into homogeneous meanings or lives. Global cultural forms still find themselves being interpreted and 'consumed' (Simmel 1971) within individual (local and personal) contexts. There is, in short, a diversity of local acts of 'appropriation' of cultural forms (Miller 1988), by which the global comes to be animated, personalized and transformed. Only a 'provisional writing' (cf. Cohen 1992b) could accommodate the plurality of symbolic orderings which the anthropologist might adduce at any one place and time: the diversity of provisional normative codes in terms of which the world is locally apprehended.

Movement and travel

'[O]ne comes to recognize the existence of an actual immortality', Nietzsche proposed (1994), 'that of motion'. The world in motion that anthropology has begun to address conceptually brings to our attention something perhaps universally true whatever the socio-cultural milieu, and whatever the conventions of representation; something which, over and against its history of conceptualization (and the will to fixed systems), is perhaps basic to the human condition. This is the relationship between knowledge (its acquisition and representation), identity, and movement: human beings conceive of their lives in terms of a moving-between – between identities, relations, people, things, groups, societies, cultures, environments and times. In and through the continuity of movement, human beings continue to construe moving accounts of their lives.

When the philosopher A.R. Louch proposed (1966: 160) that anthropology should be seen as a collection of 'traveller's tales' – and that this was perfectly fine, the tales were 'sufficient unto themselves' – few anthropologists would have been satisfied with his description. This has now changed (cf. Pratt 1986). Again in conjunction with a description of the ubiquity of movement in the world – with our heightened awareness of global interdependence, communication, diffusion, aggregation, sharing and penetration; our allowance that anthropologists are no more necessarily aware of the world cosmopolitan consciousness and its operation than their transient ethnographic subjects; and with our appreciation that there is no fixed and stable Archimedean point at which to stand and observe because we are all historico-socio-culturally situated, because all knowledge is in flux – anthropology now conceives of its enterprise very differently. There is an acceptance that cultures need to be rethought 'in terms of travel' (Clifford 1992: 101). Anthropology, in essence, is a kind of writing and itself a kind of journeying, inscribing what it was like There and Then in the categories and genres of the Here and Now (Geertz 1988: 1–5, 140–5).

In short, there is now an acceptance that anthropological knowledge derives from movement and represents itself through movement. To the travelling of 'the other', therefore, the informant (whether exile, migrant, tourist or counter-urbanite), now comes to be aligned 'the increasing nomadism of modern thought' (Chambers 1994a: 18), no longer bolstered by sites and sightings of absolutism, no longer persuaded by fixed, totalizing ways of thinking relations. So that Louch's statement is doubly true: anthropology as a study of travellers as well as by travellers.

See also: **Cybernetics, Home and Homelessness, Narrative, Non-Places, Tourism**

MYTH

Since the birth of the anthropological endeavour, myth has been, together with magic and religion, among the most assiduously explored of its subjects, which is probably more a sign of the troublesome nature of these concepts than of a disciplinary success story of problems well solved. Inherent in such a long-standing and attentive regard is the deep discomfort that anthropology still experiences about the problem of how best to treat what is, for us, other people's strange and 'exotic' statements about reality. The question that has yet to be answered is, which (and whose) reality is it that myth speaks to?

This predicament of the relationship of myth to reality is the key issue, for the anthropological focus upon myth (and also magic and religion) became one of the most potent means through which an exoticized 'anthropological other' has been created. The sharp disputes over what myth is, and the reality to which it relates, take us to the heart of broader controversies within the discipline, which in turn must be contextualized within the wider world of academic judgements over the worth of the humanities and social sciences *vis-à-vis* the natural sciences. The debates often centre on impossibly large questions, such as the relation between language and the world (of reality), and the relation of language to myth. If myth is a language of poetry, then what is the relation of poetry to reality? The most telling question of all is that of what is the relation of speaking (purportedly) *wrongly* (i.e. mythically) about reality to reality itself? What is the relation of mythopoetics to rationality and the 'progress' of reason? In the end, the issue with the real sting revolves around the question of what as bottom line any of us are willing to accept as reason or reality?

What is myth? The debate in ancient Greece

Vernant reminds us (1996: 203) that we have inherited our concept of myth from the Greeks, and also their rationalist distinction between *mythos* and *logos*. Early in Greek history, the poetic discourse of *mythos* was highly valued. Within both community life and learned society, the opposition between *mythos* and *logos* was not yet made. Through mythic narrative the speaker could captivate and charm an audience by relating the 'fantastical' adventures and misadventures of supernatural beings belonging to a different time and mode of living than ordinary people. While mythic narrative had its capacity to scandalize reason, it was also through the narration of these dramatic antics of the gods that fundamental truths of existence could be explored. According to Vernant (*ibid.*: 206–7, 220), one fundamental characteristic of the telling of myths in early Greek times was its ability to give pleasure and involve an audience emotionally. Good myths have entertainment value, for both the magic of their poetry and the power of their narrative delight the listener (cf. Overing 1985c on Amazonian narration of myths). The Greeks considered the affective, performative aspect of myth important to its power. Its dramatic appeal worked not only to enrapture an audience but to convince it.

Later in Greek history, 'myth' came to be viewed as a category of fictitious discourse. Within Greek philosophy as it developed between the eighth and fourth centuries BC, *mythos* became understood as a form of speech opposed to the reasoned discourse of *logos*. In time, myth became defined as a discourse contrary to truth (myth is fiction) and the rational (myth is absurd). *Logos*, as the arbiter of both truth and reason, served as a potent political tool in the battle to constrain the verbal freedom of wayward myth narration. Thus Thucydides, the historian, Plato, and Aristotle, devalued *mythos*, the fabulous discourse, in relation to the scientific discourse of, respectively, 'factual' history, 'truthful' speech and ostensive demonstration (see Vernant 1996: 208–9 discussion of Thucydides, and *ibid.*: 210–11 of Aristotle).

Vernant argues (*ibid.*: 207–8) that the privileging of *logos* over *mythos* was directly associated with the increasing prominence given to the written text over the tradition of oral poetry, a trend connected in Greek politics to a political process of democratizing speech. Discourse became 'common', no longer the exclusive privilege of those who possessed the gift of eloquence. All members of the community were now judged to possess equally the right to speech, and it was the rational language of *logos* that was thought to best fulfil this purpose. Thus *logos* was brought into the encounters of the public square. The reasoning used in defence of *logos* was that each man, through the faculty of reason, could fight on equal terms through discussion and counter-argument. The rules for discourse were no longer to do with overcoming an opponent through the pleasure-giving, idiosyncratic, spell-binding performance. Rather, the purpose of *logos* was to establish the truth on the basis of the 'laws of thought', and thus through logical, critical and detached intelligence alone. Everything earlier attributed to speech as the power to impress and convince was reduced to *mythos*, 'the stuff of the fabulous, the marvellous' (Vernant *ibid.*).

The battle of Greek intellectuals to destroy the respectability of *mythos* in order to privilege the rationality of *logos* in both intellectual and public discussion is a local history – and a political one. The battle was never entirely straightforward. Plato, for instance, did not entirely deny the potency of mythology, and at times used myths to elaborate his own philosophical theories (such as with the myth of Prometheus in *Protagoras*). For Plato those who were looking for the 'real truth', '*the really real*', were merely naive.

The repeat of a history: the modern West's claim to a superior rationality and knowledge

It is significant that 'myth' as a word came late into the English lexicon, appearing only in the early nineteenth century (Williams 1983a [1976]). Its entry into the language carried with it the tradition inherited from the rationalist intellectuals of Classical Greece, and their debate on the rational and the irrational in their endeavours to discover truth. The growth of the popularity of the word in the European context is most likely associated with the process of secularization, and especially the battle of the sciences for ascendancy over the church and other powers in their 'truth-claims' about reality. Thus we find that the terms 'myth' and 'mythic' have usually been used in the modern European context in a derogatory sense *with regard to other people*, to refer to a fabulous, or untrustworthy, non-rational, and even deceptive set of ideas, story, or discourse – to be found within the domain of religion, or held by a given class of society. Myth seems related to the notion of ideology, when the latter is used to mean false consciousness, and ideas that are mistaken, wrong-headed, deceptive. We find this use of the term in, for instance, Roland Barthes's fascinating study (1973) of the 'mythologies' of the French *petite bourgeoisie*. The other can be disdained *within*, and not just without.

Because the word 'myth' is used in both political and academic contexts, it is not an easy one to define. All kinds of discourse, speech, text, sets of ideas, can be deemed 'mythic', and thus its meaning depends upon the contrast frame in which it is set. Is it being contrasted with the lineal, fact-based writings of our historians? Or, the conclusions about reality proposed by our scientists? Or, the views of an opposing political voice? In each case 'mythic' almost always carries with it a connotation of irrationality, and is therefore more a judgemental than definitional or propositional procedure. Its attribution is attached to a judgement embedded in modern Western standards of truth and reality, which declare the superiority of the West with regard to rationality and knowledge. It is a judgement joined to Western metaphysical understandings of why things are as they are.

The modern West's claim to both superior knowledge and rationality can be understood only in relation to its origins in the project of the Enlightenment. As suggested, there are strong political undercurrents to this story, as there were with the ancient Greek distinction between *mythos* and *logos*. This narrative begins with the Enlightenment aim, as part of its scientific strategy, to establish civilized Europe in its role as arbiter of truth, reason and knowledge. As a central prop to this powerful story was the vision that separated 'civilized Europeans', the upholders of truth and reason, from 'ignorant pagans', who became a generalized superstitious 'other', whether from India, Africa, or ancient China. All such peoples did not have knowledge because they did not understand the rational laws of the universe (cf. Fabian 1983). Instead they defined themselves, and their relation to the cosmos, on the basis of false religions.

Enlightenment thinkers were not atheists, for the idea was that God had created the world as a perfect, rational machine that then required no further interference from Him. The Bible remained an important authoritative source from which could be derived the universal rules of knowledge. Humans, who also partake of this rationality, could perfect themselves insofar as they progressed in the knowledge of God's rational design. In other words, since God's laws of nature are rational, it is through reason that human beings can discover them (cf. Fabian *ibid.*), as Newton had done through his discovery of the mechanical laws of the universe. The global effort of the Enlightenment was to explain the postulates of other religions as false explanations. Other peoples' religious texts shed no light upon the causal laws of the world. Thus, this homologized (myth-ridden) 'other' took the form of a primitive, unenlightened, and thus backward mentality (cf. McGrane 1989; Fabian 1983). In earlier ages and other places, rationality was but imperfectly realized. The blame for other peoples' ignorance and defective rationality lay with their religious beliefs (i.e. their *myths* about reality).

It was this image of difference in mentalities that played a considerable part in the development of modern Europe's self-image, and at the same time proved to be central to its emerging intellectual and political hegemonic status in the world. By the nineteenth century, God's design tended to drop by the wayside in accordance with a secularized scientific explanation of the course of the progressive social development of humankind. All religious thought became slowly categorized as mythology. Difference between peoples became a lineal, historical difference, the basic assumption being that the human race is advancing toward a greater perfection, epitomized by Western civilization and its secularized science. In the grand evolutionary schemes of the nineteenth century, human history became transformed into laws of historical development and progress, a classification that fed into all areas of life, morality, politics, arts, technology. All existence got better over time. At the same time the key relation between development and reason was retained. Although there was no God in these schemes, they were just as certain as any religious doctrine of the great chain of being equated with the unfolding of God's reason. As Fabian notes (1983), the nineteenth-century concept of natural law was very similar to the earlier

Christian version – and just as value-laden. This myth of modern progress, which told of the West's achievements through its own rational efforts, called for an *end to all mythology*, a battle cry, so to speak, for all humankind to achieve a similar mature rationality, and through it an end to history. The bequest to us from the nineteenth century was the idea that modern man, through the realization of perfection and release from myth, could end a historical process that humankind had been undergoing through time.

An anthropological debate: myth, rationality and the savage mind

'Myth' as a term has usually been used anthropologically to refer to the narrations told by indigenous peoples about the origins of the world, and all the beings and elements that populate it. Mythic narrations are said to present a totally 'miraculous world', a 'nonsensical anti-world', the world 'as it is not', where identity is fragile and ephemeral, causality perverse, and time erased or distorted. Nonetheless, the amazing events of these narrations also tell of the circumstances in which all features of the world and forms of life came to be, especially human beings, and those agents and elements salient to them. It is through myths that cosmogonic events are unfolded and explored, and thus they relate to a people's particular metaphysical understanding of why things are as they are.

It might be thought that such a notion of myth would accord positively with an anthropological relativism because of the discipline's strong perspectival approach. However, anthropology, itself a child of the wedding of Enlightenment with nineteenth-century evolutionist thought, could hardly escape its own parents' ambitions for domination in matters of reason, truth and scientific *respectability*. It has also not been immune to the parental paradigms of rationality that sharply distinguished a healthy, adult reality from the dangerous or childish land of fantasy. Anthropologists can believe that powerful shamans are highly intelligent, but not that the shamans' stories about cosmic rays of paranoia and spirit ogres of the forest are true, or even rational. From its inception, much anthropological debate has been an attempt to deal with the dilemma of how to interpret other peoples' insistence that gods, demons and spirits exist.

Many anthropologists continue to view mythology as one of those falsities of other cultures that we anthropologists study: myths pertain to the domain of the 'fantasmogorical'; they are narratives that express the fantasy origins of a people; they contrast with history, which details 'truthfully' the real events of a people's past. This is a tradition that we have inherited from the rationalists of Classical Greece, further embellished by Enlightenment and nineteenth-century elaborations. It is unsettling that similar arguments over the respective worth of the participatory and the disengaged, the fantastical and the logical, the affective and the intellectual, the contextual and the universal, are alive and well today.

Anthropology's problem has been that it has found it difficult to shed the Enlightenment project and its specific vision of rationality. Anthropology's chosen project has been the study of the 'other', which by definition became the analysis of the mental aberrations of the 'primitive mind'. The idea of a 'primitive rationality' entails a theory of mind, and presupposes a theory of rational progress through history, within and by reason. Myths, magic and religion all provided testimony to the ways in which the 'primitive mind' was unsound in intellect, or at the least lacking in knowledge. With respect to anthropological uses of the term 'myth', it is important to note that anthropology had its beginnings not long after the word entered the English language. From the start, what anthropologists have labelled as 'myth' or 'magic' – all those irrational explanations, beliefs and practices of 'primitive' folk - have been understood as 'a problem of rationality' that must be explained. The general stance has been that while the scientist tells us of reality, the content of myths belongs to the domain of illusions.

Some twentieth-century approaches to myth

In the twentieth century, with the reappraisal of the excesses of evolutionary generalizing, myth was no longer denounced as an absurd and logical scandal. Instead its mysteries and richness became a challenge for science to unravel (cf. Vernant 1996 235). On the other hand, in this anthropological search for the logic of the myth, reason has tended to be found *elsewhere* – in the reality of the social or political structure, in psychological health, or in thought itself. The idea of the metaphysical paucity of myth itself has continued to hold sway throughout much of the century, and thus mythic statements as such have still been viewed as irrational. (On the 'rationality debate' within anthropology in respect of this assumption cf. Wilson 1970; Horton and Finnegan 1973; Overing 1985a; Hollis and Lukes 1982.)

A usual way of categorizing modern anthropological approaches to myth is to distinguish between the functionalist, symbolist and structuralist modes of analysis. Their boundaries are in fact blurred, for functionalists may speak of symbols, and we find structuralists today labelling themselves as 'symbolists'. I shall distinguish instead two broad schools of thought, those forthcoming from Durkheim, and those attached to the structuralism of Lévi-Strauss. This distinction is not wholly satisfactory because of the influence of Durkheim upon the work of Lévi-Strauss. It nevertheless pays tribute to the two powerful thinkers most responsible for the two substantial revolutions in the development of modern anthropology, that is, functionalism in its various colours and formal structural analysis.

Anthropology has been strongly affected by Durkheimian thinking about the role of myth in society. In this view, the stress is placed upon the value of myths to society. The function of myth is not to deliver 'metaphysical truth', because, while based on the reality of society itself, its content is irrational and untrue. Rather, it serves to reinforce social cohesion and unity by presenting and justifying traditional order. Mythic discourse reminds a community of its own identity through the public process of specifying and defining its distinctive social norms. Whether or not people believe the irrational content of myth is irrelevant, for its symbols have served a crucial social function in the maintenance of the given social order. The emphasis of Malinowski (1948: 84) in his discussion of the role of myth is upon its pragmatic value in enforcing belief. The narratives of myth have the function of legitimating the social structure, providing it with a charter. They especially come into play when the social or moral rule demands justification and sanctity. His stress is upon the social power of myth, and the potency of its use in matters of political concern that have to do with the legitimation of the inequities of privilege and status (*ibid.*).

The strength of the functionalist framing of myth is that it contextualizes myth within the daily social and political life of the community. Thus myth is seen as one aspect of a wider social framework. However the functionalists also insist that the meaning of myth has only to do with the arena of pragmatic socio-cultural interaction. Malinowski is very firm about the intellectual deficiency of myth: 'myth is not a savage speculation about origins of things born out of philosophic interest' (*ibid.*: 83). In other words, the 'savage's' interests are not philosophical or intellectual, but psychological and affective. In stressing the practical social use of myth, the functionalists have been able to ignore the problem of knowledge and belief, and the 'illogical', 'contradictory' material faithfully transcribed, but often hidden, in their fieldnotes. Especially in British anthropology, although the social use of myth has been given full attention, the value of its contents has tended to be denied or ignored (contrast, for example, Witherspoon 1977).

Lévi-Strauss has followed a different route from the Durkheimian one, in that he denies a one-to-one relationship of myth to a specific social world. Myth does not serve to reflect the social structure; its value instead is a cognitive one. His aim in analysing a vast corpus of native American mythology (Lévi-Strauss 1969b, 1973, 1978, 1981) was to disclose myth's *own specific features* by treating the entire body of myths as one 'objective world' that could be studied in and of itself. In developing his methodology, he drew upon structural linguistics, the allure of which was that its own methodology was acclaimed as the most 'scientific', the most akin to the natural sciences, of all the social sciences. Lévi-Strauss distinguished for myth, as the linguists did for language, its surface and underlying structures; and as did the linguists, he also privileged the latter. The meaning of myth is not then to be found on the surface level of speech, understanding and performance, but in the relationships between the myth's elements that together form an underlying structural system.

For Lévi-Strauss, mythic narrative, as narrative, provides little of value, for as illusion, or mere speech, it is not where meaning should be found. The intentional agent, as myth-teller and creator of metaphor, has no place within his structural analysis. Rather, the meaning of metaphor rests on the level of the unconscious, with metaphor being read as an unconscious, analogical process of classification. Underlying the content of myth there exists an abstract and unconscious cognitive ordering that endows the myth with rationality. The *reality* to which myth speaks is a *universal mode of thought*, and not all those stories about creation times and the origin of the world. The *story* that myth narrates is untrue.

In contrast to the functionalist approach, the major problem in Lévi-Straussian structural analysis is that myth and its meaning become decontextualized from everyday life. What myth in reality *means* becomes a topic for scientific specialist knowledge alone. The performative role and dialogics of myth narration are neglected, as are its aspects that pertain to social value, the political, the life of affect, and the (indigenous) philosophical. Because of Lévi-Strauss's particular scientific project, truth equates with the physical scientist's postulates of material reality. It also recognizes the objective reality of cognition, but not of speech, the emotions, or the world of values, which he states to be beyond the ken of scientific analysis (Lévi-Strauss 1981); contrast Overing 1985a; Leavitt 1996.

The dilemma of anthropology: the study of phantom realities

As Shweder has argued (1991b: 52–6), the anthropological dilemma is that we study phantom realities, other peoples' creations and constructions of reality. We look at their culture, their ritual, their myths. All are understood by us as belonging to the world of the imaginary. Like narrative, and as narrative, they are fictive. Words, song, ritual and the postulates of myth, all are to be viewed with mistrust, and indeed as illusory in contrast to the real, objective world of physical nature (we know that the rain which fertilizes the crops is water, not the urine of the creator god). As Shweder notes, the paradox of our work is that a large part of our task is to translate for our readers the world as the 'native' understands it. The humanist, Collingwood, taught us (1940) that the creation of skilful history requires the historian to make the effort to understand the minds of other times. Like good Collingwood historians, our chore is to get into other people's heads in order to perceive the universe as they understand it. At the same time, we are also Western academic specialists, who have inherited the Enlightenment materialist world-view. The great divide in Western theory of nature and culture ever raises its head. In the materialist example, nature is real, objectively knowable, while tradition (because of its subjectivity and diversity) is unnatural, and therefore *unreal*. One route that has been taken by anthropologists to escape the materialist predicament has been to reduce the cultural to the 'hard' facts of the natural. With this solution, we have the assumption that demons and gods have no relation to reality, while, for instance, laws of thought (which are of nature) are real, and therefore can be objectively known – the Lévi-Straussian solution.

It is this materialist world-view that creates real problems for the project of anthropology (cf. Shweder 1991b). Our view conflicts with the one we study. Another people's interpretation is that they are presenting to us their own true postulates of reality (rain really is the supreme deity urinating). For the Piaroa of the Venezuelan rain forest, what we call 'myths' belong to a genre of what they call 'old talk', or 'before-time speech', to be contrasted to the 'new talk' of today. 'Old talk' is *true* talk, and the richer the language of the myth-chanter, the more complex the metaphoricity, the *truer* it is – and the more powerful. The Piaroa express *their* strong conviction, not only in the existence of spirits and gods, but also in the efficacy of these beings. The chanter's intention is, through 'mythopoetics', to display knowledge of cosmology, of the cosmogonic events of creation-time history, and in so doing to cure illness and prevent it – and also to generate the fertility of people and the land and forest around them. The chanter of myths therefore demonstrates a deep knowledge of ontological matters, and also considerable power in dealing with them (Overing 1990, 1995). The methodological issue for anthropologists is how to reconcile these two contradictory concerns, that of translating as *they* understand, and that of how *we* understand (cf. Shweder 1991b).

Roy Wagner (1991) challenges anthropology to rid itself of the divisions of subjectivity and objectivity, to refuse *the politics of doubt* inherited from Enlightenment writers that leads us to distrust other people's certainties. As Wagner asks, how do we verify a poem? Or the design on a canoe paddle? How can we understand other people's point of view and experience in the world if our gaze is filtered through what we believe is 'the cool, aseptic skepticism of a scientist contemplating a world of stubborn fact' (Wagner 1991: 40)? For the Piaroa, the postulates of their 'old talk' are not only illuminating of everyday experience (Overing 1995), but they are also knowledge about the world. It is on this point especially that the materialist stance works against the anthropological task of understanding the judgement of knowledge made by others who patently hold different premises about existence in the world than those acknowledged by materialists.

Some new directions: from logos back to mythos

Myth and the poetics of everyday life

There is an increasing interest within anthropology to rectify the deletions and excesses of high functionalism and structuralism, along with their materialist-*cum*-rationalist world-view. The trend is to stress the foremost importance of understanding cultural expression, including the mythic, from indigenous points of view. As Malinowski observed (1926: 18), for people who engage with mythopoetics, myth is 'reality lived'. Many anthropologists now wish to understand the context of the *use* of myths in everyday life, their performative value as entertainment, as pedagogy, cure and explanation – and as evidence of knowledge and a rich poetics (cf. Brady 1991a; Turner and Bruner 1986). Anthropologists have only recently begun to pay attention to the central role of the poetic, performative side of myth in everyday life. In much of the modernist discourse of anthropology, where attention was focused upon grand theories of structure, society, or thought, there was a clear demotion of the status of the everyday. The land of the daily life, that drab place where women cook and babies cry, was of no consequence (Overing 1999). In contrast, a prevalent stance today is to recognize the salient connection of myth, poetics and aesthetics to everyday lived experiences (e.g. Witherspoon 1977; Brady 1991b; Guss 1989; Overing 1989, 1996b).

The writings of Dell Hymes (1981) on the poetics of the mythic narration of Native Americans are a ground-breaking endeavour for the enterprise of understanding everyday poetics. He unfolds the well-elaborated poetics of Native North American narrations, a poetical form neither recognized nor expected by anthropology in the past ('primitives' cannot have poetics!). His methodology is one that he frankly labels as 'structuralist', but it is a formalism that only hints at a precedent of French hue. In Hymes's hands meaning is carefully contextualized to capture its culturally specific values, ones that are also attached to the individual narrator's style and intent. Style, individual performance and the dialogics of performance, entertainment value and a moral point of view – all of these elements are necessary to understand the grammar, the co-variation of form and meaning within the poetics of Chinook mythic narration. Here, context and performance, as in Greek *mythos*, are essential to meaning.

Nowadays more anthropologists are asking about the role of myths in the framing of much of daily practice, and about the relation of the poetics of myth to indigenous understanding of the everyday. In other words, the emphasis is more upon the *conscious* use of myths through which basic (conscious) postulates of reality are also expressed, and as such made *constitutive of everyday practice*. At the same time we are questioning (as did Lévi-Strauss) a representational view of myth, the idea that there is any one-to-one relation between the myth and social structure. Myths and mythic narration are more complicated than that, in that they are often more a *reflection upon reality* than a reflection of it. As the ancient Greeks understood, myths have the capability of delivering a shock, they inspire laughter and tears, all toward the end of providing greater insight. Roy Wagner suggests that mythic narration is a creative way of standing outside of convention. In other words, myths play an innovative role in dislocating conventional orientations through a process he refers to as 'obviation' (Wagner 1978: 255).

Indigenous knowledges, and the reality of the really made up

Many anthropologists, such as Taussig (1993), are today looking at *the reality* of the really made up. It has become, for instance, steadily more obvious to Amazonian specialists that they can understand everyday behaviour of Amazonian peoples only by also learning how *they* understand and use the mythic. In other words, indigenous judgements are at last being taken seriously. The argument of Lévi-Strauss that the reality postulates of myth have no relevance to the real world refers to that actuality which is known and charted by the natural sciences. There is little reason why we should expect the two to coincide – the indigenous and the scientist's realities, since we could not but agree that in indigenous metaphysics many of the basic propositions about modes of being in the world are at variance with many of those assumed by biologists and physicists. However, do we need then to conclude that indigenous peoples in their mythology have got it 'wrong'? Our current dilemma is just this uncertainty about what it is that we wish to include in any real world. This is in contrast to the perspective of Lévi-Strauss who was more certain about such matters.

Nevertheless, current received wisdom more or less accepts two basic 'rules' for mythic interpretation: the acceptance that (1) myths express, evoke, explore and deal with, if not directly at least consciously, a people's *reality postulates* about the world, and (2) mythic truths pertain more to a *moral, evaluative, or significant universe of meanings* than to a 'natural' one (in the sense of the physical unitary world of our scientists) (Overing 1995). Increasingly, anthropologists are also accepting a third dictum, namely, that knowledge is not tied solely to reason and the material world of natural law. Rather, there are many types of knowledges: among others there are empirical, rhetorical and metaphoric, social, moral and aesthetic knowledges (cf. Goodman 1978). It is time that the power of actors thinking as social and moral beings is accepted as knowledge about the world of human sociality (Overing 1985b). For those educated within a Western tradition, myth is a strange place indeed to discover 'truth' and 'knowledge'. Nevertheless, even the most absurd of happenings, at least within Amazonian myths, has its moral and ontological implications for what it means to be a human alive today on this earth (see e.g. Overing 1985d, 1997 on the Piaroa myth telling of the day they lost their blue crystal anuses and genitals – and thereby acquired social knowledge).

Amazonian myths typically often stress modes of power. Since myth concerns the adventures and battles of heroes or gods constructing the universe in which we live, it inevitably pertains to the mighty forces of creation and destruction which have allowed for our particular humanity, and those of our enemies of whom we must beware. Often tales of great moral complexity, these mythic episodes deal with the multiple faces of power that relate to a people's images of selfhood. They state sets of identity criteria for a people and a community. Thus we find that myths of identity are equally myths of alterity, or significant otherness; for to state identity is also to speak of difference, for example between sensual and intellectual might, or the potency of the gun versus the power of thought. The images of identity and alterity that play such an important role in myth have obvious political as well as social implication. Myths are usually expressive of particular political visions that distinguish the relative worth of an array of modes of power. In these schemes the appropriateness or monstrosity of specific modes can usually be clearly spelled out (Overing 1996a). The Piaroa myths of alterity become a means through which the narrator explores the ambiguity of the human condition. While the root metaphor for alterity in Piaroa discourse is that of 'the cannibal other', such an image can hardly preclude in any absolute manner the Piaroa themselves. As eaters of animal flesh, they too are predators of the jungle. In the Piaroa highly egalitarian ontology of existence, predators are the prey of their own prey. Their mythic stress is upon the human predicament itself, and thus upon the absurdities and evil as well as the positive strengths of human power.

The Piaroa, who are very attached to their myths, live within a 'meaningful' universe, which contrasts with the unitary, objective, universe of the Western scientist. All postulates about reality in a meaningful universe, including those about physical reality, are tied explicitly to an evaluative universe. For example, personal malevolence, for the Piaroa, is ultimately the cause of all deaths. It is normal among the tropical forest peoples of the Amazon for postulates about 'physical reality' to be constitutive of other postulates which are social, moral and political in scope. This is why a main concern in anthropology today is the power of actors thinking as social and moral beings, and not as physicists.

The fact that indigenous postulates about reality are consciously not decontextualized from social, political and moral concerns, and thus from everyday practice, is not a trivial matter (Overing 1995). One methodological issue, especially pertinent for our understanding of other peoples' mythology and mythic narration, is that local metaphysical postulates about reality (e.g. sorcerers exist, as do gods; time does not flow only in a linear fashion) should not be interpreted in the same light and in accordance with the same standards as those of physics. Since they are incommensurable, have distinct concerns, and belong to separate histories, they require different standards of judgement. Or another way of putting it, is that myth and physics can equally well be treated as particular types of local knowledge. We could at the same time happily argue that one set of postulates is just as true of reality as the other. However, the expertise associated with each set deals in the main with differing aspects of reality.

NARRATIVE

Conveyed variously by way of language, image and gesture, human narratives are ubiquitous. They are to be found in myths, legends, fables, tales, novels, epics, histories, tragedies, dramas, comedies, mimes, paintings, films, photographs, stained-glass windows, comics, newspapers and conversations. Humans may be said to: dream in narrative, day-dream in narrative, believe, doubt, plan, gossip, revise, remember, anticipate, learn, hope, despair, construct, criticize, hate and love by narrative (cf. Hardy 1968). Human beings, Roland Barthes concluded (1982: 251–2), are 'narrating animals', since: 'narrative is present in every age, in every place, in every society. . . . [N]arrative is international, transhistorical, transcultural: it is simply there, like life itself.'

Notwithstanding this, narrative is one of a number of concepts which have gained prominence in anthropology primarily since the literary turn of the 1980s. Its study has accompanied an increasing appreciation within anthropology of the practice of 'writing' social reality, both by the subjects of anthropological study and by anthropologists themselves.

A definition of narrative

For a definition of narrative, one might turn to Kerby (1991: 39): 'Narrative can be conceived as the telling (in whatever medium, though especially language) of a series of temporal events so that a meaningful sequence is portrayed – the story or plot of the narrative'. A narrative account involves a sequence of two or more units of information (concerning happenings, mental states, people, or whatever) such that if the order of the sequence were changed, the meaning of the account would alter. It is this sequentiality which is used to differentiate narrative from various other forms of conveying and apprehending information about the world: from the general abstraction of 'theory', the momentariness of 'feeling', the simultaneity of 'sensation', the semantic vault of 'metaphor', and the elemental fixity of the 'model'.

Narrative is also understood as giving onto a particular way in which the world is ordered and understood: temporally. Narrative is the form of human representation concerned with expressing coherence through time; it provides human lives with a sense of order and meaning within and across time. By describing an orderly developmental sequence of events (etc.) temporal expanses are made meaningful.

Thus, narrative can be said to transform the potential discord of humanly experienced time: the experience at once of fragmentation, contingency, randomness and endlessness. But more than this, narrative makes time an aspect of socio-cultural reality; time becomes human in being articulated within a narrative sequence. Time comes to have a certain texture, a way of its being humanly experienced, due to its being home to and punctuated by a certain flow and development of events.

Again, an eventful sequentiality is key. Narrative provides a way of temporally experiencing the world by the way it records and recounts, defines, frames, orders, structures, shapes, schematizes and connects events. A beginning, a middle and an end is a common structure for events to come to possess, then, and this unitary closure assists the transformation of an inchoate sense of formlessness in experience. Furthermore, ensuring sequentiality between events also assures human lives of direction and growth. At the least, as Barthes put it (1982), what is narrated is 'hemmed in'.

The ubiquity of narrative

This makes of narrative a powerful tool, a means of eschewing the experience of fragmentation and of structuring the world over time; narrative is an instrument of doing as well as saying. Moreover, since narration presents an account of how the world is, it also represents a site of possible contest. For one narration of the world can be seen to repress or replace or otherwise obscure preceding or alternative ones. Perhaps it is the power of narrative to create temporal order coupled with the potential of narrative continually to offer new versions of that order which makes narrative so universally pervasive in human life.

Rendering experience in terms of narrative is seen as a meaning-making activity which dominates much of human practice, and (as Barthes and Hardy have noted) as taking many forms. Besides those listed above, then, writers have made distinction between real and imaginary narratives: 'histories' as distinct from 'novels' (Nash 1994); also between more and less consciously written and finished narratives: histories, novels, biographies and autobiographies which we work-up to a polish as distinct from the less conscious narratives of everyday circumstance in which we live on an ongoing basis (Kerby 1991); and again between sacred and profane narratives: ritual re-enactments of mythic, stylized, conventional and communal events, in an allusive, dramatic, corporeal language, as distinct from mundane articulations of commonsensical reality which people tell one another and themselves by way of gossip (Crites 1971). In short, within the same narrative form (and with similar power and potential) can be found a plurality of types of 'referential commitment' – epistemological, logical, make-believe, etc. 'Writing' narratives helps us to make sense of the world, but we can be aware of different kinds of possible relations between that narrated world and the actual one we live in, and maintain any number of relationships, intellectual and emotional, to the particular narratives we have made.

The argument is also made that the ubiquity of human narration, the human 'readiness or predisposition to organize experience into a narrative form' (Bruner 1990: 45), tells us something significant about human consciousness. Consciousness can itself be seen as an incipient story, and narrative as the form of its own experiencing; past, present and future are the inexorable modalities of human experience. Our present consciousness absorbs the chronicle of memory and the scenario of anticipation into a layered narrative which guides and also absorbs our present actions; in the narrative of our consciousness, action and experience meet too.

We humans are temporal beings, in short, with our perceptions, understandings and identities embedded in an ongoing story. Our conscious lives constitute dramas in which our selves, our societies and our reference groups are central characters, characters whose significance we interpret even as we live out their stories: '[N]arratives are a primary embodiment of our understanding of the world, of experience, and ultimately of ourselves. . . . It is in and through various forms of narrative emplotment that our lives – . . . our very selves – attain meaning' [Kerby 1991: 3ff.]. This is a never-finished project, and our conscious lives are taken up with self-narrating, with continuously rewriting, erasing and developing the definitions of our own stories.

The socio-cultural derivation of narrative

If narrative mediates our conscious human experience as individual sentient beings, then further argument surrounds the question of whence such narrative derives. Is it primarily socio-cultural in origin or individual? Many commentators have plumped for the first option, emphasizing the way that extant narratives precede the birth of particular individuals and influence, if not cause, their coming to selfhood. The self arises out of signifying practices, the argument runs; *contra* Cartesian or Judaeo-Christian notions of autonomous mind or soul, the self does not exist prior to its being represented. Hence, the self is given content, is delineated and embodied, primarily in narrative constructions or stories. What we understand as individual persons are simply the result of ascribing 'subject status' or selfhood to those 'sites of narration and expression' which we call human bodies (cf. Kerby 1991).

In large part, this narrative history is self-mediated; the self is a reflexive being which comes into being through its own self-narrating. In other words, individuals become human persons by means of participating in a narrative history of themselves (and to the extent that they are seen to do so). We tell the story of our lives, from the point of view of a first-person narrator, and through this description and emplotment actually create our individuality. Through our telling, in a public language, our lives emerge into meaning and reality. Furthermore, our lives maintain their coherence only to the extent that we continue to narrate them. We understand ourselves and know ourselves insofar as we construct narratives of and for ourselves which develop over time, which possess internal coherence and accessibility: we must present our stories well to ourselves.

Of course, the sense that we have of our self-identities as continuous also depends on the story we tell ourselves, and can be seen to be ethnographically variable. Over and above the fluidity and mobility which narrative identity affords – the temporal dialectic which speaks to process and change in ways that more fixed ascriptions of identity, derived from structure or substance, do not (cf. Ricoeur 1996) – use of that fluid potential will vary. It might be that one lives in a series of fragmentary, discontinuous narratives and takes oneself to be a different character at different times (to have a multiple personality). And it might be that self-scrutiny and self-narration is more of a marginal concern; there are other stories with which one is more involved (collective ones, sacred ones) and only at rites of passage or at times of personal crisis does one turn one's attention to the narrative of one's particular life.

However concerned the individual is with the narrative of self, and however coherent the result, the above line of argument is assured that social and collective practices of narration are the source. The stories individuals tell of themselves are seen as being influenced by the vocabulary and grammar of the language in which they are expressed, by the broader cultural conventions of context, style and genre of expression, and by the other stories in circulation. In this way, individuals come to consciousness within a conventional narrational context, and within a narrational space which they are expected to occupy. Indeed, even their self-narrating represents them becoming conscious of stories in which they have been narrated before their birth. Individual selves have been narrated from a third-person perspective long before they gain competence to narrate their own first-person ones. Hence individuals produce second-order stories of themselves which intersect with numerous preceding first-order ones. Indeed, even individuals' most personal stories are but segments of other stories: parents', kinsfolk's, enemies', strangers'. These other narratives set up expectations and constraints on an individual's own; at least they contribute significantly to the material from which the latter narratives derive, and at most they cause an individual's own narrative identity as such. As Barthes concludes (1982: 293), drawn from 'the centres of culture', individual narratives amount to nothing but 'a tissue of quotations'.

Within this line of argument, much anthropological work has gone into an examination of the narrative stock which a society or culture can be expected to possess (its classificatory forms and genres, its conventional structures and typical contents), the norms regarding its use, and the functional consequences of that use. Analogous to Propp's (1968) analysis of the conventional morphology of the Russian folktale and Lévi-Strauss's (1969b) analysis of South American myth, then, Labov (1972) identifies six elements of universal narrative structure: an abstract, an orientation, complicating action, an evaluation, a resolution and a coda. Barthes (1982) theorizes that all narrative contains different structural levels, specifically a horizontal plot-line in contradistinction to vertical points of punctuation into which alternative possibilities of character and action are slotted. In any particular socio-cultural setting, Greimas continues (1983), listeners will know not only the story presented to them but also reflect on the alternatives which were passed over. Any narration thereby alludes to much beyond itself – both socio-cultural situations and other narratives. In fact there are four components which will be present in any narrating situation, Bruner suggests (1990): time or sequentiality, narrative voice or 'agentivity', narrative structure or canonicality, and point of view or perspectivity. It is in an operation of contextualization, Genette explicates (1980), by which relations between these components of the 'narrating situation' come to be fully elaborated, that a sufficient analysis derives. Indeed, as Georges concludes (1969), the content of the narrative, the performance, the listeners and the knowledge, the interpretive procedures and aesthetic mechanisms which they bring, the setting, the use of the narrative to persuade or to negotiate social relations, rights or whatever, all add up to one 'storytelling event'.

The consequences of such events are seen to be that members of a society or culture come to share the same ways of organizing, presenting and remembering information, and so knowing the world. The narrative stock of a culture is thus seen as embodying what are socially recognized to be typical behaviour patterns. This will also involve assumptions for and constraints on sense-making: on the forms in which social knowledge is conventionally acquired and stored. It will further provide a framework for understanding the new, laying the grounds of future intelligibility. In short, modes of narration are seen as determining collective modes of perception, of the encoding of information, and of its remembrance and recall; in sharing the knowledge to produce and read narratives in a particular way, members of a cultural group will share ways of thinking about, of framing, schematizing, and memorizing, experience, and will thus come to share a collective memory (cf. Werbner 1991).

As Bruner concludes (1990: 96): '[t]o be in a viable culture is to be bound in a set of connecting stories'. Indeed, what cannot be narrated in terms of conventional frames and categories is either forgotten or is highlighted (routinized) as an exceptional departure from the norm. Rendering the exceptional (or even new) as deviant in this way, canonical patterns come to be reaffirmed; the exceptional is explained and simultaneously explained away. Finally, this is said to afford the narrative event a moral aspect or component. The deeply internalized narrative conceptions connect with and find support in other cultural institutions so that to focus on norms and deviations from the culturally canonical is inexorably to treat moral consequences and to adopt a moral stance. It is within a narrative understanding that moral reasoning in a particular socio-cultural setting is situated and developed.

To sum up the argument for the socio-cultural determination of narrative and narration, it is said that we perceive, anticipate, remember, tell stories and moralize from them in conventional ways. Through our narrative acts we create meaning out of experience, but only in terms of pre-existing and prescriptive categories. We can but narrate ourselves in and into socio-cultural space. Even in our autobiographies, 'the ultimate function . . . is self-location . . . in the symbolic world of culture' (Bruner and Weisser 1991: 133).

The individual derivation of narrative

What the above line of argument appears to overlook or underplay is the uniqueness of individual experience, the complexities of subjectivity and the rich subtleties of the relationship between form and meaning. On this view, whatever the seeming habituality and longevity of narrative forms, the individuals partaking of them (animating them by their mental and bodily, verbal and behavioural presence) willy-nilly find themselves cognitively apart from those forms as such.

That is, within the conventional forms of narrative, its cultural patterns of framing, organization, recitation, interpretation and evaluation, an individuality of meaning is an inevitable product. For, what participating in and performing narratives inexorably give onto are personal interpretations and understandings; individuals impart these forms with meaning which derives from unique perspectives on the world. Hence, individuals create space for themselves beyond the formal surfaces of public and collective performance. However much their narratives might be inspired by living in a particular socio-cultural environment, however much their medium might be a public and collective system of signification, and however much their structure might borrow from a conventional intertextuality, still individuals create something particular to themselves.

The ongoing engagement with narrative thus amounts to a way of proceeding actively through life, fixing personal moments of being and giving them meaning. Indeed, narrating a meaningful life and at the same time enacting the stories which they narrate make of individual lives works of art, whose character (complexity, beauty, closure) derives from a specific consciousness. Through narrational performances, conscious selves come to be maintained: selves with pasts, presents and futures; selves with world-views and identities; selves with relations and possessions; selves with knowledge, self-consciousness and understanding.

In short, the construction of personal meaning in individual narratives exhibits an originality and artistry which places them beyond the overdetermination of the language in which they are written, the collective, public forms which they employ; they are affected by these latter, in varying measure, but in no wise effects of it (cf. Rapport 1998). Through the performance of narratives, individuals write and rewrite the story of their selves and their worlds, and while the means of doing this is a *bricolage* of largely inherited cultural forms – words, images, behaviours – it is not society or culture which they embody so much as individual agency and consciousness. Narrative form becomes personalized in use, and individuals continue to write stories which depict their own world-views. Narrative comes to express nothing so well as the unique and undetermined nature of the lives lived through them.

Narrative hospitality

With the recent literary turn in anthropology, an evaluation of the conventions and responsibilities of disciplinary narratives, as well as an experimentation with new narrative possibilities, has increasingly been a feature of anthropologists' work (cf. Bruner 1986). There has been a concern both to overcome cultural assumptions (of singularity, authority and integration) which accompanied earlier narrative practices, and to benefit from the narrational potentialities of engaging with others in a situation of interpretational pluralism. An anthropological appreciation of narrative can be seen to have a number of practical consequences.

Life experiences may remain 'inalienable', Ricoeur has argued (1996), so that we cannot directly share in those of others, but using imagination and sympathy we can hope to reach out to others via our stories. We already do this for fictional and mythical characters with whom we identify in the course of a narrative telling, and we do this for ourselves as we retell our own stories and hence (re-)configure our pasts, presents and futures. In the same way, Ricoeur suggests, we may take responsibility for the stories of others and exchange with them our own.

The work of realizing the experiences of one another through our narratives is no easy task, but it is nonetheless vital. Indeed, generously extending 'narrative hospitality', in Ricoeur's terms, might be seen to be a primary ethical requirement for a world of movement and a shrinking globe. This hospitality entails at once making space for one another's narrational identities, and allowing for such identities to be fluid and plural, and matters of perspective. We must reach out for the narrated identities of others; we must expect such identities to be ongoing and changing; we must allow our own narratives and identities to be likewise retold by others; we must allow one another to reconfigure valued narrational forms in the fashion of alien logics. In this way, while not eschewing the temporal sequences of which narratives are made up, or the stories in which identities importantly reside, we can work towards achieving a space of generously plural reading. In such a hospitable ambience individuals, as world-travellers (even world-citizens), might feel free to exchange their most cherished stories, trying on one another's for fit.

See also: **Consciousness, Discourse, Literariness, Moments of Being, Myth, Writing**

NETWORK

It is said that the idea of a network for conceptualizing the connections and interconnections between individuals moving within and among different socio-cultural milieux came to John Barnes whilst undertaking fieldwork in a village of Norwegian fishermen (1954). The location is significant for understanding the history of anthropological theorizing. Kinship relations, 'genealogical method', and structural–functional assumptions of socio-cultural holism had predominated in the periods of anthropological study of distant, 'exotic' peoples. Once anthropology began to pay attention to its home environments (the Euro-American 'West'), the types of modelling it had seen fit to employ and impose elsewhere (collectivist, depersonalizing, distantiating) no longer passed muster. Too much was known, and known experientially, to talk convincingly of 'Norwegian [à la Tallensi] descent systems' or 'Norwegian [à la Sherente] structures of marital exchange'. The focus in network analysis is on individuals and their relationships, and there is an emphasis on personal behaviour and experience, on choice, action and strategy. As explained by one of its early exponents, Elizabeth Bott (1964: 159), a network of friends, neighbours, relations and particular offices and institutions conveys an appreciation of the 'primary social world' and the 'effective social environment' of individuals who may occupy the same physical space but live in different experiential worlds.

A concise definition is provided by Whitten and Wolfe (1974): 'a relevant series of linkages existing between individuals which may form a basis for the mobilization of people for specific purposes under specific conditions'. An appreciation of the social-structural as a 'contingent mobilization', and of the patterns of interpersonal relationships within a socio-cultural milieu – their formation and mobilization – as revealing the moments, range and character of that social structure, represents a radical departure from anthropological analyses which begin with notions of socio-cultural systems as overarching and *a priori*.

Attempts have been made still to treat the network model in evolutionary terms: as a methodology pertaining to the Western, the complex, large-scale and urbanized in the same way that more structural analyses (of descent, alliance, hierarchy and equilibrium) fit the traditional, rural and communitarian (cf. Sanjek 1978). However, this is to set up an unwarranted (dualistic) opposition between the way people act and interact in different socio-cultural milieux; individuals do not go about negotiating and developing relations in an ontologically different fashion because they live in rural as opposed to urban, or small-scale as opposed to large-scale environments, and so on (cf. Goody 1977: 8). Whatever the differences in formal discourse (kinship, say, as opposed to neighbourhood or occupation), the way individuals form relations with one another, and their logics for doing so, are comparable among the Tallensi, the Sherente and the Norwegians.

To regard the network model as pertaining only to certain (evolved) socio-cultural milieux is also to miss out on its full power and versatility (cf. Mitchell 1974; Boissevain 1979; Johnson 1994). The model is able to map an enormous variety of types of relationship, and network theory has concerned itself with demarcating, for instance: single-stranded relations and many-stranded, dense relations and rarefied, tightly knit and loosely knit, more clustered or overlapping or zoned relations and less so. Rather than evolutionary anchors, these have been explored in terms of individuals' different situations and purposes (cf. Barnes 1978). From types of relationship arise different types of social groups: from ego-centric to amorphous, from specific-purpose organizations to longer-lived associations, from behaviourally consensual to diverse, from those employing face-to-face dynamics to those more impersonally instituted (cf. McFeat 1974).

Network analysis is further able to tackle the old canards of the dichotomies between what informants say as distinct from what they do, and what is actually done as distinct from what is done ideally. Hence, in a celebrated study, Boissevain (1974) charted the Maltese networks claimed by a number of individuals on the island in comparison to the people whom they actually saw and engaged with on a regular basis; the 638 people claimed as part of a network of consociates by one individual translated into 128 regular interlocutors. In Bott's (1964) study of family networks in London, meanwhile, the ideal-typical relations and roles between spouses and kin were seen to be influenced if not offset by actual relations which individuals enjoyed in the personal networks which they maintained. Echoing the famous distinctions suggested by Firth (1951) between 'social structure' and 'social organization', and by Leach (1961b) between statistical and formal analyses, then, network analysis is able to provide (statistically significant) portrayals of individuals' actual behaviour – group membership as determined by the intensity of connectivity between individuals, or role-adoption as determined by the parts frequently played by individuals within a matrix of social relations. The development of computers has significantly enhanced the potential of this kind of mathematical modelling (cf. Hage and Harary 1983; Schweizer 1988).

Finally, inasmuch as, topographically speaking, the network model consists of points or nodes and the cross-cutting lines which connect them, the points and lines have also been treated metaphorically: to represent organizations, places and times as well as people, and flows of information and commodities as well as social relationships (cf. Sanjek 1974). So long as this does not eventuate in another style of reification (so long as the decision-making and agency of individuals remains the model's driving force), network analysis can in this way provide subtle and humanistic interpretations of the workings and interconnections between socio-cultural institutions.

See also **Gossip, Interaction, Transaction**

NON-PLACES

Marc Augé (1995) has suggested the notion of 'non-places' as a corrective to certain conventional conceptualizations of social milieux which are no longer persuasive. For Auge, the Durkheim–Mauss orthodoxy of 'societies' identified with geographical locations, in which are to be found representative role-players or 'persons', who belong to behavioural 'cultures' conceived of as complete wholes, can now be seen to represent an ideological conceit which had led anthropology up a blind alley. To construe a consistency and transparency between culture, society and the individual fails to provide a convincing account of the processes of identity and otherness.

No anthropologist could ever have been unaware of the contingency of socio-cultural 'places'; the image of a closed and self-sufficient world (of relations, identity and history) was never more than an instrumental semi-fantasy, a provisional myth, even for those who worked (whether inside the academy or without) towards its collective materialization. However, the organization of space etc. upon which the ideology rests is one which the world today comprehensively and irrevocably refutes. For, the measure of modern life is of movement, networks, and situations of interaction, taking place on a global stage and much in terms of 'non-places'; here are a proliferation of transit points and temporary abodes where individuals engage, without essential 'cultural' mediation, with global processes. In waiting-rooms, wastelands, building sites, refugee camps, stations, hostels and hotels, malls, thousands of individual itineraries momentarily converge as travellers break step. In these spaces individuals are at once alone and one of many; non-places are 'palimpsests on which the scrambled game of identity and relations is ceaselessly rewritten' (Auge 1995: 79).

Of course, 'non-places', too, can be construed as an ideology, no less partisan than traditional 'places'; while fixity, social relations and cultural routine (groups, gods and economies) can be seen to continue to reconstitute themselves in the world. But non-places serves the purpose of exploding the normative singularity of place; so that place and non-place represent contrastive modalities, the first never wholly constituted, the second never completely arrived at. The possibility and experience of non-place is never absent from any place, with the result that no place is completely itself and separate, and no place is completely other.

See also: **Home and Homelessness, Movement, Network, Situation and Context**

POST-MODERNISM

'[T]he will to a system is a lack of integrity', Nietzsche once aphorized (1979: 25), and there is a sense in which anthropology has always agreed. Anthropology has often felt 'uncomfortable' as a 'discipline' of study, desirous of being 'non-specialist' (Bateson 1959) in order to tackle the complexities of experience in socio-cultural milieux. In its representing of socio-cultural realities, furthermore, anthropology has pursued the polemical end of ever abnormalizing its discourse so that new possibilities can be constituted for thinking about human experience: 'constantly [building] up the conditions from which the world can be apprehended anew' (Strathern 1990a: 19). To this extent, anthropology has long practised as a 'virtual anti-discipline' (Hart 1990: 10).

In another sense, however, anthropology has seldom agreed with Nietzsche's counsel. For in any number of its paradigmatic manifestations – functionalism, structural-functionalism, structuralism, Marxism, ecologism, cognitivism, interpretivism – achieving a holistic analysis of a phenomenon conceived of as a whole – a society of institutions, a culture of representations, an environment of symbioses, a mind of schemata – has been anthropology's founding, abiding and guiding ideal.

Much 'post-modern' thinking represents a fantasia on Nietzschean themes – 'the bread and wine of modern philosophy'. (The origin of the term 'post-modern' – or one of the origins, at least – is said to be Charles Jencks's (1977) characterization of a style of contemporary architecture which offered a juxtaposition of different styles without attempting an overarching integration.) And in the same way that the relationship between anthropological practice and the above Nietzschean aphorism is an ambivalent one, anthropology's relationship to postmodernism is ambivalent too. Beginning with the writings of three of post-modernism's noted figures, this will become clear.

What should also become apparent is the difficulty of assigning 'a particular shape' to the relationship between anthropology and post-modernism at all – and again, the very post-modern nature of that ambivalence and that uncertainty. For thinking that takes as its cue the notion that 'a will to a system is a lack of integrity' is immediately caught up in a possible *reductio ad absurdum*. One seeks to avoid systematizing, because to will a system is to delimit and lack – to lack integrity (moral and ontological) – and yet to go about eschewing systems is itself systematic. So for post-modernism to have 'a nature' is for it to stop being post-modern. All that is left is its reactive character: post-modernism is not a thing but a reaction to things and thingness. In particular, post-modernism is a reaction to the propositions of thingness set out by 'modernism': of Western, Enlightenment conceptions of reason and rationality, objectivity and truth, scientific method and the progress of history and knowledge, individuality and liberal-democratic advance.

Lyotard

In *The Post-Modern Condition: A Report on Knowledge* (1986), Jean-François Lyotard describes the superficiality, the fragmentariness and the multiplicity of contemporary socio-cultural life and practice. We live in a world where there is a proliferation, even an excess, of ways and forms of knowing, speaking and gaining 'truth', Lyotard begins: from science to religion to consumerism to popular culture to multiculturalism. Each makes its own claims, posits its own values, but we are at a loss to know how to judge between them so as to grant one a superior legitimacy. Hence we arrive at no single, overarching truth, no definitive answers to our questions: is there a God? is there scientific certainty? is there artistic transcendence? is there an escape from unequal relations of power? is there an end to colonialism? In a world of excessive claims and information, we have lost faith in singularities. Not any longer knowing how to hierarchize different claims to knowledge and privilege one above others, we instead possess a 'flat' collection of types of knowledge all of which compete for our attention and among which we network, sample and drift. Each type of knowledge represents an island of determinism, its own irreducible world of order (or disorder), its own brand of (knowledge-)product, and we are travellers, shoppers, consumers amongst them. We use types of knowledges in a piecemeal and parallel fashion, trying them on for size in different situations, appreciating their usefulness for particular purposes, but not adhering exclusively to any one or believing in its overarching validity. This gives our lives a certain fragmented character. We live in episodes of particular ways of knowing but these do not last. Moreover, between our different episodes of knowing particular things in particular ways there is no necessary sequentiality, no real consequentiality. 'Things', as the (Yeatsian) title of Chinua Achebe's famous novel has it, 'fall apart', and we lead lives of contingency, chance and overriding uncertainty.

This lack of a single guiding telos to our lives, a grand or 'meta-narrative' of knowledge, identity and aspiration, Lyotard sees as an archetypically twentieth-century problem. It did not, for example, trouble Marx (Lyotard is a lapsed Marxian), for whom a distinction between truth and ideology or false consciousness was clear. After Nietzsche and Wittgenstein, however, we now recognize how all truth is discursive: a matter of conventionally normative fit between elements in a language-game. Furthermore, it is not something that particularly worries us; 'problem' is perhaps the wrong word. For we have no great nostalgia for meta-narratives or overriding truths, and probably would not recognize one as such a creature at all. We do not feel alienated by our loss (even if this was the abiding sentiment during late modernism), and are not shocked by a rule-less and directionless world which lacks a foundational moral sense. As post-moderns we simply live with our senses, and we do not attempt to make sense once and for all. The keyword is 'eclecticism': 'eclecticism is the degree zero of contemporary general culture: one listens to reggae, watches a western, eats McDonald's food for lunch and local cuisine for dinner, wears Paris perfume in Tokyo and "retro" clothes in Hong Kong; knowledge is a matter of TV games' (Lyotard 1986: 76).

Baudrillard

According to Jean Baudrillard (1989), modern culture has entered a Western-spawned age of consumerism and consumption (as opposed to the Marxian, modernist one of production). Furthermore, instead of the use- or production-value which commodities might possess in being able potentially to satisfy our basic needs, the value of commodities now derives from what they symbolize, from the images they conjure up. Commodities become encoded objects in a system of potential symbolic exchange, whose ownership we imagine as affording the possibility of being party to any number of communications and being identified with all manner of effects.

As in an age of production, however, this continues to be a wholly alienating situation. Delivered and developed by mass media with which it is impossible to engage or negotiate, the images of commodities contaminate and corrupt our lives in a number of ways. First, the images alienate us from reality and from any hope of accessing reality; so predominant and dominating is the world of images that we lose the ability to gain a perspective on our representations of reality as mere representations and to see beyond them. Instead, the images become our reality, and we lead lives of simulation surrounded by simulacra which never touch real referents. Images produce our world – absorbing any ulterior reality to themselves, appropriating reality to their ends – so that, for instance, television soap-operas become our social arenas. Our selves become merely terminals in multiple networks of moving images. Secondly, the world of images is alienating because mass media now so dominate their functions that the 'message' disappears; images become examples of pure form without any content at all. The form of the image becomes its meaning, and the world of images is a 'hyper-real' one which lacks all depth.

If we have lost control of our consumption of meaningless images, lost the distance and perspective necessary to make real meaning, or see real causes, or partake in a real history, then perhaps the only escape is into (image-less) meaninglessness. If all consumption of images is ideological, then the only route beyond the alienation of a false consciousness lies in the dissolving of Western culture and its systems of signs *per se*. And Baudrillard borrows from 'ethnography' to suggest how such escapes might seem. For instance, there is a 'beyond' Western culture, to be found in ecstatic seduction and sex, in unpredictable challenges and adventures, in meaningless catastrophes and disasters, in transcendent poetry, and in death, and there is a 'before' Western culture to be found in heterogeneous primitive systems of exchange. What is liberating about these latter is that as 'total prestations' (Mauss 1954), the items of consumption and exchange are non-monetary and non-liquid; so that a relational value between the participants (in the *kula*, in the *potlatch*) is uppermost. If such otherness can be preserved, then there might yet be an escape from Western imagism.

Foucault

Because we live our lives in terms of an exchange of images, symbols and signs which are themselves commodities of anonymous signifying systems (linguistic tokens), the real is ever epistemologically bracketed off from humanity, Michel Foucault claims (1991). We can never access reality directly, only through codes, ways of speaking and thinking, 'discourses', specific to cultural epochs. These codes or discourses, moreover, are less transparent media which provide windows onto underlying reality than creators and guarantors of specific realities. And such is the power of the unconscious workings of discourses upon the minds and bodies of those who are taught to employ them that such created realities come to be the predetermined worlds which the latter inhabit. Discourses 'imprint' themselves on users' minds and bodies so that their very beings become prison-houses. This means that human beings are not at the centre of history or in control of their lives, or even of their meanings, but are the 'effects' of discourses and particular positions within them. 'Truths' are meanings constructed in and by particular discourses, while the very notion of 'human beings' is 'a simple fold in our knowledge' (1972: 115). This also means that there can be no such things as objective knowledge or independent reasoned judgement, or autonomous individual selves, or any world that is not constructed by historically specific cultural discourses. Being, as we are, positioned effects of the anonymous play of these systems of signs, we can have no real subjective inwardness, no imagination, no original perception, no creativity. At best, we are *bricoleurs*, skilfully operating amongst networks of signs which we did not invent and do not control. What we can mean is a contingent matter dependent upon relations and differences between signs in a linguistic matrix. There is no originality here, only an endless discursive play: of signs relating to other signs in a parodic circle. There can be no escape to reality or an absolute referentiality or a real presence – God or Man – only discursive 'mimesis without origin or end'.

Finally, inasmuch as we live within (a plurality of) discourses which create socio-cultural worlds and give onto what and how we know about them, discourses are the source of knowledge, and also of great power. Or, as Foucault dubbed it, discourses are the seat of power-knowledge. Moreover, it is within power-knowledge that human beings come to consciousness. To be is to know oneself and the world in a particular way, which is to create oneself and the world in a particular way, which is to deny creating oneself and the world in other ways. Power-knowledge enables and at the same time eschews. There is no way around or outside the power-knowledge of discourse; no way of escaping its effects, but also no way of being except as one of its effects.

The reception of post-modern thinking

Differences of emphasis aside, there are clear overlaps between the above three visions: a going-beyond Marxian notions of power, relations of production and alienation; a sense of the anonymity and unreality of contemporary mass society; a feeling of 'being spoken' by languages of commodities and cultural artefacts; a sense of the impossibility of escaping back to a time of clear-cut orders and legitimacies; an awareness of a plurality of lives and worlds which can be known and related together only through the power of particular, contingent 'knowledge-practices'. As summed up pithily by Terry Eagleton (1981: 137), such post-modern exponents concur in their:

> modest disownment of theory, method and system; the revulsion from the dominative, totalizing and unequivocally denotative; the privileging of plurality and heterogeneity; the recurrent gestures of hesitation and indeterminacy; the devotion to gliding and process, slippage and movement; the distaste for the definitive.

Eagleton's description, nonetheless, is of something of which he, writing as a Marxist still, is highly critical. If the individual self of Enlightenment modernism – autonomous, active, free-willed, unified, self-identical – is emptied of psychical interiority and ethical substance, and dissolved into a network of libidinal attachments – the ephemeral function of this or that act of consumption, media experience, sexual relationship, trend or fashion – then what of the political quietism and compromise that must issue forth from it? Fragmented by institutionalized public discourses such as language, technology and consumerism, into so many pieces of 'reified technique, appetite, mechanical operation and matrix of desire', post-modernism can only supply actors whose deepest 'natures' are cultural and de-politicized (Eagleton 1988: 396; also cf. Jameson 1988: 383). More broadly, Eagleton complains of what he sees as the untenable inconsistency, the false consciousness, of remorselessly centralizing the contingent and the marginalized, of dogmatically privileging what escapes over what does not (the duplicitous and the undecidable), and of constantly dissolving and fracturing dialectical oppositions (1981: 138).

Giddens concurs (1990: 46–7). Here is the infuriating illogicality of claiming a post-modern project and epoch in a history which, it is also claimed, has no single linearity, in a world which has no one shape and therefore can be addressed by no one totalizing notion or theory. Here is a cynical scepticism, an ironic detachment, fetishizing the fragmentariness and eclecticism of present humankind while still claiming to recognize something called 'contemporary general culture', and to be able to describe a universality of change in a unifying description.

Here, Abrams concludes (1988: 273–5), is the hypocrisy of writers' preaching indeterminacy of meaning, and multiplicity of interpretation in the conventional verbal form, whilst all the time dependent upon an obvious and univocal reading of their words, and assuming the normative grammar of language to describe their points. Substantively, too, what is so new and what is so insightful in what the post-moderns have to say? There is nothing new to the West in exhibiting scepticism about extant truths; in fact, it is rather conventional. Meanwhile, is it true that meta-narratives have lost their popularity or persuasiveness? What is popular culture after all but a grand narrative, and what are religious fundamentalism, market capitalism and laboratory science? Finally, what is the picture of the modernism of the Western Enlightenment being followed by post-modernism but a meta-narrative of historical epochs in evolution?

Anthropological reactions

Anthropology's reception of post-modern thinking has been highly ambivalent, as has been mentioned. In many ways it is with an anthropologically informed awareness of socio-cultural contingency and diversity that post-modern thinking has been underpinned. Anthropological writing has been instrumental in illuminating paths beyond Western conceptions of essence, rationality, system, self, writing, language, and so on, while anthropological method (fieldwork and the dialogics of otherness) has provided the inspiration for imaging methodological progress beyond a narrowly defined scientific method. This has led to a welcoming of post-modernism in some anthropological quarters, some chagrin that the popularity of post-modern ideas has given rise to a host of new disciplines (Cultural Studies, Media Studies, Communication Studies) rather than simply an expansion of anthropology (cf. Nugent and Shore 1997), but also an acceptance that Lyotard, Baudrillard, Foucault and the like (Derrida, Lacan, Deleuze, Rorty, Bhabha) have extended anthropological insights in provocative ways. In particular, the notion of a 'literary turn' in anthropology in the 1980s, and its ramifications is a signal of the positive reception to the above ideas, at least their usefulness for thinking against (cf. Rapport 1994a).

While the names of James Clifford, Stephen Tyler, Paul Rabinow, George Marcus, Marilyn Strathern, Vincent Crapanzano and Michael Taussig stand out as writers within anthropology whose work shows some sympathetic engagement with post-modern concerns, that of Ernest Gellner stands out as a vehement critic. For Gellner (e.g. 1993), there are three basic intellectual positions (three claims to ways of knowing) which compete for our attention and loyalty in the contemporary world. These are: fundamentalist religiosity, which believes itself to be in possession of a uniquely revealed truth; post-modern relativism, which forswears the notion of unique truths and would treat each cultural and discursive vision as if true; and Enlightenment rationalism, which believes in a unique, scientific truth but never believes that we possess it definitively, only that through certain procedural rules we can continue to approach it. Gellner is a firm adherent of the last position and attacks the post-modern one (and the religious one) in some of the same terms that he maintains a long-standing opposition to a Wittgensteinian philosophy of language (1959). For, it is in part from Wittgensteinian notions that all concepts are social in nature, that speech-communities have terminal authority, and that all cultures make their own worlds, that post-modernism would conclude that everything is a text and there is no access to objective reality. Also that so-called facts and generalizations are the tools of colonial domination, that ranking kinds and ways of knowledge is wicked, and that the seemingly rational self is a product of contradictory, packaged, discursive meanings and is imprisoned in a hermeneutic circle. The popularity of these notions, Gellner surmises, derives from various failures in the social application of science this century (from the Holocaust and Hiroshima to 'mad cow' disease) and the science-like modelling of society (from Nazi Germany to Stalinist Russia), and from the difficulties of practising anthropology in a post-colonial world. These have precipitated an affirming (expiatory, sentimental and escapist) of cultural discourses as the only reality.

And yet, Gellner insists, knowledge beyond culture is possible; indeed, this is the central, most blatant, and by far the most important fact of our shared, and global, human condition today. Science, that is, represents a form of knowledge which is valid for all (its propositions and claims translatable without loss of efficacy into any socio-cultural milieu), a cognition which reaches beyond any one culture (so that new social orders spring up, sharing this new learning, in remarkably consensual ways), and an understanding of nature which leads to a universal technology for the transforming of human being. Like it or not, this is the world we live in, and the necessary starting-point of any adequate anthropology. Science represents a form of knowledge to which all cultures must and do come to terms. The world is neither one of balance nor of isolation – of culture 'A' having one version of reality, and culture 'B' having a distinct but equal one. Cognitive claims are inherently unequal – however equal people may inherently be. If post-modernism denies this, then it is a travesty:

> cognitive relativism is nonsense, moral relativism is tragic. You cannot understand the human condition if you ignore or deny

its total transformation by the success of the scientific revolution. . . . Valid knowledge ignores and does not engender frontiers. One simply cannot understand our shared social condition unless one starts from the indisputable fact that genuine knowledge of nature is possible and has occurred, and has totally transformed the terms of reference in which human societies operate.

(Gellner 1995b: 8)

Instead of pretending that knowledge of natural reality is inaccessible, anthropology should endeavour to answer why scientific modelling has proved so successful with regard to some domains and less so in others.

Post-modernism and anti-humanism

Gellner's criticisms, like those of Eagleton, Giddens, Abrams and others, are well-taken. And yet there is something in the post-modernist project which would seem to accord with contemporary experience – hence, perhaps, its persuasiveness. The oxymoronics of post-modernism, its appreciation of chaos and excess, of multiplicity, contradiction and inconsistency, its difficulties with a systematization of knowledge, all ring true.

At the same time, however, a number of key exponents of post-modernism can surely be taken to task for their illiberalism, not to say anti-humanism. (The controversy surrounding the disinterring of sympathetic writings on the Nazis by Paul de Man – a major conduit of post-modern ideas in North America – and the refusal of other post-modernist figureheads to condemn them has brought this into sharp focus.) An opposition can well be mounted against the post-modern tendency to displace ('dissolve', 'decentre') individual agency and deconstruct subjective inwardness and imagination so that social life becomes the mere playing-out of unconscious systems of signification (cf. Foucault 1972: 22).

Post-modernist thinking is right to draw attention to the difficulty, even the impossibility, of carrying through the nineteenth-century, scientistic project of making man-in-society a wholly understandable, hence controllable and directable, phenomenon. But then a critique of applying positivistic versions of systematizing science (pre-relativity theory and quantum mechanics) to the domains of human consciousness and the socio-cultural is Nietzschean, and nothing so new. Indeed, if one wishes to argue that the essence of life must always elude definition, since its circumstances are haphazard, chaotic, contradictory, irrational, unpredictable, unmanageable, and ambiguous, however simple they may superficially seem; that the nature of social reality is thus fragmentary, with perfect knowledge an illusion and immaculate perception a myth; that, furthermore, the human mind is inconsistent and eclectic, biased and situated, and its understanding of the other is only rough-and-ready, piecemeal and makeshift; and that, finally, as one cannot see things both steadily and whole, one cannot achieve a total and unequivocal interpretation of experience, it is appropriate to see them steadily and incompletely, recognizing in individuals' socio-cultural engagements not any grandiose plan but a casual disorder, a muddling-through, and representing this not in terms of closure or completion, '[n]ot rounding off but opening out' – then one need look no further than such modernist social-cum-literary commentators as E.M. Forster (1984 [1927]: 149). Post-modernism is obviously a question of emphasis, but the old Nietzschean wisdom holds the key, that 'irony is in fact of the essence' (Bradbury 1966: 130).

See also: **Discourse, Home and Homelessness, Irony, Science**

QUALITATIVE AND QUANTITATIVE METHODOLOGIES

Opposition between the concepts of the qualitative and the quantitative in research methodology points up disagreements over the nature of anthropology as such: art or science? When considering the range of methods of gathering data which anthropologists employ – participant-observation, interviews, life-histories, genealogies, censuses, questionnaires, network analysis, archival transcription – and the difficulty of deciding whether each is 'qualitative' or 'quantitative', and to what extent, it becomes clear that the latter distinction is really one of overall orientation and intention.

At the heart of the division is a disagreement over the relationship between anthropological knowledge and the replication of information. For something to be true, does it have to be observably replicated or replicatable (quantitative); and does a sample of events of the same kind have to be taken into account so that the representativeness of the new information can be ascertained? Alternatively, can one accept something is true if observed only by one person on one occasion (qualitative), both the manner of observation and the nature of the thing observed precluding replication; indeed, can something be imagined to be true if it is unique, its own kind, and while implicated in other things is not them and not like them?

Secondary oppositions then follow in the wake of this question of replication, and extend the division (cf. Filstead 1970; Johnson 1978). For instance: Is it proper to explain subjects from an independent, extraneous or etic standpoint (quantitative), or must explanation be emic, and in subjects' own terms (qualitative)? Should the researcher begin with a directing hypothesis (quantitative), or with an open mind, cleared as far as possible of preconceptions concerning the nature of his research subjects (qualitative)? Should research identify variables and causal relations which, it is hoped, possess universal provenance (quantitative), or is it sufficient to disinter substantive concepts and theories which are known to be locally grounded (qualitative)? Should the researcher restrict himself to sensory observation and the control of reason (quantitative), or allow himself to empathize, introspect and intuit meanings and relations (qualitative)?

Anthropological science?

In part, the opposition between the qualitative and the quantitative is an anachronism: a throwback to nineteenth-century conceptions of science, and attempts by social science to ape the reputed certainty of its methods of measurement and so borrow from its legitimacy and status. With the advent of twentieth-century science – Einsteinian relativity, quantum mechanics, chaos theory – comes a new ethos, however: an appreciation of the contingency, situatedness and intrusiveness – alternatively, the creativeness – of the research process as such. Conveniently summed up by Heisenberg's uncertainty principle, here is a realization that the observer is inevitably and inexorably a part of what he observes, so that what the researcher confronts is 'reality' as apprehended through his own particular prism of perception, and what he gathers as results are artefacts of the process of his observation (cf. Wiener 1949: 191). The research process is an interactive one, and the researcher, the observer, is at one and the same time an interactant, a part of the field of events under observation. Any interpretation of the information accrued, therefore, must somehow come to terms with the fact that far from being 'things-in-themselves', true for all places and all times, data are epiphenomena of their means of acquisition and their framework of representation (cf. Bellah 1977: xi). If there is no 'immaculate perception', and there are 'no facts, only interpretations', as phrased by Nietzsche (1911), then research observations, interpretations and generalizations are not so readily distinguishable from beliefs, hypotheses and evaluations (cf. Popper 1965: 36).

If there is a growing recognition in the natural sciences that proofs are learnt and respected practices common to a paradigm, and truth 'primarily a matter of fit: fit to what is referred to in one way or another, or to other renderings, or to modes and manners of organization' (Goodman 1978: 138), then anthropology has also come to accept that 'ethnographic reality is actively constructed, not to say invented' (Dumont 1978: 66). To write an authentic anthropological text is less to represent an absolute reality than to fabricate a fit of a particular generic kind between two types of conventional activity (exchanging spoken words and arranging written words), and hence to write social reality. The truth of anthropological accounts, in Wagner's celebrated formulation, is that anthropologists invent a culture for their informants: here is what they imagine to be a plausible explanation of what they understand them generally to have been doing (1977: 500–1).

This conclusion remains controversial, and much anthropological debate continues to occur concerning the nature of research processes, of research results, and of the presenting and appreciating of information. What should anthropology represent itself as if not a 'generalizing science' (cf. Ingold 1997)? Is it more than 'a collection of travellers' tales' (Louch 1966: 160)?

For some, however, this ambiguity and uncertainty is all grist to the anthropological mill. Anthropology – 'the most humanistic of the social sciences, the most scientific of the humanities' – has never been comfortably placed within certain categories of disciplinary knowledge, and, indeed, has seen its project as the exploration, and the calling-into-question, of conventional and disciplinary divisions as such. Anthropology was 'born omniform', Geertz puts it (1983: 21), and should refuse to be bound or restricted by the preconceptions of categorial knowledge. In seeking as complex an appreciation of experience as possible, an appreciation of the ambiguities concerning the nature of knowledge and truth should make anthropology 'more like itself' (cf. Rapport 1997e).

This was certainly Edmund Leach's message in his last writings. Drawing inspiration from the eighteenth-century philosopher–scientist Giambattista Vico, Leach set great store by the facility of an anthropologist's 'artistic imagination' (1982: 53). For Vico, the human imagination was to be regarded as a primary tool in a 'new science' which sought to understand the real as opposed to the outwardly observable nature of a human engagement with its environment. Such real knowledge called for an entering into the minds of other people; so that one came to know not only *that* (Caesar was dead) or *how* (to ride a bike) but *what it was like* (to be poor, to be in love, to belong to a community) (cf. Berlin 1990: 62). Moreover, it was in the nature of this imaginative knowing, or *fantasia*, that it was not analysable except in terms of itself, and it could not be identified except by examples.

Furthermore, for Leach, since 'the only ego I know at first hand is my own' (1989: 138), anthropological research was to be conceived of as a subjective process whose 'data' represented 'a kind of harmonic projection of the observer's own personality' (1984: 22). Inevitably, each anthropologist saw something which no other would recognize. But this still made the results of anthropological research admissible as knowledge because the aim was not 'objective truth' but 'insight' into behaviour, one's own as well as others': a 'quality of deep understanding' equivalent to 'fully understanding the nuances of a language [as opposed to] simply knowing the dictionary glosses of individual words' (1982: 52). This made anthropological writings 'interesting in themselves' – full of meaning, intended and unintended – and not revelatory of 'the external world' so much as of the author's reactions and interactions with it (1984: 22).

In this Leach comes close to the tenor of suggestions by physics nobel-laureate Igor Prigogine (1989). For Prigogine, an appreciation of the instability and creativity inherent in our world, the impossibility of absolute control or precise forecasting, and a clearer view of the place of human activity-within-the-world, now bring the projects of natural science and social science close to one another. In both, old notions of determinism, materialism and reductionism, of knowledge as omniscient and timeless, must give way to 'a narrative element' in the way we conceive of our knowledge, represent it, and act upon its implications. For, '[i]n effect, all human and social interaction and all literature is the expression of uncertainty about the future, and of a construction of the future' (Prigogine 1989: 389).

Anthropology as personal documentation

From qualitative versus quantitative methods of knowledge-acquisition, we have thus moved to issues of foregrounding the narrative nature of our human being-in-the-world, and coming to terms with knowledge-processes which are constructive and interpretational. For many, this self consciousness has changed radically the nature of the anthropological endeavour: given it a 'literary turn'. As urged by Needham (1978: 75–6), a 'counsel of perfection' might now see anthropologists reassessing their tasks, their standards and their ambitions, and contemplating what the discipline might become if it were to break free from its present academicism. Might not anthropology one day achieve something possessing the humane significance of metaphysics and art, Needham ponders, if ethnographic interpretations were written with the imaginative acuity, the empathetic penetration, and the literary artistry of a George Eliot, a Dostoevsky or a Woolf? Regarding method, great impetus has been given to treating culture and society and their representation as 'personal documents'. As a generic category of writing which includes diaries, autobiographies, life histories and letters (cf. Allport 1942), personal documents have long had a respected place in certain, more humanistic, versions of anthropological practice. What is different now, perhaps, is a matter of emphasis and evaluation. There is an appreciation of the 'personal document' of society and culture not as a partial component, as a biased version, as an overdetermined manifestation, as false consciousness, or whatever, but as all there is. If truth is constructive and interpretational, and a matter of narrative, then the whys and wherefores of the writing of the personal document that is an anthropological account, concerning the personal documents of those who are the subjects of the research, is all-important.

Opinion is divided, to say the least, concerning what might be described as the collapse of objectivity as a tenet in natural science (à la Heisenberg and Prigogine) and its implications for anthropology. Some see the collapse as a challenge, others as a temporary aberration to be lamented and overcome. Sharing Needham's vision, for instance, are Watson and Watson-Franke (1985: 96–7, 133) for whom

> [m]uch ethnographic research lacks a true feeling for human life as it is subjectively experienced by individuals. We know the richness and complexity of our own inner life, and when we compare this to the many tedious, dehumanizing accounts of life in other cultures . . . we may feel an acute sense of disinterest and even outright alienation. . . . All too often the real things seem to get lost in the obfuscation of the investigator playing God with his constructs. . . . To understand the individual in his human fullness we must therefore suspend total commitment to our scientific preconceptions and enter into a dialogue with the life history.

Hence, they would urge a greater appreciation in anthropology of the personal document as a means to restore to the individual actor (anthropological researcher and subject) a measure of his lost integrity, dignity and significance. For such personal documentation may be understood both as an act by which the individual constitutes his social–experiential environment, and one by which the anthropologist is able to access the individual in the act of managing his self-defined transactions with reality. While social science has tended to come to grips with experience by robbing it of its unique richness and fluidity, privileging models, quantities and the experimental testing of hypotheses, and translating experience into static and essential abstractions ('culture', 'social structure', '*habitus*', etc.), a narrative of personal documents gives onto that subjective consciousness through which the individual articulates his world. In sum, through a personal documentation the anthropologist can do justice to 'the flow of subjective experience', others' and his own, to a phenomenal consciousness as the individual himself experiences it (Watson and Watson-Franke 1985: 97; also cf. Lieblich and Josselson 1994).

For others, such as Weiner (1995), the value of personal narratives in anthropology remains low and their use is to be disparaged. For a focus on personal documents prescribes an unnecessarily narrow understanding of culture, and a reduction of social life to text. Whereas society and culture are significantly more than the stories individuals tell of them: to wit, there is the contrast between what is told and what is done, between 'what language avers and what behaviour reveals' (Weiner 1995: 5). Moreover, social practices and cultural knowledges are unevenly and restrictedly distributed, and an isolating of any one person's account will thus represent a partial understanding of the total socio-cultural repertoire of what is known. At best, Weiner concludes, 'narrated memoirs' serve to distinguish the rather feeble methodology of the oral historian from that of the social scientist; unlike the oral historian (but more like the psychoanalyst), the anthropologist should socially situate the individual narrator so as to reveal influences and constraints upon his personal documentation (whether in speech or in action) of which he himself may be unaware.

One might question whether Weiner's view of the objectivity of science and culture, and the anthropology that might emanate from their study, is outmoded. Certainly, it is arguable that it is not 'a culture' which possesses a total repertoire of things known, in the way that Weiner would portray, but rather individuals who create and possess an ongoing multitude of diverse and discrepant knowledges which they put to use in the animation of socio-cultural forms. And while it is true that there is more to observe than 'stories about social life', it is not true that these other things (from theories to sensations) are any less personal or any more objectively accessible. They are also personal documents, no less interpreted and hence narrated by the individual, and no more properly or hegemonically determinable by another. In short, what lies beyond an individual's narrations are other narrations – by the same individual and by others. The anthropologist can collect and juxtapose these in his description-analysis – as may the oral historian – but one narrative does not necessarily 'situate' another, does not give onto a superior awareness.

Literary anthropology

Because of the novelist's command of the personal life of the individual, and the former's desire to connect the externally observable with the internally responsible, Forster (1984) concluded that literature was 'truer' than social science. While each person knew from experience that there was much beyond the 'outer' evidence of observation, and while the social scientist claimed to be equally concerned to record human character, the latter appeared content to restrict himself to what could be known of its existence from scouring 'the exterior surface' of social life only, and to what could approximately be deduced from people's actions, words and gestures. Only the novelist appeared determined to accrue a fuller knowledge, and seek out 'the hidden life at its [individual] source' (Forster 1984: 55–6).

It is increasingly true that the distinction Forster would make no longer stands. In a 'biographical anthropology' of and as personal documentation, the impersonalizing impulses of an earlier social science are eschewed. It is admitted that novelists have often in the past dealt better than social scientists with 'the subtleties, inflections and varieties of individual consciousness which are concealed by the categorical masks [of membership in social and cultural groups]' (Cohen 1994: 180), and there are attempts in growing numbers to remedy the practice (cf. Rapport 1994a). Here we find the (qualitative) particularities of individual lived experience no longer necessarily eclipsed by (quantitative) generalization, or otherwise reduced, abstracted, typified or overdetermined according to the axioms of a seeming-scientific regularity, stability, order or control. Moreover, this is nothing other than that which Robert Redfield, for one, long ago urged (1960: 59):

> As soon as our attention turns from a community as a body of houses and tools and institutions to the states of mind of particular people, we are turning to the exploration of something immensely complex and difficult to know. But it is humanity, in its inner and more private form. . . . While we talk in terms of productivity, or of roles and statuses, we are . . . moving among an apparatus already removed, by our own

act of mind, from the complicated thinking and feeling of the men and women who achieve the productivity, or define and occupy the roles. But it is the thinking that is the real and ultimate raw material; it is there that events really happen. And the choice of a human biographic form for describing the whole turns us to it.

See also: **Humanism, Literariness, Narrative, Post-Modernism**

READING

An anthropological interest in reading is relatively recent, another effect, perhaps, of that shift of concern ('the literary turn') which brought into focus those practices of inscription by which anthropology as a discipline comes to produce data and reproduce itself. An anthropology of reading explores the diversity of reading traditions in the world, treats these as historically, culturally and socially situated practices, and examines the consequences of their use. Here is 'reading' as an intrinsically social exchange, historically informed, culturally specific, often collectively practised.

A diversity of reading traditions

In *The Ethnography of Reading*, edited by Jonathan Boyarin (1993), two themes predominate: the variety and the universality of reading. To study reading anthropologically is to become aware of how simplistic are such binary distinctions as literacy versus orality or individual versus collective when applied in an evolutionary or an otherwise classificatory fashion to types of societies and the reading practices to be expected within them. There never is or was an oral pastoral, for instance, while there always is a complex, multidirectional and political interplay of different forms of human communication, of which reading is frequently one. In an anthropology of reading what can be expected is a focus less on a particular technology of data-processing than a range of social acts and a specific cultural tool – of domination as well as liberation, of sociality as well as isolation, of longevity as well as recentness. Reading comes to be approached, in Boyarin's words, as a 'living textuality'.

In particular, the Boyarin volume explores the diversity of reading practices surrounding the Hebrew Bible and Talmud, ancient and contemporary; the Christian reading culture adopted by Jesus and his early followers; reading as culturally constructed in Anglo-Saxon England; the manipulation of Chinese orthography by pre-modern Japanese scribes and story-tellers; the incorporation of oral and written in the ritual and political practice of highland Colombia; the recitative reading of the Koran in Arabic (albeit incomprehensible) in village Indonesia; reading groups as sites of collective action in urban Texas; and the challenge of reading traditional (mythological) Kashaya stories in an Amerindian reservation classroom.

A reading of what these case-studies together show might conclude as follows: 'reading' in the Hebrew Bible translates as a speech act which occupies the public spaces of forum, synagogue, House of Study and court; it almost always means 'to read aloud to someone' and has immediate public consequences. Reading is here a proclamation, a declaration, a summons. Similarly, reading has a conversational character in traditional Islamic societies, where mastery of the sciences of life begins with memorization of the Koran. In the Christian West too, reading at one time had an ascetic quality and a behavioural orientation – as is yet evidenced by coenobitic monasticism: communities bound together by the oral delivery and counselling exposition of common texts.

However, by Late Antiquity reading had also become a silent and private practice of the Western study and bedroom: a meditative transaction between reader and book, and a vehicle of innerworldliness. Now we come to have a combination of textual practices, oral and literate, collective and solitary, such as we still see replicated around us today, from Indonesia to Colombia, from the anthropologist in the academy to the 'other' in the field. What is of note is less an evolution between reading practices than a dynamic tension. Indeed, to privilege one practice over another is to truncate our understanding of this tension. For, behind the private reading is always the public infrastructure which sustains literacy and legitimates solitariness, while behind the collective group of readers is the individual's reflective voice.

In short, just as there is no essential separation between the oral and the literate, so, individual and collective readings, a tradition and its performance, must also be seen in ongoing relationship. Furthermore, talking, writing and reading are significantly implicated in one another; reading is a 'kinetic art', in Stanley Fish's phrasing (1972: 401), and it is only in understanding the ways in which people move between communication in terms of talking, writing and reading that an appreciation of the significance of each in any particular historical, social and cultural situation is to be gained.

311

The agency of reading

But it is not only in its pertaining to conventions of talking and writing that the practice of reading concerns kinesis; and it is not only in terms of historico-socio-cultural milieux that reading attains to particularity. For reading is also individual and agential, and there is a vital balance to be struck between objectified reading traditions-cum-artefacts and active subjects. Reading is a kinetic art inasmuch as it concerns an individual author's textualizing and an individual reader's actualizing, and for an imaginative meeting between the two (cf. Rapport 1994a).

As living textuality, that is, the process of the origination of meaning is not restricted to the writer: it also extends to the reader. Reading is creative; it entails personalizing words, imbuing them with significance, with relevance, with life, in a particular way and at a particular time so as to make them possibly uniquely meaningful. Far from static entities, read texts represent lived works: activities which individuals perform, actively using them as instruments in their imaginative moulding of the world. This is why the written can continue to be enacted while being wholly separated from its author – 'emancipated', 'distantiated', 'decontextualized' from the psycho-sociological conditions of its production (cf. Ricoeur 1981: 91): because the reader engages in a process (comparable to the author) of imparting order and meaning to language's common symbolic forms. To read a text, in short, is to impart personality to language: to personalize verbal forms and express a personal construction of the world.

An elucidation of this point has perhaps been most clearly made by Fish (1972, 1979, 1988; also cf. Iser 1978, 1988). To begin, Fish criticizes any approach which treats the text as a self-sufficient system of signification and attempts to locate meaning in its formal features; as if meaning were something which all readers simply extracted from this repository by the same general procedures. Treating the text as a complete and stationary object in this way, as a thing-in-itself, is dangerously misleading, Fish argues, however suggestive might be the physical autonomy of printed verbal forms. For meaning must always be located in the intention of the author and thereafter in the response of the reader. The text itself is indeterminate, and meaning is re-constituted by a reader's interpretation and 'narration': making and revising assumptions, specifying causes, asking questions, solving puzzles, giving and withdrawing approval, rendering and regretting judgements, coming to and abandoning conclusions. The connectedness of the text is not so much of the text itself as the product of the reader's consciousness, outlook, past experience and expectations being brought to bear upon its raw materials. The reader transforms the text into a personal experience, the text becoming a kind of mirror of his or her dispositions. Indeed, it is the reader's interpretive assumptions, procedures and expectations which come to impart such formal features to the text as the notion of an originating 'author' with 'intentions'.

Reading is an event, in short, brought about by the reader bringing an interpretive framework (a cognitive schema, a world-view) to bear upon the text, and 'experiencing' it by constructing its meaning. The text becomes alive, and becomes concrete, when realized through the individual reader's disposition; the reading process sets the work in motion. Finally, since the meaning of a text is its experiencing by a reader, and since a reader's active and activating consciousness can be different per occasion, the meaning is fluid; there is no fixed relationship between the forms recognized in a text and the response they elicit.

Readers who share interpretive principles and strategies, who similarly constitute texts' properties and intentions, Fish describes as members of the same 'interpretive communities'; here are those who share certain structures of interpretation which make particular readings conventional, normal and obvious. But what is far more likely to happen, Fish admits, especially in modern, complex societies, is that a reader's interpretation of a text will be multiple, and often inconsistent, even at one and the same reading. Readers will oscillate between different possible organizations and interpretations of the text even as they seek consistent patterns and coherency. This is perhaps because the reader's interpretive community possesses more than one strategy for how texts are to be read – modern societies being seen as increasingly less fundamentalist, and entertaining a variety of authentic exegeses. Alternatively, a number of interpretations signals the individual reader as either belonging simultaneously to a number of different interpretive communities or else moving between them, perhaps as they grow and wane, perhaps as they compete with and complement one another.

Finally, a number of interpretations signals individual readers becoming what Nietzsche dubbed the 'wandering encyclopaedias' of the modern-day. Faced with a complex and varied repertoire of interpretive strategies and a heteroglossia of communities, individuals pick and choose, borrow and compound, negate and invent – creolize, in a word – so that the sum of strategies within their lists, and their habitual application and *bricolage*, is ultimately particular to them alone. One finds an irreducible individuality to the language-worlds interpreted by each reader whereby texts are read according to 'unique association-nets' and 'personal lexicons' (Steiner 1975: 173). To read, in short, is to translate, and to precipitate pluralism, dynamism and individuality.

Competing readings

Given the likely diversity of readings within socio-cultural milieux, both in terms of interpretive communities and of individual readers, what are the likely consequences? How might an abuttal of readings ramify into other situations. A study of such relations is offered by Eric Livingston (1995).

In *An Anthropology of Reading*, Livingston sets out to compare what he calls the 'different cultures of reading' to which professional literary critics and lay readers of English Literature belong, each laying claim to proper practice. Here are two versions of reading the same texts, and the relationship between them, Livingston argues, is fundamentally one of mistranslation. Setting out to explicate the proprieties of ordinary reading, to explain how a certain lay reading is achieved and what a proper reading should be, what literary critics in fact achieve is an alchemy of laic practices – a misconstruction and a mystification. Aiming for an understanding of 'reading *simpliciter*', the interpretive community of professional critics ends up constituting its own 'reading *cultura*'. The analytical apparatus which professional literary critics employ to uncover 'the natural rules of reading-really' actually reveal nothing but 'texts' and 'poetic objects' constructed (read) according to their own conventional practices of interpretation and criteria of propriety: to read in a cultivated, reasoned and reasonable way.

In becoming members of their interpretive community, literary critics have become instructed in the application of a 'powerful technology' of reading; the poetic object of a 'text/reading pair' emerges from a background of participatory communal work (Livingston 1995: 15). Moreover, the community of critics is an orderly and hierarchical one, and as fellow professionals, members are expected to act as implementers, purveyors and sentinels of their community's shared ways: the practice of 'reading-really' is something that all are expected to do alike. Indeed, the work of reading, the skills of 'reading pace, eye fixation, and recognition' (1995: 12) from which form and content emerge, become so learnt and ordinary that literary critics – as much as lay readers, socialized as children – do not notice their own routines. However, it is this routinization which is responsible for the mistranslation which occurs. The literary critic applies an analytical apparatus of grammar and rhetoric, and of 'reading competency' so as to disinter a 'natural' orderliness in the text. But this technological practice 'discovers' (that is, constructs) texts as always possessing certain institutional features, and misses the possibility of the text having other natures and institutionalities to discover, and emerging into other facticities. In short, the professional practice of the literary critic and the 'instructed reading' which results passes the laypractice and the ordinary reading by. Moreover, so engrossed is each in their own community constructions that their treating of 'different texts' does not become apparent. What the community of literary critics ends up studying is itself alone, while its claim to be 'reading-really' amounts to nothing more than a projection and legitimation of its own institutions.

Ultimately, Livingston's work is a critique of all professional practice. Inasmuch as literary critics work a text into affording a certain interpretation which is actually no better than another, so any reading – anthropological included – must be appreciated pragmatically: not for its absolute truth-value but for what work that reading does, for the empowerment that that particular construction of a 'true reading' achieves.

See also: **Interpretation, Literariness, Writing**

THE RURAL IDYLL

The concept of the rural idyll concerns the way that 'the rural' possesses a certain meaning and value in socio-cultural milieux which are overwhelmingly urban. It pertains to the extent to which people measure their identities and make sense of their lifestyles in terms of their purported 'rurality' or 'urbanity', and, in particular, how 'the rural' comes to be a repository for ways of life which are regarded as more natural, holistic and harmonious (cf. Strathern 1982). Among those affected in this way by notions of the rural can be included anthropologists and their depictions of village communities and of communitarianism.

The 'rural idyll' as an idiom of British social exchange provides a fitting case in point.

The British rural idyll

Since the Second World War, trips to the country from the town have become Britain's most popular recreational activity. In 1979, 37 million people took at least one trip to the countryside; by 1994 this had risen to one billion day-trips to the countryside per year overall. Next in popularity as a leisure activity comes a trip to the seaside (followed by gardening, then by walks around urban parks, trips to historic sites, museums and zoos, and sport).

When the trippers reach the countryside, they find their visit anticipated by such institutions as the National Trust, and numerous National Parks. Begun in 1895, the Trust is a charity which acts as something of a protective caretaker over British 'rural heritage': in England, some 590,000 acres of cherished countryside, 545 miles of coastline, 234 historic houses and 160 gardens, and countless archaeological sites and vernacular buildings. National Parks were set up in Britain after the Second World War, by Acts of Parliament, to ensure that areas of 'outstanding natural beauty' were conserved and their recreational enjoyment by visitors was promoted. Just over a fifth of England and Wales has now been accorded some form of official 'protection' for the 'settled harmony' of its countryside or the rarity of its wildlife.

The trippers can also anticipate the 'country life' they will find thanks to the frequent diet of rural narratives which they find on television and radio. Often seen from an urban or ex-urban point of view, these promote the image of a 'good life' to be had as a country land-owner or vet, retiree or small-holder, or simply 'A Daughter of the Dales' (Hauxwell 1991; also cf. Moggach 1996). Even if the life is one of relative hardship, it is seen to give onto an earthy, and yet a fresh and untainted, wisdom.

This is the case in an overwhelmingly urban country, where mass urbanization began more than two centuries ago, where the rural population has been outnumbered for some 150 years, and where some 90% of the population now resides in city, town or suburb. What may be described as a British love-affair with the rural continues unabated: the 'countryside' as a place of sentiment, to preserve and to visit (Palmer et al. 1977: 739). 'The rural idyll' remains one of the most widespread and abiding myths in common circulation: a romantic idea and ideal of the rural as the proper, the healthy, the original, maybe too the eventual, place of people's habitation, and which the current rural population holds in trust.

Some commentators find the roots of this anti-urban bias in the nineteenth century, and the fears of the then well-to-do that the expanding towns could become unhealthy sources of social discontent and political disorder, while the country remained a secure repository of ideal traditional values – of deferential country-folk, manors, lords and manor-houses (cf. Phillips and Williams 1984: 2–3). In Dickens's archetypal depiction of Preston (or 'Coketown') in *Hard Times* (1971: 102), the urban–industrial agglomeration also becomes home to confinement, disease, greed and the essentially unnatural:

> that ugly citadel, where Nature was as strongly bricked out as
> killing airs and gases were bricked in; at the heart of the

labyrinth of narrow courts upon courts, and close streets upon
streets, which had come into existence piecemeal, every piece
in a violent hurry for some one man's purpose, and the whole
an unnatural family, shouldering, and trampling, and pressing
one another to death.

And yet the historical source of the idyll is not so easy to isolate. Thus,
Eden can be found celebrating, in 1797, the virtue, intelligence and
independence of the healthy peasant of England's North Country as
compared with those who seek help and charity in the more familiar
regions of the populous South (cited in Dewhirst 1972: 1), while as late
as 1890 Gomme is to be found describing the village as a 'primitive
element', of necessity broken under the advance of civilization (1890:
232). Clearly, the uses to which notions of the 'rural' and the 'urban' are
put are several and complex, and more issues are involved (the question
of geographical distance, or of south Britain versus north) than simply
a blanket validation of country life at the growth of urbanization.
In other words, 'rural versus urban' is an idiom of great longevity and
common usage; Williams (1985: 1), indeed, argues for a contrast
between country and city (as fundamentally distinct ways of life) to be
seen reaching back to Classical times. Moreover, different meanings and
intents can be found adhering to the contrast in different contexts and
occasions. No doubt this is an important aspect of its continuing
popularity and power in Britain as a rhetorical strategy.

Leaving aside the question of its origin for an examination of
its contemporary provenance, perhaps the first thing to say is that
in recent decades, the British rural population has begun to rise again.
In common with other industrialized countries, there is a process of
'counter-urbanization' under way (in France it is called *rurbanisation*)
whereby the population of large cities in particular (London, Glasgow,
Birmingham), and their inner cores, has fallen dramatically. Much of
this has fed into a burgeoning suburbia on the urban peripheries (cf.
Riesman 1958), but some at least has translated into residential growth
in more remote rural districts, especially those which remain 'high
amenity environments' (Cote 1987). Accompanying the rise of new
technologies of production, then, and the growth of service industries
at the expense of manufacturing and primary production, more people
are preferring to live and work, or to retire, or at least own second
(holiday) homes, in rural areas. The English Lake District, the Yorkshire
Dales, Devon and Cornwall, as well as Wales and Scotland, each has its
share of what are sometimes dubbed 'white settlers' (Jedrej and Nuttall
1996).

Whether in search of employment, recreation, retirement, or a place from which to continue commuting to an urban job, the 'counter-urbanite', in increasing numbers, can be found to have quite a disruptive effect upon local social relations (cf. Forsythe 1980; Rapport 1993a). Often reversing more than a century of out-migration from the rural area, the urban returners also change the proportion of young to old in the community. However, the sense of vibrancy which the influx of energetic younger (often wealthier) people can bring to a place is sometimes offset by the local sense that the community – its people, its local organizations, traditions, stated values, behavioural styles and habits of interaction – is no longer quite the same. There is a felt ambivalence, born of a nostalgia for the past, a recognition, nevertheless, that past ways of life were no longer viable, and a sense of vindication that now they are being joined by ex-urbanites who seem to value what was locally possessed all along (however oddly they might seem to express it). In search of an 'authentically natural' rural community (cf. Cohen 1988), the in-comers can compete for jobs, benefits and houses, and bring with them social practices – whether of inquisitiveness, assertive leadership or conspicuous consumption – which can make the locals feel like a dispossessed minority in their own home.

It is not that 'urban refugees' resident in the country for longer or shorter periods are anything new. Country diaries over the centuries reveal a constant flow of people in both directions (e.g. Macfarlane 1970). But the quest for a rural idyll has changed in nature and number. What was once a practice of aristocratic and noble ladies and gentlemen (viewing, by appointment, artistic and horticultural displays in country 'seats', or removing to rural retreats for summer seasons), and then a perk of the burgeoning bourgeoisie, has become a populist pursuit. As Pahl describes (1968), those 'living the rural life' will now include: the traditional large property owners; the 'salariat' (middle-class professionals); ex-urban workers (retired with some capital); urban workers who continue to commute to work; local workers who also commute to jobs beyond the locale; and locals who work *in situ*.

The attempt to specify and classify in this way those who now live in the British countryside makes for a confused list, and one always open to reclassification and addition (Gypsies, hippies and new-age travellers, for instance, 'cognitive deviants' who drop-out of mainstream, urban life for the inhabiting of their own 'intentional communities' (Rigby 1974)). What is perhaps best to keep in mind is the confused sense of rural diversity: 'ruralism' and 'urbanism' no longer refer to distinct ways of life (if, in Britain, they ever did (cf. Macfarlane 1978)).

To elaborate upon Pahl's argument (1968: 269), Britain is so small geographically, so densely populated, and so socially confused, that it is as if all live in 'metropolitan villages': in cities dispersed around the country. Certainly, the urban/rural distinction, as signifying different lifestyles, different kinds of people, and different types of social relationships in different geo-physical environs, no longer makes analytic sense. What we have instead are inner cities, suburbs, garden cities, new towns, old towns, villages, hamlets, and so on, all related together in one complex process of movement and activity; here is a British population with a dispersed activity pattern, which undertakes complex movements around a 'rurban' British setting. Rather than rural/urban, and other geo-physically based representation and determination, Grillo therefore concludes (1980: 15) that we should talk instead in terms of 'centres' and 'peripheries': relative and shifting terms which can capture the ways in which local social milieux are acted upon by the supra-local and vice versa, and the way that distinct features and resources of particular habitations are matters of symbolic and attitudinal assignation.

If the urban/rural distinction makes little sense as a designation of socio-cultural difference, however, this does not necessarily lessen its sentimental or imaginative efficacy as an idiom in common usage. The 'rural' versus the 'urban' remains a highly significant polarity in terms of which people in Britain make sense of their lives, as we have seen. In Robert Park's words (1968), we are dealing with rurality and urbanity as 'states of mind': criteria by which to measure a sense of Britishness, and to chart an orderly passage of life within a British 'landscape' or milieu.

Marilyn Strathern's argument is that in the rhetoric of rurality and urbanity, and issues surrounding who 'really belongs' to rural communities (or urban ones), we are seeing ways in which people in Britain deal with 'classes in the mind' (1982: 268); what appears as a discourse concerning 'natural, 'bounded' villages is better understood as an idiom of socio-economic differentiation, and of movements of status via birth, marriage and migration. More broadly put, what appears to be a spatial division can rather be seen to signify temporal and evaluative considerations, both individual and communal. In the movement from the rural to the urban is told not only a nostalgic national story of a better and glorious past but also an individual story of a possibly better future: from urban achievement to rural retirement; from urban work to enjoying its rural fruits; from urban contest, criminality and immorality to rural peace, order and pristine nobility.

That there are different ways in which the discourse concerning the rural and the urban is phrased – rural simple-mindedness versus urban sophistication, for example – does not weaken the argument being put. So long as there is a distinction between the two modalities of existence in Britain, it is possible to garner a clear-cut view of one's life and identity, and to envisage one's progress through that life: a movement to a future, better (or worse) time and place. Moreover, one knows precisely what to expect there, because, although it will be the culmination of the passage and effort of a life-time, it will likely represent (however paradoxically) the reaching of a 'home': a certain harmony and closeness, something left behind at the beginning. In short, what we are dealing with in the British discourse on the rural idyll, and the rural/urban divide, are notions of progress and futurity, and a certain ambivalence concerning whether the movement these entail should be imagined as linear, or as a finally circular retrieval of an original home.

The anthropological rural idyll

While the argument above has concerned the rural idyll as a British discourse, the phenomenon is by no means restricted in its application. In a quest for the rural idyll there are clear overlaps with those pilgrimages made by tourists and the religious (to name but two), in search of particular 'authentic' values. Certain localities are set aside and seen as privileged sites for the attaining of experiences which are not only clearly distinct from current, everyday life but also of superior worth. These might include both the non-modern – rural, historical, natural, ethnic, exotic – and the non-human (cf. MacCannell 1989).

Also included within the 'non-modern', of course is the 'primitive', the 'exotic' and the 'ethnic', as anthropologically quested for. Perhaps the most familiar 'rural idyll' known to anthropology pertains to the bounded and homogeneous communities which anthropologists have posited, sought and found as the empirical bases of their studies. As has come to be increasingly recognized (cf. Wagner 1975; Kuper 1988), these too are idiomatic constructs which might bear little relation to the actual complexities of socio-cultural milieux in which people live.

More precisely, in the image of the 'rural community' is contained an 'idyllic notion' of a traditional, communal village life of mechanical solidarity or *Gemeinschaft* and its evolutionary supersession by atomistic urbanism and 'artificial' bases of association. Following any number of developmental dichotomies (Spencer's, or Durkheim's, or Maine's, or Weber's, or Toennies's, or Redfield's or Becker's), anthropologists have seen in the countryside a way of life and a type of social organization diametrically opposed to that of city: a traditional order and localness threatened (if not already overcome) by the massificating forces of urban change, by the universalistic structures of the modern nation-state. Hence, the rural village is depicted as close-knit and isolated, egalitarian, shunning ostentatious differentiation and esteeming conventional competencies. It is seen as embodying a culture which is consensually shared, homogeneous and uniform, and as engendering a social system which amounts to an encompassing whole and is based on status relations, multiplex roles, dense interactional networks, equilibrial social structures, and ascription (cf. Frankenberg 1966: 286–92; Harris 1974: 38–9).

In other words, the 'idyllic', rural village community has served as a dominant symbol, a verbal idiom, and a micro-institution which has played its part in the institutionalization of anthropology as a discipline of study and a tradition of writing. In the rural village community, anthropology secured for itself the possible progress towards and from a discrete, encapsulable field of study, distant and distinct both in place and in time (cf. Fabian 1983).

In contemporary anthropology (study 'in' villages, perhaps, but no longer 'of' them (Geertz 1973: 22)), idioms of idyllic otherness have become increasingly diverse. We emphasize the otherness of gender, of the body, of globality, of subalternality; we idealize ('idyll-ize') otherness *per se* (as difference, as hybridity, as Orientalism). What should be borne in mind still, however, is the gap between idyllic idioms and the empirical realities they purport to describe.

See also: **Community, Home and Homelessness, Tourism, Urbanism**

SCIENCE

Anthropological work on the concept of science has usually concerned itself with issues of the status of scientific knowledge as understood in the West, and with a comparison of forms of knowledge similarly validated elsewhere. Put succinctly: Is Western science to be treated in anthropology as a specially privileged way of knowing the world? Or is Western science equivalent (not only in its social uses but also its ontology) to religion, magic, common sense, law, aesthetics, or any other systematic fund of symbols, values and knowledge-practices shared by a community of people? A range of issues are involved here, and a range of deliberations and opinions have been aired, a sample of which includes the following.

Does science grow out of religion?

Considering the ways in which modes of thought might evolve into one another was a major preoccupation of nineteenth-century social science. Inspired by Darwin, the writings of Weber, Marx and Durkheim, Spencer, Tylor and Frazer were imbued by evolutionary schemata concerning how one kind of society with its characteristic patterns of thought and behaviour might become something other. In the early twentieth century, Levy-Bruhl and Malinowski were still famously to disagree concerning the nature of the distinction between primordial and evolved engagements with the universe. Was 'primitive man' a mystic, inhabiting a pre-logical, sentimental and personalized universe, the objective reasoning of 'modern man' only coming later (Levy-Bruhl 1985 [1910]), or did primitive spiritualism exist alongside a pragmatic and commonsensical treatment of problems (Malinowski 1926)?

By the 1930s, however, such deliberation was out of vogue. An evolutionist–temporal perspective had been substituted by a more spatial–diffusionist one, where difference (between cultures as between nation-states) was a matter of geography. To pose evolutionist questions was seen as ethnocentric and ultimately elitist, while no satisfactory criteria were likely to be agreed upon to obtain definitive answers.

And yet, differently phrased, comparable questions have again begun to be asked (cf. Macfarlane 1978; Goody 1983). Can one, for instance, chart a development in conceptions of the sacred? Without making value-judgements, or assuming necessary, singular, irreversible pathways, can one mark out an evolution in the 'set[s] of symbolic forms and acts which relate man to the ultimate conditions of his existence' (Bellah 1964: 37)?

Bellah, for one, suggests an affirmative answer (also cf. Gellner 1988). He sets out (despite some unfortunate terminology) five ideal-typical stages in whose terms 'the ultimate conditions' of human existence can be seen to compass both the religious and the scientific: 'primitive', 'archaic', 'historic', 'early modern', 'modern'. An elaboration of these need not detain us here, but the crucial transition for an understanding of the evolution of science concerns 'historic' to 'early modern'. This is characterized by the shift in Europe from Roman Catholicism to Protestantism. The Protestant Reformation, Bellah argues, amounted to an overcoming of a number of hierarchies or gradations and their replacement by more discrete distinctions; cosmology was much simplified. The legitimacy of church hierarchy, both in an institutional sense and in the sense of the church's role in structuring relations between this world and the realms of the sacred, was called into question; likewise the hierarchy of supernatural intermediary figures between the worlds: saints, angels and the Virgin Mary. Salvation from this world remained the religious end, but this was now to be achieved in terms of activities within this world (rather than withdrawal from the world) by way of a pure conscience and direct communion between autonomous, introspective individuals and an 'awful', transcendent God. Meanwhile, the vacuum created by the demise of institutional church power had enormous social repercussions; a host of secular institutions, legal, economic, educational, aesthetic and scientific, sprang up to fill the gap in meaning, knowledge and creative expression. Each of these new, humanistic forms of institutional knowing claimed its own distinct area of expertise. As Peter Berger concurs (1969: 111–26), Protestantism abolished the diverse Catholic continuities of being between the seen and unseen worlds, between humankind and the divine, so that, as Weber put it, the world became a 'disenchanted' one, no longer mediated by mysteries and miracles, sacraments and saints. A natural universe of fallen humanity as distinct from a heavenly realm of transcendent divinity was, of course, posited in Protestant cosmology by way of emphasizing the 'terrible' majesty of God, but a sky empty of angels also made room for astronomers and physicists, and an institutional and systematic, scientific exploration.

Berger and Bellah thus agree that Protestantism served as an important historical prelude to the rule of science and also the rise of secularization: to a process whereby the remaining vestige of a hierarchical, supernatural cosmology – the notion of God – becomes implausible too, and large 'sections of society and culture are removed from the domination of religious institutions and symbols' (Berger 1969: 107). In Bellah's fifth stage of religious evolution, then, 'modern', we find science answering many of the 'how' questions of the workings of the world, becoming, for many, the route to the 'sacred': to 'the ultimate conditions of human existence'. Religion is reduced to pondering the 'why' and the 'ought', although even here there are competing, secular ideologies: humanism, Marxism, cultural relativity, capitalism. Religious institutions find themselves having to mimic the argumentational styles of scientific rationalization or of commodity consumption in order to gain adherents, the latter becoming 'clients' who are 'sold' a tradition as a meaningful path to personal peace of mind (cf. Heelas 1996). Scientific knowledge via experimentation and validation is the standard for all. Not only does science grow out of religion, then, but religion now functions within the ambit of scientific method and world-view.

For some, such as Gellner (1993), this gives social science a particular, moral role to play. If science grew out of religion, if rationalism is the continuation of monotheism by other means, then it cannot overcome completely that heritage. That is, science has replaced universalistic religions (Christianity, Judaism, Hinduism, *et al.*) which themselves replaced 'tribal religions', indexically linked to certain socio-cultural spaces and relationships. Universalistic religions, transmitted by doctrine not ritual, and incarnated in movable scriptures, not local performances, claimed access to transcendental truths valid for all times and places. And this socio-culturally disembodied, religious knowledge then provided the template for autonomous scientific truth. Science has likewise come to represent itself as a form of knowledge which is valid for all: a cognition which reaches beyond any one culture, an understanding of nature giving onto a universalistic technology.

The difference, however, is that in this rationalist Enlightenment, where a sacred salvation has been replaced with a secular one, science provides no social-cum-moral vision. To complement its overcoming of a religious 'how', therefore, must be provided – by social science if not by science – the 'why' and 'ought' of the religious heritage. As Gellner concludes: '[o]ur predicament is – to work out the social options of our affluent and disenchanted condition. We have no choice about this' (1995b: 8). Perhaps social science can point the way to the institutionalization of a 'constitutional' religiosity – on a similar basis to a constitutional monarchy – which retains the ritual and symbolism of an earlier epoch but lacks any real power or consequence. So that social life and decision-making are actually run along profane, techno-scientific lines but within an idiom of traditional religious legitimations: an amalgamation of scientific cognition, order and knowledge and religious faith, aestheticism and comfort.

Are science and religion contrastive in nature?

Besides the missing moral component in a scientific world-view, how different an engagement with the world is represented by the evolution from religion to science? Are science and religion contrastive in nature?

On this point, anthropologists seem divided, as is nicely represented by a debate between John Beattie (1966) and Robin Horton (1967). For Beattie, religion should be understood as essentially expressive and dramatic behaviour more akin to art than science. Religion concerns symbolic statements, not practical procedures, and a premium is placed upon the elaboration or involution of symbolism as an end, value and beauty in itself. To the extent that religion possesses procedure – as in ritual – the efficacy of the latter resides in its expressiveness, in its being expressed and enacted in particular ways. The procedure is far from being intellectual or explanatory activity, based on experimental propositions or the testing of rationally formulated hypotheses. Religion is not grounded in a mechanistic universe at all, and to the extent that religious beliefs treat empirical facts, causes and functions ('among the Nuer, incest causes leprosy'), then these are secondary to their main purpose, and arrived at intuitively or poetically, and without theoretical or experimental mediation. The main purpose of religious ritual and belief is, rather, to influence, by imprecation, sacrifice and prayer, an intentioning universe replete with personalized beings.

In short, religion and science are like two very different, if not opposite, cultures. Religion is a kind of artistic language, a distinctive way of saying something, whose values lie in how well that thing is said. Dramatic assertion is here an end in itself, rather than aiming for any more instrumental effectiveness. Even if religion and science come to be entwined in one socio-cultural setting, then, they remain contrastive ways of imaging and engaging with the world: two types of attitude to experience, two kinds of truth, two forms of practice.

For Horton, however, this distinction between 'expressive action' and 'technical action' does not hold up. In science, religion has been replaced by a form of knowledge and construction of meanings which is basically and directly comparable: from Judaeo-Christian Genesis to the Big Bang; from God as single, absolute truth to physical nature as an objective reality; from God as disembodied agency beyond time and space to scientific reasoning and rationality.

Horton's argument against the likes of Beattie rests on four main refutations. First, religion is contrasted with science due to the claimed symbolic proliferation of the former compared to the simplicity, consistency and non-capriciousness of the latter. However, this difference is merely superficial. Whatever the elaboration of supernatural forces in religious cosmology, these come down to a relatively few kinds by whose action experience is explained. Each kind of being, moreover, will be appointed certain regular functions concerning the world of observable happenings, which a religious expert will be able to construe. This limitation in the number of kinds of ordering entity and process underlying the disorderly diversity of experience makes of religion a fundamentally explanatory phenomenon. Second, religion is as much an empirical pursuit, interested in natural causes, as is science, only the idiom is different: personalized beings as opposed to impersonal forces. In both, the visible, tangible world of commonsensical effects is superseded by reference to theoretical entities – 'the anger of spirits', 'the fusion of hydrogen nuclei' – which transcend a limited, quotidian vision and link events to more distant, antecedent causes. Third, religion, like science, possesses levels of explanation for application in different kinds of situations. Thus events can be placed in relatively limited causal contexts – one's community and one's immediate environment, say – or the widest possible – the origins of the universe or of life – as one refers, contingently, to tutelary spirits or molecules, to the supreme being or the law of gravity. Fourth, the theoretical notions which religion and science employ are in both cases transpositions of familiar analogies from commonsensical worlds. That is, given their different assumptions of where everyday order resides – the personal (religion) and the inanimate (science) – theoretical order is similarly arrived at: gods are like patriarchs or patrons; Brownian motion is like bouncing billiard balls. In both cases, too, only part of the analogy is adopted to fill out the new explanatory setting: gods are like patriarchs but not so in the patriarchs' mortality; atoms are like billiard balls but not in the balls' colouration. In each case, theoretical explanations are arrived at by abstracting from what is commonsensically known so as to provide the bedrock for the extraordinary wisdom which is demanded. Religious explanation and scientific explanation, in short, are both metaphorical in inspiration.

Differences of idiom aside, then, Horton's conclusion is that religion and science share the same explanatory nature and ethos. Any dichotomization – emotional versus intellectual engagements; mystical versus rational, fantastical versus causal, supernatural versus empirical – points up merely superficial contrasts.

How 'scientific' is science?

Horton does not suggest that religion and science are the same, however. He does recognize important differences between them, the greatest being what he calls the 'openness' of science as opposed to the 'closure' of religion: the readiness of the former, but not the latter, to accept alternatives to established doctrine and to change. As Gellner put it (1993: 76), not being revelatory, science pretends to no finality in its knowledge and shies away from no scrutiny. (Indeed, its lack of rigidity or stasis is the main reason why it is difficult tying it to moral prescriptions or an underwriting of values.) Horton (1967) then goes on to amplify the seven differences between religious and scientific systems of thought which give onto the scientific systems' distinct openness. These include the magical attitude towards words in religion, their indexical nature; the non-reflective character of religious thought, so that thoughts are not separated from occasions, and systems of thought as such are not thought about in disinterested fashion; the protective attitude to ways of knowing in religion (as opposed to the sceptical one in science) whereby predictive failure is threatening rather than challenging, and the passage of time from past to future a source of pollution and decay rather than progress and perfection; and the employment of secondary elaborations and taboos in religion to maintain questionable systems of classification instead of throwing them over.

While open versus closed may apply to science versus religion as ideal-types, Horton does however recognize that for non-specialist, lay persons living within scientific and religious systems may be more similar than dissimilar. Furnished with garbled and watered-down versions of scientific theory, that is, the grounds whereby the 'secular' layman accepts the legitimacy of scientific models may not be so different from the deferral to tradition which characterizes the non-secular religionist.

Since Horton wrote, it is such questions of the 'scienticity' of science which have represented perhaps the major avenue of anthropological exploration. Does the deployment of a scientific method and world-view operate according to scientific standards of rationality and objectivity, whether among secular laity or working scientists? Are such standards possible, and anything more than a foundation myth or ideology? Are not notions of scientific rationality, openness, scepticism and critique perhaps better seen as part-and-parcel of a 'culture of science' in which individual members, their beliefs and actions, are as constrained as in any 'traditional' religion? Heald (1991) even suggests that the specialization of knowledge and expertise in the West makes us more respectful, not less, of accepted traditions as handed to us by (say, medical) authorities 'in the know'. We cannot assess expert knowledge easily, do not expect it to be commonsensical, and hence take it largely on trust. In traditional, 'tribal' milieux, by contrast, systems of knowledge are grounded in common experience and understandings, are more concrete, less institutionalized, and are thus more easily challenged. From so-called credulous primitives to gullible moderns.

The thrust of Heald's argument – that so-called scepticism and openness are as much culturally conditioned and institutionalized as so-called closure and traditionality – has been famously generalized by the historian of science Thomas Kuhn (1970). Far from ranging openly and freely, scientific enquiry and practice is at any one time constrained by what Kuhn calls the currently dominant 'paradigm'; only at occasional, wholesale revolutions do paradigms shift and, relative to the immediate past, scientists find themselves under new dispensations. Kuhn defines a paradigm as 'the entire constellation of beliefs, values, techniques and so on, shared by the members of a given community' (1970: 175). Learnt at initiation and socially imposed thereafter, paradigms 'determine large areas of experience at the same time' (1970: 129), such that the scientist never meets objective reality directly and 'proponents of different paradigms practice their trades in different worlds' (1970: 150).

Most scientific practice is taken up with a fine-tuning of the paradigmatic model of reality, then, and only very occasionally, as anomalies gradually accrue and finally cannot be ignored, is there a crisis, a 'breakthrough', a 'discovery' — and the institutionalization of new paradigmatic theories, methods, standards and norms. At no time, however, is there no conventional paradigm guiding scientific hypothesization, experimentation and validation. And while, conventionally, the scientists' models are meant to be free-standing — the issue of discovery rather than invention — they are in fact marionettes: puppets which act according to the grace of the paradigm which determined their existence and extent. As Schuetz elaborates (1953: 37):

A total harmony has been pre-established between the determined consciousness bestowed upon the puppet and the pre-constituted environment within which it is supposed to act freely, to make rational choices and decisions. This harmony is possible merely because the puppet and its reduced environment are the creation of the scientist. And by keeping to the principles which guided him, the scientist succeeds indeed in discovering within the universe, thus created, the perfect harmony established by himself.

In other words, scientific truth, far from a solemn and severe master, may better be conceived of as a docile and obedient servant. The scientist deceives himself who sees himself stoically dedicated to its search; for he 'as much decrees as discovers the laws he sets forth, as much designs as discerns the patterns he delineates' (Goodman 1978: 18).

Human beings have a passion for world-making, Goodman elaborates, but we satisfy this passion at different times, for different purposes, in a number of different ways. Science is one such way, religion another. Science predicates itself upon observation, generalization, system, but its truths are nevertheless fabricated, not found: 'primarily a matter of fit' with a pre-existing paradigm rather than of correspondence with an objective reality (1978: 138). Scientific facts are imbued with scientific theories, in short; facts, indeed, are small theories and theories big facts. Scientific worlds, like all socio-cultural worlds are made; perceiving them consists in producing them, discovering them in drafting them; recognizing them in imposing them.

A number of well-known ethnographic studies have attempted to elucidate this process of the scientific construction of facts, often focusing their attention upon high-profile and hi-tech laboratories in which cutting-edge research is said to occur (e.g. Traweek 1988; Gusterson 1996). Studying science labs as communities of members intent upon establishing and maintaining their symbolic stature, identity, legitimacy and wealth, within a field of like communities, the broader anthropological agenda has been a querying of the equation between science and rationality (cf. Haraway 1989), and an exploring of science – sciences, better – as cultural productions (cf. Franklin 1995; Marcus 1995). Here is science as identified as tautological discourse, employing criteria for evidence and proof which are internal to itself, unable to validate itself except in terms of narratives which are socio-culturally grounded.

In *Laboratory Life* (1979), for instance, Latour and Woolgar describe how the daily activities of working scientists lead to the construction of facts in a California neuro-endocrinology laboratory. Neuro-endocrinology, as a field of study, originated in the 1940s as a result of the hybridization of the study of the nervous system and the study of the hormonal system. This precipitated a new paradigm or culture, with its own myths, precursors and revolutions, and attempts to isolate, characterize, synthesize (reproduce) and understand the modes of action and interaction of 'releasing factors': how the brain controls the hormonal system through releasing peptides comprising amino acids. Members of the California laboratory struggle to deal with a disorderly array of alternative interpretations through the application of frameworks of explanation which cut out most stimuli as noise. By and large, this is a literary exercise, constantly performing operations on literary statements: citing, enhancing, borrowing, modifying, proposing anew. An overview suggests that these scientists are constituting the truth of substances through their artful creativity.

Hundreds of statements are produced in this way in hundreds of laboratories: from scribbled results on paper, to lectures, to pre-prints, to published papers in *Nature* and *Science*. And out of the small fraction that survive uncontested and unchanged, Latour and Woolgar suggest, new 'facts' are constituted. A new statement joins the stock of taken-for-granted features which are removed from daily scientific activity, incorporated into a large body of old knowledge, and transferred to textbooks. The statement becomes 'objective reality':

> The result of the *construction* of a fact is that it appears unconstructed by anyone; the result of rhetorical persuasion in

the agonistic field is that participants are convinced that they have not been convinced; the result of *materialization* is that people can swear that material considerations are only minor components of the 'thought process'; the result of the investments of credibility is that participants can claim that economics and beliefs are in no way related to the solidity of science; as to the *circumstances*, they simply vanish from accounts.

(Latour and Woolgar 1979: 240)

Facts can be seen as consequences of scientific work rather than their cause, and 'reality' the outcome of a settling of scientific dispute.

An ancient city of knowledge-practices

In considering science as a way of knowing and a body of knowledge related to a diversity of other ways in a socio-cultural milieu, Geertz adapts a Wittgensteinian image. For Wittgenstein (1978: 8):

Our language can be seen as an ancient city: a maze of little streets and squares, of old and new houses, and of houses with additions from various periods; and this surrounded by a multitude of new boroughs with straight, regular streets and uniform houses.

For Geertz (1983: 74), 'language' in the above may be replaced by 'culture' and equal sense be made. (Wittgenstein is, after all, talking about language-games and forms of life.) Geertz's point is that within a socio-cultural milieu, as in a city, people inhabit, frequent and travel between a range of different symbol-systems or knowledge-practices; a socio-cultural milieu is made up of a number of such ways of knowing, thinking, speaking and feeling, each different in terms of its character, longevity, complexity, and the manner, time and extent in which it is used by members. Common sense might represent one such symbol-system and way of knowing, then, religion a second, art a third, science a fourth, sociology a fifth, computer studies a sixth, and so on. These boroughs or suburbs of the 'ancient city' of a culture or society exist in different and developing relations to one another (some expanding, some declining at their expense), and are visited differently by different individual members, perhaps at different times of the members' lives. Some areas are lived in every day, others only entered for special reasons and the seeking of specialist advice (medical, spiritual, financial).

This Wittgensteinian–Geertzian image is useful here for reflecting phenomenologically upon the way in which scientific thought, language and practice are experienced by individuals at particular times and places. An increasing number of anthropological studies are concerned with this, examining, for instance, the reception of science in the Third World (Goonatilake 1984), the (oracular) deployment of the lie-detector in a Western police force (Rapport 1993b), or the implications of the Human Genome Initiative (Rabinow 1996).

A particularly fruitful area of recent study has been into the representation, dissemination and local understandings of ideas surrounding new reproductive technologies (NRTs) such as *in vitro* fertilization, surrogacy and genetic counselling (Strathern 1992a; Edwards *et al.* 1993; Ginsburg and Rapp 1995; Franklin 1996). How might such scientific advances in the assisting of conception alter people's sense of the reproductive process, of kinship relations, even of a nature/culture dichotomy and relations between 'nature and nurture'? How might these senses differ in the contexts of government bureaucracies, medical clinics and family homes?

For example, in the context of the small town of Bacup in northern England, Edwards (2000) explores the extent to which discussions surrounding NRTs and their possible or actual local usage problematizes taken-for-granted ideas of ('social' or 'biological') relatedness and differentiation, and leads to new cultural practices for the reproduction and differentiation of local identities. New scientific ideas are seen to be appropriated as part of an evolving set, a diverse (and ancient) fund, which individuals variously, and contingently, employ in the continuing business of making present sense. As people consider what being 'born and Bred in bacup' – among Bacup houses, factories, local services, history, characters, dialect, churches and occupations – now entails, an ethnomethodology may be observed by which local persons and relations are created and recreated afresh.

See also: **Classification, Common Sense, Ethnomethodology, World-Making**

SITUATION AND CONTEXT

The concepts of situation and context draw attention to a number of important aspects of social life: its processual nature, its perspectival and plural quality, and the part played in its constitution and reconstitution by individual agency.

The point is made succinctly by reference to two quotations, the first from Gregory Bateson (1951: 238, 212):

> The concept of [social] reality is slippery because, always, truth is relative to context, and context is determined by the questions which we ask of events. . . . [M]an lives by those propositions whose validity is a function of his belief in them.

The second is from Edward Sapir (1956: 151):

> The true locus of culture is in the interactions of specific individuals, and, on the subjective side, in the world of meanings which each one of these individuals may unconsciously abstract for himself from his participation in these interactions.

Taken together, these point up the way in which socio-cultural reality does not exist beyond the interpretations which individuals ongoingly make of it and the extent to which they continue to act upon the assumption of its existence. It has no *sui generis* existence; it is no thing-in-itself. If individuals stop believing in socio-cultural reality and its institutions, and acting in certain routine ways *vis-à-vis* the latter, then the reality ceases to exist.

Furthermore, the interpretations of socio-cultural reality made by different individuals can be expected to be diverse, for it is in the nature of individuality that each begins from and operates with a unique perspective upon the world. And since each individual is also a unique 'energy source' (Bateson 1972: 126), each will be responsible for acting upon these interpretations in an equally unique way. Hence the importance of focusing upon moments of interaction: of the coming together of individuals in conversational and behavioural exchange. For it is here that diverse interpretations and lines of action converge and it is here that processes of social life emerge. Social organization and structure are the result of ongoing processes of negotiation between individuals operating in terms of diverse world-views and agendas. Social organization and structure continue to exist because individuals in interaction maintain the process of their reconstitution, and act on the basis of the outcome of their negotiations.

Another way of saying this is that in situations of interaction, a plurality of individual contexts come into contact, where 'context' is understood as the way an individual frames, and distinguishes between, things, people and events in the world. Context refers to the environment(s) which an individual inhabits before, during and after situations of interaction with others. These may come to be shared in long-term relationships but it is just as likely (if not more so) that they will remain individual and private. Thus, the same cognitive context may be inhabited by an individual in any number of different situations of interaction, while the seemingly 'same' interactional exchange can be cognitively contextualized in any number of different ways.

An awareness of situation and context in anthropology developed out of a reaction against those traditions which sought to reify society and culture (*après* Durkheim, Marx, Lévi-Strauss), and spoke of structure (also convention, norm, rule, role, system and class) as if possessed of its own life and momentum, and as if objective, coercive, impersonal, coherent and steady-state. An emphasis on situation and context translates as one upon those moments in which socio-cultural reality (realities, better) is ongoingly reconstituted courtesy of the decisions of individuals in interaction, acting often in concert with others but always in the context of their own interpretations and agendas.

Finally, an appreciation of situation and context gives onto a picture of social life as far from neat, settled or singular. For between moments of interaction, and between individuals in the same interactions, the meanings which are construed, and the actions consequent upon those interpretations, may be diverse. Only by a micro-social analysis of situation and context can an understanding emerge of what socio-cultural realities are being inhabited when, and by whom (cf. Scheff 1990; Briggs 1992; Rapport 1993a).

See also: **Cognition, Conversation, Interaction, Moments of Being**

SOCIETY

Throughout the modernist period, a concept of society has under-pinned the construction of all social theory, whatever its hue or denomination. If the concept of culture has played the role of queen to all analytic categories of the human sciences, the notion of society has been king. It is the master trope of high modern social thought. As such, it is nowadays considered to be a treacherous friend, a term to be used at one's risk. As Ingold (1994c: 738) has commented, the word now belongs so much to a language of argument that its use signals one contentious claim or the other about the world. We must nevertheless continue to take the term 'society' seriously, along with all the other major categories of Western sociological thought, such as 'culture', 'community' and 'collectivity', 'the individual', 'hierarchy' and 'egalitarianism'. This is because our own 'ordinary' ways of cutting up the world of the social will continue to be essential to the ethnographic process for the obvious reason that these categories remain a hidden lens through which we at first see and perhaps later judge the social lives of other peoples. The important transition for the ethnographer to make is to learn to place his or her representations of society on the *same level* as the ethnographic facts that we claim for other peoples. 'Society' and 'culture' are categories *local* to the West which other peoples may or, more than likely, may not share. Good ethnography moves back and forth between the two – ours and their view of the social – through a dialogical process that has as its reward a further unveiling of both. The aim of the dialogue is naturally to deepen our understanding of *each*. For instance an Amazonian notion of egalitarianism is hardly a mirror image of our own, but we are only able to see this discrepancy by juxtaposing the two. We come to comprehend better our categories of sociality in the process of unravelling theirs. All anthropology includes, with a greater or lesser degree of candour, an ethnography of the West.

The reason for the present-day errant status of the term 'society' is that it shares many of the same problems as its sister trope, 'culture'. It objectifies social life, with the emphasis being upon the systemic aspects of social units and the shared and distinct nature of their institutions and culture. This idea of society as a singular, self-contained, normative, bounded whole that transcends the individual is the notion that is most often cited in contemporary anthropological literature as highly suspect (cf. Strathern 1988; Fardon 1992; Ingold 1994c; Viveiros de Castro 1996; Rapport 1997a). Particularly pernicious for contemporary sensibilities is the abstract notion of society, forthcoming from Durkheimian theory, as the weighty collectivity that imposes on, opposes and constrains all those extra-social individuals who compose it. A prevalent trend in modernist thought does hold to the idea that individuals, like nature, must be mastered, developed and tamed by the greater whole in order for a progressive social order to be reached. The great debate throughout the history of the modern West has been over what this 'greater whole' should be, and who should be the object of its taming, but whatever the solution the argument has nearly always been framed in terms of the master trope, 'society'.

A very brief history of the term's use

At stake is a theory of human nature and its specific capacities for social life. This narrative of 'society' has a historical context, for it was not until the eighteenth century that the term began to be used in the modernist, general abstract sense to denote particular 'social orders'. Raymond Williams notes (1983b: 293) that this transformation of use came in the wake of the rise of the nation-state, at which time one prevailing notion of society came to denote the state's hierarchical and hegemonic institutions of control. The political turmoil of the eighteenth century played its part, for it was through thinking through the questions for a new (bourgeois) political order that the idea of society was constructed in its most general and abstract meaning (*ibid.*). This sense (e)merged with the notion of 'civil society' and the development of contract theories of the state.

In contrast to society as an abstraction, or the idea of society as that to which we all belong in an impersonal, general sense, the earlier meaning pertained to face-to-face relationships within a community, and denoted sociability, companionship, fellowship, or a mode of living (Williams 1983b: 291–2). It is this earlier meaning that many anthropologists are now saying is closer to an acceptable view. Thus instead of the term 'society', which carries still the modernist meaning of a weighty unified collectivity, many anthropologists today prefer the term 'sociality' (e.g. Strathern 1988; Ingold 1994c; Fardon 1995b), one idea being that the social requires individual agency and thus the two partake of one another.

The royal quartet, and the transformation of the normative into the universal

There are many reasons for anthropologists to question fiercely the imagery of society portrayed within the history of the field's grand narratives of social order. As the above section suggests, our own notion of society, and the elements of which it is comprised, is a product of *local* historical forces in the West, namely the rise of the nation-state, capitalism, imperialism and the colonialist endeavour. The image of society that came to be favoured in modernist social theory was one that mirrored the major shifts that had occurred in Western social life through these forces of change. Most of our analytic terms that are used for the study of 'society' reflect these historically specific transformations and revolutions that occurred in the industrial West, where over time economic life became separated from politics, political life became free of the church, and the domestic unit became detached from them all. Once these areas of life were distinguished as separate domains, it came to be seen as *natural* that 'society' should comprise these four aspects or institutions. In social theory, to understand the *order* of a society required the study of its distinct systems of economics, politics, religion and kinship. What had become normative to the West acquired the status of a universal.

Just think of all those classic monographs in anthropology, and their chapters on kinship, followed by those on economics, and then politics, and finally religion. In Schneider's critique (1984) of this royal quartet as used in anthropology, he says that each 'is conceived to be a natural, universal, vital component of society. . . . It is taken as self-evident that . . . [kinship] . . . is distinct from the other institutions, yet also related to them since they all constitute major building blocks out of which all social systems are constructed' (Schneider 1984: 187–8). Anthropologists have argued that among the peoples they most study (the 'primitives' of the world) that it is the institution of kinship that is prioritized in *their* societal ordering, as opposed to politics or economics in our own. It is kinship which serves as the salient idiom for their economic, political and religious life. Nevertheless, the very notion of a 'kinship-based society' depends analytically on distinctions that hold between each of the quartet – or, the spheres of society that European culture distinguishes. Basically Schneider is arguing that these four categories of society are local postulates of Western culture, and as such they have little analytical value when applied cross-culturally.

The evolutionary agenda of the anthropological use of the royal quartet

It is important to note the hidden political agenda to retaining our Western categories of societal ordering *as universals* in the task of understanding the sociality of other peoples. When treated not as local social facts, but as universals, the royal quartet can only serve to reflect distinctions of worth that separate the West from all the rest, and the incisive question can no longer be 'what is the character of *their* sociality?', but only 'to what degree does their social life approach or depart from *our modern Western State*?' The question, even if the overt agenda is functionalist, remains strongly coloured by evolutionism, because it asks: 'how far has a "society" progressed in its socio-cultural complexity in approximating our own'? Both description and judgement are then structured through the Western standards of normalcy. It was in the West that these spheres of life first detached from one other so that each gained independence from the authority of the next. Such detachment between institutions is understood to be one of the essential keys to progress, and to the development of the complex institutional structures of modern civilization. The category of 'primitive societies' means just that: these are societies that are simple. The hidden clause, that it is *our standards and valuations* that deem them primitive, is omitted, and thus by categorical statement they are classified as primitive. They have not developed; they do not have the institutional complexity – and therefore the development of *reason* – found in the modern West. Their political and economic spheres of life are still embedded in their kinship system. They are consequently primitive by 'scientific' standards (which in this case have their origin, it is to be remembered, in the received knowledge of *Western folk*). The only conclusion that can be forthcoming from using the royal quartet as a gauge for standards, scientific or otherwise, can be that 'primitives' are on the low rung of 'society'. However, complexity is a complex matter, its judgement being dependent upon the eyes of the beholder.

This hidden agenda of primitivism comes in a variety of colours. From its beginnings, anthropological theory has been rife with great-divide dichotomies to distinguish the primitive society from the civilized. There are the mechanical versus organic solidarities of Durkheim (1964); the cold vs. hot societies of Lévi-Strauss (1966); the pre-technological vs. technological of Gell (1992); the pre-literate/literate of Goody (1977); the holistic (collectivist) vs. individualistic of Dumont (1977); and the pre-capitalist/capitalist of Marx (1965 [1857–58]). Such generalizing classifications of difference are often more *self*-evaluative than enlightening of the practices of the other. Thus, in classifying other people through them, either positively or negatively, one is not only saying, for example, that 'they have no freedom because they have community', but also that 'we shall have no freedom if *we* value community', or '*we* can have more freedom if *we* have productive progress', or 'if *we* had no productive progress *we* would be immature and uncreative'. Each such dichotomizing tactic is in accordance with the specific Western distinctions of worth that are being evaluatively weighted to create this great divide.

It was complexity in the economic side of life, specifically its technological aspects, that until recently has been a favoured strategy used to unveil the primitive. It is not at all certain that anthropology has totally freed itself from Marx's assumption that 'simple technology' equates with 'simple minds' (Marx 1965). The grand evolutionary schemes in anthropology have principally centred attention on technology, the assumption being that technological development has causal weight in the development of the rest of society (even literacy is understood in this capacity as a 'technology of the intellect' (Goody 1977)). Thus all hunters and gatherers of the world have been lumped together as sharing a very low level of 'socio-political' progress because they only *forage* for food. Hunters and gatherers, because of their supposed ignorance of the domestication of nature, are the category of people who sit on the very lowest step of societal development. The corollary of using a 'simple' technology of hunting, fishing and food gathering is a low capability for developing the wider network of social and political ties that are necessary to the development of society (e.g. Sahlins and Service 1960; Service 1962; Woodburn 1982). 'Tribal societies' are a rung up the ladder because they have learned the technology of horticulture. Since they can create a surplus of food and also store it, they are therefore able to create more 'socio-centric' statuses through which to relate economically, and therefore politically, to wider communities of people. The idea is that it is through economic exchange that the political structures of society are created, and its hierarchical societal integration achieved. In neo-evolutionist thought (e.g. Service 1962), 'chieftainships' achieve 'higher' levels of societal integration than 'tribal' peoples because of the grand redistributive networks of goods over which the chieftain leadership has control, while the 'state', because of the complex economic powers of its executive, achieves the highest level of all. Peoples are considered to have different *degrees* of society, a judgement made according to the evolutionary progress of their hierarchical structures.

The 'domestic mode of production', and society as hierarchical ordering

In anthropology the notion of society (to be equated with 'social structure', and indeed 'the social') is usually defined by (1) structures of separation and opposition, and (2) structures of inequality, or the institutional elaboration of relations of dominance and subordination. Egalitarian peoples are considered less social than those that favour their hierarchical institutions because they have less society (e.g. Bloch 1977). The anthropological gaze upon the egalitarian ways of doing things has predominantly been one of suspicion.

Sahlins (1972) provides one of the clearest arguments for equating society *and* the social with the achievement of politico-economic hierarchical structures. He maintains that 'tribal' peoples follow a 'domestic mode of production' that is typically based on egalitarian principles that are linked to values which must be overcome in order for the social to be attained. The problem stems from the fact that the household in the 'domestic mode of production' is given economic autonomy. In contrast to the capitalist system, 'the domestic system', he says, 'entertains limited economic goals, qualitatively defined in the terms of a way of living rather than quantitatively as an abstract wealth'

338

(*ibid.*: 86). Although he makes the case that this modality leads to an 'affluent' life, in that the individual has freedom and leisure, eats well, and does not overly toil, he also argues that its social defect is that the domestic mode only serves intimate and therefore ultimately selfish familial satisfactions, and *not* those of the wider whole. As a result, production in the domestic mode, Sahlins complains, 'has all the organization of the so many potatoes in a certain famous sack of potatoes' (*ibid.*: 96) – there is a small-time anarchy lurking beneath the surface of things; there is disarray in the background.

So far perhaps so good, but Sahlins further concludes that because of its stress upon quality of life and the intimate relationship, 'the domestic mode of production' is like the state of nature. In itself, it provides no mechanisms for holding a growing community together; that is, as an economic mode of operation it has few means for coercing people to work harder. Economically, 'primitive' society is therefore founded on *anti-society* (*ibid.*: 86, 97–8, our italics). Tribal life becomes *social*, and attains *society*, only insofar as the 'economic defects' of the domestic mode of production, with its values of autonomy, equality and leisure, are overcome through the political force and economic exploitation of the chief (*ibid.*: 134). For tribal societies, Sahlins is not only opposing *domestic* and *public* domains, but he also places the first – the intimate relations of family life – within the domain of nature. Only the public domain, within which the chief operates through means of political coercion, merits in this view the label of 'social'. Collectivity, and the very possibility for its attainment, becomes by definition a matter of hierarchical structure and institutions of exchange and coercion. To be social is to engage in hierarchical relationships.

There are nuances here of ways of thinking that speak to our well-known antinomy of individual and society, where society's role is understood as a force that moves over and beyond all those egoistic and asocial individuals who make up its numbers (but see Sahlins 1999). Except here the unit of egoism is comprised of a *set* of domestic relationships. Those intimate relationships which Sahlins declares asocial are *also* those that are centred on the caring and raising of children. Even if we ignore the very questionable status of Sahlins's *isolated* household unit, which in fact for the majority of indigenous peoples sits firmly within the context of *everyday* multi-faceted relationships of community life (e.g. Overing 1993a), Sahlins's assumptions about the domestic unit fit neatly with Western ideas about society that assume an opposition between the public domains of societal importance and the asocial private domain of family and kinship life which is considered to be on the side of nature. Within the context of such a narrative, if one should categorize the economic base of 'tribal society' as 'domestic' then it is a reasonable next step to conclude that the primary thrust of 'tribal society' is asocial – and like the 'state of nature'. Such an argument would be a strong modernist formulation of primitivism.

It might, however, be wise to take a closer look at this Western dichotomy that is so denigrating of the domestic relationship. We might then understand better its tenacity within anthropological literature, as used, for instance, by Sahlins in his shaping of a 'domestic mode of production', and also the significance of the part it has played in obscuring indigenous thought and experience.

A feminist critique

It is from a feminist point of view that Marilyn Strathern provides (1988), through her studies of the peoples of Melanesia, a major critique of the construct of society as it has been prevalently used in anthropology. The feminist critique in general has played a crucial role in de-centring the construct of society as it sits within modernist social theory. In large part its success has been due to its focus upon the male bias that is embedded within the Western opposition of the domestic and the public, which, as it is argued, implicitly links women and men evaluatively to their respective places within another powerful dichotomy salient to Western thought, i.e. nature and culture. Strathern argues that the indigenous peoples of New Guinea, and in particular the Hagen with whom she worked, do not have the non-ambiguous misogynist perceptions of sociality that are characteristic of Western classifications of social order. The Hagen have no counterpart to our notion of society, with all those metaphysical problems attached to this concept, such as the idea that men complete culturally and socially what women begin naturally through childbirth. As Strathern notes, 'however useful the concept of society may be to analysis, we are not going to justify its use by appealing to indigenous counterparts' (Strathern 1988: 3).

She explains that in Western ideas of social order, the power of society is often judged by its control of extra-social individuals, who are conceived of as so much biological raw material for society to domesticate. Society's socialization of individuals becomes synonymous with the notion of its subordination of nature. There is moreover a symbolism of gender relations, and an evaluation of the respective genders, that lie at the heart of this particular model of society, for the relationship between part and whole (the biological individual with society) is envisaged as that between female and male (*ibid.*: 94). The larger whole, or the controlling collective force of society, coincides with the public domain of men, while the subordinated, individuating, familial domain of the domestic pertains to women – and their biologically based activities. Indeed, in this Western formulation of society, it is the very *separation* that holds between the dominant public domain and its subordinated private spheres of life that is thought to allow for the creation of society (*ibid.*: 94-5). *And this is the crunch.* Without the regulation and control of the wayward, non–collective and biologically based domestic domain of woman by the collectivity of men, society could not be created nor culture made (*ibid.*: 94, 318).

In this specific myth about the creation of society, 'primitives' and women hold the same symbolic position. Women, who typically relate through the individuating bonds of domestic kinship, and 'primitives', who also hold dear the domestic relations of kinship, are both metaphorically assimilated to the domain of nature. In other words, their capabilities for creating culture and society are minimal. Both are on the low end of sociality. As is true for any vision of the social, this narrative of society has its history and its own political justifications and agenda.

It is hardly surprising that Strathern, as feminist, critiques anthropological perceptions of sociality when they coincide with the above story of society. In it society is seen as a domain that is metaphorically categorized as male. Society is understood as a wider regulating sociality; it is equated with the public domain of men, who form together a collectivity of men responsible for society. This is to be contrasted to women's individuating, domestic activities which are viewed as 'the problem' for men, and thus for society at large, in that they threaten and impinge upon the solidarity of the collectivity of males (cf. Pateman (1989: 641) who observes that the Rousseau-esque social contract is for men only, with women being seen not just as excluded from it but a continual danger to society's orderly running). Strathern, as anthropologist, is most concerned to set the record straight with regard to indigenous views of sociality.

She notes that many portrayals of Melanesian sociality have followed the Western tale of society which assumes that it is the collective action of men that forms society, with male bonds of solidarity providing for its necessary cohesion. In the anthropological literature, since Malinowski's publications on the Trobrianders (1922), Melanesian peoples have been famous for their great networks of ceremonial exchange, which linked otherwise autonomous communities into greater societal structures through which big leaders could gain power and prestige. Such structures of male ceremonial exchange were analysed by anthropologists as responsible for social control, the integration of groups, and the promotion of sociability. It was the political force of ceremonial exchange that provided the unity necessary for the creation of society, which otherwise would have been impossible because of the individuating, centrifugal inclinations of individual desire. Anthropologists assumed that social structure was concerned with groups of males, and that society was a matter of male solidarity (Strathern *op. cit.*: 52). It is this popular anthropological myth about the hegemonic relation of men's collective ritual and exchange to the building of the social relations of society that Strathern wished to shatter (*ibid.*: 67–9).

According to Strathern, the indigenous view of their own sociality followed a very different sort of narrative. Among indigenous peoples of Melanesia, she says, there was no image of men ideologically promoting their own male values as those of society at large. Men did not regard female values as a mere counterpoint to their own activities. There was no simple dualistic split between the stereotypes of men and women. Male collective life did not entail a heightened sociality that served a set of male hegemonic social values, over and against those of females. Rather, both men and women were directed toward the same goal. Most of men's endeavours were 'directed towards the same production of domestic kinship, growth, and fertility as concern women' (*ibid.*: 318; cf. Overing 1999, on Amazonia). The goals of 'the collective' and 'the domestic' merged, and it is for this reason that Strathern argues that 'the forms of Melanesian collective life are not adequately described through the Western model of a society, and that however men are depicted it cannot be as authors of such an entity' (Strathern *op. cit.*: 319). Rather, collective actions in Melanesia are *one type* of sociality – they co-exist with the sociality of domestic relations; they alternate but cannot be dominant to them. Nor are men considered 'more social' than the women. In contrast to our Western image of society, the Melanesian view does not visualize sociality as a superstructural elaboration of forces, and thus the collective life of men is not understood to have a privileged vantage-point of sanctioning commentary on the 'rest' of society (Strathern *op. cit.*). In short, we must resist the anthropological tendency to conflate 'their collectivity' and 'our society', for Melanesian people do not have society as we know it. What they *do* have is sociality.

Basically, anthropologists, in objectifying the notion of society, have transformed modern Western distinctions of worth and judgement into the analytic constructs through which to gaze upon other types of socialities, and in so doing they have often been asking questions that serve to obscure rather than shed light upon indigenous experience. The big question is what does it mean to be social? If we define society as institutions of hierarchy and coercion, then it is clearly the case that many indigenous peoples do not have much of it, nor do they want it (e.g. Clastres 1977; Overing 1993b). They nevertheless are clearly social beings, and they also happen to have their own strong views about proper human sociality.

See also: **Agent and Agency, Common Sense, Culture, Gender, Humanism, Individuality, Kinship, The Unhomely**

STEREOTYPES

Stereotypes and the practice of stereotyping – attributing to all members of a category or class identical features – have not traditionally been well-received within the social sciences. Of the three broad analytic approaches, the sociological, the psychodynamic and the cognitive, all concur in linking stereotypes with pejoration and perverse inter-group relations (Ashmore and Del Boca 1981). Defined as 'relatively rigid and oversimplified conceptions of a group of people in which all individuals in the group are labelled with the group characteristics' (Wrightsman 1977: 672), and functioning as 'chunks of attributed traits [which cause] an individual's evaluations of others to come in packaged Gestalten' (Pettigrew 1981: 313–14), stereotypes are seen as deriving from hearsay and rumour rather than induction from proven fact, and from a simple projection of one's own values and expectations onto the environing world (Allport 1954). It is said that stereotypes are the resort of those lacking cognitive complexity, the penchant of those frightened by ambiguity and unsubtle in how they categorize stimuli; or else those emotionally aroused or distracted and unable to attend fully to cognitive classification; or those fixated on de-individuating themselves, and thereafter visiting the same on others (Wilder 1981: 235–40). Hence, stereotypes allow simplistic and fantastic claims to be made about a group's manifold membership, claims which are all the more ambiguous and gross the higher the societal level to which the collective label is applied.

In short, stereotypes are seen to form a discursive and conceptual fortress in which groups can barricade themselves, universally convinced of the safety, rectitude and respectability of their own traditions while at the same time aroused into making prejudiced (but self-fulfilling) responses not towards real others but towards masquerades and phantasms (Basow 1980: 3–12; also Glassman 1975: 14–20). Thus it is that stereotypes come to be decried as sources of social pathology; they are a root cause of misconception, and thus of intractable and oppressive sexism, racism and classism (Elfenbein 1989: viii, 158), of misdirected and xenophobic aggression, warring and pogrom (O'Donnell 1977: 23–4; also Lea 1978).

Traditional social-scientific appreciations of stereotypes

The origin of contemporary social-scientific interest in stereotypes is probably the work of Walter Lippmann, especially *Public Opinion* (1947 [1922]). Reality is too complex for human beings to apprehend directly, Lippmann theorized (1947: 89ff.), therefore they form mental pseudo-environments, a key part of which are stereotypes. Modern social life is hurried and multifarious, with little time or opportunity for intimate acquaintance; there is a need for economy, for seeing things as types and generalities. At the same time, there is a human love of absolutes and a dislike of constant qualification: an orderly world-view is one of clear demarcations. Hence, stereotypes represent schemata which simplify perception and cognition, and help to process information about the environment in a uniform and regular fashion. These schemata are not reached or maintained by individual testing, however. Rather they are learned as cultural practices; stereotypes come to form integral parts of individuals' world-views and yet they represent the imposition of pre-rational characterizations and classifications on data deriving from a cultural *habitus*. Stereotypes therefore rationalize 'prejudicial', pre-judgemental, cognitions and conclusions about the world.

The three main analytic approaches to stereotypes which have developed since Lippmann's day (the sociological, the psychodynamic and the cognitive) have all focused upon the factually incorrect, over-generalized and prejudicially rigid nature of stereotypes. The sociological approach (cf. Chapman 1968; McDonald 1993) focuses on the socio-cultural factors behind groups' use of and belief in stereotypes. Stereotypes are treated as temporally and regionally consistent ideological matrices which are learnt by individual members through processes of socialization. Due to the cultural mismatch of classificatory systems by which different social groups construct the world, moreover, stereotyping can be understood as an autonomous discourse which predominates within the worlds of the representers quite independently of any 'truth-value', and irrespective of any connection to those 'others' it purports to depict. Part-and-parcel of a group's 'identity rhetoric', stereotyping is a function of the social construction of group characteristics; by way of a normative treatment of others, a consensus surrounding stereotypes bolsters social solidarity and integration. Through partaking in processes of prejudicial othering, individuals can express common group membership and hope to gain the recognition of their fellows.

Psychodynamic approaches to stereotypes have centred on those instinctual and unconscious factors in the human make-up which might make for poor inter-group relations. Both the instinct for aggression *per se*, and the arising of certain personality types (authoritarian, for instance) from a dialectical interplay between particular instincts and particular agonistic social formations, are seen as motivating human beings towards prejudicial treatment of others (cf. Wrightsman 1977). Cognitive approaches, meanwhile, have tended to reject a focus upon both motive and ideology, and accepted a limited human capacity to process information and think rationally. Stereotypes here represent breakdowns in environmental perception such that experience is not cognized directly or wholly, and cognitions are not changed in the face of new data. These systematic perceptual biases are due to inevitable human fallibility. In endeavouring to reduce environmental complexity to a manageable size, when bombarded with environmental stimuli, untested cognitive short-cuts come to be employed which have a tendency to become self-fulfilling. As with 'autistic thinking' in general, stereotypes are insufficiently perspicacious to afford valid generalizations and any true relation to reality which they bear is merely by chance (cf. Klineberg 1951; Peabody 1985).

In sum, stereotypes are conventionally treated as over-generalized, overdetermined, second-hand and partial perceptions which confuse description and evaluation, which merely reflect ideological biases, instinctual motivations or cognitive limitations.

An alternative appreciation of stereotypes

This bad press can sometimes miss the mark, however. A better appreciation of the practice of stereotyping might begin by identifying just what stereotypes, as a discourse and a cognitive resort, can be said to offer.

First, then, stereotypes afford both opposition and exaggeration. From the former (from comparison and contrast), notions of being are to be gained: by continuously 'playing the *vis-à-vis*', as Boon phrases it (1982: 231), distinctions between self and other are realized. From the latter (from hyperbole), as Douglas suggests (1966: 4), clarity and definiteness are to be derived. Thus it is that in stereotypes distinct senses of identity may be seen to inhere; through the positing of stereotypical images of difference, individuals and groups can maintain their senses of belonging, while in stereotypical hyperbole differences between self and other can become ever more clear-cut. Rather than scourges of the alien, then, stereotypes may be seen as facing primarily inward: into the group and, even more, into the individual, furnishing him or her with comforting shibboleths of self.

Seen from 'inside' group boundaries, the stereotype can serve a further useful purpose; individuals can use stereotypes for cognitively mapping and then anchoring themselves within a conventional and secure social landscape. Here are cognitive 'schemata' (Neisser 1976: 53–4), which direct an exploration of the unknown and potentially chaotic in terms of the personally orderly and known. That is, stereotypes are a stable and widespread discursive currency, and they provide significant points of initial reference. They afford bearings from which to anticipate interaction, plot social relations and initiate knowing – and from a safe distance, too – however far removed their biases become from the manifold elaborations of social relationship and being which eventuate. However diversely conceived and unpredictably shifting the social universe, still an individual need never be at a loss as to what to perceive and how to commence to act; indeed, the simpler and more ambiguous the stereotype the more situations in which it can be used. Perhaps the stereotype does derive from typifying the world 'outside' in exaggerated opposition, with others' cultural traits being seen as alien and as butting against one's own, but 'inside' the stereotype still provides the cognitive furniture of a secure belonging. If two geometric axes must intersect for the identifying of a point in a plane, then in the stereotype the individual finds one ready-made cognitive axis in relation to which to gauge his or her position (cf. Price 1992: 58–9).

Moreover, stereotypes are never alone. At least one contrast is entailed and very often an entire set: 'commonsensical English' versus 'stupid Irish' versus 'mean Scots' versus 'thieving Welsh' versus 'haughty French' versus 'mystical Indians' versus 'regimented Chinese' versus 'rough-and-ready Australians', and so on. And if the stereotype is a cognitive anchor, then a set of them anchors the individual to a socio-cultural world replete with, and ready for, all manner of occurrence. Each stereotype alone may represent a corruption of an immense variety of practice, but as a set they provide a varied, rich and all-inclusive array; however fictitious and remote these labels may be from others' actual attributes and penchants, together stereotypes constitute a coherent and expectable, wider milieu, common in form to all its members.

In sum, the stereotype represents a shorthand. It is a source of consistent, expectable, broad and immediate ways of knowing of socio-cultural worlds, a ready means by which to embody and express a multitude of complex emotions, and a short-cut to generalities, to future possible regularities and uniformities. Such a foundation is very necessary not only as a bulwark against indeterminacy and unpredictability, but also as an encouragement towards action – that vital movement which, if it were not for the bias of the stereotype and the blind spots of perception it incurs, might be replaced by the self-doubt and paralysis of trying to see an environment from every point of view (cf. Lippmann 1947: 114; Rapport 1998).

The individuality of stereotypes

To stereotype is to partake of a socio-cultural discourse: to know of 'French' and 'Indians', of 'haughty' and 'mystical', and of how the words go together; also of how properly to enunciate the words, and combine them with actions, in conventional interaction. To stereotype, in short, is to evince enculturation into a set of regularly used and possibly widely shared practices.

However, an argument may be made, notwithstanding, that a discourse of stereotypes remains essentially exterior to the individual: something with which he juggles and enters into relationship. For, at the same time as the individual has recourse to stereotypes, the interpretation of experience which stereotyping affords is far from constricted. The individual can be seen adopting and yet adapting stereotypes, developing his own routine relations with them, posing one against another, personalizing what they purport in his own image. Stereotypes punctuate acts of interpretation, serving as a structure, a syntax, a cement for what is constructed, but they do not determine those constructions.

The externality of stereotypes as a discourse (and the 'internality' of their contextualization) speaks to a further feature of stereotypes: their inertia. There is wide acknowledgement of longevity of stereotypes, their persistency and consistency in the face of 'objective' contradictory claims. In this discursive stability, it might be argued, is to be found security and an assurance of one's possessing interactional currency. But besides security, it is perhaps beneath such conventional discursive forms that life can be lived most eccentrically and creatively. The very formulaicism permits the freest flights of fancy to be privately construed with the least of public consequences. As Virginia Woolf poetically phrased it (1969: 223):

one cannot despise these phrases laid like Roman roads across the tumult of our lives, since they compel us to walk in step like civilized people . . . though one may be humming any nonsense under one's breath at the same time. . . .

In short, far from the pervasiveness of stereotypes necessarily involving a retreat from subtle individual usage, experience and significance, the very opposite can be the case. Partaking in a stereotypical discourse can represent a way for the individual to secure a personal preserve: a mapping of the world, a context for action and a journeying within it which are particular to him alone. It might even be argued that the more stereotypically a milieu is imaged, the more dynamic and diverse the cognitive play which individual users may be making of it, stereotyping and personalizing being two sides of the same cognitive coin (cf. Rapport 1995).

The modernity of stereotypes

Stereotypes have been described as affording a discursive and conceptual bulwark against the randomness and complexity of the world. These static, limited, inert idioms provide beacons of constancy and recognition through which familiar cognitive order can hope to be replicated and stable collective rhythms maintained (Sherif 1967: 157–60). Indeed, as social life sees an increase in scale and pace through such 'massifying' processes as globalization, mass communication, transnationalism and travel, so the attractiveness of stereotypes might be expected also to increase. A world in movement eventuates in a heightened emphasis on the stereotyped – on the clichéd and proverbial and sloganish – in discursive and conceptual usage. One comes to be at home in stereotypical interactions as routine as one's experience is fluxional, as straitened as one's itinerary is wide (cf. Rapport 1994c).

In Zijderveld's phrasing, the contemporary world represents a 'clichégenic' condition (1979: 4–5). Cliché predominates in individual speech, thought, emotion, volition and action, and it is with the stereotypical that modern 'massificated man' feels most at home (Riesman 1958: 376–7; also cf. Drazdauskierie 1981). Social interaction becomes predominated by the verbal 'pre-fab': '[A]n enormously large part of natural language is formulaic, automatic and rehearsed, rather than propositional, creative or freely generated' (Fillmore 1976: 9). Notwithstanding, the prevalence of such stereotypic imagery may be seen as less obscurantist, less outrageous or threatening of communication and civility, when stereotypes are seen not primarily as instruments prejudicially to predominate or pre-empt others, and not as evidence of merely thinking in stale, collective terms, but rather as means for individuals rapidly to project and establish a secure personal belonging in a shifting, complicating world. Here is a cognitive resort (used in concert with possibly many other types of cognitive construction, affording very different types of environmental mapping) whose fixity and reductiveness may be a means simultaneously of conceptualizing great flux and multiplicity. Individual cognition runs to stereotypes because here is a shorthand way to order, and at the same time to juggle with, a vast array of diverse, possibly incompatible data, people, objects and events.

See also: **Classification, Cognition, Home and Homelessness, Movement**

THICK DESCRIPTION

Thick description is a concept introduced into anthropology by Clifford Geertz. It is theorized in his 1973 essay, 'Thick Description: Toward an Interpretive Theory of Culture', and perhaps best exemplified in his 1972 essay, 'Deep Play: Notes on the Balinese Cockfight' (both appearing in *The Interpretation of Cultures* 1973). The essays remain two of the central texts of what became known as 'interpretive anthropology', and figure as part of a widespread (if controversial) refocusing of anthropological interest, since the 1970s, from social structure to meaning.

The interpretation of meaning

Geertz's starting-point is Max Weber's: human beings live suspended in webs of significance which they themselves have spun and continue to spin; above all, human beings make sense, attribute meanings, of and for themselves. It is these webs of significance which are known, collectively, in anthropology, as 'culture', and whose sense is a matter of symbolism. Anthropology is, *inter alia*, the comparative study of culture, the analysis of the traffic in symbols.

But then 'culture' is the province of other academic disciplines besides: sociology, folklore, literary criticism. What distinguishes anthropological study, for Geertz, is the way that it is operationalized; what anthropologists do, first and foremost, is ethnography. And ethnography can be understood as a particular way of 'inscribing' culture, as a special kind of 'thick' writing. What anthropological analysis amounts to, in a word, is a venture in thick description.

The term, 'thick description', Geertz borrows from the philosopher Gilbert Ryle, and Ryle's disquisition on appreciating the difference between twitching and winking. In terms of overt and observable behaviours, phenomenalistic observation and superficial ('thin') description, there is no difference between a twitch and a wink; both involve contraction of the eyelid of one eye. And yet one is an involuntary movement and the other (possibly) a symbol of conspiracy to an ally; in terms of their social significance, the difference between them is vast. Nor does the matter rest there, because further complications (and significances) arise in the differences between a wink, a twitch, and the mimicking of a twitch, the parodying of a wink, the rehearsing of the parodying of a wink, the mimicking of the rehearsing of . . . , and so on. To describe this stratification of layers of significance is to describe increasingly 'thickly'. And this, Geertz advises, is the main objective of ethnography: to get beneath the surface of behaviour to the piled-up levels of inference and implication, the hierarchy of structures of meaning, in terms of which twitches, winks, burlesques and imitations are produced, perceived and interpreted.

To make out winks from twitches, furthermore, to disinter intelligible frameworks of symbolic signification, calls for a particular kind of focus: one that is microscopic and particular. Thick description is characterized by a complex specificity and a circumstantiality; and this, in turn, must originate in largely qualitative research which is participatory and long-term, and carried out in small-scale, even confined, contexts. This is not to say that anthropological study does not extend to large-scale canvases – whole villages or cities, whole societies or civilizations – but that large conclusions are characteristically drawn from small, densely textured facts, and broad abstractions grounded in narrow particulars. And as study builds on study, so anthropological analysis delves more and more deeply and finely into the underlying conceptual structures which give meaning to the symbolic usage within a socio-cultural milieu.

In explicating thick description, then, Geertz places particular and special emphasis on the notions, 'culture' and 'symbol'. Culture is to be understood as an accumulated totality of symbol-systems (religion, ideology, common sense, economics, sport, etc.) in terms of which people make sense of themselves and their world, and represent themselves to themselves and to others. Members of a culture use its symbols (winks, crucifixes, footballs, cats, collars, foods, photographs, words) as a language through which to read and interpret, to express and share meaning. And since the imposition of meaning on life is the major end and primary condition of human existence, this reading of culture (and traffic in significant symbols) is constant.

The traffic in symbols is public, but it is not thereby transparent. For symbols are inherently ambiguous, and the meanings they carry must always be interpreted before they can be read off. These readings, moreover, are not necessarily fixed or made explicit. The task of the anthropologist in inscribing a culture, therefore, is to interpret the interpretations of that culture which, at a particular moment, its members are making. It is rather like deciphering an ancient ensemble of texts at the same time as it is being read and interpreted by its current owners. An ensemble, moreover, which is often in a foreign language, incomplete in any single manifestation, scribbled over with contradictory commentaries, and written in transient behaviours, not words. Hence, Geertz's pithy conclusion: the anthropological analysis of culture is not 'an experimental science in search of law but an interpretive one in search of meaning' (1973: 5).

Interpretation as science and fiction

Writing thick description, interpreting cultural meaning as symbolized by members' behaviour, is a complex process; nevertheless, it remains a 'scientific' one, embodying objectivity and capable of being refuted.It is complex, we have seen, because the structures of meaning underlying any one social situation are multiple, partial and tangled together. Moreover, it is not only the anthropologist who is engaged in their interpretation but the members of a culture themselves; the anthropologist's inscriptions are interpretations of interpretations: constructions of members' constructions of what they and their fellow-members are engaged in doing.

Notwithstanding, the enterprise is a scientific one and suited to theoretic generalization (relating to previous cases and studies), Geertz avers (drawing on the later work of the philosopher Ludwig Wittgenstein), because meaning is inherently something public. The symbolic logic in use may be foreign to the anthropologist, and the conceptual structuring inexplicit, but these are socially established, sustained and legitimized. Moreover, they are publicly enacted; they are tied to concrete social events and occasions, and expressive of a common social world. In short, giving meaning to behaviour is not something which happens in private, in insular individual heads, but rather something dependent on an exchange of common symbols whose natural habitat is public spaces. Entering these, the anthropologist can hope to share in the symbolic traffic and so gain access to cultural meaning.

And yet, as the thick description of culture entails interpreting the momentary interpretations of systems of symbols made by a culture's members, this inscribing by the anthropologist remains an imaginative act and a fiction: something made out (even if not made up) through the inscribing process: something he or she fashions into words and fixes on the page from the flow of talk and transient behaviours. And this means that it remains incomplete and contestable. It can be refuted by events, past and future. It can always be superseded by interpretations more deeply grounded, more complexly conceptualized.

The most commonly cited exemplification of thick description remains Geertz's 'Deep Play: Notes on the Balinese Cockfight'. Much of Balinese culture 'surfaces' in a cock ring, Geertz contends, and cockfighting, a popular (if sometimes illegal) obsession, can be read as providing significant insights into what being a Balinese is really about. First, Geertz explicates how Balinese fighting cocks are locally viewed as symbolizing the ambulant genitals of their male owners. Then, he goes on to show how the ramifications of this symbolic usage touch further and further features of Balinese life; so that cocks and cock-fights come to be symbolically informed by a multiplicity of Balinese structures of signification. Precisely, here is the narcissistic male ego concretized and magnified; also, a momentary letting loose of archetypal animality; also, an oblatory blood sacrifice to cannibalistic demons and threatening powers of darkness; also, a representation of the social matrix and tensions constituting village and locale (kin-groups, irrigation societies, temple congregations and castes); also, a celebration of status rivalry, of gaining and losing esteem, honour, dignity and respect; also, an expression of leadership and loyalty; also, an opportunity to partake of the pleasures of gambling; also an art-form which renders ordinary everyday experience comprehensible, imaginable and meaningful to its own protagonists: an encompassing and displaying of the cultural themes of masculinity, pride, death, loss, rage, beneficence and chance. Here, in short, is an inscription, a fiction, a model, a metaphor, a meta-social commentary, which the Balinese construct about themselves. Spelled out publicly in a collective text, in a vocabulary of sentiment, Geertz would have read in the Balinese cockfight one expression at least of how that society is built and its individual members put together. And since to express publicly is also to realize culturally, here is Balinese temper and individual temperament being constituted and reconstituted with each performance.

For Geertz, the double task of an interpretive anthropology is to uncover the conceptual structures which inform people's acts and also to demonstrate the role that these structures play in determining human behaviour. In this venture, thick description is the *sine qua non*.

See also: **Interpretation, Literariness, Qualitative and Quantitative Methodologies, Situation and Context**

TOURISM

Tourism embodies the largest single movement of human populations around the globe outside wartime. In 1939, 1 million people are said to have travelled abroad; in 1990 this rose to 400 million. Estimates for the year 2000 are of 650 million international travellers and five times as many people travelling within their own countries.

More specifically, in 1990, 6 million people visited Hawaii; 108 people entered Notre Dame cathedral in Paris every minute, the breath and body heat of the multitudes entering the Sistine Chapel in Rome were damaging the frescos, while exhaust fumes from cars queuing to get to Alpine ski resorts were killing the local flora and causing avalanches and landslides. In a word, there is not a community, a country, an environment in the world which tourism does not affect in some degree. Sponsored by national governments, promoted by multinational enterprises, regulated by international agencies (e.g. the World Tourism Organization), engaged in by more and more of the world's population, and with an annual turnover in excess of £270 billion, it is estimated that tourism is the world's largest international industry. Latterly, tourism has also been recognized as of major conceptual concern to anthropology. (It is mooted that only the somewhat disconcerting similarities between a touristic 'quest for otherness' and that of anthropology – 'professional tourism' – explains a wariness in treating the topic sooner (cf. Crick 1989).)

Tourism and travel

Tourism is frequently differentiated from 'travel'. While travel, as Mark Twain once wrote (1869: 407), 'is fatal to prejudice, bigotry and narrow-mindedness' (*après* Augustine: 'The world is a book; he who stays at home reads only one page'), tourism has nevertheless been deemed a derisive label for those content with 'inauthentic' experiences.

'Travel', after all, has etymological connections with 'travail' – with work and activity – while tourism represents a packaged form of experience in which passivity prevails and contact with the alien and the real is avoided or prevented. Here is manufactured, emasculated travel, made safe by commercialism. Indifferent to local social reality, 'suntanned destroyers of culture' scavenge the earth intent on new pleasures, content to practise conspicuous consumption in front of the relatively deprived (cf. Turner and Ash 1976). At best, here is a short-term, instrumental relationship where tourists see locals and their culture as commodities to be bought, while locals see the visitors as resources to be milked. 'The Barbarian of yesterday is the Tourist of today', as English socialite and traveller, Nancy Mitford, quipped.

But is there more than mere snobbery to this stereotypical differentiation? Is it perhaps a question of history and of numbers? Hence, the eighteenth-century Grand Tour entailed the travel of European aristocracies in relatively small numbers, while the nineteenth-century rise of European industrialism saw the birth of bourgeois travel on a somewhat larger numerical scale. But the twentieth century has witnessed an enormous growth in people with 'annual holidays' from work, with 'times out' from the work 'treadmill', with pensionable retirements from the work 'rat-race' (cf. Graburn and Jafari 1991). In particular, in the post-Second World War West, cheaper and faster modes of transport, specialized holiday companies (*après* Thomas Cook's nineteenth-century lead), televised information on other parts of the world, and a surplus income to spend on leisure, has given rise (somewhat akin to the 'teenager') to the 'tourist' as a new category of social expectation and experience.

Smith (1989) defines the 'tourist', then, as: 'a temporarily leisured person who voluntarily visits a place away from home for the purpose of experiencing a change'. Anthropological work on these persons and the socio-cultural ramifications of their migrancy can be conveniently broken down into three main areas: economics; social and cultural change; and meanings and motivations.

Economics

In the 1960s, the primary exports of many Third World countries (coffee, and rubber, for example) declined in value; many turned to tourism as an alternative development strategy, something positively promoted by both the World Bank and the United Nations. Tourism seemed to need no vast capital-intensive infrastructural outlays but rather to rely on natural resources already in place: sun, sand and friendly people.

The experience of the past thirty years, however, has been rather different (cf. Nash 1989). First, the infrastructure (high-class hotels and restaurants, transport facilities) was by no means cheap, and once in place remained differentiated, spatially and qualitatively, from local lives; more was often spent on hotels than on state housing. Secondly, tourism turns out to be not so secure a growth industry; there are seasonal fluctuations in demand and cyclical swings outwith local control. Tourist tastes (and those of the tour operators) are fickle and faddish and destinations can succeed and fail in alternate seasons. Much decision-making rests with multi-national corporations who run hotels and car-hire firms as well as the airlines. Thirdly, most profit is 'repatriated' to First World countries; Third World access to hard currency remains restricted. Local profits tend to be restricted to local business and political elites, so that local polarizations of wealth grow. Indeed, to maintain the clean and friendly image of their countries, and their peacefulness and stability, local political regimes have become less liberal, with elites anxious to removal from the tourist gaze not merely unsightly natural detritus but also its human equivalents: political opponents, touts, beggars, slum dwellers and street children. Finally, the many local people who swopped their agricultural pursuits for work in the new tourist industries find themselves, at best, in menial service jobs; while governments often find themselves forced to import (more expensive) foodstuffs to make up for the shortfalls in production.

A caveat is necessary, however. For, an alternative weighting would emphasize the effects of tourism on countering local out-migration, and instilling a sense of pride in community and place. It can invigorate local artistic traditions and provide a market for work. It can nurture local practices of environmental up-grading, and to bring to the attention of a global audience the plight of exploited minorities, women and children (cf. Harrison 1992).

Socio-cultural change

The contact between individuals from very different socio-cultural milieux means that tourism provides anthropologists with fine examples of what was once referred to as 'processes of acculturation': the translation and mutual influencing that can occur when there is a new and rather sudden meeting between different world-views. However, since individual tourists are usually on holiday in a place for a short time while the local community may habitually have people occupying the category 'tourist', and since locals are catering for tourists in a work not a play capacity, it is often argued that borrowing is more likely (and more largely) to be seen on the part of the locals than their visitors. As the host community adapts to tourists' needs and expectations it superficially becomes, if not more like a version of the tourists' home milieux, at least a reflection of their 'holiday' expectations (cf. Urry 1990).

This has been dubbed, the 'Coca-Colanization' of the native way of life, implying both the process of Westernization (specifically American-ization) involved, and that of neo-colonialism. (In this context, the slogan of both the multi-national computer giant, IBM, and of the hotel chain, Hilton International: 'world peace through world travel' takes on a far more partisan and political colouration). It is further argued that as local people learn to market their culture 'by the pound', turning, for instance, their artistic traditions into bric-a-brac curios and 'airport art' (and themselves into queer exotics with quaint customs), so the native way of life becomes 'trinketized' (cf. Greenwood 1989). Here is the irony that having come 'visiting a place away from home so as to experience a change', tourists find something fashioned to suit their home tastes; or else a 'staged authenticity' of what tourists are thought to expect from native culture (cf. MacCannell 1989).

One of most rapid changes in local life concerns language. While few tourists may learn a native language, many locals become bilingual, those who speak more fluently then finding themselves with jobs as couriers, interpreters, tour-guides, waiters, and so on. The mediatory capacity grants them different status and more material return, which in turn may give onto a process of local polarization: a split of the host community into factions concerning attitudes towards tourists and tourism and the 'advantageous' changes in life that may accrue for some. Just as local elites are found often to share the lifestyle and aspirations of the foreigners more than those of their fellow-locals, so those who mediate with tourists at the local level are found more sympathetic regarding tourist ways than some of their erstwhile fellows.

In this way, tourism is sometimes seen to be a continuation of old-style colonialism by other means. The West takes what it wants from the Rest, while undermining local community solidarity and tradition. Thus, while Conrad Hilton claimed to be in the business of 'peace and understanding', he also boasted how each of his hotels was: 'a little America', and 'doing its bit to fight socialism'. Likewise, the vice-president of the American company, Edgar Rice Burroughs Incorporated, once expressed the desire to 'buy' the African nation-state of The Gambia; being one of a number of Third-World countries which, besides their UN ambassadors and their so-called independence, 'had absolutely nothing. No economy, nothing', the strategy would be to 'merchandise' the entire place as a series of 'Tarzan' vacation villages. However apocryphal these stories, one learns something of the context of debate in which Franz Fanon (1968) could claim that, through tourism, the West was turning the Rest of the world into its brothel (cf. Cohen 1977); the context in which the Greek Orthodox church could institute the prayer:

Lord Jesus Christ (..) have mercy on the cities, the islands and the villages of this Orthodox Fatherland . . . which are scourged by the worldly tourist wave. Grace us with a solution to this dramatic problem and protect our brethren who are sorely tried by the modernistic spirit of these contemporary Western invaders.

But words of warning are in order; the anti-tourist rhetoric, above, is as ideological as that first heard from the likes of Mitford. It is also, in both cases, somewhat reactionary: a reaction against the wherewithal of mass travel before, and a reaction against the loss of so-called community solidarity and tradition now. But this latter is a myth. Socio-cultural milieux are (and were) never isolated, bounded or homogeneous entities, but environments always involved in change and always exposed to a range of influences (economic, socio-cultural, religio-political) which might seem to be alien and new. Moreover, inasmuch as socio-cultural milieux are heterogeneous and internally fragmented, the old anthropological canards of 'culture-contact' and 'acculturation' need to be clarified and complexified.

To appreciate 'the impact' of 'tourism' upon 'Malaysian culture' for example (King 1993), is to recognize that tourism is no unitary phenomenon and that its effects will be various, first; and secondly, that Malaysian culture is an *ad hoc* assemblage of beliefs and practices pertaining in varying degrees to different people. Here is a medley or assemblage of a multitude of cultural forms (practices, objects, symbols and meanings) without common denomination in active relationship with a pot-pourri of touristic happenstances. The outcome is dynamic, ongoing and non-generalizable. Of course, some claim to be the guardians or the chief exponents of 'Malaysian culture'. But this is a rhetorical ploy, often by local elites or brokers, or those who would become such, to elevate certain partisan values to canonical status (and disseminate this information in tourist literature) for the purpose of political gain. This strategizing is an important part of the anthropological study of 'tourism' but it should not be mistaken for, say, 'the detrimental effect new touristic processes are having on local culture'. For there is no 'authentically traditional' Malaysia beyond a diversity of contesting symbolic emblemizations.

'Acculturation', in short, takes place in a complex and piecemeal fashion, and is more a matter of give-and-take between individual world-views. To talk of the 'socio-cultural changes' wrought by tourism can be a shorthand only, part of a larger understanding of the way in which, universally, people go and look beyond themselves in order to be and know themselves (cf. Boon 1982).

Meanings and motivations

'Tourism' has been anthropologically classified according to a range of types (cf. Cohen 1979): domestic, international, resort-focused, religious, adventure, ethnic, off-the-beaten-track, educational; 'tourists' likewise: from bourgeois FITs (free independent travellers), to working-class package-junkies, to latter-day hippies. What links this range, however, is the sense that tourists and tourism are concerned with a time and place beyond the ordinary and everyday: with travel, even 'pilgrimage', beyond the site of working practices and relationships. Drawing on Turnerian ideas of the way human beings organize their lives in terms of regular oscillations between periods of structure and 'liminoidal' periods of our non-structure or anti-structure (Turner 1982a), anthropologists have therefore explored the meaning of tourism as pertaining to the division of social life into periods of work and play (cf. Graburn 1983a). Tourism signals a ritual departure from the workaday world and its routinizations. One quits adult obligations, perhaps, in an experiential bubble, or 'package', where everything is provided. One plays like a child again, except with adult capacities; one enjoys extra-marital sex, nude sunbathing and drug-taking, perhaps, in a socio-cultural milieu where one knows these things are foreign. On holiday, one is a foreigner from oneself.

Combined here with the liminoidal idea of the inversion or reversal of the everyday, and an overriding of everyday distinctions and categorizations (child/adult, improper/proper) is the theme of pilgrimage; one is on holiday (etymologically, 'holy day') in spiritual quest of ultimate goods: love, oneself, one's past, one's future, the body beautiful, health, music, art, and so on (Smith 1992). Through 'play', a temporarily 'free sphere of activity' with its own distinct, captivating rhythms, which can engender the sense of the limited accomplishment of a perfect space and world (Huizinga 1980), one self-consciously quests for recreation and renewal. Relieved and rejuvenated by the experience, the performance, the tourist returns to the workaday world a new person.

Not that tourism and the annual or regular holiday is without its tensions and stresses. Not to 'go away somewhere', to 'stay home' and simply 'do nothing', must be explained by other non-routine events: the end of a relationship, a crippling overdraft. Once away, there is the pressure to 'have a good time', amid the uncertainties of weather, foreign food and germs, and the possibly unwelcome attentions of other holiday-makers, and locals.

The expectations and motivations of locals in interaction with tourists, and the pressures they feel, will be equally complex and varied. Anthropological work has explored how the tourist is locally categorized and known: from 'tourist' heard and understood as '*tous riches*' in the Seychelles, to the Trobriand Isles where the most suitable local category for the invaders was felt to be 'soldiers'. In the Simbu province of New Guinea, meanwhile (Peach 1997), the Keri speakers employed the new pidgin word, 'turis', to imply a new form of locally created wealth. In the same way that people were traditionally responsible for the axes or the salt or the pigs which they locally made or grew, so now they were proud of 'their' tourists. These were people whom they 'made' to come and partake in social relations: a form of wealth which gave onto further, intrinsically local, exchanges. For the Keri, frustration arises from the fleeting nature of the tourist presence, rather than tourists as such; the difficulty is in engendering long-term relations based on reciprocity and exchange, and so maintaining those relationships' inherent value.

European tourism

It might be thought from the above account of anthropological work that tourism entails exclusively the visitation of the West upon the Rest, the more wealthy upon the less, and with mostly unfortunate consequences. This, however, is not the case. Europe remains the world centre of international tourism, in terms of tourists' destinations as well as their origins; most tourist money is spent there and most crossing of international boundaries (cf. Bouquet and Winter 1987). Furthermore, a thriving trade in domestic tourism can be found in Japan (Hendry 1996); while traditions of 'voluntary and temporary visits to foreign places beyond workaday worlds' are probably universal. Graburn (1983b) thus discusses the difficulties of distinguishing between modern tourism and the traditions of 'temporary and voluntary movement' as pilgrimage which have characterized milieux as seemingly distinct as Australia, Arabia and Ireland for centuries.

Perhaps tourism, in this way, calls attention to the limitations of 'the West' and 'the Rest', First World and Third, as categories. At best, with the ubiquity of contemporary global movement of which tourism is such an important part, these terms can only possess metaphoric (and not geographic) referentiality. Great Britain is now the Third World, therefore, with its theme parks and the trinketization of its 'heritage', where (Conservative) politicians describe the Notting Hill Carnival, run predominantly by London's West Indian émigré communities, as 'Britain's foremost cultural festival' (cf. Cohen 1993). It is European seasides and beauty spots, likewise, which seek to accommodate themselves, economically and socio-culturally, to the wealth of the visiting hordes (cf. McDonald 1990; Rapport 1993a).

Tourism has been described as one of the keys to our consciousness of the modern world (Pollock 1994); something equivalent to past religiosity as a global experience, and to colonialism in its global consequences. Operating in a 'global ecumene' (Hannerz 1992: 34), a global socio-cultural, economic and cognitive space, tourism feeds into both the creolization of local identities and their reinventions and rebirths (cf. van den Berghe 1987). It is a potent source both of socio-cultural change and of anthropological theorizing.

See also: **Home and Homelessness, Liminality, The Rural Idyll**

TRANSACTION

According to the *bon mot*, economics is about how people make choices while sociology is about why people do not have any choices to make. An anthropological emphasis on transaction within socio-cultural milieux, and its theorization as 'transactionalism', or 'action/practice theory', amounts to an attempt to mediate between these positions.

Transactionalism has represented an important corrective to earlier functional and structural emphases which managed to reify the institutional features of social life (offices, rules, rights and duties), and essentialize corporate groups so that they somehow persisted irrespective of the actions of distinct individuals. At best, individual actors appeared as conduits of social-structural effects, their actions and 'choices' simply causing to be reproduced the systems of marital or economic (*et al.*) exchange in which they were mired; here was no individuality or will, and little change. By contrast, a transactional perspective attends to the dynamism of social process and the creation of cultural forms. Socio-cultural milieux consist of individuals in interaction, cooperation and competition, struggling to make meaning: to express themselves, to reach one another, to satisfy themselves, to control one another. Their engaging in strategic thinking, decision-making and initiative-taking, and their engagement with one another, give rise to socio-cultural processes and forms of varying duration and legitimation which are consented to and employed to varying degrees, for a variety of purposes, in various contexts. It is not system which is the *a priori* but individual agency, process and movement.

Formative development

Building upon Raymond Firth's distinction between 'social organization' and 'social structure' (1951), the former representing the present social system as derived from the sum of a series of decisions made by a group of individuals, and the latter the perduring factors which influence (constrain and direct) the choices about which individuals decide, Edmund Leach (1954, 1961b) explored the gap between behaviour as ideally prescribed by social-structural norms and that actually decided upon. The only actual socio-cultural order was statistical in nature: the patterns and changes to which a host of individual decisions incrementally and incidentally amounted. Moreover, individuals reached their decisions as a result of conscious and unconscious attempts to gain power over their lives – and thereby those of others. This, Leach concluded (following Nietzsche), was a universal human trait.

It was in the next generation of anthropological theorizing, in particular in the work of Fredrik Barth, F.G. Bailey, Robert Paine, and those associated with Max Gluckman's Manchester School and after (Clyde Mitchell, Bill Epstein, Emanuel Marx, Bruce Kapferer, Anthony Cohen and John Comaroff), that transactionalism as such was formulated.

For Barth (1959, 1966), it is necessary to collate the strategic, the symbolic and the structural components of socio-cultural systems. The first thing to be said, however, is that system – the aggregation and integration, consistency and regularity of socio-cultural phenomena – is not axiomatic and is, in fact, variable. To the extent that they exist, normative systems are generated and maintained by individual actors making strategic decisions that reflect and maximize their individual interests. The 'whole' effect is one of feedback and flow; structural arrangements are the cumulative result of a number of separate choices, made by individuals in symbolic interaction. These arrangements then serve as 'canalizing factors' for future individual decisions; the symbolic and the structural may thus be conceptualized not as somehow other than the individually strategic, or superior to it, but as different generations of it. But individuals are not determined to relate to one another; if they are constrained by their past actions and choices, then they are liberated by them too. Socio-cultural order and pattern is made up of ongoing relations between political actors, actors who can also manipulate the order, and change the pattern, in pursuit of their goals.

For Bailey (1957, 1969, 1971), through employment of a key analogy of individual actors playing a game of power, one is able analytically to account for any number of different kinds and levels of socio-cultural interaction, sociation and institution from neighbourhood and village, through regions, to nations and beyond. 'Social structure', then, can be understood as the current 'rules of the game', within which individual actors make strategic choices, which then influence the institutionalization of future rules. 'Institutions' represent the officiations of individual actors wearing masks, whose role and authority have the consent (or at least the apathy) of those other individuals who act as institution members. All the time, moreover, 'normative rules', amounting to publicly accepted customs and routines by which the game of sociation is played and evaluated, are offset by the 'pragmatic rules' of private, individual wisdom, strategy and interest. Socio-cultural exchange, in short, may be conceived of as a game which individuals make up as they go along.

Critique

Developments of transactional theory such as Bailey's and Barth's met with the reactive critique of systems analysts – from the original functionalist and structuralist camps to *arriviste* Marxian and post-structuralist ones. There was a reiteration of the belief that only some form of methodological holism could apprehend the system and structure that was culture and society (thereby reinstating the axiomatic nature of these variable and processual phenomena). Only a top-down analysis, treating overarching or underlying socio-cultural forces and factors, could account for institutional patterns of relations between (so-called) classes, castes, clans, nations, bureaucracies, roles and genders. The notion of individual actors and their agency is a culturally specific one, it was further claimed, and it is ethnocentric, not to mention unwieldy, to seek to track the interested outcomes of the rational choices which they make. As Asad put it (1972), an emphasis on the rationality and voluntariness of individuals' actions ignores the fact that outcomes are often unpredictable and unexpected. Moreover, a history of past action comes to restrict present choice, while it is the case that present action is equally, variously, compelled.

Notwithstanding that these criticisms in large part reiterated the holistic and deterministic assumptions and agenda which transactionalism had set out to reform, there was some attempt to effect a conciliation between the perspectives. Might it not be possible, Kapferer pondered for instance (1976), to bring together Barth and Asad by drawing upon Blau's (1967) notion of the 'emergent' properties of institutions, relations and organizations which, once they have been set up by individual agents, can then exert an independent effect? This might set limits upon the methodological individualism which transactionalism would entertain since structure, content and form in socio-cultural relations are now seen as operating in an (emergent) domain of their own.

However, along with other, similar (periodic) attempts to bring together agency and structure (Giddens 1976; Bourdieu 1977) – such as is also represented by a flurry of recent work on risk (Beck 1992; Douglas 1992) – the positing of 'emergence' itself runs the risk of sliding down a slippery slope to reification and essentialism. One may well talk of structural and institutional arrangements in socio-cultural milieux without the need of erecting a conceptual boundary thereby to individual agents and agency, or claiming to enter a distinct sociological domain of independent and impersonal factors and forces (cf. Blumer 1972; Cohen 1975). Indeed, it is imperative that one does talk so: this is the problem that transactionalism still poses. In the words of one of transactionalism's most famous forebears, Georg Simmel (1971 [1908]), the challenge is to describe and account for the extraordinary multitude and variety of routine interactions happening at the same time within a socio-cultural milieu, without giving 'society' or 'culture' the status of autonomous historical realities, and hypostatizing them.

The way forward Simmel believed in was to refrain from looking for a ghost in the machine; 'society exists where a number of individuals enter into interaction' (1971: 23). The interactions *are* the socio-cultural milieu – not merely its cause or consequence – and there is nothing else. A socio-cultural milieu amounts to a fluctuating field of transactions, only grasped by an analysis of the creativity and experience of its component individuals – individuals who create more or less society and culture depending on the number and types of interactions they enter into. Hence, 'any history or description of a social situation is an exercise of psychological knowledge' (Simmel 1971: 32).

See also: **Agent and Agency, Interaction, Methodological Individualism and Holism**

THE UNHOMELY

'The unhomely' is a Homi Bhabha turn of phrase (1994) which he employs to highlight the plight of 'unhomeliness' of all those people – refugees, migrants, the colonized, ex-slaves, women, gays – who have no home within 'the system'. Today, most indigenous peoples of the world also belong to this category. As a construct it refers to the state of 'hybridity' (being neither here nor there), and as such is situated within post-colonial debate. In his writings on the unhomely, Homi Bhabha is offering some good advice. By demonstrating to the powerless the unhomely territory which is singularly their own, his aim is to suggest a way through which they could begin the process of self-empowerment. He calls for the development of a 'literature of recognition', through which these peoples could find the means to signify, negate and initiate their own historic desire. By discovering their own voices, their writings could have revisionary force toward the end of destabilizing traditional relations of cultural domination. Those who have been categorized by Western civilization as beyond the pale and thus its oppositional other, could do the job themselves of translating who they are, while at the same time expressing their nausea with the linear, progressivist, rationalist claims of establishment thought. There is much at stake with this new cultural discourse that is being called for from the marginals of the world (cf. de Certeau 1997).

Anthropology, alterity and the myth of primitivism

The place of anthropology within this discussion about types of cultural discourse is hardly simple. First of all the constructs of 'the unhomely' and 'hybridity' are part of a much larger set which include other related notions that mark a Western imagery of otherness that has proven to be exceedingly powerful in Western dealings with those marginal to our own way of life. Included would be such major concepts as 'exoticism', 'primitivism', 'tribalism', all highly relevant historically to the process of 'doing anthropology'. Most of anthropology's 'technical language' has denoted primitivism (see Overing 1987). If a people were labelled as having a 'tribal' level of development, it was understood that they were 'pre-literate', 'pre-state', 'pre-technological', 'pre-industrial', that is, weak, unevolved and underdeveloped in culture, politics and technology. While 'the tribal' may be said to have the digging stick, magic and religion, we have high-tech agronomy, philosophy, ontology, epistemology and fine art! It is very clear that those who have been labelled 'tribal' have been understood as 'primitive' or even 'savage' from a perspective that is purely Eurocentric.

There is a history to such eurocentrism. Alterity in the modern West has been framed by its history of expansion and conquest, one that inscribed the relations unfolding within it as between a powerful *centre* and a *periphery* that was lacking economically, politically, culturally. In large part, the West seems to have attained its *official* identity by defining itself against its own idiosyncratic version of other peoples (cf. Brett 1991: 114) As Susan Hiller notes (1991b: 11), Western policy in its assimilation of external others has always been to consume only what could be most easily digestible. It was anthropology, the science of alterity, that provided both the technical vocabulary and the objectified imagery through which those peoples who were conquered and colonized by the Western state could be digestibly incorporated into a European mental framework.

Primitivism, exoticism and the birth of modern art

While anthropology clearly has much to answer for, its appropriation of the European other was but one force among many others involved in similar pursuit. It is not coincidental or insignificant that the concepts of 'primitivism' in art and the human sciences have the same temporal beginnings in the nineteenth century (cf. Hiller 1991b). As Kenneth Coutts-Smith, the Danish artist and sociologist of art, explains (1991 [1976]), the expanding European military and economic imperialism was paralleled with the development of structures of both cultural and intellectual colonialism. The Napoleonic adventures in Egypt concluded with the appropriation of Egyptian cultural property – all those monuments and mummies – as spoils of war. As the awareness of extra-European *cultures* rapidly increased among the European elites, all 'exotic' cultures became grist for the artist's palette as a myriad of new 'outsider' styles became ripe for the picking. Exotic cultures became a rich source for inventive Western imagery of what were considered to be signs of the raw, the truthful and the profoundly simple – or, from the Freudian point of view, the primitive monster child within.

In the early nineteenth century, the romantic movement in art concentrated upon an exoticism of the mind, a subjectivist focus through which there was an attempt, according to Coutts-Smith (1991: 24), 'to appropriate the whole twilight territory of the mind, the landscapes of dreams and fantasies, the preserves of psychology and psychopathology, the primitivism of childhood, the bizarre territories of superstition, magic, folklore, and the absurd'. However, such subjectivist concerns in art were quickly overtaken by an objectivist turn where style, not content, became paramount. As in the work of Delacroix, who captured the people of North Africa as if still-lifes of a guitar (Coutts-Smith (1991: 25), modernity in art followed the road of abstract objectivism, the powerful transformation that occurred as well in the human sciences where a potent distancing from fellow human beings became *de rigueur*. Human objects, in art as well as in anthropology, became increasingly read in ahistorical, formalist terms. There is much akin in Picasso's African masks and the structuralism of Lévi-Strauss.

The search for authenticity

The irony is that for many anthropologists and also artists their own respective 'appropriations' of the exotic was understood as *critical* strategies to protest and work against the militarist, colonialist and capitalist values of establishment views and action. Anthropologists researching in colonial Africa saw their work with 'tribals' as an ameliorating force undermining of the worst damages of colonial government. As but one example of the use of primitivism in the artistic world, the German expressionist, Emil Norde (see Lloyd 1991), began in the second decade of the twentieth century to use tribal artefacts and themes from folk art as visual models to combat the materialism and fragmentation of modernity. For Norde and many other artists the incorporating of the art styles of non-European peoples into their own work provided the means through which they could achieve an authenticity that had been lost, they felt, in the art and lifestyle of their own times (see Lloyd 1991: 96 ff.). The desire was to penetrate into the 'essential' by capturing the primal vitality of primitive hand-made production and the spontaneity and intuitive force of *child, folk* and *native* arts. Tribal, folk and child creations alike were considered to be objects that were *authentic*, and also *unalienated* (see Lloyd 1991), unsullied by the Industrial Revolution.

The goal of such primitivists was clearly political. During the first half of the twentieth century, the overt aim of the artists like Norde was to shift – through their use of primitivist styles instead of the 'sophisticated' ones they had been taught – the historicist, evolutionist categories that had become so prevalent in European thought. A similar path was followed by anthropologists who created the new ahistoricist methodologies of functionalism and structural functionalism in order to undermine prevailing evolutionist models within their own discipline. Anthropologist and artist alike, both made the political thrust of their new, anti-evolutionist styles and methods clear.

From today's point of view, it is easy to say that all these primitivist notions of 'primal vitality', 'life in the most elemental forms', all these concepts that conjoined the folk, the native and the child, so important to early-twentieth-century primitivism are just Eurocentric myths. They are a European *version* of things, providing yet more ammunition to the salient myth that tells of Europe's unique attainment of adulthood in contrast to the achievements of all other cultures in the history of the world. The artists, despite their politics, were nevertheless objectifying peoples of other lands through their elevation of style to an absolute principle, and their neglect of context and content. Likewise anthropologists were freezing 'the native' in time and space, distancing them from nowadays time through their structuralist and ahistorical methods (also see Fabian 1983; Ardener 1985). We can therefore also say that the myths of primitivism had their *danger*, for the desired 'primitive' state of authenticity pertained equally to a fantasized, savage and monstrous colonized 'other' (cf. Mason 1990; Corbey 1991).

In other hands than those of the 'right-minded' artist or anthropologist – for example the colonial administrators or other agents of nation-states – the idea of the 'simple' and the 'natural' signified as well 'the undeveloped', 'the marginal', 'the illiterate', an essential aspect of an evolutionist mentality that rationalized political domination over all those conquered territories of the Americas, Asia and Africa. Primitivism fed into a major theme of modernist ideology, one that proclaimed it to be the right of Western civilization to conduct what Bauman (1995: 166) has labelled a merciless war on the 'dead hand' of tradition. This was a war *against* cultural particularism which demanded the training, civilizing, educating, cultivating of the colonized, undeveloped other. The gigantic aim was to disqualify and uproot all those particularizing authorities (the shaman, priest, chief and king) standing in the way of an ideal order where human homogeneity could be achieved – through the subjection of all those local lifeways to the dictates of reason.

Authenticity and 'the unhomely'

By definition, 'unhomely' peoples are 'hybrids', that is, people who are no longer *authentic*. The very idea of authenticity – even when thought to be used for very positive ends – had the consequence of freezing other peoples into a mythic past, where to *remain* authentic and *thus appreciated* they could not leave. Until very recently there has been a strong code in anthropology that a *real* anthropologist did not study people who were so tainted as to wear Western clothes – men in trousers, women in skirts, rather than loincloths of beaten bark or self-spun cotton. The notion of authenticity, with all its primitivist baggage, prevailed to such an extent that the received wisdom was that only the culturally very 'pure' were worthy of anthropological attention. If a person wore Western clothes, could speak a Western language, or worked for Western masters than he or she could not be an authentic 'native'. We could study only *real* Yanomami, Dinka, or Hagen, and not any Guahibo, Ashanti, or Quechua who had become 'townies' or engaged in wage labour. It was a courageous step even as late as the 1980s for an Amazonianist to admit to working among such *in*authentic people – and to state not only the worth of such a study but also the irrelevance of our notion of 'authenticity' (see Gow 1991).

Still, times have changed, and we find that today the notion of *hybridity* is alive and well. Indeed hybridity is thought to be part-and-parcel of the post-colonial, globalized, fragmented identity – and for some (e.g. see Bauman 1995; Haraway 1990), *everyone* in the world, including both 'natives' and civil servants, have become hybrids. Thus writers within the post-colonialist tradition tend to write as if hybridity is a product of Western civilization. The present-day self is a fragmented one; we have become half humans, half machines. On the other hand, there is an anthropological view that sees *all* cultural activity as belonging to hybridity, as being a product of cultural assimilation. In other words, there has never been such a thing as an 'authentic type', or a 'pure system', for people are always exchanging, changing, processing, incorporating, elements of culture. From this perspective the position is that we have all always been hybrids. To live culturally is an ongoing, ever-shifting activity (we are the ones who place 'culture' within museums, centring, reifying, turning *it* into the matter of evolutionists' dreams).

All people, however, do not belong to Homi Bhabha's category of the 'unhomely'. Only 'marginalized' hybrids can be 'unhomely'. They are not only betwixt and between, but also have no home. They are the ones classified as *inauthentic* hybrids, and thus it is they who still suffer from the remains of early-twentieth-century Eurocentric notions of authenticity with its associated time-warp ways of thinking. There exists the strong sentiment among politicians, development agencies and even anthropologists that deprived, powerless, dominated peoples must, if they wish to be recognized, remain 'authentic' by living frozen to their past. The imagery of the 'pure' primitive goes deep, and thus has political weight today (see Overing 1998). We have the bureaucrats of Brussels promoting with perhaps the best of intentions the idea of 'the indigenous community', a dutiful salvage job for the world of nation-states. The United Nations document, 'Article 21', calls for all nation-states to *conserve* the shared cultures, the united cultures, of their respective indigenous peoples. The understanding espoused is that natives live in homogeneous communities, the members of which share identical views of the world; the nation should respect these individual cultures, these homogeneous world-views. What should we do? Should we suspect such documents? Or aid and abet them? Should we ask, as

Nicholas Thomas (1994) might do, whether such a document is yet another example of white society's *primitivism*? And, as such, an aggressive act of essentializing? Is 'Article 21' just another colonialist appropriation, with its emphasis upon the *community* of the native (we have individualism; they have community)? Yet, do we not wish to preserve the notion of community? There is the longing of Homi Bhabha (1994) for the creation of a 'community of the unhomely' to take care of the unhomely's desire for social linkage, and to join, to join . . . We find that this question of community is not very straightforward.

The importance of perspective

Similarly, Nicholas Thomas notes (1994) that despite the insidious role that 'essential discourse' has played in the colonial constructions of native identity, the notion of 'authenticity' also has its ambiguity, certainly as a political tool. To know the perspective of the user of such discourse is absolutely essential to understanding the power game at hand. We may well be offended by the 'modernized' Maori, or Aboriginal, or Native American promoting the 'authenticity' of their traditional ways. We see 'hybrids' disrupting the space of the 'authentic native'. On the other hand, what these hybrids have learned is that the very act of essentializing, as the colonial West and global capitalism has long known, is *empowering*. Thus the table can be turned. Indigenous peoples may put themselves in the studio or the museum *in order to subvert* colonialist discourse. The Maori art exhibitions capitalized on white society's primitivism, creating thereby some prestige and power for the Maori that did not exist before the 1980s. There is also the example from the Cultural Palace of the Rio Negro in Manaus, which recently engaged in a great cultural display of Amazonian ethnicity and a eulogy of its cultural authenticity in a festival entitled 'Expressions of Identity and Ethnic Affirmation'. There was an example of Yanomami shamanism, and an *ayawaska* (hallucinatory drug) ritual of the Marubo. There was myth-telling, and chanting, ritual dances performed and videos of indigenous festivals shown. A sonata was even performed by the University of Amazonas orchestra, entitled 'The Dance of the Masks'. The extent to which this display was indigenously planned and organized is unclear.

Nevertheless it is wise to remember that cultural activism on the part of the marginalized and 'discontents' of colonialist history has not been unusual. As the art critic, Guy Brett, observes (1991: 118ff.), the sheer volume of artistic critique and resistance to the colonial process on the part of the colonized has been in fact concealed in the West – or not recognized by it (cf. Gossen 1996). The mocking critiques and images of colonial masters would make, it seems, a bad fit with the widely accepted view that the colonized are uncomprehending victims. Nowadays, this art of the unhomely, which often weds a 'sophisticated' Western training in Paris or London with imagery from 'back home', tends to make explicit the dialectics of cultural discourses between centre and periphery, and their related relations of power. There have been, however, many powerful artists from countries peripheral to the great art markets who on the whole are unknown to the West, ignored by it and thereby forcibly localized (Brett 1991). Though, if known (such artists as the Russian, Malevich, or the Mexicans, Rivera and Kahlo), they are seen by Europe as mere 'primitivists'. It is, however, a particular political use of 'primitivism' that is for the most part radically different from the way it has been used in Western art (Brett 1991). We must remember that the one who does the labelling of the unhomely, the authentic or inauthentic, and the hybrids of the world – and *for whom* – makes all the difference to the game of empowerment: it follows that the flipside is disempowerment, as in the strategy of fixing ethnic identities long used by the nation-state.

The right to hybridity and the patronizing gaze

The Caribbean Nobel prize author, Derek Walcott, warns us (1996) about the dangers of the 'patronizing gaze' that insists upon the purity of culture. Walcott reminds us that a lot of defensive, aggressive academics and politicians have seized upon the definition of *folk*. He notes (1996: 271) that there is something dangerous about 'the property of reaching people and preserving what belongs to the people, all that stuff' – there is a curious kind of patronage in it. He says that he himself does not write 'folk':

> [w]hen you talk about *folk* as a writer, then the danger there is you tend to say: 'Well, we've got to preserve what we have, you've got to be rootsy, X or Y, you've got to talk that way'. You know, that kind of thing; it's all very dangerous and ephemeral, that kind of aggressiveness. It turns into anthropology; and you can't patronize genuine people by making them anthropological specimens, like saying: 'Oh, you are a great representative of the folk. Now you keep doing that. Right?' While in the meantime you've been watching a good soap opera, or singing country songs.
>
> (Walcott 1996: 271)

Walcott goes on to insist (*ibid.*) that each person has the right to go to the cinema, 'instead of being a damned representative of *folk* for the rest of his or her life. So anyway, there's that, that we have to look out for.'

Stephen Hugh-Jones (1992) makes a similar powerful plea for the right of indigenous peoples to make their own decisions about the acquisition of consumer goods. He argues that there is hypocrisy to the assumption that the integrity of Amazonian 'culture' is in jeopardy as it comes into contact with the allure of greedy market forces, which are now entering contemporary Amazonia from a myriad of directions. The idea is that Amazonian folk must not partake of, they must in fact be *protected from*, the capitalist vision of humankind's limitless needs, which are now propelling humanity to its benefit into an unbounded spiral of progress. Unlike people of the Western world, who are not beguiled by the necessary ruthlessness of market forces, indigenous peoples are portrayed as passive victims of the market economy. Yet, in the name of progress, they have been drawn into it willy-nilly at the hands of missionaries, merchants and government agents. As Hugh-Jones observes, the possibility is rarely considered that these are a people who are also fully capable of reflecting upon their relationships with the market economy, and that indeed they often well understand its risks, its dangers and its allure.

Amazonian peoples are deeply aware of the dangers of rapid economic and social development. They have suffered conditions of extreme change over the past thirty years: they have seen strangers entering their territories to take their land and destroy it. They have experienced the building on their lands of hydro-electric dams and roads, the mining of gold and the extracting of oil, the burning of forests and the creation of large cattle ranches and mono-culture plantations. They have been displaced from their up-river small villages to down-river highly populated communities. Their young people have had to enter an educational system which uses a foreign language and teaches an alien knowledge of the world. The indigenous peoples have good insight into their problems with the market economy; they know the enemy and its effect upon them. They know about the social costs of rapid change, and also the economic and personal costs of the market economy. They increasingly do not have the land to sustain indigenous practices and the type of community life which they value. To survive and feed their families they must engage in wage labour – where they can neither look nor act in accordance to their 'ordinary' (authentic?) ways of doing things. They have many skills, but not the political ones for dealing with big government or big multi-nationals which would be necessary to get their lands back, and thus their freedom for leading in one way or other their ordinary, everyday life.

Contrary to popular ideas about the matter, indigenous peoples are often quite open to change. They tend to be epistemologically open (cf. Salmond 1985), and thus, because knowledge and practice are not separate for them, they are not opposed to accepting new practices. It is not unreasonable also to say that they themselves prefer having a say in the matter in order to decide what is good or damaging to their communities, and their desired ways of living. However, the idea of self-directed change is too much of a challenge to the axiomatic premise of the Western assimilation paradigm, where all change that can be appropriate must be decided upon by the 'superior' and 'developed' form of life, which by definition 'knows best'. There are many academics, bureaucrats and politicians who believe strongly in the 'purity' of indigenous lifeways, and therefore view any sign of 'openness' to change with disdain, especially if self-directed and self-motivated. The idea of 'authenticity' is a political stance which can be used against the 'unhomely' of the world as a means to keep them within control.

Thus it is for many reasons that to question the 'authenticity' of the motivations of indigenous peoples – who wish to wear trousers, or want to make their own decisions about (or use outside expertise with regard to) their relations to the market economy and the agents of the nation-state demanding their 'development' – would border on the vacuous. However, among bureaucrats and agents of development, the pomposity, not to speak of the political weight, of their accusations of inauthenticity goes unquestioned (cf. Hobart 1993; Salmond 1995; Oldham 1996). In other words, indigenous people must not become skilled in their dealings with the world of the whites. Categorized by the state as irritating ethnic hybrids, they have no right to real hybridity which would allow them to act skilfully in both worlds. Their modern condition is precisely that which Homo Bhabha coined as 'the unhomely'.

Is an anthropology of 'the unhomely' possible?

An interesting question to be raised is whether anthropology can become one of the voices for the unhomely? Can *we* take the perspective of the unhomely? – all those blurred categories, wanderings to and fro, an unease with Western capitalism, and nausea over the structures of domination created through modernist ways of thinking and acting. However, as Zygmunt Bauman has noted (1990: 158), the premise of the assimilationist and the colonial relationship is one that has made inequality – political, social, epistemological – the axiomatic starting-point of all argument. Such assumed inequality becomes thereby secure against challenge and scrutiny, whether by the pen of governor or anthropologists. There are nevertheless possibilities for a very different type of overt engagement. One suggestion would be that the successful anthropologist of turn-of-millennium times must with full self-knowledge assume the status of *the reflexive hybrid*. In so doing he or she sheds, to the extent possible, their status as a representative (and certainly spokesperson) of a powerful nation-state and academy. Only *if necessary* strategically is it a status to be resumed in the process of dealing with governmental, multi-national and funding institutions. 'Hybridity' can take many forms. The message here is that of the novelist Walcott, that everyone has their right to hybridity – but included here is the anthropologist as well as the indigenous people.

The greatest strength of anthropologists is that we appreciate *multiperspectivism*. Within the universe of pluralities that we study, there are also plenty of 'hybrids', and 'states of hybridity'. This multi-perspectival outlook is surely anthropology's real potential. To translate all those blurred categories of human existence, now that is a worthwhile project. One way we can do this (acceptably) is systematically to undermine the exotica of Western obsessions, its use of, display of, things and peoples considered as exotic. To displace Western exotica is a worthy anthropological ambition. This is not to underplay the extent that people can differ, for perspicacious difference is the object of this message. Exotica and difference do not need to be conjoined.

We can diminish the exoticism rampant in anthropology (all that magic, all that ritual and scarification taken out of context) by focusing upon (accepting) the *everyday* of indigenous life, translating it in such a way that it becomes *familiar* to us. In other words we can become 'at home with the unhomely' (see Overing 1999). What about situated practices, their everyday ways of knowing and doing things, acting and responding? What about the sentiments and bodily styles that attract them, and those that offend? What about the *homeliness of 'the unhomely'*? It is wise to remember that indigenous peoples see what *they* do as 'everyday', 'ordinary'; for them what we do is 'exotic'. An anthropology for 'the unhomely' would be where we, on our side, transmit the message that *we too are local*, and often bizarre in our solutions. Indigenous peoples usually do not need this particular lesson about themselves, and certainly not about us. They are usually very comfortable with the idea of shared knowledges, but for obvious reasons not so keen on the idea of assimilation. They from the start, not having our hegemonic ideas about knowledge and being more tolerant about difference, are usually much more open than we.

See also: **Alterity, Culture, Gender, Home and Homelessness, Human Rights, Movement, Situation and Context, Stereotypes**

URBANISM

Do cities represent distinctive socio-cultural spaces? If so, is this because they are home to particular types of relationship, or attitude and mindset, or practices, norms, roles and ways of life? Or is it that cities are componential parts of wider social systems, regional and global, and as such are better seen as conduits in networks of relations that connect up the most localized interaction with the most far-flung? In either case, do cities play a central role in an evolutionary change of human being: from small-scale communities to ever-increasing large-scale associations?

It is questions such as these that an urban anthropology, an anthropology of urbanization and the city, has been interested to answer. For, even if 'city' is understood to be a vague concept – to demarcate simply a sizeable, dense settlement in whose more or less common physical space a relatively high level of accessibility between a relatively large number of people obtains (Hannerz 1980: 243) – it is now claimed that more than half of the world's population has become 'urban'; and with some half-a-dozen cities boasting populations of greater than 15 million, there is no sign of this trend reversing. However fuzzy the category, in short, 'city life' is difficult, anthropologically, to discount.

An urban way of life

For Simmel (1971), cities are particular because they give rise to certain common psychological traits; in cities there is an intensification of nervous stimulation, so that a lasting and predictable sequence of psychic impressions (as in rural communities) is replaced by a crowding-in of rapidly changing, unexpectable and discontinuous images. City-dwellers thus become more mentally sophisticated but also more blasé. Similarly, for Durkheim (1964 [1893]), cities represent distinct environments due to the degree of role specialization likely to be found there, and the concentration of powerful social institutions.

Extending these lines of thought in the 1920s and 1930s, the Chicago School of (ethnographic) sociologists and anthropologists famously developed the notion of an 'urban way of life' which could be expected to replace a traditional rural one, in the same way that the burgeoning city of Chicago was transmogrifying both a rural hinterland and the stream of ex-rural migrants entering its portals. Central figures in the School were Robert Park and Louis Wirth. For Park, an examination of the impact of industrial-capitalist expansion on Chicago, its suddenly large population of immigrants, entrepreneurs and hoboes, partaking of their own communities, neighbourhoods and leisure pursuits, suggested that city life amounted to a meeting and mingling of 'all sorts of people . . . who never fully comprehend one another' (1968:26). At the same time, and recalling the medieval German proverb that 'city air makes for freedom', Park concluded that: '[t]he city is . . . the natural habitat of civilized man' (1968: 3).

In a celebrated paper, 'Urbanism as a Way of Life' (1938), Wirth sought to detail just what made cities different: how a different domiciliary ecology gave rise to different types of people, identities and relationships. Defining a city as 'a relatively large, dense and permanent settlement of socially heterogeneous individuals', Wirth described the replacement of rural relations which were long-lived, knowledgeable and often derived from kinship, with urban relations which were impersonal, superficial, segmented, non-cumulative, unpredictable, and given to a faster turnover. Clearly also influenced by the nineteenth-century, premonitory writings of the likes of Henry Maine (1861– 'from status to contractual relations') and Ferdinand Toennies (1957 [1887] – 'from natural communities to artificial associations'), Wirth imaged cities as distinct social systems, and an evolutionary stage set to change rural ways of life – folkways, folklore, all that was folksy – for ever.

Renowned, Chicago-sponsored, ethnographic studies were undertaken in such evolving urban milieux by the likes of Warner and Lunt (1941, 1942) and Whyte (1943), while Robert Redfield set out to examine the transformations as they occurred at the rural end of a 'folk–urban continuum'. Communities, it was mooted, could be placed at various points along a continuum as, across time, they evolved from occupying the former pole to the latter. In studies of the Mexican village of Tepotzlan and then on the Yucatan peninsula (1930, 1941), Redfield sought to plot the urbanization of the rural in terms of the following diacritica: small-scale to large-scale; social homogeneity to social differentiation (regarding occupations, recreations, and so on); physical isolation to a predominance of networks of communication; group solidarity to individualism; personal, face-to-face relations to relations at a distance (in both physical terms and emotional); sacred experience and action to secular; illiteracy to literacy; practising Little Traditions of cultural learning to partaking of sophisticated Great Traditions.

Cities as diverse

The particularity of the city in the Chicago model was to come under increasing attack, however. Were there not many urbanisms to consider: the industrial city as distinct from the pre-industrial city, the Western city as distinct from the non-Western, the colonial as distinct from the post-colonial, and so on? And did not this diversity mitigate against reductive generalization (such as, for instance, the notion that in the city kinship as a load-bearing social institution was superseded by non-ascriptive measures)? Instead of treating the urban and the rural as two discrete (types of) social system was it not more accurate to plot their relations in one overarching set of socio-economic structures?

In a historical analysis, then, Sjoberg (1960) described the logic of the pre-industrial city as pertaining more to a concentration of govern-mental, religious and literate elites than a dense population focused upon manufacture or commerce; in its running, moreover, it continued to favour social organization along familial and ethnic lines. In a series of ethnographic critiques (1951, 1961), Oscar Lewis retraced Redfield's steps to Tepotzlan and then followed villagers from Tepotzlan to Mexico City. Not only was village life not personable and harmonic, he claimed, but urbanism did not bring about necessarily large-scale or irrevocable changes to social organization or lifestyle. Rather, people always and everywhere tend to live as members of small groups – families, neighbourhoods, associations – and not as nameless parts of amorphous masses; hence it is 'peasants in cities' that one can expect to find following processes of urbanization and migration.

In studies based in London (Wilmott and Young 1960; Young and Wilmott 1974), Washington (Hannerz 1969) and Boston (Gans 1965), comparable arguments were put forward for the existence of 'urban villagers': people partaking in face-to-face exchanges, living in relatively cohesive communities, based on kinship, familiarity and religiosity. Being encapsulated within an urban space and occupied in urban pursuits need not give rise to urbane identities. To the extent that cities-as-wholes have characters at all, they can be expected to be manifestations of the particular admixtures of the smaller and more traditional groupings that live on within them. This also calls for the study of the city within a broader context: as part of a flow of people and resources within a region and between regions.

This kind of regional emphasis was maintained in a series of studies undertaken by anthropologists working with Max Gluckman at Manchester in the 1950s and 1960s, and focused upon the urbanizing Copperbelt area of Central Africa (Mitchell 1969; Kapferer 1972). The specificity of situations rather than the particularity of cities was the logic employed here to apprehend ways of life; cities were spaces in which to undertake studies of (for instance) migration, poverty, ethnicity, networks and cultural change, rather than things to study in themselves.

Indeed, the 1960s and after have witnessed a flowering of studies of particular urban situations and topics: from urbanism and state-formation (Leeds 1994), to urbanism and musical subculture (Finnegan 1989), to urbanism and drug-gangs (Bourgois 1995). One area of special growth has been in studies of shanty-towns, and those post-colonial 'squatter cities' which have grown up in many Third World locations and today form the world's largest conurbations (Lloyd 1982; Scheper-Hughes 1992). In what are often seen as reproductions of colonial-style relations of hierarchy, exploitation and even genocide, new urban elites peripheralize the plight of those masses who move to and fro within and between urban spaces but subsist well below the poverty line. In a critique (in turn) of Lewis's notions of a 'culture of poverty' (1959), whose members are trapped in slum lives and whose fatalistic attitudes condemn them to reproduce their situation across the generations, recent study stresses the complexity of social organization and the flexibility of strategizing that goes on among shanty-town inhabitants (Wikan 1980). Not only do these latter play a vital role in the continuing wealth-creation of the elite, as cheap labour, but in an 'informal economy' (Hart 1982) beyond institutional control and official record, they engage in practices which lead to the maintenance of community ways of life against great odds.

Cities as soft

If an appreciation of the diversity of city life has mitigated against reductive generalization concerning urbanism, there are still occasional efforts to construct overviews. In *Exploring the City* (1980), Ulf Hannerz admitted that urbanism always represents the expression of a particular centripetal tendency in a particular encompassing society, but still felt it amounted to a discrete set of relations between a number of socio-cultural domains. The domains of urban life included: household and kinship, provisioning, recreation, neighbouring, and traffic with strangers; and while only the range of provisioning and the patterns of trafficking with strangers may have a specifically urban quality to them, what gave the city its character was variation on the theme of relations between these domains.

At the same time as Hannerz seeks to identify this specifically urban quality, however, he grants that cities are 'soft' environments (1980:

249): they assume shapes around individual inhabitants according to the choices which the latter make among an almost infinite and changing repertoire of possible roles. The social structures of cities are thus indeterminate and amorphous, awaiting the imprint of an individual's choice.

The notion of 'softness' comes from travel-writer Jonathan Raban (1973). An urban environment is soft, Raban suggests, in that it becomes what its inhabitants make of it; it awaits its inhabitants' consolidating it into a certain shape while embodying little in and of itself. Once they have decided, then the city assumes a certain fixity, reflecting back the identity which has been imparted to it. Should they stop imprinting themselves upon the urban environment, however, they can then easily develop the sense of being adrift since the city offers no anchors and no hard groundings of its own. Cities are plastic by nature and urban living amounts to a continual creative play.

What the notion of urban softness brings to the fore is the experiential reality and variability of the city as perceived by its inhabitants: a quality more real than the seeming hardness of the city as a fixed object of design on maps or in statistics. There are thus echoes in Raban of Park: 'every section and quarter of the city takes on something of the character and qualities of its inhabitants [becoming] inevitably stained with the peculiar sentiments of its population' (Park 1968: 6). Certainly, the city can be found home to a wide array of lives, and embodying a potential for diversity which is at once the stuff of dreams and of nightmares. For those without continued faith in their vision of their identity, or those without the resources to put their visions into effect, an urban softness may be greatly threatening. The softness of São Paulo or Manila or Cairo is such that the inhabitants of the shanty-towns can become all but invisible to the well-to-do. Within the soft city, therefore, anthropology can explore what choices are made, how choice is managed, how resisted and how competed for.

What is important to bear in mind is that, as Cohen (1993) puts it, people invest the city with culture – people enculturate the city – rather than passively responding to it as a deterministic power. As Amit-Talai concluded in her study of Armenians living in London (1989), it is in terms of a 'voluntary' involvement rather than an inherent imperative that individuals in the city can be seen acquiring the resources necessary for the development and expression of their social identities. This identity may, in Hannerz's programmatic terms (1980: 255–61), be a matter of becoming encapsulated in one social world, or else of living in a number of such worlds (with varying possible degrees of segregation or integration between them), or, finally, of living in comparative solitude without significant others. Again, at different times of their lives, individuals' choices *vis-à-vis* the above identity-types may change too. But it is wrong to envisage the city massificating and anonymizing individuals, fracturing them into roles, segmenting them *à propos* different social worlds. For this would be to reduce them to mere ciphers of the logic by which the analyst would model urban social life (and the elites control it). Focus instead on how 'people shape the city through their everyday resourcefulness' (Cohen 1993: 8), image the city in their ongoing experience of it and supply it with meaning in the contexts of their personal circumstances. Urban milieux are constituted by, not constitutive of, the selves of their individual inhabitants.

Cities as transitory

The betweenness of cities has been asserted – a space between local groupings and the wider world – and also their softness or plasticity. Another way of conceptualizing this is to consider cities as sites of transition.

People move across and within urban spaces continually, while social practices and cultural symbols are, in Hannerz's image, continuously trafficked through them, becoming transformed and creolized in the process. Cities are 'migrant landscapes' (Chambers 1994a: 14, 94), home to 'shifting, mixing, contaminating, experimenting, revisiting and recomposing': recomposing histories and traditions, shifting centres and peripheries, mixing global tendencies and local distinctions. They are sites of transformations of socio-cultural reality, transitory lives and cultural movements. A diffuse sense of mobility thus characterizes urban life as inhabitants, in transit across multiple and diverse social worlds (house and work, family and friends, religion and recreation), find connections, avoid relations, meet people, garner experiences, routinize space and escape routine.

How best can this transitoriness be apprehended anthropologically? After all, 'the crowds, the helter-skelter, and the constant buzz of joking conversation' (Geertz 1960: 49) possess an inherently elusive quality. For Hannerz, the key lies in an analysis of networks of interaction, with cities envisaged as 'networks of networks' in a shifting collage of individuals, roles, domains and situations of exchange (1980: 200; also cf. Sanjek 1978). In an ethnography of the Canadian city of St John's, Newfoundland, Rapport (1987) traced the network of links surrounding conversations about 'violence'. Tracing 'talking violence' (the violence of armed robberies, of the police, in bars, around drugs, against women, and in possible nuclear war) through different urban settings, Rapport felt he could capture the way in which people variously came together in St John's for the instigation and development of different kinds of relations, before again departing on their personal itineraries across the city. 'Violence' was a node of communication around which conversation was regularly and conveniently deployed; a catchword which made transient (potentially unsafe) conversational exchanges appear formulaic and routine. Speaking of uncertainty in a habitual fashion engendered certainty.

The picture of St John's which emerged was of a socio-cultural milieu constituted by a fund of common catchwords-in-use, and a host of changing agreements and disagreements over how individuals chose habitually to come together by way of these catchwords and converse. Dipping into this fund as they crossed urban space, individuals would develop relationships of variable verbal-cum-social closeness and complexity, and meet on varying levels of verbal-cum-social inclusivity. Here was a shifting sliding-scale of verbal sameness and difference. As a city, St John's comprised a phraseological community, catchwords, clichés and formulae of exchange being its relatively common and stable currency by which a transient population might embed itself for the purpose of local exchange.

See also: **Community, Home and Homelessness, Network, The Rural Idyll**

VIOLENCE

Raymond Williams (1983a: 329–31) described violence as a 'keyword': one of a class of concepts which seem to force themselves on our attention, invariably entering general discussion of social life. He identifies numerous denotations of the word: violence as unruly behaviour; as an infringement of property or dignity; as vehement conduct; as use of physical force; as physical assault; and as threat or dramatic portrayal of any or all of the above. In an anthropological treatment of 'violence', perhaps two features have run in tandem: difficulties in defining and circumscribing the diverse phenomenal manifestations of violence (and their 'threat' or 'portrayal'), and also the ubiquity of such phenomena.

Violence and the socio-cultural

It has been suggested (cf. Aijmer 2000) that violence and the social be seen in a mutually constitutive relationship; that, paradoxical as it may appear, violence is intrinsic to everyday social relations: an instrument or means of their propagation, as well as an idiom or mode of their expression. Violent acts and expressions are fundamental to an understanding of socio-cultural order, even while they may seem, by definition, to exist beyond the habitual, orderly and routine: as a departure-from-order, as un-order, as dis-order and as out-of-order (Stanage 1974: 229). For, as a dramatic presence, violence (including its threat and its portrayal) occasions an impulse towards the order of social practice and cultural imagery being re-constituted (cf. Gilsenan 1996).

Much anthropological writing has been concerned to explicate the precise ways in which the relationship between violence and socio-cultural order is mutually constitutive. The Durkheimian legacy has it that the social exists as a domain from which the violence of natural, individual and amoral instincts is ideally removed by socialization. Secondary social institutions, from ritual to gift-giving to feud, thereafter serve as periodic mechanisms which relieve any build-up of tensions in acceptable ways, and thus maintain the social-structural in homeostasis or equilibrium (cf. Mauss 1954; Gluckman 1956). The Marxian legacy has it that certain class-based, social-structural tensions within society will always be prone to violence and that ultimately this provides the mechanism by which the socio-cultural evolves and history proceeds down its teleological path (cf. Bloch 1986). An ethological legacy, finally, has it that violence is part and parcel of human-animal nature and cannot but express itself in the socio-cultural – which is but another idiom of expression for the instinctual (cf. Montagu 1968; Chagnon and Irons 1979).

More recent anthropological work has gone into exploring ways in which 'violence' is part of what the socio-cultural constructs rather than what it attempts to overcome. Neither a natural, a necessary or a necessarily avoided feature of human being, violence is treated as a contingent phenomenon, instrumental in achieving certain socio-cultural goals. For instance, when British football fans take part in fights with one another in order to defend and flaunt their honour and their territory – their pride in their 'Ends' of the ground (Marsh et al. 1978) – it is clear that their violence describes a social career and a social space. Marsh, Rosser and Harre identify how violence is 'grown' and then dissipated through certain stages of adolescence – as males (primarily) pass through the statuses of 'Novices', 'Rowdies' or 'Nutters', 'Town Boys' and then 'Marginals' – and how it erupts according to certain norms of dress, time, place and demeanour. The violence helps maintain a certain football subculture (in Europe as a whole) and serves to demarcate one micro-society from another (cf. Dunning et al. 1988).

Similar conclusions have come from anthropological work on violence in Northern Ireland (Feldman 1991; Jarman 1997), in the work of the British police (Young 1991, 1993), and in New Guinea (Harrison 1993).

Violence and perception

If there is a processual, mutually constitutive relationship between violence and socio-cultural order, however, then the relationship is also characterized by ambiguity. It is in the nature of all human behaviour that, in the words of the Berkeleyian motto, 'To be is to be perceived' (*Esse est percipi*); '[a]ll "phenomena" are literally "appearances"', as Bateson puts it (1972: 429). Hence, 'violence' is in the eye of the beholder, and however influential a role ethnographers may wish to attribute to it – whether in the constitution and reconstitution of the socio-cultural routines of statecraft, boundary-maintenance, ritual, punishment or sport (cf. Riches 1986) – violence can only be understood and approached as a meaningful, 'experienced reality' (Aijmer 2000).

Another way of saying this is that violence must be seen in a socio-cultural context. Violence cannot be regarded as a thing-in-itself, as an ideal-typical act, an inherently meaningful sociological condition or category of behaviour, which is directly investigatable; it cannot be defined as abnormal or pathological, or as any one thing at all. (This, as Bernard Crick puts it (1974: 2), would merely be to perpetrate a vulgar hypostatization, and to engender a 'bastard military sociology'.) Rather, violence must be seen in the context of socio-cultural interaction, and defined in terms of all the complexities of particular situations.

An insightful study in this regard is Laurie Taylor's of 'the underworld' of the professional London criminal (1984; also cf. Klockars 1975). Violence, here, was seen to accompany that which was 'out of order': behaviour which 'took liberties' with a shared code of honour, whose perpetrators needed to be reminded of 'proper respect' (Taylor 1984: 148–57). Being 'out of order' was a phrase regularly enunciated, both in connection with the dishonourable and the treatment meted out against them. It covered a diversity of non-social or anti-social acts (as defined by the criminal micro-society), and Taylor found it to be an odd understatement, seemingly employed without moral qualm. Whether expressed as an inherent part of violent acts, or as part of tales of violence recounted in later gossip, being 'out of order' and hence subject to violence was something phenomenally bleached of all moral colouring. The violent acts themselves, matter-of-fact and routine, were simply the instrumental means by which departures-from-order were socio-culturally inscribed and overcome.

Also significant in the above ethnography is the impossibilty of differentiating between violence as a physical act and its symbolization: between 'doing violence' and 'talking violence'. Talking is a form of doing in the London underworld, and doing a mode of expression. This insight warrants being put on a wider footing. The socio-cultural context of violence may be expected always to encompass both the done and the said, such that no ontological disjunction is positable between 'real' violence and 'symbolic' violence, between the physical and the merely figurative.

Clear-cut and universal distinctions have been anthropologically sought, notwithstanding, between the violence of words and of action, between violent expression by tongue and by fist, these distinctions then implying others: 'verbal-cum-symbolic violence implies no neurological change in the perpetrator, self-control not yet giving way to rage (real, physical violence)'; or 'verbal-cum-symbolic violence implies upper-class socialization rather than plebeian, where tongue-lashing is likely to give way to physical beating' (cf. May 1972). These kinds of reductionist and deterministic theorizations show little respect for the ethnographic record, however, and do not stand close empirical inspection. The symbolical and the physical are inextricable in human behaviour. Certainly, resort to physical violence cannot be correlated with alienation from, or negation of, language; there is no possible or necessary differentiation (and hence relation) between them such that 'symbolic' violence negates 'real' violence, or 'figurative' violence makes 'physical' violence more likely (cf. Wertham 1971; Frank 1976). To appreciate the complexities of particular situations is to see any combination of behaviours (of the so-called symbolic/figurative/lingual as opposed to the real/physical/fistical) as being possibly negotiable in the constitution of routine social relations, and any number of means and modalities by which they can be 'violated' – and violence done to them (cf. Rapport 1987).

'Democratic' versus 'nihilistic' violence

A more fruitful avenue of enquiry than that of attempting to understand violence either as specific behaviours, or as a relationship between behavioural types, is perhaps to explore issues of predictability: violence as a matter of behavioural expectability rather than explosiveness. Here, 'violence' is understood as a decision to negate a relationship of reciprocal predictability and orientability, or to refuse to enter into one:

violence as a deliberate negating of formal routine and a refusal to enter into relations of mutual expectability through the perpetration of 'disorderly' and unoriented behaviours which go beyond them. The keyword here is 'routine', while 'violence' is that which makes civil relations in socio-cultural milieux impossible.

Drawing upon an Existential legacy (Nietzsche, Camus), Edmund Leach theorized upon the fundamental role that doing violence to extant social-structural relations and norms plays in the constitution of human being. '[A]ll of us are criminals by instinct', Leach suggested (1977: 19), and it is 'part of our very nature', 'the very essence of being a human being', to resent the domination of customary social practices and imagine their creative rewriting: '[A]ll creativity, whether it is the work of the artist or the scholar or even of the politician, contains within it a deep-rooted hostility to the system as it is' (1977: 20). Nevertheless, by distinguishing between the outward *form* of socio-cultural relations and their inward *content*, it is possible to prescribe an accommodation between the intrinsic, human–natural violence which Leach describes – ubiquitous, creative, individual, 'democratic' – and another, 'nihilistic' kind, that which destroys the possibility of a creative engagement with social structure in an individual constitution of self, or indeed of any kind of ongoing (civil) socio-cultural relations.

Social structure may be described as a set of discursive idioms in terms of which individuals meet, for the purpose of expressing, constructing, fulfilling and extending their personal world-views (cf. Rapport 1993a). Meeting in terms of common, shared, often formulaic behavioural forms (verbal and non-verbal), individuals are able to make meaningful interpretations of their worlds and selves of great personality and diversity.

A.F.C. Wallace spoke of 'the organization of diversity' which social structure entails (1964: *passim*). Each individual may inhabit what amounts to a private world, and may rarely if ever achieve 'cognitive communality' or mutual identification with another. What is necessary for individuals regularly to engage in routine interactions with one another is mutual predictability. Individual A knows that when she perpetrates action a1 then individual B, in all probability, will perpetrate action b1, which will lead to her doing a2, *et cetera*. Meanwhile, individual B knows that when he perpetrates action b1, individual A responds with a1, which he follows with b2. In other words, individuals A and B need not concur on when precisely the interaction begins and whose action is perpetrated first – on who acts and who reacts – never mind concurring on the content of their interaction. Rather, Wallace's image of the orderly relationships which constitute stable socio-cultural systems is of what he calls 'equivalence structures' or sets of equivalent behavioural expectancies. Social structures are jointly held notions of relations, and something which individuals establish for the mutual facilitation of their separate strivings.

What is crucial in the above, to repeat, is expectability. However different and diverse the interpretations of individuals who partake of the 'contractual' relations of exchanging common social forms – however creative and new – so long as each can predict, each can expect, certain behaviours from the other, then the relationship is able to continue – as can the underlying diversity. Expectability means that each individual is able to continue to find the behaviour of the other(s) understandable, meaningful. Even to the extent that *had each understood the actual meanings of the other*, then they might have felt violated.

A 'democratic violence' may be described, then, as one which does not deny or negate the possibility and ability of fellow-interactants to go on interpreting and meaning as they choose, even as the meanings which each construes in the interaction might be found to violate the others'. 'Democratic violence' enables individual creativity to live beneath an ambiguous surface of social-structural calm and within a form of behavioural norms which individuals continue to share. If the *sine qua non* of the social contract is individuals' possession of mutual expectations which allow them to orient their behaviour to one another in a particular relationship or kind of relationship, then the stability of such expectations is not threatened by a violent diversity of individual interpretations which do not breach the civil surface of the exchange.

A 'nihilistic violence', on the other hand, may be described as behaviour which deliberately or unintentionally disorients others in the relationship such that the latter's acts of prediction and interpretation are made impossible. Nihilistic violence despoils the shared forms of behaviour, such that orientation towards it by others, and their development of stable expectations with regard to it, are prevented (cf. Johnson 1982: 8).

In this conceptualization, violence might be morally neutral, a fact of the individual (creative) interpretation of social exchange. It is 'a sort of constant' (Aijmer 2000) around which the social is organized. Furthermore, violence need not be tied only to particular behaviours and excepted from others: violence does not correspond to brutality or physicality or the absence of empathy; violence is not precluded by the presence of empathy or the expression of love, for instance. Rather, it is violence of a particular, 'nihilistic' kind to which others cannot adapt: behaviour which others cannot expect or predict and find meaningful in some way. Only nihilistic violence makes mutual expectation and diversity impossible by violating any practicable norms of exchange and hence denying the possibility of a civil relationship of mutual predictability and orientability.

Such denial may take a variety of forms and degrees. Random sounds, silences and actions will preclude viable interactions of a routine and ongoing kind, and hence deny others the opportunity of making sense, of making meaningful interpretations of the particular exchange. But then maiming or killing will preclude viable interaction and meaningful interpretation henceforward and in general. Thus, a sliding-scale of nihilistic violence may be introduced, the severity adjudged in terms of the intended or received injury to others' ability to make sense, to create meaning, at that time and henceforth.

'Violence' and schizophrenia

While 'democratic' violence gives onto diverse individual meanings, 'nihilistic' violence negates common forms of exchange; it entails the violating of existing or practicable norms of behaviour. If society is seen to encompass individuals' coming together to constitute manifold types of relationship, using common cultural institutions both to communicate their relationships and to create and express their personal meanings, then there are some individuals who refuse such communication: they do violence to others' possible perception of routine. Such individuals excommunicate themselves, placing their behaviour beyond the bounds of expectability, orientability and interpretation, and in the process render impossible or ineffectual the communication of others.

This portrayal recalls Bateson *et al.*'s conception of the schizophrenic (1974: 32–4). He is the individual who fails to communicate because he does not 'correctly' (conventionally) label or channel his meanings, and does not correctly interpret the labels and channels of others' messages. The difference is that the nihilistically violent individual may be described as arriving at such a situation by intention. Deliberately he negates and eschews those regularities through which relationships, as contractual equivalence structures, are possible.

See also: **Form and Content, Interaction, The Unhomely**

VISUALISM

It is perhaps ironical that at the same time as there has been an anthropological desire to deconstruct the central place given in the West to vision as a form of knowing (where 'I see' is synonymous with 'I understand') (cf. Ong 1969; Dias 1994), and to recognize an array of other senses and forms (Stoller 1989b), visual anthropology has also grown into a methodological specialism – albeit one seeking to redress a traditional (Western) emphasis on the written word as a form of representing anthropological knowledge. Nor has the irony gone unnoticed. Indeed, visual anthropology has been critiqued from two vantage-points: the 'traditional', in whose view anthropology must perforce remain a logocentric discipline because of the need to convey abstraction and theory, and there being no clear route from the particularities of the image to the generalities of a holistic social structure (cf. Bloch 1988); and the 'post-colonial', in whose view the technologies of filmic representation are unavoidably corrupted by their being Western practices with a history and continuing provenance of ideological control.

Notwithstanding this, visual anthropology, the employment of pictorial media as means to communicate anthropological knowledge, has continued to grow; it has challenged notions that anthropological knowledge must needs be seen either as holistic or as hegemonic. It has argued that there are important contributions to be made via pictorial media to the study of the audio-visual dimensions of human behaviour, of culture as manifested in visible symbols and audible sounds – as gesture, script, oration, dance, ceremony, ritual, art-work, craft and material artefact.

'Pictorial media' has come generally to mean film and video, although there have been significant anthropological forays into study of and by other visual forms such as photography (Bateson and Mead 1942; Pinney 1990) and television (Intintoli 1984; Liebes and Katz 1990). (The anthropology of artistic-cum-visual forms has tended to represent another specialism again, linked with issues of aesthetics (cf. Layton 1981; Coote and Shelton 1991).) Even here, however, and with film and video being such accepted representational genres outwith anthropology, definitional problems have arisen concerning what is truly or distinctively 'anthropological' or 'ethnographic' in the pictorial. How seriously are aesthetic, emotional and sentimental registers to be taken as filmic components? How should documentation be validated, and how balanced with narrational needs? What poetic, even surrealistic, strategies are to be permissible in the conveying of subjects' inner experiences? In short, how, and to what extent, should 'ethnography' take precedence over cinematography? Through a number of celebrated films – Robert Gardner's *Dead Birds* (1963) and *Forest of Bliss* (1985); Jean Rouch's *Jaguar* (1965) – these issues have been brought to a head (cf. Heider 1976; Stoller 1992). Perhaps the best that can be said, following Sol Worth (1981), is that a film or video is anthropological if an anthropologist chooses to treat it as such, a judgement likely to be made on the basis of the extent to which the 'screen-play' can be seen to be informed by local ethnographic knowledge, while the subject-matter is local behaviour which is normative (whether spontaneous or scripted) in a particular socio-cultural milieu.

History

The history of a visual appreciation in anthropology, and its filmic representation, goes back to the very beginnings of modern field-research. An argument can be made, in fact, that in W.H.R. Rivers's conception of field-research (before a Malinowskian format became paradigmatic), a visual record and an appreciation of otherness were seen to be inextricably tied (cf. Grimshaw 1994). Since then, the nature of visual representation and what it should purport anthropologically to be has undergone a number of transformations: from a romantic capturing of the exotic and anachronistic, to positivistic observation, to realistic dramatization, to surrealistic fictionalization, to reflexive and subjective construction, to collaborative textualization (cf. Marks 1995).

However, a number of key dates and occasions, linking the above developments, stand out:

- 1895: Felix Regnault films a Wolof woman in Paris making a clay pot.
- 1898: Alfred Haddon takes a cine-camera with him (and Rivers) on the Cambridge University expedition to the Torres Straits.
- 1901: Baldwin Spencer films Aboriginal dances.
- 1914: Edward Curtis produces the exotic Kwakiutl movie *In the Land of the Head-hunters*.
- 1922: Robert Flaherty releases the Eskimo drama *Nanook of the North* (followed by *Man of Aran* (1934)).
- 1930: H. Carver directs *The Silent Enemy: An Epic of the American Indian* with an all-Amerindian cast, one of a number of 'rescue' films depicting native and peasant populations, in costume, proudly enacting their everyday lives, rituals and adventures for posterity.
- late-1930s: Gregory Bateson and Margaret Mead undertake a photo-graphic project on national character and cultural ethos as they are revealed in social interaction, culminating in analytical films such as *Childhood Rivalry in Bali and New Guinea* (1951).

- 1940s onwards: Jean Rouch begins a series of influential cinematographic narratives, located in Africa and France, such as *Les Maîtres
Foux* (1953) and *Chronique d'un été* (1960), which experiment with
plot and genre.
- 1950s: the Goettingen *Institut fuer den Wissenschaftlichen Film* launches
its 'Encyclopaedia Cinematographica' project and archive.
- 1960s: advances in camera technology (colour reproduction, sound-
synchrony and video) lead to a great expansion in the number of
films made by such luminaries as David and Judith MacDougall,
Timothy and Patsy Asch, Melissa Llewelyn-Davies, Paul Henley,
and (the Oscar-nominated) Dan Marks.
- 1970s onwards: the release of a number of ethnographic film series
on prime-time television: Granada's *Disappearing World*; PBS's
Odyssey; BBC's *Face Values* and *Worlds Apart*.
- 1980s onwards: universities offer specialist courses in visual anthropology (Manchester, New York, Southern California).

Issues

Visual anthropology has succeeded in bringing into focus, throwing
significant light upon or putting into interesting perspective, a number
of key issues in contemporary anthropology. These include:

Fieldwork method: Making films in the field elucidates the processes
by which field data are elicited through the anthropologist's presence
and the particular relations in which he or she is enmeshed. As a
medium of record and reportage, film can be particularly reflexive,
making explicit field methodology, subjectivity and intersubjectivity.
As provocation, the camera can cause people to articulate taken-for-
granted aspects of their culture (cf. Ruby 1980; MacDougall 1995).

Teaching methods: Timothy Asch, in collaboration with John Marshall,
has made over 20 films on the !Kung San, and, with Napoleon
Chagnon, over 35 films on the Yanomami (such as *Ax Fight* (1975)),
primarily as teaching-aids. Might not filmic immediacy elicit a sense
of ethnographic immersion? Then again, might not students used to
film-as-entertainment receive the filmic text as an affirmation of prior
prejudices (cf. Martinez 1992; Asch and Asch 1987)?

Advocacy: As a new means of communication, one which bypasses the
state and also the need for literacy, can film offer a medium for resistant
local voices? Via projects such as *Navaho Film Themselves*, sponsored by
Worth and Adair (1972; also Michaels among Aborigines (cf. 1987) and
Turner among Kayapo (cf. 1992)), locals who are given the chance to
film themselves produce cultural documents which reveal aspects of an

indigenous world as seen through local eyes. This may culminate, as in the British 'Black Audio Collective', in a forum for grass-roots political critique.

Intellectual property rights: The distribution and reproduction of film calls into question rights of ownership of footage. A film made by Timothy Asch and Asen Balikci on nomads in Afghanistan – produced by the Canadian Film Board as *Sons of Haji Omar*, then sold to the BBC, who add a political commentary concerning the role of the protagonists in the (1980s) Afghan war, before releasing it as a finished product – ends up endangering the lives of those originally filmed.

Contested discourses: A growing realization that the camera is more than simply a window on the world – a neutral, transparent, objective unimpeachable medium – brings to the fore questions of its ideological nature: of filming as the pronouncements of the ideology of the film-makers upon that of the filmed. To film is to have the power, the technology, the operational knowledge and the marketing control *to* film, and to abide by certain hegemonic conventions of producing the 'filmic gaze'. But all this is also contestable by its consumers (cf. Minh-ha 1989; Crawford and Turton 1992).

Kinaesthetics: Film is ideally equipped for the study of body movement, whether as dance or as everyday gesture, and the socio-cultural spaces in which this takes place. It records the proxemics of interaction, and can call into question their overdetermination as so-called cultural *habitus* (cf. Birdwhistell 1970).

Globalization: Film is part of a globalization of technology, of translocal and transnational production and consumption. As such it provides a test case of how a Western cultural artefact and practice is advertised and sold, and also how it is locally transformed (cf. Armes 1987; Appadurai 1991b).

Mass media: Many questions surround the relationship between contemporary mass media and their importance in social life, and the formation of cultural identities. Via film one is able to explore the construction of local identity as part-and-parcel of its being represented (cf. Musello 1980; Kottak 1990).

Reflexivity: From film of people watching themselves on film, to film-makers' making their presence behind the camera felt in front of it, film can show up the constructed nature of all texts, the individual artistry and the collaboration that goes into their final forms (cf. Loizos 1993).

Individuation: Inasmuch as film captures the transience of particular moments of interaction – between film-maker and local, between local and local, between film-maker and film-maker – it is individual actors and their practices which are focused upon. Thus film can help rectify tendencies to generalization, collectivization and abstraction which have plagued traditional ethnography and given rise to brands of fictional holism (cf. Asch and Asch 1988).

See also: **Literariness, Post-Modernism, Qualitative and Quantitative Methodologies**

WORLD-MAKING

No socio-cultural version of reality is entirely original, according to David Parkin (1987: 66), and no socio-cultural practices or expertise wholly pristine (cf. Strathern 1991: 14). And yet innovative reworking continually creates realities and practices which are new and distinct, as an inherent individual creativity engages in innovative dialogue with conventional socio-cultural forms. Moreover, while each new reality might borrow from, adapt and parody a myriad of previous ones, it can yet do so without being predictable, encompassed or otherwise predetermined. As new formal worlds (new objects and relations) are created from old, so culture becomes a constantly reworked product, a workaday *bricolage*, not only without beginning but also without end.

Nelson Goodman, in a celebrated essay (1978), dubbed this process 'world-making'. The facts of a world, its objects and relations, are fabricated, not found, Goodman begins. Any order we experience in the world does not simply 'lie there ready-made to be discovered'; nor is not determined by passive observation. Rather, order is reached by painstaking fabrication: 'imposed by world-versions we contrive – in the sciences, the arts, perception, and everyday practice' (1984: 21). Goodman then identifies some five ways in which a contriving of world-versions, via a reworking (and recreating) of the extant, frequently occurs (1978: 7–16). The first he calls 'Composition and Decomposition'. Here, old worlds are taken apart (wholes divided into sections, parts into subsections, complexes into components) and then new entities are composed through different connections being made. (In anthropology, we find the world of Lévi-Straussian structuralism, for instance, composed from decomposed aspects of Boasian culturalism, Saussurean and Prague School linguistics, and binary-code computer logic.)

A second way of world-making, Goodman calls 'Weighting'. Here, a current world is made anew by a different accentuating: by giving different relative prominence to certain of its features. (Anthropological functionalism, then, becomes neo-functionalism by a different weighting of social disorder, conflict and competition, dynamic equilibrium and disequilibrium.) Thirdly, there is 'Reordering'. By ordering differently the elements of a world-view, the meaning of each element becomes different, and their aggregation amounts to a different systemic. (It is by a reordering of this kind, then, that anthropology moves between being conceived of as an empirical pursuit and a rationalist one: 'a problematic in the data eventuates in an explanatory model' versus 'an explanatory model eventuates in a problematic in the data'.) Fourthly, there is 'Deletion and Supplementation'. Here, worlds are made out of each other by the excision of certain elements and the introduction of others from elsewhere. (Neo-Marxian anthropology deletes the notion that economic relations of production always and alone represent the foundational infra-structure of a society, then, and allows the supplementation that in primitive social formations such relations may be expressed through kinship.) And finally, new worlds can be made by way of 'Deformation'. A world is renewed by distorting, reducing or elaborating upon, some of its elements, and by making variations on its themes. (A Foucauldian deconstruction of society deforms the Marxian critique, for instance, by elaborating upon the themes of power and ideology to the extent that every interaction and every body is implicated; the result is that any overarching system of control fragments into a palimpsest of parodic, ultimately uncontrollable moments.)

The above represents a sample of ways of world-making, not an exhaustive set, Goodman admits (1978: 17–20). New ways are always being created, and since these can also occur in combination and in layers, change can also issue from more than one process at the same time. Moreover, worlds can be made up from different kinds of symbolic forms: words, numerals, pictures, sounds, smells, or any combination of these; and the translation of one kind of symbolic notation into another is also tantamount to the creation of a new world. Finally, since there is no direct way of translating between different versions of the same symbolic notation, say from Chagall's version of the pictorial to Stanley Spencer's (never mind from the written in anthropology to the written in anthroposophy), any attempt to say the same thing in a different way can be seen as in fact amounting to saying a different thing.

Goodman concludes that: 'comprehension and creation go on together' in the human mind (1978: 22). Our 'facts' would be better conceived of as small 'theories' – and our theories big facts; (après Goethe: 'the highest wisdom would be to understand that every fact is already theory'). What we know is what we make and use in socio-cultural milieux. For the truth of the world, as Goodman puts it, is a docile and obedient servant, mediated by the questions we ask of the world and by the way we participate in it. 'Truth' does not derive from correspondence between perception and a finished, ready-made universe; rather, 'truth' derives from a correspondence between perception and a humanly made system of conception. Hence: perceiving is producing, recognizing is imposing, discovering is drafting, is finding a fit. 'Truth', indeed, becomes the name for the perfect fit, the perfect tailoring and fabricating of the universe, the perfect designing of its laws and patterns.

But if there is nothing absolutely solid underneath us then there is nothing stolid either: worlds are continuously made from other worlds and in such a way that any one is radically different from any other and irreducible to it. What is striking is how worlds abound, how a vast variety of versions and visions, of symbolic realities, of cultural worlds, are in existence at one time, each advocated by a different science or scientist, or painter or school of art, or politician, or political interest, or ethnic group, or religious denomination, or poet or farmer or man-in-the-street. These different world-versions (concerning both the stuff which the world is made of and the things it contains) are inherently irreducible; at best, they can be transformed into one another only with great difficulty and corruption. What this speaks of, to repeat, is the prevalence of individual creativity reworking collective forms: refiguring the funds of forms to which cultures amount, and refashioning the social interaction to which the routine exchange of such forms gives rise.

Imagination of worlds

The quality necessary for an individual to conceive of such refiguring and refashioning is imagination. This is a quality different from 'knowing how' or 'knowing what', what Edward Ions refers to as 'a third way of knowing' (1977: 152–3), pertaining not to hypothetico-deduction but to intuition. What is essential is the forming of mental concepts, schemata, projects, for what is not present. Imagination deals not with extant observable systems but with the unseen; it is the quality of thinking, feeling, knowing oneself and one's world as other, the intentional stepping away from the extant.

Individuals may dwell within certain epistemological frameworks, habitually embodying themselves and becoming embodied in terms of paradigms, pre-understandings, which are conventional and collective. Nevertheless, through their imagination individuals also have the capability of questioning the present and opening out their horizons (cf. Gadamer 1975: 238). The relationship between the imagined and the present is thus metaphoric rather than metonymic, entailing the potentiality of an epistemological leap rather than simple reflection or extension.

Complementary to Goodman's account of the various processes of creative world-making is Preston's attempt (however seemingly oxymoronic), then, to describe the inventive qualities of the imagination (1991). The imagination commonly transforms the world along four dimensions, Preston suggests: the spatial, the temporal, the morphological and the comprehensive. Within each of these dimensions, there then exists a variety of possible processes of transformation, which can occur singly or together. For example, 'spatially' an existing world might be imaginatively transformed through 'magnification' and 'miniaturization', through 'condensation' (as in a shorthand), or through 'translocation' (of the viewing eye). 'Temporally', a world might be imaginatively transformed through 'montage' (as discrete events are made kaleidoscopic), through 'simultaneity' (as different events are juxtaposed), and through 'progression' and 'retrogression' (with the inclusion of wholly new events in future and past). Again, a world might be 'morphologically' transformed through 'transmutation' of its shapes and structures, through 'animation' and 'materialization' of its being, or through 'complementarization' of its relationships (the changing of its symmetries and asymmetries). And finally, a world might be 'comprehensively' transformed in terms of its overall 'chromatics' (its colouration and light), in terms of one's 'focal depth' (one's particular concentration), one's 'distortions' (and various enhancements), or one's decisions on overall 'composition' (the balancing of all of the above means of construction).

Preston's attempt is inevitably inconclusive; what surpasses the present cannot adequately be described. Nevertheless, his account emphasizes the perspectival nature of socio-cultural reality, and the transformatory quality of individual imagination. His conclusion neatly sums up the discussion: imagination is the capacity to give reality to culture, and to keep inventing social worlds anew.

See also: **Agent and Agency, Interpretation, World-View**

WORLD-VIEW

'World-view' is the common English translation of the German word *Weltanschauung*, meaning overarching philosophy or outlook, or conception of the world. The original loan status of 'world-view' has led to a conceptual usage which is particularly broad.

In an early anthropological usage, Robert Redfield (1952, 1960) argued for the importance of accessing 'the peasant world-view' if the anthropologist was to be able to appreciate responses to change in traditional 'little communities' on the road to modernization and urbanization. Without an understanding of peasant notions of 'limited good' (Foster 1965) and the 'amoral familism' which comes to characterize peasant social interaction (Banfield 1958), the anthropologist would be able neither to make sense of, nor predict, behaviour in a community under study and its relations to the outside world.

In this usage, 'world-view' is employed to point up diacritical features of cognition and perception which then give onto certain behaviours. 'World-view' represents fundamental conceptions of the world, conceptions which ramify into all other thoughts and feelings about the world, and conceptions which directly influence how people behave in the world. Furthermore, 'world-view' is used to point up critical differences between groups of people: here, between peasants and moderns (urbanites and cosmopolitans), based on how they view the world.

Clearly, there are overlaps between 'world-view', as used here, and at least two other common anthropological concepts: cosmology and ideology. Treated in 'vertical' orientation, as it were, 'world-view' (like 'cosmology') covers those relations between group, world and cosmos. Treated in more 'horizontal' orientation, 'world-view' (like 'ideology') covers that outlook on the world which guides behaviour within a particular social group, perhaps obscuring or imperfectly mediating a 'true' or more beneficial version of relations between that group and others. Indeed, if understood broadly as 'a particular system of values, beliefs and attitudes held by a specific group (based on locality, age, class, status, ethnicity, nationality or religion)', there is little to choose between 'world-view' as a concept and traditional anthropological conceptions of 'culture' or 'sub-culture'.

To begin to narrow the matter down, one can say that 'world-view' focuses on thought and feeling in distinction from behaviour, also in a sense as prior to behaviour. There is a theorization of causation and sequence implied by the concept such that behaviour is not seen as automatic or as meaningless, as *sui generis* or as *a priori*; behaviour is what world-view gives onto if the latter is translated into action. Kearney (1984) adds a qualification to this understanding, and would define 'world-view' as tacit knowledge about their worlds as distinct from those thoughts and feelings which people are willing or able to make explicit (cf. Sperber 1975: x–xi).

Geertz (1973), meanwhile, adapts an earlier usage of Bateson's (1936) and differentiates 'world-view' from 'ethos', this being tantamount to a distinction between thought and feeling. For Geertz, 'world-view' refers to an intellectual understanding of the world, a way of thinking about the world and its workings, which is common amongst a particular group, while 'ethos' refers to an emotional appreciation, a way of feeling about and evaluating the world. It is the work of religious rituals, Geertz concludes, to assure that world-view and ethos have a mutually supportive relationship (and hence that the culture remains integrated): what is thought remains emotionally acceptable and what is felt remains intellectually reasonable.

Psychic unities

Perhaps the most common matter that 'world-view' has been called upon anthropologically to signal has been the relationship between psyche and society or culture, and questions of psychic unity. To what extent, in short, are cognition and perception socially or culturally determined, and to what extent are social or cultural groups psychically homogeneous, consensual or harmonious?

Four positions obviously suggest themselves (cf. Hunt 1967). In the first, the realms of society and culture on the one hand and individual psyche on the other are separate and distinct, and must be analytically treated as such. One can recall in this connection Durkheim (1966), and his insistence upon a distantiation of sociology from psychology since the 'social fact' of the *conscience collective* made psychic variables irrelevant. The second position is perhaps a derivative of this, as expounded by Boas and his descendants. This sees the socio-cultural as determinant of the psychical: the psyche is culture writ small (Benedict 1934), as effected, for example, by a culture's linguistic grammar and lexicon (Whorf 1956), or other 'primary institutions' such as type of subsistence, household pattern and methods of child-training (Kardiner and Linton 1939). As summed up by Sacks (1974: 218): 'the fine power of a culture [is such that it] does not, so to speak, merely fill brains in roughly the same way, it fills them so that they are alike in fine detail'.

The third position concerning the relationship between the socio-cultural and the psychical reverses the relation of determinacy and sees the latter as causative of the former: culture is psyche writ large. In some of Malinowski's notions regarding the route from individually felt anxiety to collective rites of religious assuagement one finds this conclusion (1939; also cf. Homans 1941). As with the second position, there is a positing of psychic unity, not now eventuating from some standardized conditioning but responsible for joint socio-cultural procedures. Finally, the fourth position, as advocated by the likes of Bateson, Wallace (1961) and Schwartz (1978a), argues that the socio-cultural and the psychical are distinct but interdependent and mutually influencing realms. To the extent that one can analytically identify a particular ethos (emotional tone) or eidos (cognitive style) in a particular society or culture, one must also recognize the individual as a distinct 'energy source' whose metabolic processes give rise to the constant possibility of perceiving and cognizing random, new objects and relations in the external world (Bateson 1972: 126).

This fourth position adds a creative tension or dialectic to the picture which the others lack. It presumes neither psychic unity nor difference, and generalizes on the basis neither of determinism nor irrelevancy; rather, it allows for an analytical appreciation of the relationship between the individual and the socio-cultural which is subtle and variable. As Schwartz puts it (1975: 128), the relationship is dynamic and unresolved; or again (1978a: 430–2), culture is no more a shared totality than psychical contents are confined or unique to different individuals. Rather, think of individual psyches or 'ideoverses' (1978a: 429) as different versions or portions of a culture. Individuals will have different cognitive, affective and evaluative mappings of the world, in terms both of the structure of events and their classification; here are cultural constructs as experientially discovered and individually transformed. What becomes significant for anthropological analysis is the way different individuals' 'personal constructs' (Kelly 1969) variously intersect and play around structures of commonality by which degrees of inter-personal communicability and coordination are maintained.

In this 'distributive' picture, then, world-view does not amount to something either essentially uniform or necessarily shared but to a sum of diversities. The focus has also shifted, from an assumption that 'cultures' or 'societies' eventuate in common world-views to an exploration of how a diversity of world-views can co-exist within 'single' socio-cultural settings.

'The organization of diversity'

These ideas have found their fullest elaboration in the theorizing of Anthony Wallace (1961, 1962, 1964). Certainly, it is his work which is most frequently referred to in connection with attempts to come to terms with a dynamic relationship between the psychical and the socio-cultural (cf. Goodenough 1963; Szwed 1966; Paine 1974; Schwartz 1978b).

Wallace's opening premise is that the cultural does not form a closed system; it is always engaged with non-cultural factors such as the psychological. Moreover, the dialectical relations between the cultural and the psychological eventuate not in a replication of psychological uniformity within a social group, in personalities sharing a homogeneous 'cultural' character, but rather in an organization of diversity. Individuals in any one society need not be found 'threaded like beads on a string of common motives'; they can still interact in a stable and mutually rewarding fashion, and organize themselves culturally into orderly, expanding, changing societies in spite of their having radically different interests, habits, personalities, customs, and despite there being no one cognitive map that members share.

Indeed, the world-view or 'mazeway' of each individual – that mental map of values, plans, techniques, people and things; that organized totality of meanings which each maintains at a given time and which is regularly evoked by perceived or remembered stimuli – may be unique. Each individual may possess a complex cognitive system of interrelated objects which amount to a private world, and may rarely if ever achieve 'cognitive communality' or mutual identification with another. To this extent, all human societies are plural societies. Indeed, Wallace goes on to suggest that cognitive non-uniformity may be a 'functional desideratum' of social structure, a necessary condition of making social coordination possible, and that if all participants were to share a common knowledge of the social system, or indeed the burden of knowing their differences, then the system would not work.

Wallace's image of the orderly relationships which constitute stable socio-cultural systems is of what he calls 'equivalence structures' or sets of equivalent behavioural expectancies: individuals regularly engaging in routine interactions with one another because they have developed a capacity for mutual prediction whereby the specific behaviour of one is highly likely to eventuate in the specific response of another, and so on. That is, individuals organize themselves, integrate their behaviours into reliable and joint systems, not by developing uniform cognitive maps or possessing equivalent motives but by learning that under certain circumstances others' behaviour is predictable, and can be confidently interrelated with actions of their own. This system of organizing relations, Wallace suggests, fits interactions of different levels and types: between the American Indians and the Whites, for instance, trading and fighting for years without mutual comprehension; between different social classes, who may not share ideologies; and between bus drivers and passengers, whose interests in avoiding traffic jams may be very different and whose cognitive worlds, especially in large and complex societies, may be 'uniquely private'.

Nonetheless, what the bus driver and passengers do share is something very precise. Their interests in keeping to timetables overlap, their motives in riding the bus are complementary, and they possess detailed, mutual behavioural expectancies. Moreover, the relations are standardized between any driver and any passenger within the urban or regional or national system. Wallace calls this a 'contract': something where the equivalent roles are specified and available for implementation to any parties whose motives make their adoption promising. At other times, Wallace also calls it a 'meta-calculus': something which is the sum of at least two parties' particular 'calculi', or recipes of behaviour. And he goes on to say that a culture may be described as a 'family of meta-calculi': a set of standardized models of contractual relationships: a system of interlinking equivalence structures.

In fact, culture becomes a consummate equivalence structure over the diverse whole: the sum of all the diverse world-views of a society's particular sub-groupings and individuals. In this way, Wallace concludes, individuals can together produce a socio-cultural system which is beyond the comprehension of any single one of them. The contracts which they establish for the mutual facilitation of their separate strivings amount to a structured whole, however tacitly and gradually concocted, which is more complex than the cognitive map of any of its members: a world-view of world-views.

A critique of Wallace

Despite his insistence that his portrayal of a socio-cultural system as an organization of a diversity of individual world-views does not amount to the positing of a distinct, superorganic entity in the Durkheimian sense of something *sui generis*, Wallace still opens himself up to criticism in this vein. In allowing that individual contracts and group policies give onto a system at another and higher level of complexity and organization, a socio-cultural whole which functions beyond the comprehension of individual participants, we begin to slide towards Durkheimian notions of organicism, of the socio-cultural determining the psychical.

Wallace would probably object to this, saying that he sees culture and personality as constructs of different Russellian logical types – personality signifying cognitive diversity, and culture merely amounting to shared expectations – and that it would be using the wrong metaphors to talk of individuals 'internalizing' a culture, or a culture 'moulding' the personalities of its members; almost as if one were to talk of a circle moulding the individual points that constitute its circumference. And yet, Wallace's model *does* take on this character, and must do so, in order to describe the circle of interactions, the holistic system of interlocking parts, to which individual behaviours come to amount.

For the principle of socio-cultural organization in Wallace's model is the institutionalized meta-calculus or macro equivalence structure, whereby almost any individuals, any assemblage of world-views, can work as interchangeable components of the system. And one must explain how this institutionalization comes about and how it is maintained. Wallace's answer must be that culture is the driving force: cultural forms, standardized contracts, becoming autonomous and maintaining themselves by teaching members the mutually predictable behaviours necessary to their functioning on different occasions. More than this, culture would also appear to provide members with their diverse world-views: it teaches sets of equivalent meanings by which individuals can predictably define stimuli and, just as predictably, act before one another over wide situational parameters. Far from culture's emerging from individual invention and continuing decisions about practice, then, it is culture which now acts, and in peremptory fashion, taking advantage of individual cognitive tendencies to make possible a maximal organization of motivational diversity. Thus, notwithstanding his initial renunciation of socio-cultural determinism, we come to find Wallace talking about diverse individual cognitions being articulated by a society into functional equivalence structures, and a culture as an organization which is responsible for coordinating its disparate elements and shaping them into relatively consistent patterns; it is very much to a separate societal domain that these elegant meta-calculi belong.

In short, a diversity of individual world-views becomes, for Wallace, a cultural task, a social tool. Sometimes this diversity is culturally forbidden, he explains, and uniformity is socialized into individual members and rewarded. On other occasions it is 'in the interests of the survival of the culture' to encourage randomness and not to organize individuals at all. But most 'solutions', Wallace concludes, fall between the two: in one or more of four universal mechanisms ('Inclusive Structures' – where a subordinate interactional partner bows to the calculus, the plan, of a superordinate – 'End-Linkage' – where a precise articulation of the calculi of equals in different domains of expertise, a division of labour, occurs – 'Ad Hoc Communication' – where a warding-off of centrifugal calculi and societal dissolution takes place through constant casual intercourse – and 'Administration' – where a group of experts undertakes to check the large numbers of the above three types of contract in operation, adjusting individual members' calculi as necessary), diversity comes to be socio-culturally organized and used.

In sum, with his image of a circle in whose circumference individual points of difference join and submerge, Wallace himself comes full circle:

to a Durkheimian picture of individual diversity as a form of (organic) socio-cultural integration. Individual world-views have ceased to have any real relevance and are succeeded by a picture of socio-cultural harmony: a system with a structure of interdependent parts, maintained by standardized behaviours, ensuring at least some degree of social stability and cultural unity.

Wallace's work deserves its recognition because of his appreciation of psychic diversity within socio-cultural commonality and his efforts to keep the two analytically in relationship. He shows how individuals might meet in interaction while at the same time executing moves, achieving positions, proclaiming successes, and so on, in private and possibly very different game-plans; so that individual views of social worlds may have tangential connections, colliding and co-evolving without amounting to a single or even compatible world of meaning. He recognizes, in short, that social systems can exist without consisting of replications of uniformity and that cultures need not represent standards, norms, practices, rules, views or beliefs which are shared alike by all members.

What is less sympathetic in Wallace's portrayal is the way in which individual agency comes to be replaced by that of a cultural force which is seen as accountable for order and responsible for behavioural predictability. The diversity of behavioural contracts between people comes to amount to one, neatly integrated, social system, and a multitude of individual requirements and interests comes to translate into those of socio-cultural organization. We seem to trade (psychical) world-views for (socio-cultural) World-view.

And yet, behavioural complementarity need not entail organizational hierarchy; individual behaviours can be complementary without being integrated together or otherwise subsumed within a structure which is more complex than each. Muddle, moreover, can be a more appropriate keynote than organization.

World-views and context

This is certainly the conclusion of an ethnographic study of world-views in the English village of Wanet (Rapport 1993a). Here, a multitude and diversity of world-views, both within and between individual psyches, could be seen to give onto no overarching or singular socio-cultural system. Rather, the expression and realization of a diversity of world-views, in an aggregation of behavioural contracts, amounted to a chaotic array. Here is life in a socio-cultural milieu very much portrayed as a momentary muddling-through.

To elaborate, briefly, at one point in his discussion of the individuation of language, the way in which each speaker possesses an 'idiolect' of finally irreducible personal meanings, George Steiner speaks of the unique 'association-net' of individual consciousness (1975: 173). It is in the way that different individuals associate words with one another that the key to the uniqueness of individual meanings and memory is to be found. Focusing on the everyday expression of a few close informants, it was the phenomenon of idiolect or association-net (a verbal form of Wallace's 'mazeway' or Schwartz's 'ideoverse') that Rapport's work in Wanet arrived at as outward expression of an individual's world-view.

The daily utterances or 'speech-acts' (Searle 1973) of different individuals Rapport found to consist of certain sets of phrases, routinely repeated. Each individual speaker possessed a number of verbal loops, of words and phrases which they habitually associated together, and which they regularly expressed. In different moments of interaction, greater or lesser lengths of different strings or loops of an individual's habitually associated words and phrases would be enunciated.

But it was not simply a matter of words. For Rapport noted that each verbal loop also entailed a particular mood, humour or outlook, a particular identity or persona, which the individual speaker appeared to assume for the length of the particular verbal expression. It was as if the verbal phrasing and the tenor of its expression were part-and-parcel of one phenomenon: a particular outlook on the world which the individual adopted, and a particular identity which accompanied that outlook.

Finding himself able to piece together the habitually linked phrases of his informants, the verbal building blocks of their utterances, into longer and longer strings, so that aggregated words became great chains, Rapport determined to call these association-nets of words, feelings and outlook, 'world-views'. For, in its entirety (a form actually unlikely to be expressed in any one speech-act), each association-net traversed an amassment of opinion, detailed and rich: a seemingly whole world around which its owner might cognitively travel. The strings of verbal associations, that is, translated into assemblages of ideas, identities and behaviours which found their owners experientially located in distinct, self-contained worlds of people, events, values, norms and constraints.

Moreover, different sets of linked words and phrases (whether of the same or different individual speakers) resulted in an outlook on the world, a world-view, possibly very different from that constructed from another set. Even though the same individual words cropped up in different world-views, when related and contrasted to other words, to form a cognitive set, their meanings became different. Hence, opinions expressed would differ, as would expectations and evaluations of behaviour – definitions of behaviour *per se* and the people and events it was deemed relevant to consider. Inasmuch as each individual possessed a number of verbal loops, then, the 'same' individual would also possess a number of different world-views; from one close informant Rapport discovered nine world-views, and from another, seven. It was as if his informants were habitually living and talking in a number of different, bounded, socio-cultural environments at one and the same time, and were different people in each. Moreover, the set of worlds in which one individual lived was not necessarily the same or even consistent with that of others.

Furthermore, linking together in this way the sets of preferred phrasal associations of different individual speakers, the snippets of world-views that speakers would reveal in different utterances, Rapport felt was more a process of recontextualizing than decontextualizing people's words. It was as though he were returning the words from the momentary interactions in which he had heard the words expressed to the larger worlds of opinion, the cognitive homes, from which individual speakers had initially extracted their words for the mundane and rushed business of everyday conversation. To the extent that speakers partook of a common behavioural contract to meet, talk and work together, this was more a matter of partial overlaps, of individuals' construing the 'same' events rather differently (fulfilling 'different' contracts) than their being organized into one common, socio-cultural context. It was beneath the surface of ambiguous conversational exchanges, in their series of diverse world-views, in which speakers lived more fully (intellectually and emotionally).

Inasmuch as world-views gave onto context, then, the latter should be understood as something internal: something originating in individual cognition rather than immanent in, or emanating from, an interactional setting. Context was something *prior* to interaction, something which individuals brought to it and employed within it. Context was the way individual speakers internalized words and related them to others in their heads so as to accrue meaning. Hence, the same cognitive context could reappear in any number of externally different situations, and vice versa, the same interactional setting being cognitively contextualized in any number of different ways. This was not to say that there could be no regularity or consistency between cognitive definition and external setting, that an individual did not possess a number of routine ways of behaving when talking in a particular setting, but that the decision was an individual and possibly private one.

In short, it was within individual world-views that the significance of socio-cultural exchanges lay; it was their diverse world-views which individuals used in constructing, populating and anticipating the social worlds around them, and these furnished them with their expectations before meeting with other people in interaction, their opinions during such meetings, and their conclusions afterwards.

Representation and analysis

A conclusion to be drawn from focusing upon world-views as contexts of individual significance in socio-cultural milieux is that the anthropologist is not able to give just one neat and consistent account of socio-cultural interaction or exchange. Not only do individual world-views fail to gave onto a set of common-denominational, community-wide perspectives, but this individual diversity refuses to be tied to objectively defined situations. The logic behind these cognitive contexts is subjective and particular.

The analytical value of focusing on world-views would seem to depend on refusing to corrupt this logic: refusing to impose a spurious unity upon informants, singly or collectively, in the name of clarity or generalization. The aspiration must be to an understanding of internal judgements and definitions, so that the integrity of world-views is maintained over and above dubious leap of abstraction to socio-cultural (or psychical) wholes. In spite of the chaotic aggregations which may result, it is a diversity of individual orderings of particular landmarks in idiosyncratic landscapes that the analyst determines to convey. The commonalities of exchange – the sharing of abstract codes, of a grammar of interaction, and of regular occasions on which it is exchanged – can then be recast as moments in which a diversity of individual meanings and motivations find expression, realization and fulfilment. It is through the working-out of these individual world-views that the fate and development of the contractual commonalities lie.

See also: **Cognition, Individuality, Interaction, Situation and Context**

WRITING

Raymond Williams once commented on the way in which the process of writing has become social-scientifically 'naturalized' in the Western academy (1983c: 1). We ask 'what is the writing about?', 'what knowledge, facts and experience does it contain?', but we treat the process itself as non-problematic: as transparent and commonsensical, once the skills of writing have been acquired in childhood.

Writing and literacy

Anthropologists, perhaps, have been less prone than others to this lapse, since they more often treat those who do not and may not seek to acquire the writing technique to which Williams refers. Hence, treating writing as a marker of literacy, anthropology has emphasized the historico-cultural specificity of such writing, and the effects which its arrival precipitates. Anthropology has postulated, *inter alia*, that the technique of writing represents an objectification of speech and a proliferation of words and meanings which causes more layering and less indexicality in socio-cultural milieux, so that individual members become palimpsests who participate less fully and more sceptically, less securely and more selectively, in their traditions (Goody and Watt 1968: 57–8); writing affords that socio-cultural alienation and distance out of which a sense of greater unities comes, and an evolution in consciousness, science and technology in terms of encyclopaedic composition and sequentiality (Ong 1977: 47). Here is a technique for the fixing of discourse, preserving it as a possible archive of later analysis and translation, and the creating of a quasi-separate world of texts which comes to eclipse the circumstantial world of orality (Ricoeur 1981: 145–9); writing is a means of keeping present moments at bay and at the same time preserving them, recontextualizing them, as ongoing, univocal, unifocal and reconsultable (Clifford 1990: 57–64). Or again, here is a technology which lends itself to the social institutions of its time and place so as to serve a number of possible functions (hierarchical, educational), and thus to structure a particular ideological reality for those who employ (rather, are employed by) it (Street 1984: 8; and cf. Herzfeld 1993: 116). In short, in anthropology, writing comes to be conceived of not so much as a neutral medium of knowledge, facts and experience, a window onto an independent reality, than as a way of knowing in itself.

Writing as a mode of cognition

Nevertheless, there is a sense in which writing has still become 'naturalized' in this anthropological appreciation. For, writing has been treated wholly as a particular technique or technology: writing as the inscription of words or forms on a page or material surface. However, writing could profitably be regarded as something far broader: the orderly inscription of words or forms *per se*, whatever the precise technique and technology of that inscription. Hence: words in phrases and sentences, but also musical notes in chords and phrases, daubs of paint in shapes and relations, religious icons in mouldings and arrays, physical behaviours in habits and routines, prescribed roles in institutions and hierarchies. Inscription, moreover, might take place on any number of surfaces: fields, houses, footballs, spaces, bodies and memories, as well as pages. Here is writing understood as 'the orderly use of symbolic forms (that is, forms which carry meaning for their user) for the making of orderly worlds'; writing conceived of not as a technique of communication but as 'a mode of cognition which makes experience meaningful'.

To elaborate, briefly, writing entails the separating of experience from its ratiocination (Stock 1983: 531). Writing is an experiencing of experience, a meta-experience; it is the considered ordering of experience in symbolic form, and the conscious production of meaning from it. Understood in its fullest form, writing is the practice of symbolically reflecting on, and making sense of, experience.

Furthermore, since symbols are simply 'vehicles for a conception' (Geertz 1973), the outward manifestations of such writing may be highly diverse. Diaries and novels, of course, monographs and theses, poems, songs and plays; but also the shapes of field-systems and the patterns of their ploughing; also ways of shaping, carrying, tattooing and clothing bodies; also forms of dancing and politicking, orating and marketing and warring. All these may serve as mnemonics by which messages about life's order and meaning may be inscribed, retained and recalled. A definition of writing in this conceptualization would be, then: the composition, in symbolic form, of a sequence of thoughts and ideas and senses such that a set of meanings is created and retained from passing experience for further possible retrieval, amendment and elaboration. The practice of written reflection remains a constant even as the forms of its expression vary.

Writing as universal

Writing, in this way, can be appreciated as a universal: a ubiquitous and constant part of human being. It is the special preserve neither of certain cultures and times (literate versus non-literate), nor of certain social classes and occupations (professionals versus workers); it is practicable and practised by all (cf. Berger 1979: 6).

Certainly, both in socio-cultural milieux which practise largely oral techniques of communication and those which prefer scriptural ones, there will flourish the practice of scrutinizing and abstracting from experience so as to produce orderly accounts. Orality and literacy do not necessarily entail different habits of thought. As Shweder comments (1991a: 14), if we use the word 'civilized' to describe those people who can explain their practices far better and with more imagination than the anthropologist, then the 'primitive' who leads an unexamined life does not exist. 'There is no "primitive"', Rabinow concurs (1977: 151–2), '[t]here are other men living other lives.'

Writing, text and self

Another way of saying this is that every socio-cultural milieu is a textual milieu, where 'text' (from the Latin root) implies a 'weaving' of language into patterned compositions, whether spoken or scripted or both (Stock 1990). Every milieu has its meaningful, inscribed narratives.

It is in this sense, too, that one can understand Bruner and Weisser's claim (1991: 133) that: '"lives" are texts: texts that are subject to revision, exegesis, reinterpretation, and so on'. For, one comes to know one's life through 'never-ending textualization', through the formulation and reformulation of a conceptual and narrative account of what that life is about. The individual constitutes himself for himself (and as a self) in an ongoing story; carried in memory, such textualization represents the primary process of 'self-accounting'.

The textual account of self might be verbalized (voiced or unvoiced) or it might be otherwise imagined, it might be enunciated as shorter or longer versions of itself, it might be to some extent unified, but it is always evolving and always referred to, whether implicitly or explicitly. Cognitive writing, in short, is a constant process. As Bruner and Weisser sum up (1991:136): 'The process of life-textualization is . . . a never-ending interpretation and reinterpretation. Its textual status is not in the strict sense determined exclusively by acts of speaking and writing, but depends instead upon acts of conceptualization.'

Writing and coherency

By writing a text, Augustine argued (1907), one is able to hold together the fragments of consciousness and hence make meaning and some kind of order in one's life. In a sense, he felt, such autobiography is fictional since one is attempting the impossible: to know oneself from amid one's life and story as if from without; to see as whole and complete – as 'God's eternal now' – what is still becoming. Nevertheless, the structured nature of our ongoing cognitive writing, and the supposition that in our autobiography we are holding the truth of the self, is a fiction which is 'life-preserving' (Nietzsche 1973). It saves us from the inevitable discontinuities of our experience, the disorder and entropy, and enables us to go on acting and experiencing (cf. Chambers 1994a).

It also enables a meeting between people. People can meet through a telling of their own and others' writings or stories, and through according to others an imaginative and sympathetic hearing (cf. Ricoeur 1996: 6–7). If the essence of coherent structures of social relations are 'emotional bonds' (Oz 1975: 115) then the fact that individuals are in the process of constantly writing stories of their lives which they can tell others and which others can recount can be appreciated as a major criterion of the possibility of sociation.

Indeed, an argument can be made that such writing was fundamental to the evolution of our humanity; that reflecting on and giving meaning to experience in a sequential fashion enabled our forebears better to image, project and hence predict the possible behaviour of peers, based on a sense of their own narrational progression, an appreciation of the meanings behind their own actions (Humphrey 1982: 476–7; Lewin 1988: *passim*). Certainly, stepping back from experience and looking at it askance, as an object, affords an individual the possibility of seeing his life as others might see it; he can relate the plot or plan of his life to the life-course or life-cycle which others might anticipate or provide for him, and then act upon that knowledge. He can negotiate his passage through the course of ageing which family and friends might wish for him (cf. Hockey and James 1993); he can better marry his autobiography with the biography of a family or group (cf. Werbner 1991).

The essence of writing, it has been suggested, is the practice of giving meaning to experience: of stepping back from the present, scrutinizing a given moment and connecting it to others in an ongoing text. Writing is experience-once-removed, or meta-experience. For experience in and of itself is incoherent and meaningless; as Existentialism has it, the truly empirical 'being-in-itself' is 'absurd' (cf. Lyman 1984). Hence, meaning is given to experience through its being cognitively 'written up' as part of an ever reconstituted comprehensible world.

See also: **Cognition, Moments of Being, Narrative**

BIBLIOGRAPHY

Abrahams, R. (1990) 'Chaos and Kachin', *Anthropology Today* 6, 3: 15–17.

Abrams, M. (1988) 'The Deconstructive Angel', in D. Lodge (ed.) *Modern Criticism and Theory*, London: Longman.

Abu-Lughod, L. (1990a) 'Shifting Politics in Bedouin Love Poetry', in C. Lutz and L. Abu-Lughod (eds) *Language and the Politics of Emotion*, Cambridge: Cambridge University Press.

—— (1990b) 'Writing against Culture', in R. Fox (ed.) *Recapturing Anthropology*, Sante Fe, N.Mex: School of American Research Press.

—— (1999) 'Comments upon Christoph Brumann's "Writing for Culture: Why a Successful Concept should not Be Discarded"', *Current Anthropology* 40, Supplement, 13–15.

Aijmer, G. (2000) 'Introduction', in G. Aijmer and J. Abbink (eds) *Meanings of Violence: Symbolism and Structure in Violent Practice*, Oxford: Berg.

Allport, G. (1942) *The Use of Personal Documents in Psychological Science*, New York: Social Science Research Council.

—— (1954) *The Nature of Prejudice*, Reading, Mass.: Addison-Wesley.

American Anthropological Association (1947) 'Statement on Human Rights', *American Anthropologist* 49, 4: 539–43.

Amit-Talai, V. (1989) *Armenians in London: The Management of Social Boundaries*, Manchester: Manchester University Press.

Amit-Talai, V. and Wulff, H. (eds) (1996) *Youth Cultures*, London: Routledge.

Anderson, B. (1983) *Imagined Communities*, London: Verso.

Appadurai, A. (1990) 'Disjuncture and Difference in the Global Cultural Economy', in *Public Culture* 2, 2: 1–24.

—— (1991a) 'Global Ethnoscapes. Notes and Queries for a Transnational Anthropology', in R. Fox (ed.) *Recapturing Anthropology*, Sante Fe, N.Mex: School of American Research Press.

—— (1991b) 'Marriage, Migration and Money', *Visual Anthropology* 4: 95–102.

Ardener, E. (1975) 'Belief and the Problem of Women', in S. Ardener (ed.) *Perceiving Women*, London: Malaby Press. Originally in Jean La Fontaine (ed.), 1972, *The Interpretation of Ritual*. London: Tavistock.

—— (1985) 'Social Anthropology and the Decline of Modernism', in J. Overing (ed.) *Reason and Morality*, London: Tavistock.

—— (1987) '"Remote Areas": Some Theoretical Considerations', in A. Jackson (ed.) *Anthropology at Home*, London: Routledge.

Ardener, S. (ed.) (1975a) *Perceiving Women*, London: Malaby Press.

—— (1975b) 'Introduction', in S. Ardener (ed.) *Perceiving Women*, London: Malaby Press.

Armes, R. (1987) *Third World Film-Making and the West*, Berkeley: University of California Press.

Asad, T. (1972) 'Market Model, Class, Structure and Consent: A Reconsideration of Swat Political Organization', *Man* 7, 1: 74–94.

—— (ed.) (1975) *Anthropology and the Colonial Encounter*. London: Ithaca Press and Humanities Press.

Asch, T. and Asch, P. (1987) 'Images that Represent Ideas', in M. Biesele *et al.* (eds) *The Past and the Future of !Kung Ethnography*, Hamburg: Buske.

—— (1988) 'Film in Anthropological Research', in P. Hockings and Y. Omori (eds) *Cinematographic Theory and New Directions in Ethnographic Film*, Osaka: National Museum of Ethnology.

Ashley, K. (1990) 'Introduction', in K. Ashley (ed.) *Victor Turner and the Construction of Cultural Criticism. Between Literature and Anthropology*, Bloomington, Indiana University Press.

Ashmore, R. and Del Boca, F. (1981) 'Conceptual Approaches to Stereotypes and Stereotyping', in D. Hamilton (ed.) *Cognitive Processes in Stereotyping and Intergroup Behavior*, Hillsdale, NJ: Erlbaum.

Atran, S. (1993) 'Whither "Ethnoscience"?', in P. Boyer (ed.) *Cognitive Aspects of Religious Symbolism*, Cambridge: Cambridge University Press.

Auge, M. (1995) *Non-places: Introduction to an Anthropology of Supermodernity*, London: Verso.

Augustine of Hippo (1907) *The Confessions*, London: Dent.

Austin, J. (1971) 'Performative–Constative', in J. Searle (ed.) *The Philosophy of Language*, Oxford: Oxford University Press.

—— (1975) *How to Do Things with Words*, Oxford: Oxford University Press.

Austin-Smith, B. (1990) 'Into the Heart of Irony', *Canadian Dimension* 27, 7: 51–2.

Avruch, K. (1981) *American Immigrants in Israel*, Chicago: University of Chicago Press.

Ayer, A. (1968) 'Can There Be a Private Language?', in G. Pitcher (ed.) *Wittgenstein*, London: Macmillan.

Bachelard, G. (1994) *The Poetics of Space*, Boston: Beacon.

Baier, A. (1994) *Moral Prejudices*, Cambridge, Mass.: Harvard University Press.

Bailey, F. (1957) *Caste and the Economic Frontier*, Manchester: Manchester University Press.

—— (1969) *Stratagems and Spoils*, Oxford: Blackwell.

—— (ed.) (1971) *Gifts and Poison*, Oxford: Blackwell.

Bakhtin, M. (1981) *The Dialogic Imagination*, Austin: University of Texas Press.

—— (1984) *Problems of Dostoevsky's Poetics*, Minneapolis: University of Minnesota Press.

Ballard, R. (1987) 'The Political Economy of Migration: Pakistan, Britain, and the Middle East', in J. Eades (ed.) *Migrants, Workers and the Social Order*, London: Tavistock.

Banfield, E. (1958) *The Moral Basis of a Backward Society*, New York: Free Press.

Barfield, T. (ed.) (1997) *The Dictionary of Anthropology*, Oxford: Blackwell.

Barnard, A. and Spencer, J. (eds) (1996) *Encyclopedia of Social and Cultural Anthropology*, London: Routledge.

Barnes, J. (1954) 'Class and Committees in a Norwegian Island Parish', *Human Relations* 7: 39–58.

—— (1978) 'Neither Peasants nor Townsmen: a Critique of a Segment of the Folk–Urban Continuum', in F. Barth (ed.) *Scale and Social Organization*, Oslo: Greig.

Barth, F. (1959) *Political Leadership among the Swat Pathans*, London: Athlone.

—— (1966) *Models of Social Organization*, London: RAI Occasional Paper 23.

—— (1969) *Ethnic Groups and Boundaries*, Boston: Little, Brown.

—— (1992) 'Towards a Greater Naturalism in Conceptualising Societies', in A. Kuper (ed.) *Conceptualising Society*, London: Routledge.

Barthes, R. (1973 [1957]) *Mythologies* (orig. pub. in French, Paris: Editions du Seuil), London: Paladin.

—— (1982) 'Introduction to the Structural Analysis of Narratives', in S. Sontag (ed.) *A Barthes Reader*, London: Cape.

Bartlett, F. (1932) *Remembering*, Cambridge: Cambridge University Press.

Basow, S. (1980) *Sex-Role Stereotypes*, Monterey: Brooks/Cole.

Bateson, G. (1936) *Naven*, Cambridge: Cambridge University Press.

—— (1951) (with J. Ruesch) *Communication*, New York: Norton.

—— (1958) 'Language and Psychotherapy', *Psychiatry* 21: 96–100.

—— (1959) 'Anthropological Theories', *Science* 129: 294–8.

—— (1972) *Steps to an Ecology of Mind*, London: Paladin.

—— (1974) (with D. Jackson, J. Haley and J. Weakland) 'Towards a Theory of Schizophrenia', in D. Jackson (ed.) *Communication, Family and Marriage*, Palo Alto, Calif.: Science and Behavior Books.

—— (1980) *Mind and Nature: A Necessary Unity*, Glasgow: Fontana.

Bateson, G. and Mead, M. (1942) *Balinese Character. A Photographic Analysis*, New York: New York Academy of Sciences (Special Publications 2).

Baudrillard, J. (1989) *Selected Writings*, Cambridge: Polity.

Bauman, R. and Briggs, C. (1990) 'Poetics and Performance as Critical Perspectives on Language and Social Life', *Annual Review of Anthropology* 19: 59–88.

Bauman, R. and Sherzer, J. (eds) (1974) *Explorations in the Ethnography of Speaking*, Cambridge: Cambridge University Press.

Bauman, Z. (1990) 'Modernity and Ambivalence', *Theory, Culture and Society* 7: 143–69.

—— (1995) *Life in Fragments: Essays in Postmodern Morality*, Oxford: Blackwell.

Beattie, J. (1964) *Other Cultures*, London: Cohen & West.

—— (1966) 'Ritual and Social Change', *Man* 1: 60–74.

Beck, U. (1992) *Risk Society*, London: Sage.

Becker, H. (1964) 'Problems in the Publications of Community Studies', in A. Vidich, J. Bensman and M. Stein (eds) *Reflections on Community Studies*, New York: Wiley.

—— (1977) *Sociological Work: Method and Substance*, New Brunswick, NJ: Transaction.

Belaunde, E. (1992) *Gender, Commensality and Community among the Airo-Pai of West Amazonia (Secoya, Western-Tukanoan Speaking)*, PhD Thesis, University of London.

—— (1994) 'Parrots and Oropendolas: The Aesthetics of Gender Relations among the Airo-Pai of the Peruvian Amazon', *Journal de la Société des Américanistes*, 80: 95–111.

Bellah, R. (1964) 'Religious Evolution', *American Sociological Review* XXIX: 358–74.

—— (1977) 'Foreword', in P. Rabinow, *Reflections on Fieldwork in Morocco*, Berkeley: University of California Press.

Benedict, R. (1934) *Patterns of Culture*, Boston: Houghton Mifflin.
—— (1938) 'Continuities and Discontinuities in Cultural Conditioning', *Psychiatry* 1: 161–7.
Benhabib, S. (1992) *Situating the Self: Gender, Community and Postmodernism in Contemporary Ethics*, Cambridge: Polity.
Berger, J. (1975) *A Seventh Man*, Harmondsworth: Penguin.
—— (1979) *Pig Earth*, London: Writers & Readers.
—— (1984) *And Our Faces, My Heart, Brief as Photos*, London: Writers & Readers.
—— (1994) *A Telling Eye: The Work of John Berger*, BBC 2, 30 July.
Berger, P. (1963) *Invitation to Sociology: A Humanistic Perspective*, Harmondsworth: Penguin.
—— (1969) *The Social Reality of Religion*, London: Faber.
—— (1970) 'Identity as a Problem in the Sociology of Knowledge', in J. Curtis and J. Petras (eds) *The Sociology of Knowledge*, London: Duckworth.
Berger, P. and Luckmann, T. (1966) *The Social Construction of Reality*, New York: Doubleday.
—— (1969) 'Sociology of Religion and Sociology of Knowledge', in R. Robertson (ed.) *Sociology of Religion*, Harmondsworth: Penguin.
Berger, P., Berger, B. and Kellner, H. (1973) *The Homeless Mind*, New York: Random House.
Berlin, B. (1992) *Ethnobiological Classification: Principles of Categorization of Plants and Animals in Traditional Societies*, Princeton, NJ: Princeton University Press.
Berlin, B. and Kay, P. (1969) *Basic Color Terms: Their Universality and Evolution*, Berkeley: University of California Press.
Berlin, I. (1990) *The Crooked Timber of Humanity*, London: Murray.
Bernstein, B. (1964) 'Aspects of Language and Learning in the Genesis of the Social Process', in D. Hymes (ed.) *Language in Culture and Society*, New York: Harper & Row.
—— (1972) 'A Sociolinguistic Approach to Socialization: With some Reference to Educability', in J. Gumperz and D. Hymes (eds) *Directions in Sociolinguistics*, New York: Holt, Rinehart & Winston.
—— (1973) *Class, Codes and Control*, St. Albans: Paladin.
Bhabha, H. (1990) *Nation and Narration*, London: Routledge.
—— (1994) *The Location of Culture*, London: Routledge.
Birdwhistell, R. (1970) *Kinesics and Context*, Philadelphia: University of Pennsylvania Press.
Blakemore, C. (1988) *The Mind Machine*, London: BBC.
Blau, P. (1967) *Exchange and Power in Social Life*, New York: Wiley.
Bloch, M. (1975) 'Introduction', in M. Bloch (ed.) *Political Language and Oratory in Traditional Society*, London: Academic Press.
—— (1977) 'The Past and the Present in the Present', *Man* n.s. 12, 2: 278–92.
—— (1986) *From Blessing to Violence*, Cambridge: Cambridge University Press.
—— (1988) 'An Interview with Maurice Bloch' (ed. G. Houtman), *Anthropology Today* 4, 1: 18–21.
—— (1998) *How We Think They Think. Anthropological Approaches to Cognition, Memory and Literacy*, Boulder, Colo.: Westview.
Bluebond-Langner, M. (1978) *The Private Worlds of Dying Children*, Princeton, NJ: Princeton University Press.
Blumer, H. (1969) *Symbolic Interactionism*, Englewood Cliffs, NJ: Prentice-Hall.

—— (1972) 'Society as Symbolic Interaction', in A. Rose (ed.) *Human Behaviour and Social Processes*, London: Routledge & Kegan Paul.

Boas, F. (1886) 'The Limitations of the Comparative Method of Anthropology', *Science* 4, no. 103.

—— (1911) *The Mind of Primitive Man*, New York: Macmillan.

Bohannan, P. and Middleton, J. (eds) (1968) *Kinship and Social Organization*, Garden City, NY: Natural History Press.

Boissevain, J. (1974) *Friends of Friends*, Oxford: Blackwell.

—— (1979) 'Network Analysis: A Reappraisal', *Current Anthropology* 20: 392–4.

Boon, J. (1982) *Other Tribes, Other Scribes*, Cambridge: Cambridge University Press.

Boonzaier, E. and Sharp. J. (eds) (1988) *South African Keywords: The Uses and Abuses of Political Concepts*, Cape Town: Philip.

Bott, E. (1964) *Family and Social Network*, London: Tavistock.

Boulware-Miller, K. (1985) 'Female Circumcision: Challenges to the Practice as a Human Rights Violation', *Harvard Women's Law Journal* 8: 155–77.

Bouquet, M. and Winter, M. (eds) (1987) *'"Who From their Labours Rest?" Conflict and Practice in Rural Tourism'*, Aldershot: Avebury.

Bourdieu, P. (1977) *Outline of a Theory of Practice*, Cambridge: Cambridge University Press.

Bourgois, P. (1995) *In Search of Respect*, Cambridge: Cambridge University Press.

Boyarin, J. (ed.) (1993) *The Ethnography of Reading*, Berkeley: University of California Press.

Bradbury, R. (1966) 'Howards End', in M. Bradbury (ed.) *Forster*, Englewood Cliffs, NJ: Prentice-Hall.

Brady, I. (ed.) (1991a) *Anthropological Poetics*, Savage, Md: Rowman-Littlefield.

—— (1991b) 'Harmony and Argument: Bringing Forth the Artful Science', in I. Brady (ed.) *Anthropological Poetics*, Savage, Md: Rowman-Littlefield.

Brady, I. and Turner, E. (eds) (1994) 'Humanism and Anthropology', *Anthropology and Humanism* (Special Issue) 19: 1–103.

Brett, G. (1991) 'Unofficial Versions', in S. Hiller (ed.) *The Myth of Primitivism*, London: Routledge.

Briggs, J. (1970) *Never in Anger*, Cambridge Mass.: Harvard University Press.

—— (1992) 'Mazes of Meaning: How a Child and a Culture Create Each Other', in W. Corsaro and P. Miller (eds) *Interpretive Approaches to Children's Socialization*, San Francisco: Jossey-Bass.

—— (1998) *Inuit Morality Play: The Emotional Education of a Three-Year-Old*, New Haven, Conn.: Yale University Press.

Brown, G. and Yule, G. (1983) *Discourse Analysis*, Cambridge: Cambridge University Press.

Brown, P. and Levinson, S. (1978) 'Universals in Language Usage', in E. Goody (ed.) *Questions and Politeness*, Cambridge: Cambridge University Press.

Bruner, E. (ed.) (1983) *Text, Play and Story*, Washington: American Ethnological Society.

—— (1986) 'Ethnography as Narrative', in V. Turner and E. Bruner (eds) *The Anthropology of Experience*, Urbana: University of Illinois Press.

Bruner, J. (1990) *Acts of Meaning*, Cambridge, Mass.: Harvard University Press.

Bruner, J. and Haste, H. (eds) (1987) *Making Sense. The Child's Construction of the World*, London: Methuen.

Bruner, J. and Weisser, S. (1991) 'The Invention of Self: Autobiography and its

Forms', in D. Olson and N. Torrance (eds) *Literacy and Orality*, Cambridge: Cambridge University Press.

Burke, K. (1973) *The Philosophy of Literary Form: Studies in Symbolic Action*, Berkeley: University of California Press.

Burridge, K. (1979) *Someone, No One. An Essay on Individuality*, Princeton, NJ: Princeton University Press.

Callaway, H. (1992) 'Ethnography and Experience: Gender Implications in Fieldwork and Texts', in J. Okely and H. Callaway (eds) *Anthropology and Autobiography*, London: Routledge.

Campbell, A. (1989) *To Square with Genesis: Causal Statements and Shamanic Ideas in Wayãpí*, Edinburgh: Edinburgh University Press.

—— (1995) *Getting to Know WaiWai. An Amazonian Ethnography*, London: Routledge.

Caplan, P. (ed.) (1987) *The Cultural Construction of Sexuality*, London: Tavistock.

Carrier, J. (ed.) (1995) *Occidentalism*, Oxford: Oxford University Press.

Carrithers, M., Collins, S. and Lukes, S. (eds) (1985) *The Category of the Person. Anthropology, Philosophy, History*, Cambridge: Cambridge University Press.

Carsten, J. (1991) 'Children in Between: Fostering and the Process of Kinship in Pulau Langkawi, Malaysia', *Man* 26, 3: 425–43.

Carsten, J. and Hugh-Jones, S. (eds) (1995) *About the House*, Cambridge: Cambridge University Press.

Carter, P. (1992) *Living in a New Country. History, Travelling and Language*, London: Faber.

Cerroni-Long, E.L. (1999) 'Comments upon Christoph Brumann's "Writing for Culture: Why a Successful Concept should not Be Discarded"', *Current Anthropology*, 40, Supplement, 15–16.

Chagnon, N. and Irons, W. (1979) *Evolutionary Biology and Human Social Behavior*, North Scituate, Mass.: Duxbury.

Chalmers, D. (1996) *The Conscious Mind*, Oxford: Oxford University Press.

Chambers Twentieth Century Dictionary (1966) ed. W. Geddie, Chambers: Edinburgh.

Chambers, I. (1994a) *Migrancy Culture Identity*, London: Routledge.

—— (1994b) 'Leaky Habitats and Broken Grammar', in G. Robertson *et al.* (eds) *Travellers' Tales. Narratives of Home and Displacement*, London: Routledge.

Chapman, D. (1968) *Sociology and the Stereotype of the Criminal*, London: Tavistock.

Cheater, A. (1987) 'The Anthropologist as Citizen: The Diffracted Self?', in A. Jackson (ed.) *Anthropology at Home*, London: Routledge.

Chodorow, N. (1994) 'Reflections on Personal Meaning and Cultural Meaning', paper presented at the American Anthropological Association Meeting, Atlanta, Ga.

Churchland, P.S. (1994) 'Can Neurobiology Teach us Anything about Consciousness?', *Proceedings and Addresses of the American Philosophical Association* 67, 4: 23–40.

Cixous, H. (1990) *The Body and the Text* (ed. H. Wilcox *et al.*), London: Harvester Wheatsheaf.

Clastres, P. (1977) *Society against the State: the Leader as Servant and the Humane Uses of Power among the Indians of the Americas*, Oxford: Basil Blackwell.

Claxton, G. (1979) 'Individual Relativity: The Model of Man in Modern Physics', *Bulletin of the British Psychological Society* 32: 414–18.

Clay, J. (1988) 'Anthropologists and Human Rights – Activists by Default?', in

T. Downing and G. Kushner (eds) *Human Rights and Anthropology*, Cambridge, Mass.: Cultural Survival.

Clifford, J. (1986) 'Introduction: Partial Truths', in G. Marcus and J. Clifford (eds) *Writing Culture*, Berkeley: University of California Press.

—— (1988) *The Predicament of Culture: Twentieth-Century Ethnography, Literature and Art*, Cambridge, Mass.: Harvard University Press.

—— (1990) 'Notes on (Field)notes', in R. Sanjek (ed.) *Fieldnotes, The Making of Anthropology*, Ithaca, NY: Cornell University Press.

—— (1992) 'Travelling Cultures', in L. Grossberg, C. Nelson and P. Treichler (eds) *Cultural Studies*, London: Routledge.

Cohen, A. (1982) 'Drama and Politics in the Development of a London Carnival', in R. Frankenberg (ed.) *Custom and Conflict in British Society*, Manchester: Manchester University Press.

Cohen, A.P. (1975) *The Management of Myths*, Manchester: Manchester University Press.

—— (1985) *The Symbolic Construction of Community*, Chichester: Horwood.

—— (1987) *Whalsay. Symbol, Segment and Boundary in a Shetland Island Community*, Manchester: Manchester University Press.

—— (1989) 'Opposing the Motion that "Social Anthropology Is a Generalising Science or it Is Nothing"', *Group for Debates in Anthropological Theory*, Department of Social Anthropology, University of Manchester.

—— (1992a) 'Self-conscious Anthropology', in J. Okely and H. Callaway (eds) *Anthropology and Autobiography*, London: Routledge.

—— (1992b) 'Post-fieldwork Fieldwork', *Journal of Anthropological Research* 48: 339–54.

—— (1993) 'Introduction', in A.P. Cohen and K. Fukui (eds) *Humanising the City? Social Contexts of Urban Life at the Turn of the Millennium*, Edinburgh: Edinburgh University Press.

—— (1994) *Self Consciousness. An Alternative Anthropology of Identity*, London: Routledge.

Cohen A.P. and Rapport, N.J. (1995) 'Introduction: Consciousness in Anthropology', in A.P. Cohen and N.J. Rapport (eds) *Questions of Consciousness*, London: Routledge.

Cohen, E. (1977) 'Arab Boys and Tourist Girls in a Mixed Arab/Jewish Community', *International Journal of Comparative Sociology* 12, 4: 217–33.

—— (1979) 'A Phenomenology of Tourist Experiences', *Sociology* 13: 179–201.

—— (1988) 'Authenticity and Commoditization in Tourism', *Annals of Tourism Research* 15: 371–86.

Collier, J.F. and Yanagisako, S.J. (eds) (1987) *Gender and Kinship: Essays toward a Unified Analysis*, Stanford, Calif.: Stanford University Press.

Collingwood, R.G. (1940) *Essays on Metaphysics*, Oxford: Clarendon Press.

Colson, E. (1953) *The Makah Indians*, Manchester: Manchester University Press.

Conklin, B. (1998) 'Cannibalism in Europe and South America: Comparative Political Economies of Body Parts', paper presented at the American Anthropological Association meeting, Philadelphia, Pa.

Conquergood, D. (1988) 'Health Theatre in a Hmong Refugee Camp', *Journal of Performance Studies* 32: 174–208.

Coote, J. and Shelton, A. (eds) (1991) *Anthropology, Art and Aesthetics*, Oxford: Oxford University Press.

Corbey, R. (1991) 'Freud's Phylogenetic Narrative', in R. Corbey and J. Leerssen (eds) *Alterity, Identity, Image: Selves and Others in Society and Scholarship*, Amsterdam, Atlanta, Ga: Rodopi.

Corbey, R. and Leerssen, J. (1991) 'Studying Alterity: Backgrounds and Perspectives', in R. Corbey and J. Leerssen (eds), *Alterity, Identity, Image: Selves and Others in Society and Scholarship*, Amsterdam, Atlanta, Ga.: Rodopi.

Cornwell, J. (1994) 'Is Mind Really Matter?', *The Sunday Times* 15 May: 10/4–10/6.

Cote, D. (1987) 'Valle d'Aosta and the Lake District: A Comparison of Issues and Approaches to Recreational and Residential Growth', in M. Bouquet and M. Winter (eds) *'Who From their Labours Rest?' Conflict and Practice in Rural Tourism*, Aldershot: Avebury.

Coulter, J. (1979) 'Beliefs and Practical Understanding', in G. Psathas (ed.) *Everyday Language: Studies in Ethnomethodology*, New York: Irvington.

Coutts-Smith, K. (1991 [1976]) 'Some General Observations on the Problem of Cultural Colonialism', in S. Hiller (ed.) *The Myth of Primitivism*, London: Routledge.

Cranston, M. (1953) *Freedom*, London: Longmans, Green.

Crapanzano, V. (1980) *Tuhami: Portrait of a Moroccan*, Chicago: University of Chicago Press.

Crawford, J. (ed.) (1988) *The Rights of Peoples*, Oxford: Clarendon.

Crawford, P. and Turton, D. (eds) (1992) *Film as Ethnography*, Manchester: Manchester University Press.

Crick, B. (1974) *Crime, Rape and Gin*, London: Elek.

Crick, F. (1994) *The Astonishing Hypothesis. The Scientific Search for the Soul*, New York: Simon & Schuster.

Crick, M. (1989) 'Representations of International Tourism in the Social Sciences: Sun, Sex, Sights, Savings and Servility', in *Annual Review of Anthropology* 18: 307–44.

Crites, S. (1971) 'The Narrative Quality of Experience', *Journal of the American Academy of Religion* XXXIX: 291–311.

Crocker, J.C. (1977) 'My Brother the Parrot', in J.D. Sapir and J.C. Crocker (eds) *The Social Use of Metaphor*, University of Pennsylvania.

—— (1985) *Vital Souls: Bororo Cosmology, Natural Symbolism, and Shamanism*, Tucson: University of Arizona Press.

Csordas, T. (1994) *Embodiment and Experience: The Existential Grounds of Culture and Self*, Cambridge: Cambridge University Press.

Culler, J. (1981) *The Pursuit of Signs: Semiotics, Literature, Deconstruction*, Ithaca, NY: Cornell University Press.

Dasen, P. (1994) 'Culture and Cognitive Development from a Piagetian Perspective', in W. Lonner and R. Malpass (eds) *Psychology and Culture*, Boston: Allyn & Bacon.

D'Andrade, R. (1984) 'Cultural Meaning Systems', in R. Shweder and R. LeVine (eds) *Culture Theory: Essays on Mind, Self, and Emotion*, Cambridge: Cambridge University Press.

de Certeau, M. (1997) *Culture in the Plural*, Minneapolis: University of Minnesota.

DeLillo, D. (1991) 'The Word, the Image and the Gun', *Omnibus*, BBC 1 Television, 27 September.

Dennett, D. (1991) *Consciousness Explained*, London: Penguin.

Descola, P. (1994) *In the Society of Nature: A Native Ecology in Amazonia*, Cambridge: Cambridge University Press.

—— (1996) *The Spears of Twilight: Life and Death in the Amazon Jungle*, London: Harper Collins.

Devereux, G. (1978) *Ethnopsychoanalysis*, Berkeley: University of California Press.

Dewhirst, I. (1972) *Gleanings from Victorian Yorkshire*, Driffield: Ridings.

Dias, N. (1994) 'Looking at Objects: Memory, Knowledge in Nineteenth Century Ethnographic Displays', in G. Robertson *et al.* (eds) *Travellers' Tales. Narratives of Home and Displacement*, London: Routledge.

Dickens, C. (1971) *Hard Times*, Harmondsworth: Penguin.

di Leonardo, M. (1998) *Exotics at Home: Anthropologies, Others, American Modernity*, Chicago: University of Chicago Press.

Douglas, J. and Johnson, J. (eds) (1977) *Existential Sociology*, Cambridge: Cambridge University Press.

Douglas, M. (1966) *Purity and Danger*, London: Routledge & Kegan Paul.

—— (1991) 'The Idea of Home: A Kind of Space', *Social Research* 58, 1: 287–307.

—— (1992) *Risk and Blame*, London: Routledge.

Downing, T. and Kushner, G. (eds) (1988) *Human Rights and Anthropology*, Cambridge, Mass.: Cultural Survival.

Drazdauskierie, M-L. (1981) 'On Stereotypes in Conversation, their Meaning and Significance', in F. Coulmas (ed.) *Conversational Routine*, The Hague: Mouton.

Dreitzel, H.-P. (1970) 'Introduction', in H.-P. Dreitzel (ed.) *Patterns of Communicative Behaviour*, London: Collier-Macmillan.

Drummond, L. (1980) 'The Cultural Continuum: A Theory of Intersystems', *Man* 15: 352–74.

Du Bois, C. (1944) *The People of Alor*, Minneapolis: University of Minnesota Press.

Duerr, H.P. (1985) *Dreamtime: Concerning the Boundary between Wilderness and Civilization*, tr. F. Goudman, Oxford: Blackwell.

Dumont, J.-P. (1978) *The Headman and I*, Austin: University of Texas Press.

Dumont, L. (1953) 'The Dravidian Kinship Terminology as an Expression of Marriage', *Man* LIII, 224: 143.

—— (1977) *From Mandeville to Marx: The Genesis and Triumph of Economic Ideology*, Chicago: University of Chicago Press.

—— (1986) *Essays on Individualism*, Chicago: University of Chicago Press.

Dunning, E., Murphy, P. and Williams, J. (1988) *The Roots of Football Hooliganism*, London: Routledge.

Durkheim, E. (1964 [1893]) *The Division of Labor in Society*, New York: Free Press.

—— (1966 [1895]) *The Rules of Sociological Method*, New York: Free Press.

—— (1973 [1925]) *Moral Education*, New York: Free Press.

Durkheim, E. and Mauss, M. (1970 [1903]) *Primitive Classification*, London: Routledge.

Dwyer, K. (1982) *Moroccan Dialogues*, Baltimore: Johns Hopkins University Press.

Eade, J. and Sallnow, M. (eds) (1991) *Contesting the Sacred*, London: Routledge.

Eagleton, T. (1981) *Walter Benjamin or Towards a Revolutionary Criticism*, London: New Left Books.

—— (1988) 'Capitalism, Modernism and Postmodernism', in D. Lodge (ed.) *Modern Criticism and Theory*, London: Longman.

Eccles, J. (1994) *How the Self Controls Its Brain*, London: Springer-Verlag.

Edelman, G. (1989) *The Remembered Present. A Biological Theory of Consciousness*, New York: Basic Books.

—— (1992) *Bright Air, Brilliant Fire. On the Matter of the Mind*, Harmondsworth: Penguin.

417

Edwards, J. (2000) *Born and Bred: Idioms of Relatedness in Late-Twentieth Century England*, Oxford: Oxford University Press.

Edwards, J., Franklin, S., Hirsch, E. and Strathern, M. (1993) *Technologies of Procreation: Kinship in the Age of Assisted Conception*, Manchester: Manchester University Press.

Elfenbein, A. (1989) *Women on the Color Line*, Charlottesville: Virginia University Press.

Eliade, M. (1954) *The Myth of the Eternal Return, or Cosmos and History*, Princeton, NJ: Princeton University Press.

—— (1959) *The Sacred and the Profane*, New York: Harcourt, Brace.

Ellen, R. (1993) *The Cultural Relations of Classification*, Cambridge: Cambridge University Press.

—— (1997) 'Classification', in A. Barnard and J. Spencer (eds) *Encyclopedia of Social and Cultural Anthropology*, London: Routledge.

Eller, J.D. (1997) 'Anti-anti-multiculturalism', *American Anthropologist* 99: 249–60.

Ellmann, R. (1977) *The Consciousness of Joyce*, London: Faber.

Ennew, J. (1986) *The Sexual Exploitation of Children*, Cambridge: Polity.

Erickson, V. (1988) '*Buddenbrooks*, Thomas Mann and North German Social Class: An Application of Literary Anthropology', in F. Poyatos (ed.) *Literary Anthropology*, Amsterdam: Benjamins.

Erikson, E. (1977) *Childhood and Society*, St. Albans: Paladin.

Evans-Pritchard, E. (1950) *Witchcraft, Oracles and Magic among the Azande*, Oxford: Oxford University Press.

—— (1962) 'Social Anthropology: Past and Present'. in E.E. Evans-Pritchard, *Social Anthropology and Other Essays*, New York: Free Press.

Ewing, K. (1990) 'The Illusion of Wholeness: Culture, Self and the Experience of Inconsistency', *Ethos* 18: 251–78.

Fabian, J. (1983) *Time and the Other: How Anthropology Makes its Object*, New York: Columbia University Press.

—— (1998) *Moments of Freedom: Anthropology and Popular Culture*, Charlottesville: University Press of Virginia.

Falk, R. (1980) 'Theoretical Foundations of Human Rights' in P. Newberg (ed.) *The Politics of Human Rights*, New York: New York University Press.

Fanon, F. (1968) *The Wretched of the Earth*, New York: Grove.

Fardon, R. (1992) 'Postmodern Anthropology? Or, an Anthropology of Postmodernity?', in J. Doherty, E. Graham and M. Malek (eds) *Postmodernism and the Social Sciences*, London: Macmillan.

—— (ed.) (1995a) *Counterworks: Managing the Diversity of Knowledge*, London: Routledge.

—— (1995b) 'Introduction: Counterworks', in R. Fardon (ed.) *Counterworks: Managing the Diversity of Knowledge*, London: Routledge.

Favret-Saada, J. (1980) *Deadly Words*, Cambridge: Cambridge University Press.

Featherstone, M. (1990) 'Global Culture: An Introduction', in M. Featherstone (ed.) *Global Culture: Nationalism, Globalisation and Modernity*, London: Sage.

Feldman, A. (1991) *Formations of Violence*, Chicago: University of Chicago Press.

Felstiner, J. (1994) *Paul Celan*, New Haven, Conn.: Yale University Press.

Fernandez, J. (1971) 'Persuasions and Performances: Of the Beast in Every Body . . . and the Metaphors of Everyman', in C. Geertz (ed.) *Myth, Symbol and Culture*, New York: Norton.

—— (1977) 'Poetry in Motion: Being Moved by Amusement, by Mockery and by Mortality in the Asturian Countryside', *New Literary History* VIII, 3: 459–83.

—— (1982) *Bwiti. An Ethnography of the Religious Imagination in Africa*, Princeton, NJ: Princeton University Press.

—— (1985) 'Macrothought', *American Ethnologist* 12, 4: 749–57.

—— (1986) *Persuasions and Performances: The Play of Tropes in Culture*, Bloomington: Indiana University Press.

—— (1992) 'What it Is like to Be a Banzie: On Sharing the Experience of an Equatorial Microcosm', in J. Gort, H. Vroom, R. Fernhout and A. Wessels (eds) *On Sharing Religious Experience*, Amsterdam: Rodopi.

—— (1993) 'Ceferino Suarez: A Village Versifier', in S. Lavie, K. Narayan and R. Rosaldo (eds) *Creativity/Anthropology*, Ithaca, NY: Cornell University Press.

—— (1995) 'Amazing Grace: Meaning Deficit, Displacement and New Consciousness in Expressive Interaction', in A.P. Cohen and N.J. Rapport (eds) *Questions of Consciousness*, London: Routledge.

Feyerabend, P. (1975) *Against Method*, London: New Left Books.

Fillmore, C. (1976) *Statistical Methods in Linguistics*, Stockholm: Skriptor.

—— (1979) 'On Fluency', in C. Fillmore, D. Kempler and W. Wang (eds) *Individual Differences in Language Ability and Language Behavior*, New York: Academic Press.

Filstead, W. (ed.) (1970) *Qualitative Methodology*, Chicago: Markham.

Finnegan, R. (1977) *Oral Poetry*, Cambridge: Cambridge University Press.

—— (1989) *The Hidden Musicians*, Cambridge: Cambridge University Press.

Firth, R. (1951) *Elements of Social Organization*, London: Watts.

Fish, S. (1972) *Self-Consuming Artefacts*, Berkeley: University of California Press.

—— (1979) 'Normal Circumstances, Literal language, Direct Speech-Acts, the Ordinary, the Everyday, the Obvious, What Goes Without Saying, and Other Special Cases', in P. Rabinow and W. Sullivan (eds) *Interpretive Social Science*, Berkeley: University of California Press.

—— (1988) 'Interpreting the *Variorum*', in D. Lodge (ed.) *Modern Criticism and Theory*, London: Longman.

Flanagan, O. (1992) *Consciousness Reconsidered*, Cambridge, Mass.: MIT Press.

Forster, E.M. (1950) *Howards End*, Harmondsworth: Penguin.

—— (1961) *Collected Short Stories*, Harmondsworth: Penguin.

—— (1984 [1927]) *Aspects of the Novel*, Harmondsworth: Penguin.

Forsythe, D. (1980) 'Urban Incomers and Rural Change. The Impact of Migrants from the City on Life in an Orkney Community', *Sociologia Ruralis* XX: 287–307.

Fortes, M. (1969) *Kinship and the Social Order: the Legacy of Lewis Henry Morgan*, London: Routledge & Kegan Paul.

—— (1970) *Time and Social Structure, and Other Essays*, London: Athlone.

Foster, G. (1965) 'Peasant Society and the Image of Limited Good', *American Anthropologist* 67: 293–314.

Foucault, M. (1972) *The Archaeology of Knowledge*, New York: Harper & Row.

—— (1973) *The Order of Things*, New York: Vintage.

—— (1977) *Discipline and Punish*, New York: Pantheon.

—— (1991) *The Foucault Reader* (ed. P. Rabinow), Harmondsworth: Penguin.

Fox, R. (1967) *Kinship and Marriage: an Anthropological Perspective*, Harmondsworth: Penguin.

Frake, C. (1964) 'Notes on Queries in Ethnography', in J. Gumperz and D. Hymes

(eds) *The Ethnography of Communication*, Washington: American Anthropological Association.
—— (1980) *Language and Cultural Description*, Stanford, Calif.: Stanford University Press.
Frank, A.G. (1965) *Capitalism and Underdevelopment in Latin America*, New York: Monthly Review Press.
Frank, A.W. (1976) 'Making Scenes in Public', *Theory and Society* 3, 3: 395–416.
Frankenberg, R (1957) *Village on the Border*, London: Cohen & West.
—— (1966) *Communities in Britain*, Harmondsworth: Penguin.
Franklin, S. (1995) 'Science as Culture, Cultures of Science', *Annual Reviews in Anthropology* 24: 163–84.
—— (1996) *Embodied Progress: A Cultural Account of Assisted Conception*, London: Routledge.
Fratto, T. (1976) 'Toward an Anthropological Humanism', *Anthropology and Humanism* 1, 1: 1–5.
Freeman, D. (1983) *Margaret Mead and Samoa*, Cambridge, Mass.: Harvard University Press.
Friedman, J. (1994) *Cultural Identity and Global Process*, New York: Basic Books.
Gadamer, H.-G. (1975) *Truth and Method*, New York: Seabury.
—— (1976) *Philosophical Hermeneutics*, Berkeley: University of California Press.
Gans, H. (1965) *The Urban Villagers: Group and Class in the Life of Italian-Americans*, New York: Free Press.
Gardner, K, (1995) *Global Migrants, Local Lives*, Oxford: Clarendon.
Garfinkel, H. (1964) 'Studies of the Routine Grounds of Everyday Activity', *Social Problems* 11: 225–50.
—— (1967) *Studies in Ethnomethodology*, Englewood Cliffs, NJ: Prentice-Hall.
—— (1968) 'Conditions of Successful Status-Degradation Ceremonies', in J. Manis and B. Meltzer (eds) *Symbolic Interaction*, Boston: Allyn & Bacon.
—— (1972) 'Remarks on Ethnomethodology', in J. Gumperz and D. Hymes (eds) *Directions in Sociolinguistics*, New York: Holt, Rinehart & Winston.
Gassen, K. and Landmann, M. (eds) (1958) *Buch des Dankes an Georg Simmel*, Berlin: Verlagsbuchhandlung.
Geertz, C. (1960) *The Religion of Java*, Glencoe, Ill.: Free Press.
—— (1970) 'The Impact of the Concept of Culture on the Concept of Man', in E. Hammel and W. Simmons (eds) *Man Makes Sense*, Boston: Little, Brown.
—— (1971) *Islam Observed*, Chicago: University of Chicago Press.
—— (1973) *The Interpretation of Cultures*, New York: Basic Books.
—— (1976) 'From the Native's Point of View: On the Nature of Anthropological Understanding', in K. Basso and H. Selby (eds) *Meaning in Anthropology*, Albuquerque: University of New Mexico Press.
—— (1983) *Local Knowledge*, New York: Basic Books.
—— (1986) 'The Uses of Diversity', *Michigan Quarterly Review* 25: 105–22.
—— (1988) *Works and Lives: The Anthropologist as Author*, Cambridge: Polity.
—— (1995) *After the Fact*, Cambridge, Mass.: Harvard University Press.
Gell, A. (1992) *An Anthropology of Time*, Oxford: Berg.
Gellner, E. (1959) *Words and Things*, London: Gollancz.
—— (1970) 'Concepts and Society', in B. Wilson (ed.) *Rationality*, Oxford: Blackwell.
—— (1988) 'Origins of Society', in A. Fabian (ed.) *Origins*, Cambridge: Cambridge University Press.

—— (1993) *Postmodernism, Reason and Religion*, London: Routledge.

—— (1995a) *Anthropology and Politics*, Oxford: Blackwell.

—— (1995b) 'Anything Goes: The Carnival of Cheap Relativism which Threatens to Swamp the Coming *Fin de Millenaire*', *Times Literary Supplement* 4811: 6–8.

—— (1998) *Language and Solitude*, Cambridge: Cambridge University Press.

Genette, G. (1980) *Narrative Discourse*, Ithaca, NY: Cornell University Press.

Georges, R. (1969) 'Toward an Understanding of Storytelling Events', *Journal of American Folklore* 82: 313–28.

Giddens, A. (1976) *New Rules of Sociological Method*, London: Hutchinson.

—— (1984) *The Constitution of Society: Outline of the Theory of Structuration*, Cambridge: Polity.

—— (1990) *The Consequences of Modernity*, Stanford, Calif.: Stanford University Press.

Gilad, L. (1990) *The Northern Route: An Ethnography of Refugee Experiences*, St. John's, Nfld: ISER Press, Memorial University.

—— (1996) 'Cultural Collision and Human Rights', in W. Giles, H. Moussa and P. Van Esterik (eds) *Development and Diaspora: Gender and the Refugee Experience*, Dundas, Ont.: Artemis.

Gilligan, C. (1982) *In a Different Voice*, Cambridge, Mass.: Harvard University.

Gillison, G. (1980) 'Images of Nature in Gimi Thought', in C. MacCormack and M. Strathern (eds), *Nature, Culture and Gender*, Cambridge: Cambridge University Press.

—— (1993) *Between Culture and Fantasy: A New Guinea Highlands Mythology*, Chicago: University of Chicago Press.

Gilsenan, M. (1996) *Lords of the Lebanese Marches: Violence and Narrative in an Arab Society*, London: Tauris.

Ginsburg, F. and Rapp, R. (eds) (1995) *Conceiving the New World Order: The Global Politics of Reproduction*, Berkeley: University of California Press.

Glassman, B. (1975) *Anti-Semitic Stereotypes without Jews*, Detroit: Wayne State University Press.

Gluckman, M. (1956) *Custom and Conflict in Africa*, Oxford: Blackwell.

—— (1959) *Custom and Conflict in Africa*, Glencoe, Ill.: Free Press.

—— (1963a) *Order and Rebellion in Tribal Africa*, New York: Free Press.

—— (1963b) 'Gossip and Scandal', *Current Anthropology* 4, 3: 307–15.

Gluckman, M. and Devons E. (1964) 'Introduction', in M. Gluckman (ed.) *Closed Systems and Open Minds: The Limits of Naivety in Social Anthropology*, Chicago: Aldine.

Gmelch, G. (1980) 'Return Migration', *Annual Review of Anthropology* 9: 135–59.

Goffman, E. (1972) *Encounters*, London: Penguin.

—— (1978) *The Presentation of Self in Everyday Life*, Harmondsworth: Penguin.

Goldschlaeger, A. (1985) 'On Ideological Discourse', *Semiotica* (special issue: 'The Rhetoric of Violence') 54, 1/2: 165–76.

Gomme, G.L. (1890) *The Village Community*, London: Scott.

Gonzalez, N. (1992) *Dollar, Dove and Eagle: One Hundred Years of Palestinian Migration to Honduras*, Ann Arbor: University of Michigan Press.

Goodenough, W. (1963) *Cooperation in Change*, New York: Sage.

Goodman, N. (1978) *Ways of Worldmaking*, Hassocks: Harvester.

—— (1984) *Of Mind and Other Matters*, Cambridge, Mass.: Harvard University Press.

Goodman, R. (1993) *Japan's International Youth*, Oxford: Oxford University Press.

Goody, E. (ed.) (1978) *Questions and Politeness: Strategies in Social Interaction*, Cambridge: Cambridge University Press.

—— (1982) *Parenthood and Social Reproduction*, Cambridge: Cambridge University Press.

Goody, J. (1977) *The Domestication of the Savage Mind*, Cambridge: Cambridge University Press.

—— (1983) *The Development of the Family and Marriage in Europe*, Cambridge: Cambridge University Press.

Goody, J. and Watt, I. (1968) 'The Consequences of Literacy', in J. Goody (ed.) *Literacy in Traditional Societies*, Cambridge: Cambridge University Press.

Goonatilake, S. (1984) *Aborted Discovery. Science and Creativity in the Third World*, London: Zed.

Gordon-Grube, K. (1988) 'Anthropophagy in Post-Renaissance Europe: The Tradition of Medicinal Cannibalism', *American Anthropologist* 90: 405–9.

Gossen, G. (1996) 'Animal Souls, Co-essences, and Human Destiny in Mesoamerica', in A.J. Arnold (ed.) *Monsters, Tricksters, and Sacred Cows: Animal Tales and American Identities*, Charlottesville: University Press of Virginia.

Gow, P. (1991) *Of Mixed Blood*, Oxford: Clarendon.

Graburn, N. (1983a) *To Pray, Pay and Play*, Aix-en-Provence: Centre des Hautes Etudes Touristiques.

—— (1983b) 'The Anthropology of Tourism', *Annals of Tourism Research* 10, 1: 9–33.

Graburn, N. and Jafari, J. (eds) (1991) *Annals of Tourism Research* (special issue: 'Tourism Social Sciences') 18, 1.

Greenwood, D. (1989) 'Culture by the Pound. An Anthropological Perspective on Tourism as Cultural Commoditization', in V. Smith (ed.) *Hosts and Guests*, Oxford: Blackwell.

Greimas, A. (1983) *On Meaning*, Minneapolis: University of Minnesota Press.

Grillo, R. (1980) 'Introduction', in R. Grillo (ed.) *'Nation' and 'State' in Europe*, London: Academic Press.

—— (1985) *Ideologies and Institutions in Urban France*, Cambridge: Cambridge University Press.

Grimshaw, A. (1992) *Servants of the Buddha*, London: Open Letters.

—— (1994) 'The Eye in the Door. Anthropology, Film and the Exploration of Interior Space', unpublished paper, Dept of Social Anthropology, Manchester University.

Gumperz, J. (1970) 'Linguistic and Social Interaction in Two Communities', in E. Hammel and W. Simmons (eds) *Man Makes Sense*, Boston: Little, Brown.

—— (1972) 'Introduction', in J. Gumperz and D. Hymes (eds) *Directions in Sociolinguistics*, New York: Holt, Rinehart & Winston.

Gumperz, J. and Hymes D. (1972) 'Editorial Introduction', in *Directions in Sociolinguistics*, New York: Holt, Rinehart & Winston.

Gumperz, J. and Tannen, D. (1979) 'Individual and Social Differences in Language Use', in C. Fillmore, D. Kempler and W. Wang (eds) *Individual Differences in Language Ability and Language Behavior*, New York: Academic Press.

Gusfield, J. (1975) *Community*, Oxford: Blackwell.

Guss, D. (1989) *To Weave and to Sing: Art, Symbol, and Narrative in the South American Rain Forest*, Berkeley: University of California Press.

Gusterson, H. (1996) *Nuclear Rites*, Berkeley: University of California Press.

Hage, P. and Harary, F. (1983) *Structural Models in Anthropology*, Cambridge: Cambridge University Press.

Handler, R. and Segal D. (1990) *Jane Austen and the Fiction of Culture: An Essay on the Narration of Social Realities*, Tucson: University of Arizona Press.

Hanke, L. (1959) *Aristotle and the American Indians: A Study of Race Prejudice and the Modern World*, London: Hollis and Carter.

Hannerz, U. (1969) *Soulside*, New York: Columbia University Press.

—— (1980) *Exploring the City*, New York: Columbia University Press.

—— (1987) 'The World in Creolization', *Africa* 57, 4: 546–59.

—— (1992) 'The Global Ecumene as a Network of Networks', in A. Kuper (ed.) *Conceptualising Society*, London: Routledge.

—— (1993) 'The Cultural Role of World Cities', in A.P. Cohen and K. Fukui (eds) *Humanising the City?*, Edinburgh: Edinburgh University Press.

Haraway, D. (1989) *Primate Visions: Gender, Race and Nature in the World of Modern Science*, New York: Routledge.

—— (1990 [1985]) 'A Manifesto for Cyborgs: Science, Technology, and Socialist Feminism in the 1980s', in L. Nicholson (ed.) *Feminism/Postmodernism*, London: Routledge.

Hardy, B. (1968) 'Towards a poetics of Fiction: 3. An Approach through Narrative', *Novel* 2, 1: 5–14.

Harkness, S. and Super, C. (eds) (1996) *Parents' Cultural Belief Systems*, New York: Guilford.

Harrell-Bond, B. (1986) *Imposing Aid*, Oxford: Oxford University Press.

Harries-Jones, P. (ed.) (1991) *Making Knowledge Count: Advocacy and Social Science*, Montreal and Kingston: McGill-Queens University Press.

—— (1995) *A Recursive Vision. Ecological Understanding and Gregory Bateson*, Toronto: University of Toronto Press.

Harris, C. (1974) *Hennage*, New York: Holt, Rinehart & Winston.

Harris, R. (1981) *The Language Myth*, London: Duckworth.

Harrison, D. (ed.) (1992) *Tourism and the Less Developed Countries*, New York: Wiley.

Harrison, S. (1993) *The Mask of War*, Manchester: Manchester University Press.

Hart, K. (1982) *The Political Economy of West African Agriculture*, Cambridge: Cambridge University Press.

—— (1990) 'Swimming into the Human Current', *Cambridge Anthropology* 14, 3: 3–10.

Hastrup, K. (1995a) 'The Inarticulate Mind: The Place of Awareness in Social Action', in A.P. Cohen and N.J. Rapport (eds) *Questions of Consciousness*, London: Routledge.

—— (1995b) *A Passage to Anthropology: Between Experience and Theory*, London: Routledge.

Hastrup, K. and Olwig, K.F. (eds) (1997) *Siting Culture*, London: Routledge.

Hauxwell, H. (1991) *Daughter of the Dales*, London: Arrow.

Haviland, J. (1977) *Gossip, Reputation and Knowledge in Zinacantan*, Chicago: University of Chicago Press.

Hayek, F.A. (1946) *Individualism*, Oxford: Blackwell.

—— (1969) *Individualism and Economic Order*, Chicago: University of Chicago Press.

Heald, S. (1991) 'Divinatory Failure: The Religious and Social Roles of Gisu Diviners', *Africa* 61, 3: 299–317.

Heath, S. (1983) *Ways with Words*, Cambridge: Cambridge University Press.

Hebdige, D. (1979) *Subculture*, London: Methuen.

Heelas, P. (1996) *The New Age Movement*, Oxford: Blackwell.

Heider, K. (1976) *Ethnographic Film*, Austin: University of Texas Press.

Heilman, S. (1978) *Synagogue Life*, Chicago: University of Chicago Press.

Heller, J. (1961) *Catch-22*, Jonathan Cape.

Hendry, J. (1996) 'Who Is Representing Whom? Gardens, Theme Parks and the Anthropologist in Japan', in A. James, J. Hockey and A. Dawson (eds) *After Writing Culture*, London: Routledge.

Herskovits, M. (1937) *Life in a Haitian Valley*, New York: Knopf.

Herzfeld, M. (1993) *The Social Production of Indifference*, Oxford: Berg.

Hiller, S. (ed.) (1991a) *The Myth of the Primitivism*, London: Routledge.

—— (1991b) 'Editor's Introductions', in S. Hiller (ed.) *The Myth of Primitivism*, London: Routledge.

Hillery, G. (1955) 'Definitions of Community: Areas of Agreement', *Rural Sociology* 20: 116–31.

Hirschon, R. (1989) *Heirs of the Greek Catastrophe*, Oxford: Clarendon.

Hobart, M. (1993) 'Introduction: The Growth of Ignorance?', in M. Hobart (ed.) *An Anthropological Critique of Development*, London: Routledge.

Hobsbawm, E. (1991) 'Introduction', *Social Research* 58, 1: 65–8.

Hobsbawm, E. and Ranger, T. (eds) (1983) *The Invention of Tradition*, Cambridge: Cambridge University Press.

Hockey, J. and James, A. (1993) *Growing Up and Growing Old*, London: Sage.

Hoebel, E. and Wallace, E. (1958) *The Comanches*, Norman: University of Oklahoma Press.

Hoggart, R. (1966) 'Literature and Society', in N. Mackenzie (ed.) *A Guide to the Social Sciences*, London: Weidenfeld & Nicolson.

Hollis, M. (1982) 'The Social Destruction of Reality', in M. Hollis and S. Lukes (eds) *Rationality and Relativism*, Oxford: Blackwell.

Hollis, M. and Lukes, S. (eds) (1982) *Rationality and Relativism*, Oxford: Blackwell.

Holy, L. (1996) *Anthropological Perspectives on Kinship*, London and Chicago: Pluto.

Holy, L. and Stuchlik, M. (1981) 'The Structure of Folk Models', in L. Holy and M. Stuchlik (eds) *The Structure of Folk Models*, London: Academic Press.

Homans, G. (1941) 'Anxiety and Ritual: The Theories of Malinowski and Radcliffe-Brown', *American Anthropologist* 43: 164–72.

Horton, R. (1967) 'African Traditional Thought and Western Science', *Africa* 37, 1/2: 50–71, 155–87.

—— (1979) 'Material-Object Language And Theoretical Language: Towards a Strawsonian Sociology of Thought,' in S. Brown (ed.) *Philosophical Disputes in the Social Sciences*, Brighton: Harvester.

Horton, R. and Finnegan, R. (eds) (1973) *Modes of Thought*, London: Faber & Faber.

Hough, G. (1969) *Style and Stylistics*, London: Routledge & Kegan Paul.

Hugh-Jones, C. (1979) *From the Milk River*, Cambridge: Cambridge University Press.

Hugh-Jones, S. (1992) 'Yesterday's Luxuries, Tomorrow's Necessities: Business and Barter in Northwest Amazonia', in C. Humphrey and S. Hugh-Jones (eds) *Barter, Exchange and Value: An Anthropological Approach*, Cambridge: Cambridge University Press.

Hughes-Freeland, F. (ed.) (1997) *Ritual, Performance, Media*, London: Routledge.
Huizinga, J. (1980) *Homo Ludens*, London: Routledge & Kegan Paul.
Hulme, P. (1986) *Colonial Encounters: Europe and the Native Caribbean 1492–1979*, London: Methuen.
Humphrey, N. (1982) 'Consciousness: A Just-so Story', *New Scientist* 95: 474–8.
—— (1983) *Consciousness Regained*, Oxford: Oxford University Press.
Hunt, R. (1967) 'Introduction', in R. Hunt (ed.) *Personalities and Cultures*, New York: Natural History Press.
Hutcheon, L. (1994) *Irony's Edge*, London: Routledge.
Hymes, D. (1972) 'Models of Interaction of Language and Social Life', in J. Gumperz and D. Hymes (eds) *Directions in Sociolinguistics*, New York: Holt, Rinehart & Winston.
—— (1973a) 'Towards Ethnographies of Communication: The Analysis of Communicative Events', in P. Giglioli (ed.) *Language and Social Context*, Harmondsworth: Penguin.
—— (1973b) 'An Ethnographic Perspective on "What Is Literature?"', *New Literary History* V, 1: 431–57.
—— (1979) 'Sapir, Competence, Voices', in C. Fillmore, D. Kempler and W. Wang (eds) *Individual Differences in Language Ability and Language Behavior*, New York: Academic Press.
—— (1981) *'In Vain I Tried to Tell You.': Essays in Native American Ethnopoetics*, Philadelphia: University of Pennsylvania.
Ingold, T. (1986) *The Appropriation of Nature*, Manchester: Manchester University Press.
—— (1990) 'An Anthropologist Looks at Biology', *Man* 25, 2: 208–29.
—— (1992) 'Technology, Language, Intelligence: A Reconsideration of Basic Concepts', in K. Gibson and T. Ingold (eds) *Tools, Language and Cognition in Human Evolution*, Cambridge: Cambridge University Press.
—— (ed.) (1994a) *Companion Encyclopedia of Anthropology*, London: Routledge.
—— (1994b) 'Introduction to Culture', in T. Ingold (ed.) *Companion Encyclopedia of Anthropology: Humanity, Culture and Social Life*, London and New York: Routledge.
—— (1994c) 'Introduction to Social Life', in T. Ingold (ed.) *Companion Encyclopedia of Anthropology: Humanity, Culture and Social Life*, London and New York: Routledge.
—— (ed.) (1997) *Key Debates in Anthropology*, London: Routledge.
Intintoli, M. (1984) *Taking Soaps Seriously*, New York: Praeger.
Ions, E. (1977) *Against Behaviourism*, Oxford: Blackwell.
Irigaray, L. (1985) *Speculum of the Other Woman*, Ithaca, NY: Cornell University Press.
—— (1991) *Marine Lover of Friedrich Nietzsche*, New York: Columbia University Press.
—— (1993) *An Ethics of Sexual Difference*, Ithaca, NY: Cornell University Press.
Iser, W. (1978) *The Act of Reading*, London: Routledge & Kegan Paul.
—— (1988) 'The Reading Process: A Phenomenological Approach', in D. Lodge (ed.) *Modern Criticism and Theory*, London: Longman.
Jackson, A. (1987) 'Reflections on Ethnography at Home and the ASA', in A. Jackson (ed.) *Anthropology at Home*, London: Routledge.
Jackson, M. (1989) *Paths toward a Clearing. Radical Empiricism and Ethnographic Inquiry*, Bloomington: Indiana University Press.

—— (ed.) (1996) *Things as They Are: New Directions in Phenomenological Anthropology*, Bloomington: Indiana University Press.

James, A. (1986) 'Learning to Belong', in A.P. Cohen (ed.) *Symbolising Boundaries*, Manchester: Manchester University Press.

—— (1993) *Childhood Identities*, Edinburgh: Edinburgh University Press.

James, A. and Prout, A. (eds) (1990) *Constructing and Reconstructing Childhood*, London: Falmer.

James, A., Jencks, C. and Prout, A. (1997) *Theorizing Childhood*, Oxford: Blackwell.

James, W. (1961[1892]) *Psychology*, London: Harper & Row.

Jameson, F. (1981) *The Political Unconscious: Narrative as a Socially Symbolic Act*, Ithaca, NY: Cornell University Press.

—— (1988) 'The Politics of Theory: Ideological Positions in the Postmodern Debate', in D. Lodge (ed.) *Modern Criticism and Theory*, London: Longman.

Jarman, N. (1997) *Material Conflicts*, Oxford: Berg.

Jedrej, C. and Nuttall, M. (1996) *White Settlers: The Impact on Rural Repopulation in Scotland*, Luxemburg: Harwood.

Jencks, C. (1977) *The Language of Post-Modern Architecture*, London: Academy.

Jenkins, R. (1982) *Hightown Rules. Growing up in a Belfast Housing Estate*, Leicester: National Youth Bureau.

—— (1983) *Lads, Citizens and Ordinary Citizens: Working-Class Youth Life-Styles in Belfast*, London: Routledge & Kegan Paul.

—— (1992) *Pierre Bourdieu*, London: Routledge.

Johnson, A. (1978) *Quantification in Cultural Anthropology*, Stanford, Calif.: Stanford University Press.

Johnson, C. (1982) *Revolutionary Change*, Stanford, Calif.: Stanford University Press.

Johnson, J. (1994) 'Anthropological Contributions to the Study of Social Networks: A Review', in S. Wasserman and J. Galaskiwicz (eds) *Advances in Social Network Analysis*, Thousand Oaks, Calif.: Sage.

Jordanova, L.J. (1980) 'Natural Facts: A Historical Perspective on Science and Sexuality', in C. MacCormack and M. Strathern (eds) *Nature, Culture and Gender*, Cambridge: Cambridge University Press.

Kapferer, B. (1972) *Strategy and Transaction in an African Factory*, Manchester: Manchester University Press.

—— (1976) 'Transactional Models Reconsidered', in B. Kapferer (ed.) *Transaction and Meaning*, Philadelphia: ISHI.

—— (1983) *A Celebration of Demons*, Bloomington: Indiana University Press.

Kardiner, A. and Linton, R. (1939) *The Individual and His Society*, New York: Columbia University Press.

Karstens, M. (1991) 'Alterity as Defect: On the Logic of the Mechanism of Exclusion', in R. Corbey and J. Leerssen (eds) *Alterity, Identity, Image: Selves and Others in Society and Scholarship*, Amsterdam and Atlanta, Ga: Rodopi.

Kateb, G. (1991) 'Exile, Alienation and Estrangement', *Social Research* 58, 1: 135–8.

Kearney, M. (1984) *World View*, Novato, Calif.: Chandler & Sharp.

—— (1986) 'From the Invisible Hand to Visible Feet: Anthropological Studies of Migration and Development', *Annual Review of Anthropology* 15: 331–61.

Kearney, R. (1988) *The Wake of Imagination. Ideas of Creativity in Western Culture*, London: Hutchinson.

Keesing, R. (1987a) 'Anthropology as Interpretive Quest', *Current Anthropology* 28: 161–9.

—— (1987b) *'Ta'ageni: Women's Perspective on Kwaio Society'*, in M. Strathern (ed.)

Dealing with Inequality: Analysing Gender Relations in Melanesia and Beyond, Cambridge: Cambridge University Press.

Kelly, G. (1969) *Clinical Psychology and Personality* (ed. B. Maher), New York: Wiley.

—— (1970) 'A Brief Introduction to Personal Construct Theory', in D. Bannister (ed.) *Perspectives in Personal Construct Theory,* London: Academic Press.

Kerby, A. (1991) *Narrative and the Self,* Bloomington: Indiana University Press.

Kidd, S. (1999) *Love and Hate among the People without Things: the Social and Economic Relations of the Enxet People of Paraguay,* PhD Thesis, University of St Andrews.

King, V. (1993) 'Tourism and Culture in Malaysia', in M. Hitchcock, V. King and M. Parnwell (eds) *Tourism in South-East Asia,* London: Routledge.

Klineberg, O. (1951) 'The Scientific Study of National Stereotypes', *UNESCO Social Science Bulletin* III, 3: 505–11.

Klockars, C. (1975) *The Professional Fence,* London: Tavistock.

Knapp, S. and Michaels, W. (1982) 'Against Theory', *Critical Inquiry* 8,4: 723–42.

—— (1988) 'Against Theory 2: Hermeneutics and Deconstruction', *Critical Inquiry* 14,1: 51–70.

Kotarba, J. and Fontana, A. (eds) (1984) *The Existential Self in Society,* Chicago: University of Chicago Press.

Kottak, C. (1990) *Prime-Time Society,* Belmont, Calif.: Wadsworth.

Kristeva, J. (1984) *Revolution in Poetic Language,* New York: Columbia University Press.

Kuhn, T. (1970) *The Structure of Scientific Revolutions,* Chicago: University of Chicago Press.

Kundera, M. (1990) *The Art of the Novel,* London: Faber.

Kuper, A. (1988) *The Invention of Primitive Society,* London: Routledge.

Labov, W. (1972) *The Language of the Inner City,* Philadelphia: University of Pennsylvania Press.

Lacey, C. (1971) *Hightown Grammar: The School as a Social System,* Manchester: Manchester University Press.

La Fontaine, J. (1985a) *Initiation Ritual, Drama and Secret Knowledge across the World,* Harmondsworth: Penguin.

—— (1985b) 'Person and Individual: Some Anthropological Reflections', in M. Carrithers, S. Collins and S. Lukes (eds) *The Category of the Person,* Cambridge: Cambridge University Press.

Lagrou, E. (1998) *Cashinahua Cosmovision: A Perspectival Approach to Identity and Alterity,* PhD Thesis, University of St Andrews.

Laing, R.D. (1968) *The Politics of Experience,* Harmondsworth: Penguin.

—— (1976) *The Divided Self,* Harmondsworth: Penguin.

Langer, S. (1964) *Philosophical Sketches,* New York: Mentor.

Langness, L. and Frank, G. (1981) *Lives,* Novato, Calif.: Chandler & Sharp.

Latour, B. and Woolgar, S. (1979) *Laboratory Life: The Social Construction of Scientific Facts,* London: Sage.

Layton, R. (1981) *The Anthropology of Art,* London: Granada.

Lea, C. (1978) *Emancipation, Assimilation, and Stereotypes,* Bonn: Grundmann.

Leach, E.R. (1954) *The Political Systems of Highland Burma,* London: Athlone.

—— (1961a) *Rethinking Anthropology,* London: Athlone.

—— (1961b) *Pul Eliya,* Cambridge: Cambridge University Press.

—— (1968) 'Anthropological Aspects of Language: Animal Categories and Animal

Abuse', in E. Lenneberg (ed.) *New Directions in the Study of Language*, Cambridge, Mass.: MIT Press.

—— (1969) *A Runaway World?*, London: Oxford University Press.

—— (1976a) *Culture and Communication*, Cambridge: Cambridge University Press.

—— (1976b) 'Humanism', public lecture delivered at the Humanism Society, University of Cambridge.

—— (1977) *Custom, Law and Terrorist Violence*, Edinburgh: Edinburgh University Press.

—— (1982) *Social Anthropology*, London: Fontana.

—— (1984) 'Glimpses of the Unmentionable in the History of British Social Anthropology', *Annual Review of Anthropology* 13: 1–23.

—— (1989) 'Writing Anthropology: A Review of Geertz's *Works and Lives*', *American Ethnologist* 16, 1: 137–41.

Leavis, F.R. (1972) *Nor Shall My Sword. Discourses on Pluralism, Compassion and Social Hope*, London: Chatto & Windus.

Leavitt, J. (1996) 'Meaning and Feeling in the Anthropology of Emotions', *American Ethnologist* 23: 514–39.

Leeds, A. (1994) *Cities, Classes, and the Social Order*, Ithaca, NY: Cornell University Press.

Lévi-Strauss, C. (1963) *Structural Anthropology*, New York: Basic Books.

—— (1966) *The Savage Mind*, Chicago: University of Chicago Press.

—— (1969a [1949]) *The Elementary Structures of Kinship*, London: Eyre and Spottiswoode.

—— (1969b [1964]) *The Raw and the Cooked: Introduction to a Science of Mythology: 1* (orig. pub. as *Le Cru et le Cuit*, Paris: Librairie Plon), New York: Harper & Row.

—— (1970 [1961]) *Tristes Tropiques*, New York: Atheneum.

—— (1973 [1966]) *From Honey to Ashes: Introduction to a Science of Mythology: 2* (orig. pub. as *Du Miel aux Centres*, Paris: Librairie Plon), New York: Harper & Row.

—— (1978 [1968]) *The Origin of Table Manners: Introduction to a Science of Mythology: 3* (orig. pub. as *L'Origine des Manières de Table*, Paris: Librarie Plon), London: Jonathan Cape.

—— (1981 [1971]) *The Naked Man: Introduction to a Science of Mythology: 4* (orig. pub. as *L'Homme nu*, Paris: Librairie Plon), New York: Harper & Row.

LeVine, R. (1982) *Culture, Behavior and Personality: An Introduction to the Comparative Study of Psychosocial Adaptation*, Chicago: Aldine.

Levinson, D. and Ember, M. (eds) (1996) *Encyclopedia of Cultural Anthropology*, New York: Holt.

Levy, R. (1978) 'Tahitian Gentleness and Redundant Controls', in A. Montagu (ed.) *Learning Non-aggression*, Oxford: Oxford University Press.

Levy-Bruhl, L. (1985 [1910]) *How Natives Think*, Princeton, NJ: Princeton University Press.

Lewin, R. (1988) *In the Age of Mankind*, Washington: Smithsonian.

Lewis, H. (1982) *The Elusive Self*, London: Macmillan.

Lewis, I.M. (1971) *Ecstatic Religion*, Harmondsworth: Penguin.

Lewis, O. (1951) *Life in a Mexican Village*, Urbana: University of Illinois Press.

—— (1959) *Five Families: Mexican Studies in the Culture of Poverty*, New York: Basic.

—— (1961) *The Children of Sanchez*, New York: Random House.

Liebes, T. and Katz, E. (1990) *The Export of Meaning*, New York: Oxford University Press.

Lieblich, A. and Josselson, R. (eds) (1994) *Exploring Identity and Gender. The Narrative Study of Lives*, London: Sage.

Lienhardt, G. (1985) 'Self: Public, Private. Some African Representations', in M. Carrithers, S. Collins and S. Lukes (eds) *The Category of the Person*, Cambridge: Cambridge University Press.

Lindqvist, S. (1996 [1992]) *Exterminate All the Brutes*, London: Granta Books.

Lippmann, W. (1947 [1922]) *Public Opinion*, New York: Macmillan.

Little, K. (1948) *Negroes in Britain*, London: Routledge & Kegan Paul.

Littlewood, R. (1993) *Pathology and Identity*, Cambridge: Cambridge University Press.

Livingston, E. (1995) *An Anthropology of Reading*, Bloomington: Indiana University Press.

Lloyd, G. (1993) *Being in Time. Selves and Narrators in Philosophy and Literature*, London: Routledge.

Lloyd, J. (1991) 'Emil Nolde's "Ethnographic" Still Lifes: Primitivism, Tradition, and Modernity', in S. Hiller (ed.) *The Myth of Primitivism*, London: Routledge.

Lloyd, P. (1979) *Slums of Hope: Shanty Towns in the Third World*, Manchester: Manchester University Press.

—— (1982) *A Third-World Proletariat?*, London: Allen & Unwin.

Lodge, D. (1977) *The Modes of Modern Writing*, London: Arnold.

Loizos, P. (1993) *Innovation in Ethnographic Film*, Manchester: Manchester University Press.

Louch, A. (1966) *Explanation and Human Action*, Oxford: Blackwell.

Lounsbury, F. (1968) 'The Structural Analysis of Kinship Semantics', in P. Bohannan and J. Middleton (eds) *Kinship and Social Organization*, Garden City NY: Natural History.

Lukes, S. (1968) 'Methodological Individualism Reconsidered', *British Journal of Sociology* 19: 119–29.

—— (1990) *Individualism*, Oxford: Blackwell.

Lyman, S. (1984) 'Foreword', in A. Kotarba and A. Fontana (eds) *The Existential Self in Society*, Chicago: University of Chicago Press.

Lyotard, J.-F. (1986) *The Post-Modern Condition: A Report on Knowledge*, Manchester: Manchester University Press.

McCallum, C. (1989) *Power, Gender and Social Organisation among the Cashinahua of Brazil*, PhD Thesis, University of London.

MacCannell, D. (1989) *The Tourist: A New Theory of the Leisure Class*, New York: Schocken.

MacCormack, C. (1980) 'Nature, Culture and Gender: A Critique', in C. MacCormack and M. Strathern (eds) *Nature, Culture and Gender*, Cambridge: Cambridge University Press.

McDonald, M. (1990) *We Are not French! Language, Culture and Identity in Brittany*, London: Routledge.

—— (1993) 'The Construction of Difference: An Anthropological Approach to Stereotypes', in S. Macdonald (ed.) *Inside European Identities*, Oxford: Berg.

MacDougall, D. (1995) 'The Subjective Voice in Ethnographic Film', in L. Devereaux and R. Hillman (eds) *Fields of Vision*, Berkeley: University of California Press.

Macfarlane, A. (1970) *The Family Life of Ralph Josselin, a Seventeenth-Century Clergyman*, Cambridge: Cambridge University Press.
—— (1978) *The Origins of English Individualism*, Oxford: Blackwell.
McFeat, T. (1974) *Small-Group Cultures*, New York: Pergamon.
McGinn, C. (1992) *The Problem of Consciousness*, Oxford: Blackwell.
McGrane, B. (1989) *Beyond Anthropology: Society and the Other*, New York: Columbia University.
McInnis, R. (1991) 'Series Foreword', in R. Winthrop *Dictionary of Concepts in Cultural Anthropology*, Westport, Conn.: Greenwood.
MacIntyre, A. (1985) *After Virtue: A Study in Moral Theory*, second edition, London: Duckworth.
MacIver, A. (1961) 'Historical Explanation', in A. Flew (ed.) *Logic and Language (second series)*, Oxford: Blackwell.
Maine, H. (1861) *Ancient Law*, London: Murray.
Malinowski, B. (1922) *Argonauts of the Western Pacific*, London: Routledge & Kegan Paul.
—— (1926) *Myth in Primitive Psychology*, London, reprinted in B. Malinowski, *Magic, Science and Religion, and Other Essays*, 1948.
—— (1930) 'Kinship', *Man* 30: 9–29.
—— (1939) 'The Group and the Individual in Functional Analysis', in *American Journal of Sociology* 44: 938–64.
—— (1948) *Magic, Science and Religion, and Other Essays*, Glencoe, Ill.: Free Press.
—— (1989) *A Diary in the Strict Sense of the Term*, Stanford, Calif.: Stanford University Press.
Malkki, L. (1995) *Purity and Exile*, Chicago: University of Chicago Press.
Mandelbaum, D. (1966) 'Transcendental and Pragmatic Aspects of Religion', *American Anthropologist* 68: 1174–91.
Mannheim, K. (1952) *Ideology and Utopia*, London: Routledge & Kegan Paul.
Manning, F. (ed.) (1983) *The Celebration of Society*, Bowling Green, Ohio: Popular Press.
Marcus, G. (1980) 'Rhetoric and Ethnographic Genre in Anthropological Research', *Current Anthropology* 21, 4: 507–10.
—— (ed.) (1995) *Technoscientific Imaginaries*, Chicago: University of Chicago Press.
Marcus, G. and Clifford, J. (eds) (1986) *Writing Culture. The Poetics and Politics of Ethnography*, Berkeley: University of California Press.
Marcus, G. and Fischer, M. (1986) *Anthropology as Cultural Critique. An Experimental Moment in the Human Sciences*, Chicago: University of Chicago Press.
Marks, D. (1995) 'Ethnography and Ethnographic Film: From Flaherty to Asch and after', *American Anthropologist*, 97, 2: 339–47.
Marsella, A., De Vos, G. and Hsu, F. (eds) (1985) *Culture and Self: Asian and Western Perspectives*, New York: Tavistock.
Marsh, P., Rosser, E. and Harre, R. (1978) *The Rules of Disorder*, London: Routledge & Kegan Paul.
Martin, G. (1983) 'The Bridge and the River. Or the Ironies of Communication', *Poetics Today* 4, 3: 415–35.
Martinez, W. (1992) 'Who Constructs Anthropological Knowledge? Towards a Theory of Ethnographic Film Spectatorship', in P. Crawford and D. Turton (eds) *Film as Ethnography*, Manchester: Manchester University Press.
Marx, E. (1987) 'Labour Migrants with a Secure Base: Bedouin of South Sinai', in J. Eades (ed.) *Migrants, Workers and the Social Order*, London: Tavistock.

Marx, K. (1965 [1857–58]) *Pre-capitalist Economic Formations*, (ed. C.J. Arthur), London: Lawrence & Wishart.

Mason, P. (1990) *Deconstructing America: Representations of the Other*, London: Routledge.

Mauss, M. (1954) *The Gift*, London: Routledge & Kegan Paul.

—— (1985) 'A Category of the Human Mind: The Notion of Person, the Notion of Self', in M. Carrithers, S. Collins and S. Lukes (eds) *The Category of the Person*, Cambridge: Cambridge University Press.

May, R. (1972) *Power and Innocence*, New York: Norton.

Mead, M. (1928) *Coming of Age in Samoa*, New York: Morrow.

Meillassoux, C. (1981 [1975]) *Maidens, Meal and Money. Capitalism and the Domestic Community* (orig. pub. as *Femmes, greniers et capitaux*, Paris: Librairie François Maspero), Cambridge: Cambridge University Press.

Meløe, J. (1988a) 'Some Remarks on Agent Perception', in L. Hertzberg and J. Pietarinen (eds), *Perspectives on Human Conduct*, Leiden: E.J. Brill.

—— (1988b) 'The Two Landscapes of Northern Norway', *Inquiry* 31: 387–401.

Messer, E. (1993) 'Anthropology and Human Rights', *Annual Review of Anthropology* 22: 221–49.

Messerschmidt, D. (ed.) (1981) *Anthropologists at Home in North America: Methods and Issues in the Study of One's Own Society*, Cambridge: Cambridge University Press.

Michaels, E. (1987) *For a Cultural Future*, Sydney: Art Space (Art and Criticism series 3).

Mill, J.S. (1875) *Autobiography*, London: Longmans Green & Reader & Dyer.

Miller, D. (1988) 'Appropriating the State on the Council Estate', *Man* 23: 353–72.

Minar, D. and Greer, S. (1969) *The Concept of Community*, Chicago: Aldine.

Minh-ha, T. (1989) *Woman, Native, Other*, Bloomington: Indiana University Press.

—— (1994) 'Other than Myself/My Other Self', in G. Robertson *et al.* (eds) *Travellers' Tales. Narratives of Home and Displacement*, London: Routledge.

Mitchell, J. (ed.) (1969) *Social Networks in Urban Situations*, Manchester: Manchester University Press.

—— (1974) 'Social Networks', *Annual Review of Anthropology* 3: 279–99.

Moerman, M. (1988) *Talking Culture. Ethnography and Conversation Analysis*, Philadelphia: University of Pennsylvania Press.

Moggach, D. (1996) 'How I Learnt to Be a Real Countrywoman', in D. Spears (ed.) *Woman's Hour Fiftieth Anniversary Short Story Collection*, BBC: London.

Mommsen, W. (1965) 'Max Weber's Political Sociology and his Philosophy of World History', *International Social Science Journal* XVII: 1–27.

Montagu, A. (ed.) (1968) *Man and Aggression*, New York: Oxford University Press.

Moore, H. (1988) *Feminism and Anthropology*, Cambridge: Polity.

—— (1994a) *A Passion for Difference*, Cambridge: Polity.

—— (1994b) 'Understanding Sex and Gender', in T. Ingold (ed.) *Companion Encyclopedia of Anthropology*, London: Routledge.

Moore, S. (1987) 'Explaining the Present: Theoretical Dilemmas in Processual Ethnography', *American Ethnologist* 14, 4: 727–36.

Moravec, H. (1988) *Mind Children*, Cambridge, Mass.: Harvard University Press.

Morgan, L.H. (1871) *Systems of Consanguinity and Affinity of the Human Family*, Washington DC: Smithsonian.

Morris, B. (1991) *Western Conceptions of the Individual*, Oxford: Berg.

Moskos, C. (1989) *Greek Americans*, New Brunswick, NJ: Transaction.

Moskovitz, M. (1968) *The Politics of Human Rights*, Dordrecht: Kluwer.

Musello, C. (1980) 'Studying the Home Mode', *Studies in Visual Communication* 6: 23–42.

Myerhoff, B. (1974) *Peyote Hunt. The Sacred Journey of the Huichol Indians*, Ithaca, NY: Cornell University Press.

—— (1978) *Number Our Days*, New York: Simon & Schuster.

Naipaul, V.S. (1987) *The Enigma of Arrival*, Harmondsworth: Penguin.

Nash, C. (ed.) (1994) *Narrative in Culture. The Uses of Storytelling in the Sciences, Philosophy, and Literature*, London: Routledge.

Nash, D. (1989) 'Tourism as a Form of Imperialism', in V. Smith (ed.) *Hosts and Guests*, Oxford: Blackwell.

Needham, R. (1964) 'Descent, Category, and Alliance in Siriono Society', *Southwestern Journal of Anthropology* XX: 229–40.

—— (1970) 'Introduction', in E. Durkheim and M. Mauss, *Primitive Classification*, London: Routledge & Kegan Paul.

—— (1971) 'Remarks on the Analysis of Kinship and Marriage', in R. Needham (ed.) *Rethinking Kinship and Marriage*, London: Tavistock.

—— (1975) 'Polythetic Classification', *Man* 10: 349–69.

—— (1978) *Primordial Characters*, Charlottesville: Virginia University Press.

—— (1979) *Symbolic Classification*, Santa Monica, Calif.: Goodyear.

—— (1985) *Exemplars*, Berkeley: University of California Press.

Neisser, U. (1976) *Cognition and Reality*, San Francisco: Freeman.

Nietzsche, F. (1911) 'On Truth and Falsity in their Ultramoral Sense (1873)' in *Early Greek Philosophy, and Other Essays*, London: Foulis.

—— (1968) *The Will to Power* (ed. W. Kaufmann), New York: Random House.

—— (1973) *Beyond Good and Evil*, Harmondsworth: Penguin.

—— (1979) *Twilight of the Idols*, Harmondsworth: Penguin.

—— (1994) *Human, All Too Human*, Harmondsworth: Penguin.

Nkosi, L. (1994) 'Ironies of Exile: Post-colonial Homelessness and the Anticlimax of Return', *Times Literary Supplement* 4748: 5.

Nugent, S. and Shore, C. (eds) (1997) *Anthropology and Cultural Studies*, London: Pluto.

Oakeshott, M. (1962) *Rationalism in Politics and Other Essays*, London: Methuen.

O'Donnell, E. (1977) *Northern Ireland Stereotypes*, Dublin: College of Industrial Relations.

Okely, J. (1992) 'Anthropology and Autobiography: Participatory Experience and Embodied Knowledge', in J. Okely and H. Callaway (eds) *Anthropology and Autobiography*, London: Routledge.

—— (1996) *Own or Other Culture*, London: Routledge.

Oldham, P. (1996) *The Impacts of Development and Indigenous Responses among the Piaroa of the Venezuelan Amazon*, PhD Thesis, University of London.

Ong, W. (1969) 'World as View and World as Event', *American Anthropologist* 71: 634–47.

—— (1977) *Interfaces of the Word. Studies in the Evolution of Consciousness and Culture*, Ithaca, NY: Cornell University Press.

Oppenheimer, P. (1989) *The Birth of the Modern Mind. Self, Consciousness and the Invention of the Sonnet*, New York: Oxford University Press.

Ortega y Gasset, J. (1956) *The Dehumanization of Art and Other Writings on Art and Culture*, New York: Doubleday.

Ortner, S. (1974) 'Is Female to Male as Nature is to Culture?', in M. Rosaldo and

L. Lamphere (eds) *Woman, Culture and Society*, Stanford, Calif.: Stanford University Press.

Ortner, S. and Whitehead, H. (eds) (1981) *Sexual Meanings: The Cultural Construction of Gender and Sexuality*, Cambridge: Cambridge University Press.

Overing, J. (ed.) (1985a) *Reason and Morality*, London: Tavistock.

—— (1985b) 'Introduction', in J. Overing (ed.) *Reason and Morality*, London: Tavistock.

—— (1985c) 'Today I shall Call him "Mummy": Multiple Worlds and Classificatory Confusion', in J. Overing (ed.) *Reason and Morality*, London: Tavistock.

—— (1985d) 'There Is no End of Evil: The Guilty Innocents and their Fallible God', in D. Parkin (ed.) *The Anthropology of Evil*, Oxford: Basil Blackwell.

—— (1986) 'Men Control Women? The "Catch 22" in the Analysis of Gender'. *International Journal of Moral and Social Studies*,1, 2: 135–56.

—— (1987) 'Translation as a Creative Process: The Power of the Name', in L. Holy (ed.) *Comparative Anthropology*, Oxford: Basil Blackwell.

—— (1989) 'The Aesthetics of Production: The Sense of Community among the Cubeo and Piaroa', *Dialectical Anthropology* 14: 159–75.

—— (1990) 'The Shaman as a Maker of Worlds: Nelson Goodman in the Amazon', *Man* 25, 4: 602–19.

—— (1993a) 'The Anarchy and Collectivism of the "Primitive Other": Marx and Sahlins in the Amazon', in C. Hann (ed.) *Socialism: Ideals, Ideologies, and Local Practice*, ASA Monographs 31, London: Routledge.

—— (1993b) 'Death and the Loss of Civilized Predation among the Piaroa of the Orinoco Basin', *L'Homme* 126–8: 191–212.

—— (1995) 'O mito como historia: um problema de tempo, realidade e outras questões' (Myth and history: a problem of time, reality and other matters), *Mana* 1, 1: 107–40.

—— (1996a) 'Who Is the Mightiest of them All? Jaguar and Conquistador in Piaroa Images of Alterity', in J. Arnold (ed.) *Monsters, Tricksters and Sacred Cows*, Charlottesville, Virginia: University Press of Virginia.

—— (1996b) 'Aesthetics is a Cross-cultural Category: Against the Motion', in T. Ingold (ed.) *Key Debates in Anthropology*, London: Routledge.

—— (1997) 'The Role of Myth: An Anthropological Perspective, or: "The Reality of the Really Made-up"', in G. Hosking and G. Schöpflin (eds) *Myths and Nationhood*, London: Hurst and Company.

—— (1998) 'Is an Anthropological Translation of the "Unhomely" Possible, or Desirable?', in M. Bal *et al.* (eds) *Intellectual Traditions in Movement*, ASCA Yearbook, Amsterdam: ASCA Press.

—— (1999) 'Elogio do cotidiano: a confiança e a arte da vida social em uma comunidade amazônica' (In praise of the everyday: trust and the art of sociality in an Amazonian community), *Mana* 5, 1: 81–108.

Overing Kaplan, J. (1975) *The Piaroa, a People of the Orinoco Basin: A Study in Kinship and Marriage*, Oxford: Clarendon.

—— (1981) 'Review Article: "Amazonian Anthropology"', in *Journal of Latin American Studies* 13, part 1.

Oz, A. (1975) *Touch the Water, Touch the Wind*, London: Chatto & Windus.

Pagden, A. (1982) *The Fall of Natural Man: The American Indian and the Origins of Comparative Ethnology*, Cambridge: Cambridge University Press.

Pahl, R. (1968) 'The Rural–Urban Continuum', in R. Pahl (ed.) *Readings in Urban Sociology*, Oxford: Pergamon.

Paine, R. (1967) 'What Is Gossip About? An Alternative Hypothesis', *Man* 2, 2: 272–85.

—— (1971) 'A Theory of Patronage and Brokerage', in R. Paine (ed.) *Patrons and Brokers in the East Arctic*, St. John's, Nfld: ISER Press, Memorial University.

—— (1974) 'Second Thoughts about Barth's Models', *Royal Anthropological Institute Occasional Papers* 32.

—— (1976) 'Two Modes of Exchange and Mediation', in B. Kapferer (ed.) *Transaction and Meaning*, Philadelphia: ISHI.

—— (1981) 'When Saying is Doing', in R. Paine (ed.) *Politically Speaking*, St. John's, Nfld: ISER Press, Memorial University.

—— (1992) 'The Marabar Caves, 1920–2020', in S. Wallman (ed.) *Contemporary Futures*, London: Routledge.

Palmer, C., Robinson, M. and Thomas, R. (1977) 'The Countryside Image: An Investigation of Structure And Meaning', *Environment and Planning* A9: 739–50.

Park, G. (1974) *The Idea of Social Structure*, New York: Doubleday.

Park, R. (1968) 'The City', in R. Park, E. Burgess and R. McKenzie (eds) *The City*, Chicago: University of Chicago Press.

Parkin, D. (1969) *Neighbours and Nationals in an African City Ward*, London: Routledge & Kegan Paul.

—— (1987) 'Comparison as a Search for Continuity', in L. Holy (ed.) *Comparative Anthropology*, Oxford: Blackwell.

Parsons, T. (1977) *Social Systems and the Evolution of Action Theory*, New York: Free Press.

Passes, A. (1998) *The Hearer, the Hunter, and the Agouti Head: Aspects of Inter-communication and Conviviality among the Pa'ikwené of French Guiana*, PhD Thesis, University of St Andrews.

Pateman, C. (1989) *The Disorder of Women*, Cambridge: Polity Press.

Peabody, D. (1985) *National Characteristics*, Cambridge: Cambridge University Press.

Peach, P. (1997) 'Making *Turis*: Tourism, Identity and Material Culture in a Highland New Guinea Village', *Journal of Performance Research*, summer.

Peacock, J. (1986) *The Anthropological Lens*, Cambridge: Cambridge University Press.

Peacock, M. (1896) 'Executed Criminals and Folk Medicine', *Folklore* (London Folklore Society) 7: 268–83.

Pelto, P, and Pelto, G. (1978) *Anthropological Research: The Structure of Inquiry*, Cambridge: Cambridge University Press.

Penrose, R. (1990) *The Emperor's New Mind*, London: Vintage.

Percy, W. (1958) 'Symbol, Consciousness and Intersubjectivity', *Journal of Philosophy* 55: 631–41.

Pettigrew, T. (1981) 'Extending the Stereotype Concept', in D. Hamilton (ed.) *Cognitive Processes in Stereotyping and Intergroup Behavior*, Hillsdale, NJ: Erlbaum.

Phillips, D. (1993) *Looking Backward. A Critical Appraisal of Communitarian Thought*, Princeton, NJ: Princeton University Press.

Phillips, D. and Williams, A. (1984) *Rural Britain*, Oxford: Blackwell.

Pike, K.L. (1964) 'Toward a Theory of the Structure of Human Behavior', in D. Hymes (ed.) *Language in Culture and Society*, New York: Harper & Row.

Pine, F. (1996) 'Gender', in A. Barnard and J. Spencer (eds) *Encyclopedia of Social and Cultural Anthropology*, London: Routledge.

Pinney, C. (1990) 'Classification and Fantasy in the Photographic Construction of Caste and Tribe', *Visual Anthropology* 3: 259–88.

Pitt-Rivers, J. (1974) *The People of the Sierra*, Chicago: University of Chicago Press.

Pocock, D. (1961) *Social Anthropology*, London: Sheed & Ward.

—— (1986) 'The Ethnography of Morals', *International Journal of Moral and Social Studies* 1, 1: 3–20.

Pollock, G. (1994) 'Territories of Desire: Reconsiderations of an African Childhood', in G. Robertson *et al.* (eds) *Travellers' Tales. Narratives of Home and Displacement*, London: Routledge.

Popper, K. (1965) 'Unity of Method in the Natural and Social Sciences', in D. Braybrooke (ed.) *Philosophical Problems of the Social Sciences*, New York: Macmillan.

—— (1966) *The Open Society and its Enemies (volume 2)*, Princeton, NJ: Princeton University Press.

Porter, R. (1994) 'A Mind and its Meanings', *Times Literary Supplement* 4772: 6–7.

Pratt, M. (1986) 'Fieldwork in Common Places', in G. Marcus and J. Clifford (eds) *Writing Culture. The Poetics and Politics of Ethnography*, Berkeley: University of California Press.

—— (1992) *Imperial Eyes*, London: Routledge.

Prattis, I. (1985) *Reflection, the Anthropological Muse*, Washington: American Anthropological Association.

—— (1996) 'Reflexive Anthropology', in M. Ember and D. Levinson (eds) *Encyclopedia of Cultural Anthropology*, New York: Holt.

Preston, J. (1991) 'The Trickster Unmasked: Anthropology and the Imagination', in I. Brady (ed.) *Anthropological Poetics*, Savage, Md: Rowman-Littlefield.

Price, V. (1992) *Communication Concepts 4: Public Opinion*, Newbury Park, Calif.: Sage.

Prigogine, I. (1989) 'The Philosophy of Instability', *Futures* August: 396–400.

Propp, V. (1968) *Morphology of the Folk Tale*, Austin: University of Texas Press.

Prott, L. (1988) 'Cultural Rights as Peoples' Rights in International Law', in J. Crawford (ed) *The Rights of Peoples*, Oxford: Clarendon.

Psathas, G. (1973) 'Introduction', in G. Psathas (ed.) *Phenomenological Sociology*, New York: Wiley.

Raban, J. (1973) *Soft City*, Harmondsworth: Penguin.

Rabinow, P. (1977) *Reflections on Fieldwork in Morocco*, Berkeley: University of California Press.

—— (1996) *Essays on the Anthropology of Reason*, Princeton, NJ: Princeton University Press.

Radcliffe-Brown, A.R. (1953) 'Dravidian Kinship Terminology', *Man* LIII, 169: 112.

—— (1965 [1952]) *Structure and Function in Primitive Society*, New York: The Free Press.

Radin, P. (1927) *Primitive Man as Philosopher*, New York: Appleton.

Rappaport, R. (1968) *Pigs for the Ancestors: Ritual in the Ecology of a New Guinea People*, New Haven, Conn.: Yale University Press.

Rapport, N.J. (1987) *Talking Violence. An Anthropological Interpretation of Conversation in the City*, St. John's, Nfld: ISER Press, Memorial University.

—— (1990) 'Ritual Speaking in a Canadian Suburb. Anthropology and the Problem of Generalisation', *Human Relations* 43, 9: 849–64.

—— (1993a) *Diverse World-Views in an English Village*, Edinburgh: Edinburgh University Press.

—— (1993b) 'A Policeman's Construction of "the Truth": Sergeant Hibbs and the Lie-Detector Machine', in W. Haviland and R. Gordon (eds) *Talking about People: Readings in Contemporary Cultural Anthropology*, Mountain View, Calif.: Mayfield.

—— (1994a) *The Prose and the Passion. Anthropology, Literature and the Writing of E.M. Forster*, Manchester: Manchester University Press.

—— (1994b) 'Trauma and Ego-Syntonic Response. The Holocaust and the "Newfoundland Young Yids", 1985', in S. Heald and A. Duluz (eds) *Anthropology and Psychoanalysis*, London: Routledge.

—— (1994c) '"Busted for Hash": Common Catchwords and Individual Identities in a Canadian City', in V. Amit-Talai and H. Lustiger-Thaler (eds) *Urban Lives. Fragmentation and Resistance*, Toronto: McClelland & Stewart.

—— (1995) 'Migrant Selves and Stereotypes: Personal Context in a Postmodern World', in S. Pile and N. Thrift (eds) *Mapping the Subject: Geographies of Cultural Transformation*, London: Routledge.

—— (1997a) *Transcendent Individual: Towards a Liberal and Literary Anthropology*, London: Routledge.

—— (1997b) 'Hard-Sell. Commercial Performance and the Narration of the Self', in F. Hughes-Freeland (ed.) *Ritual, Performance, Media*, London: Routledge.

—— (1997c) 'The "Contrarieties" of Israel. An Essay on the Cognitive Importance and the Creative Promise of Both/And', *Journal of the Royal Anthropological Institute* 3, 4: 653–72.

—— (1997d) 'Edifying Anthropology: Culture as Conversation: Representation as Conversation', in A. James, A. Dawson and J. Hockey (eds) *After Writing Culture*, London: Routledge.

—— (1997e) 'Opposing the Motion that "Cultural Studies will Be the Death of Anthropology"', *Group for Debates in Anthropological Theory*, Department of Social Anthropology, University of Manchester.

—— (1998) 'Problem-solving and Contradiction: Playing Darts and Becoming Human', *Self, Agency and Society* 2, 1: 81–101.

—— (1999) 'The Narrative as Fieldwork Technique: Processual Ethnography for a World in Motion', in V. Amit-Talai (ed.) *Constructing the Field: Ethnographic Fieldwork at the End of Century*, London: Routledge.

Rapport, N.J. and Dawson, A. (eds) (1998) *Migrants of Identity. Perceptions of Home in a World of Movement*, Oxford: Berg.

Read, K. (1955) 'Morality and the Concept of the Person among the Gahuku Gama', *Oceania* 25(4).

Redfield, R. (1930) *Tepotzlan*, Chicago: University of Chicago Press.

—— (1941) *The Folk Culture of Yucatan*, Chicago: University of Chicago Press.

—— (1952) 'The Primitive World View', *Proceedings of the American Philosophical Society* 96: 30–6.

—— (1960) *The Little Community, and Peasant Society and Culture*, Chicago: University of Chicago Press.

Reichel-Dolmatoff, G. (1971) *Amazonian Cosmos: The Sexual and Religious Symbolism of the Tukano Indians*, Chicago: University of Chicago Press.

Richards, A. (1982) *Chisungu*, London: Routledge.

Riches, D. (ed.) (1986) *The Anthropology of Violence*, Oxford: Blackwell.

Ricoeur, P. (1981) *Hermeneutics and the Human Sciences*, Cambridge: Cambridge University Press.

—— (1996) *Paul Ricoeur: The Hermeneutics of Action* (ed. R. Kearney), London: Sage.

Riesman, D. (1954) *Individualism Reconsidered, and Other Essays*, Glencoe, Ill.: Free Press.

—— (1958) 'The Suburban Sadness', in W. Dobriner (ed.) *The Suburban Community*, New York: Putnam.

Riffaterre, M. (1978) *Semiotics of Poetry*, Bloomington: Indiana University Press.

Rigby, A. (1974) *Communes in Britain*, London: Routledge & Kegan Paul.

Rivière, P. G. (1969) *Marriage among the Trio: A Principle of Social Organisation*, Oxford: Clarendon.

—— (1971) 'Marriage: A Reassessment', in R. Needham (ed.) *Rethinking Kinship and Anthropology*, London: Tavistock.

—— (1984) *Individual and Society in Guiana*, Cambridge: Cambridge University Press.

Rorty, R. (1980) *Philosophy and the Mirror of Nature*, Princeton, NJ: Princeton University Press.

—— (1986) 'On Ethnocentrism: A Reply to Clifford Geertz', *Michigan Quarterly Review* 25 (Winter): 525–34.

—— (1991) *Objectivity, Relativism, and Truth*, Cambridge: Cambridge University Press.

—— (1992) *Contingency, Irony, and Solidarity*, Cambridge: Cambridge University Press.

Rosaldo, M. (1974) 'Woman, Culture, and Society: A Theoretical Overview', in M. Rosaldo and L. Lamphere (eds), *Woman, Culture and Society*, Stanford, Calif.: Stanford University Press.

Rosaldo, M. and Lamphere, L. (eds) (1974) *Woman, Culture and Society*, Stanford, Calif.: Stanford University Press.

Rosaldo, R., Lavie, S. and Narayan, K. (1993) 'Introduction: Creativity in Anthropology', in S. Lavie, K. Narayan and R. Rosaldo (eds) *Creativity/Anthropology*, Ithaca, NY: Cornell University Press.

Ruby, J. (1980) 'Exposing Yourself: Reflexivity, Film and Anthropology', *Semiotica* 3: 153–79.

Rykwert, J. (1991) 'House and Home', *Social Research* 58/1: 51–62.

Ryle, G. (1971) *Collected Papers, Volume 2: Essays 1929–1968*, London: Hutchinson.

Sacks, H. (1974) 'On the Analysability of Stories by Children', in R. Turner (ed.) *Ethnomethodology*, Penguin: Harmondsworth.

Sahlins, M. (1968) *Tribesmen*, Englewood Cliffs, NJ: Prentice-Hall.

—— (1972) *Stone Age Economics*, Chicago: Aldine.

—— (1976) *Culture and Practical Reason*, Chicago: University of Chicago Press.

—— (1994) 'Goodbye to Tristes Tropes: Ethnography in the Context of Modern World History', in R. Borofsky (ed.) *Assessing Cultural Anthropology*, New York: McGraw-Hill.

—— (1996) *Waiting for Foucault*, Cambridge: Prickly Pear Press.

—— (1999) 'Two or Three Things I Know about Culture', *JRAI* 5, 3: 399–422.

Sahlins, M. and Service, E.R. (eds) (1960) *Evolution and Society*, Ann Arbor: University of Michigan Press.

Said, E. (1978) *Orientalism*, London: Penguin.

Salmond, A. (1985) 'Maori Epistemologies', in J. Overing (ed.) *Reason and Morality*, London: Tavistock.

—— (1995) 'Self and Other in Contemporary Anthropology', in R. Fardon (ed.) *Counterworks: Managing the Diversity of Knowledge*, London: Routledge.

Sangren, S. (1988) 'Rhetoric and the Authority of Ethnography: Post Modernism and the Social Reproduction of Texts', *Current Anthropology* 29, 3: 415–24.

Sanjek, R. (1974) 'What Is Network Analysis, and What Is it Good For?', *Reviews in Anthropology* 1: 588–97.

—— (1978) 'A Network Method and its Uses in Urban Ethnography', *Human Organization* 37: 257–68.

Sapir, E. (1956) *Culture, Language and Personality*, Berkeley: University of California Press.

Sartre, J.-P. (1972) *The Psychology of Imagination*, New York: Citadel.

—— (1997) *Existentialism and Humanism*, London: Methuen.

Saussure, F. de (1983) *Course in General Linguistics*, London: Duckworth.

Scheff, T. (1990) *Microsociology: Discourse, Emotion and Social Structure*, Chicago: University of Chicago Press.

Scheffler, H. W. (1966) 'Ancestor Worship in Anthropology; Or, Observations on Descent and Descent Groups', *Curent Anthropology* VII: 541–51.

—— (1978) *Australian Kin Classification*, Cambridge: Cambridge University Press.

Schegloff, E.A. (1972) 'Sequencing in Conversational Openings' in J. Gumperz and D. Hymes (eds) *Directions in Sociolinguistics*, New York: Holt, Rinehart & Winston.

Scheper-Hughes, N. (1985) 'Culture, Scarcity and Maternal Thinking: Maternal Detachment and Infant Survival in a Brazilian Shantytown', *Ethos* 13, 4: 291–317.

—— (1992) *Death without Weeping*, Berkeley: University of California Press.

Schildkrout, E. (1978) 'Roles of Children in Urban Kano', in J. La Fontaine (ed.) *Sex and Age as Principles of Social Differentiation*, New York: Academic.

Schiller, N., Basch, L. and Blanc-Szanton, C. (eds) (1992) *Towards a Transnational Perspective on Migration*, New York: New York Academy of Sciences.

Schneider, D. (1968) *American Kinship*, Chicago: University of Chicago Press.

—— (1976) 'Notes toward a Theory of Culture', in K. Basso and H. Selby (eds) *Meaning in Anthropology*, Albuquerque: University of New Mexico Press.

—— (1984) *A Critique of the Study of Kinship*, Ann Arbor: University Press of Michigan.

Scholte, B. (1969) 'Toward a Reflexive and Critical Anthropology', in D. Hymes (ed.) *Reinventing Anthropology*, New York: Pantheon.

Schuetz, A. (1944) 'The Stranger: An Essay in Social Psychology', *American Journal of Sociology* 49, 6: 499–507.

—— (1953) 'Common Sense and Scientific Interpretation of Human Action', *Philosophy and Phenomenological Research* 14, 1: 1–37.

Schwartz, R. (1987) 'Crazy Machines', *Telos* 70: 125–37.

Schwartz, T. (1975) 'Cultural Totemism', in G. de Vos and L. Romanucci-Ross (eds) *Ethnic Identity*, Palo Alto, Calif.: Mayfield.

—— (1978a) 'Where Is the Culture? Personality as the Distributive Locus of Culture', in G. Spindler (ed.) *The Making of Psychological Anthropology*, Berkeley: University of California Press.

—— (1978b) 'The Size and Shape of a Culture', in F. Barth (ed.) *Scale and Social Organisation*, Oslo: Greig.

Schwartzman, H. (1978) *Transformations*, New York: Plenum.

Schweizer, T. (1988) 'Detecting Positions in Networks', *American Anthropologist* 88: 313–38.

Searle, J. (1973), 'What Is a Speech-Act?', in P. Giglioli (ed.) *Language and Social Context*, Harmondsworth: Penguin.

—— (1977) 'Reiterating the Differences: A Reply to Derrida', *Glyph* 1: 198–208.

—— (1992) *The Rediscovery of the Mind*, Cambridge, Mass.: MIT Press.

Service, E.R. (1962) *Primitive Social Organization: An Evolutionary Perspective*, New York: Random House.

Seymour-Smith, C. (1986) *Macmillan Dictionary of Anthropology*, London: Macmillan.

Shankman, P. (1984) 'The Thick and the Thin. On the Interpretive Theoretical Program of Clifford Geertz', *Current Anthropology* 25, 3: 261–80.

Shanon, B. (1993) *The Representational and the Presentational: An Essay on Cognition and the Study of Mind*, New York: Harvester Wheatsheaf.

Shelley, P.B. (1954) *Shelley's Prose*, Albuquerque: University of New Mexico Press.

Sherif, M. (1967) *Social Interaction*, Chicago: Aldine.

Shostak, M. (1983) *Nisa. The Life and Words of a !Kung Woman*, Harmondsworth: Penguin.

Shuman, A. (1996) 'Narrative', in D. Levinson and M. Ember (eds) *Encyclopedia of Cultural Anthropology*, New York: Holt.

Shweder, R. (1991a) *Thinking through Cultures*, Cambridge, Mass.: Harvard University Press.

—— (1991b) 'Post-Nietzschean Anthropology: The Idea of Multiple Objective Worlds', in R.A. Shweder, *Thinking through Cultures*, Cambridge, Mass.: Harvard University Press.

Silverstone, R., Hirsch, E. and Morley, D. (1994), 'Information and Communication Technologies and the Moral Economy of the Household', in R. Silverstone and E. Hirsch (eds), *Consuming Technologies. Media and Information in Domestic Spaces*, London: Routledge.

Simmel, G. (1971 [1908]) *On Individuality and Social Forms* (ed. D. Levine), Chicago: University of Chicago Press.

—— (1980) *Essays on Interpretation in Social Science* (ed. G. Oakes), Totowa, NJ: Rowman-Littlefield.

—— (1984) *Georg Simmel: On Women, Sexuality and Love* (ed. G. Oakes), New Haven, Conn.: Yale University Press.

Sjoberg, G. (1960) *The Pre-Industrial City*, New York: Free Press.

Skinner, D. and Holland, D. (1996) 'Schools and the Cultural Production of the Educated Person in a Nepalese Hill Community', in B. Levinson, D. Foley and D. Holland (eds) *The Cultural Production of the Educated Person*, Albany: State University of New York Press.

Smith, V. (1989) 'Introduction', in V. Smith (ed.) *Hosts and Guests*, Oxford: Blackwell.

—— (1992) 'Pilgrimage and Tourism: The Quest in Guest', *Annals of Tourism Research* 19, 1.

Specht, E. (1969) *The Foundations of Wittgenstein's Late Philosophy*, Manchester: Manchester University Press.

Spencer, J. (1989) 'Anthropology as a Kind of Writing', *Man* 24: 145–64.

Sperber, D. (1975) *Rethinking Symbolism*, Cambridge: Cambridge University Press.

—— (1985) 'Anthropology and Psychology: Towards an Epidemiology of Representations', *Man* 20: 73–89.

Spiro, M. (1958) *Children of the Kibbutz*, Cambridge, Mass.: Harvard University Press.

—— (1982) *Oedipus in the Trobriands*, Chicago: University of Chicago Press.

Stanage, S. (1974) 'Violatives: Modes and Themes of Violence', in S. Stanage (ed.) *Reason and Violence*, Totowa, NJ: Littlefield/Adams.

Stein, M. (1964) *The Eclipse of Community*, New York: Harper.

Steiner, G. (1975) *After Babel*, London: Oxford University Press.

—— (1978) 'The Distribution of Discourse', in *On Difficulty and Other Essays*, Oxford: Oxford University Press.

Stirrat, R. (1984) 'Sacred Models', *Man* 19: 199–215.

Stock, B. (1983) *The Implications of Literacy*, Princeton, NJ: Princeton University Press.

—— (1990) *Listening for the Text*, Baltimore: Johns Hopkins University Press.

Stocking, G. (1992) *The Ethnographer's Magic and Other Essays in the History of Anthropology*, Madison: University of Wisconsin Press.

Stoller, P. (1989a) *Fusion of the Worlds*, Chicago: University of Chicago Press.

—— (1989b) *The Taste of Ethnographic Things: The Senses in Anthropology*, Philadelphia: University of Pennsylvania Press.

—— (1992) *The Cinematic Griot: The Ethnography of Jean Rouch*, Chicago: University of Chicago Press.

—— (1997) *Sensuous Scholarship*, Philadelphia: University of Pennsylvania Press.

Storrie, R. (1999) *Being Human: Personhood, Cosmology and Subsistence for the Hoti of Venezuelan Guiana*, PhD Thesis, University of Manchester.

Strathern, M. (1972) *Women in Between*, London: Seminar Press.

—— (1980) 'No Nature, No Culture: The Hagen Case', in C. MacCormack and M. Strathern (eds), *Nature, Culture and Gender*, Cambridge: Cambridge University Press.

—— (1981) 'Self-interest and the Social Good: Some Implications of Hagen Gender', in S. Ortner and H. Whitehead (eds) *Sexual Meanings: The Cultural Construction of Gender and Sexuality*, Cambridge: Cambridge University Press.

—— (1982) 'The Village as an Idea', in A.P. Cohen (ed.) *Belonging*, Manchester: Manchester University Press.

—— (1984) 'Domesticity and the Denigration of Women', in D. O'Brien and S. Tiffany (eds), *Rethinking Women's Roles: Perspectives from the Pacific*, Berkeley: University of California Press.

—— (1987) 'The Limits of Auto-anthropology', in A. Jackson (ed.) *Anthropology at Home*, London: Routledge.

—— (1988) *The Gender of the Gift. Problems with Women and Problems with Society in Melanesia*, Berkeley: University of California Press.

—— (1990a) *Partial Connections*, Savage, Md: Rowman-Littlefield.

—— (1990b) 'Proposing the motion that "The Concept of Society is Theoretically Obsolete"', *Group for Debates in Anthropological Theory*, Department of Social Anthropology, University of Manchester.

—— (1991) 'Why Anthropology? Why Kinship?', paper presented at the ESRC Seminar, 'Kinship and New Reproductive Technologies: Anthropological Perspectives on Assisted Kinship', University of Manchester, September.

—— (1992a) *Reproducing the Future: Anthropology, Kinship and the New Reproductive Technologies*, Manchester: Manchester University Press.

—— (1992b) *After Nature: English Kinship in the Late Twentieth Century*, Cambridge: Cambridge University Press.

—— (1995) *The Relation*, Cambridge: Prickly Pear Press.

Street, B. (1984) *Literacy in Theory and Practice*, Cambridge: Cambridge University Press.

Szwed, J. (1966) *Private Cultures and Public Imagery*, St. John's, Nfld: ISER Press, Memorial University.

Tambiah, S. (1989) 'Ethnic Conflict in the World Today', *American Ethnologist* 16, 2: 335–49.

Tannen, D. (1989) *Talking Voices* Cambridge: Cambridge University Press.

Taussig, M. (1993) *Mimesis and Alterity: A Particular History of the Senses*, New York, London: Routledge.

Taylor, C. (1985) *Philosophical Papers 1 and 2*, Cambridge: Cambridge University.

Taylor, L. (1984) *In the Underworld*, Oxford: Blackwell.

Tedlock, B. (1996) 'Diasporas', in D. Levinson and M. Ember (eds) *Encyclopedia of Cultural Anthropology*, New York: Holt.

Tedlock, D. (1979) 'The Analogical Tradition and the Emergence of a Dialogical Anthropology', *Journal of Anthropological Research* 35: 387–400.

—— (1983) *The Spoken Word and the Work of Interpretation*, Philadelphia: University of Pennsylvania Press.

Teixeira-Pinto, M. (1997) *Ieipari*, São Paulo: ANPOCS/HUCITEC.

Thomas, D. (1982) *Order without Government*, Urbana: University of Illinois Press.

Thomas, N. (1994) *Colonialism's Culture*, Cambridge: Polity Press.

Thornton, R. (1991) 'The End of the Future?' *Anthropology Today* 7, 1: 1–2.

—— (1992) 'The Chains of Reciprocity: The Impact of Nietzsche's *Genealogy* on Malinowski's *Crime and Custom in Savage Society*', *The Polish Sociological Bulletin* 1: 19–33.

Todorov, T. (1987) *The Conquest of America*, tr. Richard Howard, New York: Harper & Row.

Toennies, F. (1957 [1887]) *Community and Society*, New York: Harper.

Tonkin, E. (1992) *Narrating our Pasts*, Cambridge: Cambridge University Press.

Toren, C. (1983) 'Thinking Symbols: A Critique of Sperber (1979)', *Man* 18, 2: 260–8.

—— (1993) 'Making History: The Significance of Childhood Cognition for a Comparative Anthropology of Mind', *Man* 28: 461–78.

Traweek, S. (1988) *Beamtimes and Lifetimes: The World of High Energy Physicists*, Cambridge, Mass.: Harvard University Press.

Turner, L. and Ash, J. (eds) (1976) *The Golden Hordes: International Tourism and the Pleasure Periphery*, New York: St. Martin's.

Turner, T. (1992) 'Defiant Images: The Kayapo Appropriation of Video', *Anthropology Today* 8, 6: 5–16.

Turner, V. (1964) 'Symbols in Ndembu Ritual', in M. Gluckman and E. Devons (eds) *Closed Systems, Open Minds*, Chicago: Aldine.

—— (1967) *The Forest of Symbols*, Ithaca, NY: Cornell University Press.

—— (1974) *Dramas, Fields, Metaphors*, Ithaca, NY: Cornell University Press.

—— (1976) 'African Ritual and Western Literature: Is a Comparative Symbology Possible?', in A. Fletcher (ed.) *The Literature of Fact*, New York: Columbia University Press.

—— (1982a) *The Ritual Process*, Ithaca, NY: Cornell University Press.

—— (1982b) *Celebration: A World of Art and Ritual*, Washington: Smithsonian Journal.

—— (1986) *The Anthropology of Performance*, New York: Performing Arts Journal.

Turner, V. and Bruner, E. (eds) (1986) *The Anthropology of Experience*, Urbana, Ill: University of Illinois Press.

Twain, M. (1869) *The Innocents Abroad* vol. 2, New York: Harper & Row.

Tyler, S. (1986) 'Post-Modern Ethnography: From Document of the Occult to Occult Document', in G. Marcus and J. Clifford (eds) *Writing Culture*, Berkeley: University of California Press.

Urry, J. (1990) *The Tourist Gaze*, London: Sage.

van den Berghe, P. (1987) *The Ethnic Phenomenon*, New York: Praeger.

van Gennep, A. (1960 [1909]) *The Rites of Passage*, London: Routledge & Kegan Paul.

van Velsen, J. (1967) 'The Extended-case Method and Situational Analysis', in A. Epstein (ed.) *The Craft of Social Anthropology*, London: Tavistock.

Vernant, J.P. (1996 [1974]) *Myth and Society in Ancient Greece* (orig. pub. as *Mythe et société en Grèce ancienne*, Paris: Librarie François Maspero), New York: Zone Books.

Viveiros de Castro, E. (1992) *From the Enemy's Point of View: Humanity and Divinity in an Amazonian Society*, Chicago: University of Chicago Press.

—— (1996) 'Society', in A. Barnard and J. Spencer (eds) *Encyclopedia of Social and Cultural Anthropology*, London: Routledge.

Wagner, R. (1975) *The Invention of Culture*, Englewood Cliffs, NJ: Prentice Hall.

—— (1977) 'Culture as Creativity', in J. Dolgin, D. Kemnitzer and D. Schneider (eds) *Symbolic Anthropology*, New York: Columbia University Press.

—— (1978) *Lethal Speech: Daribi Myth and Symbolic Obviation*, Ithaca, NY: Cornell University Press.

—— (1986) *Symbols that Stand for Themselves*, Chicago: University of Chicago Press.

—— (1991) 'Poetics and the Recentering of Anthropology', in I. Brady (ed.) *Anthropological Poetics*, Savage, Md: Rowman-Littlefield.

Walcott, D. (1996) 'Afterword: Animals, Elemental Tales, and the Theater', in A.J. Arnold (ed.) *Monsters, Tricksters, and Sacred Cows*, Charlottesville: University Press of Virginia.

Wallace, A.F.C. (1961) 'The Psychic Unity of Human Groups', in B. Kaplan (ed.) *Studying Personality Cross-Culturally*, New York: Harper & Row.

——(1962) 'Culture and Cognition', *Science* 135: 351–7.

——(1964) *Culture and Personality*, New York: Random House.

Wallerstein, I. (1974/1980) *The Modern World-System*, volumes I and II, New York: Academic Press.

Wallman, S. (ed.) (1992) *Contemporary Futures. Perspectives from Social Anthropology*, London: Routledge.

Warner, W.L. (1941) 'Social Anthropology and the Modern Community', *American Journal of Sociology* 46: 785–96.

—— (1959) *The Living and the Dead: A Study of the Symbolic Life of Americans*, New Haven, Conn.: Yale University Press.

Warner, W.L. and Lunt, P. (1941) *The Social Life of a Modern Community*, New Haven: Yale University Press.

—— (1942) *The Status System of a Modern Community*, New Haven, Conn.: Yale University Press.

Watkins, J. (1953) 'Ideal Types and Historical Explanation', in H. Feigl and M. Brodbeck (eds) *Readings in the Philosophy of Science*, New York: Appleton-Century-Crofts.
—— (1959) 'Historical Explanation in the Social Sciences', in P. Gardiner (ed.) *Theories of History*, London: Allen & Unwin.
Watson, L. and Watson-Franke, M.-B. (1985), *Interpreting Life-Histories*, New Brunswick, NJ: Rutgers University Press.
Watt, I. (1979) 'Literature and Society', in R. Wilson (ed.) *The Arts in Society*, New York: Arno.
Weber, M. (1964) *The Theory of Social and Economic Organization*, New York: Free Press.
Wedgwood, C. (1932–34) Wedgwood Personal Archives, University Archives, University of Sydney.
Weiner, A. (1976) *Women of Value, Men of Renown*, Austin: University of Texas Press.
Weiner, J. (1991) *The Empty Place*, Bloomington: Indiana University Press.
—— (1995) 'Anthropologists, Historians and the Secret of Social Knowledge', *Anthropology Today* 11, 5: 3–7.
Weisner, T. (1989) 'Social Support for Children among the Abaluyia of Kenya', in D. Belle (ed.) *Children's Social Networks and Social Supports*, New York: Wiley.
Weisner, T. and Gallimore, R. (1977) 'My Brother's Keeper: Child and Sibling Caretaking', *Current Anthropology* 18: 169–90.
Weisner, T., Mathoson, C. and Bernheimer, L. (1996) 'American Cultural Models of Early Influence and Parent Recognition of Development Delays', in S. Harkness and C. Super (eds) *Parents' Cultural Belief Systems*, New York: Guilford.
Weissbrodt, W. (1988) 'Human Rights: An Historical Perspective', in P. Davies (ed.) *Human Rights*, London: Routledge.
Werbner, R. (1989) *Ritual Passage, Sacred Journey: The Process, Form and Organization of Religious Movement*, Manchester: Manchester University Press.
—— (1991) *Tears of the Dead*, Edinburgh: Edinburgh University Press.
Wertham, F. (1971) 'The Goddess of Violence', in G. Estey and D. Hunter (eds) *Violence*, Waltham, Mass.: Xerox.
Whitaker, M. (1997) 'Reflexivity', in A. Barnard and J. Spencer (eds) *Encyclopedia of Social and Cultural Anthropology*, London: Routledge.
White, H. (1987) *The Content of the Form*, Baltimore: Johns Hopkins University Press.
Whitehead, A. (1925) *Science and the Modern World*, New York: Macmillan.
Whiting, J. and Child, I. (1953) *Child Training and Personality*, New Haven, Conn.: Yale University Press.
Whitten, N. and Wolfe, D. (1974) 'Network Analysis', in J. Honigmann (ed.) *Handbook of Social and Cultural Anthropology*, Chicago: University of Chicago Press.
Whorf, B.L. (1956) *Language, Thought and Reality* (ed. J. Carroll), Cambridge, Mass.: MIT Press.
Whyte, W.F. (1943) *Street Corner Society*, Chicago: University of Chicago Press.
Wiener, N. (1949) *Cybernetics*, New York: Wiley.
Wikan, U. (1980) *Life among the Poor in Cairo*, London: Tavistock.
Wilder, D. (1981) 'Perceiving Persons as a Group', in D. Hamilton (ed.) *Cognitive Processes in Stereotyping and Intergroup Behavior*, Hillsdale, NJ: Erlbaum.

Wilk, S. (1991) *Humanistic Anthropology*, Knoxville: University of Tennessee Press.

Williams, R. (1983a [1976]) *Keywords*, London: Flamingo.

—— (1983b) 'Society', in R. Williams, *Keywords*, London: Flamingo.

—— (1983c) *Writing in Society*, London: Verso.

—— (1985) *The Country and the City*, London: Hogarth.

Willis, P. (1978) *Learning to Labour*, Farnborough: Saxon House.

Wilmott, P. and Young, M. (1960) *Family and Class in a London Suburb*, London: Routledge & Kegan Paul.

Wilson, B. (1970) (ed.) *Rationality*, Oxford: Blackwell.

Wilson, R. (1997) *Human Rights, Culture and Context: Anthropological Perspectives*, London: Pluto.

Winch, P. (1970) *The Idea of a Social Science, and its Relation to Philosophy*, London: Routledge & Kegan Paul.

Winthrop, R. (1991) *Dictionary of Concepts in Cultural Anthropology*, Westport, Conn.: Greenwood.

Wirth, L. (1938) 'Urbanism as a Way of Life', *American Journal of Sociology* 44.

Witherspoon, G. (1977) *Language and Art in the Navajo Universe*, Ann Arbor: University of Michigan Press.

Wittgenstein, L (1978) *Philosophical Investigations*, Oxford: Blackwell.

Wolf, E. (1974) *Anthropology*, New York: Norton.

Wolfram, S. (1985) 'Facts and Theories: Saying and Believing', in J. Overing (ed.) *Reason and Morality*, London: Tavistock.

—— (1988) *'Human Rights': Commentary*, in T. Downing and G. Kushner (eds) *Human Rights and Anthropology*, Cambridge, Mass.: Cultural Survival.

Woodburn, J. (1982) 'Egalitarian Societies', *Man* 17: 431–51.

Woolf, V. (1969) *The Waves*, Harmondsworth: Penguin.

—— (1976) *Moments of Being*, Falmer: Sussex University Press.

—— (1978) *Jacob's Room*, San Diego: Harcourt Brace Jovanovich.

—— (1980) *The Diary of Virginia Woolf. Volume III: 1925–1930*, London: Hogarth.

Worth, S. (1981) *Studying Visual Communication*, Philadelphia: University of Pennsylvania Press.

Worth, S. and Adair, J. (1972) *Through Navaho Eyes*, Bloomington: Indiana University Press.

Wright, G. (1991) 'Prescribing the Model Home', *Social Research* 58, 1.

Wrightsman, L. (1977) *Social Psychology*, Monterey, Calif.: Brooks Cole.

Yamba, C.B. (1992) 'Going There and Getting There: The Future as a Legitimating Charter for Life in the Present', in S. Wallman (ed.) *Contemporary Futures*, London: Routledge.

Young, M. (1991) *An Inside Job*, Oxford: Oxford University Press.

—— (1993) *In the Sticks*, Oxford: Oxford University Press.

Young, M. and Wilmott, P. (1974) *Family and Kinship in East London*, Harmondsworth: Penguin.

Zijderveld, A. (1979) *On Clichés*, London: Routledge & Kegan Paul.

INDEX